TRADEMARK LAW AND THE

RESEARCH HANDBOOKS IN INTELLECTUAL PROPERTY

Series Editor: Jeremy Phillips, *Intellectual Property Consultant, Slaughter and May and Professorial Fellow, Centre for Commercial Law Studies, Queen Mary, University of London, UK*

Under the general editorship and direction of Jeremy Phillips comes this important new Handbook series of high quality, original reference works that cover the broad pillars of intellectual property law: trademark law, patent law and copyright law – as well as less developed areas, such as geographical indications, and the increasing intersection of intellectual property with other fields. Taking an international and comparative approach, these Handbooks, each edited by leading scholars in the respective field, will comprise specially commissioned contributions from a select cast of authors, bringing together renowned figures with up-and-coming younger authors. Each will offer a wide-ranging examination of current issues in intellectual property that is unrivalled in its blend of critical, innovative thinking and substantive analysis, and in its synthesis of contemporary research.

Each Handbook will stand alone as an invaluable source of reference for all scholars of intellectual property, as well as for practising lawyers who wish to engage with the discussion of ideas within the field. Whether used as an information resource on key topics, or as a platform for advanced study, these Handbooks will become definitive scholarly reference works in intellectual property law.

Titles in the series include:
Copyright Law
A Handbook of Contemporary Research
Edited by Paul Torremans

Trademark Law and Theory
A Handbook of Contemporary Research
Edited by Graeme Dinwoodie and Mark D. Janis

Trademark Law and Theory

A Handbook of Contemporary Research

Edited by
Graeme B. Dinwoodie

Professor of Law, Associate Dean, and Director, Program in Intellectual Property Law, Chicago-Kent College of Law, USA and Professor of Intellectual Property Law, Queen Mary, University of London, UK

and

Mark D. Janis

Professor of Law and H. Blair and Joan V. White Chair in Intellectual Property Law, University of Iowa College of Law, USA

RESEARCH HANDBOOKS IN INTELLECTUAL PROPERTY

Edward Elgar
Cheltenham, UK • Northampton, MA, USA

© The Editors and Contributors Severally 2008

All rights reserved. No part of this publication may be reproduced, stored in a retrieval system or transmitted in any form or by any means, electronic, mechanical or photocopying, recording, or otherwise without the prior permission of the publisher.

Published by
Edward Elgar Publishing Limited
Glensanda House
Montpellier Parade
Cheltenham
Glos GL50 1UA
UK

Edward Elgar Publishing, Inc.
William Pratt House
9 Dewey Court
Northampton
Massachusetts 01060
USA

A catalogue record for this book
is available from the British Library

Library of Congress Control Number: 2008924976

ISBN 978 1 84542 602 6

Typeset by Cambrian Typesetters, Camberley, Surrey
Printed and bound in Great Britain by MPG Books Ltd, Bodmin, Cornwall

Contents

List of contributors vii
Introduction ix

PART I   METHODOLOGICAL PERSPECTIVES

1 From communication to thing: historical aspects of the
   conceptualisation of trade marks as property   3
   Lionel Bently
2 The semiotic account of trademark doctrine and trademark
   culture   42
   Barton Beebe
3 A search-costs theory of limiting doctrines in trademark law   65
   Stacey L. Dogan and Mark A. Lemley
4 Trade mark bureaucracies   95
   Robert Burrell
5 The political economy of trademark dilution   132
   Clarisa Long

PART II   INTERNATIONAL AND COMPARATIVE DIMENSIONS

6 Fundamental concerns in the harmonization of (European)
   trademark law   151
   Annette Kur
7 Substantive trademark law harmonization: on the emerging
   coherence between the jurisprudence of the WTO Appellate
   body and the European Court of Justice   177
   Gail E. Evans
8 The free movement (or not) of trademark protected goods
   in Europe   204
   Thomas Hays
9 The trademark law provisions of bilateral free trade agreements 229
   Burton Ong

PART III   CRITICAL ISSUES

Section A   **Trademarks and speech**
10   Reconciling trademark rights and expressive values: how to stop worrying and learn to love ambiguity   261
   Rochelle Cooper Dreyfuss
11   Truth and advertising: the Lanham Act and commercial speech doctrine   294
   Rebecca Tushnet
12   Restricting allusion to trade marks: a new justification   324
   Michael Spence

Section B   **Limiting the scope of trademark rights**
13   Protecting the common: delineating a public domain in trade mark law   345
   Jennifer Davis
14   Tolerating confusion about confusion: trademark policies and fair use   368
   Graeme W. Austin
15   Online word of mouth and its implications for trademark law   404
   Eric Goldman

Section C   **Trademarks and traditional knowledge**
16   Trademarks and traditional knowledge and cultural intellectual property rights   433
   Susy Frankel
17   Culture, traditional knowledge and trademarks: a view from the South   464
   Coenraad Visser

Section D   **The edges of trademark protection**
18   Of mutant copyrights, mangled trademarks, and Barbie's beneficence: the influence of copyright on trademark law   481
   Jane C. Ginsburg
19   Signs, surfaces, shapes and structures – the protection of product design under trade mark law   498
   Alison Firth

Index   523

Contributors

Graeme W. Austin, J. Byron McCormick Professor of Law, James E. Rogers College of Law, University of Arizona, USA.

Barton Beebe, Associate Professor of Law, Benjamin N. Cardozo School of Law, Yeshiva University, USA.

Lionel Bently, Herchel Smith Professor of Intellectual Property and Information Law, University of Cambridge, UK.

Robert Burrell, Associate Professor and Associate Director, Australian Centre for Intellectual Property in Agriculture, TC Beirne School of Law, University of Queensland, Australia.

Jennifer Davis, Dr and Newton Trust Lecturer, The Faculty of Law, Cambridge University, UK.

Graeme B. Dinwoodie, Professor of Law, Associate Dean, and Director, Program in Intellectual Property Law, Chicago-Kent College of Law, USA and Professor of Intellectual Property Law, Queen Mary, University of London, UK

Stacey L. Dogan, Professor of Law, Northeastern University School of Law, USA.

Rochelle Cooper Dreyfuss, Pauline Newman Professor of Law, New York University School of Law, USA.

Gail E. Evans, Reader in International Trade and Intellectual Property Law, Queen Mary, University of London, UK.

Alison Firth, Professor of Commercial Law, University of Newcastle upon Tyne, UK.

Susy Frankel, Professor of Law, Victoria University of Wellington, New Zealand.

Jane C. Ginsburg, Morton L. Janklow Professor of Literary and Artistic Property Law, Columbia University School of Law, USA.

Eric Goldman, Assistant Professor of Law and Director, High Tech Law Institute, Santa Clara University School of Law, USA.

Thomas Hays, PhD (Cambridge); Lewis Silkin LLP, London; CIER, the Molengraaff Institute, Utrecht, Netherlands.

Mark D. Janis, Professor of Law and H. Blair and Joan V. White Chair in Intellectual Property Law, University of Iowa College of Law, USA.

Annette Kur, Professor and Research Fellow, Department of Intellectual Property and Competition Law, Max Planck Institute for Intellectual Property, Munich, Germany.

Mark A. Lemley, William H. Neukom Professor of Law, Stanford Law School, USA; of counsel, Keker & Van Nest LLP.

Clarisa Long, Max Mendel Shaye Professor of Law, Columbia Law School, USA.

Burton Ong, Faculty of Law, National University of Singapore.

Michael Spence, Head of Social Sciences Division and CUF Lecturer, The Faculty of Law, Oxford University, UK.

Rebecca Tushnet, Professor of Law, Georgetown University Law Center, USA.

Coenraad Visser, Professor of Intellectual Property Law, Head of Department of Mercantile Law, University of South Africa, Pretoria, South Africa.

Introduction
Graeme B. Dinwoodie and Mark D. Janis

In the mid-twentieth century, many countries revised and restated their trademark laws. Although the revised statutes, and the debates that produced them, reflected a certain willingness to begin thinking about trademarks in a new way, traditional practices still predominated. Trademarks were still widely understood as primarily serving the traditional purpose of source identification. And trademark law's purposes were still articulated in familiar rhetorical overtones. For example, according to the U.S. Senate, U.S. trademark law circa 1946 was intended to 'protect the public so that it may be confident that, in purchasing a product bearing a particular trademark which it favorably knows, it will get the product which it asks for and which it wants to get', while also ensuring that 'where the owner of a trademark has spent energy, time and money in presenting to the public the product, he is protected in his investment from its appropriation by pirates and cheats'.[1]

Trademark law has maintained its grasp on tradition, but much has changed in the past half-century: the consumer economy has become globalized, making international trademark negotiations more significant; image has become pervasive in popular culture; intellectual property has emerged as among the most vital of private assets; and the range of symbols that might function as marks has expanded to include additional non-verbal indicia. Firms now use trademarks – their own and those of their competitors – in new and varying ways, reflecting a greater diversity in consumer perceptions. Along many dimensions, the story of trademarks is becoming richer, and, correspondingly, trademark law is becoming more subtle and complex.

In this volume, we seek to demonstrate that contemporary trademark law scholarship can take the lead in laying out a more robust, multi-faceted theoretical foundation for this the new era of trademark law. In light of that goal, we have organized the contributions to this book in three parts: the new diversity in methodologies for analyzing trademark law (Part I); current international considerations in trademark law (Part II); and the evolving relationships between trademark law and other bodies of law triggered by the multivariate functions that trademarks now play in the modern economy (Part III). Part I

---

[1] S. Rep. No. 1333, 79th Cong., 2d Sess. 3 (1946).

includes chapters that illustrate both the continuing significance of historical perspectives,[2] and the fresh insights to be found in disciplines such as semiotics,[3] economics,[4] and political science.[5] Part II explores the harmonization of substantive trademark law[6] as well as the dynamic relationship between trademark law and global trade,[7] reflecting the need for trademark law to become better attuned to international considerations. Part III covers the growing complexity of relationships between trademark law and various areas of concern: speech;[8] the public domain and concerns about enabling free competition;[9] the protection of traditional knowledge,[10] and adjacent areas of intellectual property law such as copyright, moral rights, and design protection.[11]

Although we have organized the book into three discrete groups of chapters, there are a number of cross-cutting themes. One such theme is the concern about articulating limits on trademark rights. Some scholars propose

---

[2]   Lionel Bently, *From Communication to Thing: Historical Aspects of the Conceptualisation of Trade Marks as Property,* Chapter 1, *infra.*

[3]   Barton Beebe, *The Semiotic Account of Trademark Doctrine and Trademark Culture,* Chapter 2, *infra.*

[4]   Stacey L. Dogan & Mark A. Lemley, *A Search Costs Theory of Limiting Doctrines in Trademark Law*, Chapter 3, *infra.*

[5]   Robert Burrell, *Trademark Bureaucracies*, Chapter 4, *infra*; Clarisa Long, *The Political Economy of Trademark Dilution*, Chapter 5, *infra.*

[6]   Annette Kur, *Fundamental Concerns in the Harmonization of (European) Trademark Law*, Chapter 6, *infra*; Gail E. Evans, *Substantive Trademark Law Harmonization: On the Emerging Coherence Between the Jurisprudence of the WTO Appellate Body and the European Court of Justice*, Chapter 7, *infra.*

[7]   Thomas Hays, *The Free Movement (or not) of Trademark Protected Goods in Europe*, Chapter 8, *infra*; Burton Ong, *The Trademark Law Provisions of Bilateral Free Trade Agreements*, Chapter 9, *infra.*

[8]   Rochelle Cooper Dreyfus, *Reconciling Trademark Rights and Expressive Values: How to Stop Worrying and Learn to Love Ambiguity*, Chapter 10, *infra*; Rebecca Tushnet, *Truth and Advertising: The Lanham Act and Commercial Speech Doctrine*, Chapter 11, *infra*; Michael Spence, *Restricting Allusion to Trade Marks – A New Justification*, Chapter 12, *infra.*

[9]   Jennifer Davis, *Protecting the Common: Delineating a Public Domain in Trademark Law*, Chapter 13, *infra*; Graeme W. Austin, *Tolerating Confusion About Confusion: Trademark Policies and Fair Use*, Chapter 14, *infra*; Eric Goldman, *Online Word of Mouth and Its Implications for Trademark Law*, Chapter 15, *infra.*

[10]   Susy Frankel, *Trademarks and Traditional Knowledge and Cultural Intellectual Property Rights*, Chapter 16, *infra*; Coenraad Visser, *Culture, Traditional Knowledge, and Trademarks: A View from the South*, Chapter17, *infra.*

[11]   Jane C. Ginsburg, *Of Mutant Copyrights, Mangled Trademarks and Barbie's Beneficence: The Influence of Copyright on Trademark Law*, Chapter 18, *infra*; Alison Firth, *Signs, Surfaces, Shapes and Structures – The Protection of Product Design Under Trademark Law*, Chapter 19, *infra.*

to define limits that are inspired by an economic approach to the trademark system. Thus, Dogan and Lemley argue that the search-costs rationale that supports the existence of trademark rights also generates important limits on those rights.[12] Others would determine limits by affirming the expressive values of free speech. Rochelle Dreyfuss argues that unauthorized third-party uses of trademarks serve important social goals that trump concerns that trademark law may have.[13] Rebecca Tushnet elevates these concerns to the constitutional level.[14] Michael Spence reaches somewhat similar conclusions by introducing a broader range of philosophical values – in particular, the value of autonomy.[15] Jennifer Davis argues that important limits already inhere in existing doctrine, and those limits should be given weight in order to preserve a vibrant commons.[16] Finally, authors such as Graeme Austin would assign greater sophistication to the consumer in analysing key theories like confusion, thus producing less expansive trademark protection.[17]

A second theme is the broadening circle of stakeholders in trademark law. Susy Frankel and Coenraad Visser demonstrate that trademark law should be sensitive to the cultural heritage of indigenous peoples.[18] Jane Ginsburg shows that authors' interests may be served as effectively through trademark and unfair competition principles as through the traditional vehicle of copyright, especially in an environment that is suspicious of claims of moral rights.[19] And Alison Firth reminds us that designers must continue to rely on trademark and unfair competition theories even as they invoke protections from other regimes, including *sui generis* design protection.[20]

Another theme – related to the notion of the broadening circle of stakeholders – is the continued re-evaluation of the effectiveness of particular institutions of the trademark system, and continued assessment of the allocation of power among those institutions. The institutional perspectives are most salient in Robert Burrell's chapter, in which he argues that the role of the trademark office as an administrative actor has shaped the nature of trademark and unfair competition law, such that trademark law can be seen as a bureaucratic property.[21] Clarisa Long's chapter highlights that increased legislative intervention

---

[12] See infra Chapter 3.
[13] See infra Chapter 10.
[14] See infra Chapter 11.
[15] See infra Chapter 12.
[16] See infra Chapter 13.
[17] See infra Chapter 14.
[18] See infra Chapters 16–17.
[19] See infra Chapter 18.
[20] See infra Chapter 19.
[21] See infra Chapter 4.

in trademark law is unlikely to diminish judicial appetite for common law development of trademark law consistent with core principles of competition and speech.[22] Gail Evans' chapter, analyzing the case law of the WTO Appellate Body and the ECJ, reminds us that the types of 'courts' that will develop trademark law are likely to change as trademark law internationalizes.[23]

Another theme is the extent to which trademark law is currently being driven by concerns that are external to the conventional account of the trademark right. Annette Kur takes up this theme, observing that the direction in which trademark law has developed in the European Union has as much to do with the context of harmonization of laws as with development of ideal trademark principles.[24] Burton Ong addresses a similar dynamic occurring in a slightly different international context, highlighting the *realpolitik* of bilateral free trade negotiations.[25] Thomas Hays gives an account of issues concerning parallel imports, which, as always, implicates concerns about international competition.[26] And Barton Beebe urges us to reconsider trademark law through the lens of semiotics.[27]

A final theme brings us back to the topic of change. All of the contributors to this volume deal with the rapidity of change in the modern trademark system. Some raise pointed questions about whether the rapid change is desirable. For example, Eric Goldman urges us to apply traditional principles of trademark law developed offline by analogy to online word-of-mouth marketing, thus immunizing much of that activity from scrutiny under the trademark laws.[28] And Lionel Bently wonders whether one rhetorical (or conceptual) change – a trend towards viewing trademarks as property – is in fact the change that its critics fear it to be.[29] As he points out, history suggests that it is not.

Completing a project like this one has reinforced our faith in the vitality of contemporary trademark law scholarship. The community of trademark law scholars around the world is dynamic and creative, and the leadership of that community is well represented in this volume. It has been our pleasure to work with such an outstanding group of scholars on this project.

---

[22] See infra Chapter 5.
[23] See infra Chapter 7.
[24] See infra Chapter 6.
[25] See infra Chapter 9.
[26] See infra Chapter 8.
[27] See infra Chapter 2.
[28] Chapter 15.
[29] See infra Chapter 1.

We also received excellent support for this project at our respective institutions. At Iowa, research assistants Erica Andersen, Liz Dlouhy, and Julie Mowers provided expert editorial support, and the indefatigable Kati Jumper provided her customary top-notch secretarial support. At Chicago-Kent, Jason Du Mont, Jayne Hoffman, Emily Monteith, and Laura Cederberg were invaluable.

PART I

METHODOLOGICAL PERSPECTIVES

1 From communication to thing: historical aspects of the conceptualisation of trade marks as property

Lionel Bently[1]

It is a common criticism of contemporary trade marks law (and one almost certainly represented by chapters in this volume) that legislatures and judges have expanded the rights of trade mark owners too far, at the expense of the needs or interests of other traders and the public interest.[2] More specifically, it is argued that trade marks are granted too readily, that the rights granted to trade mark owners are too strong, that the situations in which trade mark rights are capable of being invalidated or revoked are too limited, and that the grounds on which a defendant can escape liability are too narrowly formulated or restrictively interpreted. For many of these commentators, the criticism is normative: positive law now affords trade marks owners broader and stronger rights than can be justified by reference to principle or policy. Sometimes, however, commentators attempt to explain the dynamics that have led to this (undesirable) expansion of trade mark rights.[3] Chief amongst these explanatory narratives is the assertion that one of the root causes of expansion is that

---

[1] Herchel Smith Professor of Intellectual Property and Information Law, University of Cambridge. A version of this chapter was previously presented at the ATRIP meeting in Parma in September 2006, at the London School of Economics in March 2007, at New York University's Symposium on Innovation Law and Policy and the Fordham International Intellectual Property Law and Policy Conference in April 2007. I am grateful particularly to Anne Barron, Andrew Bridges, Robert Burrell, Graeme Dinwoodie, Dev Gangee, Justin Hughes, Mark Janis, Phill Johnson and Jamie Stapleton for their comments. Thanks also to Doug MacMahon for research assistance.

[2] Rochelle Cooper Dreyfuss, "Expressive Genericity: Trademarks as Language in the Pepsi Generation" (1990) 65 *Notre Dame L. Rev.* 397, 399 ("the changing legal climate has tended to grant trademark owners ever greater control over their marks"); in the UK, see Jennifer Davis, "European Trade Mark Law and the Enclosure of the Commons" (2002) *IPQ* 342; "To Protect or Serve? European Trade Mark Law and the Decline of the Public Interest" (2003) *EIPR* 180–7.

[3] Jennifer Davis, "European Trade Mark Law and the Enclosure of the Commons" (2002) *IPQ* 342.

trade marks are increasingly described as "property".[4] Trade marks law, originally conceived as a legal mechanism for preventing fraud or protecting consumers, has been reconceptualised as "property",[5] and this, in turn, has caused the law to shed traditional limits on the regulation of the use of trade marks. At the same time, the property label exerts an irresistible force towards expansion of trade mark rights from rights to prevent uses of signs which are likely to confuse consumers' understandings of the origin of the goods bearing the sign to what Blackstone described as full despotic dominion,[6] and what Professor Honoré referred to famously as the full liberal conception of ownership.[7] The power of the proprietary model of trade marks is to cause its metamorphosis into "strong, unfettered property rights".[8]

In this chapter I want to set this analysis of contemporary developments in some historical context, particularly that of the second half of the nineteenth century. During this period, English law witnessed the conceptualisation of trade mark protection as property. At mid-century, there were many laws, some general and some specific, which regulated the uses of signs in trade, but the most important was the general protection provided by the Common Law

---

[4] For example, Glynn Lunney, "Trademark Monopolies" (1999) 48 *Emory L.J.* 367 (identifying a shift from viewing a trade mark as a source of information about a product ("deception-based trademark") to viewing the trade mark as the product ("property-based trademark"), and suggesting that such "property mania" has induced "a radical and ongoing expansion of trademark protection, both in terms of what can be owned as a trademark and in terms of what trademark ownership entails."); Mark Lemley, "The Modern Lanham Act and the Death of Common Sense" 108 *Yale L.J.* 1687, 1687 ("Commentators and even courts increasingly talk about trademarks as property rights; as things valuable in and of themselves"); id. at 1697 ("Courts seem to be replacing the traditional rationale for trademark law with a conception of trademarks as property rights, in which trademark 'owners' are given strong rights over the marks without much regard for the social costs of such rights.").

[5] Lunney, for example ("Trademark Monopolies" (1999) 48 *Emory L.J.* 367 at 417), states that "Originally, trademark law was justified on grounds of preventing consumer deception." Lemley ("The Death of Common Sense" (1999) 108 *Yale L.J.* 1687, at 1697) also refers to the courts "replacing the traditional rationale for trademark law with a conception of trademarks as property." These appeals to "original conception" and "tradition" are problematic in the face of the history, which is certainly messy.

[6] W. Blackstone, *Commentaries on the Laws of England, A Facsimile of the First Edition of 1765–1769* (Chicago: University of Chicago Press, 1979) Book II, Ch. 1, p. 2.

[7] "Ownership" in A.G. Guest (ed.), *Oxford Essays in Jurisprudence* (Oxford: Clarendon, 1961) 107, 113 (the right to possess, use, manage, receive income, to capital, to security; the power of transmissibility; the absence of term; the prohibition on harmful use; liability to execution; and the incident of residuarity).

[8] Lemley, Mark, "The Modern Lanham Act and the Death of Common Sense" (1999) 108 *Yale L.J.* 1687, 1694.

and the supplementary protection of the Chancery courts against misrepresentation in trade.[9] The protection afforded by both sets of courts was communication-based: the Common Law action, understood by courts and commentators in this period to have derived from deceit,[10] requiring a demonstration of an intention to deceive, the Chancery regime requiring a misrepresentation, that is, a communicative act, of the defendant likely to mislead. However, during the 1860s a debate emerged as to whether trade marks were to be seen as property. In the judicial field, as also amongst legal commentators, the question arose in the context of the expanded protection afforded by the Chancery courts (as opposed to the Common Law courts) after *Millington v Fox*. The question for these jurists was whether this extended protection rendered the signs "property" and with what consequences. The question of "property" took on further significance in the discussions over the Trade Mark Registration Bill of 1861 which proposed that trade marks that were registered be property. This proposal was met with opposition in the Select Committee of 1862,[11] on the assumption that such a characterisation would render trade marks a mechanism for perpetrating (rather than preventing) fraud. As a result of case-law developments, particularly during the 1860s, and finally the adoption of a Trade Mark Registration Act in 1875, trade marks came to be widely recognised as property.

There seems no doubt that certain consequences flowed from the fact that

---

[9] See L. Bently, "The Making of Modern Trade Marks Law: The Construction of the Legal Concept of Trade Mark (1860–80)" in L. Bently, J. Davis & J. Ginsburg (eds.), *Trade Marks and Brands: An Interdisciplinary Critique* (Cambridge: CUP, 2008).

[10] Cresswell J. characterised the action as one for deceit in *Crawshay v Thompson* (1842) 4 Man & G 356, 385–6. The issue was raised in *Rodgers v Nowill* (1847) 5 CB 109, 116 by Maule J, Montagu Chambers responding that "there is no other title under which such an action shall be classed". See also F. Lloyd, "On the Law of Trade Marks No. I" (11 May, 1861) *Sol Jo & Rep* 486; F. Lloyd, "On the Law of Trade Marks No. II" (25 May, 1861) *Sol Jo & Rep* 523; *Cartier v Carlile* (1862) 31 Beav 292, 296–7 (counsel for the defendant); *Edelsten v Edelsten* (1863) 1 De G J & S 185, 199 (Lord Chancellor Westbury stating that "[a]t law the proper remedy is by an action on the case for deceit.").

Whether the early cases were really actions for deceit is a topic worthy of serious investigation (but unfortunately is one beyond the scope of this chapter). Most accounts of the history of the common law of deceit suggest that deceit was handled largely as part of what we would consider the law of contract until *Pasley v Freeman* (1789) 3 TR 51: see e.g. S.F.C. Milsom, *Historical Foundations of the Common Law* (2d ed. London: Butterworths, 1981) 361–6. If this is so, it is difficult to see how the action for wrongful use of a trade mark might have been considered as deceit.

[11] Select Committee on Trade Marks Bill and Merchandize Marks Bill, Report, Proceedings and Minutes of Evidence (1862) 12 *Parliamentary Papers* 431.

trade marks were widely accepted as property by the mid-1870s. For example, trade marks started to be treated as part of a law of "industrial property", included in legislation relating also to patents and designs, and, before long, in the first significant multilateral international treaty, the Paris Convention. Moreover, perceived as "property", trade marks were frequently compared and contrasted by commentators with analogous but distinct laws of patents and copyright. Courts too occasionally were prepared to reason from an understanding of trade marks as property when developing applicable rules, for example, on "abandonment".[12] But while designation of trade marks as "property" was important, no one in the 1870s or 1880s would have inferred from this that trade-mark rights extended to the use of the protected sign on dissimilar goods.

Revisiting this period of the historical development of trade marks in the light of today's commentaries on the significance of property rhetoric in current developments in the law of trade marks clearly raises certain questions.[13] If the mere designation of trade marks as "property" has the power attributed to it, why has trade-marks jurisprudence taken so long to develop into its maximal incarnation? Have the consequences attributed to the notion of "property" changed in the intervening 130 or so years? Or has the "handling" of the concept of property by the courts (and policy-makers) altered in that time? Alternatively, does the history suggest that contemporary accounts overemphasise the role of property rhetoric as a causal factor in the expansion of trade-marks law? In my conclusion, I will return to some of these questions.

I. The emergence of trade marks law prior to 1860: trade marks as communications

At mid-century, the most significant laws regulating misrepresentation in

---

[12] *Mouson v Boehm* (1884) 26 Ch D 398 (Chitty J) (drawing analogy with easements and goods).

[13] For a comparable analysis of US history, see Mark McKenna, "The Normative Foundation of Trademark Law" (2007) 82 *Notre Dame L. Rev.* 1839 (where the author revisits the history to contradict the commonplace account that trade-mark law has expanded in the light of a normative shift from a goal of protecting consumers to protecting traders). McKenna's account claims that the history shows that trademark protection was always concerned with protecting producers against diversion of sales, so that the transformation in trade-mark protection cannot be explained by reference to such a shift. The parallel between McKenna's argument, and the one offered here which uses history to contradict accounts of trade-mark laws' expansive tendencies by reference to a shift to property, is self-evident. For a sceptical view of claims that copyright law's expansion is attributable to "propertization" see Justin Hughes, "Copyright and Incomplete Historiographies: Of Piracy, Propertization and Thomas Jefferson" (2006) 79 *S. Cal. L. Rev.* 993.

trade were the action on the case (it seems, for deceit) at Common Law, and Equity's intervention by way of injunction in support of the Common Law right in plain cases.[14] Both regimes were premised on the idea that the courts should intervene where one trader fraudulently used a mark associated with another.

The Common Law action preventing use of a mark associated with one trader by another has often been traced back to the late sixteenth century case of *JG v Samford*, a Common Pleas decision of 1584 where two of the presiding judges stated that an action would lie against use on inferior cloth of a mark which had been used by another manufacturer who had gained great reputation for his cloth.[15] While the significance of *Samford* (or rather its subsequent citation in 1618 in *Southern v How,* a case brought by a purchaser of counterfeit jewels against the vendor) is heavily contested,[16] it seems clear that by the late eighteenth century the Common Law courts were prepared to permit traders to bring actions based on intentional, damaging, misrepresentations of this sort.[17] Lord Mansfield's manuscripts contain details of two

---

[14] For discussion of the wide array of other laws protecting specific designations in particular trades, as well as criminal remedies, see L. Bently, "The Making of Modern Trade Marks Law: The Construction of the Legal Concept of Trade Mark (1860–80)" in L. Bently, J. Davis & J. Ginsburg (eds.), *Trade Marks and Brands: An Interdisciplinary Critique* (Cambridge: CUP, 2008).

[15] J.H. Baker & S.F.C. Milsom, *Sources of English Legal History: Private Law to 1750* (London: Butterworths, 1986) 615–8; J.H. Baker, *An Introduction to English Legal History* (4th ed. London: Butterworths, 2002) 459. The two other judges argued that it was legitimate for a trader to use whatever mark he wished. The *Samford* case was referred to in *Southern v How* (1656) Pop R. 144 where it is stated that Doderidge J. held that the action would lie, and it was this source that caused it to be later relied on. The report of *Southern* in Cro Jac 471 has the action being brought by the purchasers of cloth.

[16] Schechter, in his *The Historical Foundations of the Law Relating to Trade-Marks* (New York: Columbia, 1925), argues that *Southern v How* is a dubious authority for the modern law of passing off: "the sole contribution of that case was at best an irrelevant dictum of a reminiscent judge that he remembered an action by one clothier against another for the mis-use of the former's trade-mark". But the case was cited in a number of cases, as well as influential commentaries, and thus cannot be so readily ignored: *Blanchard v Hill* (1742) 2 Atk 484; *Crawshay v Thomson* (1842) 4 Man & G 357, 386 per Cresswell J; *Burgess v Burgess* (1853) 3 De G M & G 896, 902 per Knight Bruce LJ; *Hirst v Denham* (1872) LR 14 Eq Cas 542; E. Lloyd, "On the Law of Trade Marks No. I" (May 11, 1861) *Sol Jo & Rep* 486 (stating that the case "gives us all the elements of the law which governs this subject").

[17] J.H. Baker (*An Introduction to English Legal History* (4th ed. London: Butterworths, 2002) 459) also refers to two seventeenth century cases that are mentioned in Girdler's manuscripts in Cambridge University Library: one, *Waldron v Hill* (1659) in which a scythe-maker brought an action for use of his mark; the other, *W.E. v R.M.* (1670), relating to cheese-making.

actions by a London chemist relating to his lozenges: *Greenough v Dalmahoy* in 1769, where the plaintiff recovered £50 damages and *Greenough v Lambertson in 1777* in which he was awarded £20.[18] In the first reported case, *Singleton v Bolton*, the claimant failed in his action to prevent the defendant from using the designation "Dr Johnson's Yellow Ointment" for his medicine, but Lord Mansfield conceded that "if the defendant had sold a medicine of his own under the plaintiff's name or mark, that would be a fraud for which an action would lie".[19]

Two cases from the Common Law courts in the first decades of the nineteenth century are notable because they extended the action significantly beyond the circumstances in *Southern v How*. First, in *Sykes v Sykes*,[20] a King's Bench decision of 1824, the Court held that the action could be brought against a defendant manufacturer who sold products, bearing a mark generally associated with the plaintiffs, to retailers all of whom knew that the products they were buying were not made by the plaintiffs. The plaintiffs had stamped their goods, shot-belts and powder flasks, with the mark "Sykes Patent" and the defendant made an inferior version marked with the same terms in the same way. The retailers themselves sold the marked goods to customers "as and for the goods manufactured by the plaintiffs", and the plaintiffs' sales declined. The Court took the view that providing the fraudulently-marked goods to a third party so that the third party could sell them as the genuine goods, was "substantially the same thing" as selling the goods directly to those customers. Secondly, in *Blofield v Payne*,[21] the Common Law courts granted relief even where the claimant failed to prove damage to its reputation. The Court of King's Bench affirmed a decision finding in favour of the plaintiff manufacturer of metal hones for sharpening razors and against a defendant who sold its hones in plaintiff's packaging – envelopes resembling those of the plaintiff and containing the same words – even

---

[18] J. Oldham (ed.), *The Mansfield Manuscripts and the Growth of English Law in the Eighteenth Century* (Chapel Hill: University of North Carolina Press, 1992) Vol. I, pp. 741, 746 (transcriptions of Mansfield's notes and accounts of reports in the *London Chronicle*, December 14, 1769, and *Morning Chronicle*, December 23, 1777); J. Adams, "Intellectual Property Cases in Lord Mansfield's Court Notebooks" 7 *Jo Leg Hist* 18 (1987).

[19] 3 Douglas 293 (1783) ("Dr Johnson's Yellow Ointment"); V. Ludlow & H. Jenkins, *A Treatise on the Law of Trade-Marks and Trade-Names* 10 (London: W. Maxwell & Son, 1873) (describing *Singleton* as "[t]he first reported case of any real importance"). Although the designation had been used by his father prior to his death the plaintiff failed to establish that the father's rights passed to him.

[20] (1824) 3 B & C 541; 107 ER 834.

[21] (1833) 4 B & Ald 410; 110 ER 509.

though claimant had failed to prove damage by showing that defendant's hones were inferior.[22]

After some hesitation,[23] the Equitable action was developed in support of the extended Common Law action for deceit. The advantage of suing in Equity was the possibility of injunctive relief, a remedy not available in the Common Law courts. The first recorded case in which such relief was granted was *Day v Day*, in 1816, where a manufacturer of blacking was ordered to refrain from using labels in imitation of those employed by the plaintiff.[24] By 1841 Maule

---

[22] Other reported cases involving actions at Common Law are *Morison v Salmon* (1841) 2 Man & G 385; *Crawshay v Thompson* (1842) 4 Man & G 356; *Rodgers v Nowill* (1847) 5 CB 109; *Lawson v The Bank of London* (1856) 18 CB 84.

[23] The first trade-mark case in Chancery is often thought to have been *Blanchard v Hill* (1742) 2 Atk 484, in which Lord Hardwicke declined to grant an injunction preventing the defendant from using Blanchard's mark, a picture of the "Great Mogul", the emperor of Delhi, with the words "The Great Mogul" above, on playing cards. The report, in Atkyns' reports, is particularly unclear and the refusal of injunctive relief by Lord Hardwicke, a judge sympathetic to developing equitable principles to prevent fraud, has puzzled scholars. The case has now been subjected to a fascinating analysis by Norma Dawson ("English Trade Mark Law in the Eighteenth Century: *Blanchard v Hill* Revisited – Another 'Case of Monopolies'?" 24(2) *Journal of Legal History* 111, 125 (2003)), who not only places it in the context of the regulation of heraldry by the court of Chivalry, but also through a close analysis of the pleadings, explains why Lord Hardwicke found as he did, rather than adopting the Attorney General's arguments (which were based on *Southern v How*). These pleadings reveal that Blanchard based his title to the mark on the rules of the Company of the Makers of Playing Cards in the City of London, granted by Charles I on 22 October, 1628. Indeed, Blanchard had, prior to seeking the assistance of the Court of Equity, already sought the assistance of the Court of the Company, and the pleadings were interpreted by the defendant, and Lord Hardwicke, as an attempt to enforce the judgment of the Company court. Lord Hardwicke saw the Charter as an illegitimate monopoly, and as the claim was directly based on the rules and practices under the Charter he refused to grant injunctive relief.

[24] *See* R.H. Eden, *A Treatise on the Law of Injunctions* (London: Butterworth, 1821) p. 314. *Canham v Jones* (1813) 2 V & B 218 mentions an earlier case, *Sedon v Senate*, in which Grant MR enjoined the defendant having sold a medicine to the plaintiff, set up another [business] under a similar description, and in his advertisement adopted verses which had been attached to the "original medicine." Assuming that Grant MR's order followed the determination of the legal rights in *Seddon v Senate* (1810) 13 East 63, the action was based on contractual rights to use the recipe, the name of Dr Senate and the name PASTILLES MARTIALLES DE MONTPELLIER. In *Wilkie v m'Culloch* (1823) 2 Court of Session 369, an interdict was granted in favour of the claimant, Wilkie, who had invented a type of plough preventing the defendant from selling plough boards stamped WILKIE. J.E. Hovenden, *A General Treatise on the Principles and Practice by Which Courts of Equity Are Guided as to the Prevention or Remedial Correction of Fraud* (London: S. Sweet, 1825) Vol. II, p. 70, without citing authority, states that "Equity will restrain a fraudulent attempt by one man to invade another's property, or to appropriate the benefit of a valuable interest, in the nature of

J could state that applications "are frequently made to the Court of Chancery to enjoin one manufacturer from imitating the mark of another".[25] However, Equity only acted in such cases in aid of evident legal right:[26] any doubt over the right led the Chancery judges to require an action at law first.[27] Consequently, for the most part, Equity acted upon the same principles as the Common Law courts. Importantly, prior to 1860, the basis for the action was explicitly described in terms of fraud (not property).

Lord Langdale MR, who was Master of the Rolls from 1836 to 1851,[28] gave five decisions in which he explicitly based Equity's interference in support of the Common Law action by reference to the prevention of fraud. In the first case, *Knott v Morgan*,[29] he granted an injunction preventing a coach

---

goodwill, consisting in the reputation of his trade or production. Or, the encroaching party, by representing himself to be the same person, or his trade or production to be the same as that first established, combines imposition on the public with injury to the individual." J. Chitty, *The Law and Practice of the Law in All Its Principal Departments* (2d ed. London: Butterworth, 1834) 721 refers to another case of injunctive relief, *Gout v Aleopogla* (1833) 6 Bea 69 note, in which the defendant was enjoined from exporting to Turkey watches with the term "Pessendede" (which means "warranted") thereon "in imitation of the watches of the plaintiff, by which they had for very many years been distinguished, and by which he had obtained great credit in the Turkish trade".

See also, Hogg v Kirby (1803) 8 Ves 215 per Lord Eldon LC (restraining use of magazine title).

[25] *Morison v Salmon* (1841) 2 Man & G 385, 394.

[26] See "On Fraudulent Trade Marks" (1861) *Sol Jo & Rep* 820 reporting paper of John Morris given to the Metropolitan and Provincial Law Association, Worcester ("the Court of Chancery rarely ever grants an injunction until the legal right to the trade mark has been established by an action or issue at law"). Cf. Anon, Untitled Article, 17 *The Jurist* (April 23, 1853) 141 ("in cases of infringement of trade marks, Courts of Equity do not proceed on the doctrine of relief being only ancillary to legal title, but on the doctrine of prevention of fraud, quite independently of legal title").

[27] *Farina v Silverlock* (1855) 1 K & J 509, 517, 69 ER 560, 56; (1856) 6 De G M & G 214, 43 ER 1214 (on appeal, Lord Cranworth dissolving injunction with liberty to the plaintiff to bring an action at law); for injunction following success at law, see 4 K & J 650 (1858) 70 ER 270. *See also Pidding v How* (1836) 3 Sim 477; *Motley v Downman* (1837) 3 My & Cr 1, 14; *Perry v Truefitt* (1842) 6 Beav 66, 49 ER 749; *Spottiswoode v Clark* (1846) 1 Coop. T. Cott 254; *Welch v Knott* (1857) 4 K & J 747, 753, 70 ER 310; *Brook v Evans* (1860) *The Times*, July 12, 1860.

[28] At this stage, the Master of the Rolls was a first instance judge in Chancery. The appellate position of the Master of the Rolls dates from 1881. The position of Vice-Chancellor was created in 1814, and two further Vice-Chancellors were added from 1841. The Lord Chancellor operated primarily at an appellate level from 1851, when a court of appeal was established from the Master of the Rolls or the Vice-Chancellors, comprising two Lord Justices of Appeal or the Lord Chancellor or the three combined.

[29] (1836) 2 Keen 213. The decision was affirmed on appeal by Lord Chancellor Cottenham: *see* (1836) 2 Keen 213 at 220.

company from operating an omnibus service in imitation of the plaintiff's LONDON CONVEYANCE COMPANY. In the second, *Perry v Truefitt*,[30] he declined to grant a hairdresser who had for six years sold hair-grease as Perry's MEDICATED MEXICAN BALM relief against a rival hairdresser and perfumer selling hair-grease as TRUEFITT'S MEDICATED MEXICAN BALM. In the third, *Croft v Day*,[31] an injunction was granted to the executors of Day, a well-known maker of blacking, preventing the deceased's nephew from selling blacking under the same name, DAY AND MARTIN. In the fourth case, *Franks v Weaver*,[32] an injunction was granted preventing the defendant from selling medicine with various testimonials which referred favourably to the claimant's product, FRANKS' SPECIFIC SOLUTION OF COPAIBA, even though the defendant's product used the descriptive name CHEMICAL SOLUTION OF COPAIBA. The testimonials were "so craftily employed as to be calculated to produce, in the minds of ordinary readers, the impression that the . . . solution . . . sold by the defendant is . . . the . . . solution of the Plaintiff". Finally, in *Holloway v Holloway*,[33] Lord Landgale enjoined the defendant Henry Holloway from selling pills as H. HOLLOWAY'S PILLS in boxes and with labels similar to those of the claimant, Thomas Holloway, who had for some years previously sold pills as HOLLOWAY'S PILLS AND OINTMENTS.

In all these five cases, Lord Langdale grounded the intervention of Equity in fraud.[34] In *Knott*,[35] the question was whether "the defendant fraudulently imitated the title and insignia used by the Plaintiffs for the purpose of injuring them in their trade", and he found it had. In *Perry*, he indicated that he did not think "a man can acquire property merely in a name or mark"; but he had "no doubt that another person has not a right to use that name or mark for the purposes of deception, and in order to attract to himself that course of trade or that custom which, without that improper act, would have flowed to the person

---

[30] (1842) 6 Beav 66, 49 ER 749. Relief was refused because the claimant's sign itself misrepresented the product as Mexican.
[31] (1843) 7 Beav 84. The defendant, whose name was Day, had found a partner named Martin to help him justify using the name DAY AND MARTIN.
[32] (1847) 10 Beav 297.
[33] (1850) 13 Beav 209.
[34] In a sixth case, *Clark v Freeman* 11 Beav 112, 8 Law Magazine p. 236, where the defendant sold its goods as "Sir J. Clarke's Consumption Pills", and the defendant's actions were characterised as "disgraceful", Lord Langdale MR nevertheless rejected Clark's claim on the basis that the action required damage "to property by the fraudulent misuse of the name of another, by which his profits are diminished." If Clark had been "in the habit of manufacturing and selling pills" that property would have existed. However, he was not. Langdale said that the gist of Clark's complaint was thus "in the way of slander" and the Court had no jurisdiction "to stay the publication of a libel."
[35] (1836) 2 Keen 213, 219.

who first used or was alone in the habit of using the particular name or mark". In *Croft v Day*,[36] he explained again that "no man has a right to sell his own goods as the goods of another" for "it is perfectly manifest, that to do [so] . . . is to commit a fraud, a very gross fraud". Given that the defendant shared the name Day with the deceased, Lord Langdale reiterated that the basis of intervention was not "any exclusive right . . . to a particular name, or to a particular form of words" but a right "to be protected against fraud". In *Franks v Weaver*, the Master of the Rolls characterised the "crafty adaptation" of the testimonials as a kind of fraud, a concept he famously explained as being indefinable because "it is so multiform". And in *Holloway*, while noting that the defendant was perfectly entitled "to constitute himself a vendor of Holloway's pills", "he has no right to do so with such additions to his own name as to deceive the public and make them believe he is selling the Plaintiff's pills": the "law protects persons from fraudulent misrepresentations" and the evidence revealed "as clear . . . a fraud as I ever knew".

Lord Langdale MR's analysis was adopted by Page-Wood V-C, who from 1853 to 1868 was one of three Vice-Chancellors sitting in the Courts of Chancery,[37] and who over his career was to decide at least forty-five trade mark cases.[38] (The late 1850s and 1860s witnessed a surge in case law on trade marks, fuelled by important economic and social shifts.[39]) In *Collins Co. v*

---

[36] (1843) 7 Beav 84, 88.

[37] The two other Vice-Chancellors were Kindersley and Stuart.

[38] The numbers are derived from an examination of the cases digested in L.B. Sebastian, *A Digest of Cases of Trade Mark, Trade Name, Trade Secret, Goodwill etc* (London: Stevens & Sons, 1879). Page-Wood V-C was made Lord Chancellor in 1868 and thereafter was known as Lord Hatherley. In this capacity he presided in *Wotherspoon v Currie* (1871–72) L.R. 5 H.L. 508. For biographical background relating to Page-Wood, including an incomplete autobiographical sketch, see W.R. Stephens, *A Memoir of Lord Hatherley* (London: R. Bentley & Sons, 1883).

[39] In 1850 a writer in *The Jurist* attributed the rise in the importance of trade marks to "the progress of the useful arts", and predicted increased importance "as national and international intercourse extends the value of commercial and manufacturing character, and consequently, of the mark or sign by which it is denoted and guaranteed": Anon, "Trades Marks" (1850), 14(2) *The Jurist*, 223. There is plenty of evidence in the 1862 Select Committee that adoption of trade marks was, for many businesses, a relatively new phenomenon. One factor, prompting more widespread use of trade marks, was growth in advertising associated with the expansion of newspapers, and, in turn, the removal of newspaper duty from 1855. See T.R. Nevett, *Advertising in Britain: A History* (North Pomfret, Vt: David & Charles, 1982); Roy Church, "Advertising Consumer Goods in Nineteenth Century Britain: Re-interpretations" (2000) 53(4) *The Economic History Review* 621–45. On more general changes, in the US context, see Robert Bone, "Hunting Goodwill: A History of the Concept of Goodwill in Trademark Law" (2006) 86 *Boston University L. Rev.* 549, 576–9.

Brown,[40] for example, the claimant, an edge-tool manufacturer from Connecticut, brought an action against a Sheffield-based defendant complaining that the latter had been stamping its goods with the plaintiff's designation. The defendant demurred, arguing that the American claimant had no property right. Page Wood V-C held that it was "settled law that there is no property whatever in a trade mark" and that the right to prevent others using a mark was based on fraud "and any fraud may be redressed in the country in which it is committed, whatever may be the country of the person who has been defrauded". He therefore found for the claimant.[41]

Although Equitable jurisdiction, like its Common Law counterpart, was widely justified on the basis of preventing fraud, theoretical problems with this approach were raised by Lord Cottenham's 1839 decision in *Millington v Fox*.[42] This case was brought by a firm of steel-makers, which had been operating for over fifty years, and one of whose businesses was known as "The Crowley Works". The plaintiff sold steel bearing the signs CROWLEY, CROWLEY MILLINGTON and I.H. The defendant, sometime steel-makers and vendors, sold steel bearing these signs, with the addition of their own mark FOX BROTHERS, and the plaintiffs sought equitable relief in the form of injunction, account and delivery up. The defendants argued that the term CROWLEY was understood as synonymous with the word "faggot" and not as designating the manufacture of any particular trader. Equally, CROWLEY MILLINGTON, it was contended, had been used generally to refer to a kind of steel. Some witnesses gave evidence in support of these claims. (In modern trade-mark parlance, the argument was that the signs had become "generic", that is, they

---

[40] (1857) 3 K & J 423. See also *Edelsten v Vick* (1853) 11 Hare 78, 84 ("there must be an intention to deceive the public or this Court will not interfere"); *Dent v Turpin* (1861) 2 J & H 139, 144 ("each of the persons entitled to the mark has a right of action for the fraud, . . . a right which this Court would struggle to protect . . . by granting an injunction"); *Woolam v Ratcliff* (1863) 1 H & M 259 (refusing injunction in case of imitation of trade dress (tying up of silk), stating that the "Court is not to presume a fraudulent intention unnecessarily").

[41] A similar position was reached in the United States in *Taylor v Carpenter* (1844) 3 Story's Rep 450 (Cir. Ct. Mass.), and *Taylor v Carpenter* (1845) 2 Woodbury & Minot 1, 2 Sand. Ch. R. 603 (Court of Chancery of New York) (Court of Errors), but was not regarded by Francis Henry Upton as inconsistent with his treatment of trade marks as property. F. Upton, *A Treatise on the Law of Trade Marks* (Albany: Weare C. Little, 1860) 19–21. For a later discussion of the rights of foreign trade-mark owners in England, see "Foreign Trade-Marks in England" (April 12, 1884) *Solicitors Journal* 423–4, (April 19, 1884) *Solicitors Journal* 439–41.

[42] (1838) 3 Myl & Cr 338, 40 ER 956. In principle, as Lord Chancellor, Lord Cottenham's views carried more authority than those of Lord Langdale MR or the Vice-Chancellors (from whom the Lord Chancellor would hear appeals), but in *Millington* he, too, was sitting at first instance.

14 *Trademark law and theory*

no longer indicated a product from a particular source, but rather a genus of product.) The Lord Chancellor granted an injunction, explaining that although the defendant had not acted fraudulently,[43]

> there is no evidence to shew that the terms "Crowley" and "Crowley Millington" were merely technical terms, yet there is sufficient to shew that they were very generally used, in conversation at least, as descriptive of particular qualities of steel. In short, it does not appear to me that there was any fraudulent intention in the use of the marks. That circumstance, however, does not deprive the Plaintiffs of their right to the exclusive use of those names.

The decision in *Millington v Fox* that injunctive relief was available to a claimant even where there was no reason for thinking that there had been any fraudulent use by the defendant was a radical extension of the Equitable action from its Common Law origins. Such an extension raised difficult questions of principle, particularly about the relationship between Law and Equity,[44] and the status of the case as an authority was by no means secure.[45] In *Perry v Truefitt*,[46] for example, Lord Langdale MR seemed to cast doubt on *Millington* when he said he was "not aware that any previous case carried the principle to that extent" and in *Edelsten v Vick* Page-Wood V-C had stated that "there must be an intention to deceive the public, or this Court will not interfere".[47] Nevertheless, *Millington* was not over-ruled, and by the 1860s was regarded,

---

[43] (1838) 3 Myl & Cr 338, 352, 40 ER 956, 962.

[44] Subsequent case law reiterated the orthodoxy that Equity acted only in an ancillary role, and that relief was contingent on establishing a case at law; *Rodgers v Nowill* (1846) 6 Hare 325 (Wigram V-C). In *Welch v Knott* (1857) 4 K & J 747, 751, 70 ER 310, 312, Page-Wood V-C recognised the problem of reconciling these positions ("How far that doctrine is capable of being reconciled with cases at law in which the *scienter* has been held to be essential in order to enable the Plaintiff to recover, it is not material to consider . . .").

[45] *Crawshay v Thomson* (1842) 4 Man & G 357, 383 per Maule J (distinguishing *Millington*); *Dixon v Fawcus* (1861) 3 El & El 537 per Crompton J, at 546 ("That decision . . . has been questioned in subsequent cases . . ."), Hill J, at 547 ("*Millington v Fox* which, however much it may have been questioned, has not been overruled"); Anon, Untitled Article, 17 *The Jurist* (April 23, 1853) 141 ("the authority of that case [*Millington v Fox*] has been doubted"). But cf. Vice-Chancellor Bacon, writing two decades later in *Singer Manufacturing Co v Loog* (1879) 18 Ch D 395 at 407, stating that *Millington* "has never been questioned".

[46] (1842) 6 Beav 66, 73, 49 ER 749, 752. C.S. Drewry, "Points on the Law and Practice of Injunctions" (1846) 10(2) *The Jurist* 230, 231 (noting Lord Langdale MR's criticism of *Millington* and observing that "It will not, however, be forgotten, that that case was most fully argued, and that the judgment is one of the most careful of the many elaborate judgments delivered by the eminently cautious judge who pronounced it").

[47] (1853) 11 Hare 78, 84. No mention is made of *Millington* in that case.

at the very least for that reason, as binding authority in Chancery by Page-Wood V-C in *Welch v Knott*,[48] and even a court of Common law held it good law in *Dixon v Fawcus*.[49] Page-Wood V-C, in particular, thought the inconsistency between *Millington* and the idea that Equitable jurisdiction was based on fraud was more apparent than real, arguing on a number of occasions that even if a defendant was innocent when it commenced use of a particular mark, by the time Equity interfered to grant injunctive relief the defendant could no longer plead ignorance, and any continued use of a sign which misled consumers would thereafter amount to fraud. In other words, both Common Law and Equitable jurisdictions were based on fraud, but in the case of the Common Law, which was concerned with the status of past acts and the damage they might have caused, it was necessary to establish the defendant's knowledge and intent; whereas because Equity was concerned with future behaviour, the fact that the proceedings indicated that the continued use of the signs would be likely to deceive the public was sufficient to establish the requisite fraud.[50]

II. Towards trade marks as property

Understood as being based in the law of deceit, the rationale for the protection of signs used in trade derived from their communicative significance: were the signs intended to, and likely to, deceive?[51] Would their continued use be likely to deceive the "ordinary run of persons",[52] so that a court of Equity should step

---

[48] (1857) 4 K & J 747. 751, 70 ER 310, 312 ("In this Court the rule is clear as laid down in *Millington v Fox*"). The case was cited with approval in *Clement v Maddick* (1859) 5(1) Jur. 592 (Stuart V-C).

[49] *Dixon v Fawcus* (1861) 3 El & El 537, per Crompton J, at 546, that "That decision . . . has never been overruled; and is binding in this Court"; Hill J, at 547 ("*Millington v Fox* . . . has not been overruled, is a direct authority that the plaintiff was liable to a suit in equity").

[50] See *Leather Cloth v American Leather Cloth Co* (1863) 1 H & M 271. Sir John Romilly MR in *Cartier v Carlile* (1862) 31 Beav 292, 297 stating "I consider the rule at law and in equity to be the same" and awarded an account of profits against innocent defendant. It seems that Sir John Romilly's understanding that the rules were the same had a different basis, namely that in Equity an intention to deceive would be imputed from the determination that the defendant's mark was a colourable imitation of that of the claimant. Anon, Untitled Article, 8(2) *The Jurist* (October 18, 1862) 471. *See also Singer v Wilson* (1877) LR 3 HL 376, 400 per Lord Blackburn.

[51] "Fraud in law consists in knowingly asserting that which is false in fact, to the injury of another": *Crawshay v Thompson* (1842) 4 Man & G 357, 387 (Cresswell J).

[52] *Croft v Day* (1843) 7 Beav 84; *Shrimpton v Laight* (1854) 18 Beav 164 (Sir John Romilly MR, clarifying that the relevant persons were the public rather than manufacturers themselves); *Singer v Wilson* (1876) LR 2 Ch Div 434, 447 per Jessel MR (consider "ordinary English people" rather than "fools or idiots"), (1877) LR 3 HL

16   *Trademark law and theory*

in and prevent such frauds? However, in the 1860s, this communication-based model started to be challenged by a model of protection based upon ideas of property. That is, trade-mark law started to be reconceptualised as protecting a trade mark as an asset, rather than fixing on particular qualities of communicative act. The transformation occurred in the context of calls for legislative protection of traders, in developing case law, and in the increasing number of commentaries.

A.   *Legislative activity: the 1861 Bills, the Select Committee and the 1862 Act*

Calls for recognition of trade marks as property first emerged in the late 1850s as part of a more general campaign for legislation strengthening the rights of traders against piracy.[53] In 1862, a Bill (the so-called "Sheffield Bill", so named because it was drafted on behalf of the Sheffield Chamber of Commerce) was introduced into the House of Commons that proposed that trade marks be expressly recognised as "property". Clause 9 stated that a registered trade mark "shall be deemed the personal property of the proprietor, and shall be transmissible according to the ordinary rules of law affecting personal property".[54] The Government of the day considered that the issue of trade-mark protection generally warranted further investigation, and a Select

---

376, 390 (Lord Cairns referring to the need to consider the reactions not merely of experts on sewing machines but also "the case of the common workman and workwomen having very few and very limited ideas, and a very imperfect knowledge upon the subject of such machines"), 392 (Lord Cairns referring to "unwary purchasers"), 394 (Lord O'Hagan suggesting that the "multitudes who are ignorant and unwary . . . should be regarded in considering the interests of traders who may be injured by their mistakes"); *Singer v Loog* (1882) LR 8 HL 15 at 18 (Lord Selborne referring to misleading of the unwary rather than "a person who carefully and intelligently examined and studied" the trade mark).

[53]   The main lobbyists were the Chambers of Commerce, particularly those in the industrial centres of Sheffield and Birmingham. See e.g. "Trade Marks" (1858) *Journal of the Society of Arts* 595 (August 20, 1858) (reporting meeting of Birmingham Chamber of Commerce unanimously approving motion that improper use of trade marks was wrong and should be discouraged in every way by the Chamber); A. Ryland, "The Fraudulent Imitation of Trade Marks" (1859) *Transactions of the National Association for the Promotion of Social Science* 229, with responses at 269. *See* "On Fraudulent Trade Marks" (1861) *Sol Jo & Rep* 820 reporting paper of John Morris given to the Metropolitan and Provincial Law Association, Worcester; and "The Registration of Trade Marks" (1861) *Sol Jo & Rep* 839 reporting paper by Arthur Ryland to the same Association.

[54]   A Bill to Amend the law relating to the counterfeiting or fraudulent use or appropriation of trade marks, and to secure to the proprietors of trade marks in certain cases the benefit of international protection, Bill No 17 (February 18, 1862), Parliamentary Papers, Bills (Public) Vol. 5

Committee was convened.⁵⁵ The Select Committee, comprising "lawyers and mercantile men of great experience and representing different interests",⁵⁶ met and heard evidence from a wide range of traders, merchants, bureaucrats, and lawyers.

The question whether trade marks should be regarded as property was a key issue in the Select Committee investigation. The frequently expressed concern with recognising trade marks as property was not (as might be expected) consequences in terms of the potential breadth of the rights, but rather related to the issue of transferability. If trade marks were property, it was assumed (indeed, the Sheffield Bill was explicit) that the trade mark would be transferable.

Many of those who gave evidence were concerned about this notion. In particular, it was objected that a law that purported to be designed to suppress fraudulent practices would be transformed into one that would facilitate such practices. This was because most witnesses understood a trade mark as a sign or emblem that goods came from a particular trade source (or place): if the rights in the sign associated with trader A could be transferred "as personal property" to another trader, trader B, members of the public who continued to rely on the mark as an indication that the goods came from the former owner (A) would be induced into buying the goods of B. For most of those who gave evidence to the Committee, such action was not merely likely to give rise to disappointment on the part of the public, but to truly amount to a fraud on them.⁵⁷ As John Dillon (of the London dealers in female attire, Morrison, Dillon & Co) explained, a mark implied "a certain fact, that it is an established manufacture by a certain man or firm, at a certain place. If you alter the place

---

⁵⁵ Hansard (1862) 165 *Parliamentary Debates* 1231 (March 7, 1862), 1280 (March 10, 1862), 1489 (March 13, 1862).

⁵⁶ Poland, H.B. (1862), *The Merchandise Marks Act 1862*, London: J. Crockford, p. 7, chaired by John Arthur Roebuck, MP for Sheffield (d. 1879), the Committee comprised three barristers (Selwyn, Hugh Cairns and Sir Francis Goldsmid, a lawyer – indeed the first Jewish barrister and MP for Reading (d. 1878)); in England two members of the government (Milner Gibson, President of the Board of Trade, and Sir William Atherton, the Attorney General); manufacturers (Sir Francis Crossley, a carpet manufacturer and MP for Halifax (d. 1872, MP for Halifax from 1852, liberal); Alderman William Taylor Copeland, Alderman in Bishopsgate, a pottery manufacturer and MP for Stoke (d. 1868); Edmund Potter, a calico printer and MP for Carlisle (d. 1883); George Moffatt, a tea-broker and MP for Dartmouth, Ashburton, Honiton and Southampton (1810–78; 1845–52, Dartmouth; 1852–9, Ashburton; 1860–5 Honiton; 1865–8, Southampton, a liberal); Humfrey Crum Ewing, MP for Paisley (1802–87, elected 1857, a radical).

⁵⁷ Select Committee, Q. 2280 (Dillon: "the trade mark ought to be a mark only, and not a property which a man can sell and dispose of"); Q. 2435 (Morley: "I confess that I rather tremble at the consequences of universally making a property out of those miserable marks, as some of them are"); Q. 2657 (Travers Smith); Q. 2773 (Hindmarch: "unnecessary to begin with and I think it is fraught with mischief").

or the person, that destroys the mark. I have heard of people attempting to sell their trade marks, but I should as soon think of a soldier selling his medal."[58] Likewise, seeing trade marks as indicators of origin from which purchasers could infer quality, solicitor Joseph Travers Smith argued that transferability "might be productive of very considerable danger" because "the trade mark ceases to be any guarantee of origin": "I do not say that in every case it must be so; but that if a trade mark were made personal property, it would be open to serious risk." In his view it would be immoral for the Legislature to render trade marks vendible as property, since this would "allow the perpetration of a fraud with a statutory sanction".[59]

While it was argued by the proponents of the Bill that in fact the public could be equally "defrauded" if the original trader altered the quality of the goods (and noone was suggesting that a trader who used a mark would be bound thereafter to retain exactly the same quality standards or systems of production), the Committee was considerably more nervous about the prospect of such "misrepresentations" being carried out by transferees. The argument that all that a trade mark indicated was that the sign had been placed on the goods with the agreement of whoever happened to be the current legal owner of the trade mark rights made sense to very few.[60]

Following its deliberations the Committee decided not to press the Sheffield Bill,[61] but to back the Government's suggested alternative which created new criminal offences for uses of misdescriptions in trade with intent to defraud, and specifically referred to misuse of trade marks, which were defined broadly.[62] The Act was, at least to contemporary thinkers, consistent with a view of trade-mark protection as a communication-based wrong, rather than a proprietary offence. A proprietary wrong pointed conventionally to civil relief rather than criminal:[63] but "there is no real distinction between using the

---

[58] Select Committee, Q. 2282.
[59] Select Committee, Q. 2655, 2665, 2667.
[60] Ludlow & Jenkyns, *A Treatise on the Law of Trade-Marks and Trade-Names* 2 (London: W. Maxwell & Son, 1873) ("A trade-mark . . . may signify no more than this . . . that the article to which it is affixed has passed into the market through the hands of the person entitled to use the mark . . .").
[61] Hansard (1862) 167 *Parliamentary Debates* 1418 (July 4, 1862).
[62] Merchandize Marks Act 1862, s. 1: "any Name, Signature, Word, Letter, Device, Emblem, Figure, Sign, Seal, Stamp, Diagram, Label, Ticket or other Mark of any other Description lawfully used by any person to denote any chattel, to be the Manufacture, Workmanship, Production or Merchandise of such Person".
[63] John Morris, in a paper delivered to the Metropolitan and Provincial Law Association, Worcester: "A trademark is a species of private property and there certainly seems no more reason why that should be protected by the criminal law than copyright, patents or designs". (1861) *Sol Jo & Rep* 820 (October 26, 1861).

name of another in a bill of exchange with the intention to defraud, and using the trade-mark of another for a similar purpose; if there is any distinction it is merely one of degree – both offences come under the same categories – they are forgeries".[64]

B. *Internationalisation*

A second arena in which the description of trade marks as "property" was becoming increasingly common was in governmental circles involved in claiming protection for British trade marks abroad. From as early as 1858, British traders had sought the assistance of the government in gaining some sort of international recognition of their rights. The primary concern was preventing use of British trade marks abroad, especially in Germany. In a document submitted by various representatives of the Sheffield steel goods trade to the Secretary of State for the Foreign Office, the Earl of Malmesbury, the petitioners expressed the desire of securing for themselves and successors the honourable reputation and just rewards for their efforts, claiming that *"the law of England regards and defends [trade marks] as private property"*.[65] The Foreign Office responded by conducting a detailed inquiry into the laws of foreign states through the network of consuls and embassies. The resulting picture was uneven, with most laws seemingly based in ideas of forgery, counterfeiting and deceit. The terms on which such protection was made available was unclear, and the Foreign Office decided to negotiate protection of British traders through bilateral treaties, following the model of the existing copyright bilaterals.[66] In this process, the language of property became more and more prevalent, even featuring in a number of bilateral treaties.[67] The Austrian Treaty of 16 December 1865, for example, declared that "[t]he subjects of one of the Two High Contracting parties shall, in the dominions of the other, enjoy the same protection as native subjects in regard to the rights of property in trade marks and other distinctive marks",[68] while the US Treaty 1877 gave

---

[64] Anon, Untitled, 8(2) *The Jurist* (October 18, 1862) 471, 472.

[65] *Robert Jackson, Hobson Smith, William Matthews to Earl of Malmesbury*, 13 May 1858, NA: FO 83/211.

[66] See Treaty Stipulations between Great Britain and Foreign Powers on the Subject of Trade Marks (1872) (C.633) 54 *Parliamentary Papers* 673.

[67] Other treaties avoided such language. For example, the treaty with Russia, dated 11 July 1871, stated that "the offering for sale or the placing in circulation of goods bearing counterfeit British or Russian Trade marks, wherever fabricated, shall be considered as a fraudulent operation, prohibited within the territory of the two states . . .". See C.412 (1871) 72 Parliamentary Papers 393.

[68] Treaty Stipulations between Great Britain and Foreign Powers on the Subject of Trade Marks (1872) (C.633) 54 *Parliamentary Papers* 673, at 675. See also Treaty of Commerce and Navigation between Her Majesty and the King of the Belgians,

20   *Trademark law and theory*

subjects and citizens of the US the same rights as British citizens "in everything relating to property in trade marks and trade labels".[69]

C. Judicial activity
While the attempt to obtain legislative recognition for trade marks as property had (temporarily) failed, Richard Bethell, who from 1861 was Lord Chancellor Westbury, elaborated a theory of trade marks as property in a series of cases beginning with *Edelsten v Edelsten*.[70] In so doing, he expressly rejected the analysis of Lord Langdale MR and Page-Wood V-C, and provided an explanation for *Millington v Fox*.[71]

In *Edelsten v Edelsten*,[72] the plaintiff was a manufacturer of wire, and from 1852 adoped the device of an anchor as his trade mark, which he stamped upon the metal labels ("tallies") attached to each bundle of wire. The claimant's wire thus came to be known as "Anchor Brand Wire". Suspecting that the defendant, a Birmingham firm (coincidentally, it seems, called Edelsten Williams and Edelsten) was selling wire as "Anchor Brand Wire", the plaintiff asked one of his travellers to order some such wire from the defendants. By so doing it became clear that the defendants were using a mark comprising a crown and an anchor, and the claimant brought an action for an

---

signed at London, July 23, 1862, Art 16, in ibid. at 676 ("all that relates to property in trade marks"); Treaty of Commerce between Her Majesty and the Emperor of France, Paris, 23 January 1860, Article XX in ibid at 679 ("the rights of property in trademarks"); Declaration between Great Britain and Denmark for the Protection of Trade Marks, Copenhagen, November 28, 1879 ("everything relating to property in trademarks and trade-labels"); Declaration between G.B. and Spain for Protection of Trade Marks, London, December 1875 (1876) 84 *Parliamentary Papers* 105 ("everything relating to property in manufacturing or Trade Marks").

[69]   (1878) (C.1901) 80 *Parliamentary Papers* 439. The first US treatise, Francis Upton's *A Treatise on the Law of Trade Marks* (1860) declared that the "right of property in trade marks has now become firmly established".

[70]   Westbury gave decisions in *Edelsten* v *Edelsten* (1863) 1 De G J & S 185; *Hall v Barrows* (1863) 4 De G J & S 150; *M'Andrew v Basset* (1864) 4 De G J & S 380, as well as in the House of Lords in *Leather Cloth* and *Wotherspoon v Currie* (1871–2) L.R. 5 H.L. 508.

[71]   Other cases hinting at proprietary analysis include *Clement v Maddick* (1859) 5(1) Jur. 592 (Stuart V-C) (granting injunction in favour of proprietor of BELL'S LIFE IN LONDON against defendants who were selling magazine as THE PENNY BELL'S LIFE magazine, stating that "he considered this application in the light of one to support a right of property"); *Cartier v Carlile* (1862) 31 Beav 292, 298, per Sir John Romilly MR (Where the defendant's mark is found to be a colourable imitation of the claimant's trade mark, "there must be imputed to a person imitating a trade mark a desire to gain the advantages which are attached to the use of that particular trade mark, and which is the private property of another person").

[72]   (1863) 1 De G J & S 185, 199.

injunction and an account of profits. The defendant sought to argue that an anchor was a common mark, and that the crown and anchor sign was readily differentiable from it. Lord Westbury LC took the opportunity provided to state the law of trade marks in proprietary terms: "The questions are whether the Plaintiff had property in the trade mark . . . and, if so, whether the mark of the Defendants is substantially the same as the trade mark of the Plaintiff, and therefore an invasion of his property". He continued by observing that while "[a]t law the proper remedy is by action on the case for deceit: and proof of fraud on the part of the Defendant is of the essence of the action" but that the Court of Equity "will act on the principle of protecting property alone, and it is not necessary for the injunction to prove fraud in the Defendant". Having stated these principles, Lord Westbury LC found that the defendant knew of the claimant's mark and had deliberately adopted an essential part of it for use in relation to the defendant's wire,[73] and this was "piracy" of the plaintiff's trade mark.

Westbury reiterated his treatment of trade marks as property in *Hall v Barrows,* a case which arose from dissolution of a partnership. The partnership deed had specified that when one partner died, the other could purchase all the stock, and this was defined to include "property belonging to the business". The Master of the Rolls, Sir John Romilly, had ordered a sale,[74] but on appeal Lord Chancellor Westbury considered the scope of any valuation, in particular whether it was to include the trade mark BBH surrounded by a crown. He said that *Millington* indicated "the principle that the jurisdiction of the Court in the protection of trade marks rests upon property, and that fraud in the Defendant is not necessary for the exercise of that jurisdiction . . .".[75] The Lord Chancellor then reviewed the history of the trade mark in question, namely the letters BBH surrounded by a crown. BBH had stood for Bradley, Barrows and Hall, but had long since stopped indicating that goods were manufactured by that partnership – it had been used by Hall and Barrows since 1847, and had, according to the evidence, only ever been understood as a "brand of quality". According to Westbury the trade mark "is a valuable property of the partnership as an addition to the Bloomfield Works and may be properly sold with the works, and therefore properly included as a distinct subject of value in the valuation of the surviving partner". Westbury explained statements that there is no property in a trade mark, as merely indicating that "there can be no right to the exclusive ownership of any symbols or marks universally in the abstract". But he reiterated that there could be property in

---

[73] (1863) 1 De G J & S 185, 201–2. These findings might appear to render the rest of Lord Westbury LC's judgment obiter.
[74] 11 WR 525; (1863) 32 LJ Ch 548.
[75] (1863) 4 De G J & S 150, 156.

the sense that "a trade mark consists in the exclusive right to the use of some name or symbol as applied to a particular manufacturer or vendible commodity": "such exclusive right is property". Imposition on the public – the communicative aspect of trade marks – was "the test of the invasion by the Defendant of the Plaintiff's right of property . . . but the true ground of this Court's jurisdiction is property . . .".

On the same day as Westbury decided *Hall v Barrows*, he also decided the appeal from Page-Wood V-C's decision of July 1863 in *Leather Cloth Co v American Leather Cloth*.[76] However, in contrast with *Hall*, this decision was further appealed to the House of Lords, which thus had its first opportunity to explain the law of trade marks, and to indicate whether it preferred Lord Westbury's proprietary analysis to that of Page-Wood V-C.[77] Curiously, Lord Westbury himself was one of the three-judge tribunal.

In this case, the claimant claimed protection of the court for a mark comprising a circle including the words "Crockett International Leather Cloth Co. Excelsior. Tanned leather cloth, patented Jan 24 1856. JR & CP CROCKETT & Co Manufacturers, Newark NJ USA West Ham England". Crockett had invented "leather cloth" and as of 1855 manufactured the product both in New Jersey and in West Ham, through a company called The Crockett International Leather Cloth Co. Although one of Crockett's partners had developed a patent for tanning leather cloth, which was assigned to the Company, this had been allowed to expire. In 1857, the Crockett Company sold all its plant and property in West Ham to the plaintiff, including its goodwill and the right of using the trade mark. Soon after, two of Crockett's former agents established a competing "leather cloth" business in the Old Kent Road, and on the dissolution of this, the defendant manufactured leather cloth from the same premises. Its device was a semi circle including the words "American Leather Cloth Company. Superior, Leather Cloth Manufactured by their Manager Late with JR & CP Crockett 12 Yds Old Kent Road, London." Wegelin, the defendant's manager, had been employed by Crockett for six months in 1856–7. The claimant brought an action seeking injunctive relief. Three matters called for decision: whether the claimant could rely on rights in the trade marks developed by Crockett; whether the plaintiff's and defendant's marks were sufficiently similar to raise a question of infringement; and whether the plaintiff was disentitled to relief on the basis that its marks referred to patents which had lapsed.

At first instance, Page-Wood VC held for the claimant. First, he rejected the view that it was not possible to transfer the right to use the trade mark. The

---

[76] 1 H & M 271 (Page Wood V-C).
[77] *Leather Cloth v American Leather Cloth Co* (1865) 11 HLC 523.

plaintiff was the only person in England using the mark to attract themselves customers. The question was not one of property but whether the act of the defendant is such as to hold out his goods as the goods of the plaintiff.[78] He insisted that even in cases where the defendant was innocent "the ground of the interference is still fraud" because if the defendant continues to do the act, although previously done innocently, he will be committing a fraud. In this case, the plaintiff "having purchased the business, are perfectly entitled to use the trade mark formerly used by their vendors". Second, the Vice-Chancellor compared the signs, holding in various respects that they were similar, particularly as regards the defendant's reference to Crockett, which he held was unjustified on the facts. Thirdly, he examined whether the plaintiff had disentitled himself to relief for lack of good faith in his reference to the patent. He thought it would have been better had this not been used on untanned leather, but that in such cases no one would be deceived.

On appeal,[79] Lord Westbury reversed, finding for the defendant, primarily because in his view the plaintiff had made significant misrepresentations to the public. However, before discussing these objections to the plaintiff's claim, Lord Westbury was quick to correct the "uncertainty and want of precision . . . as to the ground on which a Court of Equity interferes to protect the enjoyment of a trade mark, and also on the question whether the right to use a trade mark admits of being sold and transferred by one man to another". In particular, Lord Westbury contradicted existing analysis of trade mark protection as based on fraud rather than property (which he attributed to both Lord Langdale MR and Page-Wood V-C). While Westbury admitted that at law the remedy "for the piracy of a trade mark" was deceit, a remedy "founded on fraud", in Equity the remedy was based not on fraud but on property. This was indicated by two facts: first, because the remedy was not available for fraud alone but required "some pecuniary loss or damage",[80] and, secondly, because the remedy was available even where there was no "fraud or imposition practised by the Defendant at all".[81] While it was necessary for the defendant to use the mark on the same goods as the plaintiff so that it may be mistaken in the market for the plaintiff's, "imposition on the public, becomes the test of property in the trade marks having been invaded and injured, and not the ground on which the Court rests its jurisdiction". The "exclusive right . . . to use any particular mark or symbol" in "connection with the sale of some commodity" was property, and "the act of the

---

[78] (1863) 1 H & M 271, 286.
[79] (1863) 4 De G J & S 136.
[80] Citing *Clark v Freeman* 11 Beav 112.
[81] Citing *Millington v Fox* and *Welch v Knott*.

Defendant is a violation of such right of property, corresponding with the piracy of copyright or the infringement of the patent. I cannot therefore assent to the dictum that there is no property in a trade mark."

Having set the record straight as to the jurisdictional basis and nature of trade-mark protection, Lord Westbury LC held that the plaintiff's mark contained five misrepresentations,[82] the most significant of which were that the goods were tanned and patented. He rejected Page-Wood VC's analysis that the representation as to tanning in relation to untanned goods would not deceive anyone, taking the view that a person should be responsible for even those falsehoods which were "so gross and palpable" that noone would be deceived by them. Given all the misrepresentations, it could not be said that the plaintiff had "clean hands" and relief was refused.

On appeal,[83] the (three-judge) House of Lords affirmed Westbury LC's decision, Lord Cranworth and Lord Kingsdown both employing the language of property. Lord Cranworth acknowledged Lord Westbury's concern that the law of trade marks "has not been well-defined, and has not been made to rest on any satisfactory principles", and importantly affirmed the use of the language of property. Lord Cranworth stated that if the word property was aptly used in relation to copyright, he could see no reason for objecting to the use of the term in relation to trade marks. Moreover, he stated that the right to a trade mark "may, in general, treating it as property or as an accessory to property, be sold and transferred upon a sale and transfer of the manufactory of the goods on which the mark has been used to be affixed, and may be lawfully used by the purchaser".[84] While thus seemingly giving his imprimatur to the conception of trade marks as property, he in fact chose to affirm Westbury LC's decision on a different basis from that of the Lord Chancellor: namely that the plaintiff and defendant's marks were not so similar as "to deceive a purchaser using ordinary caution":[85] "to any one at all acquainted with the Plaintiff's trade mark in this case, I can hardly think that even on the

---

[82] Namely, that the articles were the goods of Crockett International; that they had been made by JR & CP Crockett; that they were tanned leather cloth; that the articles were patented; and that they were made in the USA or in West Ham.

[83] (1865) 11 HLC 523. Lord Westbury also gave a speech, affirming his own decision, but agreeing with his colleagues specifically on the point that the defendant's label was not so similar as to amount to infringement of the plaintiff's label. The claimant later succeeded on the basis of contract: *The Leather Cloth Co v Lorsont*, *The Times*, November 13, 1869, p. 11 b (James V-C).

[84] (1865) 11 HLC 523, 534.

[85] *Cf. Glenny v Smith* (1865) 2 Dr & Sm 476, 481 per Kindersley V-C (test is whether the "unwary, the heedless, the incautious portion of the public would be likely to be misled"). Lord Cranworth, as Lord Chancellor, reiterated the "ordinary purchaser acting with ordinary caution" test in *Seixo v Provezende* (1866) LR 1 Ch Apps 192, 196.

most cursory glance there could be any deception." One was a circle, the other semi-circular; both contained representations of eagles, but each very different from the other; both contained the name and address of the manufacturers, but these were different. Lord Kingsdown agreed that the appeal should be dismissed on the ground that the defendant's trade mark did not resemble the plaintiff's closely enough as to be calculated to deceive incautious purchasers and also on the basis that the plaintiff's mark contained misstatements of material facts which were calculated to deceive the public. Although Lord Kingsdown provided no lengthy exegesis on the conceptual nature of trade marks, he acknowledged in passing that "a man may have property in a trade mark, in the sense of having a right to exclude any other trader from the use of it in selling the same description of goods". Given that the third member of the Lords was Lord Westbury LC himself, the overall tenor of *Leather Cloth* amounted to a ringing endorsement of trade marks as property.

D. *Responses of commentators*

Even before Lord Westbury's judicial intervention, proprietary analysis of trade marks had gained support amongst commentators. In one of the earliest systematic commentaries on trade marks serialised in the *Solicitors Journal and Reporter* for 1861–2, Edward Lloyd observed that the fraud model of trade mark protection was still being held fast to by the courts. He explained that

> the constant leaning of the Court of Equity has been to protect the right to use a trade mark on the ground not of the existence of any property in a mark or name; for it holds that any manufacturer has a right to use whatever mark or name he pleases to distinguish his manufacture, but with this limitation, he must not use such a distinctive mark as will induce a purchaser to buy his article on the supposition that it is the manufacture of another man.[86]

In contrast with the judiciary's "anxiety to guard against anything like a recognition of property in a trade-mark",[87] Lloyd himself advocated recognition that the equitable action was based on protection of some kind of "quasi-property".[88] Lloyd explained that while there is no property in a mark by itself,

---

[86] E. Lloyd, "On the Law of Trade Marks No. IX" (January 4, 1862) *Sol Jo & Rep* 153.

[87] E. Lloyd, "On the Law of Trade Marks No. V" (July 6, 1861) *Sol Jo & Rep* 613 ("no one who reads their decisions will fail to be struck by a species of timidity in their expressions, by an anxiety to guard against anything like a recognition of property in a trade-mark").

[88] Lloyd's opinions were influenced by US case law, which he describes in E.

when a mark is associated with a trader's goods a "compound property" emerges.[89] After examining *Millington v Fox,* he concluded that

> There is therefore sufficient authority for saying that in consideration of the court of equity the right of property in a trade-mark is something more direct and specific than it can be deemed to be at law. At law it consists of a right to be protected against fraud; in equity it challenges some of the peculiar characteristics of property; but as it has been laid down more than once that a person cannot acquire property in a mere name, it must be deemed a species of property qualified rather than absolute; still sufficiently precise to enable the subject to obtain a substantial protection.[90]

After 1863 most commentators were quick to embrace Lord Westbury LC's theory of trade marks as property. Writing in 1864, the *Solicitors' Journal* welcomed Lord Westbury's contribution to the jurisprudence relating to trade marks, asserting that "under his authority, the extent of the jurisdiction of courts of equity in granting injunctions has been defined in a broad and philosophical manner".[91] The journal acknowledged that the decision in *Millington* "can only be explained on the principle that the plaintiffs had an exclusive right of property in the name which has been violated",[92] and concluded that with Lord Westbury's decisions "the doctrine that the exclusive use of a trade name or mark in connexion with a particular article of manufacture is rightly classed under the head of 'property' [was] thus established by the highest authority".

Two other commentators in the 1860s, E.M. Underdown and Wybrow Robertson, also reiterated the proprietary conception of trade marks. In a paper to the Royal Society of Arts in 1866,[93] Underdown, a barrister, stated that

> all lawyers knew how that principle had been fought through every court – how gravely one decision after another had been given that there was no property in such things – and how the House of Lords had, in the case of the *Leather Cloth Company,*

Lloyd, "On the Law of Trade Marks No. V" (July 6, 1861) *Sol Jo & Rep* 613. In particular, he describes *Partridge v Menk,* 2 Sand Ch 622, where he says it was held that "the right of a trader in the use of his mark is regarded as a species of goodwill which he acquires in his business (which is undoubtedly a proprietary right)". The first trademark treatise written in the United States, Francis Henry Upton's *A Treatise on the Law of Trade Marks* (Albany: Weare C. Little, 1860), refers to rights in relation to trade marks as property (e.g. pp. 3, 10, 13, 14), albeit one with "peculiar character" (p. 4).

[89] E. Lloyd, "On the Law of Trade Marks" (May 11, 1861) *Sol Jo & Rep* 486.
[90] E. Lloyd, "On the Law of Trade Marks" (May 11, 1861) *Sol Jo & Rep* 486.
[91] "Trade Names and Marks" (1864) *Sol Jo & Rep* 175, 177.
[92] (1864) *Sol Jo & Rep* 176.
[93] E.M. Underdown, "On the Piracy of Trade Marks" (1866) 14 *Journal of Society of Arts* 370.

decided that there was such a distinct property in trade marks. If there was such a property established, the common law of England would come to protect it.

Commenting on Underdown's paper,[94] the patent lawyer, Thomas Webster, approving of the reinterpretation of the action as based on property, indicated that the next essential step was legislative action to reinforce the interest thus recognised through a register.[95] Three years later, in 1869, Wybrow Robertson, gave a further paper on trade marks to the Society,[96] observing that

> A most important point for notice is that a trade mark is property. Since 1863, it has been clearly laid down . . . that the right to a trade mark is a right to the exclusive use of it; that it is, therefore, property and will be protected by the court as if it were property . . [97]

Finally, in the early 1870s, two textbooks appeared on the law of trade marks, both recognising that trade marks were property. In the first, Ludlow and Jenkins[98] described a trade mark as a "*jus in rem*" because, even though it has no "material subject", it imposes duties on all men.[99] They rejected the "fraud" analysis as unhelpful because the fraud is on the public not the trader. In the second text, Frank Mantel Adams observed that "there can be no doubt at the present day that the true ground for interference of a court of equity for the

---

[94] In a similar vein, another barrister, Edward Daniel QC, 14 *Journal of Society of Arts* 370, 377 stated that "Lord Cottenham . . . established as a principle of law that there was property in trade-marks, when he held that an individual who innocently and unknowingly adopted a mark which belonged to another could not continue to use it. That principle had been followed up by Lord Westbury, when he held that if a man had a particular emblem by which he denoted the results of his own labour, the law protected him in the exclusive use of that emblem, and to that extent it became a property."

[95] Thomas Webster, *Journal of Society of Arts*, **14**, 370, 375: "It was truly stated that this was a question of property . . . Property was an empty name unless it was protected by law . . . the great objects to be sought were a proper record of the property in trade marks and proper remedies in cases of infraction . . . of that property."

[96] "On Trade Marks" (1869) *Journal of Society of Arts* 414.

[97] Note the qualification: "But though a trade mark is undoubtedly property, it is not so for all purposes; for a proprietor of a trade mark cannot prevent another person from using the same mark for other description of goods; and, even when applied to the same goods, he must show in an action at law that there has been a false representation, calculated to mislead the public."

[98] H. Ludlow & H. Jenkins, *A Treatise on the Law of Trade-Marks and Trade-Names* (London: W. Maxwell & Son, 1873) 3–6.

[99] The authors added that one cannot assume "anything as to the general transferableness of a trade mark or as to the remedy of a person whose right is infringed" from this designation: ibid. p. 5.

protection of a trade mark is, with respect to the plaintiff, property and the protection of property".[100]

E. Legislative activity: the 1875 Act

The property analysis seemed to have come to be accepted by the late 1860s, and was reinforced by the passage of the 1875 Act which established a registration system for trade marks, and made the existence of such registration equivalent to public use.[101] It is important to note that, in contrast with later trade-marks Acts, this one did not purport to establish a self-contained or exhaustive scheme. Rather, the 1875 Act built upon the existing common law system – the Act led to a presumption of public use, but the consequences of such public use for other traders remained governed wholly by the judicially-developed law of trade marks.[102] In contrast with the 1862 Sheffield Bill, this instrument did not expressly declare registered trade marks to be "personal property" and while it permitted assignments of trade marks, section 2 of the Act limited transmissibility of a registered mark "only in connexion with the goodwill of the business concerned in such particular goods or classes of goods".

While the 1875 Act did not declare trade marks to be property, it did introduce proprietary language: the registrant became the registered proprietor of the trade mark, the relationship being described in the language of "title".[103] Consequently, it was widely understood as reinforcing the reconceptualisation (developed particularly by Lord Westbury) of trade marks as property.[104]

---

[100] F.M. Adams, *A Treatise on the Law of Trade Marks* (London: 1874) 13. But Adams was quick to qualify this, adding that such "property is not the ownership of the symbols which constitute the trade mark, but that which is the result of the exclusive right to apply them to a particular class of goods". Ibid at p. 16.

[101] An Act to Establish a Register of Trade Marks (1875) 38 & 39 Vict. c. 91.

[102] The rights of owners of registered trade marks were first defined by statute in the Trade Marks Act 1905.

[103] Trade Mark Registration Act 1875, ss. 2 and 3.

[104] Some commentators saw judicial recognition of trade marks as property as a prerequisite for the legislative enactment of a registration system. Consequently, it was said that one of the reasons why a registration system could not be adopted in 1862 was that too much uncertainty hung over the legal status of trade marks. See, for example, the comments of Dundas Gardiner in (1866) *Journal of Society of Arts* at 376 that he "thought he could understand how it was that the registration of trade marks had been so long postponed. He believed it was owing to the fact that up to a recent period the law courts were divided in opinion as to whether or not there was any property in them . . .". Certainly, judicial recognition buttressed the claim for registration. In a similar vein, Thomas Webster argued that judicial recognition that trade marks were property was a first step, and that legislative action was required to establish a "proper record of the property in trade marks and proper remedies in cases of infraction . . . of that property".

Moreover, the effect of the introduction of the bureaucratic structure was to cement the previously recognised status of trade marks as property (as well as to alter certain of the dynamics of that property).[105] Indeed, the use of the registration system gave a sense of closure and certainty to the subject matter of protection: being defined through the representations required by the Registry, trade marks appeared as visualised forms, capable of allocation as "objects" to particular owners. Trade marks evolved from communications to things.[106]

The Times welcomed the new Registration Act in the language of property, referring to the great assistance it would be in alleviating "the enormous costs incurred by owners of trade-marks in their attempts *to defend their property*."[107] Similarly, J. Seymour Salaman, solicitor to the Trade Mark Protection Society, which had lobbied for the Act, claimed that "[r]egistration gives a parliamentary property in a trade mark",[108] "a thoroughly valuable right and property not again liable to be interfered with . . .". Edward Morton Daniel, in his commentary on the 1875 Act, stated that the 1862 and 1875 Acts had "established in the most solemn manner the right of property of this description". He elaborated, "the species of property possessed by a man in the signs or means by which he indicates to the public that certain goods are sold with any reputation he may have acquired pledged to them, has become in many cases of great importance, and has received full recognition in the Courts of Justice and in Parliament".[109]

---

[105] Lloyd predicted in 1862 that registration would consolidate and affirm the status of trade marks as property: "By registration I have no doubt many frauds that are now attempted would be restrained, and the adoption of such a system would afford a reasonable ground for giving new legal forms of protection to a species of property which would then be recognised and defined by a specific enactment" E. Lloyd, *Solicitors Journal and Reporter*, January 4, 1862, p. 154. *See also Bow v Hart* [1905] KB 592, 598 (per Vaughan Williams LJ) (the 1883 Act "assumes that in a sense there may be property in a trade mark, and provides for the protection of that property by a statutory system of registration").

[106] B. Sherman & L. Bently, *The Making of Modern Intellectual Property Law: The British Experience, 1760–1911* (Cambridge: CUP, 1999) 197–8. For a nuanced criticism and elaboration of this argument, see Robert Burrell, "Trademark Bureaucracies", in this volume, Chapter 4.

[107] *The Times*, September 10, 1875 p. 8A (emphasis added).

[108] J.S. Salaman, *A Manual of the Practice of Trade Mark Registration* (London: Shaw and Son, 1876) 31.

[109] E.M. Daniel, *The Trade Mark Registration Act 1875* (London: Stevens & Haynes, 1876) 2; M.E. Bigelow, *Elements of the Law of Torts* (Cambridge: CUP, 1889) 50 n. 2 ("The subject of trade marks is being gradually assimilated to the law of property, and actions for deceit are apparently becoming infrequent under the influence of a better right"); L.C. Innes, *The Principles of the Law of Torts* (London: Stevens, 1891) 247, para 225.

Looking back from the mid-1880s,[110] Lowry Whittle, who had been the Assistant Registrar of Trade Marks and Designs from 1876, remarked that:

> The nature of this property being once established, the next step was to give it statutory recognition, and supply facilities for securing its protection, and this Lord Cairns undertook in the Trade Marks Act 1875, which for the first time established a system of Registration of Trade Marks in accordance with the practice of Foreign countries, in which perhaps English Trade Marks are, from the reputation of the English manufacturer, a property more important even than in the British dominions.

III. The significance of trade marks as property

If the period between 1860 and 1875 witnessed a transformation in the way in which trade marks were conceived – from one example of fraudulent trading to objects of property – one might have expected that transformation to bring with it significant consequences. Indeed, in *The Making of Modern Intellectual Property Law*,[111] Brad Sherman and I identified this shift as one component that informed the evolution of the modern categorical schema of intellectual property, with its familiar tri-partite division into copyright, patents and trade marks. We argued that registration of trade marks,[112] and their conceptualisation as property, enabled the law of trade marks to be perceived first as part of a law of industrial property and then as a category of intellectual property – a process of categorisation which would have been less fluid (if at all possible) as long as trade-marks law was seen as concerned with deceit, forgery, fraud or communication more generally.

---

[110] J. Lowry Whittle, "The Late Earl Cairns" (1885–6) 11 *Law Mag & L Rev* (5th ser.) 133, 150.

[111] Sherman & Bently, *The Making of Modern Intellectual Property Law* (Cambridge: CUP, 1999) 196–9. Giving evidence to the Herschell Committee in 1887, Whittle referred to "this ideal property, which is not chattels and is not real property." *Report of a Commission Appointed by the Board of Trade to Inquire into the Duties, Organisation and Arrangements of the Patent Office under the Patents, Designs and Trade Marks Act 1883, so far as relates to Trade Marks and Designs* (C.5350) (1888), 81 *Parliamentary Papers* Q. 1728.

[112] A tri-partite scheme of "intellectual property", we argued, could be seen to develop around about the 1840s and 1850s, but the three categories of intellectual property were copyright, patents *and designs*. By the end of the century, the three main categories of intellectual property had transformed into copyright, patents *and trade marks*. In part, this was because through the establishment of a registration system, trade marks had started to look like patents and designs. All defined their objects through processes of representative registration. This was reinforced by the fact that the registries for patents, designs and copyright were all located in the same buildings (the Trade Mark Office had been at Quality Court, Chancery Lane under the superintendence of the Commissioner of Patents; in 1881 it was moved to the Patent Office in Southampton Buildings), and, in 1883, became governed by the same body of legislation (until 1905).

While the shift to property may have been important in the context of the fabrication of legal categories, what seems remarkable to the modern commentator is how little effect this shift seems to have had on substantive legal doctrine. Inevitably, it is difficult to establish a method by which to gauge the impact of a particular conceptual scheme on the development of substantive law (especially in an era where the detailed application of the law was still in the process of being elaborated), so that the following analysis is as much one of impression as anything else. Nevertheless, it seems that reconceptualising trade marks as property had no significant impact on the delineation of rights or breadth of protection conferred on trade-marks owners. Despite widespread use of proprietary language,[113] over the two decades following Lord Westbury LC's intervention, the rights of trade-mark owners and the breadth of protection remained limited. Attempts by plaintiffs to expand these rights often employed the rhetoric of property, but were readily rebuffed.

Perhaps the best example of the limited effect of proprietary rhetoric can be seen in the House of Lords decision in *Singer v Loog*,[114] where it was argued that the use of the description SINGER SYSTEM on circulars, invoices, instructions for use and price lists directed at wholesalers, infringed the plaintiff sewing machine manufacturer's rights in the word SINGER. In effect, the claimant was seeking to prevent all trade uses of the word SINGER, not just those in which the mark was applied to goods in a way that indicated trade origin to the relevant audience. Counsel for Singer focused on the existing judicial recognition of trade marks as property to argue that these kinds of uses should be prohibited unless the defendant could provide a justification – which might either be based on a right to use the name or use in a descriptive fashion (where a person is unable to designate the article in any other way than by its known name). At first instance, Vice-Chancellor Bacon was persuaded by the property analysis.[115] He concluded that "the Plaintiffs are entitled to an

---

[113] *Maxwell v Hogg* (1867) LR 2 Ch App 307, 310 (Cairns LJ), 313–14 (Turner LJ); *Cheavin v Walker* (1876) 5 Ch D 850, 858 (Bacon V C) ("That a trade-mark is property cannot reasonably be doubted") (rev'd on appeal, on different grounds); *Singer v Wilson* (1876) LR 2 Ch D 434, 454 (Mellish LJ) ("no doubt there is in a certain sense a property in a trade mark") (1877) LR 3 HL 376, 396 (Lord O'Hagan); *Orr Ewing v Registrar of Trade-Marks* (1879) LR 4 HL 479, 494 (Lord Blackburn, "The exclusive right to use a trade-mark was a right of property"); *Singer v Loog* (1882) LR 8 HL 15, 33 (Lord Blackburn); *Watt v O'Hanlon* (1886) 4 RPC 1, 5, 13 ("the right to a trade mark is a right of property"); *Somerville v Schembri* (1887) 4 RPC 180 (Lord Watson, Privy Council); *Oakey and Son v Dalton* (1887) 4 RPC 313, 315.
[114] (1879) LR 18 Ch Div 395, 398–9; (1882) LR 8 HL 15.
[115] (1879) LR 18 Ch Div 395, 402, 403. He treated the historical basis of the common law action as an action for trespass (rather than deceit).

injunction which will protect them in the enjoyment of the property which has been theirs all these years, against which, neither by their negligence nor acquiescence, has any other person acquired a title."[116] On appeal, however, the decision was reversed. James LJ quickly got to the point: "there is no such thing as a monopoly or a property in the nature of a copyright, or in the nature of a patent, in the use of any name."[117] The House of Lords too reiterated that even though a trade mark might be regarded as property,[118] the test of infringement remained (as it had always been) one of deception.[119] The defendant's use of the term SINGER was not likely to cause any such deception: first, because the material was aimed at wholesalers who would understand the product was not manufactured by the Singer Manufacturing Co; and secondly because these uses themselves were not ones that suggested the machines had been made by Singer.[120] Relief was thus denied to the plaintiff.

The second situation in which proprietary language seems to have no significant impact on the scope of trade-mark rights relates to the question of use on different goods. While it is a key claim of contemporary academic commentators that the "property" conception of trade marks is linked with the expanded protection of trade-mark rights to encompass uses on dissimilar goods where there is dilution or tarnishment, no such tendencies are discernible in the 1870s or 1880s. To say that a trade mark used by a trader on one particular good was property, did not mean that he could stop another trader using the same mark on different goods. In *Leather Cloth Co v American Leather Cloth*,[121] for example, Lord Westbury stated that "there is no exclusive ownership of the symbols which constitute a trade mark apart from the use or application of them",[122] and the right was only invaded by use on "the same kind of goods" in such a way as to cause "buyers in the market" to mistake the defendant's goods for those of the trade-mark owner.[123] Elaborating on this, he explained that "property in a trade mark is ... the right

---

[116] (1879) LR 18 Ch Div 395, 411.
[117] (1879) LR 18 Ch Div 395, 412.
[118] (1882) LR 8 HL 15, 33 (Lord Blackburn) ("I think it settled by a series of cases, of which *Hall v Barrows* is, I think, the leading one, that both trade-marks and trade-names are in a certain sense property").
[119] (1882) LR 8 HL 15, 39 (Lord Watson).
[120] (1882) LR 8 HL 15, 20 (Lord Selborne LC).
[121] (1863) 4 De G J & S 136. *See also Hall v Barrows*, in which Lord Westbury said that there could be property in the sense that "a trade mark consists in the exclusive right to the use of some name or symbol as applied to a particular manufacturer or vendible commodity" and that "there can be no right to the exclusive ownership of any symbols or marks universally in the abstract".
[122] (1863) 4 De G J & S 136, 142.
[123] (1863) 4 De G J & S 136, 141.

to the exclusive use of some mark, name or symbol in connection with a particular manufacture or vendible commodity. Consequently, the use of the same mark in connection with a different article is not an infringement of such right of property."[124] Page-Wood V-C, although by the late 1860s prepared to acknowledge (as precedent required of him) that trade marks had been recognised as property, gave a clear example of the limited breadth of the property rights in *Ainsworth v Walmsley*:[125] "If he does not carry on a trade in iron, but carries on a trade in linen, and stamps a lion on his linen, another person may stamp a lion on iron."

In fact, it is notable that just as there are uses of the "property" concept to attempt to expand protection, there were also cases where attempts were made to use the concept to limit the availability of protection. One example of this was *M'Andrew v Bassett*.[126] Here the claimant was a manufacturer of liquorice and from August 1861 had stamped the liquorice with the word ANATOLIA, an area where liquorice-root was grown. In September the defendant, also liquorice makers, received an order from a third party for 5 cwt of liquorice and a request that it be marked ANATOLIA, which the defendants did. The plaintiffs brought an action, and the defendants sought to argue that insufficient use of the mark had been made by the plaintiffs to establish it as property. Lord Westbury LC was quick to reject the argument: the mark had been applied by the claimant, reached the market, and was now being imitated, so these facts themselves led to the conclusion that the trade mark was property. Moreover, he rejected any argument that the sign, being geographical, was a word common to all. He referred to a fallacy that he had "frequently had occasion to expose":

> property in a word for all purposes cannot exist; but property in that word, as applied by way of a stamp upon a particular vendible article, as a stick of liquorice, does exist the moment the article goes into the market so stamped, and there obtains acceptance and reputation whereby the stamp gets currency as an indicator of superior quality, or of some other circumstance which renders the article so stamped acceptable to the public.

IV. Conclusion

The contrast between the limited impact of proprietary language in the late nineteenth century, and its supposed effects in recent trade-marks jurisprudence, prompts two further potential lines of enquiry. The first is to revisit the critical accounts of contemporary trade-marks law and consider whether these

---

[124] (1863) 4 De G J & S 136, 144.
[125] (1866) LR 1 Eq 518.
[126] (1864) 4 De G J & S 380, 10 LT(NS) 445.

attribute too much causal power to proprietary language. If so, what are the real causes of the expansionist tendencies in trade-marks law? The second line of enquiry is to consider why it is that proprietary language has so much more impact today than in previous periods?

An historical investigation such as this is not the place to assess whether contemporary critics of trade-mark expansionism are attributing too much power to the language of property, though there do seem to be a number of more obvious factors contributing to expansion of trade-marks law than the language of property. In so far as expansion is a consequence of legislation implementing newly-agreed international norms (as with, for example, Articles 15–21 of the TRIPs Agreement), or harmonised laws (such as the EC's 1989 Trade Marks Directive), more obvious influences on expansion are likely to have been corporate self-interest, national trade interest, and the one-directional logic of harmonisation.[127] In other respects, the expansion of trade-mark rights has been linked to the emergent rhetoric of "brands", and associated commercial practice of "brand extension".[128] As businesses have come to understand brand values as capable of attaching to a range of disparate products, pressure has come to be exerted to extend the protection given to established trade marks to include the right to prevent unauthorised use on even dissimilar products.[129] Others explain expansion of trade-mark rights in terms of conventional understandings.[130] Given these other, more obvious, explanations for the expansion of trade-mark rights, it seems plausible that contemporary accounts are attributing too much influence to the rhetoric of property. Perhaps the more interesting question, and one which historical material can help with, is why acceptance of trade marks as property did not

---

[127] Of course, "property" rhetoric may well have played a part in the formulation of these international or regional norms (and, importantly, the tendency to harmonise up rather than down is attributable in part to the idea that it is inappropriate to deprive private parties of vested legal rights).

[128] A good starting point for those interested in this topic is Jennifer Davis, "The Value of Trade Marks: Economic Assets and Cultural Icons" in Y. Gendreau (ed.), *Intellectual Property: Bridging Aesthetics and Economics—Propriété intellectuelle: Entre l'art et l'argent* (Montreal: Editions Themis, 2006) 97–125.

[129] For a sociological perspective, see C. Lury, "Trade Mark Style as a Way of Fixing Things" in L. Bently, J. Davis & J. Ginsburg (eds.), *Trade Marks and Brands: An Interdisciplinary Critique*, Ch. 9 (Cambridge: CUP, 2008).

[130] Certainly, there are commentators who have argued that some of the developments are justifiable under traditional understandings of trade-marks function. For example, Robert G. Bone has argued that many of the recent expansions of trade-marks law in the United States fit "core information transmission policies" when those policies are supplemented by a concern about limiting high enforcement costs. Robert G. Bone, "Enforcement Costs and Trademark Puzzles" (2004) 90 *Va. L. Rev.* 2099, 2121–2.

have a particularly radical transformative effect on the scope of protection in the late nineteenth century. One reason is because, at least for some jurists, such as Page-Wood V-C, the property analysis remained unpersuasive and the real basis for intervention was fraud. While in the decisions he gave as Vice-Chancellor after *Leather Cloth* he acknowledged that trade marks must be treated as property,[131] once he was himself elevated to Lord Chancellor (Hatherley), the use of the word "property" is conspicuously absent. In *Wotherspoon v Currie*,[132] eight years after *Leather Cloth*, the House of Lords heard its second trade-mark case. The plaintiff, who had formerly manufactured starch from the Scottish village of Glenfield but had since moved to Paisley, had an established reputation as the maker of GLENFIELD STARCH. The plaintiff sought an injunction to prevent the defendant from selling its CURRIE ROYAL PALACE STARCH with the word GLENFIELD prominently on the label. The defendant claimed he was entitled to do so on the basis that he himself resided in Glenfield, but the defendant's business address was in fact elsewhere. The House of Lords had no hesitation in granting relief. What is interesting for our purposes is that while Lord Westbury described the designation GLENFIELD for starch as being the property of the claimant, so the sole question was whether the property had been infringed, Lord Hatherley nowhere referred to property, consistently being interested in the honesty of the defendant and the deception likely to result from its behaviour.

Other judges may well have shared Lord Hatherley's scepticism.[133] Certainly, towards the end of the century a different justification for equitable intervention emerged in place of the idea of property in the mark itself, namely that of protecting the trader's goodwill – a proprietary interest distinct from any in the mark itself. After Lord Parker's famous speech in *Spalding v*

---

[131] *M'Andrew v Basset* (1864) 33 LJ Ch 561; *Ainsworth v Walmsley* (1866) LR 1 Eq 518.
[132] (1872) LR 5 HL 518.
[133] *See also Singer v Wilson* (1877) LR 3 HL 376, 400 (Lord Blackburn) (declining to determine whether the basis of the action was fraud or property, and asserting that "[n]either position has ... ever been the ground on which a decision of this House has proceeded"). But see Lord Blackburn in *Orr Ewing v Registrar of Trade-Marks* (1879) LR 4 HL 479 (referring to the protection of trade marks as "property") and in *Singer v Loog* (1882) LR 8 HL 15, 33 (conceding that it was well settled that trade marks were property). Note also *Singer v Loog* (1880) LR 8 Ch D 395, 412 per James LJ (no property in the use of any name equivalent to the property granted by copyright), 425 per Lush LJ (emphasising fraud as basis of action). Later scepticism was exhibited by Lord Herschell in *Reddaway v Banham* [1896] AC 199, 209–10 ("The word 'property' has been sometimes applied to what has been termed a trade mark at common law. I doubt myself whether it is accurate to speak of there being property in such a trade mark, though, no doubt some of the rights which are incident to property may attach to it.").

Gamage in 1915,[134] this idea that protection of trade marks at common law was really a mechanism for protecting "goodwill" as property became the orthodoxy in England (as indeed it did in the United States). While US scholar Bob Bone argues that it was the fluidity that the concept of goodwill provided that enabled trade marks law to commence down its expansionist road, the importance of this later transformation here is that it indicates that there was a level of discomfort with the analysis of trade marks as property developed in the 1860s. How deep, widespread or longstanding was this scepticism about trade marks being property is difficult to gauge.

A less sceptical, but perhaps more prevalent and influential, view of Lord Westbury's property analysis was that it was really a matter of form rather than substance. Not long after *Edelsten* and *Hall v Barrows*, Page-Wood V-C had referred to the use of the term "property" to describe trade marks[135] as "a mere question of nomenclature" or, as a commentator in the *Law Times* of 1864 put it, a "point of legal science." [136] In other words, the "difference between the Lord Chancellor's view and the view taken by preceding judges appears . . . to be theoretical rather than practical. After all, the property in a trade-mark is not absolute like other property . . .".[137] The adoption of the language of property (at least for some time) may have had little substantive impact because it was recognised that the "property" label was just that, a label. It was a label adopted to solve a specific problem: that of explaining Equity's extended jurisdiction beyond that of the Common Law and the availability of injunctive relief at all. Adoption of that label did not mean that trade marks were property, like land or goods, or even like copyright or patents. Indeed, in *Leather Cloth*, Lord Cranworth indicated that the term property was used "in a sense very different from what is meant by it when applied to a house or a watch".[138] Later, Mellish LJ and Lord Blackburn would describe trade marks as property but only "in a certain sense".[139]

---

[134] (1915) 32 RPC 273.

[135] *M'Andrew v Basset*, (1864) 33 LJ Ch 561 (ANATOLIA for liquorice) ("Whether it is property or not is not material.")

[136] (1864) *Law Times*. Charles Stewart Drewry, *The Law of Trade Marks* (London: Knight, 1878) p. xi ("But from recent decisions, it is now to be collected that the right to a trade mark is a right of property. It is not however always practically of much importance whether a trade mark is legally property or not.")

[137] Anon, "The Marking of Merchandise in Equity" (January 16, 1864) *The Law Times* 123. *See also* the commentary on *M'Andrew v Bassett* (June 4, 1864) *The Law Times* 348.

[138] (1865) 11 HLC 523, 533.

[139] *Singer v Wilson* (1876) LR 2 Ch D 434, 454 (Mellish LJ); *Singer v Loog* (1882) LR 8 HL 15, 33 (Lord Blackburn).

To say that the question was merely one of "nomenclature" or "legal science" may also be to suggest that the property designation was understood, for the most part, as a matter of analytic rather than normative jurisprudence. That is, the property designation was adopted to explain existing characteristics of trade-marks law, particularly the case law holding innocent traders liable where use of a mark was liable to confuse the public, or the fact that infringement could result in injunctive relief. Although there are a few scattered examples of jurists (notably Lord Westbury LC himself) and commentators who suggest trade-mark protection is justified on the same basis as protection of other properties, such as protecting the products of labour and effort,[140] or natural rights in one's name, for the most part the normative justifications of trade-mark protection are not linked to the normative justification of copyright, patents or property in tangibles and realty.

A further factor that may have limited the possible impact of proprietary language is the very different context of the second half of the nineteenth century. In many ways that was a period when free-trade ideology was at its zenith, and when intellectual property rights were under attack. The free-traders had campaigned for the outright abolition of patents and, while the campaign failed in the United Kingdom, it had succeeded elsewhere.[141] During the 1870s the copyright system was subjected to heavy criticism, with proposals being made by members of the Royal Commission to replace copyright as a proprietary right with a system of remuneration.[142] It is surprising then that trade marks should have emerged as properties. But as emergent

---

[140] For example, Richard Bethell, then a leading Chancery barrister and MP, later Attorney General and Lord Chancellor, Lord Westbury, commented publicly in 1859 that counterfeiting "is in effect theft . . . The thief obtains at once the fruits, probably, of a life of labour, invention and industry . . ." "Fifteenth Ordinary Meeting" (1859) *Journal of the Society of Arts*, 262, 268. The comments were made in his capacity of Chairman at a meeting of the Royal Society of Arts at which Professor Leone Levi gave a paper highlighting deficiencies in the existing legal protection of trade marks. Speaking at the Royal Society of Arts in 1866, Daniel QC stated that "Lord Westbury . . . held that if a man had a particular emblem by which he denoted *the results of his own labour*, the law protected him in the exclusive use of that emblem, and to that extent it became a property."

[141] See, (1866) **14**, *Journal of the Society of Arts*, 370, 377. F. Machlup & E. Penrose, "The Patent Controversy in the Nineteenth Century" (1950) 10 *Journal of Economic History* 1; M. Coulter, *Property in Ideas: The Patent Question in Mid-Victorian Britain* (Kirksville, Mo: Thomas Jefferson University Press, 1991).

[142] *Rep. of the Commissioners Appointed to Make Inquiry with Regard to the Laws and Regulations Relating to Home, Colonial and Int'l Copyright*, 1878, c. 2036, 24 British Parl. Papers 163 (1878); Minutes of Evidence, with Appendix, 1878, c. 2036–1, 24 British Parl. Papers 253 (1878). *See also* Paul Saint-Armour, *Intellectual Property and the Literary Imagination* (Ithaca: Cornell University Press, 2003).

38 *Trademark law and theory*

properties in an environment that was highly sceptical of the benefits of monopolies over intangibles, the conditions were anything but favourable for an expansive interpretation of the rights.

The final reason why the property analysis of trade marks may have had so little impact in this period is because judges and commentators were scrupulous first to distinguish this property from others (whether copyright, patents, or more importantly tangibles and land);[143] and secondly, to emphasise that while a right may have some of the characteristics of property, one could not conclude from this designation that it would carry other such consequences. Property had a number of functions, and many jurists were capable of distinguishing, and alert to distinguish, between them. In the context of trade marks, "property" variously was significant in determining: whether injunctive relief was available;[144] whether the right was enforceable against innocent third

---

[143] *Singer v Loog* (1880) LR 8 Ch D 395, 412 per James LJ (trade marks not property in sense of patents and copyrights). Some differentiated between "qualified" property and "absolute" property. See, e.g., E. Lloyd, *Sol Jo & Rep* May 25, 1861 p. 523 (calling trade marks "qualified property", "quasi-property"). *See also* Lionel B. Mozley, *Trade Marks Registration. A Concise View of the Law and Practice* (London, 1877), ("It is settled, at any rate, that there is a certain qualified right of property in a trade mark, as applied to particular goods or articles, and that it possesses many of the ordinary incidents of property, such as that of being made the subject of a sale, except where it is a personal trade mark . . . And there are dicta in certain decisions . . . which would lead to the conclusion that there is an absolute property in a trade mark, so that no one else may use the mark as applied to the goods in connection with which it is used, whether he does so honestly or in a way intended to deceive or not . . .".)

[144] In the high-profile decision in *Emperor of Austria v Day and Kossuth* (1861) 3 De G F & J 217, 45 ER 861 the Court of Chancery reiterated that it could only grant injunctions in protection of property rights. The facts of the case had little to do with trade marks, the action being brought by the King of Hungary to restrain the defendant from having notes manufactured purporting to be money usable in Hungary. The notes, which were not imitations of any notes circulating already in Hungary, were created on behalf of Kossuth (formerly Minister of Finance to Ferdinand V), an exile who claimed the government in Hungary was unconstitutional and who hoped to make the notes usable after a revolution. Lord Campbell, the Lord Chancellor, considered whether this matter was one over which the Court of Chancery had jurisdiction by injunction, noting that while the Court could not prevent crimes nor libels, "this Court has jurisdiction by injunction to protect property from an act threatened, which if completed would give a right of action", ibid. at 240, 870. The issue of the money was regarded as just such an act. Turner LJ reasoned to the same end that the King could bring an action on behalf of his subjects where there was impending injury to the private property rights of those subjects, and found the possible introduction of the currency to be just such a threat. This was because the introduction of the currency was likely to endanger the existing currency, and thus to affect directly all the holders of Austrian bank notes, and indirectly, if not directly, all the holders of property "in the State." (ibid. at 253, 875).

parties;[145] whether the interest was capable of assignment; whether the right to sue for infringement survived on the death of the trade-mark owner;[146] whether the rights could be raised in an English court,[147] and, if so, whether this included the County Court; whether a defendant had to produce a justification for using the mark;[148] and, of course, the scope of protection.[149] Decisions over whether a trade mark was property for each purpose, or what it meant for a trade mark to be property in such a respect, was (perhaps surprisingly) one over which judges and jurists took considerable care.[150]

This was true even (or perhaps, particularly) of the great property advocate, Lord Westbury. In *Hall v Barrows*, for example, Westbury was keen to ensure that his judgment, forthright and categorical as it was, could not be taken to indicate that trade marks could be sold "in gross":

> Nothing that I have said is intended to lead to the conclusion that the business and iron works might be put up for sale by the Court in one lot, and the right to use the trade mark might be put up as a separate lot, and that one lot might be sold and transferred to one person and the other lot sold and transferred to another, the case requiring only that I should decide that the exclusive right to this trade mark belongs to the partnership as part of its property and might be sold with the business and works and as a valuable right, and if it might be sold it must be included in the valuation to the surviving partner.

Similarly, in *Leather Cloth Co v American Leather Cloth*,[151] Lord Kingsdown stated that "Though a man may have property in a trade mark, in the sense of having a right to exclude any other trader from the use of it in selling the same description of goods, it does not follow that he can in all cases give another person the right to use it, or to use his name."

---

[145] Lionel B. Mozley, *Trade Marks Registration. A Concise View of the Law and Practice* (London: 1877) ("Much discussion has taken place as to whether a trade mark can be said to be property, or to speak more correctly, whether a right of property exists in a trade mark. The importance of the distinction arises from the fact that if it is property, strictly so called, the owner is entitled to be protected in the enjoyment of it absolutely, but if it is not property he must obtain a remedy on some other ground, such as that of fraud.") *See also Watt v O'Hanlon* (1886) 4 RPC 1, 13 (linking "property" to absence of need to prove fraud).

[146] *Oakey and Son v Dalton* (1887) 4 RPC 313 (Chitty J).

[147] *Collins Co. v Brown* (1857) 3 K & J 423.

[148] On abandonment, see *Mouson v Boehm* (1884) 26 Ch D 398 (Chitty J).

[149] For example, whether protection extended to sale of labels.

[150] While some US academics, such as Professor Bone ("Hunting Goodwill: A History of the Concept of Goodwill in Trademark Law" (2006) 86 *Boston University L. Rev.* 549, 562), have been quick to accuse the nineteenth century's jurists of formalism, the evidence from the UK points towards the opposite view.

[151] (1865) 11 HLC 523.

Most jurists had a similar propensity to scrupulousness, distinguishing between the various ways in which the label of property might be used. In 1866, Wybrow Robertson highlighted the limited nature of the property right, saying that while "a trade mark is undoubtedly property, it is not so for all purposes; for a proprietor of a trade mark cannot prevent another person from using the same mark for other description of goods."[152] In their treatise,[153] Ludlow and Jenkyns, who argued that a trade mark was a "ius in rem" wanted to make clear the limits of this analysis, in particular, that it would not be right to assume from this "anything as to the general transferableness of a trade mark or as to the remedy of a person whose right is infringed". If formalistic reasoning was a characteristic of late-nineteenth century reasoning, it is notably absent from virtually all discussion of trade marks as property.

Perhaps the most articulate example of the judicial rejection of formalistic analysis was in the Court of Appeal in the first English *Singer* decision, *Singer Manufacturing v Wilson*.[154] As with *Singer v Loog* (discussed previously) this case concerned use of the name SINGER on price-lists, though not on the defendant's machines, which were marked with its mark of St George and the Dragon and name Newton Wilson & Co. Jessel MR, at first instance, found that the plaintiff had not established a prima facie case and declined to hear the arguments of the defendant. He explained that where a sign was not being applied to the goods themselves, it was for the claimant to establish that deception had occurred and that fraud existed. The public, reading the price-lists, would appreciate that these machines had been manufactured by the defendant rather than the Singer Manufacturing Co. The Court of Appeal affirmed, on this occasion not bothering to hear the arguments of the respondent, the defendant. Mellish LJ highlighted the dangers:[155]

---

[152] Wybrow Robertson, "On Trade Marks" (1869) JSA 414.

[153] H. Ludlow & H. Jenkins, *A Treatise on the Law of Trade-Marks and Trade-Names* (London: W. Maxwell & Son, 1873) 5. *Cf.* (1864) *Sol Jo & Rep* 177, ("The doctrine that the exclusive use of a trade name or mark in connexion with a particular article of manufacture is rightly classed under the head of 'property' being thus established by the highest authority, it must be accepted with all its consequences. The proprietary right must carry with it the right of alienation. *Cujus est dare ejus est disponere*.")

[154] (1876) LR 2 Ch Div 434; (1877) LR 3 HL 376.

[155] (1876) LR 2 Ch Div 434, 456. Mellish LJ could see that formalistic reasoning was deployed in an attempt by traders to broaden protection beyond what he considered to be justified: "although it is perfectly right to protect the use of of trade-marks and trade-names, yet it is impossible not to see that persons do try to use their right in trade-marks and trade-names for the purpose of getting a monopoly in particular articles, just as if they had a patent for the goods they manufacture."

> You first say the right to use the name or the mark can be made the subject of purchase, and therefore, it is a property, and then you proceed to draw the further inference, that, as it is a property, whether it is used in a way that is calculated to deceive or not, you can prevent anyone else from using it. That, to my mind, would be going further than the English courts have ever gone.

Although the House of Lords overturned the decisions of the Court of Appeal and Jessel MR, this was done on the basis that the courts had mistakenly distinguished tests applicable for liability through applying a mark to goods and other uses, requiring a demonstration of fraud in the latter cases.[156] The majority of the members of the House did not think fraud was a requirement and took the view that on the proper test a prima facie case has been made out.[157] The House said nothing to cast doubt on Mellish LJ's criticism of formalistic reasoning, and Lord Cairns reiterated the test of liability as to whether the advertisements "were calculated to mislead an unwary purchaser of the machines."

If these reasons help us to understand how the "property" conceptualisation of trade marks in the late nineteenth century did not bring with it any obvious expansion in trade-mark rights, they may simultaneously point towards possible explanations for such expansionist tendencies (in as much as they exist) today. If property rhetoric has had the influence that commentators like Lemley and Lunney claim, is it because judges and policy-makers are less careful, and more susceptible to formalism than their nineteenth century precursors? Or is it because they consider trade marks as property normatively, as a product of labour deserving strong protection, rather than in terms of legal nomenclature? Or is it, perhaps, because those in the judiciary now understand property to mean something else than it once did? At least in the United States, where neo-liberal economics has become a judicial orthodoxy, there seems to be a new vision of property that implies the private appropriation of virtually all value. If the expansion of trade-marks rights is in any way attributable to the use of property rhetoric (a question about which I remain agnostic), the historical record suggests that it was less the adoption of that rhetoric than a transformation of its meaning that has brought about the change.

---

[156] (1876) LR 2 Ch Div 434, 452 (James LJ).
[157] (1877) LR 3 HL 376, 396 (fraud not necessary). Cf. Lord Blackburn at 400.

2 The semiotic account of trademark doctrine and trademark culture
Barton Beebe

I. Introduction

Semiotics is the study of signs and sign systems. While linguistics concerns itself specifically with human speech, semiotics investigates "the processes and effects of the production and reproduction, reception and circulation of meaning in all forms, used by all kinds of agent[s] of communication."[1] Semiotic thought developed into its own distinctive field of inquiry in the late-nineteenth and early-twentieth centuries at a time strangely coincident with the development of modern trademark doctrine.[2] It was during this period that the Swiss linguist Ferdinand de Saussure projected a bold extension of his research in structural linguistics: "A science that studies the life of signs within society is conceivable ... I shall call it semiology (from Greek semeîon 'sign'). Semiology would show what constitutes signs, what laws govern them."[3] Since Saussure's time, semiotics (or semiology) has developed into a sophisticated systems-theoretical field of knowledge of enormous reach and ambition. The semiotic tradition forms the foundation of the past century's structuralist and poststructuralist thought across the humanities.[4]

In this short chapter, I will seek to show how semiotic concepts can be applied to clarify and ameliorate fundamental areas of trademark doctrine and policy. Elsewhere I have set forth at length a semiotic analysis of trademark law.[5] My purpose here is not to reprise that account, nor is it simply to cele-

---

* Associate Professor of Law, Benjamin J. Cordozo School of Law, Yeshiva University.

[1] ROBERT HODGE & GUNTHER KRESS, SOCIAL SEMIOTICS 261 (1988).

[2] *See generally* JOHN DEELY, INTRODUCING SEMIOTIC: ITS HISTORY AND DOCTRINE (1982); WINFRIED NÖTH, HANDBOOK OF SEMIOTICS (1990).

[3] FERDINAND DE SAUSSURE, COURSE IN GENERAL LINGUISTICS 16 (Charles Bally & Albert Sechehaye eds., Wade Baskin trans., 1959) (1916) [hereinafter SAUSSURE (Baskin)].

[4] *See generally* JONATHAN CULLER, ON DECONSTRUCTION: THEORY AND CRITICISM AFTER STRUCTURALISM (1982); JONATHAN CULLER, STRUCTURALIST POETICS: STRUCTURALISM, LINGUISTICS AND THE STUDY OF LITERATURE (1975).

[5] *See generally* Barton Beebe, *The Semiotic Analysis of Trademark Law*, 51 UCLA L. REV. 621 (2004) [hereinafter Beebe, *Semiotic Analysis*].

brate, as a matter of intellectual history, the parallel development of, and many striking homologies between, semiotic thought and trademark doctrine. Nor do I seek to suggest that the law should simply defer to the authority of the semiotic—rather than the economic—tradition. Instead, my purpose is more pragmatic. It is to demonstrate that the semiotic account of trademark law is worthwhile because, as a descriptive matter, it explains many areas of trademark doctrine better than other accounts and because, as a normative matter, it recommends practical and sensible improvements in the doctrine that other accounts are unable—or unwilling—to recommend.[6] To demonstrate this, I will set forth here only the most basic of semiotic concepts because that is all that is needed to achieve this goal.

Readers familiar with trademark scholarship and the trademark case law may already wonder about the value of this enterprise. After all, it is generally thought, at least in the United States, that we already have a "theory" of trademark law that explains everything. To be sure, the economic account of trademark law, if not of commercial semiosis more generally, is a powerful one.[7] Its expositors have applied the rhetoric of what is "optimal" to explain many aspects of trademark doctrine, and in their positivism, they will likely have little patience in what follows for the fuzzy abstraction of much of semiotic thought. Nevertheless, when the economic account turns to certain foundational concepts in trademark doctrine, such as trademark "distinctiveness" or trademark "dilution," the account either fails to persuade or, more often, is simply no longer a positive economic account—indeed, it begins to sound like semiotics, and quite rudimentary semiotics at that. The point, then, of this chapter is not to argue that the semiotic account should *replace* the economic account. On the contrary, I accept, at least for the purposes of this chapter, the key descriptive (and prescriptive) insight of the economic account, that trademarks and trademark law function primarily—though not entirely—to minimize consumer search costs. The purpose of this chapter is simply to argue that the semiotic account is a necessary supplement to the economic account,

---

[6] Graeme Dinwoodie is altogether justified in questioning the extent to which the descriptive and prescriptive can be separated in any discussion of trademark law, and particularly in this one, which employs a body of thought whose "descriptive" claims about language and culture seem so often to comport, at least superficially, with the political agenda of the Left. Still, the semiotic account may at least be employed as a counterweight in this regard to the economic account. *See* Graeme B. Dinwoodie, *What Linguistics Can Do For Trademark Law*, in TRADE MARKS AND BRANDS: AN INTERDISCIPLINARY CRITIQUE (Lionel Bently, Jennifer Davis & Jane Ginsburg eds., 2007) ("[L]inguistic unerstanding of key terms of art in trademark law illustrates the inevitable prescriptive content of supposedly descriptive assessments of trademark claims.").

[7] *See, e.g.*, William M. Landes & Richard A. Posner, *Trademark Law: An Economic Perspective*, 30 J.L. & ECON. 265 (1987).

if only because it furthers the very purpose—a more "efficient" legal regime—that the economic account seeks to achieve.[8]

To defend this claim, I will proceed as follows. First, I will set forth and defend the utility of a structural model of the trademark. I will then invoke various semiotic concepts to clarify the meaning of trademark "distinctiveness" and consider the implications of this clarification for trademark doctrine. Finally, I will briefly survey the semiotic account of the role of trademarks and trademark law in culture.

II. The internal structure of the trademark

Semiotics' fundamental object and instrument of analysis is the "sign," which Charles Sanders Peirce defined quite broadly as "something which stands to somebody for something in some respect or capacity."[9] To explain how signs and sign systems operate, semiotic inquiry typically proceeds from a theory of the internal structure of the sign. This theoretical emphasis on intrasign structure is crucial. It is what has made semiotic inquiry possible. A variety of conceptual problems continue to confound trademark law because it has yet fully to appreciate that the trademark, like the sign, also possesses an internal structure. As with the sign's structure, each element of the trademark's structure performs a specific role in preserving the stability of the structure and must be kept separate from the others lest the structure of the trademark, if not of trademark doctrine more generally, collapse in on itself. In this part, I seek to show how a semiotically-informed awareness of the trademark's internal structure helps to resolve or at least clarify various doctrinal conundrums in trademark law. To begin, I turn first to a brief discussion of semiotic theories of intrasign structure.

A. Semiotic sign structurations

Semiotic thinking typically subscribes to one or the other of two leading structural models of the sign.[10] The triadic model of the sign holds that the sign consists of three subsign elements: a "signifier" (the perceptible form of the sign, *e.g.*, the sound of the word "book" or "*Buch*" or "*livre*"), a "signified" (the meaning to which that perceptible form refers, *e.g.*, the idea of a book), and a "referent" (*e.g.*, a tangible book itself).[11] The dyadic model holds that

---

[8] *See generally* Giovanni B. Ramello, *What's in a Sign? Trademark Law and Economic Theory*, 20 J. ECON. SURVEYS 547 (2006) (assessing trademark law from an economic and semiotic perspective).

[9] 2 CHARLES SANDERS PEIRCE, COLLECTED PAPERS OF CHARLES SANDERS PEIRCE ¶ 228 (Charles Hartshorne & Paul Weiss eds., 1934).

[10] *See* NÖTH, *supra* note 2, at 83–91.

[11] *See, e.g.*, PEIRCE, *supra* note 9, at ¶ 228 (setting forth a triadic model of the sign).

the sign consists of two subsign elements: the signifier and the signified.[12] For various reasons that need not detain us, the dyadic model "brackets" or excludes the referent.[13]

One aspect of semiotics' effort to model intrasign structure will be relevant to our discussion below. In speaking of the internal structure of the sign, semiotic thought has long struggled with the ambiguity of the term "sign."[14] In semiotic thinking, the sign consists of and the term "sign" refers to more than simply a signifier. The sign is a relational system, only one element of which is the perceptible form of the sign. Each element of this system is mutually constitutive of and interdependent with the others. To refer to the signifier as the sign, as is common in everyday language, is to mistake the part for the whole and to suggest that the part, the signifier, can exist separate from the whole, the sign. It is like using the term "water" to refer only to hydrogen.[15] Nevertheless, semiotic thinkers have long recognized that everyday language, if not everyday thought, has damaged beyond repair the distinction between "sign" as signifier and "sign" as relational system and often fails to honor the distinction itself.[16]

B. The triadic structure of the trademark

Though perhaps not altogether consciously, trademark commentary has traditionally conceived of the trademark as a three-legged stool, consisting of a signifier (the perceptible form of the mark), a signified (the semantic content of the mark, such as the goodwill or effect to which the signifier refers), and a referent (the product or service to which the mark refers).[17] Consider, for example, J. Thomas McCarthy's description of the requirements that a trademark must meet to qualify for protection:

---

[12] *See, e.g.*, SAUSSURE (Baskin), *supra* note 3, at 67 (explaining that "the sign is the whole that results from the associating of the signifier with the signified").

[13] For a sophisticated analysis of Saussure's exclusion of the referent, see PAUL J. THIBAULT, RE-READING SAUSSURE: THE DYNAMICS OF SIGNS IN SOCIAL LIFE (1997).

[14] *See* NÖTH, *supra* note 2, at 79.

[15] *Cf.* SAUSSURE (Baskin), *supra* note 3, at 103. Saussure writes:

> The two-sided linguistic unit has often been compared with the human person, made up of the body and the soul. The comparison is hardly satisfactory. A better choice would be a chemical compound like water, a combination of hydrogen and oxygen; taken separately, neither element has any of the properties of water.

[16] *See id.* at 67.

[17] *Cf.* Jason Bosland, *The Culture of Trade Marks: An Alternative Cultural Theory Perspective* (working paper on file with the author) (applying Roland Barthes' theory of the sign to the trademark).

The requirements for qualification of a word or symbol as a trademark can be broken down into three elements: (1) the tangible symbol: a word, name, symbol or device or any combination of these; (2) type of use: actual adoption and use of the symbol as a mark by a manufacturer or seller of goods or services; (3) the function: to identify and distinguish the seller's goods from goods made or sold by others.[18]

Here, the triadic structure of the mark becomes apparent. First, the trademark must take the form of a "tangible symbol." When courts speak of the trademark as, in the Third Circuit's lexicon, a "signifier of origin"[19] or, in the Seventh Circuit's, a "signifier[ ] of source,"[20] they mean by the term "signifier" to refer specifically to the perceptible form of the mark. Some courts use the more general term "symbol."[21] Second, the trademark must be used in commerce to refer to goods or services. These goods or services constitute the trademark's referent, as when Judge Zobel explained that "a descriptive mark describes a property or ingredient of its referent."[22] Third and finally, the trademark must "identify and distinguish" its referent. Typically, the trademark's signifier does so by identifying the referent with a specific source and that source's goodwill.[23] This source and its goodwill constitute the trademark's signified.[24]

The triadic structure is also apparent in the syntax of trademark talk, which

---

[18] 1 J. THOMAS MCCARTHY, MCCARTHY ON TRADEMARKS AND UNFAIR COMPETITION § 3.01 (4th ed. 2002).

[19] A & H Sportswear, Inc. v. Victoria's Secret Stores, Inc., 237 F.3d 198, 222 (3d Cir. 2000).

[20] Publ'ns Int'l, Ltd. v. Landoll, Inc., 164 F.3d 337, 343 (7th Cir. 1998).

[21] *See, e.g.*, Warner Bros., Inc. v. Gay Toys, Inc. 724 F.2d 327, 332 (2d Cir. 1983); Boston Prof'l Hockey Ass'n, Inc. v. Dallas Cap & Emblem Mfg., 510 F.2d 1004, 1011 (5th Cir. 1975).

[22] Diversified Funding Inc. v. Diversified Mortgage Co., 1994 WL 129602, at *1 (D. Mass., March 29, 1994); *see also In re* DC Comics, Inc., 689 F.2d 1042, 1044 (C.C.P.A. 1982).

[23] The question of whether the trademark's signifier should be understood to refer specifically to the trademark's referent or to the trademark's signified raises the question, in semiotic terms, of intrasign "mediation." This issue is dealt with in detail in Beebe, *Semiotic Analysis, supra* note 5, at 651–3.

[24] At least two trademark commentators have previously conceived of the trademark in structuralist terms. In his work on trade dress, Tom Bell has outlined a structural model of the trademark that takes into account the distinction between the signifier and the referent within the trademark structure. Specifically, Bell invokes Gottlob Frege's division of sense and reference to criticize the legal protection of the new "virtual trade dress," which "merg[es] sense and reference completely." Tom W. Bell, *Virtual Trade Dress: A Very Real Problem*, 56 MD. L. REV. 384, 413 (1997). Per Mollerup has also developed a highly sophisticated triadic model of the mark. *See generally* PER MOLLERUP, MARKS OF EXCELLENCE: THE HISTORY AND TAXONOMY OF TRADEMARKS (1999).

tends to refer to a signifier x for a referent y (*e.g.*, the trademark "FORD for cars" or the trademark "ACE for hardware, but not for bandages") and, in doing so, implies the existence of a third, unmentioned variable, z, the source of the product and the goodwill associated with that source. As such, the triadic structure underlies the law's simple two-dimensional model of trademark infringement, which conceives of any given trademark as forming a point in a two-dimensional features space consisting of a signifier dimension and a referent dimension. The closer the point formed by the defendant's signifier-referent combination is to the point formed by the plaintiff's signifier-referent combination, the greater is the likelihood that consumers will assume that both points refer to the same source, z.[25]

One implication of this structural model must be emphasized from the outset. A trademark consists of more than simply its signifier. It is more than simply the term "NIKE" or "APPLE." Rather, a trademark, like a sign, is a relational system consisting of a signifier, a signified, and a referent, and of the three relations among these interdependent elements.[26] This bears emphasis because the term "trademark" suffers from the same ambiguity as the term "sign." Trademark lawyers and scholars, myself included, tend to use the term "trademark" to refer either to the trademark's signifier specifically, to the "brand name," or to the overall relational system, to the "brand." For example, we invoke the first meaning of the term ("trademark" as signifier) when we speak of the various forms of word, image, or shape that a trademark may take, of the similarities of sound, sight, and meaning among trademarks, or of the literal meaning or functionality of a trademark. We invoke the second meaning of the term ("trademark" as relational system) when we speak of trademark rights or trademark infringement, or more recently in the internet context, of "trademark use."[27] By trademark rights, for example, we do not mean the exclusive right to use a signifier in itself. Rather, we mean the exclusive right to use a signifier in connection with a specific signified goodwill and referenced good or service. We mean, in other words, the exclusive right to use a relational system of meaning, a sign. The ambiguity of the term "trademark"

---

[25] *See* Beebe, *Semiotic Analysis*, *supra* note 5, at 653–6.

[26] *Cf.* 1 MCCARTHY, *supra* note 18, at § 18:2 ("Good will and its trademark symbol are as inseparable as Siamese Twins who cannot be separated without death to both.").

[27] *See generally* Margreth Barrett, *Internet Trademark Suits and the Demise of "Trademark Use."* 39 U.C. DAVIS L. REV. 371 (2005); Stacey L. Dogan & Mark A. Lemley, *Trademark and Consumer Search Costs on the Internet*, 41 HOUS. L. REV. 777 (2004); Uli Widmaier, *Use, Liability and the Structure of Trademark Law*, 33 HOFSTRA L. REV. 603 (2004); Graeme B. Dinwoodie & Mark D. Janis, *Confusion Over Use: Contextualism in Trademark Law*, 92 IOWA L. REV. 1597 (2007).

has long caused a great deal of trouble in the doctrine. To expand the scope of their property rights, trademark owners have sought to define their property right as an exclusive right to the signifier in itself. This is nowhere more evident than in recent internet contextual advertising case law.[28] The ambiguity of the term "trademark" invites this slippage in the doctrine towards "in gross" rights.

It should also be emphasized that the economic account of trademark law assumes, though not explicitly, that the trademark (as relational system) is triadic in structure. According to the economic account, the primary functions of the trademark and of trademark protection are to promote efficient markets by minimizing consumer search costs and to promote consumer welfare by enabling producers to capture the reputation-related rewards of investments in quality.[29] Quite obviously, consumer search costs are minimized only to the extent that the trademark (as signifier) actually refers to a product or source for which the consumer is searching. Similarly, product quality is enhanced only to the extent that the owner of a trademark attaches that trademark (as signifier) to products whose quality it actually controls. Both the semiotic and economic accounts of trademark law are concerned with the informational efficiency and integrity of the trademark system, and both assume that the sign must be intact for this efficiency and integrity to obtain.

C. The breakdown of the triadic structure of the trademark

We are in a position now to recognize that much of trademark doctrine is designed to preserve the traditional triadic structure of the mark, specifically,

---

[28] *See, e.g.*, Edina Realty, Inc. v. TheMLSonline.com, No. Civ. 04-4371, 2006 WL 737064 (D. Minn. Mar. 20, 2006); GEICO v. Google, Inc., 330 F. Supp. 2d 700 (E.D. Va. 2004). In such cases, the plaintiff asserts that the defendant is using the plaintiff's "trademark," the defendant asserts that it is not using the plaintiff's "trademark," and both parties are correct—though, of course, they mean different things by the term "trademark." As Dinwoodie and Janis have recently explained, *see* Dinwoodie & Janis, *supra* note 27, at 1662, the likelihood of consumer confusion rather than any "formal notion of trademark use" should guide the court's analysis of such cases. Indeed, to the extent that consumers are confused as to source by the defendant's use of the plaintiff's trademark, then we can conclude that the defendant was making use of the trademark "as a mark," *i.e.*, as a relational system. But to the extent that consumers are not confused, we can conclude that the defendant's use was merely nominative. That is, the defendant was not perceived to have applied a signifier to a referent in such a way that improperly associated that signifier and referent with the plaintiff's signified. *See* 1-800Contacts, Inc. v. WhenU.com, 414 F.3d 400, 409 (2d Cir. 2005) (explaining that the defendant's "conduct simply does not violate the Lanham Act, which is concerned with the use of trademarks in connection with the sale of goods or services in a manner likely to lead to consumer confusion as to the source of such goods or services").

[29] *See, e.g.*, Qualitex Co. v. Jacobson Prods. Co., 514 U.S. 159, 164 (1995).

to preserve both the linkages among the three elements of the mark's structure and the separations among these elements. The doctrine seeks to preserve the triadic structure in an effort to further the basic informational purposes of the trademark and trademark protection. We can see, furthermore, that recent developments in the doctrine should be resisted to the extent that they threaten to break down the mark's traditional triadic structure. Here, the synergy between the semiotic and economic accounts should be apparent. A breakdown in the semiotic structure of the mark signals a breakdown also in the basic economic functions of the mark—just as a breakdown in the grammar of a language tends to signal a breakdown in the communicative capacity of the language itself.

1. Trademark use doctrine Consider, for example, the various rules that make up the doctrine of trademark use. These rules are intended to preserve each of the three linkages among the trademark's elements. In recent times, however, they have increasingly failed to do so. First, the linkage between the signifier (the perceptible form of the mark) and the signified (the source and goodwill of the mark) is regulated by assignment doctrine. Traditionally, trademark law will deny protection to a trademark that has been assigned "in gross," separate from the ongoing business that is the source of the mark's goodwill.[30] Yet, as several commentators have noted, the rule against assignment in gross is now a rule more honored in the breach.[31] Second, the linkage between the signified (the source and goodwill of the mark) and the referent (the product to which the mark is attached) is regulated by licensing doctrine and, specifically, by the rule against "naked licensing."[32] Traditionally, if the source represented by the signifier fails to control the quality of the goods to which the signifier is attached, the trademark will be deemed abandoned. Yet here also, enforcement of the naked licensing rule is now practically non-existent.[33] Third, the linkage between the signifier and the referent is regulated by the affixation and use in commerce requirements.[34] A trademark will not receive protection unless it is affixed to a good or service offered in

---

[30] *See, e.g.*, Green River Bottling Co. v. Green River Corp., 997 F.2d 359, 362 (7th Cir. 1993).
[31] *See generally*, Pamela S. Chestek, *Who Owns the Mark? A Single Framework for Resolving Trademark Ownership Disputes*, 96 TRADEMARK REP. 681 (2006).
[32] *See, e.g.*, Société Comptoir de L'Industrie Cotonnière Etablissements Boussac v. Alexander's Dep't Stores, Inc., 299 F.2d 33 (2d Cir. 1962).
[33] *See* Kevin Parks, *"Naked" is Not a Four-Letter Word: Debunking the Myth of the "Quality Control Requirement" in Trademark Licensing*, 82 TRADEMARK REP. 531 (1992).
[34] *See generally* 1 MCCARTHY, *supra* note 18, at § 16.

commerce. Nevertheless, the case law has substantially liberalized both requirements, most notably in the context of internet contextual advertising.[35]

The trademark, in short, is falling apart. In the process, it is less and less able to accomplish what the economic account claims to be its primary functions. Consumer search costs are not minimized when the mark no longer refers to the source for which consumers are searching, and quality is not fostered by a regime in which the licensor of a mark need not control the quality of the goods to which the licensee affixes it.

2. Merchandising doctrine and Dastar   Other areas of trademark doctrine are designed to prevent the *merger* of intramark elements, and these areas too are under attack. Functionality doctrine has largely failed to prevent the merger of the signifier and the referent, while merchandising doctrine has yielded to the merger of the signified and the referent. In both situations, in acquiring the exclusive right to use the trademark, the trademark owner also acquires the exclusive right to produce the "actual benefit that the consumer wishes to purchase."[36] I consider here in more detail the current condition of merchandising doctrine.

Two assumptions underpin the traditional triadic structure of the mark. The first is that consumers consume things rather than signs, tangible goods or services rather than the intangible meanings of those goods or services. The second and related assumption is that trademark law merely protects the means of consumption rather than the ends of consumption. Trademark law only protects signs, the economic value of which is exhausted once the thing to be consumed is found, while the protection of consumable things themselves—the "actual benefit the consumer wishes to purchase"—is left to patent or perhaps to copyright law. These strangely materialist assumptions came to the fore quite recently in the Supreme Court opinion in *Dastar Corp. v. Twentieth Century Fox Film Corp.*[37] The *Dastar* Court stated that a trademark refers to "the producer of the *tangible* product sold in the marketplace"[38] or possibly to the "trademark owner who commissioned or assumed responsi-

---

[35] *See* David J. Kera & Theodore H. Davis, *The Fifty-Second Year of Administration of the Lanham Trademark Act of 1946*, 90 TRADEMARK REP. 1, 68–70 (2000) (discussing cases liberalizing trademark use and affixation requirements); *The United States Trademark Association Trademark Review Commission Report and Recommendations to USTA President and Board of Directors*, 77 TRADEMARK REP. 375, 396 (1987) ("There is already considerable relaxation of the affixation requirement in Section 45 . . . .").

[36] Int'l Order of Job's Daughters v. Lindeburg & Co., 633 F.2d 912, 917 (9th Cir. 1980).

[37] 539 U.S. 23 (2003).

[38] *Id.* at 31 (emphasis added).

bility for ... production of the *physical* product."[39] The trademark does not, however, signify the origin of the "ideas or communications that 'goods' embody or contain."[40]

In recent decades, trademark producers have made a mockery of the assumptions that underpin the trademark's triadic structure and the Court's reasoning in *Dastar*. Producers have discovered in the trademark a remarkably productive tool for the commodification of "ideas [and] communications." For such producers, the "mark *is* the product."[41] This is clearly the case, for example, when one buys a shirt bearing the ARSENAL or BATMAN logo at three times the price of a shirt without the logo. In such a situation, the "physical product," of whose source the consumer is ostensibly being informed by the trademark, is reduced to a nullity. The trademark's goodwill is commodified and sold as its own product. In effect, we are left with a purely linguistic, purely textual trademark, a dyadic relational system of meaning consisting only of a signifier and a signified.

The law thus grants exclusive rights in the ends of consumption under the guise of granting exclusive rights in the means of consumption. In the past, conscientious judges have recognized this problem and sought to deal with it in a variety of ways.[42] More recently, important scholarship has explained why, as an economic matter, merchandising rights impair competition.[43] This scholarship has proposed that disclaimers be the sole or at least the leading remedy available to plaintiffs in merchandising cases.[44] The problem is that we currently have no reliable method of distinguishing between merchandising fact-patterns and non-merchandising fact-patterns.[45] This is because all

---

[39] *Id.* at 32 (emphasis added).
[40] *Id.*
[41] Stacey L. Dogan & Mark A. Lemley, *The Merchandising Right: Fragile Theory or Fait Accompli?*, 54 EMORY L.J. 461, 472 (2005).
[42] *See* Beebe, *Semiotic Analysis*, *supra* note 5, at 657–61.
[43] Robert G. Bone, *Enforcement Costs and Trademark Puzzles*, 90 VA. L. REV. 2099 (2004). *See* Dogan & Lemley, *supra* note 41.
[44] *See* Bone, *supra* note 43, at 2182–3; Dogan & Lemley, *supra* note 41, at 489.
[45] Perhaps I should be allowed to sell unlicensed ARSENAL merchandise if I state prominently on the merchandise that it is not "officially licensed," *cf.* Arsenal Football Club plc v Reed [2003] R.P.C. 696 (C.A.), but may I do the same with merchandise bearing such trademarks as FERRARI (in support of the racing team if not also the automobile) or RED BULL (in support of the soccer team if not also the "utility drink")? And what, then, about unofficial merchandise bearing prominent disclaimers under such marks as BATMAN or even CHANEL? All of these are essentially nominative uses. All of them enable consumers to avail themselves of the goodwill, the "ideas [and] communications," and the "surplus meaning," that the trademark embodies. On "surplus meaning" in trademark law, see Rochelle Cooper Dreyfuss, *Expressive Genericity: Trademarks as Language in the Pepsi Generation*, 65 NOTRE DAME L. REV. 397 (1990).

trademark uses are now essentially merchandising uses. They are all celebrity endorsements of one stripe or another. Contrary to the quite outdated views of the *Dastar* Court, trademarks do not signify the origin of the goods to which they are affixed so much as they signify the origin of themselves, of the "ideas [and] communications" that they embody. To profit from their ownership, the owners of trademarks will confer these "ideas [and] communications" on suitable goods. Ultimately, then, the modern trademark does not function to identify the true origin of goods. It functions to obscure that origin, to cover it over with a *myth* of origin.[46] The modern trademark facilitates the fetishism of commodities by suggesting that brands, rather than actual human beings, produce commodities.[47] In other words, the modern trademark encourages the belief that both the tangible and intangible things that we consume all come from one "anonymous source"[48] or another.

III. The semiotic account of trademark "distinctiveness"

The concept of distinctiveness is the hinge on which trademark law turns. Yet for all of its importance—or perhaps precisely because of its importance—distinctiveness has never been adequately theorized. Traditional notions of "inherent" and "acquired" distinctiveness tend to confuse more than they clarify. This part argues that trademark law should reconceptualize trademark distinctiveness as consisting of *source distinctiveness* and *differential distinctiveness*. Corresponding to the semiotic relation of "signification," source distinctiveness describes the extent to which a trademark's signifier is distinctive *of* its signified. Corresponding to the semiotic relation of "value," differential distinctiveness describes the extent to which a trademark's signifier is distinctive *from* other signifiers in the trademark system. This reconceptualization recommends, among other things, an altered approach to trademark infringement analysis and a revised theory of trademark dilution. To explain why such a reconceptualization is worthwhile, I turn first to a discussion of the Saussurean concepts of "signification" and "value."

A. Signification and value

At the core of Saussure's structural linguistics is the distinction between signification and value. In brief, signification describes the vertical, intrasign rela-

---

[46] *See* Jessica Silbey, *Origin Stories and Other Tales: Mythical Beginnings of Intellectual Property* (working paper on file with the author).

[47] *Cf.* Dastar Corp. v Twentieth Century Fox Film Corp., 539 U.S. 23, 36 (2003) ("We do not think the Lanham Act requires this search for the source of the Nile and all its tributaries.").

[48] On the anonymous source theory, *see* 1 MCCARTHY, *supra* note 18, at § 3.9.

tions between signifier and signified.[49] Value describes the horizontal, intersign relations among signifiers, signifieds, and signs generally across the system of values, of "reciprocal delimitation[s],"[50] of "articulations,"[51] that constitute a language system. Whereas signification refers to the positive meaning of the sign, value refers to the negative difference or distinctiveness of the sign as against all other signs. Signification is one-dimensional equivalence; value is n-dimensional difference. To the extent that "differences carry signification,"[52] value is that by virtue of which signification occurs. Signification, in other words, cannot obtain without value; identity cannot obtain without difference.

Signification would appear to be an easily understood concept. The meaning of signification is ultimately based on the meaning of value, however, and value is probably the most obscure and unstable concept in all of Saussurean semiotics. It is also the most important (and of utmost importance to an understanding of the concept of distinctiveness in modern trademark doctrine). In general terms, value is a consummately structuralist notion. It conceives of identity not as something intrinsic, but rather as something dependent entirely on extrinsic, oppositional relations, that is, on relations of differential value to other identities in a system. "A language is a system of interdependent elements in which the value of any one element depends on the simultaneous coexistence of all the others."[53] Value describes place-value, context, and situation: "Signs function . . . not through their intrinsic value but through their relative position."[54] Intersign relations of value are necessary to perfect signification by delimiting it, by placing it within everything that is outside of and different from it: "[W]hatever distinguishes one sign from [another] constitutes it."[55] Value is thus not intrinsic to the sign but issues from the values of all other signs. "[E]verywhere and always there is the same complex equilibrium of terms that mutually condition each other."[56]

---

49 *See* ROLAND BARTHES, ELEMENTS OF SEMIOLOGY 48 (Annette Lavers & Colin Smith trans., 1967) (1964) (noting that "*signification* can be conceived as a process; it is the act which binds the signifier and the signified, an act whose product is the sign").
50 FERDINAND DE SAUSSURE, COURSE IN GENERAL LINGUISTICS 110 (Charles Bally & Albert Sechehaye eds., Roy Harris trans., 1990) (1916) [hereinafter SAUSSURE (Harris)].
51 SAUSSURE (Baskin), *supra* note 3, at 112.
52 SAUSSURE (Harris), *supra* note 50, at 118.
53 *Id*. at 159.
54 SAUSSURE (Baskin), *supra* note 3, at 118.
55 *Id*. at 121.
56 *Id*. at 122.

B. Source distinctiveness and differential distinctiveness

For too long, trademark law has improperly conflated its analysis of the *subject matter* of trademark protection with its analysis of the *scope* of trademark protection. The law has conflated, in other words, its analysis of eligibility with its analysis of strength, as when Judge Friendly, in his highly influential opinion in *Abercrombie & Fitch v Hunting World*,[57] analyzed at once the mark's "eligibility to trademark status and degree of protection accorded."[58] The law has made this mistake because it has failed to appreciate the difference between the semiotic relation of signification and the semiotic relation of value. The question of subject matter, of eligibility, is a binary question that considers whether or not a sufficient proportion of relevant consumers perceive a relation of signification between the trademark's signifier and signified. It is a simple matter: a trademark qualifies as protectable subject matter if the trademark's signifier is perceived as distinctive of its signified source and does not if the trademark's signifier is not perceived as distinctive of its signified source. To suggest, as the *Abercrombie* opinion does, that one trademark is "more eligible" for trademark protection than another because it is "more distinctive of source" than another makes no more sense than to suggest that one trademark (say, NIKE) is "more of a trademark" than another (say, ADIDAS). The question of scope, in contrast, is more complicated. It is a continuous question which considers the differential value of the mark, the degree to which it is distinctive, to which it stands out, to which it is salient, as against the multitude of other trademarks in the trademark system. Consumers are more likely to be confused by the appearance of a new mark which is similar to a pre-existing mark that is highly distinctive in this manner. Here, it is appropriate to conclude that one trademark (*e.g.*, COKE) may deserve a wider scope of protection than another trademark (*e.g.*, IGOR) because it is stronger and more distinctive as against other marks.

The root of the problem is that trademark doctrine's understanding of semiosis, of the operation of sign systems, fails to recognize the interdependence of signs. It has always given priority to the semiotic relation of signification and considered the semiotic relation of value as an afterthought, if at all. It assumes, in short, that identity precedes difference. This is reflected in the common belief that "distinctiveness" simply refers to source distinctiveness. But a mark's distinctiveness of source is only made possible by its distinctiveness from other marks. Relations of value, that is, facilitate relations of signification. Indeed, relations of value are what make relations of signification possible. There is no identity without difference, no source distinctiveness

---

[57] 537 F.2d 4 (2d Cir. 1976).
[58] *Id.* at 9.

without differential distinctiveness. The binary distinction of kind, between marks which are and are not source distinctive, is properly understood as merely the first in a continuum of distinctions of degree, along which are arrayed marks of more or less differential distinctiveness. Put in terms that any trademark lawyer will understand, if a mark is strong, it is necessarily eligible for trademark protection, but if a mark is eligible for trademark protection, it is not necessarily strong.

Consider the problem of the relation between the concepts of "secondary meaning" and strength. Students of trademark law often question whether there is any difference between these concepts. Though courts and commentary often use the terms interchangeably,[59] I suggest that there is a difference between them. Secondary meaning goes to the question of eligibility: does the non-inherently distinctive mark possess secondary meaning as a designation of source? But it makes little sense to then ask for purposes of scope analysis, to what *extent* does the mark possess secondary meaning? This is like asking to what extent your name refers to you. Perhaps your name may refer to other people as well, but to determine if this is the case, we must look to the context in which the sign used as your name appears. We must compare the sign to other signs around it, both syntactically and in its "sign field." We must, in other words, gauge the "value" of the sign to understand the nature of its signification. The analysis of trademark strength is ultimately an analysis of the extent of difference, of distinctiveness *from*, while the analysis of secondary meaning is an analysis of the existence of identity or reference, of distinctiveness *of*. The former analysis necessarily incorporates the latter analysis. Differential distinctiveness necessarily incorporates source distinctiveness.

Consider also the *Abercrombie* spectrum of marks. Empirical evidence suggests that most U.S. courts no longer rely on this regrettable area of trademark doctrine.[60] The semiotic account encourages us to abandon it entirely. For purposes of determining a trademark's eligibility for protection, it should not matter whether a mark is fanciful, arbitrary, suggestive, or descriptive. Nor does it necessarily matter whether the mark's distinctiveness of source is inherent or acquired.[61] All that matters is whether, for a sufficient proportion

---

[59] *But see* 1 MCCARTHY, *supra* note 18, at § 11.82 (emphasizing that the terms "secondary meaning" and "strength" are not interchangeable).

[60] *See* Barton Beebe, *An Empirical Study of the Multifactor Tests for Trademark Infringement*, 95 CAL. L. REV. 1581, 1634–40 (2006) (reporting that of 331 district court opinions sampled applying the multifactor test for consumer confusion, only 193 or 58% made some use of the *Abercrombie* spectrum).

[61] To be sure, as a policy matter, courts may wish to give a broader scope of protection to marks that are inherently distinctive in order to encourage the adoption of inherently distinctive marks rather than those that are not inherently distinctive. But if

of the relevant consumer population, the mark is or is not distinctive of source. For these consumers, does the relation of signification obtain? If the mark is inherently distinctive, we can rely on an irrebuttable presumption that this relation does obtain; if the mark is not inherently distinctive, then the owner must present evidence of the existence of the relation. For purposes of determining the scope of protection, the *Abercrombie* spectrum is also of little help. The question here is not whether the mark is distinctive of source, but to what extent it is distinctive from other marks. *Abercrombie* analyzes the nature of the intramark relation of signification, but our concern here is with the intermark relation of value. A signifier may be fanciful or arbitrarily related to its signified or referent in such a way that consumers perceive the signifier as a designation of source, but this usually tells us little about the degree to which the mark actually stands out from the noise of the marketplace as against other designations of source. More important by far is the degree of the mark's actual acquired distinctiveness in the marketplace, which will, in any event, necessarily incorporate any effect of the mark's inherent distinctiveness. Again, empirical evidence suggests that, in practice, most U.S. courts already recognize this; in their confusion analysis, courts' assessment of a mark's actual strength almost invariably trumps their assessment of a mark's inherent strength.[62]

C. *The infringement of source distinctiveness and the dilution of differential distinctiveness*

1. Trademark infringement The semiotic distinction between the relation of signification and the relation of value, and the corresponding legal distinction between source distinctiveness and differential distinctiveness, is recapitulated in the difference between the prohibition against trademark infringement and the prohibition against trademark dilution. The former prohi-

---

this is the course that they are pursuing, then courts should say so explicitly, perhaps by separating the issue from their assessment of the mark's strength and establishing it as a completely independent factor in the multifactor analysis for the likelihood of confusion. At present, when courts give an added bonus to inherently distinctive marks in their assessment of those marks' strength, they allow policy goals, however worthy, improperly to skew what they otherwise claim to be a strictly empirical assessment of the strength of the mark.

[62] *See id.* at 1636 (reporting that of twenty-three opinions in which courts found the mark to be inherently weak but commercially strong under the strength factor of the multifactor test for consumer confusion, twenty-two found that the strength factor favored a finding of confusion, and that of the twenty-seven opinions in which courts found the mark to be inherently strong but commercially weak, twenty-four found that the strength factor disfavored a finding of confusion).

The semiotic account of trademark doctrine 57

bition is a prohibition against interference in the intramark relation of signification between a trademark's signifier and its signified. Notwithstanding its name, trademark infringement is not infringement of a "trademark," if by trademark we mean simply the trademark's perceptible form, its signifier. Rather, trademark infringement is a trespass on goodwill, one which is accomplished by means of a confusingly similar signifier (and referent). The engrafting onto trademark doctrine of the syntax of copyright law has long confused this matter. The mere "reproduction, counterfeit, copy, or colorable imitation" of a trademark's signifier is not in itself trademark infringement,[63] nor, in fact, is the mere creation of confusion, mistake, or even deception. These are highly probative tests of whether trademark infringement has occurred, but they are not bases for relief. Copyright law prohibits the infringement of the signifier. Trademark law, in contrast, prohibits the infringement of the signified. Anti-infringement protection ultimately seeks to protect exclusive rights in the idea, not the expression.

To determine whether a defendant has infringed a plaintiff's trademark, a court should thus proceed in two steps. First, the court should determine whether or not the plaintiff's trademark is distinctive of source and thus eligible for trademark protection. Underlying this inquiry is the assumption that if the plaintiff's signifier-referent combination is not itself distinctive of the plaintiff's signified, then no similar signifier-referent combination will also be distinctive of, and thus trespass upon, that signified. The eligibility determination is not difficult to make. An eligible mark is either inherently source distinctive or acquires its source distinctiveness. Either form of distinctiveness will do; neither is privileged. Having determined that the plaintiff's signifier-referent combination is itself distinctive of the plaintiff's signified, the court should then determine whether the defendant's signifier-referent combination is sufficiently similar to the plaintiff's as also to be distinctive of the plaintiff's signified. Here, the court should consider not the source distinctiveness of the plaintiff's mark, but its differential distinctiveness, the distance between it and the nearest, most similar marks, other than the defendant's, in trademark features space. Consumer confusion surveys, as opposed to secondary meaning surveys, test for precisely this form of distinctiveness. Such surveys are essentially tests of comparative similarity. In the absence of reliable survey evidence, the most important factor in estimating the differential distinctiveness of the plaintiff's signifier is its acquired distinctiveness, in other words, its fame, renown, or salience.

---

[63] Quality Inns Int'l v. McDonald's Corp., 695 F. Supp. 198, 218 (D. Md. 1988) ("Unlike a copyright, mere reproduction of a trademark is not an infringement.").

2. *Trademark dilution* Dilution is as difficult a concept to understand in trademark law as value is in semiotic thought. This is not surprising. The law's recognition of the phenomenon of dilution is essentially the law's recognition of the semiotic relation of value. While trademark infringement involves the infringement of source distinctiveness, trademark dilution involves the dilution of differential distinctiveness, of a trademark signifier's set of relations of difference with all other signifiers in the trademark system. Antidilution protection entails a commitment to global, systemic, and absolute protection of those relations of difference. As Frank Schechter recognized, it entails a commitment to the "uniqueness" of the mark, to protecting the degree to which the mark is, as Schechter put it, "actually unique and different *from other marks.*"[64]

Trademark dilution occurs when, because two signifiers are similar, they lessen each other's differential distinctiveness. (We conventionally say that the junior signifier dilutes the distinctiveness of the senior signifier, though, strictly speaking, dilution occurs as to both signifiers; they are engaged in a zero-sum struggle.) In the typical dilution situation, the plaintiff's and the defendant's signifiers are very near, if not identical, to each other on the signifier dimension, but because their referents are sufficiently different, consumers are not confused as to source, with the result that no infringement action will lie. In this sense, trademark dilution constitutes not a trespass on the plaintiff's signified, but rather a kind of nontrespassory nuisance as to the plaintiff's signifier. The action for trademark dilution is designed to prevent such nuisances and, in doing so, to preserve the differential distinctiveness of the plaintiff's signifier, regardless of to what referent it is affixed. The prohibition against dilution is thus a prohibition against interference in intermark relations of value between the plaintiff's signifier and all other signifiers in the trademark system. If protection from trademark infringement prohibits synonyms (two different signifiers pointing to the same signified), protection from trademark dilution prohibits homonyms (two closely similar signifiers pointing each to its own signified). Antidilution protection ultimately seeks to protect exclusive rights in the expression, not the idea.

The semiotic account asserts, controversially, that dilution is not "blurring." The blurring theory of dilution put forward by the economic account is quite easily understood, which may account for its success as doctrine. Blurring occurs when consumers are aware that similar or identical marks refer to different sources, as in BASS for ale and BASS for leather goods. In such a situation, the link between the signifier BASS and the particular signified to

---

[64] Frank I. Schechter, *The Rational Basis of Trademark Protection*, 40 HARV. L. REV. 813, 831 (1927).

which it refers is blurred by the existence of an alternative link to an alternative signified.[65] The form of distinctiveness that is blurred is the mark's distinctiveness *of source*. The economic harm thus takes the form of an increase in search costs. As Judge Posner has explained, "[a] trademark seeks to economize on information costs by providing a compact, memorable and unambiguous identifier of a product or service. The economy is less when, because the trademark has other associations, a person seeing it must think for a moment before recognizing it as the mark of the product or service."[66] Conceived of as it is here as an impairment of the immediacy of the relation of signification between the signifier and the signified, dilution is essentially an inverted theory of trademark infringement. Where anti-infringement protection is a shield that prevents consumer confusion as to source, antiblurring protection is a sword that promotes consumer identification as to source. The blurring theory of dilution seeks to give the consumer better than twenty/twenty vision.

The most significant problem with the blurring theory of dilution is that it fails to comprehend, as a semiotic matter, what antiblurring protection fully entails and thus presents antidilution protection as no less benign than simple anti-infringement protection. Here again, conventional trademark doctrine is semiotically quite naive. The blurring theory of dilution conceives of the trademark as simply the union of a certain signifier with a certain source. In doing so, it isolates the trademark from the trademark system. But to protect relations of signification, one must protect relations of value. Distinctiveness *of source* requires distinctiveness *from other marks*, and while the first form of distinctiveness is by its nature limited to relations within the mark, the second form of distinctiveness is not. Thus, to prevent blurring, the law must preserve the differential distinctiveness of the mark as against all other marks. This means absolute, in gross protection that impacts the whole of the trademark system. Stated differently, blurring is a symptom of dilution, but it is not dilution itself. It is merely one effect of the dilution of the uniqueness of the mark as against all other marks. To prevent blurring, therefore, one must prevent dilution, and to prevent dilution, one must grant the owner of the mark absolute property rights, against the world, in that mark.

IV. The semiotic account of trademark culture

Trademark policy is, among other things, cultural policy. Trademarks utterly

---

[65] *See* Michael Pulos, *A Semiotic Solution to the Propertization Problem of Trademark*, 53 UCLA L. REV. 833, 854 (2006) (discussing dilution as "delay in signification").

[66] Richard Posner, *When Is Parody Fair Use?*, 21 J. LEGAL STUD. 67, 75 (1992).

dominate the lived experience of modern commercial culture. They fill that culture with their particular brand of distinctiveness. This is regrettable. To the extent that trademark law countenances at once the breaking apart of the trademark and the merging together of its various elements, it only facilitates the emptying out of meaning of the most pervasive signs around us and the production of the superficiality of "floating signifiers." The world in which we live and which constructs us as consumers and citizens is the lesser for it. Lacking the tools to confront them, the economic theory of trademark law is simply dismissive of such concerns. The semiotic account, in contrast, considers such concerns to be of crucial importance. I briefly survey here certain semiotic concepts that may help to clarify the cultural implications of the modern trademark and modern trademark law.

A. *The floating signifier and the hypermark*

Saussure himself would not likely have accepted the proposition, but Saussurean semiotics has since his time explored the possibility that while signification cannot obtain without value, value can nevertheless obtain without signification. From this follows the radical hypothesis that a signifier can be articulated, can achieve form, without being connected to any particular signified. Such an "empty" or "floating signifier" may refer to, or at least imply, a signified, but that signified is so indefinite or contested as to constitute an "empty category."[67] In such a situation, a sign "only means that it means."[68]

The phenomenon of the floating signifier is most readily identifiable in the context of nonrepresentational art and modernist literary texts (or indeed in ideological categories such as race,[69] democracy,[70] "1968,"[71] or "post-

---

[67] JOHN LECHTE, FIFTY KEY CONTEMPORARY THINKERS: FROM STRUCTURALISM TO POSTMODERNITY 64 (1994). *See also* Graeme B. Dinwoodie, *The Death of Ontology: A Teleological Approach to Trademark Law*, 84 IOWA L. REV. 611, 653 n. 174 (1999) (discussing the strategy of "weak advertising" by which "producers deliberately use 'weak' advertising texts that by their openness invite a 'strong' reading on the part of the recipient," and "by which producers hope consumers will project their own positive meanings on to the producer's goods").

[68] ROBERT GOLDMAN & STEPHEN PAPSON, SIGN WARS: THE CLUTTERED LANDSCAPE OF ADVERTISING 81 (1996).

[69] *See* Videotape: Race, the Floating Signifier (Media Education Foundation 1996).

[70] *See* Ernesto Laclau, *Politics and the Limits of Modernity*, *in* POSTMODERNISM: A READER 329, 334–5 (Thomas Docherty ed., 1993) (discussing "democracy" as a floating signifier).

[71] *See* Terry Eagleton, *12 Great Thinkers of Our Time–Jacques Derrida*, NEW STATESMAN, July 14, 2003, at 31, 32 ("Nineteen sixty-eight lives on in a fantasy of the floating signifier, but not as political possibility.").

modernity"). It is also increasingly identifiable in modern visual culture, particularly in the rapid succession of provocative, obscurely meaningful images that characterizes music video and some motion pictures, and in modern celebrity culture. As Jean Baudrillard has written, the increasingly common condition of Disney-like hyperreality, in which reality itself is constructed of simulations of imagined realities that themselves never existed, is especially conducive to the "floatation" of the signifier and the liberation of value from signification, of difference from identity:

> Referential value is annihilated, giving the structural play of value the upper hand. The structural dimension becomes autonomous by excluding the referential dimension, and is instituted upon the death of reference.... The emancipation of the sign: remove this archaic obligation to designate something and it finally becomes free, indifferent and totally indeterminate, in the structural or combinatory play which succeeds the previous rule of determinate equivalence.... The floatation of money and signs, the floatation of needs and ends of production, the floatation of labor itself.... the real has died of the shock of value acquiring this fantastic autonomy.[72]

In a condition of hyperreality, in other words, differences are not built upon designation, upon the equivalence of signifier and signified. There is only distinctiveness *from*, not *of*. This involves more than simply the "bracketing of the referent." It involves the bracketing of reference altogether, of any intrasign relation among subsign elements.

In theory, trademark law will not tolerate the semiotic condition that Baudrillard describes. The law still insists on reference, on source, however "anonymous." But in recent decades, there has emerged a truly radical structure of the mark, what might be termed the monadic structure. In such a structure, the trademark signifier has broken free from its moorings in a signified or referent. It signifies still, but signifies nothing. Such hypermarks—and Times Square is filled with them—are not designations of source, but commodified *simulations* of such designations. They are commodified fictions masquerading as trademarks and protected as trademarks. Mass produced, nonrepresentational canvases of great value, they invest the products, if any, to which they are affixed with pure unarticulated distinctiveness—distinctiveness of nothing, distinctiveness from everything. They represent the total collapse—the "implosion," Baudrillard might say—of the triadic structure.

B. *Sign value*

What is the purpose of such marks? Their purpose is to convey "sign value."

---

[72] JEAN BAUDRILLARD, SYMBOLIC EXCHANGE AND DEATH 6–7 (Ian Hamilton Grant trans., Sage Publ'ns 1993).

The concept of "sign value" is distinct from but based upon the Saussurean concept of "value." In everyday speech, the term "sign value" is typically used to refer to the capacity of status goods to signal high status, their "expression and mark of style, prestige, luxury, power, and so on."[73] Thus, it is said that the BMW has sign value and the DODGE does not. This definition of sign value descends from our notions of use value and exchange value, both of which draw upon essentially utilitarian conceptions of the term "value" ("worth in usefulness or importance to the possessor"[74] or "[m]onetary or material worth"[75]), rather than upon, say, a painterly conception of "value" ("the relative darkness or lightness of a color," "the relation of one part or detail in a picture to another with respect to lightness and darkness"[76]). In this utilitarian sense, sign value is understood as a special form of use value—a commodity may have various use values, one of which may be that it signals high status.

This is not the definition of sign value that I want to apply to trademark doctrine, where it will yield few nonobvious insights. Rather, I want to establish here the concept's more technical meaning, particularly as it is set forth in the early work of Jean Baudrillard. To develop the concept of sign value, Baudrillard works not from the classical economic notions of use value and exchange value, but from the linguistic, Saussurean notion of value, that is, value as relational difference. In Baudrillard's social-semiotic theory, sign value describes a commodity's differential value as against all other commodities, and thus the commodity's capacity to differentiate its consumer. Sign value does not necessarily involve the conspicuous display of prestige or wealth or of scarce positional goods. Rather, it involves something more essential: the conspicuous display of distinctions, of "marginal differences."[77] Sign value is Saussurean structural value made explicit, signaled, displayed. It is formal, differential value performed. It is the abstract essence of what Justice Frankfurter called a trademark's "commercial magnetism,"[78] and it is exactly what Frank Schechter had in mind when he spoke of the need to

---

[73] Douglas Kellner, *Introduction: Jean Baudrillard in the Fin-de-Millennium*, in BAUDRILLARD: A CRITICAL READER 4 (Douglas Kellner ed., 1994).

[74] THE AMERICAN HERITAGE DICTIONARY OF THE ENGLISH LANGUAGE 1972 (3d ed. 1992).

[75] *Id.*

[76] *Id.*

[77] *See* JEAN BAUDRILLARD, THE CONSUMER SOCIETY: MYTHS AND STRUCTURES 90 (Chris Turner trans., Sage Publ'ns 1998) (1970) [hereinafter BAUDRILLARD, CONSUMER SOCIETY].

[78] Mishawaka Rubber & Woolen Mfg. Co. v. S.S. Kresge Co., 316 U.S. 203, 205 (1942).

protect the mark's "arresting uniqueness,"[79] its "singularity"[80] and "identity."[81] To be sure, connotations of prestige may and often do issue from difference, but such connotations are merely an effect of sign value; they are not sign value itself. Such connotations merely give content to the differential form.

Placing this in more concrete terms, it is marketing orthodoxy that a trademark's most important quality is not the "esteem" in which it is held by consumers or its "relevance" to the lives of consumers, nor is it the "knowledge" consumers have of what the mark stands for. Rather, strong brands are characterized above all by "differentiation."[82] Distinction is their lifeblood and arguably the primary characteristic they offer for consumption. As Schechter recognized, it is their distinction that generates "selling power." This is the lesson of *BusinessWeek*[83] as much as it is of Baudrillard.[84]

C. *Sign value and consumer culture*
In a modern industrialized mass society, particularly a wealthy one, perhaps the most pressing scarcity that the individual faces is the scarcity of distinction—distinction not in the sense of prestige, but in the sense simply of difference that conduces to identity. Trademarks provide this difference and they do so through their sign value. It has long been a cliché, of social theory as much as of advertising practice, that consumers communicate with each other by the objects they consume. Of late, however, commodity culture has begun to unburden itself of the object language of material commodities. The trademark system has developed as an alternative language of consumption, and its development has been rapid indeed. No other language in history, and certainly no other language of distinction, has experienced such explosive growth, both extensively and intensively, in so short a time. The trademark system's classificatory scheme now orders culture as much as the market— and, in doing so, evidences the degree to which the two fields have merged. To be sure, it is not the only such classificatory system, but none exercises its classifying function so exoterically, in terms so easily and widely understood. Where other systems of distinction are opaque, even unknowable except to those whom they privilege, the power of the trademark scheme resides in its emphatic transparency.

---

[79] Schechter, *supra* note 64, at 830.
[80] *Id.* at 831.
[81] *Id.* at 827.
[82] *See* DAVID A. AAKER, BUILDING STRONG BRANDS 304 (1996).
[83] *See* Gerry Khermouch, *The Best Global Brands*, BUS. WK., Aug. 6, 2001, at 50.
[84] *See* BAUDRILLARD, CONSUMER SOCIETY, *supra* note 77, at 88 (discussing "the industrial production of differences").

While the semiotic analysis—or the economic analysis, for that matter—may go far towards explaining how the trademark system has evolved as it has, it will not ultimately explain why. Underlying the semiotic logic of the trademark system and of trademark law is a more profound logic, what Baudrillard has termed the "social logic of differentiation."[85] This logic meets "an objective social demand for signs and differences,"[86] for "the distinguishing processes of class or caste which are fundamental to the social structure and are given free rein in 'democratic' society."[87] The trademark system is ultimately both an agent and an object of "classification struggle":[88] an agent in its own struggle to establish itself as the pre-eminent system of classification, and an object in the struggle by producers and consumers within the trademark system to bend its classificatory scheme to their own economic or cultural ends. The culture industries—and what industries aren't?—have long sold trademarks as commodities in their own right. Entire areas of trademark doctrine cannot be understood except as systems of rules designed to facilitate the commodification—indeed, the "industrial production"[89]—of social distinction.

V. Conclusion

For all of our efforts to reform trademark law, it is unlikely that any reform of the law itself will alter its underlying social logic. Perhaps we can fortify the defense of fair use or expand the functionality bar to protection. Perhaps we can persuade courts that consumers do not so easily confuse two similar, but not identical marks and thus bring about a limiting of the scope of anti-infringement protection. Perhaps we can somehow even cabin the notion of trademark dilution. But none of these reforms will stem the cultural, "semiurgic" tide. More likely, the further rationalization of the law will only quicken it. Consumers will continue to demand signs, distinctions, differences. As presently conceived, the goal of trademark law is to meet that demand as efficiently as possible. Whether we can conceive of a different goal for trademark law remains an open question. This is not a question of law or economics, however, but ultimately one of aesthetics and politics.[90]

---

[85] *See id.* at 74.
[86] *Id.*
[87] *Id.*
[88] *See* PIERRE BOURDIEU, DISTINCTION: A SOCIAL CRITIQUE OF THE JUDGMENT OF TASTE 479–81 (1984).
[89] *See* BAUDRILLARD, CONSUMER SOCIETY, *supra* note 77, at 88.
[90] *See, e.g.*, Sonia K. Katyal, *Semiotic Disobedience*, 84 WASH. L. REV. 489 (2006); Llewellyn Joseph Gibbons, *Semiotics of the Scandalous and the Immoral and the Disparaging: Section 2(A) Trademark Law After* Lawrence v. Texas, 9 MARQ. INTELL. PROP. L. REV.

3 A search-costs theory of limiting doctrines in trademark law[1]

Stacey L. Dogan and Mark A. Lemley

Twenty years have passed since William Landes and Richard Posner wrote their classic economic defense of trademark laws.[2] Under Landes and Posner's "search costs" theory, trademarks have value because they reduce consumer search costs and thus promote overall efficiency in the economy. Over the past two decades, the search costs theory of trademark law has attracted a substantial following among both commentators and courts.[3]

While the search costs theory provides a compelling argument for trademark rights, it also compels an equally important – but often overlooked – set of principles for defining and limiting those rights. Certainly, trademark laws can make it easier and cheaper for consumers to locate products with desired qualities,

---

[1] © 2007 Stacey L. Dogan & Mark A. Lemley. This chapter is a continuation of a larger project on trademarks, and portions of the text are adapted from our article *Trademarks and Consumer Search Costs on the Internet,* 41 Hous. L. Rev. 777 (2004) [hereinafter Dogan & Lemley, *Search Costs*]. Thanks to Graeme Dinwoodie, Eric Goldman, Rose Hagan, Laura Heymann, Justin Hughes, Mark Janis, Ariel Katz, Doug Lichtman, Peter Menell, Michael Meurer, Sandra Rierson, Peter Swire, Rita Weeks and participants in workshops at the 2004 IPIL/Houston Santa Fe Conference: *Trademark in Transition,* Boston University Law School, the Intellectual Property Scholars' Conference at DePaul College of Law, George Washington University National Law Center, Stanford Law School, Thomas Jefferson School of Law, and the University of San Diego Law School for discussions and comments on this or that earlier project.

[2] William M. Landes & Richard A. Posner, *Trademark Law: An Economic Perspective,* 30 J. L. & Econ. 265 (1987).

[3] *E.g.,* Qualitex Co. v Jacobson Prods. Co., 514 U.S. 159, 163–4 (1995); Brennan's, Inc. v Brennan's Restaurant, L.L.C., 360 F.3d 125, 132 (2d Cir. 2004); Ty Inc. v Perryman, 306 F.3d 509 (7th Cir. 2002); New Kids on the Block v News Amer. Pub., Inc., 971 F.2d 302, 305 & n.2 (9th Cir. 1992); Clarisa Long, *Dilution,* 106 Colum. L. Rev. 1029, 1056–9 (2006); Maureen A. O'Rourke, *Defining the Limits of Free-Riding in Cyberspace: Trademark Liability for Metatagging,* 33 Gonz. L. Rev. 277, 306–7 & n. 114 (1997–8); Margreth Barrett, *Internet Trademark Suits and the Demise of "Trademark Use,"* 39 U.C. Davis L. Rev. 371, 376–8 (2006). *But see* Mark P. McKenna, *The Normative Foundations of Trademark Law,* 82 Notre Dame L. Rev. 1839 (2007) (challenging search costs rationale and pointing to an amorphous concept of unfair competition as the predominant driving force behind trademark law).

thus making markets more competitive. Yet if carried too far, trademark law can do the opposite: it can entrench market dominance by leading firms and make it harder for competitors to crack new markets. The evolution of trademark law reflects a continual balancing act that seeks to maximize the informational value of marks while avoiding their use to suppress competitive information.

Most of the literature on the search costs theory of trademark law has focused on the theory as a rationale for trademark protection. In this chapter, we examine its role in supporting limiting doctrines in trademark law.[4] We find that some limiting doctrines unambiguously lower consumer search costs and thus promote the goals of trademark law. Another group of doctrines, however, involves behavior that increases consumer search costs for some individuals even as it improves economic conditions for others. We believe that these latter doctrines – genericness, functionality, and abandonment – may sometimes go too far in accepting increased consumer search costs as the cost of achieving competition. Rather than the all-or-nothing approach suggested by these doctrines, we suggest that consumers would benefit from a more nuanced approach in their application.

I. Trademarks and information

A. Economic theory – trademarks and search costs

Most people think of trademark law in terms of what it forbids: the use of another party's trademark, or something resembling it, in a way that will cause confusion among consumers in the marketplace. Courts commonly describe the goal of trademark law as avoiding consumer confusion, which has the corollary effect of preventing the appropriation of a producer's goodwill.[5]

---

[4] By and large, these limiting doctrines are defenses. However, some of the doctrines we discuss here have a more complex relationship to the prima facie case of trademark infringement. There is controversy over whether the trademark use requirement is a defense or a part of the trademark owner's affirmative case, for example, and the doctrine of functionality is sometimes a defense and sometimes a part of the prima facie case, depending on which section of the Lanham Act is invoked. We have chosen the term "limiting doctrines" to avoid any confusion on this point. We also wish to make it clear that we have chosen only a subset of those doctrines for discussion in this chapter.

[5] See, e.g., Park 'N Fly, Inc. v Dollar Park & Fly, Inc., 469 U.S. 189, 197–8 (1985) (noting that the goal of trademark protection is to protect the consumer's ability "to distinguish among competing producers"); Ty Inc. v Perryman, 306 F.3d 509, 510 (7th Cir. 2002) (noting that the central concern of trademark law is to provide consumers with "a concise and unequivocal identifier of the particular source of particular goods").

Both consumers and producers, these courts point out, benefit when the public has access to truthful information about the source of products and services.[6]

In economic terms, trademarks contribute to economic efficiency by reducing consumer search costs.[7] Rather than having to inquire into the provenance and qualities of every potential purchase, consumers can look to trademarks as shorthand indicators. Because this shorthand information is less expensive

---

[6] *See Qualitex*, 514 U.S. at 163–4; *Park 'N Fly*, 469 U.S. at 197–8 (considering the benefits to consumers and producers that motivated Congress to pass the Lanham Act); *Perryman*, 306 F.3d at 510.

[7] *See* WILLIAM M. LANDES & RICHARD A. POSNER, THE ECONOMIC STRUCTURE OF INTELLECTUAL PROPERTY LAW 167–8 (2003); Nicholas S. Economides, *The Economics of Trademarks*, 78 TRADEMARK REP. 523, 525–7 (1988) (discussing the economic benefits of marks that apprise consumers of products' unobservable features); Nicholas S. Economides, *Trademarks*, in 3 THE NEW PALGRAVE DICTIONARY OF ECONOMICS AND THE LAW 602 (Peter Newman ed., 1998) [hereinafter Economides, *Trademarks*] (describing the savings for consumers in product searches as one of "[t]he primary reasons for the existence and protection of trademarks"); Brian A. Jacobs, *Trademark Dilution on the Constitutional Edge*, 104 COLUM. L. REV. 161, 164 (2004) (noting search costs rationale); Landes & Posner, *supra* note 2, at 268–70 (identifying the lowering of brand recognition costs to consumers as the justification for trademark law); Mark A. Lemley, *The Modern Lanham Act and the Death of Common Sense*, 108 YALE L.J. 1687, 1690–94 (1999) [hereinafter Lemley, *Modern Lanham Act*] (describing economic justifications for trademarks and advertising); I.P.L. Png & David Reitman, *Why Are Some Products Branded and Others Not?*, 38 J.L. & ECON. 207, 208–11, 218 (1995) (analyzing empirical search cost data and suggesting that "consumers of products subject to performance uncertainty will pay for brand-name assurance"); John F. Coverdale, Comment, *Trademarks and Generic Words: An Effect-on-Competition Test*, 51 U. CHI. L. REV. 867, 869–70 (1984) (noting that trademark law encourages competition, which potentially decreases the cost to consumers); *see also Qualitex*, 514 U.S. at 163–4 (explaining that trademark law "reduce[s] the customer's costs of shopping and making purchasing decisions," and "helps assure a producer that it (and not an imitating competitor) will reap the financial, reputation related rewards associated with a desirable product" (internal quotation marks omitted) (alteration in original)); Union Nat'l Bank of Tex., Laredo v Union Nat'l Bank of Tex., Austin, 909 F.2d 839, 844 (5th Cir. 1990) ("The idea is that trademarks are 'distinguishing' features which lower consumer search costs and encourage higher quality production by discouraging free-riders."). *Cf.* Mishawaka Rubber & Woolen Mfg. Co. v S.S. Kresge Co., 316 U.S. 203, 205 (1942) ("A trade-mark is a merchandising shortcut which induces a purchaser to select what he wants, or what he has been led to believe he wants.").

For other applications of the search costs theory of trademarks, *see, e.g.*, Michael Grynberg, *The Road Not Taken: Initial Interest Confusion, Consumer Search Costs, and the Challenge of the Internet*, 28 SEATTLE U. L. REV. 97 (2004). To be sure, there have been other explanations offered for trademark law. We analyze and critique several of them in Dogan & Lemley, *Search Costs, supra* note 1.

than detailed inquiries, consumers can more easily obtain and process it and will arguably become better informed, resulting in a more competitive market.[8] This system works, of course, only if consumers can trust the accuracy of trademarks, and this is where the law comes in.[9] By protecting established trademarks against confusing imitation, the law ensures a reliable vocabulary for communications between producers and consumers. Both sellers and buyers benefit from the ability to trust this vocabulary to mean what it says. Sellers benefit because they can invest in goodwill with the knowledge that others will not appropriate it.[10] Consumers benefit because they don't have to do exhaustive research or even spend extra time looking at labels before making a purchase; they can know, based on a brand name, that a prod-

---

[8] *See* HAL R. VARIAN, MICROECONOMIC ANALYSIS 82 (2d ed. 1984) (describing "perfect information" as one of the characteristics of a competitive market). To some extent, the brand-based product differentiation encouraged by trademark law arguably runs in tension with the law's information-facilitating goals. Ralph Brown famously argued that strong trademark protection has the effect of misallocating resources toward advertising, "[m]ost [of which], however, is designed not to inform, but to persuade and influence." Ralph S. Brown, Jr., *Advertising and the Public Interest: Legal Protection of Trade Symbols*, 57 YALE L.J. 1165, 1169 (1948) (footnote omitted). Furthermore, "[c]onsidering the economic welfare of the community as a whole, to use up part of the national product persuading people to buy product *A* rather than product *B* appears to be a waste of resources." *Id.* Yet trademarks undeniably provide value in conveying information about products and sources. Thus, "the only sensible conclusion, and the one eventually reached, was that trademark protection can both advance and disserve the development of an efficient and desirably competitive market." Glynn S. Lunney, Jr., *Trademark Monopolies*, 48 EMORY L.J. 367, 370 (1999). The key was to craft rules that minimized trademarks' anticompetitive effects. *Id.* at 371.

The separate question of when and how consumers seek and process information is a complex one, drawing from neuroscience as well as marketing theory. For glimpses, *see, e.g.*, Eric Goldman, *Deregulating Relevancy in Internet Trademark Law*, 54 EMORY L.J. 507 (2005); Rebecca Tushnet, *Gone in 60 Milliseconds: Trademark Law and Cognitive Science*, 86 TEX. L. REV. 507 (2008); Thomas Lee, *Trademarks, Consumer Psychology, and the Sophisticated Consumer*, available at http://papers.ssrn.com/sol3/ papers.cfm?abstract_id=967742 (working paper 2007).

[9] *See* Landes & Posner, *supra* note 2, at 270 ("If the law does not prevent it, free riding will eventually destroy the information capital embodied in a trademark, and the prospect of free riding may therefore eliminate the incentive to develop a valuable trademark in the first place.").

[10] By preserving the integrity of brands and advertising, trademark protection has a corollary effect of creating incentives to maintain high quality products. *See* Robert G. Bone, *Enforcement Costs and Trademark Puzzles*, 90 VA. L. REV. 2099, 2108 (2004) ("[I]f consumers lacked the ability to distinguish one brand from another, firms would have no reason to create brands with more costly but higher quality characteristics.").

uct has the features they are seeking.[11] Trademark law, in other words, aims to promote rigorous, truthful competition in the marketplace by preserving the clarity of the language of trade.[12]

While the reduction of consumer search costs and the encouragement of goodwill investment represent critical intermediate objectives of the trademark system, neither of these goals is an end in itself. The law reduces consumer search costs in order to facilitate the functioning of a competitive marketplace. Informed consumers will make better-informed purchases, which will increase their overall utility and push producers to develop better quality products.[13] Trademark law, then, aims to promote more competitive markets by improving the quality of information in those markets.[14]

Trademark law therefore represents an affirmation of, rather than a departure from, the competitive model that drives the United States economy. It is in this respect distinct from the rest of intellectual property (IP) law, which departs from the competitive norm in order to encourage investment in invention and creation.[15] Like antitrust laws, false advertising laws, and other

---

[11] *See* Smith v Chanel, Inc., 402 F.2d 562, 566 (9th Cir. 1968) ("Preservation of the trademark as a means of identifying the trademark owner's products . . . makes effective competition possible in a complex, impersonal marketplace by providing a means through which the consumer can identify products which please him and reward the producer with continued patronage. Without some such method of product identification, informed consumer choice, and hence meaningful competition in quality, could not exist.").

[12] *See* Economides, *Trademarks*, *supra* note 7, at 602 (stating that trademarks "facilitate and enhance consumer decisions"); William P. Kratzke, *Normative Economic Analysis of Trademark Law*, 21 MEMPHIS ST. U. L. REV. 199, 214–17 (1991) (arguing that trademarks are highly efficient means of conveying product information); Phillip Nelson, *Advertising as Information*, 82 J. POL. ECON. 729, 729–31, 743–52 (1974) (arguing that the simple fact that a product is advertised conveys information about the "experience qualities" of that product); Phillip Nelson, *Information and Consumer Behavior*, 78 J. POL. ECON. 311, 323–5 (1970) (comparing the advantages of national-brand versus retail advertising); George J. Stigler, *The Economics of Information*, 69 J. POL. ECON. 213, 220–24 (1961) (arguing that, although imperfect, advertising is a valuable means to reduce consumer ignorance).

[13] Indeed, classical economics requires fully informed buyers and sellers as a condition for a perfectly competitive economy. *See* Maureen A. O'Rourke, *Shaping Competition on the Internet: Who Owns Product and Pricing Information?*, 53 VAND. L. REV. 1965, 1968 (2000) (describing conditions for perfectly competitive market).

[14] *Cf.* Landscape Forms, Inc. v Columbia Cascade Co., 113 F.3d 373, 379 (2d Cir. 1997) ("[T]he Lanham Act must be construed in light of a strong federal policy in favor of vigorously competitive markets, which is exemplified by the Sherman Act and other anti-trust laws.").

[15] *See, e.g.*, Mark A. Lemley, *The Economics of Improvement in Intellectual Property Law*, 75 TEX. L. REV. 989 (1997).

consumer protection statutes, trademark law both draws from and reinforces the notion that competitive markets, under ordinary circumstances, will ensure efficient resource allocation and bring consumers the highest quality products at the lowest prices.[16]

B. Some limiting rules of trademark law and their search costs rationale

The pro-information, pro-competition goal of trademark law has several important implications for the scope of trademark protection, particularly in comparison to other areas of IP law. Overly restrictive trademark law has the potential to stifle competition rather than to facilitate it. Particularly when trademark holders have economic power, giving them absolute control over uses of their marks could erect significant barriers to entry for competitors seeking to describe their own products.[17] Even in less differentiated markets, strong trademark rights come at a cost because they have the potential to remove words from our language and product features from competition.[18] One task of trademark law, then, is to preserve the informative role of trademarks while minimizing these downside risks. One way trademark law does this is by granting trademark owners rights that are less than absolute.

First and most generally, trademarks are not property rights in gross, but limited entitlements to protect against uses that diminish the informative value of marks.[19] Trademark law historically limited itself to preventing uses of

---

[16] *See generally* Mark A. Lemley, *Property, Intellectual Property, and Free Riding*, 83 TEX. L. REV. 1031 (2005).

[17] *See* Lunney, *supra* note 8, at 421 (noting that trademark protection may encourage monopolistic behavior).

[18] *See* Rochelle Cooper Dreyfuss, *Expressive Genericity: Trademarks as Language in the Pepsi Generation*, 65 NOTRE DAME L. REV. 397, 398–9 (1990) (noting that current jurisprudence deals poorly with the evolving significance of trademarks as a part of language).

[19] *See* Beanstalk Group, Inc. v AM Gen. Corp., 283 F.3d 856, 861 (7th Cir. 2002) (stating that "a trademark is an identifier, not a freestanding piece of intellectual property; hence the rule that a trademark cannot be sold in gross, that is, without the assets that create the product that it identifies"); Marshak v Green, 746 F.2d 927, 929 (2d Cir. 1984) (invoking the rule against assignments of trademarks in gross, which states that "[a] trade name or mark is merely a symbol of goodwill; it has no independent significance apart from the goodwill it symbolizes"). *See generally* ETW Corp. v Jireh Publ'g, Inc., 332 F.3d 915, 922 (6th Cir. 2003) (differentiating between trademarks and patents because the latter confer a property right in gross rather than a limited interest). Professor Landes and Judge Posner explain that the rule against the transfer of trademarks in gross is important to prevent consumer deception during a "last-period" game, in which the company is going out of business and wishes to spend its goodwill; the long-term effect of permitting confusion of consumers in this way would be to increase aggregate search costs. *See* LANDES & POSNER, *supra* note 7, at

marks that "defraud[ed] the public"[20] by confusing people into believing that an infringer's goods were produced or sponsored by the trademark holder.[21] Likelihood of confusion does not necessarily follow every time a party adopts another's trademark; it turns on a complex analysis that considers competitive proximity, consumer sophistication, and other factors that explore whether a use will truly create a false association in the minds of consumers, and thus taint the information marketplace.[22] Although Congress recently added a

---

185–6; *see also* Kratzke, *supra* note 12, at 247–9 (offering an economic rationale for the rule "that a trademark user cannot assign the trademark in gross"); Stephen L. Carter, *The Trouble With Trademark*, 99 YALE L.J. 759, 786 (1990) (arguing that the prohibition on assignments in gross is consistent with trademark theory properly understood) [hereinafter Carter, *Trouble With Trademark*]. *Cf.* Lemley, *Modern Lanham Act*, *supra* note 7, at 1709–10 (criticizing trends in trademark law that permit transfers in gross). *But see* Allison Sell McDade, Note, *Trading in Trademarks—Why the Anti-Assignment in Gross Doctrine Should Be Abolished When Trademarks Are Used as Collateral*, 77 TEX. L. REV. 465 (1998) (proposing that in gross assignment rights be permitted when the assignment is offered as collateral for a loan).

[20] Taylor v Carpenter, 23 F. Cas. 742, 744 (C.C.D. Mass. 1844) (No. 13,784).

[21] The most significant exception to this rule may be the merchandising cases, in which some courts have allowed trademark holders to prevent use of their marks as products, rather than as indicators of the brand or source of products. *See, e.g.*, Boston Athletic Ass'n v Sullivan, 867 F.2d 22, 35 (1st Cir. 1989) (finding infringement in unauthorized sale of "Boston Marathon" t-shirts, reasoning that "when a manufacturer intentionally uses another's mark as a means of establishing a link in consumers' minds with the other's enterprise, and directly profits from that link, there is an unmistakable aura of deception"). The Fifth Circuit ushered in this trend in the *Boston Hockey* opinion, which found infringement in the absence of any confusion as to source or sponsorship:

> The confusion or deceit requirement [of the Lanham Act] is met by the fact that the defendant duplicated the protected trademarks and sold them to the public knowing that the public would identify them as being the teams' trademarks. The certain knowledge of the buyer that the source and origin of the *trademark symbols* were in plaintiffs satisfies the requirement of the act.

Boston Prof'l Hockey Ass'n v Dallas Cap & Emblem Mfg., Inc., 510 F.2d 1004, 1012 (5th Cir. 1975) (emphasis added). But at least as many courts have rejected the merchandising theory, and it is likely the U.S. Supreme Court would do so as well. *See* Stacey L. Dogan & Mark A. Lemley, *The Merchandising Right: Fragile Theory or Fait Accompli?*, 54 EMORY L.J. 461, 496–505 (2005) [hereinafter Dogan & Lemley, *Merchandising*]; *see also* Lemley, *Modern Lanham Act*, *supra* note 7, at 1706–09 (criticizing the merchandising right cases).

[22] *See* Polaroid Corp. v Polarad Elecs. Corp., 287 F.2d 492, 495 (2d Cir. 1961) (establishing factors of likelihood of confusion between different products in the Second Circuit); *see also* AMF Inc. v Sleekcraft Boats, 599 F.2d 341, 348 & n.11, 349 (9th Cir. 1979) (identifying likelihood of confusion factors in the Ninth Circuit).

federal cause of action based on the "dilution" of famous trademarks,[23] the statute focuses on uses that increase consumer search costs, either by "blurring" the significance of a unique mark[24] or by giving such a mark a negative association,[25] and to permit uses such as commentary and comparative advertising that actually facilitate consumer search.[26] Like the more traditional likelihood of confusion analysis, therefore, dilution – at least as properly understood[27] – turns on injury to the informative value of a mark.[28]

---

[23] See Federal Trademark Dilution Act of 1995, 15 U.S.C. § 1125(c) (2000) (providing federal cause of action for trademark dilution). Congress revised the statute in 2006 to modify the standard for establishing dilution and to clarify the scope of dilution defenses. See Federal Trademark Dilution Revision Act of 2006, P.L. 109-312, 120 Stat. 1730.

[24] 15 U.S.C. § 1125(c)(2)(B) (defining "dilution by blurring" as "association arising from the similarity between a mark or trade name and a famous mark that impairs the distinctiveness of the famous mark"). At least in the case of truly singular marks, such dilution by blurring can increase consumer search costs by making consumers look further for context, rather than immediately associating the trademark with its sole owner. See O'Rourke, *Defining the Limits*, supra note 3 at 291–5 & n. 65 (1997) (noting the harms of dilution). If consumers hear the term "Exxon," they think immediately of the oil company. If they hear "National" or "United," by contrast, they need context to understand what is being referred to. The risk of blurring is precisely that unique terms will over time be relegated to context-specific terms. *Id.*; Dogan & Lemley, *Merchandising*, supra note 21, at 493–5 (explaining how dilution is consistent with the search costs rationale). One might reasonably question how much of an increase in search costs this represents, however. See Tushnet, *supra* note 8 (doing so).

[25] 15 U.S.C. § 1125(c)(4) (defining dilution by tarnishment as "association arising from the similarity between a mark or trade name and a famous mark that harms the reputation of the famous mark").

[26] 15 U.S.C. § 1125(c)(3) (exempting parody, comparative commercial advertising, noncommercial use, and news reporting from a claim of trademark dilution). The Supreme Court further limited the original dilution law by interpreting it to require actual injury to the source-identifying function of a famous trademark. See Moseley v V Secret Catalogue, Inc., 537 U.S. 418, 432–4 (2003) (holding that 15 U.S.C. § 1125(c)(1) "requires a showing of actual dilution, rather than a likelihood of dilution"). Whether requiring actual harm was in fact in the public interest is open to question, because the federal dilution statute generally limits remedies to prospective injunctive relief. See 15 U.S.C. § 1125(c)(2). And indeed Congress changed the standard to likelihood of confusion in its 2006 revisions. But the Court's instinct that the law must limit the scope of dilution is in some ways undoubtedly correct, and the 2006 revisions also made it more difficult to qualify for dilution protection and expanded the defenses for those whose use of a mark was actually reducing, rather than increasing, search costs.

[27] Although courts seem to understand the concept of blurring the distinctiveness of a formerly unique mark, they occasionally have more difficulty with dilution by tarnishment. In theory, tarnishment applies only where the defendant brands its own goods with the plaintiff's mark, and where those goods are inferior in quality to or less reputable than the plaintiff's unrelated goods. See L.L. Bean, Inc. v Drake Publishers,

Second, trademark law rewards – and provides incentives for – investment in goodwill, but does not provide rights to all of the economic value that derives from that goodwill. Our competitive economy is based on the premise that competitors can generally appropriate ideas for products and services, as long as they are doing so in a non-deceptive way and are not infringing some other exclusive right, such as copyright or patent.[29] The patent and copyright

---

Inc., 811 F.2d 26, 31 (1st Cir. 1987) (noting that "[a] trademark is tarnished when consumer capacity to associate it with the appropriate products or services has been diminished [by being] linked to products which are of shoddy quality"). For example, if a defendant sells Toyota-brand pornography, those who encounter the use may think less highly of the Toyota brand name because they subconsciously associate it with pornography, even if they understand that the car company did not itself sponsor the materials.

Courts applying the tarnishment doctrine have sometimes used it to target criticism or derogatory speech about the trademark owner, a result that finds little justification in the search costs rationale. *See, e.g.*, Deere & Co. v MTD Prods., Inc., 41 F.3d 39, 44–6 (2d Cir. 1994). Most courts, however, properly distinguish the two. *See, e.g.*, Mattel, Inc. v Walking Mountain Prods., 353 F.3d 792, 812 (9th Cir. 2003) (holding that noncommercial parody is protected by the First Amendment and not subject to trademark dilution claims); MasterCard Int'l, Inc. v Nader 2000 Primary Comm., Inc., 70 U.S.P.Q. 2d 1046, 1053–5 (S.D.N.Y. 2004) (determining that Nader's political advertisements in the 2000 presidential campaign were not commercial in nature and thus not actionable dilution).

[28] *See Moseley*, 537 U.S. at 433–4 (stating that under the FTDA, mental association with another product does "not necessarily reduce the capacity of the famous mark to identify the goods of its owner"); Louis Vuitton Malletier S.A. v Haute Diggity Dog, LLC, 507 F.3d 252, 267–68 (4th Cir. 2007) (concluding that parody of famous trademark is unlikely to impair the distinctiveness of the mark); *see also* Stacey L. Dogan, *An Exclusive Right to Evoke*, 44 B.C. L. Rev. 291, 315–16 (2003) (interpreting *Moseley* to limit the federal antidilution statute to uses that reduce the "singularity" of famous marks).

[29] *See* TrafFix Devices, Inc. v Mktg. Displays, Inc., 532 U.S. 23, 29 (2001) ("[C]opying is not always discouraged or disfavored by the laws which preserve our competitive economy."); Deere & Co. v Farmhand, Inc., 560 F. Supp. 85, 98 (S.D. Iowa 1982) ("It is not only fair to imitate non-patented functional products, it is necessary to our form of economy."). When copying unprotected product features, competitors must sometimes take extra steps to protect against consumer confusion—for example, prominently using their own trademarks in marketing the copied product. *See, e.g.*, Kellogg Co. v Nat'l Biscuit Co., 305 U.S. 111, 120 (1938) ("Kellogg Company was free to use the pillow-shaped form, subject only to the obligation to identify its product lest it be mistaken for that of the plaintiff."); Fisher Stoves, Inc. v All Nighter Stove Works, Inc., 626 F.2d 193, 195 (1st Cir. 1980) (determining that the defendant took the necessary precautions to avoid consumer confusion by clearly displaying its name and logo on the product). In this way, the courts protect the competitive marketplace while at the same time keeping search costs to a minimum. *Cf.* Sears, Roebuck & Co. v Stiffel Co., 376 U.S. 225 (1964). Although states "may, in appropriate circumstances, require that goods . . . be labeled or that other precautionary steps be taken to prevent customers from being misled as to the source," they "may not, when the article is unpatented and uncopyrighted, prohibit the copying of the article itself." *Id.* at 232–3.

systems represent a response to the potential market failure that can result from the copying of public goods.[30] By contrast, trademark law is avowedly *not* designed to resolve any perceived failure in the market for quality products and services, but instead addresses failure in the market for information about those goods and services.[31] Thus, trademark law is reluctant to provide protection for product configurations (where the shape is both the product and "information") because doing so may give the trademark owner control not just over search characteristics, but also over the intrinsic value of the product itself.[32] Only where the product configuration has an established meaning as a brand in the minds of consumers is it entitled to protection.[33] Even then, protection does not extend to "functional" features that would limit competition on the merits in a particular product market.[34]

The limitations we have considered in this section stem from the search-cost-reducing goal of trademark law. When a word or product feature does not inform consumers about the product's source or sponsorship, legal protection for that word or feature would not reduce consumer search costs and is therefore denied.[35] Even when a mark is protected, the law quite reasonably permits uses of the mark that do not make a consumer's search more difficult, either by confusing the consumer or reducing the capacity of the mark to identify goods. Absent some legitimate reason to prevent such use, trademark law

---

[30] In economic terms, a public good is both nonrivalrous and nonexcludable, meaning that after it has been created and released, many parties can possess it simultaneously and the original creator cannot physically exclude others from doing so. *See* Bruce Abramson, *Promoting Innovation in the Software Industry: A First Principles Approach to Intellectual Property Reform*, 8 B.U. J. SCI. & TECH. L. 75, 92 (2002). U.S. copyright and patent law rest on the notion that, absent some form of legal protection, creators will under-invest in public goods such as useful inventions, art, and music. *See, e.g.*, Wendy J. Gordon, *Asymmetric Market Failure and Prisoner's Dilemma in Intellectual Property*, 17 U. DAYTON L. REV. 853, 854–5 (1992); Wendy J. Gordon, *Fair Use as Market Failure: A Structural and Economic Analysis of the* Betamax *Case and its Predecessors*, 82 COLUM. L. REV. 1600, 1610–11 (1982).
[31] *See TrafFix Devices*, 532 U.S. at 29 (noting that certain types of copying, such as reverse engineering, are fundamental to the workings of our competitive economy).
[32] *See* Wal-Mart Stores, Inc. v Samara Bros., 529 U.S. 205, 212–14 (2000) (pointing out that most design configurations reflect functional purposes rather than a means of identification for consumers).
[33] *Id.* at 212.
[34] *See, e.g., TrafFix Devices*, 532 U.S. at 29. *But cf.* Bone, *supra* note 10, at 2175–81 (noting that inquiry in functionality cases does not focus on the effect on competition in particular product markets, largely because of the difficulty of defining relevant markets).
[35] For this reason, descriptive terms, like product configurations, merit protection only after they have acquired secondary meaning. *See, e.g.*, Zatarain's, Inc. v Oak Grove Smokehouse, Inc., 698 F.2d 786, 790 (5th Cir. 1983).

accepts the core premise that unfettered competition will generate the best results for consumers.

II. Search costs and trademark limiting doctrines

The rule that trademark law is designed to reduce search costs justifies not just boundaries on the affirmative scope of trademark rights but doctrines that carve out limits from the ordinary scope of those rights. In the most straightforward of the trademark limiting doctrines, a party's truthful use of a mark unambiguously lowers search costs and thus deserves protection. Other doctrines, however, involve more uncertain informational effects. We consider both types of doctrines in this section.

A. *Limiting doctrines that unambiguously lower search costs*

The first group of trademark doctrines is fairly straightforward. In these cases, the defendant's use of a mark is a truthful one that gives consumers valuable information, and so permitting the use is consistent with the goal of lowering consumer search costs.

1. *Comparative and other truthful advertising* One example is truthful advertising about the nature and source of the product. Resellers of new, used, and refurbished products have a right to use trademarks to accurately identify the original source of the goods.[36] The fact that these parties advertise using the trademark is not illegal because they have legitimate reasons to attract the attention of those seeking the trademarked good.[37] "The result is, of course, that the second-hand dealer gets some advantage from the trade mark. But . . . that [rule] is wholly permissible so long as the manufacturer is not identified with the inferior qualities of the product resulting from wear and tear or the reconditioning by the dealer."[38]

---

[36] *See, e.g.*, Scott Fetzer Co. v House of Vacuums Inc., 381 F.3d 477 (5th Cir. 2004) (permitting resale and repair shop to use the names of the brands it supplied); Nitro Leisure Prods., L.L.C. v Acushnet Co., 341 F.3d 1356, 1364–5 (Fed. Cir. 2003) (permitting a refurbisher of used golf balls to sell them under their original brand name); Bijur Lubricating Corp. v Devco Corp., 332 F. Supp. 2d 722, 730–31 (D.N.J. 2004) (permitting resellers of used and refurbished goods to sell their wares as used or refurbished under the original trademark); Bumble Bee Seafoods, L.L.C. v UFS Indus., 71 U.S.P.Q. 2d 1684 (S.D.N.Y. 2004) (permitting tuna-salad maker that used Bumble Bee tuna in its salad to advertise that fact).
[37] *Scott Fetzer Co.*, 381 F.3d at 439 ("Independent dealers and repair shops may use a mark to advertise truthfully that they sell or repair certain branded products . . . ."); *Bijur Lubricating Corp.*, 332 F. Supp. at 731 (permitting the use of the trademark in metatags).
[38] Champion Spark Plug Co. v Sanders, 331 U.S. 125, 130 (1947). In cases

The right to engage in truthful advertising extends beyond the resale of the trademark owner's products. Competitors have an affirmative right to use others' trademarks to capture public attention and attempt to divert it to their own products by providing useful information that compares those products. As long as they do not mislead people into presuming some kind of affiliation between themselves and the trademark holder, competitors may use the mark to explain that their product imitates or aspires to the qualities of the trademark holder's goods.

In *Saxlehner v Wagner*,[39] for example, the Supreme Court allowed a natural water producer to use its competitor's mark to identify the product that it was copying.[40] Justice Holmes explained that as long as the defendants did not create confusion about the real source of their product, they were free "to tell the public what they are doing and to get whatever share they can in the popularity of the [trademarked product] by advertising that they are trying to make the same article and think that they succeed."[41] The Court distinguished between deceptive appropriation of goodwill and legitimate comparative advertising, concluding that by flagging its product as an imitator of the original, "they are not trying to get the good will of the name, but the good will of the goods."[42]

Similarly, in *Smith v Chanel, Inc.*,[43] the court allowed a knock-off perfume manufacturer to advertise that its perfume smelled like Chanel No. 5.[44] The court dismissed Chanel's argument "that protection should also be extended to

---

involving used or reconditioned products, courts require disclosure of that fact rather than preventing the seller from using the manufacturer's trademark. *Id.*; *cf.* Rolex Watch, U.S.A., Inc. v Michel Co., 179 F.3d 704, 709–10 (9th Cir. 1999) (refusing to allow reseller to use Rolex mark when modifications to watches were so substantial that they "result[ed] in a new product").

[39] 216 U.S. 375 (1910).
[40] *Id.* at 379–80.
[41] *Id.* at 380.
[42] *Id.* at 380–81.
[43] 402 F.2d 562 (9th Cir. 1968).
[44] The defendant's advertisements included at least two references to Chanel No. 5. In one reference, the defendant challenged consumers: "'We dare you to try to detect any difference between Chanel #5 (25.00) and Ta'Ron's 2nd Chance. $7.00.'" *Id.* at 563. The corresponding order form listed "Second Chance" with "*(Chanel #5)" just below it. *Id. Accord* Calvin Klein Cosmetics Corp. v Lenox Labs., Inc., 815 F.2d 500, 503–04 (8th Cir. 1987) (upholding competitor's use of the Calvin Klein mark OBSESSION if used in a nondeceptive, comparative manner); G.D. Searle & Co. v Hudson Pharm. Corp., 715 F.2d 837, 842 & n. 12 (3d Cir. 1983) (generic manufacturer could advertise that its product was "[e]quivalent to" plaintiff's if accompanied by a disclaimer); Upjohn Co. v Am. Home Prods. Corp., 598 F. Supp. 550, 561 (S.D.N.Y. 1984) (permitting maker of Advil to advertise Advil's equivalent strength to Motrin by using the MOTRIN mark).

the trademark's commercially more important function of embodying consumer good will created through extensive, skillful, and costly advertising," reasoning that "[t]he courts . . . have generally confined legal protection to the trademark's source identification function for reasons grounded in the public policy favoring a free, competitive economy."[45] Landes and Posner explain that the result in *Chanel* is entirely consistent with the search-costs rationale: "It would have been very costly for consumers to acquire such information [about the smell of the original perfume and the copy] before purchasing the copier's perfume because the perfume was sold through the mail."[46] But the search costs justification for comparative advertising is even stronger than they suggest. Truthful information about the similarities between two products lowers consumer search costs even if other ways of providing that information are not particularly costly. Trademarks work as signifiers precisely because they are a particularly efficient means of conveying information. They are useful in making comparisons for the same reason.

The same rationale has led courts to allow generic manufacturers to imitate branded trade dress in a way that evokes but does not confuse.[47] These cases, like those involving comparative advertising, emphasize that the public benefits from having fuller information about the products available in the marketplace.[48] The connection to search costs may be less obvious than in the comparative advertising case, but it is just as compelling: by providing

---

[45] *Chanel*, 402 F.2d at 566.
[46] LANDES & POSNER, *supra* note 7, at 206.
[47] *See* Am. Home Prods. Corp. v Barr Labs., Inc., 656 F. Supp. 1058, 1068 (D.N.J. 1987) (construing New Jersey and federal trademark statutes to render unlicensed imitation "irrelevant unless confusion also is shown"); *see also* Conopco, Inc. v May Dep't Stores Co., 46 F.3d 1556, 1565 (Fed. Cir. 1994) (finding no infringement when private label retailer "packages its product in a manner to make it clear to the consumer that the product is similar to the national brand, and is intended for the same purposes").
[48] *Am. Home Prods.*, 656 F. Supp. at 1068.

> The resemblance between two products can alert consumers to the functional or utilitarian equivalence between them, to the fact that one product may be substituted for the other in the ultimate uses for which the products are intended. The free flow of information regarding the substitutability of products is valuable to individual consumers and to society collectively, and by providing it a supplier engages in fair competition based on those aspects – for example, price – in which the products differ.

Id. Not all countries protect comparative advertising to the same degree as the United States. *See, e.g.*, Warren S. Grimes, *Control of Advertising in the United States and Germany: Volkswagen Has a Better Idea*, 84 HARV. L. REV. 1769, 1787 (1971) (discussing limitations on comparative advertising in Germany). But with the passage of the Comparative Advertising Directive, Directive 97/55/EC (Oct. 6, 1997), law in the EU began to improve.

consumers with visual indicators of a relationship between the product in question and branded products with which they have experience, the practice gives them a quick and easy way to comparison shop. Certainly, imitating the color of a box or the shape of a package operates at the level of subconscious attention-gathering rather than conscious comparison. But consumer search is by no means a process that always involves a conscious consideration of clearly identified criteria; it often turns on more subconscious judgments based on experience with particular products or brands.[49] Making it easier for consumers to find like products will thus sometimes mean permitting manufacturers to make them look alike as well as describing their similarities, for example by using gold coloration on cola cans to indicate that the cola is caffeine-free.[50]

Finally, competitors may use descriptive marks in their non-trademark sense to describe the features or qualities of their own products.[51] "In essence,

---

[49] For discussion of the extensive literature on this point in cognitive psychology, *see, e.g.*, Goldman, *supra* note 8; Barton Beebe, *The Semiotic Analysis of Trademark Law*, 51 UCLA L. REV. 621 (2004); Tushnet, *supra* note 8. Indeed, one author has gone so far as to argue that trademark law as a whole should be understood as "designed to accommodate and even harness non-rational human thought processes, rather than suppress or eradicate them." Jeremy N. Sheff, *The (Boundedly) Rational Basis of Trademark Liability: Reconciling the Federal Trademark Dilution Act and the Lanham Act*, 15 TEX. INTELL. PROP. L.J. 331, 334 (2007). To be sure, this fact is sometimes used as an argument in favor of stronger trademark protection by those who contend that a mere mental association between two products will either confuse consumers or dilute the strength of a trademark. *See, e.g.*, Jacob Jacoby, *The Psychological Foundations of Trademark Law: Secondary Meaning, Genericism, Fame, Confusion, and Dilution*, 91 TRADEMARK RPTR. 1013 (2001); Jerre B. Swann & Theodore H. Davis, Jr., *Dilution, An Idea Whose Time Has Gone; Brand Equity As Protectable Property, The New/Old Paradigm*, 84 TRADEMARK RPTR. 267 (1994). But as long as consumers are capable of distinguishing between the two products, there is no reason to believe that the evocation will have any negative effect on the strength or quality of the original brand. Indeed, the fact that one product references the other may strengthen the brand association in the minds of consumers. *See* Chi-Ru Jou, *The Perils of a Mental Association Standard of Liability: The Case Against the Subliminal Confusion Cause of Action*, 11 VA. J. L. & TECH. 2, ¶58–60 (2006); *see also* Louis Vuitton Malletier S.A. v Haute Diggity Dog, LLC, 507 F.3d 252, 268 (4th Cir. 2007) (finding no dilution by use, 'designed . . . to imitate and suggest, but not *use* the marks' at issue).

[50] We are indebted to Ariel Katz for this example.

[51] *See* 15 U.S.C. § 1115(b)(4) (2000) (providing a defense to infringement when a term is used "fairly and in good faith . . . to describe the goods or services of [the] party"); *Zatarain's, Inc.*, 698 F.2d at 791 (describing the "fair-use" defense); *see also* Car-Freshner Corp. v S.C. Johnson & Son, Inc., 70 F.3d 267, 269 (2d Cir. 1995) ("[I]t should make no difference whether the plaintiff's mark is to be classed on the descriptive tier of the trademark ladder . . . . What matters is whether the *defendant* is using the protected word or image descriptively, and not as a mark.").

[this] fair use defense prevents a trademark registrant from appropriating a descriptive term for its own use to the exclusion of others, who may be prevented thereby from describing their own goods."[52] Again, the interest protected is informational: trademark holders may not interfere with the ability of others to describe their products in truthful, non-deceptive ways.

2. *Trademark use*[53]   The trademark use doctrine attempts to ensure that the trademark grant does not stifle informative speech by non-competitors. To infringe a trademark, a defendant must "use [ ]" a mark "in commerce" "on or in connection with any goods or services."[54] Courts historically insisted that trademark "use" required that the defendant market goods or services under the mark.[55] As the Eighth Circuit recently explained, "the mark holder is generally not entitled to relief unless the defendant advertises or otherwise promotes [the actual mark] *thereby causing the public to **see** the protected mark and associate the infringer's goods or services with those of the mark holder*."[56] Defendants who do not themselves "use" a mark in commerce can

---

[52]   *Zatarain's*, 698 F.2d at 791.
[53]   For reasons we have explained elsewhere, we believe trademark use is an affirmative part of a plaintiff's trademark case, not a defense. *See, e.g.,* Stacey L. Dogan & Mark A. Lemley, *Grounding Trademark Law Through Trademark Use,* 92 IOWA L. REV. 1669 (2007) [hereinafter Dogan & Lemley, *Grounding*]. Our discussion here is a necessarily truncated one; for a fuller justification for the doctrine, see that article.
[54]   15 U.S.C. § 1125(a)(1) (2000); *see also id.* § 1114(a)(1). The act defines "use in commerce" as "the bona fide use of a mark in the ordinary course of trade, and not made merely to reserve a right in a mark." 15 U.S.C. § 1127. A use qualifies as a use in commerce on goods only when

> (A) it is placed in any manner on the goods or their containers or the displays associated therewith or on the tags or labels affixed thereto, or if the nature of the goods makes such placement impracticable, then on documents associated with the goods or their sale, and
> (B) the goods are sold or transported in commerce.

Id. For services, a use qualifies "when it is used or displayed in the sale or advertising of services and the services are rendered in commerce." *Id.*
[55]   *See* Felix the Cat Prods. v New Line Cinema Corp., 54 U.S.P.Q. 2d (BNA) 1856, 1858 (C.D. Cal. 2000) ("Use of the character as an expression of an idea or device to 'set the mood' of the Picture does not qualify as use of the mark 'to identify or distinguish' goods 'to indicate their source' as required to fall under the purview of trademark law."). As we explain elsewhere, the issue rarely arose until recently because trademark owners did not even try to claim ownership over the sorts of uses they now seek to prevent. *See* Dogan & Lemley, *Grounding, supra* note 53, at 1669.
[56]   DaimlerChrysler AG v Bloom, 315 F.3d 932, 939 (8th Cir. 2003) (emphasis added). Many courts adopting the trademark use doctrine have relied upon the "in connection with" language in the Lanham Act. *See, e.g.*, Bosley Med. Inst., Inc. v Kremer, 403 F.3d 672, 679–80 (9th Cir. 2005) (finding the appropriate inquiry in evalu-

80   *Trademark law and theory*

face liability for another's infringement only if they actively induce that infringement or knowingly help to bring it about.[57]

The trademark use doctrine is under attack in the Internet context,[58] and we

---

ating the "in connection with" requirement, as "whether [defendant] offers *competing* services to the public"); Holiday Inns, Inc. v 800 Reservation, Inc., 86 F.3d 619, 623–6 (6th Cir. 1996) (holding that the use of a telephone number that translated into 1-800-H0LIDAY–with a zero in place of the "O"–was not trademark "use" within the Lanham Act because the defendant had not advertised its services under the offending alphabetical translation). Others have relied on the "use in commerce" language. *See, e.g.*, 1-800 Contacts, Inc. v WhenU.com, Inc., 414 F.3d 400, 407–11 (2d Cir. 2005) (relying on the "use in commerce" requirement to find no direct infringement by a party selling pop-up advertisements); Karl Storz EndoscopyAm., Inc. v Surgical Techs., Inc., 285 F.3d 848, 855 (9th Cir. 2002) ("'[U]se in commerce' appears to contemplate a trading upon the goodwill of or association with the trademark holder."); Site Pro-1, Inc. v Better Metal, LLC, No. CV-06-6508, 2007 WL 1385730, at *4 (E.D.N.Y. May 9, 2007); Best Western Int'l, Inc. v Doe, No. CV61537PHXDGC, 2006 WL 2091695, at *5 (D. Ariz. July 25, 2006); *cf.* Hamzik v Zale Corp., No. 3:06-cv-1300, 2007 WL 1174863, at *3 (N.D.N.Y. April 19, 2007) (finding potential trademark use by a keyword advertiser that displayed plaintiff's trademark in the text of its ad). Still others have held that the trademark use doctrine bars claims without specific reference to statutory language. *See, e.g.*, Universal Comm. Sys., Inc. v Lycos, Inc., 478 F.3d 413, 424 (1st Cir. 2007) (rejecting a state dilution claim because "Lycos might profit by encouraging others to talk about UCS under the UCSY name, but neither that speech nor Lycos's providing a forum for that speech is the type of use that is subject to trademark liability"); Nautilus Group, Inc. v Icon Health & Fitness, Inc., No. CO2242ORSM, 2006 WL 3761367, at *5 (W.D. Wash. Dec. 21, 2006) (holding that an advertiser's use of a keyword to generate a sponsored link to run a comparative advertisement was not a trademark use for dilution purposes); Merck & Co., Inc. v Mediplan Health Consulting, Inc., 431 F. Supp. 2d 425, 428 (S.D.N.Y. 2006); Rescuecom Corp. v Google, Inc., 456 F. Supp. 2d 393, 398–403 (N.D.N.Y. 2006) (finding that sale of keyword-based advertising does not constitute "trademark use"); Lucasfilm Ltd. v High Frontier, 622 F. Supp. 931, 934–5 (D.D.C. 1985).

57   *See* Inwood Labs., Inc. v Ives Labs., Inc., 456 U.S. 844, 853–4 (1982) (concluding that manufacturers and distributors are liable for harm resulting from their intentional inducement of another to engage in trademark infringement).

58   *See, e.g.*, Playboy Enters., Inc. v Netscape Communications Corp., 354 F.3d 1020 (9th Cir. 2004) (holding that search engine could face liability as direct infringer for selling keyword-based advertisements); Government Employees Insurance Co. v Google Inc., No. 1:04CV507LMBTCB, 2004 WL 1977700 (E.D. Va. Aug. 25, 2004) (same); Google, Inc. v Am. Blind & Wallpaper, No. C-03-5340JF (RS), 2007 WL 1159950, at *6 (N.D. Cal. Apr. 18, 2007) (holding that a search engine's sale of keyword-based advertising can constitute trademark use under the Lanham Act); 800-JR Cigar, Inc. v GoTo.com, Inc., 437 F. Supp. 2d 273, 282–93 (D.N.J. 2006) (allowing trademark claims against a pay-for-priority search engine based on its "sale" of keywords in exchange for prominent placement in search results); Merck & Co., Inc. v Mediplan Health Consulting, Inc., 431 F. Supp. 2d 425, 426–8 (S.D.N.Y. 2006) (rejecting a trademark claim based on keyword-based advertising because defendant did not make trademark use); Rescuecom Corp. v Google, Inc., 456 F. Supp. 2d 393, 397–404 (N.D.N.Y. 2006) (same); Edina Realty, Inc. v TheMLSonline.com, No. Civ. 04-

have elsewhere offered a detailed defense of the doctrine.[59] For now, suffice it to say that limiting trademark rights to a right to prevent confusing uses of the mark as a brand helps to ensure that trademark rights remain tied to their search costs rationale—only those individuals or companies who are using the mark to advertise their own products or services have the motive and opportunity to interfere with the clarity of the mark's meaning in conveying product information to consumers, and so only those uses ought to be of concern to trademark law.[60] And by limiting trademark claims to those who themselves

---

4371JRTFLN, 2006 WL 737064, at *1–2 (D. Minn. Mar. 20, 2006) (allowing a trademark claim based on keyword-based advertising); Buying for the Home, LLC v Humble Abode, LLC, 459 F. Supp. 2d 310, 321–4 (D.N.J. 2006) (same); Int'l Profit Assocs., Inc. v Paisola, 461 F. Supp. 2d 672, 676–80 (N.D. Ill. 2006) (enjoining keyword advertising by a gripe site); *cf.* 1-800 Contacts, Inc. v WhenU.com, Inc., 414 F.3d 400, 408–12 (2d Cir. 2005) (rejecting infringement claim based on pop-up advertisements); Google v American Blind & Wallpaper Factory, 74 U.S.P.Q. 2d 1385 (N.D. Cal. 2005) (denying a motion to dismiss a keyword advertising complaint based on trademark use). *Cf.* 1-800 Contacts, Inc. v WhenU.com, Inc., 414 F.3d 400 (2d Cir. 2005) (finding that "use" of trademark to generate pop-up ads did not constitute trademark use and could not be basis for direct infringement claim); Wells Fargo & Co. v WhenU.com, Inc., 293 F. Supp. 2d 734 (E.D. Mich. 2003) (same); U-Haul International, Inc. v WhenU.com, Inc., 279 F. Supp. 2d 723 (E.D. Va. 2003) (same).

[59] Dogan & Lemley, *Search Costs, supra* note 1; Dogan & Lemley, *Grounding, supra* note 53.

[60] The Federal Trademark Dilution Act until 2006 required a "commercial use in commerce of a mark or trade name," 15 U.S.C. § 1125(c)(1) (2005), a standard that more explicitly incorporated the use requirement by applying only to "commercial speech" as that term is defined in First Amendment jurisprudence–speech that proposes a commercial transaction. H.R. REP. NO. 104–374, at 4 (1995), *reprinted in* 1995 U.S.C.C.A.N. 1029, 1031; *see also* Mattel, Inc. v MCA Records, Inc., 296 F.3d 894, 905–06 (9th Cir. 2002), *cert. denied*, 537 U.S. 1171 (2003) (explaining that "noncommercial use" under the Federal Trademark Dilution Act "refers to a use that consists entirely of noncommercial, or fully constitutionally protected, speech"). While the inartful phrase "commercial use in commerce" was removed from the statute in the 2006 revision, the current language of the statute makes it clear that the defendant must use the plaintiff's term as a mark in order to be liable for dilution. It speaks expressly of the effect of the defendant's "mark or trade name," one that exists separately from the plaintiff's "famous mark." 15 U.S.C. § 1125(c)(1) (2006).

The trademark use doctrine is even more important in dilution than in ordinary trademark infringement, because trademarks are often what Barton Beebe calls "floating signifiers" that can have multiple meanings, not all of which the trademark owner is entitled to control. Beebe, *supra* note 49, at 628–83. The Visa credit card network may have a famous mark entitled to dilution protection, for instance, but that doesn't give it the right to prevent uses of the English word "visa" in connection with travel services companies. The trademark use doctrine helps prevent dilution from swallowing language in cases such as these. For a discussion of how, see Stacey L. Dogan & Mark A. Lemley, 'The Trademark Use Requirement in Dilution Cases', *Santa Clara Comp. & High Tech. L.J.* (forthcoming, 2008).

use marks in a way that suggests some affiliation between themselves and the trademark holder (and to others intimately involved in their infringing activities), the law ensures that information facilitators, publishers, and others who bear only a tangential relationship to trademark infringement can go about their business without the responsibility of having to police all of the parties with whom they have commercial relations.

3. Prohibitions on naked licensing and assignments in gross[61] Unlike copyrights and patents, which have the alienability attributes of real property,[62] trademarks have never been freely alienable.[63] Indeed, selling a trademark without the accompanying business assets or goodwill is called "assignment in gross," and it can lead to the invalidation of the trademark.[64] Unsupervised licensing of a trademark can invalidate it as well.[65] The rationale for preventing free alienation of trademarks is closely tied to the search-costs theory of trademarks.[66] It is hard to see how the goals of preventing consumer confusion and encouraging investments in product quality would be furthered by allowing a company to sell the rights to a mark to another who will not make the same products at all or who will make products of different quality. If anything, assignments in gross are vehicles for *adding to* consumer confusion, not reducing it.[67]

---

[61] Portions of this section are adapted from Lemley, *Modern Lanham Act, supra* note 7.

[62] *See* 17 U.S.C. § 201(d)(e) (1994); 35 U.S.C. § 261 (2000).

[63] *See* Kenneth L. Port, *The Illegitimacy of Trademark Incontestability*, 26 IND. L. REV. 519, 553 (1993) ("Trademarks, on the other hand, enjoy none of the 'bundle of rights' that other forms of property enjoy. . . . Mark holders do not possess a property right in the mark itself, because trademarks are nothing when devoid of the goodwill they have come to represent or the product on which they are used.").

[64] The Lanham Act provides that the trademark owner can assign the mark along with the accompanying goodwill. *See* 15 U.S.C. § 1060 (1994). The negative implication is that it cannot be assigned otherwise. *See* Pepsico v Grapette Co., 416 F.2d 285, 289–90 (8th Cir. 1969) (invalidating a trademark assigned in gross). For a discussion of the rule against assignment in gross, see 2 J. THOMAS MCCARTHY, TRADEMARK AND UNFAIR COMPETITION § 18.01, at 18–14 to 18–16. For criticism of the rule, *see, e.g.*, Irene Calboli, *Trademark Assignment "with Goodwill": A Concept Whose Time Has Gone*, 57 FLA L. REV. 771 (2005); McDade, *supra* note 19.

For an interesting example of assignments in gross, see Lisa Lerer, *Bringing Back the Dead*, INTELL. PROP. L. & BUS., June 2006, at 28 (discussing RiverWest Brands, which buys defunct brand names and markets products under those marks).

[65] *See, e.g.*, Stanfield v Osborne Indus., 52 F.3d 867, 871–2 (10th Cir. 1995); Dawn Donut Co. v Hart's Food Stores, 267 F.2d 358, 366 (2d Cir. 1959).

[66] Indeed, the Supreme Court in *American Steel Foundries v Robertson*, 269 U.S. 372 (1926), expressly traced the reasons for the rule to the fact that trademarks were only symbols of goodwill, rather than property in and of themselves. *Id.* at 380.

[67] *See, e.g.*, Carter, *Trouble with Trademark, supra* note 19, at 786 ("The dete-

Landes and Posner point out that trademark owners will frequently have an incentive to maintain the quality of goods they sell even after a transfer of trademark rights in gross. Only in "final period" cases, where a company might want to spend down its stock of goodwill, will a transfer pose risks that a buyer will deliberately sell shoddy goods.[68] Whether or not a transfer is part of a final period game, however, the mental association a consumer has between a trademark and a particular product will generally be weakened by assignments in gross, and search costs will accordingly go up. Indeed, Landes and Posner themselves note that an assignment in gross itself makes economic sense primarily when it will involve confusing a significant number of consumers.[69]

The law does not prevent all deceptions of consumers by the mark owner during such a last period problem. If Coca-Cola wanted to spend down its goodwill by cheapening Coke, it could do so, and people would buy the product for a little while. But the fact that the law doesn't prohibit all possible ways a trademark owner might deceive its own consumers for profit doesn't mean that it must permit transactions that seem primarily designed to do so. Not only are assignments in gross unsupported by the traditional economic rationale for trademarks, but they do active damage to the goals of trademark law. The mental associations consumers make between trademarks and products are weakened by such transfers.[70]

The rule against naked licenses and assignments does create a problem for search costs theory, however, because the remedy for such assignments – invalidation of the trademark, so that anyone is free to use it – is hardly likely to avoid confusing consumers of that product. This is an area in which the law has taken a long-term rather than a short-term view, concluding that invalidating trademarks that are assigned in gross will discourage such assignments, and therefore will reduce consumer confusion on average, even though the remedy doesn't eliminate confusion in the particular case before it.

---

rioration of the prohibition on transfers in gross is a reflection of the continuing judicial misunderstanding of the theoretical underpinnings of trademark law. As a matter of theory, the prohibition on transfers in gross should be a firm one."); Kratzke, *supra* note 12, at 247–9 (offering an economic rationale for the rule against assignments in gross).

68 Landes & Posner, *supra* note 2, at 274–5.
69 *See id.* at 285.
70 There is a positive economic case to be made for free alienability in general. Restraints on alienation generally interfere with the operation of the market and may prevent assets from being put to their highest and best use. While this is a powerful argument when applied to most assets, it is weaker when applied to trademarks, since the asset is defined by – indeed, consists of – the connection between goods and their particular manufacturer.

B. Doctrines with ambiguous search-cost effects

The doctrines we discussed in the previous section further the search costs rationale of trademark law in a straightforward way – they permit third parties to give consumers accurate information about products or the cultural significance of brand names. But trademark law's procompetitive objectives sometimes require more. In the doctrines we consider in this section, the law limits a trademark holder's rights even when competitors might appear to receive a windfall or some consumers may be confused as a result. The law does this for one of two reasons – either because *overall* search costs would be higher without the limitation on trademark rights, or because recognizing trademark rights would impede the ability of competitors to enter markets and compete. In either case, however, at least some consumers will suffer higher search costs as a result of the limitation. The genericness, functionality, and abandonment doctrines present "hard cases" precisely because there are search cost rationales on both sides of the argument.

For the most part, the courts have resolved these hard cases in favor of the defendant, withdrawing trademark protection entirely in cases in which doing so facilitates search for the majority of consumers, or where it ensures competitive access to particular product markets. In other words, when market access and competition run in tension with the trademark holder's interests in protecting its product-associated goodwill, the competitive interests generally trump.[71]

From a search costs perspective, the automatic preference given to one group of consumers over another can be troubling. True, there will be times when the law must choose a rule that will disadvantage some consumers in order to protect others, and if there really is no alternative, courts must choose the rule that benefits most consumers. But the law's preference for all-or-nothing rules is a poor fit for these hard cases, and the courts can and should apply some of these limiting doctrines with greater nuance.

Several venerable doctrines of trademark law fall into this ambiguous-case category. We consider three such doctrines, and how the law might be modified to minimize consumer harm in each case.

1. Genericide The genericness doctrine prevents a party from claiming

---

[71] See *Kellogg Co.*, 305 U.S. at 122.

Kellogg Company is undoubtedly sharing in the goodwill of the article known as "Shredded Wheat"; and thus is sharing in a market which was created by the skill and judgment of plaintiff's predecessor and has been widely extended by vast expenditures in advertising persistently made. But that is not unfair. Sharing in the goodwill of an article unprotected by patent or trade-mark is the exercise of a right possessed by all—and in the free exercise of which the consuming public is deeply interested.

rights to a term "that refers, or has come to be understood as referring, to the genus of which the particular product is a species."[72] Genericness arises in two different situations. Some terms are born generic, and the law refuses ever to grant them protection. No one is free to claim the term "Computer" as its exclusive trademark for computers, preventing competitors from using the normal term by which the public refers to the entire class of goods.[73] Other terms are legitimate trademarks for many years, but come over time to be associated in the minds of the public not just with the trademark owner or its products but with the entire class of goods itself. When that happens, the law withdraws the protection it once granted. "Aspirin," "thermos," and "escalator" are all terms that were once trademarks but suffered this "genericide."[74] When a term has come to signify a class of goods, competitors have the right to explain what they are selling, even when their use of the generic term clearly piggybacks on the efforts of the party that first introduced the product.[75]

The genericness doctrine arises out of a concern for consumer search costs: Consumers will be misled if what they believe is a generic term is in fact a product sold by only one company.[76] And if competitors cannot use the generic term to describe their own products, consumers will incur unnecessary expense in trying to locate the competitors' versions. At the same time, the

---

[72] Abercrombie & Fitch Co. v Hunting World, Inc., 537 F.2d 4, 9 (2d Cir. 1976).

[73] McCarthy, *supra* note 64, § 12:1; *see* Gruner + Jahr USA Publ'g. v Meredith Corp., 991 F.2d 1072, 1078 (2d Cir. 1993) (holding that PARENTS magazine could not prevent use of the name PARENTS' DIGEST because "registering the proper noun 'Parents' as a trademark scarcely can be held to have removed it from being available for use by others, or grant exclusive possession of this property right to the trademark registrant" (internal citation omitted)); *see also* J. Kohnstam, Ltd. v Louis Marx & Co., 280 F.2d 437, 440 (C.C.P.A. 1960) (denying the exclusivity of the word "matchbox" as used to describe a type of toy).

[74] *See* McCarthy, *supra* note 64, § 12:1; *cf.* Union National Bank of Tex., Laredo, Tex., v Union National Bank of Tex., Austin, Tex., 909 F.2d 839, 844 (5th Cir. 1990) ("The English language, more than most, is in a constant state of flux. A word which is today fanciful may tomorrow become descriptive or 'generic')".

[75] *See, e.g., Kellogg Co.*, 305 U.S. at 122; *cf. Abercrombie & Fitch*, 537 F.2d at 9 ("[N]o matter how much money and effort the user of a generic term has poured into promoting the sale of its merchandise and what success it has achieved in securing public identification, it cannot deprive competing manufacturers of the product of the right to call an article by its name.").

[76] *See* Bayer Co. v United Drug Co., 272 F. 505, 509, 510–11 (S.D.N.Y. 1921) (analyzing whether aspirin had become a generic term to consumers); Landes & Posner, *supra* note 2, at 296; Ralph H. Folsom & Larry L. Teply, *Trademarked Generic Words*, 89 Yale L.J. 1323, 1337, 1342–43 (1980) (suggesting that hybrid terms would raise consumer search costs if they were granted continuing protections despite becoming generic).

genericide branch of the genericness doctrine can impose substantial search costs on consumers, particularly when a once-famous mark such as "aspirin" or "thermos" becomes generic.[77] Consumers who associate the famous mark with the company that uses it may well be confused when competitors begin using the mark as a generic term.[78]

The law is willing to make that sacrifice if enough consumers treat the term as generic, because the harm to consumers who associate the term with the entire class of goods outweighs the harm to the diminishing number who view it only as a mark.[79] But because there are consumers on both sides who may be confused, the law has traditionally required significantly more evidence of genericide than it does for consumer confusion. While courts will enjoin a defendant's use of a mark on a showing of as little as 10 percent consumer confusion,[80] they will not declare an existing mark generic unless a "substantial majority of the public" believes it describes a class of goods rather than a species within that class.[81]

Even with this accommodation to the interests of those who have come to

---

[77] *See Bayer Co.*, 272 F. at 514–15; Am. Thermos Prods., Inc. v Aladdin Indus., Inc., 207 F. Supp. 9, 14 (D. Conn. 1962).

[78] For discussion of the loss of producer goodwill when a mark is declared generic, see Stephen L. Carter, *Does It Matter Whether Intellectual Property Is Property?*, 68 CHI.-KENT L. REV. 715, 722 (1993). On the interrelationship between genericide and patent protection, *see Kellogg Co.*, 305 U.S. at 116–18 (noting that because the term "shredded wheat" is generic, "the original maker of the product acquired no exclusive right to use it"); *cf.* Gideon Parchomovsky & Peter Siegelman, *Towards an Integrated Theory of Intellectual Property*, 88 VA. L. REV. 1455, 1461 (2002) (commenting on the brand loyalty that remained with Bayer decades after "aspirin" became generic).

[79] *See* Folsom & Teply, *supra* note 76, at 1340–41; Landes & Posner, *supra* note 2, at 291–2; *see also* Justin Hughes, *The Philosophy of Intellectual Property*, 77 GEO. L.J. 287, 315–23 (1988) (noting that generic terms are "extraordinary ideas" that should remain open for all to use).

[80] *See* Henri's Food Prods., Co. v Kraft, Inc., 717 F.2d 352, 358 (7th Cir. 1983) (holding that 7.6% confusion was insufficient to establish likelihood of confusion, but collecting authorities finding likelihood of confusion based on surveys showing as low as 8.5% confusion among consumers); Grotrian, Helfferich, Schulz, Th. Steinweg Nachf. v Steinway & Sons, 365 F. Supp. 707, 716 (S.D.N.Y. 1973), *mod. on other grounds*, 523 F.2d 1331 (2d Cir. 1975) ("7.7% ... perceived a business connection between the two companies and 8.5% confused the names"); Jockey International, Inc. v Burkard, 185 U.S.P.Q. 201, 205 (S.D. Cal. 1975) (stating that the survey showed that "11.4 percent of the universe ... would associate defendant's JOCK SOCK underwear package with plaintiff"); Exxon Corp. v Texas Motor Exchange of Houston, 528 F.2d 500, 507, 208, U.S.P.Q. 384, 390 (5th Cir.1980) (stating that 15% was sufficient).

[81] Murphy Door Bed Co. v Interior Sleep Sys., Inc., 874 F.2d 95 (2d Cir. 1989); King-Seeley Thermos Co. v Aladdin Indus., 321 F.2d 577, 579 (2d Cir. 1963).

understand the term as a mark, the all-or-nothing nature of the genericide determination is somewhat troubling from a search costs perspective. Consumers do not simply flip a switch in their minds and go from thinking of a term as signifying a product to thinking of it as signifying a class of products. Some may strongly hold one view or the other, but others may occupy a middle state, in which a term like "Kleenex" can signify a trademark in certain contexts at the same time that it is used in casual conversation in a generic way.[82] A legal determination of genericide is an instantaneous elimination of the associations between mark and product built up in the minds of consumers. As such, it cannot help but confuse some – even some who also use the term in a generic sense in some contexts.[83]

We think that a legal doctrine designed to minimize consumer search costs should respond to the complex of consumer interests on both sides of a genericide case by tending towards standards rather than absolute rules.[84] Trademark's fair use doctrine serves as an example.[85] Under that doctrine, competitors are free to use descriptive terms that have acquired secondary meaning, but only in contexts in which they use those terms for their descriptive rather than their trademarked meaning, and only if the defendant uses the term in good faith.[86] Whether that use is permissible will depend on the strength of the mark, the nature of the use and of the goods on which it was made, the defendant's use of a separate brand to identify and distinguish its own goods, and other factors. Courts applying the defense will tolerate some consumer confusion among the plaintiff's customers in order to permit the defen-

---

[82] *See* Beebe, *supra* note 49 (noting the ability to hold several meanings for terms in the mind simultaneously); Deven R. Desai & Sandra L. Rierson, *Confronting the Genericism Conundrum*, 28 CARDOZO L. REV. 1789, 1803 (2007) (stating that "trademarks function differently for different people in different contexts and are capable of different yet simultaneous uses"); Folsom & Teply, *supra* note 76, 1339–42 (noting that many, and perhaps most, generic marks are hybrids with both trademark and generic meanings, and explaining the costs that such hybrids can impose on consumers).

[83] *See* Jerre B. Swann, *Genericism Rationalized*, 89 TRADEMARK RPTR. 639, 653 (1999) ("Consumer confusion is virtually a dictated consequence whenever a word used by one firm is declared generic . . .").

[84] *See also id.* at 655 ("[T]he line between a fringe generic and a naturally descriptive term is far too thin and inconsequential to justify the expenditure of enormous judicial resources to ferret out its placement."); Vanessa Bowman Pierce, *If It Walks Like a Duck and Quacks Like a Duck, Shouldn't It Be A Duck?: How a "Functional" Approach Ameliorates the Discontinuity Between the "Primary Significance" Tests for Genericness and Secondary Meaning*, 37 N.M. L. REV. 147 (2007).

[85] 15 U.S.C. § 1115(b)(4) (2000).

[86] *See, e.g., Zatarain's, Inc.*, 698 F.2d at 791.

dant's customers to easily find the products they are looking for, but the fact and extent of such confusion is relevant in deciding whether to permit the use.[87]

Something similar to the fair use doctrine might well serve consumers better than the all-or-nothing rule regarding genericide. Rather than immediately halting trademark protection as soon as 51 percent of the public views a former trademark as generic, the law could take a more case-by-case approach that focuses on the relationship between the plaintiff's interest and the defendant's use. If a substantial portion of the public still views the term as a trademark, but the majority views it primarily as a generic term, then both of these sets of consumers would benefit from an approach that allowed competitors to use the term in its generic sense, but prevented its use as a trademark by anyone other than the original trademark holder and required those who did use the term to try to avoid confusing consumers who thought of it as a mark. Courts, in other words, could permit uses of the generic term to describe the class of goods, while at the same time prohibiting competitors from adopting the term as a mark, or minimizing their own mark in an effort to confuse the consumers who still think of the mark as signifying a particular product. To be sure, courts today sometimes take steps to protect trademark owners in this situation – for example, by establishing rules requiring competitors who adopt a generic term that was once a protectable trademark to take steps to minimize confusion with the former mark owner.[88] But the approach is neither systematically adopted nor consistent with the general thrust of genericide, which holds generic marks completely without protection. A better approach would recognize that the confusing use of even generic terms can constitute unfair competition under section 43(a) of the Lanham Act[89] when the generic term has trademark significance among some portion of the public and the defendant's use capitalizes on that trademark meaning. Cases like *Genesee* are on the right track in effectively treating genericide as a continuum rather than a threshold.[90]

---

[87] *See* KP Permanent Makeup Inc. v Lasting Impression I, 543 U.S. 111 (2004) (finding that the fair use defense presupposes tolerating some confusion), *on remand,* KP Permanent Makeup Inc. v Lasting Impression I, 408 F.3d 596 (9th Cir. 2005) (finding that confusion is still relevant in determining whether the fair use defense applies).

[88] Genesee Brewing Co. v Stroh Brewing Co., 124 F.3d 137, 150 (2d Cir. 1997) (concluding that plaintiff's mark HONEY BROWN for its ale was generic, but defendant could still be liable if it did not use "every reasonable means to prevent confusion" in using the generic term) (quoting *Kellogg Co.*, 305 U.S. at 121); *see also, e.g.,* Home Builders Ass'n v L & L Exhibition Mgmt., Inc., 226 F.3d 944, 950 (8th Cir. 2000); Forschner Group, Inc. v Arrow Trading Co., 124 F.3d 402, 408–09 (2d Cir. 1997).

[89] 45 U.S.C. § 1125(a) (2004).

[90] *Cf.* Desai & Rierson, *supra* note 82, at 1855 (contending that genericness determination should turn on mark's significance in the commercial marketplace, rather than in common language or parlance).

We think a standard rather than an absolute rule is also appropriate in those rare instances in which a term that was born generic comes over time to signify a single source of goods. From a search costs perspective, the situation is simply the inverse of genericide – a group of consumers have treated the term as generic, but over time another group – sometimes the vast majority – comes to understand it as a trademark. Microsoft's "Windows" is an obvious example. There is good evidence that at the time Microsoft adopted the term in 1983, it was in general use to describe graphical user interface-based computer operating systems.[91] But by this century, the vast majority of computer users likely think of the term as signifying only Microsoft's operating system. Under current law, the only relevant question in such a case seems to be what consumers thought in 1983 when the term was adopted.[92] But from a search costs perspective, marks should be able to lose their generic character as well as gain it, depending on the reactions of consumers.[93] And just as we think the transition need not be an on-off switch for genericide, so too courts can apply a continuum in deciding whether a once-generic term has come over time to serve as a mark.

Treating genericness as a sliding scale rather than an absolute bar may have other salutary effects as well. Right now, trademark owners go to great lengths to prevent genericide.[94] They constrain the way they use their mark, never treating it as a noun or a verb, but only as an adjective.[95] They run advertisements to try to influence the way a mark is used in conversation.[96] They send threatening or cajoling letters to dictionaries, newspapers, and artists, encouraging them to modify their use or description of a trademarked term.[97] They have even come up with a (mythical) cause of action called "contributory dilution" that would allow them to sue dictionaries or ordinary

---

[91] *See, e.g.*, Microsoft Corp. v Lindows.com, Inc., 2002 WL 32153471 (W.D. Wash. May 13, 2002).

[92] *Id.* (marshalling evidence from that period).

[93] *See* Anti-Defamation League of B'Nai B'Rith v Arab Anti-Defamation League, 340 N.Y.S.2d 532, 543 (N.Y. Sup. Ct. 1972) (suggesting that generic term can acquire secondary meaning and thus become a protectable mark).

[94] *See* Desai & Rierson, *supra* note 82, at 1834–6 (making this point, and exploring in detail the socially wasteful expenditure of resources to avoid genericide).

[95] This particular piece of advice, widespread in the trademark bar, appears to be based on a myth. No court has ever held a mark generic because it was used as a verb. *See* Rose A. Hagan, *The Myths of Genericide*, 22:2 ABA INTELL. PROP. L. NEWSLETTER 13 (2004), available at http://www.abanet.org/intelprop/bulletin/winter_04.pdf .

[96] *See, e.g.*, ROBERT P. MERGES *ET AL.*, INTELLECTUAL PROPERTY IN THE NEW TECHNOLOGICAL AGE 679 (3d ed. 2003) (reproducing ad by Xerox corporation).

[97] For one cartoonist's amusing response to such a letter, see http://extlab1.entnem.ufl.edu/IH8PCs/vol3/V3N2.html.

citizens for misusing "their" term in dialogue.[98] All of these expenditures are socially wasteful, and if they are successful, the resulting restraint on speech may do even more harm to society. They are a function of the mark owners' fear of the catastrophic loss of genericide. These expenditures would be largely unnecessary if courts were to adopt a fact-specific approach to genericide, because the focus would be on the defendant's use in context rather than on what the public or dictionaries say.

2. *Functionality* The functionality doctrine, like the genericness doctrine, prevents parties from claiming trademark rights in a product feature that "'is essential to the use or purpose of the article or if it affects the cost or quality of the article.'"[99] But while genericness generally applies to word marks, functionality applies to product configuration and occasionally packaging. Like genericness, functionality is a threshold rather than a linear variable in existing law.[100] Even when consumers have come to associate a particular product feature with a single seller, that feature cannot serve as a trademark if exclusive use of it would put competitors at a non-reputation-related disadvantage. The U.S. Supreme Court recently emphasized, for example, that even if the public associates a particular feature with its first producer, the Lanham Act

---

[98] *See* Jerre B. Swann, *The Validity of Dual Functioning Trademarks, Genericism Tested By Consumer Understanding Rather Than By Consumer Use*, 69 TRADEMARK RPTR. 357, 375 (1979). We want to emphasize that there is no such contributory dilution theory in the law today. No appellate court has ever adopted such a theory, and the Lanham Act provides no statutory support for the theory. *See* Lockheed Martin Corp. v Network Solutions, Inc., 194 F.3d 980, 986 (9th Cir. 1999) (rejecting claim of "contributory dilution" and noting that no court has ever adopted it); Ty, Inc. v Perryman, 306 F.3d 509, 512 (7th Cir. 2002) (noting that the case law doesn't support this broader conception of dilution, and questioning the desirability of creating such a doctrine); Freecycle Network v Oey, 2007 WL 2781902 (9th Cir. Sept. 26, 2007) (finding there is no cause of action for "disparagement" of a mark by using it generally; *but cf.* Kegan v Apple Computer, Inc., 1996 WL 667808 (N.D. Ill. 1996) (finding genuine issue of fact as to contributory dilution claim, suggesting that "encouragement" of dilution could constitute contributory dilution). Still, the fact that the argument is made is a testament to the lengths to which trademark owners will go to try to avoid genericide.

[99] *TrafFix Devices, Inc.*, 532 U.S. at 32–3 (quoting *Qualitex*, 514 U.S. at 165). Strictly speaking, after Congressional action in the late 1990s functionality is no longer a defense but rather a part of a trademark owner's affirmative case in actions brought under § 43(a). 15 U.S.C. § 1125(a)(3); *see* Tumblebus Inc. v Cranmer, 399 F.3d 754, 768 (6th Cir. 2005).

[100] But also like genericide, there is some support for preventing confusing uses under section 43(a) in a few cases that find functionality but are concerned with the confusion that might result. *See* Graeme B. Dinwoodie, *The Death of Ontology: A Teleological Approach to Trademark Law*, 84 IOWA L. REV. 611, 746–51 (1999).

does not prevent others from copying that feature if it is part of what makes the product work.[101]

The connection between the functionality doctrine and a functioning market is even more fundamental than search costs – consumers cannot choose between competing products if one manufacturer can use a law designed to facilitate an efficient market to eliminate competing products altogether. Preventing trademark owners from protecting functional aspects of their products is therefore consistent with a search costs rationale. Indeed, one might think of it as a precondition to consumer search. While this is easiest to see with technological functionality – imagine the seller of a wheel claiming the round design as a trademark and preventing competitors from making round wheels – it is also true of aesthetic functionality.[102] A design feature is aesthetically functional if it causes the product to be more desirable not because of a reputational connection, but because it is intrinsically attractive. Many goods are purchased on aesthetics in whole or in part. Allowing someone who develops an attractive style of painting or a sleek design for a product to prevent others from using it interferes with the market for the product and generally serves no trademark-related purpose.

As with genericide, however, there is a problem. Because functional characteristics, aesthetic appeal, and source-identifying information may sometimes be lumped together in the same product – think of the Ferrari[103] – strict application of the functionality doctrine also has the potential to increase rather than decrease consumer search costs in some cases.[104] When a functional product feature has achieved secondary meaning, for example, some consumers might assume that all products with that feature come from a single

---

[101] See *TrafFix Devices, Inc.*, 532 U.S. at 34–5 ("The Lanham Act . . . does not protect trade dress in a functional design simply because an investment has been made to encourage the public to associate a particular functional feature with a single manufacturer or seller."). On the contours of trademark functionality doctrine, see Mark Alan Thurmon, *The Rise and Fall of Trademark Law's Functionality Doctrine*, 56 FLA. L. REV. 243 (2004); Robert C. Denicola, *Freedom to Copy*, 108 YALE L.J. 1661, 1670–74 (1999).

[102] See *Abercrombie & Fitch*, 537 F.2d at 9.

[103] See Ferrari S.p.A. Esercizio v Roberts, 944 F.2d 1235, 1246–7 (6th Cir. 1991) (holding that the exterior design of the Ferrari is nonfunctional).

[104] See Peter E. Mims, Note, *Promotional Goods and the Functionality Doctrine: An Economic Model of Trademarks*, 63 TEX. L. REV. 639, 658–9 (1984) (recognizing the role that the functionality doctrine plays in lowering search costs, but arguing that the doctrine of aesthetic functionality interferes with that role). For academic commentary on the functionality doctrine and the tradeoffs it embodies, see Maury Audet, *Wilhelm Pudenz v Littlefuse, Inc.: Next Replace Misnomer "Incontestable" with "Conclusive"*, 40 IDEA 473, 483–7 (2000); Dinwoodie, *supra* note 100, at 699–701; Thurmon, *supra* note 101, at 244–53.

source. If others can copy that feature, those who make such an assumption will be confused; if not, those who just want the product for its intrinsic value will lose the benefit of competition to produce the product.[105]

Unlike genericide, a sliding scale is harder to imagine with functional products, because the consumer interest in use of the product is not simply avoiding confusion as to source, but access to the product itself. But that doesn't mean that nothing can be done to limit the potentially confusing consequences of a finding of functionality. As with some cases involving generic marks, some courts have responded to these risks not by prohibiting use of the feature, but by requiring competitors to "use reasonable care to inform the public of the source of [their] product[s]."[106] To the extent that the use may even then mislead some members of the public, the functionality doctrine presupposes that the harm to consumers in these cases is outweighed by the greater availability of competitive products in the first place. Given what's at stake, that seems to us the right balance.

3. Abandonment Trademarks are protected so long as the mark owner uses them in commerce. When use stops for good, the trademark is deemed abandoned.[107] The abandonment rule is designed to release marks back to the public for use by others, preventing companies from "warehousing" marks.[108] But releasing marks back to the open market can have a rather significant

---

[105] Robert Bone points out that courts in functionality cases have to decide between two different economic costs: the increase in consumer search costs if the trade dress is denied protection, balanced against the increase in price that might occur if the originator has exclusive rights over the product feature. *See* Bone, *supra* note 10, at 2180 ("The goal of the functionality doctrine is to strike a balance between limiting the acquisition of market power and reducing information-related consumer harms. This means that a functionality analysis should tolerate market power over price when doing so is justified by the information-related consumer harms that trade dress protection avoids.").

[106] Gum, Inc. v Gumakers of Am., Inc., 136 F.2d 957, 960 (3d Cir. 1943) (citing *Kellogg Co.*, 305 U.S. at 120); Am. Greetings Corp. v Dan-Dee Imps., Inc., 807 F.2d 1136, 1141 (3d Cir. 1986) ("[I]f the functional feature or combination is also found to have acquired secondary meaning, the imitator may be required to take reasonable steps to minimize the risk of source confusion."); *cf.* Am. Fork & Hoe Co. v Stampit Corp., 125 F.2d 472, 475 (6th Cir. 1942) ("[I]n order to establish even the limited right of compelling appellant to take positive steps to avoid confusion, the existence of secondary meaning must plainly appear.").

[107] 15 U.S.C. § 1127 (providing that abandonment occurs when "use has been discontinued with intent not to resume such use," or when the mark hasn't been used for three years).

[108] *See* Major League Baseball Properties, Inc. v Sed Non Olet Denarius, Ltd., 817 F. Supp. 1103 (S.D.N.Y. 1993).

negative impact on consumer search. If a company builds up substantial goodwill before going out of business, that goodwill will often persist long after the company and its products disappear. The abandonment rule, and in particular the three-year presumption of abandonment, permits new trademark owners to capitalize on that goodwill, creating confusion or at the least causing cognitive dissonance within the minds of consumers who remember a mark as signifying one product and must now relearn it as signifying a different product in the same field. Examples abound, and include the reappearance of both FRONTIER and PAN AM as airline names and a race to claim DURAFLAME as a trademark for fake fire logs.[109]

To be sure, some – though hardly all – courts seem willing to avoid finding abandonment based on an involuntary cessation of business, and continuing goodwill in the mark is one reason they do so.[110] But those courts do so only when a company ceases business involuntarily, and under the statutory framework they can do even that only for three years. Goodwill in a major mark can persist long after that, particularly in cases where a company changes its name but continues in business. Federal Express changed its name to FedEx several years back, and it is the new name that appears on the Web site and on all packaging. But we doubt seriously that consumers would benefit should the name be deemed abandoned, permitting a competitor to use it.[111]

The statutory framework seems to serve little purpose within the search costs framework, and can affirmatively increase consumer search costs. We think the statute should be revised to preclude others from adopting a mark in any case in which significant brand recognition remained in the old name, even after it is abandoned.[112] The result may be that no one is entitled to use

---

[109] California Cedar Prods. Co. v Pine Mountain Corp., 724 F.2d 827 (9th Cir. 1984).

[110] *See, e.g.*, Pan Am. World Airways, Inc. v Panamerican Sch. of Travel, Inc., 648 F. Supp. 1026, 1031 (S.D.N.Y.), *aff'd*, 810 F.2d 1160 (2d Cir. 1986); Am. Int'l Group v American Int'l Airways, Inc., 726 F. Supp. 1470 (E.D. Pa. 1989). *But see Major League Baseball*, 817 F. Supp. at 1128–9 & n. 20 (refusing to protect "Brooklyn Dodgers" mark after the team's move to Los Angeles despite presence of significant name recognition).

[111] In fact, FedEx has likely retained some use of the FEDERAL EXPRESS mark to avoid just such an outcome. Whether that will be effective is open to question, though. *See* Exxon v Humble Exploration, Inc., 695 F.2d 96 (5th Cir. 1983) (finding that a token continuing use of Humble Oil name after name change was not sufficient to avoid abandonment).

[112] Cf. Stanley A. Bowker, Jr., Note, *The Song Is Over But the Melody Lingers On: Persistence of Goodwill and the Intent Factor in Trademark Abandonment*, 56 FORDHAM L. REV. 1003, 1006–07 (1988).

a particular mark after a well-known owner abandons it, but that result is the one that is least likely to confuse consumers.[113]

III. Conclusion

Economists have long recognized that the goal of facilitating the free exchange of goods requires consumers to be able to find what they are looking for quickly and cheaply. Reducing consumer search costs, in turn, is the primary traditional justification – and still the best one – for having trademark law. What we have shown in this chapter is that the search-costs rationale justifies not only the affirmative rights trademark law confers, but also the limits the law places on those rights. To a large extent, existing doctrine is consistent with trademark theory. But a few doctrines – notably genericness, functionality and abandonment – can have the unintended consequence of increasing rather than reducing consumer search costs. We suggest ways those doctrines can be modified so all aspects of trademark law – the grant of rights and the limitation on those rights – serve the purposes of that law.

---

[113] There is some question who would enforce such a right in the case of common-law usage as opposed to an effort to register the abandoned mark. We think the former owner of the abandoned mark should have a right to seek injunctive relief, but not damages, in such a case. While one might reasonably wonder whether a company that abandoned the mark would have any such incentive, the fact that there are a sizeable number of cases involving abandoned marks suggests that, for whatever reason, they often do.

4 Trade mark bureaucracies
Robert Burrell*

I. Introduction

Academic discussions of the justifications for trade mark protection have focused on the arguments that trade marks reduce consumer search costs[1] and protect against misappropriation of other traders' labour and investment.[2] One thing that is striking about these justifications, however, is that they provide little explanation of trade mark *registration*. This disjuncture between the standard justifications for trade mark protection and the existence and operation of registered trade mark systems is significant, because having a registered trade mark system requires a substantial expenditure of resources. Most obviously, a registered trade mark system requires the existence of a bureaucracy to process applications for registration. Less obvious costs flow from having a special class of lawyers (that is, "trade mark agents" or "trade mark attorneys") who

---

* Associate Professor and Associate Director for Australian Centre for Intellectual Property in Agriculture, the University of Queensland, TC Beirne School of Law. My thanks go to Graeme Austin, Lionel Bently, Michael Handler, Charles Lawson and Kimberlee Weatherall.

[1] *See, e.g.*, WILLIAM LANDES & RICHARD POSNER, THE ECONOMIC STRUCTURE OF INTELLECTUAL PROPERTY LAW Ch. 7 (2003); Nicholas Economides, *The Economics of Trademarks*, 78 TRADEMARK REP. 523, 525–6 (1988); I.P.L. Png & David Reitman, *Why Are Some Products Branded and Others Not?*, 38 J.L. & ECON. 207 (1995). By allowing consumers to identify products they have enjoyed in the past, trade marks also, on this view, provide traders with incentives to compete on grounds other than price by developing products with particularly desirable properties. It should also be noted that some of the more recent law and economics literature seeks to go beyond the consumer confusion/search cost argument and suggests that trade mark protection provides incentives for traders to invest in the development of new signs. The most sophisticated version of this argument is presented by Vincent Chiappetta, *Trademarks: More than Meets the Eye*, [2003] U. ILL. J.L. TECH. & POL'Y 35. *But see also* LANDES & POSNER, *id.* at 168–72; Megan Richardson, *Trade Marks and Language*, 26 SYDNEY L. REV. 193 (2004).

[2] *See, e.g.*, ANSELM KAMPERMAN SANDERS, UNFAIR COMPETITION LAW: THE PROTECTION OF INTELLECTUAL AND INDUSTRIAL CREATIVITY (1997). In this category can also be placed work that seeks to justify trade mark protection on the ground that trade marks are important cultural artefacts, *e.g.*, Massimo Sterpi, *Trademarks as Social Characters: The New Legal Issues of Identity Protection*, Address at the Twelfth Annual Fordham Intellectual Property Conference, (Apr. 15–16, 2004).

are only licensed to practise in the registered trade mark field and even in having university courses and books that deal exclusively or predominately with the law of registered trade marks. The mere fact that registration systems are now largely self-funding (that is, the fees paid by trade mark applicants cover the salaries of those working within trade mark offices in most countries) should not blind us to the fact that the resources expended on the trade mark bureaucracy and on the other activities mentioned above could be employed in other ways.

It is notable that the function of registration tends to be much better addressed in relation to other intellectual property rights than it is in the trade mark context.[3] For example, it is commonly understood that patent registration forms part of the "bargain" between the inventor and the public, with the patentee being required to disclose the invention to the public through the registration process in return for the grant of the patent.[4] It is also notable that patent protection seems inevitably to require the existence of a registration

---

[3] It is possible to draw a further distinction between the function of "registration" and the function of "examination". This is not, however, a distinction on which this chapter will dwell. As is explained below, a "bare registration" or "deposit" system would be incompatible with the information function of the trade mark register.

[4] Clarisa Long has argued that this explanation of the role of registration has obscured the "signal value" of patents, that is, that obtaining patents can be a cost effective way of transmitting information to third parties (in particular, to potential investors), for example, as to the vitality of a firm's research and development programme. *See* Clarisa Long, *Patent Signals*, 60 U. CHI. L. REV. 625 (2002). The possibility that trade mark registration might perform a similar signalling function is not explored at length in this essay. It might be noted, however, that it is not immediately obvious that trade mark registration provides the sort of signal that Long describes. It is possible that the number of trade marks registered by a firm might be treated as a surrogate marker for a firm's commitment to brand development or to innovation in product design or marketing strategy. However, there would have to be robust evidence that potential investors look at registered trade marks in this way before a plausible case for registration could be built around signal value. Still more importantly, it would also be necessary to demonstrate that investors are right to treat registered trade marks in this way. That is, it would be necessary to demonstrate that trade mark registration does not, in fact, provide misleading information about a firm's underlying characteristics or performance. *Cf.* Long, *supra.* at 660–63. For example, it would be necessary to show that a multiplicity of registrations does not indicate a lack of marketing focus or a confused approach to brand development, rather than a commitment to innovation. Moreover, it might well be the case that there are more efficient and reliable ways for firms to communicate to the market their commitment to brand building, innovation in marketing and so forth: it is far from obvious that the number of trade mark registrations provides a better surrogate marker for these aspects of a firm's performance than details of advertising and marketing budgets, *etc. Cf.* Long, *id.*, for a discussion of the difficulty of communicating information about research performance in the absence of patent protection.

system, or at least there seems to be a broad consensus to the effect that insofar as patent protection is justifiable at all, it ought to depend on the would-be owner of the invention lodging an application with a central registry.[5] In contrast, it is clearly possible to devise robust legal mechanisms to protect trade marks that are not dependent upon registration—most countries already provide protection for unregistered marks through one means or another.

If a registered trade mark system creates costs of various kinds, and if there are perfectly good methods of protecting trade marks that do not require marks to be registered, there is a clear need for attention to be given to reasons why providing a facility for trade mark registration might be thought desirable. In this respect trade mark and designs law share something in common, since many countries have systems for protecting both registered and unregistered designs that sit alongside one another. Significantly, the existence of these dual forms of protection has drawn attention to the merits of requiring or providing a facility for design registration.[6] A similar debate needs to take place in relation to trade marks.

The difficulty is that it is hard to find a truly convincing justification for trade mark registration. This is not to say that registration fails to perform any useful function, but rather that the public benefits offered by registration do not seem sufficient to justify the elaborate edifices that registered trade mark systems have become. It might, therefore, be possible to make a case for the abolition of trade mark registration. However, given that trade mark registration now forms an integral part of commercial life in most developed countries, it would be both premature and, from a practical perspective, pointless to call for the abolition of trade mark registration. Recognition of the problematic nature of trade mark registration ought instead to be treated as a spur for thinking about how trade mark registration can best be made to serve useful ends. Such an assessment requires careful attention to be paid to the way registered trade mark systems function. Specifically, this means that consideration needs to be given to the way trade mark bureaucracies operate and to how such

---

[5]   Indeed, dating back to the mid-nineteenth century, when nations began to establish modern patent systems, there does not seem to have been any sustained interest in moving patent protection to a more copyright-like model (although, as is noted below, support has been expressed at times for greater reliance on a petty patent model, that is, a system in which examination is deferred until it is requested by the owner, for example, because the owner wishes to commence infringement proceedings).

[6]   See, e.g., Report of the Committee to Consider the Law on Copyright and Designs 1977 (Cmnd. 6732) ¶ 131 (UK); Lionel Bently, *Requiem for Registration? Reflections on the History of the United Kingdom Registered Designs System*, in 1 PERSPECTIVES ON INTELLECTUAL PROPERTY: THE PREHISTORY AND DEVELOPMENT OF INTELLECTUAL PROPERTY SYSTEMS (Alison Firth ed., 1997); UMA SUTHERSANEN, DESIGNS LAW IN EUROPE 103–07 (2000).

bureaucracies interact with courts, other government agencies, users of the trade mark system and their legal representatives. Unfortunately, such an analysis suggests that there are likely to be significant obstacles to ensuring that trade mark registration becomes better focused on achieving publicly desirable goals. Whilst recognition of such obstacles undermines further the case for registration, it is only once we have reached this point that we can gain a clear picture of the consequences of providing protection for trade marks as a species of bureaucratic property.

II. The clearance cost argument for registration

To the extent that the role of trade mark registration is ever addressed, it is usually done so in terms of the advantages that registration confers on the registered proprietor. For example, it is often pointed out that compared to relying on unfair competition law or a passing off action or some similar mechanism, it is relatively easy to establish infringement of a registered mark. Similarly, in the context of US law, it is pointed out that the conferral of incontestability on a registered mark that has been in continuous use for five consecutive years confers a significant quiet title benefit on the registered owner.[7] The advantages conferred by registration provide an incentive for traders to register their marks, but such incentives are only desirable if the registered trade mark system ultimately confers a benefit on the public. As with other intellectual property systems, the public benefits that might be said to flow from registration lie, for the most part, in the value of the trade mark register as a source of information. For example, one can defend registration on the basis that the trade mark register provides valuable information about the ownership of trade signs, as is discussed below. The strongest informational argument for the value of trade mark registration, however, is that it enables those engaged in trade, and the public more generally, to discover quickly and cheaply which signs third parties have already claimed. In order for a trade mark register to perform its function effectively on this view, it is essential that it reflect, as accurately as possible, marks that enjoy legal protection.

As regards the final point about the need for the trade mark register to convey accurate information, one might at first think that much the same could be said in relation to other intellectual property rights. It is important, however, to appreciate that there are significant differences between the nature of the information communicated by the trade mark system and the nature of the information communicated by other intellectual property registration systems. In the case of trade marks, registration ought to make it easier for third parties to ascertain whether a mark enjoys legal protection. The benefits

---

[7] *See* 15 U.S.C. § 1065 (2000).

of registration come in the form of reduced clearance costs, but such benefits will only manifest themselves to the extent that those consulting the register are able to rely on the information contained therein. If the register misinforms, by failing to record marks that enjoy legal protection or by incorporating marks that would not survive a legal challenge, the function of registration is undermined— it will still be necessary to conduct searches for marks that are protected in the marketplace but do not appear on the register and/or to look behind the registration to see whether the mark ought really to be on the register.

The information communicated by patent and design registers is, in contrast, quite different. The value of the information contained on such registers lies in the record they provide of novel technologies and innovations in design. The fact that some inventions and designs will inevitably remain unregistered means that the information on patent and designs registers will always be incomplete, but this does not call into question the value of the information that is included on the register. The same is true even as regards poor quality or "invalid" patents (also read designs) that find their way onto the register. Whilst such patents may create a net social cost, viewed solely from the perspective of the information function of the register, they only detract from the value of the register insofar as they clutter it and make it more difficult to search. Moreover, even the point about poor quality patents cluttering the register must be treated with caution, since it is perfectly possible that such patents will contain information useful to those consulting the register, even if it would have been better overall if the office had never issued the patents.

Differences between the nature of the information communicated by trade mark registers on the one hand and patent (and design) registers on the other also mean that there is much less scope for arguing that the costs expended on rigorous assessment of validity are better deferred until infringement proceedings. In the patent context, some scholars have argued that because relatively few patented inventions have commercial value, it makes little sense to police all applications vigorously. Rather, it has been said that inevitably costly inquiries as to validity should be postponed until a patent is litigated.[8] In the trade mark context, however, deferring questions of validity in this way would largely remove the benefits of registration for both third parties and owners. Those consulting the register would have no certainty that the mark was valid; a "bare" or "deposit" system for trade mark registration would be incompatible with a doctrine of incontestability and with many of the rules that make it easier to prove infringement of registered as opposed to unregistered marks.

---

[8] *See, e.g.,* F. Scott Kieff, *The Case for Registering Patents and the Law and Economics of Present Patent-Obtaining Rules,* 45 B.C. L. REV. 55 (2003); Mark Lemley, *Rational Ignorance at the Patent Office,* 95 NW. U. L. REV. 1495 (2001).

In summary, in order to be justified on the ground that registration reduces clearance costs, the registered trade mark system 1) would have to provide a comprehensive picture of signs that are protected in the marketplace; and 2) would have to ensure a much higher level of fidelity in the information contained on the register than is true in the case of other forms of registered intellectual property. Unless the system meets these objectives, providing a facility for registering trade marks will not significantly reduce clearance costs (and might even increase such costs). At present it is clear that registered trade mark systems are failing to achieve either of these goals, with the result that what initially appears to be the strongest argument for registration breaks down. One can best illustrate the unreliability of the information communicated by the trade mark register by taking as a starting point the hypothetical person who searches the register regularly with a view to determining whether it is safe to use particular signs in the course of trade. This person will soon discover that searches of the trade mark register generate frequently both false negative results (that is, cases where the search fails to reveal that a legally protected, confusingly similar, sign is already in use in the marketplace) and false positive results (that is, cases where the search identifies a mark that has been incorrectly entered or maintained on the register).

A. *The problem of false negatives*

Most jurisdictions recognise that trade mark registration must be a voluntary act—there are few (if any) countries that require trade mark registration as a precondition to being allowed to trade. In and of itself, this fact limits the utility of the trade mark register as a source of information. This is because, leaving aside any question of potential legal liability, a trader might wish to consult the register with a view to ensuring that it chooses a sign that will help position itself some distance from its competitors. However, consulting the register would only provide a very limited picture of what is occurring in the marketplace, and a trader motivated by the desire to ensure that it adopts an "original" sign would have to investigate the market for itself.

The voluntariness of registration would inevitably limit the ability of the register to provide an accurate reflection of what is occurring in the marketplace, but the position is made much worse by the fact that few countries require registration even as a precondition for trade mark protection. Rather, unregistered trade marks are protected through a variety of mechanisms—through specific legislative provision,[9] through general unfair competition

---

[9] For example, in the United States, the Lanham Act makes express provision for the protection of both registered and unregistered trade marks.

laws[10] or through common law actions such as the tort of passing off. It is important to emphasise that there are good arguments of principle for protecting unregistered marks. Most obviously, a failure to provide such protection might lead to significant consumer confusion. In addition, protection for unregistered marks recognises that some traders will inevitably remain unaware of the benefits of registration or will be unable or unwilling to incur the expense of registration. However, whilst there is a strong case for the protection of unregistered marks, such protection has the potential to undermine significantly the effectiveness of the registered trade mark system as a source of information. A trader who consults the register in order to determine whether it is safe to use a particular sign can never safely rely on a finding that no confusingly similar sign has been registered. The trader will still need to conduct expensive and time-consuming searches in order to determine which other signs may enjoy protection in the marketplace. Accordingly, the information provided by the trade mark register would only be of limited use to the hypothetical trader who was making decisions about how to position itself within the market or who was concerned about its potential legal liability. Consequently, the claim that trade mark registration reduces business clearance costs needs to be treated with considerable caution.

When one takes account of how real market actors are likely to behave, the argument that trade mark registration lowers clearance costs seems even less convincing. Although there is a need for more empirical research to be conducted into how different types of business use registered trade mark systems, the evidence that is available suggests that many small and medium-size enterprises undertake few formal steps to check for the existence of prior conflicting trade marks.[11] Rather, firms often assume that registration of a business or company name provides immunity from a claim of trade mark infringement, reflecting considerable confusion about the rules of both trade mark acquisition and trade mark infringement.[12] The fact that small and medium-size enterprises often have little understanding of the mechanics of trade mark protection casts further doubt on the usefulness of the register as a source of information. But beyond this there is a case to be made that trade mark registration may in fact create additional dangers for the types of business that are

---

[10] For example, it is possible to prevent the unauthorised use of an unregistered trade mark in Australia by reference to the Trade Practices Act 1974 (Cth), § 52.
[11] See Australian Advisory Council on Intellectual Property, *A Review of the Relationship between Trade Marks and Business Names, Company Names and Domain Names* (March 2006), *available at* http://www.acip.gov.au. This report draws on evidence from a range of countries and on the results of specially commissioned market research.
[12] *Id.* at 1, 27, 29–30.

unlikely to consult the register. In many jurisdictions protection for unregistered marks is geographically limited and only arises once a mark is in use and has begun to attract consumer recognition. In contrast, registered trade mark rights normally apply throughout the jurisdiction in question[13] and the vast majority of countries now provide for the registration of marks whose use has not yet commenced. This means that small and medium-size enterprises are much more likely to be caught out by the registered trade mark system than they are by protection for unregistered marks. Traders who know their market well are likely to have a fair degree of awareness of the marks their competitors are using and may well have a general sense that choosing to employ a sign similar to one that is already in use would be a risky business strategy. Such traders are much more likely to fall foul of a mark that has been registered by a business that only operates on the other side of the country or by a mark which has been registered but whose use has not yet commenced than they are by any rights that may subsist in an unregistered mark.

If small and medium-size enterprises often make little use of the information provided by the trade mark register and if trade mark registration might, in fact, create significant additional risks for such enterprises, registration would at least seem to provide important information to larger businesses and other businesses that are particularly well informed. But, to reiterate, any business falling into this category is also going to know that it will not be safe to rely on the results of a search of the register alone. Nevertheless, one might defend the register as providing businesses that consult it with an early indication of marks that it will not be safe to use. In other words, even if it will always be necessary to investigate whether a confusingly similar mark is protected at common law, at least this inquiry can be commenced from a much higher knowledge base. However, even this argument cannot be accepted at face value, since it ignores the possibility that the register will misinform by containing illegitimate marks—the chance that a search of the register may produce a "false positive" result.

B. *The problem of false positives*

It is important to emphasise that the danger that the register will contain marks that ought never to have been registered or that ought not to be maintained on the register is not merely a product of human fallibility; the problem goes beyond the fact that some unregistrable marks will inevitably slip through the net. Nor is the problem simply that some of the factors that determine regis-

---

[13] Some countries do, however, make special provision to deal with marks that have only enjoyed "localised use." *See, e.g.,* Trade Marks Act 1995 (Cth), §§ 44(3), 102 (Australia).

trability, such as the levels of inherent and acquired distinctiveness enjoyed by a mark, are inherently uncertain in their application. Rather, as is discussed below, the attitude of the bureaucracy means that the registry is unlikely to prove as diligent in preventing invalid marks from getting onto the register as might be expected.[14] Moreover, in addition to such institutional considerations, there are elements of the legislative frameworks that govern registered trade marks that make it almost inevitable that large numbers of invalid marks will be sitting on the register at any given time.

One reason why searches of the register will not infrequently produce false positive results flows from the way that trade mark systems deal with the requirement that trade marks be used in order to remain on the register. As has been explained in detail elsewhere, the principal justifications for trade mark protection (that is, to reiterate, that trade marks reduce consumer search costs and protect against misappropriation of another's labour and investment) suggest that only marks that are being actively exploited in the marketplace should remain on the register.[15] Most countries do impose a requirement of use in order for a mark to remain on the register. However, there appears to be a growing sense that registers are becoming cluttered with unused marks and that this is beginning to create significant problems for legitimate traders. It is notable, for example, that in recent reviews of the registered trade mark system in Australia the problem of non-use has been much discussed,[16] and that this issue has even attracted some attention in the general press in the UK.[17]

Growing concern about the problem of non-use is unsurprising given that the procedural mechanisms for detecting and cancelling unused marks are often unsatisfactory. For example, the trade mark rules in many countries draw no distinction at the point of application between marks that are already in use and marks that are being applied for on the basis of "intent to use."[18]

---

[14] *See infra* Section IV.

[15] *See* Lionel Bently & Robert Burrell, *The Requirement of Trade Mark Use*, 13 A.I.P.J. 181, 185–6 (2002).

[16] *See* Australian Advisory Council on Intellectual Property, *Review of Enforcement of Trade Marks*, Feb. 2002 at 27–9; *Review of Trade Mark Enforcement*, Apr. 2004 at 25, *available at* http://www.acip.gov.au; IP Australia, *Trade Marks Legislation Review—Paper 2*, Mar. 2004 at 7–9; *Trade Marks Legislation Review—Paper 3*, Sept. 2004 at 23–7, *available at* http://www.ipaustralia.gov.au.

[17] *See Getting Back Proper Brand Names*, THE TIMES, Feb. 13, 2006.

[18] It might be noted, however, that a distinction will subsequently be drawn during the examination process in cases where the registry treats the mark as lacking inherent distinctiveness. *See, e.g.*, Australian Trade Marks Act 1995 (Cth) §§ 41(3) (no need to provide any details of intent to use or evidence of actual use in cases where the mark is "inherently adapted to distinguish"; 41(5) (details of intent to use and/or

Consequently, in many countries there is no requirement that applicants prove that use has started within a reasonable period in intent-to-use cases. This leaves the system open to abuse by those who are prepared to lodge speculative trade mark applications in the hope of selling marks to traders who are later inconvenienced by the registrations in question. Mechanisms for detecting marks that have been registered and used, but whose use has stopped, are similarly unsatisfactory in many jurisdictions: registration lasts for a long period of time, registrars are generally not given *ex officio* powers to initiate revocation proceedings for non-use,[19] renewal costs tend to be low, there is generally no requirement of proof of use on renewal and, in some countries at least, minimal use is sufficient to maintain a mark on the register.[20]

The most obvious response to the problem of non-use is to suggest that there ought to be a fundamental overhaul of existing mechanisms for detecting unused marks and removing them from the register. Reforms of this type certainly merit serious consideration. However, it is important to note that the international conventions governing trade mark law make dealing with the problem of non-use difficult, perhaps in no small part because the function of trade mark registration is so poorly understood. For example, these conventions require that the initial period of trade mark protection and each renewal last for a significant period of time: seven years in the case of TRIPS,[21] ten years in the case of the Trademark Law Treaty.[22] Equally importantly, the Trademark Law Treaty prohibits making renewal dependent upon the owner providing a declaration or evidence of use.[23]

It is also worth saying something about the extent of the problem in the United States. For many years the United States has adopted a robust approach to ensuring that only marks that are being actively exploited remain on the register. Specifically, until relatively recently it was not possible to register a mark prior to its actual use. Although it is now possible to lodge an application on the basis of intent to use, registration is still dependent on proof of

---

evidence of actual use required in cases where the mark is "to some extent inherently adapted to distinguish the designated goods or services"; 41(6) (evidence of actual use before the filing date required in cases where the mark is "not to any extent inherently adapted to distinguish the designated goods or services").

[19] *But see* Trade-marks Act, R.S.C, c. T-13, § 45(1) (1985) for the position in Canada. *See also* Sheldon Burshstein, *Trade Mark "Use" in Canada: The Who, What, When, Why and How (Part II)*, 12 I.P.J. 75, 97–9 (1998).

[20] All of these defects characterise the present position in Australia. *See* Robert Burrell, *The Requirement of Trade Mark Use: Recent Developments in Australia*, 16 A.I.P.J. 231 (2005).

[21] TRIPS Agreement, art. 18. (1994).

[22] Trademark Law Treaty, art. 13(7) (1994), *see also* Singapore revision, art. 13(5) (2006).

[23] Trademark Law Treaty at art. 13(4), *see also* Singapore revision, art. 13(2).

actual use.²⁴ The United States also continues to require owners to provide periodically affidavits of use, and failure to do so results in cancellation of the registration.²⁵ Yet despite this robust approach to the problem of non-use, there is reason to suggest that very significant numbers of unused marks sit on the register for long periods of time in the United States—for example, in view of a 1987 report estimating that 23% of registrations over six years old represented unused "deadwood."²⁶ It seems reasonable to suggest that if the United States has been unsuccessful in keeping unused marks off the register, and if the international conventions prohibit the adoption of the type of draconian measures that would be probably be required to really get on top of the problem (such as requiring annual renewal coupled with a requirement that the owner provide evidence of actual use over the previous twelve months), it seems inevitable that large numbers of unused marks will remain registered around the world.

Searches will thus not infrequently reveal marks that ought to be struck off the register for non-use. False positive results of this type are particularly problematic, since in these cases the register is actively misinforming the public. The presence of the mark on the register may well be sufficient to deter any further inquiry and, even if the person who discovers the registration then goes on to investigate what is occurring in the marketplace, the position will only be rectified if that person takes the trouble to launch non-use proceedings. The register may thus not merely fail to reduce clearance costs, it may actually increase the costs of doing business.

The failure of registries to deal adequately with the problem of non-use provides a fairly straightforward illustration of why searches of the register will produce false positive results. It is also worth pointing out, however, that false positive results can be generated by the presence of marks on the register that are vulnerable to cancellation because they conflict with some earlier

---

[24] Although it is also worth noting that the United States does not require use prior to issuing a registration for an application that was based on Article 6^{quinquies} of the Paris Convention for the Protection of Industrial Property (1883) (the "telle quelle" provision) or on the Protocol Relating to the Madrid Agreement Concerning the International Registration of Marks (1989). *See* 15 U.S.C. § 1126 (2000).

[25] There is a strong argument that this requirement is incompatible with the Trademark Law Treaty. See P. Jay Hines, *The Trademark Law Treaty, The Trademark Law Implementation Act, and Changes in United States Trademark Practice*, 90 TRADEMARK REP. 513, 525 (2000).

[26] *Trademark Review Commission Report*, 77 TRADEMARK REP. 375 (1987); *see also* Stephen Carter, *The Trouble with Trademark*, 99 YALE L.J. 759, 779–81 (1990) (arguing that the subsequent amendments to US law that allowed intent-to-use applications were designed to allow trade mark owners to warehouse marks for up to two years).

mark. Once again, part of the problem flows from that fact that unregistered marks can attract legal protection. Many trade mark systems provide accordingly a facility for cancelling a registered mark on the basis that it conflicts with an earlier unregistered mark.[27]

At first sight, the fact that a registered mark might be vulnerable to challenge by the owner of an earlier unregistered mark would seem to have little bearing on the information function of the register. The fact that a third party might have better title to a mark than the registered owner would not appear to impact adversely on a person searching the register. If anything, such a registration might be thought to help inform the person conducting the search of the need to steer clear of a particular mark, even if the register attributes the rights in the mark to the wrong person. It must be remembered, however, that it is highly unlikely that the scope of the registration will coincide exactly with the scope of protection enjoyed by the third party owner of an unregistered right. Thus a person who searches the register and discovers a mark of interest must ensure that they do not act on the basis of this information alone. In particular, it would be dangerous to seek to work around the registered mark without taking into account the scope of the rights that a third party might have in an unregistered mark. Equally importantly, it must be remembered that the person conducting the search might wish to approach the registered owner with an offer to purchase the mark in question or to enter into a division of use agreement. In such a case, the potential purchaser/party to a division of use agreement would have to investigate carefully the possibility that the mark might be vulnerable to a challenge from the proprietor of an earlier unregistered mark, a potentially time consuming and expensive inquiry. Whilst it would be possible to characterise these problems as merely another aspect of the false negative problem, at the very least it should be noted that the existence of the later, potentially invalid, registration will complicate the picture and make it more difficult for the would-be market entrant to work out which marks it will be safe to (contract to) use.

The problematic relationship between registered and unregistered marks creates some risk that a search of the register will produce a false positive result, but problems can also arise in cases of conflicts between two registered marks. This is particularly true in countries that place the burden of preventing the registration of confusingly similar marks solely on trade mark owners.[28] There are a number of reasons for doubting the wisdom of not citing

---

[27] *See, e.g.*, Council Directive 89/104/EEC, art. 4(4); Council Regulation (EC) No. 40/94, arts. 8(2)(c), 8(4), 52(1) (EU); Trade Marks Act 1995 (Cth), §§ 42(b), 43, 58, 60, 88(2)(a) (Australia).

[28] This description characterises, *e.g.*, the trade mark registration system in the United Kingdom from Oct. 1, 2007. See Trade Marks (Relative Grounds) Order 2007 (S.I. 2007 No. 1976).

prior conflicting marks as a bar to registration, but, in terms of the information function of the register, the principal potential problem with such a system is that it may result in the register providing a somewhat unstable record of protected marks. This possibility arises because owners of earlier marks may fail to commence opposition proceedings on time or may decide initially to allow the later mark to proceed to registration, only to later seek cancellation of the mark. In many jurisdictions the owner will have several years in which to decide whether to bring an action for cancellation[29] and it may take many months for such proceedings to be brought to a conclusion. Consequently, there is a real risk that the register will provide a less stable record of protected trade marks than in countries where the office cites prior conflicting marks as a bar to registration. In the period between a mark being entered onto the register and it being removed at the conclusion of cancellation proceedings, it will be capable of generating false positive results that will shape the decisions of parties searching the register.

C. *Other quality concerns*

If searches can generate both false negative and false positive results, it is also worth saying something about the quality of the information communicated by the register in cases where the search results are accurate. Insofar as the nature of the information communicated by the register is ever discussed, it seems to be assumed that the register is capable of providing information of a type that will allow members of the public, and potential competitors in particular, to determine the scope of the rights enjoyed by the registered owner. The decision of the European Court of Justice (ECJ) in *Sieckmann v Deutsches Patent- und Markenamt*[30] best illustrates this assumption. That case marked the first attempt by the ECJ to develop a set of rules to determine how the graphic representation requirement is to be applied under EU law. These rules help control the form in which marks appear on trade mark registers in Europe, and it is significant that the ECJ took as its starting point the ideas that marks must appear on the register in a form that allows the public to "receive relevant information about the rights of third parties" and to "determine the precise subject of the protection."

---

[29] *See, e.g.*, Trade Marks Act 1994, s. 48(1) (UK) ("Where the proprietor of an earlier trade mark . . . has acquiesced for a continuous period of five years in the use of a registered trade mark in the United Kingdom, being aware of that use, there shall cease to be any entitlement on the basis of that earlier trade mark . . .—(a) to apply for a declaration that the registration of the later trade mark is invalid.") Moreover, it might be noted that this section goes on to provide that this five-year limitation period does not apply if the "later trade mark was applied for in bad faith."
[30] [2002] E.C.R. I-11737.

The suggestion that the register allows members of the public to determine what rights third parties enjoy is much more problematic than it may at first appear. In order to establish the scope of third party rights it would be necessary to have a fairly detailed knowledge of the rules governing infringement. Infringement of a registered trade mark is generally not confined to use of a mark identical to that which is registered, nor even to a mark which has been colourably altered. Rather, infringement extends to the use of "similar" marks, a concept that has been given a broad interpretation in many jurisdictions.[31] Moreover, infringement can also extend to cases where the defendant's use is on goods or in relation to services that are dissimilar to those for which the mark is registered.[32] In other words, the scope of the trade mark owner's property can extend well beyond the mark as registered to include the exclusive right to use a (not all that) similar mark on wholly different goods or services. This might well not be obvious to a person searching the register and there is thus a danger that the register will create overconfidence as regards the scope of third party rights. The register will only perform effectively if the hypothetical trader has its hypothetical lawyer on hand to explain what the information on the register means.

A still more significant problem is posed by the fact that determining the scope of a third party's rights will at times require an investigation of what is occurring in the marketplace. This is most obviously true in cases where the person searching the register is concerned to know whether a mark might be protected against use on dissimilar goods. In many countries, protection of this type is confined to marks that "have a reputation" or are "well-known."[33] However, it will not be clear from the face of the register whether a mark meets the relevant threshold; this can only be determined by investigating conditions in the marketplace. More generally, when determining whether a trade mark has been infringed, courts tend to place a good deal of weight on evidence of actual confusion.[34] Actual confusion depends, of course, upon

---

[31] *See, e.g.*, Claudia Oberhauser v OHIM [2003] E.T.M.R. 58; Sabel v Puma [1998] E.T.M.R. 1 (EU); Effem Foods v Wandella Pet Foods [2006] F.C.A. 767; Coca-Cola v All-Fect Distributors (1999) 47 I.P.R. 481; Seven Up v Bubble Up (1987) 9 I.P.R. 259 (Australia).

[32] *See, e.g.*, Council Directive 89/104/EEC, art. 5(2); Council Regulation (EC) No. 40/94, art. 9(1)(c) (EU); Trade Marks Act 1995 (Cth), § 120(3) (Australia).

[33] *Id.*

[34] The European v The Economist [1998] F.S.R. 283, 291 (evidence of actual confusion not always significant, but required to displace trial judge's view); Claudius Ash v Invicta Manufacturing (1912) 29 R.P.C. 465, 476 (per Ld MacNaghten) (UK); Australian Woollen Mills v Walton (1937) 58 C.L.R. 641, 658 (Australia); *see also* Paul Scott, *A Tale of Confusion: How Tribunals Treat the Presence and Absence of Evidence of Actual Confusion in Trade Mark Matters*, [2001] VICT. U. WELL. L. REV. 5.

confusion between the marks used in the marketplace. Courts are thus likely to determine whether infringement has occurred not merely by the similarity of the signs, but also by the appearance of the goods and how the parties have marketed the goods. Courts will therefore determine in part questions of infringement (and hence the scope of trade mark owners' property rights) by reference in part to factors that are unconnected to how a mark appears on the register.

D. What is left of the search cost argument?
As demonstrated above, registration will only ever provide a partial record of signs that enjoy protection in the marketplace and, as regards those marks that are on the register, it must be kept in mind that a registration may be invalid. Moreover, even if a mark has been properly registered, the register only provides a signpost as to the scope of the owner's monopoly. Only a person armed with a fairly developed understanding of trade mark infringement would be able to get a proper sense of the scope of the owner's rights, and building a complete picture would require investigation into how the sign has been used by its proprietor and the level of consumer recognition it enjoys. This final point leads into a more general problem with the limited information provided by the register, namely, that in order to get more accurate information it will often be necessary to investigate conditions in the marketplace. Such an investigation will involve incurring broadly similar costs as would arise if trade marks were only protected by legal mechanisms that do not require registration.

Trade mark systems thus perform poorly when judged against the argument that registration helps reduce traders' clearance costs. This does not, however, mean that the clearance cost justification for registration can be dismissed entirely. It is plain that trade mark registers do have the capacity to provide some information that traders find useful. It might, therefore, be possible to claim that registration allows searches of what is occurring in the marketplace to be targeted somewhat more accurately than might otherwise be the case. Equally, however, it must also be remembered that in practice many businesses make little use of the information provided by the trade mark system. Consequently, it is difficult to escape the conclusion that registration is an elaborate and expensive system for achieving the limited goal of reducing modestly the clearance costs of well-advised businesses.

III. Other justifications for trade mark registration
If the clearance cost argument for trade mark registration is unpersuasive, it is important to consider whether a registration system might be justifiable on some other ground. Two arguments present themselves: first, it might be said

110   *Trademark law and theory*

that registration is important because it provides a mechanism by which marks can be protected prior to their establishing marketplace recognition; second, it might be said that registration is important insofar as it serves to create property rights in trade signs. It will be seen that whilst neither of these arguments can be dismissed entirely, nor do they provide a convincing justification for trade mark registration.

A.   *Protection prior to use*

If trade mark protection is normally only justified if a mark is in use, it may initially seem strange to suggest that providing a facility for protecting marks whose use has not yet commenced might provide a justification for the entire trade mark registration system. Such an argument is likely to sound particularly strange to American ears, given that intent-to-use applications are a relatively recent feature of the registration system in the United States. Nevertheless, it might be possible to construct an argument along the following lines. Traders about to embark on a new business venture benefit from the security that comes from being able to reserve for themselves the use of a sign prior to investing in the design of packaging and advertising and promotional material. Registration provides this security. In contrast, in a significant number of countries, particularly those with a British common law tradition, protection for unregistered marks only arises once the mark has begun to enjoy consumer recognition. This leaves a period during which a trader may find that its investment has been undermined by another party who, deliberately or otherwise, adopts a confusingly similar sign.

In order to demonstrate the problems with the above argument, it is necessary to distinguish between two different scenarios. The first such scenario concerns a situation where a mark has not yet been exposed to the public at all. In such a case trade mark protection is not required to prevent a rival trader from deliberately copying the mark. Such copying could only occur if information about the planned launch were leaked to the rival trader and, in many countries, it would already be possible to protect against such leaks through legal regimes that protect against the misuse of commercially sensitive information.[35] In contrast, it is by no means clear that the law ought to provide a remedy as against an innocent trader who coincidentally chooses to use a confusingly similar mark. It can be argued that the law should give priority no more to the interests of the person who applies first to register the mark than it should to the interests of the person who first uses the mark in the market-

---

[35]   For example, through an action for breach of confidence. There are also cases in which the owner would be able to rely on copyright in the mark to prevent it from being copied by a rival trader.

place. In either case the consequence is to give one party exclusive rights in the sign at the expense of another party who will find that its investment has been wasted.[36]

The second scenario concerns a situation where a rival trader begins to use a confusingly similar mark shortly after the first mark has been exposed to the public and before it has begun to attract public recognition. As discussed above, in countries with a British common law tradition, there will be a gap between the point at which use of unregistered mark commences and the point at which it attracts legal protection. Consequently, it can be said that registration helps protect trade mark owners against unscrupulous rivals during the early days of a new business venture. Again, however, on closer examination this argument appears problematic. The fact that inherently distinctive marks do not automatically attract protection at the point they are exposed to the public is a product of the way that the action for passing off evolved. There is nothing inevitable about this limitation, as United States law demonstrates. There, inherently distinctive, unregistered marks attract protection from the moment they are exposed to the public.[37]

An important variant on the argument that registration is justified because it allows protection prior to use, concerns the situation in which a trader plans to expand gradually the geographical area across which a mark is used.

---

[36] In reply, it might be said that the first to register rule is more effective at "minimiz[ing] wasteful duplicative parallel investment by giving advance notice to competitors through registration records." Chiappetta, *supra* note 1, at 67. However, this argument rests on the sort of unwarranted faith in the ability of the register to communicate information to rival traders that was criticised above. Furthermore, it might be noted that trade mark systems are far from consistent in how they resolve the tension between first registration and first use. In Australia, for example, upon discovering an application to register, a trader with advanced plans to use a confusingly similar sign might be better advised to dash to market than to abandon its plans: if the use were such as to attract consumer recognition the trader might have a ground of opposition/cancellation under § 42(b) of the Trade Marks Act 1995 (Cth). *See* Robert Burrell & Michael Handler, *The Intersection Between Registered and Unregistered Trade Marks* 35 FED. L. REV. 375, 386–7 (2007).

[37] It might be noted that this formulation is somewhat simplistic, since pre-launch advertising exposes the mark to the public, but is not sufficient to establish rights in an unregistered mark in the United States, and may not be sufficient in the United Kingdom, even if the advertising is such as to generate goodwill: *cf.* BBC v Talbot [1981] F.S.R. 228, but many commentators doubt whether this case was decided correctly, *e.g.*, LIONEL BENTLY & BRAD SHERMAN, INTELLECTUAL PROPERTY LAW 716–17 (2d ed. 2004). But, again, there is nothing inevitable about the conclusion that consumer recognition generated through pre-trade advertisement cannot form the basis of an action. In Australia it would almost certainly be possible to bring an action under § 52 of the Trade Practices Act 1974 (Cth) in such circumstances.

Registration "reduce[s] the uncertainties of future regional contests."[38] This claim can be made both in relation to the expansion of trade within a country and to trade across national boundaries, but the latter perhaps provides the simpler example. Where a trader is planning to market a product internationally it may be necessary to stagger its release—the trader may need commercial success in one country before launching the product elsewhere, administrative hurdles or problems finding appropriate premises or staff may delay a launch in one country but not another. By allowing a trader to obtain protection for a mark in a number of countries simultaneously (something that the international conventions relating to intellectual property are intended to facilitate) trade mark registration aids the transnational marketing of goods.

There is something in the argument that registration provides security to traders planning to expand the geographical reach of their activities over time, but it is important not to overstate the argument. Registration is not, for example, necessary to prevent traders from exploiting "spill over" goodwill. If a trader has established a reputation amongst consumers it ought not to matter that the product has not yet been marketed in the territory in question; the mark under which the product is sold should still attract protection. Any other outcome would create a real risk of consumer confusion and would allow a third party to trade off the owner's investment.[39] Trade mark registration is thus only important in cases where the use of a similar sign occurs at a time before the mark has acquired a spill over reputation amongst consumers. The question of whether the law should provide a remedy in these circumstances is, however, rather less clear cut.[40] There will be no immediate risk of consumer confusion and thus no immediate impact on consumer search costs

---

[38] Chiappetta, *supra* note 1, at 66. *See also* Peter Jaffey, *The New European Trade Marks Regime*, 28 I.I.C. 153, 159–60, 161 (1997).

[39] UK cases such as Anheuser-Busch v Budejovicky Budvar [1984] F.S.R. 413 and Bernardin v Pavilion Properties [1967] R.P.C. 581, which indicate that a trader cannot maintain an action for passing off unless it is trading in the jurisdiction, should thus be regarded as wrongly decided. It is notable that the position in other Commonwealth countries is different. *See, e.g.*, ConAgra v McCain Foods (1992) 23 I.P.R. 193 (Federal Court of Australia—Full Court); *see also* Allison Coleman, *Protection of Foreign Business Names and Marks under the Tort of Passing Off*, 6 LEG. STUD. 70 (1986).

[40] It is interesting to note in this context the outcome in Dawn Donut Company v Hart's Food Stores, 267 F.2d 358 (2d Cir. 1959) (refusing injunctive relief in a situation where there was little likelihood that the plaintiff would expand into the defendant's trade area). *See also* Thomas L. Casagrande, *The "Dawn Donut Rule": Still Standing (Article III, that is) Even with the Rise of The Internet*, 90 TRADEMARK REP. 723 (2000); Jaffey, *supra* note 38, at 178–80.

in such a case;[41] whilst the first trader's interests may be harmed in the sense that its preparations for release in the territory in question will be upset, the second trader will not be benefiting from the first trader's investment, such that the misappropriation argument for trade mark protection is only weakly implicated.

The argument that registration is required in order to allow trade mark owners to expand gradually the geographical scope across which a mark is used is thus far from conclusive, particularly when one bears in mind the impact registration may have on innocent traders who do not think to check the register. Moreover, it must also be remembered that registration creates an opening for the making of speculative trade mark applications on the part of those who have no intention of using a mark, such that (absent strong mechanisms to detect and remove marks whose use has never commenced) a registration facility may actually hinder traders who wish to expand into new markets.[42]

B. The property argument

In many jurisdictions registration plays a key role in creating property rights in trade signs. That is, it can safely be said that registration serves to confer more property-like characteristics on trade marks in most countries, without plunging into conceptual disagreements about when, precisely, it is appropriate to classify trade mark rights as "property" rights.[43] Thus, insofar as the "propertisation" of trade marks produces desirable outcomes, this provides a *prima facie* justification for trade mark registration. Writing within the British common law tradition, Brennan argues that registration is important because

---

[41] It might nevertheless be possible to argue that the wider the geographical reach of a mark, the more consumer search costs are reduced, an argument that it would be tempting to reinforce by reference to the increased mobility of consumers and to the possibility that consumers will benefit from the economies of scale offered to producers who are able to produce and market goods on a global basis. It is important, however, to treat claims about increased consumer mobility with a considerable degree of scepticism. *See* Carter, *supra* note 26, at 789–92. The weak nature of the product guarantee function of trade marks must also be kept in mind: there is nothing that requires trade mark owners to produce identical products across national boundaries and, in practice, traders are often forced to adapt their products to take account of local sensibilities and tastes.

[42] *See also* Graeme Dinwoodie, *Trademarks and Territory: Detaching Trademark Law from the Nation-State*, 41 HOUS. L. REV. 885, 898 (2004), noting that the use of registration to create uniform rights throughout a territory will tend to seem particularly attractive in the context of conscious efforts to create a common market, but pointing out that the broad protection conferred by registration can also increase market clutter and hence act as a barrier to trade.

[43] As to which, *see, e.g.*, Lionel Bently's chapter in this volume.

the property form provides owners with extra security as against misuse and future claims to ownership made by licensees. Registration therefore helps ensure that the law is neutral as between the vertical integration of a business through ownership (the creation, in ordinary parlance, of "a firm") and the vertical integration of business through contract (the creation of a "firm-like" structure).[44] Rather more obviously, the shift to the property form might be thought desirable because it often makes it easier to transfer title to a mark. More specifically, in many countries it is not possible to assign unregistered marks separately from the business to which the goodwill attaches,[45] and it may not be possible to transfer a mark at all if it is taken to represent a personal connection between the original owner of the mark and the goods.[46]

The suggestion that registration is desirable in order to secure the propertisation of marks is, however, not free from difficulty. First, there is no consensus that trade mark law ought to be moving in this direction. In particular, despite the international trend towards allowing trade marks to be assigned in gross,[47] such assignments remain controversial.[48] The United States still prohibits the selling of a trade mark without its associated goodwill,[49] and questions remain about how the judiciary is likely to respond even where the legislative regime seems to permit assignments in gross.[50] Second, and more

---

[44] David Brennan, *The Trade Mark and the Firm*, [2006] I.P.Q. 283; *see also* Shelley Lane, *Goodwill Hunting: Assignments and Licences in Gross after* Scandecor, [1999] I.P.Q. 264 (distinguishing "fact based" and "rule based" approaches to determining ownership of goodwill); and Chestek, *infra* n. 52.

[45] *See, e.g.*, Scandecor v Scandecor [2001] E.T.M.R. 74, 809–10; Barnsley Brewery v RBNB [1997] F.S.R. 462, 469; Pinto v Badman (1891) 8 R.P.C. 181, 194–5 (UK).

[46] *Scandecor* [2001] E.T.M.R. 74, 810 (giving the example of a mark used by an artist).

[47] TRIPS Agreement, art. 21; Trademark Law Treaty, art. 11(4)(iv), *see also* Singapore revision, art. 11(3)(iv).

[48] Compare Carter, *supra* note 26, at 785–6; Mark Lemley, *The Modern Lanham Act and the Death of Common Sense*, 108 YALE L.J. 1687, 1701–10 (1999); and Michael Pulos, *A Semiotic Solution to the Propertization Problem of Trademark*, 53 UCLA L. REV. 833, 861–3 (2006); with Allison McDade, *Trading in Trademarks— Why the Anti-Assignment in Gross Doctrine Should be Abolished when Trademarks are Used as Collateral*, 77 TEX. L. REV. 465 (1998), and Irene Calboli, *Trademark Assignment "With Goodwill": A Concept whose Time has Gone*, 57 FLA. L. REV. 771 (2005).

[49] 15 U.S.C. § 1060 (2000).

[50] *See, e.g.*, Heintzman v 751056 Ontario (1990) 34 C.P.R. (3d) (Federal Court of Canada, Trial Division) (holding that assignment in gross had deprived the mark of distinctiveness); Elizabeth Emanuel v Continental Shelf 128 [2006] E.T.M.R. 56 (ECJ) (emphasising that, on the facts, the goodwill associated with the mark had been assigned together with the business making the goods). In Australia there is uncertainty

importantly for present purposes, there is only a weak connection between registration and the conferral of property-style protection. The refusal of the common law to recognise a true proprietary right in unregistered marks is, at least on one interpretation, merely an historical accident, a product of the fact that the passing off action has its origins in the tort of deceit. Thus, if one were to accept Brennan's argument that the law should provide "structure neutral choices" to traders as regards the mode of vertical integration they employ,[51] it would be a relatively simple matter to achieve this by reconceptualising the person to whom goodwill accrues for the purposes of the tort of passing off.[52] Similarly, if one were to conclude that marks ought to be assignable in gross, there would be no insurmountable obstacle to allowing unregistered marks to be assigned in this way.

Even if there is only a weak link between registration and the conferral of property-type rights on marks, registration might still be said to be important insofar as it provides a mechanism to record ownership of marks and transactions therewith. That is, registration might be thought desirable because it creates a publicly accessible record of the rights that subsist in marks, in much the same way that land registers are intended to provide reliable information about rights over land. On closer inspection, however, the analogy with land registration quickly breaks down.[53] First, it is important to remember that registration does not even provide a guarantee that the property exists at all—large numbers of invalid marks will be sitting on the register at any given time. Secondly, even when we turn to the recording of interests in trade marks, we find that trade mark registers do poorly when judged against the record they provide of entitlements over signs.

In the United Kingdom there is no obligation to register any form of transaction involving a trade mark. Admittedly, there are a number of significant advantages to such registration, in particular, as regards the vulnerability of

---

about how § 52 of the Trade Practices Act 1974 (Cth) (which prohibits traders from engaging in conduct that is likely to mislead or deceive) intersects with § 106 of the Trade Marks Act 1995 (Cth) (which allows marks to be assigned "with or without the goodwill of the business concerned").

[51] Brennan, *supra* note 44, at 209.

[52] *Cf.* Pamela Chestek, *Who Owns the Mark? A Single Framework for Resolving Trademark Ownership Disputes*, 96 TRADEMARK REP. 681, 703–05 (2006) (arguing for what might be described as a mixed approach to determining ownership issues (*cf.* Lane, *supra* note 44) and insisting that, in essence, the same rule should apply to both registered and unregistered marks).

[53] *See* BENTLY & SHERMAN, *supra* note 37, at 953 ("The [trade marks] register cannot be said to operate as a 'mirror' of legal rights over trade signs in the way the Land Registration system purports to be a reflection of proprietary rights over real property.").

unregistered transactions to later dealings,[54] but such a system hardly seems compatible with the claim that the registration system is justified primarily on the basis of the information that registration provides about dealings in respect of trade marks. In the United States recordation of assignments is also purely voluntary, but, again as in the United Kingdom, is advisable in order to protect the assignee against later *bona fide* purchasers.[55] As regards the registration of security interests in trade marks, however, it is unclear whether the proper approach is to record the interest with the US Patent and Trademark Office or to record the interest using the state Uniform Commercial Code procedure.[56] In Australia transfers of title (whether through assignment or by operation of law) only take effect once an application to register the transfer is lodged with the registry.[57] However, there is no requirement under the Trade Marks Act to register other types of transaction and although other types of interests can be registered, the Act specifically provides that registration does not provide "proof or evidence that the [registrant] has that right or interest"[58]—the registry refuses to take any responsibility for policing the accuracy of the register in this respect. Significantly, the Australian Corporations Act 2001 (Cth) does require charges over intangible assets (including trade marks) to be registered,[59] but registration in this context means registration with the Australian Securities and Investment Commission, not with the trade marks office. The trade mark register is thus not even the best source of information as to some of the interests that may subsist in a mark in Australia. Consequently, although trade mark registers do play a role in providing a record of entitlements over trade signs, this role appears to be very much a secondary consideration in most jurisdictions. The information provided by the register will often be incomplete and trade mark registers are not always the most appropriate vehicle for recording certain types of transaction and hence may not even provide the most comprehensive source of information as to earlier dealings.

C. Thinking about reform

Trade mark registration cannot be dismissed as performing no useful function. However, taken individually, the potentially valuable roles that registration performs—in providing information about whether a sign is protected, in

---

[54] Trade Marks Act 1994, § 25(3).
[55] 15 U.S.C. § 1060(4) (2000).
[56] J. THOMAS MCCARTHY, 3 MCCARTHY ON TRADEMARKS AND UNFAIR COMPETITION ¶ 18.7 (2007).
[57] Trade Marks Act 1995 (Cth), §§ 107, 110.
[58] *Id.* § 116.
[59] § 262(1)(e).

providing a mechanism for protecting marks prior to use, and in providing a record of entitlements over trade signs—do not explain trade mark registration systems as they exist at present. It is also important to avoid the temptation of leaping to the conclusion that an adequate explanation for registration can be found once the potential benefits offered by registration systems are viewed collectively. This would feel too much like a desperate attempt to cobble together an *ex post* justification for a system whose abolition is, practically speaking, more or less unimaginable. Nevertheless, even if we accept that we might well choose not to create a facility for trade mark registration if we were to start with a blank slate, given that registration is here to stay, it makes sense to seek to ensure that it works as effectively as possible.

Some of the problems that detract from the utility of the register are, admittedly, not capable of resolution. The only way to ensure that the register provides a comprehensive picture of signs that enjoy legal protection would be to remove protection for unregistered marks, a drastic step that would open the door to unscrupulous traders. Moreover, it would only be possible to determine the precise scope of the owner's rights from the face of the register if the scope of the trade mark monopoly were narrowed to the point that it would no longer provide adequate protection against confusion or misappropriation. It is precisely for this reason that the author remains sceptical about the ultimate value of registration. Nevertheless, there are things that could be done to ensure that the register serves publicly desirable ends, most of which relate to ensuring that the register acts as a valuable source of public information. For example, implicit in what has already been said, is that in order for the public benefits of registration to be maximised, the registry would have to pay significant attention to ensuring that, where possible, unregistered marks were taken into account when assessing registrability, would have to ensure that only genuine intent-to-use applicants were accepted, would have to have rigorous procedures for detecting and removing unused marks from the register, and would have to take much greater responsibility for recording interests in marks.

The analysis presented in the next section does not, however, focus on what, precisely, would need to be done to improve the operation of the register (this would vary from country to country, but in most cases would probably require a mix of legislative reform and a willingness to use existing powers rather differently). Nor does it provide a detailed account of the ways in which present registry performance is unsatisfactory—it will, however, provide some examples of this type and it is hoped that these examples, together with some of the material presented earlier, are sufficient to make the case that, in theory, there is considerable room to improve how registries function. The remainder of this chapter will concentrate instead on why trade mark registries are unlikely to embrace the necessary changes, irrespective of whether these changes come in the form of proposals for legislative reform[60] or exhortations to alter registry practice. Taking Australia as a case study, it will be argued that recent management reforms, the way in which registries interact with government, and the financial interests of registries all push in the opposite direction. Inevitably, this analysis causes this chapter to touch upon more general concerns about the way in which trade mark offices are applying registrability criteria at present. Insofar as possible, however, the analysis will remain focused on those areas that impact most directly on the question of whether the registry serves any useful function (that is, to reiterate, non-use, speculative trade mark applications, the relationship between registered and unregistered marks and the recording of interests in marks), rather than, say, on the question of whether the registry has relaxed the distinctiveness requirement over recent years.

The material that follows is not, of course, to suggest that the attitude of the intellectual property bureaucracy is the only factor that is likely to shape the future development of the trade mark system. But it is to suggest both that the bureaucracy needs to be taken seriously as a site of power within the intellectual property system and that not all of the negative developments that have taken place in intellectual property law over recent years can be put down to the effects of lobbying by powerful interests.[61]

IV. The role of the trade mark bureaucracy

A. *The financial imperative*

The suggestion that the bureaucracy is likely to resist attempts to refocus its efforts on ensuring that the register serves publicly desirable ends chimes with a popular critique of the operation of intellectual property offices, namely, that the increasing expectation that such offices will be self-funding has resulted in a decline in the quality of the subject matter accepted for registration. More specifically, it is said that because intellectual property offices derive much of

---

[60] Part of the analysis presented below is therefore premised on the belief that the intellectual property bureaucracy has a significant degree of influence over the legislative process (something that is certainly now true in Australia and is quite probably true in other parliamentary democracies) and/or will be able to exert considerable control over how intellectual property legislation is interpreted and applied, an issue that goes to the relationship between the courts and the bureaucracy. *See infra* Section IV(D).

[61] In this respect the author would add his voice to those who are calling for greater attention to be paid to the role that national intellectual property offices play in negotiating international treaties and in driving a process of "soft" harmonisation. *See, e.g.*, Peter Drahos, *Death of a Patent System—Introduction, in* 11 PERSPECTIVES ON INTELLECTUAL PROPERTY: DEATH OF PATENTS (Peter Drahos ed., 2005), at 4.

their income from the fees paid by users, there is a financial imperative to accept as many applications as possible. This both ensures that applicants are encouraged to come forward in the future and enables offices to generate income from renewal fees.[62] This analysis certainly has some resonance in Australia, where there has been an expectation that the intellectual property bureaucracy, now officially entitled "IP Australia," would be a "full-cost recovery" arm of government since at least the mid-1990s. Consequently, IP Australia is now expected to be almost entirely self-funding, using the revenue it receives in fees to fund its operations.[63] It would also be obtuse to deny that running or being a senior manager within a self-funding arm of government must be an attractive proposition—self-funding brings with it a degree of autonomy that any bureau chief would be loath to surrender.

It is important, however, to be careful to define what, precisely, we mean by a decline in trade mark quality and to be clear about the manner in which this decline has manifested itself. Taking the latter point first, in order to demonstrate convincingly that the need to increase fee income has led to a decline in trade mark quality, it would be necessary to show that pressure is being brought to bear on examiners to let through as many applications as possible. Yet, as far as the author has been able to determine, the internal performance review criteria for trade mark examiners in Australia focus on the speed and quality of decision-making, not on number of acceptances per se. Moreover, to turn to the first point, if anything there seems to have been a real drive to increase quality control over recent years, with significant changes taking place in supervision, auditing and training. Additionally, the suggestion that those working within IP Australia see their job as being to maximise revenue sits very uncomfortably alongside the impression the author has formed of how individuals working within the trade mark office perceive their roles.

This is not to suggest that the expectation that IP Australia will be self-funding is of no importance, but rather that this expectation has a much less direct impact than is sometimes presumed. Generally speaking, therefore, it would probably be more accurate to treat the need to generate revenue from applicants as a background influence that feeds into the way in which the trade mark office and the rest of IP Australia sees its role. The funding arrangements for IP Australia help to underpin the customer service mentality which, it will be argued below, is antithetical to reforming how the system operates. This

---

[62] *See, e.g.*, PETER DRAHOS & JOHN BRAITHWAITE, INFORMATION FEUDALISM: WHO OWNS THE KNOWLEDGE ECONOMY (2002).
[63] *The Department of Industry, Tourism and Resource's Annual Report 2004–2005: IP Australia's Financial Statements* 308, available at http://www.itr.gov.au.

mentality has not resulted in a failure to monitor the quality of individual decisions (far from it), but rather in the registry refusing to accept that it bears any responsibility at all for investigating or policing certain matters.

The indirect influence that questions of finance have on how IP Australia perceives its role can be illustrated by noting the way in which IP Australia's funding arrangements structure its reporting requirements. In order to enable IP Australia to fund its own activities, it was necessary to set up a "special account" within the meaning of the Financial Management and Accountability Act 1997 (Cth). Such accounts record rights to draw money from the Consolidated Revenue Fund—in the case of IP Australia an amount that matches the fee income it generates.[64] Importantly for present purposes, however, the 1997 Act also imposes particular obligations on chief executives who administer special accounts, including a requirement that they promote "efficiency" and "cost effectiveness."[65] These requirements are reflected in the way IP Australia evaluates its performance and presents its annual report. Inevitably these requirements push IP Australia towards a focus on enumerable outcomes that allow comparisons to be made over a number of years—how many applications were received, how long did it take to process them, what was the cost to applicants, did the system generate a profit—and away from an emphasis on the importance of professional judgment and maintaining the quality of the information communicated by the register.

B. IP Australia and the new public management

The fact that IP Australia now sees its role in terms of providing a service to its "customers" would come as no surprise to anyone familiar with the direction of reforms within the Australian public service over the past twenty or so years.[66] Australia, like many other Western countries, has embarked upon a prolonged series of reforms that have been heavily influenced by the "new public management" agenda, under which the government attempts to apply the language, goals and management techniques of the private sector to the

---

[64] This somewhat circuitous arrangement is required in order to comply with §§ 81 and 83 of the Constitution, which control how the Commonwealth raises and distributes revenue.

[65] Financial Management and Accountability Act 1997 (Cth), § 44.

[66] *See generally*, as to the reforms that have taken place in the Australian Public Service during this period, ANDREW KORAC-KAKABADSE & NADA KORAC-KAKABADSE, LEADERSHIP IN GOVERNMENT: STUDY OF THE AUSTRALIAN PUBLIC SERVICE 106–16 (1998); ALEXA TURNER, AN ANALYSIS OF CHANGES TO THE AUSTRALIAN PUBLIC SERVICE UNDER THE COALITION GOVERNMENT 1996–2001 (2001); SPENCER ZIFCAK, NEW MANAGERIALISM: ADMINISTRATIVE REFORM IN WHITEHALL AND CANBERRA (1994).

delivery of public services.⁶⁷ Even a cursory glance at the IP Australia website shows the depth of influence of the new public management agenda. IP Australia has a mission statement: it defines its role by reference to five goals, four of which would not look out of place in promotional material for a private corporation;⁶⁸ it emphasises its commitment to monitoring and improving "customer satisfaction;" and the very first piece of "information" that it provides about trade marks is that they "may be your most valuable marketing tool."

Not all of the consequences of the adoption of a new public management ethos are to be lamented. As was noted above, there has been an increased emphasis on quality control over recent years and there are now internal audit processes that focus on such things as how examiners conduct their research, whether they correctly identify earlier conflicting marks and whether applications are being passed on to examiners who dealt previously with earlier or similar marks. In other respects, however, the adoption of the new public management agenda is likely to act as a significant bar to reform. Some of the most powerful critiques of the new public management agenda are that increased responsiveness "is likely to expand citizens' demands for non-beneficial public services"⁶⁹ and has the potential to impact adversely on policy coherence.⁷⁰ These critiques should be borne in mind when thinking about how changes in management practices within IP Australia might detract from the rigorous policing of applications and the ability of the register to serve the public interest.

It was suggested above that the drive to measure performance by reference to clearly identifiable and quantifiable outputs means that things like increases

---

⁶⁷ In addition to the sources cited below, *see, e.g.*, David Farham & Sylvia Horton, *The New Public Sector Managerialism: An Assessment, in* MANAGING THE NEW PUBLIC SERVICES (David Farham & Sylvia Horton eds., 1993); Robert Schwartz, *Accountability in New Public Management: An Elusive Phenomenon?, in* PUBLIC ADMINISTRATION—AN INTERDISCIPLINARY CRITICAL ANALYSIS (Eran Vigoda ed., 2002) [hereinafter VIGODA]; Christopher Hood & Guy Peters, *The Middle Aging of New Public Management: Into the Age of Paradox*, 14 J. PUB. ADMIN. RES. THEORY 267 (2004); Kenneth Kernaghan, *The Post-Bureaucratic Organization and Public Service Values*, 66 INT. REV. ADMIN. SCI. 91 (2000).

⁶⁸ These include the goals of "provid[ing] our customers with quality services that meet their needs;" and ensuring that "our operations are cost effective." The exception is the goal of ensuring that "the international IP system meets the needs of Australians."

⁶⁹ Rivka Amado, *New Ethical Challenges under the New Reform Movements in the Public Administration Sector, in* VIGODA, *supra* note 67, at 147.

⁷⁰ B. Guy Peters, *The Search for Coordination and Coherence in Public Policy: Return to the Center?*, available at http://web.fu-berlin.de/ffu/akumwelt/bc2004/download/peters_f.pdf.

in the number of applications and renewals and decreases in the amount of time it takes to process applications will always be treated as evidence of success. In contrast, the new public management agenda provides a strong disincentive for the registry to take responsibility for things that are not capable of easy measurement. Most importantly for present purposes, it provides a disincentive for the registry to do its best to identify potential conflicts between the mark applied for and earlier unregistered marks. In theory, there would be nothing to prevent examiners from devoting a given amount of time (say thirty minutes per application) searching for prior conflicting unregistered marks by conducting internet searches, looking through trade directories, and so on. Even if the results of such inquiries were only communicated to applicants, something that would be entirely consistent with treating applicants as "customers," the quality of the register would be improved, since some applicants would inevitably choose to abandon or modify their plans rather than persisting with applications for marks that might well be vulnerable to a subsequent challenge. However, if the registry were to accept that it ought to be checking for potential conflicts between registered and unregistered marks, it would then be necessary to design a set of performance indictors against which to measure the quality of registry "outputs."[71] The idea that examiners should do their best when dealing with unregistered marks given limited time and resources is simply not the sort of devolved decision-making process encouraged by an approach to public administration that denigrates the importance of professional judgment.[72]

Still more importantly, the new public management agenda carries with it a heavy emphasis on customer satisfaction. Whilst it is extremely difficult to chart how an institutional ethos impacts on specific outcomes, the concern must be that pressure to keep customers happy will deter the office from making inquiries that could be construed as intrusive or hostile or from taking on or exercising powers that might bring the office into conflict with applicants and owners. For example, it is worth noting in this context that the Registrar has the power under the Act to decline an application in cases where

---

[71] *Cf.* Patrick Dunleavy et al., *New Public Management is Dead—Long Live Digital-Era Governance*, 16 J. PUB. ADMIN. RES. THEORY 467, 473 (2006) (noting that "perverse incentives may . . . arise in highly measured performance systems").

[72] Amado, *supra* note 69, at 140 ("Under the new reform movement, professional judgment is to be superseded by client preferences."); MICHAEL POWER, THE AUDIT SOCIETY: THE RITUALS OF VERIFICATION 119 (2d ed. 1999) ("The power of auditing is . . . to construct concepts of performance in its own image."); *also see generally,* JAMES SCOTT, SEEING LIKE A STATE Ch. 9 (1998) (arguing that market-driven standardisation and other "high-modernist schemes" suppress the common sense and experience needed to underwrite complex activities).

the person does not intend to start using the mark,[73] but it seems that this power is almost never exercised—the office is not prepared to inquire as to the applicant's intentions, even if the examiner has reason to doubt whether the application has been made in good faith, for example, because the applicant has a history of making speculative applications.[74]

Similarly, it is notable that under current arrangements the registry does not have the power to register a mark subject to a mandatory disclaimer for the non-distinctive elements of a mark. This devalues still further the information communicated by the register about the scope of trade mark rights and it is therefore unsurprising that a recent review of the Trade Marks Act recommended the reintroduction of mandatory disclaimers.[75] Tellingly, IP Australia came out against this recommendation and one of the reasons it gave for so doing was that the benefits offered by mandatory disclaimers have to be "balanced against . . . [the] significant administrative difficulties posed by the reluctance of applicants to use disclaimers."[76] In the context of a discussion of *mandatory* disclaimers, it is difficult to see how administrative "difficulties" could be caused by the reluctance of applicants to "use" disclaimers other than through consumer dissatisfaction.

To take a final example, the desire not to upset its customers is another factor that inevitably steers IP Australia away from seeking to do more to identify and resolve conflicts between registered and unregistered marks. Perhaps the best system for dealing with this issue would be for the registry to spend a given amount of time per application searching for possible conflicts of this type. In addition to informing the applicant of the results of this search (as suggested above), examiners might be expected to take reasonable steps to contact persons who seem likely to have an interest in a conflicting unregistered mark and invite them to make submissions about whether the application should be accepted. However, applicants might well perceive such a system as hostile, and hence it would be incompatible with IP Australia's customer service ethos.

C. *Constructing the trade mark office client*

The need to identify a discrete group of clients, whose "satisfaction levels" can be surveyed, inevitably steers government agencies away from seeking to present the importance of their mission in terms of the general public interest

---

[73] *See* Trade Marks Act 1995 (Cth), §§ 27, 33.
[74] *See* Burrell, *supra* note 20, at 232.
[75] *Review of Trade Mark Enforcement*, *supra* note 16, at 14–15.
[76] *Government's Response to the Review of Trade Mark Enforcement conducted by the Advisory Council on Intellectual Property (ACIP)* 3, *available at* http://www.ipaustralia.gov.au.

or from seeking to present the public at large as their client base. It makes any attempt to explain the value of intellectual property registration systems on the basis that such systems provide valuable information to the public much less attractive. It makes it difficult to argue that the persons served by the registration system include traders who would be inconvenienced if certain types of mark were accepted onto the register, traders who may well be blissfully unaware that the trade mark office is working on their behalf. But beyond this, new public management has very little to say about how the clients of a government agency are to be identified. Indeed, the fact that government agencies might have some scope for constructing their clients in different ways is an issue that seems to have received surprisingly little attention in the new public management literature.

Implicit in what has been said thus far is that IP Australia takes the view that its core clients, whose needs and expectations inform how the agency conducts itself, are businesses that are either existing intellectual property owners or are seeking to register a new right.[77] In fact, this is now so well established it is easy to lose sight of the fact that there are other ways in which IP Australia could conceptualise its client base. IP Australia could, alternatively, take the position that its core clients include financial institutions and, most significantly, members of the legal profession who have dealings with the office.[78] That IP Australia has sought to construct its clients as owners and applicants is unsurprising. Government agencies need to communicate with politicians who "may not listen to details," consequently "officials must resort to short-cut methods, [t]hey invent and develop bureaucratic ideologies, that is, images of each bureau's aspirations stated in terms of ultimate policy objectives."[79] When IP Australia is faced with the need to "sell" its role to politicians, it is almost inevitable that this will be done in terms of the services that it provides to businesses whose innovation and marketing success can be said to be essential to the Australian economy. Telling politicians that the role of

---

[77] See, e.g., IP Australia's Customer Service Charter Report for Apr.–June 2006, available at http://www.ipaustralia.gov.au.

[78] IP Australia does, admittedly, include "Attorneys and other IP professionals" (at the bottom) of its list of potential clients in its Customer Service Charter. Moreover, some senior trade mark practitioners are given an opportunity to provide input into IP Australia's policy formation through the Combined Interest Group (CIG) and the Executive Relationship Group (ERG) that meet regularly with IP Australia (disgracefully, very little public information is available about the CIG or the ERG or about the content of these meetings). Overall, however, the point remains that the legal profession is not within IP Australia's core conception of who its clients are and it is interesting to note that there are now plans to include owner representatives on both the CIG and ERG.

[79] ANTHONY DOWNS, INSIDE BUREAUCRACY 237–8 (1967).

the office is to serve the needs of the legal profession and the banking sector can hardly seem like an attractive alternative.

The importance of IP Australia's decision to define its client base narrowly should not, however, be underestimated. Most importantly for present purposes, this decision means that the views of groups who might be expected to take a broad view of how the trade mark system ought to function are not always heard. In other words, it results in the partial exclusion of groups whose views might to some degree act as a surrogate marker for ensuring that the trade mark system is achieving publicly desirable ends. That this has occurred cannot be explained solely by reference to IP Australia's adoption of the new public management agenda. But this in turn means that the obstacles to persuading the bureaucracy to refocus its efforts go beyond the fact that this would run counter to the thrust of recent management reforms. These reforms have required the bureaucracy to identify specific clients. The bureaucracy has adapted to this by sharpening its bureaucratic ideology—the intellectual property system promotes economic growth by providing a service to business; to change this would impact upon the way the intellectual property bureaucracy communicates with the rest of government.

In order to help demonstrate that government agencies have some scope for constructing their clients in different ways and in order to begin the process of identifying the consequences of IP Australia's decision to define its client base narrowly, it is perhaps worth drawing a contrast between the position occupied by the legal profession in relation to IP Australia and the position occupied by solicitors in relation to the Land Registry for England and Wales. The Land Registry has always had to ensure that its practices found favour with the legal profession and hence it has always seen the maintenance of a good relationship with the legal profession as essential to the performance of its role.[80] The creep of the language of new public management into the UK Land Registry's publications and pronouncements has not done much to alter the position— members of the legal profession have simply been relabelled as one of the Land Registry's core group of "customers."[81] The fact that the legal profession sits close to the heart of the operation of the land registration system in the United Kingdom may help explain why maintaining the accuracy and reliability of the register has remained central to the Land Registry's mission.[82]

---

[80] For an historical analysis, *see* Alain Pottage, *The Originality of Registration*, 15 O.J.L.S. 371 (1995).

[81] Information about how the Land Registry constructs its client base can be gleaned from its *Customer Service Statement*, from the way it conducts its customer-service surveys, and from the training programmes it offers. *See* http://www.land registry.gov.uk.

[82] *See* Nicola Jackson, *Title by Registration and Concealed Overriding*

There are, of course, other factors that may help explain why the UK Land Registry has not lost sight of its central purpose, including the fact there is no obvious, more politically attractive, alternative way in which the Land Registry could present its role. Special mention should also be made in this context of the interest that financial institutions have as mortgagees in ensuring that the Land Register is functioning effectively. But equally, it might be noted that such institutions have precisely the same interest in ensuring that the rights recorded on the trade mark register are stable and that the ownership details, including the existence of any encumbrances, are recorded accurately. Admittedly, such institutions have much less at stake in the case of trade mark registers than they do in the case of land registers, but when thinking about why the register does not provide a more accurate reflection of the interests that subsist in marks, it is worth remembering that financial institutions are largely excluded from Australia's understanding of who its clients are.

IP Australia's decision to define its core clients as applicants and owners has also had other important consequences. This logic has, for example, led IP Australia to expend considerable resources developing self-filing support services for trade mark applicants: its clients ought to be able to avoid expensive legal fees. Still more importantly, this logic means that customer satisfaction is always judged from one narrow perspective. This point is best illustrated by thinking about what customer satisfaction might be taken to mean if members of the legal profession were to be treated as IP Australia's principal client group. It has to be remembered that legal practitioners have to appear before the trade mark office in a range of capacities (they will not always be acting for a party seeking registration). Thus if legal practitioners were to be treated as IP Australia's core clients, this would inevitably lead to the performance of the trade mark office to be judged against a wider set of criteria.[83]

More generally, and despite what academic commentators sometimes intimate, in the author's experience legal practitioners are often concerned about

---

Interests: The Cause and Effect of Antipathy to Documentary Proof [2003] L.Q.R. 660, for a discussion of recent legislative reforms.

[83] It might be objected that IP Australia's larger clients (in particular) will interact with the office in a range of capacities and thus can also be expected to adopt a broad view of the functioning of the trade mark system. The response is that IP Australia views its relationship with its clients in terms of individual interactions, rather than in terms of developing a good long-term relationship with its most important clients. Any other approach would create the suspicion that the office was favouring big business at the expense of small and medium-size enterprises and would leave it open to significant criticism. This further reinforces the point that account must be taken not only of the development of a customer service ethos, but also of the political considerations that lead IP Australia to construct its client base in a particular manner.

the overall shape and health of the trade mark system.[84] Combined with the fact that some practitioners are increasingly seeing their clients being inconvenienced by marks that are not in use or that ought to be struck off the register for some other reason, it is unsurprising that lawyers have not universally welcomed the shift towards a more applicant- and owner-friendly stance. For example, it is interesting to note that in their submissions to recent reviews of the operation of the Trade Marks Act, major law firms in Australia have, *inter alia*, expressed their support for the introduction of a requirement of proof of use on renewal, opposed any increase in the cost of bringing a non-use application, and argued that the office is being overly generous when granting trade mark owners extensions of time in which to provide evidence of use.[85] Similarly, it should be noted that some senior trade mark practitioners in Australia have become concerned about a possible decline in the number of successful oppositions over recent years and that the legal community has expressed strong support for the reintroduction of mandatory disclaimers.[86]

On a rather different note, it is worth saying something about how IP Australia's focus might have an indirect effect on how segments of the legal profession are regulated. IP Australia has considerable input into the regulation of trade mark (and patent) attorneys. Strictly speaking, the Professional Standards Board for Patent and Trade Mark Attorneys is an independent body, which is responsible for regulating the professional conduct of trade mark attorneys. In practice, however, there is an extremely close relationship between the Board and IP Australia. The administrative support staff who assist the Board are IP Australia employees and the Director General of IP Australia is an ex-officio member of the Board. The other members of the Board are appointed by the Minister for Industry Tourism and Resources, the Minister to whom IP Australia reports, and it seems likely that the Director General of IP Australia is asked to recommend names to the Minister.

The Professional Standards Board has developed and administers a *Code of Conduct* that is designed to provide ethical guidance to trade mark attorneys.[87] Unfortunately, however, this code deals almost exclusively with the relationship between attorneys and their clients; it fails to provide any express acknowledgement of the duties attorneys might owe to third parties or to the

---

[84] The author has formed this view from conversations and other dealings with lawyers who practise predominantly in the intellectual property field. Trade mark practitioners who are members of that elusive species *homo economicus* may well take a different view.
[85] *See* Burrell, *supra* note 20, at 245–6 and the sources cited therein.
[86] *See Review of Trade Mark Enforcement*, *supra* note 16, at 14–15.
[87] *Available at* http://www.psb.gov.au/complaints.htm.

public generally. Consequently, the code contains no clear statement to the effect that trade mark attorneys must not help their clients to apply for intellectual property rights that they know beyond reasonable doubt ought not to be granted.[88] Consequently, trade mark attorneys are not clearly prohibited from applying for a mark after a client has disclosed that she does not intend to use it or from applying to renew a mark that the attorney knows has not been in use for many years. Given the nature of the relationship between IP Australia and the Professional Standards Board, it seems reasonable to suggest that IP Australia's customer service ethos may have spilt over into the way in which trade mark attorneys are regulated.

More generally, IP Australia plays an important role in shaping elements of intellectual property practice. Its focus on meeting the needs of its customers and its accompanying reluctance to probe into certain issues (such as intent to use) is hardly a stance that is likely to encourage trade mark attorneys or, for that matter, solicitors to resist client pressure to apply for or renew marks which they know to be invalid, particularly at a time when there is widespread concern that changes in the nature of legal practice may themselves have undermined ethical standards.[89]

In summary, IP Australia's decision to construe its client base narrowly leads to two different, but ultimately interconnected, problems. First, it leads IP Australia to adopt an overly narrow view of its role and how to measure its performance. The emphasis it places on meeting the needs of applicants and owners does not, of course, mean that the trade marks office lets every application that comes before it proceed to registration, nor does it mean that hearing officers consciously favour applicants and owners in opposition and non-use proceedings. Rather, the point is that the institutional focus may help to create a culture or a mindset within the office that is antithetical to ensuring that the trade mark register is as accurate a source of information as possible. It feeds into and helps underpin the refusal of the office to make even cursory inquiries about whether an applicant intends to start using a mark or to do as much as reasonably possible to take unregistered marks into account when assessing registrability; it leads the office to give little attention to function of the register in providing a stable and comprehensive record of the rights that subsist in a mark. Secondly, although, generally speaking, members of the legal profession can be expected to do more than focus on the needs of applicants and owners, when it comes to the question of whether lawyers are likely

---

[88] Such a duty can, at best, be inferred from an attorney's general duty not to engage in "practices which are misleading or deceptive": *Code of Conduct* ¶ 4.2.9.

[89] See, e.g., Donald Nicolson, *Making Lawyers Moral: Ethical Codes and Moral Character*, 25 LEGAL STUD. 601, 625–6 (2005).

to resist client pressure to apply for or renew marks that they know are invalid, the regulatory framework governing trade mark attorneys and the broader working environment in which legal professionals are operating (into which IP Australia's customer service ethos feeds) makes such resistance less likely than might otherwise be the case.

D. *The role of the courts and bureaucratic resistance*
No attempt to take account of the influence of the bureaucracy's attitudes and ideology on the trade mark system could be complete without also considering how the courts and the bureaucracy interact. This is a potentially mammoth inquiry. The analysis presented here will therefore concentrate solely on why it is important not to assume that the courts will be able to ensure that the trade mark registration system meets publicly desirable ends, irrespective of the attitude of the bureaucracy. The most serious problem with this proposition is that it assumes that the courts will be able to force an alternative view of the objects of the trade mark system on the registry, ignoring the possibility that the registry may resist any such shift. The way in which registries react to, distil and use court judgments is an issue to which far too little attention has been paid. The author's impression is that conscious resistance to court decisions is a surprisingly rare occurrence in most countries—registries might be expected to take a rather dimmer view of the courts meddling with "their" system than generally seems to be the case. Nevertheless, active resistance to court decisions can and does occur. Moreover, it is perhaps most likely to arise in response to cases in which the courts are demanding a fundamental shift in registry work practices of the type that would be required in order to refocus the trade mark system on achieving publicly desirable ends.[90]

The reaction of the Australian trade mark office to the decision of the Federal Court in *Advantage-Rent-A-Car v Advantage Car Rental*[91] provides a nice illustration of bureaucratic resistance and of the manner in which it can manifest itself. The background to that case was that, during opposition proceedings, the registry had taken the view that it could not be required to determine an issue of law other than in the field of registered trade marks. Consequently, the registry had refused to consider the opponent's argument that the application should have been rejected because use of the mark would amount to an infringement of copyright and hence "would be contrary to

---

[90] Jay Thomas has made the related point in the patent context that "reforms that heighten examiner burdens will be employed grudgingly or not at all." John R. Thomas, *The Responsibility of the Rulemaker: Comparative Approaches to Patent Administration Reform*, 17 BERKELEY TECH. L.J. 727, 750 (2002).

[91] [2001] F.C.A. 683.

law."⁹² In rejecting the registry's argument, Mr Justice Madgwick made it clear that by adopting such an approach the registry was failing in its duty, and that a court could not condone "reticence on the part of an administrative decision-maker to express an opinion on a matter of law."⁹³

The potential significance of the *Advantage* decision should not be underestimated. Read naturally, the case seems to require the registry to take account of not only copyright protection, but also, much more importantly, the possibility that the mark applied for might conflict with an earlier unregistered mark.⁹⁴ The registry, however, has displayed a rugged determination to place the narrowest construction possible on the *Advantage* decision. For example, the registry has taken the position that because *Advantage* was only concerned with opposition proceedings, it is entitled to take a narrow view of the factors that might make a mark unregistrable at the examination stage. But in order to justify this approach the registry relies on an argument of bureaucratic convenience,⁹⁵ which was precisely the argument that was rejected in *Advantage*. Similarly, the registry has seized on the fact that all of the examples developed by Madgwick J as to the scope of the registry's obligation to determine whether use of the mark would be contrary to law concerned the operation of other statutory provisions. Consequently, the registry still adopts the position that, even in opposition proceedings, it is not required to consider potential conflicts between the mark applied for and common law rights, including those that arise by reference to the tort of passing off.⁹⁶

Given the tiny proportion of cases that reach the courts, the possibility that registries will actively resist the implications of a decision like *Advantage* creates a significant limit on the courts' ability to refocus the trade mark system. To this can be added the fact that developments that run contrary to the bureaucracy's ethos may be greeted by a form of subconscious resistance, manifested in a "that couldn't possibly be what the judge intended" mentality. When one also takes account of the fact that decisions may be handed down by non-expert judges who may see little reason to challenge the registry's

---

⁹² *See* Trade Marks Act 1995 (Cth), § 42(b).
⁹³ *Advantage-Rent-A-Car* [2001] F.C.A. 683 ¶ 26.
⁹⁴ This is because of the potential breadth of § 42(b) of the 1995 Act.
⁹⁵ *See Australian Trade Marks Office Manual of Practice and Procedure* ¶ 30.3.2, *available at* http://www.ipaustralia.gov.au/resources/manuals_trademarks.shtml.
⁹⁶ *Id.* Registry decisions are not entirely consistent in adopting this position, but it is nevertheless fair to treat this as the registry's dominant approach. A review of opposition decisions in this area reveals that opponents have only rarely sought to rely on passing off in the context of § 42(b), Burrell & Handler, *supra* note 36, at 383, presumably because their lawyers have been guided by this statement in the *Manual*.

approach or by judges who, for whatever reason, are unwilling to unsettle entrenched registry practice, there is little reason to be sanguine about the ability and willingness of the courts to control the overall direction and function of the trade mark regime.

V. Conclusion

The analysis presented here has, for the most part, been negative: it is difficult to find a convincing justification for trade mark registration; any attempt to get the system working as efficiently as possible is likely to encounter formidable obstacles, but there is no realistic prospect of trade mark registration being abolished. To finish on a more positive note, it is hoped that the final section of this chapter will help create discussion about the role and influence of the trade marks bureaucracy. This is clearly an area in which a good deal of work remains to be done. In particular, more consideration needs to be given to the relationship between the courts and the bureaucracy, but the other relationships touched upon here (for example, the relationships between the bureaucracy and the legal profession and the bureaucracy and government) also merit further analysis. In addition, it might be noted that more could be done to probe the relationship between the development of a bureaucratic ethos and the behaviour of individuals. Some reference was made here to internal systems for monitoring staff performance, but a range of other issues also deserve attention, including the possibility that staff within the bureaucracy who have internalised a traditional public service ethic may seek to resist changes in institutional culture. It is nevertheless hoped that readers will see this chapter as an initial attempt to chart how bureaucratic culture affects the operation of the trade mark system, and as an effort to focus attention on the fact that, in most countries at least, the paradigmatic form of protection for trade marks is as a species of bureaucratic property that is difficult to justify.

5 The political economy of trademark dilution
*Clarisa Long**

The development of federal trademark dilution law over the past decade is unusual, perhaps even unique, among the various intellectual property regimes. What is notable about the evolution of this form of trademark protection is the relative balance of power between Congress and the courts as these two bodies have expanded and contracted the scope of protection, respectively, for famous marks. Patent law, by contrast, has been influenced mostly by courts, most notably the U.S. Court of Appeals for the Federal Circuit, which has increased the strength of the underlying rights.[1] Copyright law has been dominated by Congress, but the trajectory of its development is much the same: protection has increased in length and strength.[2]

When it was first added to the Lanham Act in 1996, the Federal Trademark Dilution Act ("FTDA") sparked much academic and legal commentary.[3] Commentators were concerned about the apparent power the statute conferred on the holders of famous trademarks.[4] This is not surprising considering the

---

* Max Mendel Shaye Professor of Law, Columbia Law School.

[1] *See, e.g.*, State Street Bank & Trust Co. v Signature Fin. Group, Inc., 149 F.3d 1368, 1375–6 (Fed. Cir. 1998) (declaring business methods to be patent-eligible subject matter). Recently the Supreme Court has started to take a more active role in shaping patent law. *See, e.g.*, Microsoft Corp. v AT&T Corp., 127 S. Ct. 1746 (2007) (limiting extraterritorial reach of patent protection); KSR Int'l Co. v Teleflex Inc., 127 S. Ct. 1727 (2007) (making it easier to invalidate patents for being obvious); MedImmune, Inc. v Genentech, 127 S. Ct. 764 (2007) (allowing patentees to challenge the validity of the patents they have licensed); eBay, Inc. v MercExchange, 547 U.S. 388 (2006) (rejecting the general rule that patent infringement should be enjoined).

[2] *See, e.g.*, Sonny Bono Copyright Term Extension Act, Pub. L. No. 105-298, 112 Stat. 2827 (codified at 17 U.S.C. §§ 301–04 (amended 2002)) (extending term of copyright protection by twenty years).

[3] *See* Sara Stadler Nelson, *The Wages of Ubiquity in Trademark Law*, 88 IOWA L. REV. 731, 732 (2003) ("Courts and scholars have spilled a great deal of ink on the subject of trademark dilution").

[4] *See e.g.,* Barton Beebe, *The Semiotic Analysis of Trademark Law*, 51 UCLA L. REV. 621, 684 (2004) ("[a]ntidilution protection is by its nature absolute and unlimitable."); Wendy J. Gordon, *Introduction*, 108 YALE L.J. 1611, 1614–15 (1999) (expressing concern about dilution law's ability to undermine comparative advertising and parody); Mark A. Lemley, *The Modern Lanham Act and the Death of Common*

FTDA's departure from trademark law's traditional requirement that a third party's unauthorized use of a trademark create a likelihood of confusion before a trademark holder could recover. Instead, the FTDA provided an injunctive remedy against a third party's commercial use of a famous mark, regardless of the presence or absence of confusion as to whose mark was whose.[5]

Over the next decade, however, various aspects of the FTDA proved unpopular with the federal judiciary, and courts cut back the reach of the statute.[6] The most notable trimming came in 2003 when the Supreme Court in *Moseley v V Secret Catalog* raised the bar by holding that parties seeking to recover under the FTDA had to prove actual dilution rather than a likelihood of dilution.[7] Some circuits placed the bar for protection higher than mere distinctiveness, even though the statute stated that a mark need merely be "distinctive,"[8] whereas others suggested that trade dress might be beyond the scope of the FTDA, even though once again the statute contained no such restriction.[9] In response to these and other moves by the federal courts to limit protection, Congress passed the Trademark Dilution Revision Act of 2006 ("TDRA").[10] Among other things, the TDRA mandated a likelihood of dilution standard and expanded protection to include marks that have obtained secondary meaning.[11] Congress's amendments have restored the statute in many respects almost to the point it was at ten years ago before the courts started cutting it back.

Sense, 108 YALE L.J. 1687, 1698 (1999) ("dilution laws represent a fundamental shift in the nature of trademark protection"); Gerard N. Magliocca, *From Ashes to Fire: Trademark and Copyright in Transition*, 82 N.C. L. REV. 1009, 1033 (2004) (dilution "is now a powerful alternative to the traditional model of trademark protection"); David S. Welkowitz, *The Supreme Court and Trademark Law in the New Millennium*, 30 WILLIAM MITCHELL L. REV. 1659, 1681 (2004) (describing this form of protection as "immensely popular").

[5] 15 U.S.C. § 1125(c)(5) (stating that "the owner of the famous mark shall be entitled to injunctive relief").

[6] *See* Clarisa Long, *Dilution*, 106 COLUM. L. REV. 1029 (2006).

[7] 537 U.S. 418, 432 (2003). Until then the federal appellate courts, as well as many states, had been divided upon the appropriate standard for establishing dilution.

[8] *See, e.g.*, TCPIP Holding Co. v Haar Commc'ns Inc., 244 F.3d 88, 98 (2d Cir. 2001) ("Because TCPIP's mark, 'The Children's Place,' as a designator of stores for children's clothing and accessories, is descriptive, and thus, lacks inherent distinctiveness, it cannot qualify for the protection of the Dilution Act."); I.P. Lund Trading ApS v Kohler Co., 163 F.3d 27, 46–7 (1st Cir. 1998) (stating that something more than evidence of secondary meaning was required in order to show fame).

[9] *See, e.g.*, Planet Hollywood, Inc. v Hollywood Casino Corp., 80 F. Supp. 2d 815, 898–900 (N.D. Ill. 1999) (holding that trade dress is not protected by FTDA).

[10] Trademark Dilution Revision Act of 2006, Pub. L. No. 109-312, 120 Stat. 1730 (2006) (codified at 15 U.S.C. § 1125(c)).

[11] 15 U.S.C. § 1125(c)(1) (2006) (distinctiveness may be inherent or acquired).

What is notable about the evolution of this form of trademark protection is the relative balance of power between courts and Congress. From the perspective of holders of famous marks, what Congress giveth, the courts taketh away – and Congress restoreth, at least in part. (Congress also codified some of the courts' attempts to limit the reach of federal dilution law, such as eliminating from the ambit of the statute marks that had achieved fame only in a niche market.[12]) In this chapter I explore the political economy of federal trademark dilution law. What can public choice theory tell us about the inclusion of dilution in the Lanham Act? Why would courts want to trim back the statute? And why would Congress move to expand the statute back almost to its reach in 1996?

I. The Federal Trademark Dilution Act

In the first fifty years of its existence, the Lanham Act followed the consumer protection model of trademark rights, prohibiting the use of a trademark "where such use is likely to cause confusion, or to cause mistake, or to deceive."[13] Congress consistently rejected language supporting the fundamental premise of dilution law – that a mark holder could suffer harm even when consumers were not confused as to whose mark was whose – into federal trademark law.[14] Courts interpreted the Lanham Act likewise. As one court opined: "The Lanham Act rejects the dilution doctrine as a basis of relief in trademark cases in placing the burden on the trademark owner claiming infringement to at least prove the likelihood of confusion."[15]

The FTDA changed this. The statute barred the use of a mark that diluted the distinctiveness of a famous mark even in the absence of a likelihood of consumer confusion. Dilution law's underlying assumption is that the unauthorized use of a famous mark by another entity can diminish the mark's selling power and value because the mark is no longer associated with a single source.[16] Congress put a distinctly producer-oriented spin on this addition to

---

12 *Id.* at § 1125(c)(2)(A) (stating that "a mark is famous if it is widely recognized by the general consuming public of the United States").

13 15 U.S.C. § 1114(1)(a) (2006).

14 *See, e.g.,* H.R. 11592, 72d Cong. (1932) for a pre-Lanham Act example, and S. 1883, 100th Cong. (1988) for a later example.

15 *See* Avon Shoe Co., Inc. v David Crystal, Inc., 171 F. Supp. 293, 299 (S.D.N.Y. 1959).

16 15 U.S.C. § 1127 (2000) (defining dilution as "lessening of the capacity of a famous mark to identify and distinguish goods or services, regardless of the presence or absence of (1) competition between the owner of the famous mark and other parties, or (2) likelihood of confusion, mistake, or deception"). The TDRA defined "dilution by blurring" as the "association arising from the similarity between a mark or trade name and a famous mark that impairs the distinctiveness of the famous mark." 15 U.S.C. § 1125(c)(2)(B) (2006).

the Lanham Act when it specified that "dilution recognizes the substantial investment the owner has made in the mark and the commercial value and aura of the mark itself, protecting both from those who would appropriate the mark for their own gain."[17] When it enacted the FTDA, Congress emphasized that it was trying to protect the goodwill, or "aura" surrounding famous marks.[18] As a result, a famous mark could be protected against trademark dilution if a similar mark was used to identify completely unrelated goods.

Dilution is a more exclusionary version of the trademark entitlement than the classic likelihood-of-confusion variant. As a result, owners of famous marks have trademark rights closer to traditional property rights than to classic trademark rights. If classic trademark infringement can be analogized to the law of nuisance in real property, dilution has more trespass-like elements. Dilution law also represents an accession model of exclusionary rights.[19] Accession models allow the owner of a *res* in one context or market to capture revenues resulting from the use of that *res* in another context or market.[20] Thus the FTDA represented, at least on paper, a significant expansion in the power of trademark protection for holders of famous marks and the potential to capture revenue from the use of the mark when the trademark holder expanded into a new market. In this respect, protection was even broader than that envisioned by Frank Schechter, who initiated the concept of dilution.[21] According to one interpretation, Schechter intended his original proposal to apply to trademarks used with a single product or product class, not to those used in multiple product markets.[22]

Dilution as it appeared in the FTDA posed several problems. First of all,

---

[17] H.R. REP. No. 104-374, at 3 (1995), *reprinted in* 1995 U.S.C.C.A.N. 1029, 1030.

[18] *See id.* at 1030 (stating that the FTDA would "create a federal cause of action to protect famous marks from unauthorized users that attempt to trade upon the goodwill and established renown of such marks").

[19] I am grateful to my colleague Tom Merrill for this observation.

[20] *See, e.g.*, State v Hagerty, 251 I a 477 (1967) (stating that the doctrine of accession mandates that "[t]he ownership of a thing, whether it be movable or immovable, carries with it the right to all that the thing produces").

[21] *See* Frank I. Schechter, *The Rational Basis of Trademark Protection*, 40 HARV. L. REV. 813, 828–31 (1927) (proposing a form of dilution law limited to conflicts between identical marks, where the plaintiff's mark was not only famous but also arbitrary, and where the defendant's use of the mark was on noncompeting and nonsimilar goods).

[22] *See* Sara Stadler Nelson, *supra.* note 3 ("Schechter intended his remedy to apply not to famous marks, but to a select class of highly distinctive (indeed, for the most part, inherently distinctive) trademarks that were, like most trademarks of his day, synonymous with a single product or product class.").

it's not clear what "dilution of a mark" even is. The FTDA defined dilution as a "lessening of the capacity of a famous mark to identify and distinguish goods or services" but gave little guidance as to how this occurred or how to identify such an outcome.[23] The TDRA recognized two forms of dilution: "dilution by blurring" and "dilution by tarnishment," but even today there is no single accepted mechanism by which dilution occurs.[24] Another difficult problem under the FTDA was identifying the nature of the harm that arises when a mark is diluted.[25] Following from this was the related problem of how to prove harm.[26] Moreover, even when the alleged harm is a loss of goodwill, in all but the most straightforward of cases, commentators have found it hard to articulate exactly how the unauthorized but nonconfusing third-party use of a mark damages the mark's goodwill.

In light of these and other problems, federal dilution law was not popular with many commentators. Some found its "seductive appeal" troubling.[27] Others called it "absolute and unlimitable," "powerful," and a "disaster."[28] Others noted that it represented an expansion in property rights at the expense of the public domain.[29] Still others worried about its potential to stifle expression, hamper commercial communication, or reduce competition.[30]

Despite its vagaries, flaws, and eventual unpopularity with commentators,

---

[23] 15 U.S.C. § 1127 (2000).
[24] *See* 15 U.S.C. § 1125(c)(2)(B) (C) (mentioning blurring and tarnishment as theories of dilution).
[25] Dilution is a concept whose harm has been called "dauntingly elusive." Ringling Bros.-Barnum & Bailey Combined Shows, Inc. v Utah Div. of Travel Dev., 170 F.3d 449, 451 (4th Cir. 1999). Commentators generally agree. *See, e.g.*, Robert N. Klieger, *Trademark Dilution: The Whittling Away of the Rational Basis for Trademark Protection*, 58 U. PITT. L. REV. 789, 822 (1997); David S. Welkowitz, *Reexamining Trademark Dilution*, 44 VAND. L. REV. 531, 543 (1991).
[26] *Id.* (requiring that plaintiffs under the FTDA prove actual harm rather than just a likelihood of dilution).
[27] *See* Richard A. Posner, *Misappropriation: A Dirge*, 40 HOUS. L. REV. 621, 623 (2003).
[28] *See* Beebe, *supra.*, note 4, 684 ("[a]ntidilution protection is by its nature absolute and unlimitable."); Gordon, *supra.*, note 4, at 1614–15 ("One can only hope that Congress's recent decision to allow the owners of famous marks to sue in the absence of 'consumer confusion' will not prove a disaster"); Magliocca, *supra.*, note 4, at 1033 (dilution "is now a powerful alternative to the traditional model of trademark protection").
[29] *See* Margaret Jane Radin & R. Polk Wagner, *The Myth of Private Ordering: Rediscovering Legal Realism in Cyberspace*, 73 CHI.-KENT L. REV. 1295, 1305 n. 29 (1998) ("Modern trademark law is moving ... towards a ... property rights regime.").
[30] *See, e.g.*, Gordon, *supra* note 4, at 1614–15 (expressing concern about dilution law's ability to undermine comparative advertising and parody); Mark A. Lemley,

the FTDA passed readily. The House of Representatives approved the Act on a voice vote, and the Senate took up the House bill by unanimous consent, passing it on a voice vote without hearings or floor debate.[31] Indeed, not everyone apparently understood that the FTDA represented a new justification for protecting certain trademarks. One Congressional press release described the FTDA as "another . . . legislative effort to protect consumers."[32]

Public choice theory can help us understand some of the circumstances behind the passage of the FTDA. Indeed, the story we can tell about the addition of dilution to the Lanham Act is a straightforward one. Public choice theory posits that groups have the incentive to lobby for passage of legislation that will confer concentrated benefits on the group.[33] So long as the costs the legislation imposes on others are dispersed, opponents will have less incentive to oppose the legislation. As a result, legal rules can be expected to favor the interests of well-organized and politically influential interest groups at the expense of more diffuse groups.

By limiting protection to famous marks, the dilution entitlement protects a subset of all trademark holders who can identify themselves fairly readily. All else equal, holders of famous marks will have more at stake than holders of relatively unknown marks. Thus dilution law creates a benefit for a group of holders of high-value trademarks. It is less clear who bears the costs of the legislation. Entities who might be sued for dilution of famous marks will have a hard time identifying themselves in advance. They have less at stake and less incentive to organize to oppose legislation that exposes them to liability. Indeed, the entities testifying in support of the FTDA fit the profile of holders of a large portfolio of valuable trademarks: Reebok International, Campbell Soup Company, Warner Brothers, and the Samsonite Corporation.[34] As one would expect, witnesses downplayed the potential costs of the statute and even presented dilution law as preventing broader *social* harm, not just harm to a trademark. For instance, Warner Brothers' witness used the case of a third

---

Romantic Authorship and the Rhetoric of Property, 75 TEX. L. REV. 873, 900 (1997) (stating that trademark owners "are well on their way to owning the exclusive right to pun").

[31] *See* Robert N. Klieger, *Trademark Dilution: The Whittling Away of the Rational Basis for Trademark Protection*, 58 U. PITT. L. REV. 789, 839 (1997).

[32] Sen. Orrin G. Hatch, President Signs Hatch Trademark Bill Into Law, Cong. Press Releases (Jan. 18, 1996).

[33] *See* JAMES BUCHANAN & GORDON TULLOCK, THE CALCULUS OF CONSENT: LOGICAL FOUNDATIONS OF CONSTITUTIONAL DEMOCRACY 287–8 (1962); *see also* STEPHEN M. BAINBRIDGE, CORPORATION LAW AND ECONOMICS 22–3 (2002).

[34] *See Madrid Protocol Implementation Act and Federal Trademark Dilution Act of 1995: Hearing on H.R. 1270 and 1295 Before the Subcomm. on Courts and Intellectual Property of the House Comm. on the Judiciary*, 104th Cong. 109 (1995).

party showing Bugs Bunny smoking a marijuana cigarette as an example of trademark dilution, but described it as a "counterfeit" product rather than tarnishment of the mark.[35]

Similarly, the other witnesses – Philip G. Hampton II, Assistant Commissioner for Trademarks of the U.S. Patent and Trademark Office; Thomas E. Smith, Chair of the section of Intellectual Property Law of the American Bar Association; and Jonathan E. Moskin, an attorney with Pennie & Edmonds – all represented interests that could benefit from an expanded trademark law, and all testified in favor of the statute.[36] No witnesses testified against the Act or even expressed serious reservations about it.[37]

II. Courts' reaction to federal dilution law

If federal dilution law was not popular with commentators, it was not a hit with many courts either.[38] In the early years of federal dilution law, courts often enforced the statute as written. In the decade after passage of the FTDA, however, the statute became increasingly unpopular in the federal courts. From 1996 to 2006, federal courts began to deny relief more frequently for federal dilution claims.[39] By 2006, the dilution claims that did get injunctive relief often involved counterfeit goods.[40]

Not only did courts decline to enforce dilution claims at a greater rate over time, but they also created statutory limitations and erected barriers to recov-

---

[35] *See id.* at 103, 111 (Statement of Nils Victor Montan, Vice President and Senior Intellectual Property Counsel, Warner Bros.).

[36] *See id.* (statement of Philip G. Hampton that "The Administration strongly supports providing protection on the federal level for famous marks and supports amending the Trademark Act of 1946 to add a remedy against dilution of the reputation of a famous mark.").

[37] *Moseley v V Secret Catalogue Inc.* 537 U.S. 418, 431 (2003) (stating that "No opposition to the bill was voiced at the hearing and, with one minor amendment that extended protection to unregistered as well as registered marks, the subcommittee endorsed the bill and it passed the House unanimously.").

[38] This section draws on my previous work on how the federal courts became increasingly unwilling to enforce federal dilution law as written from 1996 to 2006. *See* Long, *supra* note 6 (empirically showing how federal courts became increasingly less willing to grant injunctions on dilution claims in the decade after the FTDA was created).

[39] *See id.*

[40] *See, e.g.*, Gen. Motors Corp. v Autovation Techs., Inc., 317 F. Supp. 2d 756, 764–5 (E.D. Mich. 2004) (enjoining defendant's use of General Motors' trademark on counterfeit automobile parts); Nike, Inc. v Variety Wholesalers, Inc., 274 F. Supp. 2d 1352, 1374 (S.D. Ga. 2003) (enjoining defendant's use of NIKE mark on counterfeit socks and clothing.

ery.[41] Some of this was driven by the vagaries of the statute itself. As written, the FTDA granted protection against a broad range of potential uses of a trademark by a non-owner.[42] Not all third-party uses of a famous trademark are harmful, but the FTDA contained little guidance on which uses ought to be enjoined. Forced to look outside the few limitations of the statute to find reasons to justify recovery in one circumstance but not another, various circuits created their own ways to shut down many of the dilution claims that came before them. As a result, dilution law evolved differently in each circuit.[43]

If interpreted exactly as written, the FTDA allowed injunctions for many instances of third-party trademark use that did not present clear cases of harm. In the early years of the FTDA, such outcomes were not uncommon, as courts issued injunctions against third parties whose use of another's mark created only ambiguous harm under dilution law.[44] The circuits soon split on whether the FTDA required actual harm or whether a likelihood of dilution was sufficient. The Supreme Court granted certiorari in *Moseley v V Secret Catalogue, Inc.* to resolve that split.[45] In *Moseley*, the Court held that a plaintiff bringing a dilution claim must show "actual dilution," or a lessening of the famous mark's capacity to distinguish goods and services. The court reasoned that when the U.S. Congress and state legislatures wanted to indicate a likelihood of something occurring under the trademark laws, they did so. The Lanham Act refers to a "likelihood of confusion" and state dilution statues generally refer to the "likelihood of dilution," whereas the FTDA referred only to "dilution," not a

---

[41]   *See, e.g.*, I.P. Lund Trading ApS v Kohler Co, 163 F.3d 27 (1st Cir. 1998) (denying protection against dilution to product shape).

[42]   15 U.S.C. § 1125(c) (allowing an injunction "against another person's commercial use [of a famous mark] if such use begins after the mark has become famous and causes dilution").

[43]   *See* Nabisco, Inc. v PF Brands, Inc., 191 F.3d 208, 216 (2d Cir. 1999) ("It is quite clear that the statute intends distinctiveness, in addition to fame as an essential element."); *I.P. Lund Trading ApS*, 163 F.3d at 45 (dilution "applies to a famous 'mark' and does not restrict the definition of that term to names or traditional marks. In the absence of such a restriction, the Act applies to all types of marks recognized by the Lanham Act, including marks derived from product designs.").

[44]   In many of these cases, the alleged harm appeared to stem from consumer confusion rather than a loss of distinctiveness, despite the statements of the court to the contrary. *See, e.g.*, Wawa Inc. v Haaf, 40 U.S.P.Q. 2d (BNA) 1629, 1633 (E.D. Pa. 1996) (expressing concern that "the sophistication of convenience store customers, in general" was such that they would be unable to distinguish HAHA mark from WAWA mark); Gazette Newspapers, Inc. v New Paper, Inc., 934 F. Supp. 688, 696–7 (D. Md. 1996) (finding "Frederick Gazette" to infringe upon GAZETTE mark for chain of newspapers on a confusion theory).

[45]   537 U.S. 418 (2003).

likelihood of dilution. The Court concluded that trademark holders had to prove actual dilution, but courts and commentators quickly lamented that the Court did not indicate what evidence was needed to prove dilution.[46] The upshot was that it became more difficult for a trademark holder to prevail on a dilution claim. *Moseley* became a major factor limiting recovery under the FTDA.

Moseley also hinted in dicta that tarnishment – the use of a trademark by a third party in a way that creates a negative impression of the trademark in the minds of consumers[47] – might not be a viable theory of dilution under the FTDA.[48] The Court noted that tarnishment was a popular theory of dilution allowed under many state statutes, but "[w]hether it is actually embraced by the statutory text [of the FTDA], however, is another matter."[49] By questioning whether one of the two most long-standing justifications for recovery was covered by the FTDA, the Court further weakened the structure of federal dilution law.

Courts similarly made recovery more difficult by ramping up the standard a mark had to meet in order to be declared famous and therefore qualify for protection. Fame was the one attribute Congress explicitly required marks to possess in order to qualify for protection under the FTDA. Congress then declined to define exactly what made a mark famous, instead setting forth eight factors for courts to consider.[50] Some of the factors, such as fame in a product niche market, tip in favor of marks qualifying for protection under the FTDA. Other factors, such as "the geographical extent of the trading area in which the mark is used" could be used to nudge marks in or out of protection. In the decade after passage of the FTDA, courts came to focus on those factors that tended to make fame more difficult to establish. While early cases allowed a regional mark to be declared famous, later cases generally declared mere regional fame insufficient.[51] Cases decided soon after the FTDA was passed held that fame in a product niche market was sufficient to establish fame for protection against trademark dilution, but most later courts came out the other

---

[46] *See, e.g.*, Thomas R. Lee, *Demystifying Dilution*, 84 B.U. L. REV. 859, 863 (2004) ("*Moseley* raises at least as many questions as it answers. Its core holding is inherently unstable.").

[47] *See* 4 J. THOMAS MCCARTHY, TRADEMARKS AND UNFAIR COMPETITION, § 24:94, at 24–160 (defining blurring); *id.* at § 24:95, at 24–165 (defining tarnishment).

[48] *Moseley*, 537 U.S. at 432.

[49] *Id.*

[50] *See* 15 U.S.C. § 1125(c)(1)(A)–(H).

[51] *Compare Wawa, Inc.*, 40 U.S.P.Q. 2d (BNA) at 1630 (WAWA famous in Pennsylvania and surrounding states) *with TCPIP Holding Co.*, 244 F.3d at 98 (rejecting regional fame as sufficient to establish fame under the FTDA).

way.⁵² By raising the bar for a mark to qualify as famous, courts made it harder for trademark holders to prevail on dilution claims.

In addition to confining protection to a subset of all types of marks, over time some circuits came to confine protection to marks that are "inherently distinctive," or generally speaking, memorable enough to be associated with a particular product in consumers' minds from the very start of the mark's use.⁵³ If the mark had merely established "distinctiveness," or had become recognizable to consumers over time, this was not enough to qualify for protection, even if the trademark holder's claim was that dilution began after the mark became distinctive.⁵⁴ Under this interpretation, marks that established recognition over time, and thus were distinctive but had secondary meaning, failed to qualify for dilution protection. Sometimes a mark's lack of inherent distinctiveness was used as a basis for declaring it nonfamous.⁵⁵ The FTDA did not require marks to be inherently distinctive, but rather merely said that a mark must be distinctive.⁵⁶ All trademarks must be distinctive in order to qualify for protection, with inherently distinctive marks being a subset of all distinctive marks. Distinctiveness simply means consumers associate a mark with a product. By requiring inherent distinctiveness (consumer recognition from day one) when the statute demands only distinctiveness (consumer recognition), courts were able to narrow the set of marks to which the FTDA applied.

So long as a trademark is famous, nothing in the FTDA limits protection to any particular kind of trademark. Early interpretation of dilution law applied

---

⁵² *Compare* Advantage Rent-A-Car v Enterprise Rent-A-Car, 238 F.3d 378 (5th Cir. 2001); Times Mirror Magazines Inc. v Las Vegas Sports News, 212 F.3d 157 (3rd Cir. 2000) *with TCPIP Holding Co.*, 244 F.3d at 99 (doubting that Congress intended to protect "marks that have enjoyed only brief fame in a small part of the country, or among a small segment of the population"); *I.P. Lund Trading ApS*, 163 F.3d at 58 (stating that famousness requires "national renown"); Heidi Ott A.G. v Target Corp., 153 F. Supp. 2d 1055 (D. Minn. 2001) (citing concerns that fame based on a niche market would overprotect trademarks).

⁵³ *See, e.g.*, New York Stock Exchange, Inc. v New York Hotel, 293 F.3d 550, 556 (2d Cir. 2002) (stating that "marks that are not inherently distinctive but that have acquired secondary meaning" are not subject to dilution protection); *TCPIP Holding Co.*, 244 F.3d at 98; *I.P. Lund Trading ApS*, 163 F.3d at 58 (citing Restatement (Third) of Unfair Competition § 25 cmt e). In *TCPIP*, the court stated, "Because TCPIP's mark, 'The Children's Place,' as a designator of stores for children's clothing and accessories, is descriptive, and thus, lacks inherent distinctiveness, it cannot qualify for the protection of the Dilution Act." *Id.*

⁵⁴ "The mark's deficiency in inherent distinctiveness is not compensated by the fact that TCPIP's mark has achieved a significant degree of consumer recognition." *Id.*

⁵⁵ *See* Savin Corp. v Savin Group, 391 F.3d 439 (2d Cir. 2004).

⁵⁶ 15 U.S.C. § 1125(c) (permitting an injunction against third party use of a mark that "causes dilution of the distinctive quality of the mark").

it across the board to a range of trademarks. The Second Circuit upheld a preliminary injunction granted to protect the shape of a cracker from alleged dilution.[57] Many courts including the Second Circuit in later cases, however, limited the subject matter to which they would apply dilution protection. Circuits that have considered the issue will hesitate before granting dilution protection for anything that is not a word, logo, symbol, or picture.[58] For example, in *I.P. Lund Trading ApS v Kohler Co.*, the First Circuit declined to apply dilution law to product design – in this case the shape of a bathroom faucet – stating that "[w]e doubt that Congress intended the reach of the dilution concept to extend this far."[59] The court justified its move by explaining that "[w]here words are the marks at issue it is easy to understand that there can be blurring and tarnishment [the two prevailing theories of dilution]. . . . What is much more difficult is to see how dilution is to be shown where some of a design is partially replicated."[60]

Why did the courts trim back dilution law? Courts are not subject to the pressures of lobbying and interest groups in the same way Congress is.[61] This is not to say that judges remain uninfluenced by outside forces, however. Judges may be concerned about their reputations, or want to maximize their leisure time by clearing their dockets as quickly as possible, or may be motivated by any number of things. A cynical answer, therefore, is that even though dilution claims are almost always pleaded in conjunction with nondilution claims, trimming back the statute made it easier for courts to dispose of cases by denying relief on the dilution claims.[62] Another response could be that courts had long been used to having broad authority to interpret the Lanham Act and were not about to cede that authority to Congress. A less cynical answer, and one supported by the resulting cases, is that judges were often balancing the harms and benefits of enjoining unauthorized third party use of a mark and attempting to grant injunctions when the private and social

---

[57] *See* Nabisco, Inc. v PF Brands, Inc., 191 F.3d 208 (2d Cir. 1999) (comparing Pepperidge Farm's Goldfish crackers with Nabisco's CatDog cracker).
[58] *See, e.g., I.P. Lund Trading ApS*, 163 F.3d at 27 (denying protection to product shape).
[59] *Id.* at 50.
[60] *Id.*
[61] *See* RICHARD A. POSNER, ECONOMIC ANALYSIS OF LAW 505 (1986) (stating that "judges, like other people, seek to maximize a utility function that includes both monetary and non-monetary elements (the latter including deciding the case, leisure, prestige, power, and aversion to reversal)."; *see also* Richard A. Posner, *What Do Judges and Justices Maximize? (The Same Thing Everybody Else Does)*, 3 SUP. CT. ECON. REV. 1, 14–15 (1993).
[62] *See* Long, *supra* note 6 at 1054 (showing that dilution claims are rarely brought alone).

benefits of doing so outweighed the private and social costs.[63] In other words, judges wanted to get dilution law right in the cases that came before them.[64]

If interpreted exactly as written, the FTDA allowed courts to enjoin many instances of unauthorized trademark use that did not present clear cases of harm. When harm is as ambiguous as it was under the FTDA, and given that the statute did not contain many limitations or other tools to help courts distinguish unauthorized uses that presented net positive social benefits from those that did not, it is not surprising that courts began reading limitations into the statute in order to identify cases of clear private or social harm and deny relief when the harm from authorized use was not clear.

One circumstance in which the net social benefits of dilution enforcement will often outweigh the net social costs arises when an accused infringer is using a counterfeit mark. The social benefits from falsely labeling generic shoes NIKE are likely to be outweighed by the social costs resulting in the diminution in value of the mark when attached to genuine NIKE brand shoes. Setting aside parody, satire, and other forms of truthful communication that involve unauthorized commercial use of the mark, in most cases the harm trademark holders will suffer from the counterfeit uses of their marks will be positive whereas consumers will experience small net social benefits at best. Counterfeiting cases, therefore, present one example where injunctive relief on a dilution claim ought to be granted. In the few years leading up to the revision of the FTDA, the dilution claims for which injunctive relief was granted often involved counterfeit goods.[65]

III. Congress's reinvigoration of federal dilution law

Holders of famous marks were understandably upset, not just by the result in *Moseley*, but by courts' treatment of the FTDA generally. A decade after dilution law was first added to the Lanham Act, trademark holders had come to agree with commentators (albeit for different reasons) that federal dilution law was a "mess."[66] Interest groups began to petition Congress to "repair" federal

---

[63] *See id.*

[64] *See* THOMAS E. BAKER, RATIONING JUSTICE ON APPEAL: THE PROBLEMS OF THE U.S. COURTS OF APPEALS 172 (1994) (stating that judges "are very independent, highly motivated, individual decisionmakers who feel a great responsibility to 'get it right'").

[65] *See, e.g.*, GMC v Autovation Techs., Inc., 317 F. Supp. 2d 756 (E.D. Mich. 2004) (defendant's use of General Motors' trademark on counterfeit automobile parts enjoined); Nike Inc. v Variety Wholesalers, Inc., 274 F. Supp. 2d 1352 (S.D. Ga. 2003) (defendant's use of NIKE mark on counterfeit socks and clothing enjoined).

[66] *See, e.g., Trademark Dilution Revision Act of 2005: Hearing on H.R. 683 Before the Subcomm. on Courts and Intellectual Property of the House Comm. on the Judiciary*, 109th Cong. at 6 (Feb. 17, 2005) (testimony of Ann Gundelfinger, President, International Trademark Ass'n) ("trademark dilution law in the United States is in need of repair") [hereinafter *TDRA Hearing on H.R. 683*].

dilution law and rewrite the FTDA to resolve circuit splits because courts' whittling back the statute had made it "ambiguous, at best, and at worst, ineffective."[67]

In response, Congress passed the Trademark Dilution Revision Act of 2006 ("TDRA"), which revised the FTDA.[68] The TDRA made a number of changes to federal dilution law, the most important of which I will discuss here. First, it overturned *Moseley* by allowing injunctions to be granted to protect famous marks from dilution "regardless of the presence or absence of actual or likely confusion, of competition or of actual economic injury."[69] Congress explicitly made the new standard one of likelihood of dilution, thereby making it easier for holders of famous marks to get injunctive relief. The House Judiciary Committee's report on the bill declared that *Moseley*'s standard created an "undue burden" for trademark holders, because in many cases injunctive relief would be ineffective by the time the trademark holder could prove that actual dilution had occurred.[70]

Second, Congress specified that blurring and tarnishment were both definitions of dilution covered by the statute, thus undercutting the Supreme Court's dicta in *Moseley* questioning tarnishment as a theory of dilution. The TDRA defines blurring as "association arising from the similarity between a mark or trade name and a famous mark that impairs the distinctiveness of the famous mark."[71] The statute suggests that courts may refer to factors such as the degree of similarity between the allegedly violating mark and the famous mark, and the degree of distinctiveness of the famous mark. The definition of tarnishment is more succinct although no less broad, covering any "association arising from the similarity between a mark or trade name and a famous mark that harms the reputation of the famous mark."[72] The statutory revisions eliminated any third basis of dilution, such as free riding, which was one theory that had been suggested by some courts.[73] The definitions are both sweeping, and potentially cover a wide range of behavior.

---

[67] *Id.* (stating that "hundreds of cases after the FTDA was enacted, virtually everyone – courts, litigants, commentators alike – agree that the law is a mess.").

[68] Trademark Dilution Revision Act of 2006, Pub. L. No. 109-312, 120 Stat. 1730 (codified as amended at 15 U.S.C. § 1125(c)).

[69] 15 U.S.C. § 1125(c)(1) (2006).

[70] Trademark Dilution Revision Act of 2005, H.R. Rep. No. 109-23, at 5 (March 17, 2005).

[71] 15 U.S.C. § 1125(c)(2)(B).

[72] 15 U.S.C. § 1125(c)(2)(C).

[73] *See, e.g.*, Ty Inc. v Perryman, 306 F.3d 509, 512 (7th Cir. 2002) (noting the possibility that free riding might be a basis for dilution law but doubting the "validity of the rationale"); *see also* David J. Franklyn, *Debunking Dilution Doctrine: Toward a Coherent Theory of the Anti-Free-Rider Principle in American Trademark Law*, 56

Third, Congress defined a famous mark as one that is "widely recognized by the general consuming public of the United States as a designation of source of the goods or services" and reduced the number of suggested famousness factors from eight to three: the duration and reach of publicity of the mark, the volume and extent of sales, and actual recognition of the mark.[74] By incorporating into the TDRA much of the courts' definition of fame as developed under the FTDA in the previous decade, Congress eliminated niche market fame as sufficient to qualify for protection under the Act.

Fourth, the new legislation specified that it does not matter whether the mark's distinctiveness is inherent or acquired, thus undoing courts' insistence that a mark be inherently distinctive in order to be protected.[75]

Finally, the TDRA recognized that dilution protection could apply to trade dress, although plaintiffs alleging dilution of famous trade dress would have to prove more than a plaintiff seeking to enforce protection for a word or logo.[76] Specifically, plaintiffs alleging famous but unregistered trade dress would have to prove that the trade dress was still famous in the absence of any marks or logos that might appear in context with it.[77] This eviscerated the rulings of the circuits that had confined protection to words, logos, symbols, and pictures.

Unlike in the hearings regarding the FTDA, testimony regarding the TDRA paid more attention to the potential social costs of the legislation. For example, the American Civil Liberties Union expressed concern about the First Amendment implications of dilution law, stating that "The idea that trademark owners would use the FTDA to stifle criticism is far from a fanciful notion," and successfully urged an exemption for third party uses of a trademark that extended beyond noncommercial use.[78] Similarly, Professor Mark A. Lemley stated that the goal of the TDRA should be to "strike a balance between the

---

HASTINGS L. J. 117 (2004) (stating that "while American dilution law purports to be about preventing dilutive harm, it really is about preventing free-riding on famous marks").

[74] 15 U.S.C. § 1125(c)(2)(A).
[75] *Id.* § 1125(c)(1).
[76] *Id.* § 1125(c)(4).
[77] *Id.* (stating that "if the claimed trade dress includes any mark or marks registered on the principal register," the trade dress holder must prove that the unregistered trade dress "taken as a whole, is famous separate and apart from any fame of such registered marks.").
[78] *TDRA Hearing on H.R. 683, supra* note 66, at 33 (testimony of Marvin A. Johnson, Legislative Counsel, American Civil Liberties Union). The exemption appears in 15 U.S.C. § 1125(c)(3)(A)(ii) (protecting third party uses "identifying and parodying, criticizing, or commenting on the famous mark owner or the goods or services of the famous mark owner").

interests of trademark owners and the interests of consumers."[79] Despite some reservations being expressed about various aspects of the TDRA, the legislation passed easily in the House of Representatives with a vote of 411 to 8, and in the Senate by unanimous consent.[80]

The outcome, both regarding the TDRA and with respect to the evolution of federal dilution law from 1995 onward, should not surprise us. Most of the changes the TDRA made to dilution law expanded the scope of protection back almost to what it had been in 1995. This is no accident. (Unsurprisingly, Congress did not frame the changes as an expansion of the scope of dilution protection but rather as a clarification of the law.[81]) Once again, public choice theory can help us understand many of these changes. Four of the five revisions I noted above favor holders of famous marks and undo the courts' trimming of the statute: requiring trademark holders to demonstrate a likelihood of dilution rather than actual dilution, explicitly establishing tarnishment as a justification for dilution protection, specifying that marks need not be inherently distinctive, and protecting trade dress.

What about the remaining change – raising the bar for fame so that a mark needed to have national recognition? To be sure, this incorporates the courts' treatment of fame in the decade after the FTDA was passed into the new statute and shrinks the number of trademark holders who could potentially recover. But the excluded trademark holders – which will often be mom-and-pop style establishments that have fame in their local community but not beyond – were not lobbying Congress to amend the statute, nor were they likely to have the wherewithal to organize to seek protection for themselves. Once again, as with the FTDA, the TDRA protects a subset of all trademark holders who can identify themselves fairly readily, who will have the most at stake, and who have the resources to organize and to protect their interests.

IV. Conclusion

It remains to be seen how courts will interpret the TDRA over the coming years. The pressures to reform dilution law are not as great as they once were, and judicial evolution of the law usually moves incrementally if not glacially. One thing can be said with confidence, however. Courts are not subject to the

---

[79] *Id.* at 18 (testimony of Mark A. Lemley, William H. Neukom Professor of Law, Stanford University).

[80] *See* GovTrack.us, *available at* http://www.govtrack.us/congress/bill.xpd?bill=h109-683.

[81] *See TDRA Hearing on H.R. 683, supra* note 66, at 2 ("For the most part, I do not believe the bill breaks new precedential grouns. Rather [it] represents a clarification of what Congress meant when it passed the dilution statute almost a deade ago.") (remarks of Rep. Smith).

same pressures as Congress, and trademark dilution law has been an area in which the judiciary has not hesitated to leave its imprint. Even after passage of the TDRA, key elements of federal dilution law remain uncertain, such as how consistently to identify the harm created by a third party's nonconfusing use. If past history is any guide, we can expect that the courts will continue to act as a counterweight to Congress and play an active role in the evolution of this area of intellectual property law.

PART II

INTERNATIONAL AND COMPARATIVE DIMENSIONS

6 Fundamental concerns in the harmonization of (European) trademark law
Annette Kur*

I. The roots and the upshot

When the European Economic Communities were founded fifty years ago,[1] the trademark laws applying in the member countries[2] were far from homogeneous. Some of those differences were of a rather technical nature, but others reflected basically divergent attitudes towards the very foundations of trademark law. For instance, from a French point of view, it was taken for granted that the rights vested in a trademark owner were not essentially different from those accorded by other intellectual property rights: just as in patent or copyright law, the proprietor must be entitled to enjoin any kind of unauthorized use, no matter for which purpose. In Germany, on the other hand, trademark law and doctrine were strictly founded on the origin function, which was held to constitute the sole and mandatory guideline regarding the acquisition as well as the protection of marks. Based on its common law tradition, the UK[3] endorsed still another approach – one which was less dogmatic than the German, and more competition-friendly than the French. And finally, the Benelux countries added strong new colours to the overall picture when they enacted a uniform law[4] incorporating features like protection beyond the risk of confusion, which at the time were seen as strikingly modern.[5]

---

*   Professor and Research Fellow, Department of Intellectual Property and Competition Law, Max Planck Institute for Intellectual Property, Munich, Germany.
[1] The "Treaties of Rome", i.e. the Treaty establishing the European Economic Community (EEC) and the Treaty establishing the European Atomic Energy Community (Euratom), were signed in Rome in May 1957 and entered into force on 1 January 1958. The beginnings of what has now become the EU can even be dated back further, to the Treaty establishing the European Coal and Steel Community (ECSC), which was signed in Paris on 18 April 1951 and entered into force on 24 July 1952.
[2] The founding members were France, Italy, Germany, and the Benelux countries.
[3] This is also true for Ireland as another country with a common law tradition. The UK and Ireland joined the EEC in 1974.
[4] Benelux Merkenwet (BMW), enacted 1975.
[5] The Benelux law was considered and advertised by those who created it as an obvious model for European harmonization, an ambition proving at least partly successful.

152 *Trademark law and theory*

The efforts to harmonize trademark law in the European Union were not triggered by an academic desire to overcome those conceptual divergences. Instead, they were driven by the pragmatic wish to improve the proper functioning of the Common Market. Trademarks, like other IP rights, made their first prominent appearance on the European legal scene in the context of what is usually referred to as the parallel import cases[6] – attempts by IP right holders to use their exclusive territorial rights in order to block unauthorized traffic over intra-Community borders. Although those attempts were stopped in their tracks when the European Court of Justice ("ECJ") developed the principle of Community-wide exhaustion,[7] a persistent problem was that whenever the right to the same or a similar sign belonged to different persons in different Member States, each proprietor was entitled to oppose the movement of goods into the country where he or she was in a position to claim a better right.

This problem gave rise to the view that impediments to the free movement of goods resulting from the territorial nature of intellectual property should ultimately be overcome by the creation of unitary rights,[8] to be acquired through one single act taken out *vis-à-vis* one single authority, and having legal effect throughout the whole Community (one application, one office, one right). Trademarks were the first, and today still are the most important, category of IP rights where this vision has finally been realized (with the adoption of the Trademark Regulation, or "CTMR").[9]

As to national trademark law, it was decided that it should coexist with the Community system, and that the national rules should be harmonized in order

---

[6] See in particular ECJ decisions C-56/64 & 58/64, *Etablissements Consten Sarl and Grundig VerkaufsGmbH/Commission*, [1966] ECR 299, 385; C-24/67 *Parke Davis/Centrafarm*, [1968] ECR 55; C-40/70, *Sirena/Eda*, [1971] ECR 69; C-78/70, *Deutsche Grammophon Ges./Metro*, [1971] ECR 487; C-15/74 *Centrafarm B.V./Sterling Drug*, [1974] ECR 1147; C-16/74 *Centrafarm/Winthrop*, [1974] ECR 1183; C-51/75 *EMI Record/CBS*, [1976] ECR 1183.

[7] This means that the owner of a trademark (or any other intellectual property right) cannot object to further circulation within the Community of goods that have been released by himself or with his consent on the market in a Member State. The principle is now embedded in Art. 7 of the trademark directive (104/89/EEC).

[8] S. Hans von der Groeben, *Rechtsangleichung auf dem Gebiet des gewerblichen Rechtsschutzes im Rahmen der Europäischen Wirtschaftsgemeinschaft* (Harmonisation of laws in the framework of the European Economic Communities), GRUR Int. 1959, 629 *et seq.*, stating the necessity to create a European (i.e. Community) trademark, patent, and design regime. Von der Groeben was a member of the Commission at the time.

[9] The same idea was developed at the same time in patent law, without those dreams having come true until now. On the other hand, it has been relatively easy to implement the same concept in industrial design law, where a harmonization directive and a Community design regulation were enacted in 1998 and 2002 respectively.

to remove obstacles to free trade resulting from existing disparities.[10] In its content, the directive was made congruent with the core provisions in the Community trademark regulation.[11] Apart from working efficiency, this had the advantage that it prevented national legislatures from engaging in "unfair competition" with the Community system, by granting more favourable conditions for the acquisition and scope of rights.

The substantive rules of the directive and the CTMR were both finalized in the late 1980s. While the directive went into force in 1989, it took five more years for the CTMR to become enacted, due to political quarrels concerning the official languages of the Community system and the seat of the central trademark office. However, implementation of the directive in all countries that were members of the EU at the relevant time was not fully completed until 1996, when the new Irish trademark act (TMA) went into force. In the same year, the Office for Harmonisation in the Internal Market (OHIM) started to accept and process CTM applications, so that at the time of writing,[12] both the directive and the CTM system can look back on ten years of full-blown activities.

II. The system in operation

A. Actors and stages

Due to its double-tier structure, the practical development of European trademark law occurs on two stages. A number of actors involved in the play – the national authorities and courts in the Member States, the OHIM and its appeal boards, and the two courts in Luxembourg[13] – impact each other and the process as a whole. And, of course, each one of these consists of a plurality of individuals with as many independent minds, fostering their own ideas of what exactly should be the meaning and content of European trademark law.

This concerns not least the OHIM in Alicante, with the office and its appeal boards forming a congregation of individuals from all EU countries. At least in the beginning, when virtually everything the office did and decided was new and unsettled, the diversity of legal backgrounds – in a nutshell, a clash of legal cultures – must have fuelled a plethora of internal debates concerning the correct interpretation of both substantive law and procedural issues. It is particularly noteworthy in the latter regard that a number of details in the

---

[10] Council Directive 89/104/EC of 21 December 1988.
[11] Council Regulation (EC) No. 40/94 of 20 December 1993.
[12] The original version of this manuscript was completed in autumn 2006.
[13] The Court of First Instance (CFI), established in 1998, is competent *inter alia* to decide appeals against decisions of the OHIM appeal boards, and its decisions are subject to revision on legal grounds by the ECJ.

implementing regulations to the CTMR were left open, with the task being imposed on OHIM and its Appeal Boards to develop, on the basis of procedural principles generally accepted in the Member States, their own rules of procedure. Given the range of difficult questions this posed, it was certainly a most valuable exercise and a pioneering task, involving a good deal of comparative legal work with immediate practical relevance.

Similar problems accrued in the practice of the Court of First Instance (CFI) and the European Court of Justice (ECJ), in particular in the latter Court. The mere fact that a compromise had to be found between styles of decision-writing which are as diverse as the British and the French tradition offers a glimpse of how difficult it must have been to establish a well-functioning judiciary. As ECJ decisions are rendered *per curiam* only and do not allow for individual judges to state their own views, the task is rendered even more delicate. It is claimed that in critical cases, a frequently used technique involves deleting from the reasoning those passages that have proven most controversial, so that dissenting judges, although not fully satisfied with the result, at least do not appear to have supported a text to which they are completely opposed. While resort to such a technique is understandable given the difficulties mentioned above, the method typically entails a risk that the full grounds originally stated for the decision are severely curtailed. If true, this might furnish one explanation for the fact that ECJ decisions are sometimes surprisingly brief, even concerning rather complex issues.[14]

Due to the ECJ's unique position, its decisions are of paramount importance for the development of European trademark law. The Court is competent both to adjudicate cases coming up from OHIM and to give authoritative answers to questions regarding the directive referred to it by national courts on the basis of Art. 234 of the EC Treaty. This double function makes the ECJ the only institutional link between the genuine Community system governing registration of CTMRs, and the national judicial systems.[15] ECJ decisions therefore have an immediate effect on several levels, thus multiplying the potentially detrimental effects of unclear or ambiguous reasoning.

---

[14] Even worse, in some of its more recent decisions, the ECJ has shown a tendency to answer the questions posed simply by quoting or paraphrasing the text of the legal provision at stake, without providing the national court with guidelines for interpretation. This tendency can be observed in C-48/05, Judgment of 25/01/2007, *Opel/Autec* (regarding the interpretation of Art. 5(2)) and C-17/06, Judgment of 11/09/2007, *Céline SARL/Céline SA* (regarding Art. 6(1)(a)).

[15] Disputes regarding national trademark laws remain fully within the national court system. As to CTMs, infringement and – if possible under national law – counterclaims for invalidity are adjudicated in so-called Community trademark courts (Art. 91 CTMR), which, despite their name, remain fully part of the national judicial system. *See also* Section III.1.

Fundamental concerns in the harmonization of trademark law 155

At least in the initial phase, practically all decisions of the ECJ immediately attained the status of landmark cases, as they were addressing core issues of trademark law where the text of the CTMR and the directive did not provide clear guidance.[16] While this might be attributable to the poor quality of legislative drafting – a suggestion most would be inclined to deny – it could also result from the fact that in spite of the efforts vested in the harmonization project during the years of negotiation, it has not been possible to resolve all issues resulting from the inherent complexities of the subject-matter, and to overcome the fundamental differences in national attitudes towards the underlying objectives of trademark protection briefly sketched above.[17] We shall come back to this later.

The fact that the ECJ's judgments are of such crucial importance for trademark law has created a novel situation in civil law countries where, traditionally, wisdom to be found in books is valued more than judges' deliberations. Especially in a country like Germany, which has always boasted a very complex and refined legal doctrine in the field, supported by bookshelves full of specialized literature, it has been difficult and sometimes even painful to accept that the thousands of pages which have been written in German, from a German legal perspective, have no more – and sometimes even less – impact on the ECJ, and thereby on the actual state of trademark law, than a single, well-written decision by the British High Court. Indeed, the strength inherent in a thoroughly developed, systematic approach can turn out to be a disadvantage, in so far as it is understood merely by specialists and cannot be communicated in simple words and comprehensible terms to judges who are not experts in the field. Rather than lamenting these developments, however, it is better in this situation to attempt to reduce rather than further enhance the complexity and refinement of national legal doctrines, and to try to convey one's own ideas in a manner which can easily be grasped by persons who have not grown up in one's own system, instead of using language which is hardly apt for communication outside an exclusive circle of fellow disciples.

---

[16] It is also noteworthy that the ECJ's trademark jurisprudence has been extremely rich in number of cases compared to other (harmonized) fields of IP law, most notably in comparison with copyright, where seven harmonization directives have been adopted. In patent law, Community legislation only concerns a few specific fields, like the directive on biotechnological inventions and the regulations on supplementary protection certificate for inventions in the pharmaceutical and the agro-chemical sector.

[17] *See supra* text accompanying notes 3–5 (discussing the fundamental question of whether trademarks enjoy full protection as a "normal" property right against any use which has not been authorized by the owner, or whether protection should in principle be restricted, unless extended protection is expressly granted, to the capacity of the mark to furnish a correct indication of the commercial origin of the merchandise to which it is applied).

156 *Trademark law and theory*

B. Problems and tendencies in substantive law

1. Likelihood of confusion (including association) As stated above, the frequency of the ECJ being asked for preliminary rulings in core matters of trademark law indicates that the texts of the directive and CTMR are not as clear as might be desired. Indeed, the formulation of certain provisions reflects the outcome of a political compromise rather than the thoroughly founded decision of a "wise lawmaker". Beneath the camouflage, the original diversities linger on and are bound to surface sooner or later.

One well-known example of such a situation is the debate concerning the interpretation of Art. 5(1)(b) of the directive[18] according to which likelihood of confusion includes the risk of association between conflicting signs. The wording was adapted in order to meet, on the one hand, a demand by the Benelux countries that the provision should embrace the notion of non-origin confusion, which had been developed in Dutch court practice and formed part of the 1975 Benelux trademark law. On the other hand, the expansion of the scope of trademark protection that this would entail was firmly opposed by other countries.[19] The compromise reflected in Art. 5(1)(b), where account is taken of both positions, with the narrower notion of confusion including the broader concept of association, was bluntly characterized by commentators as "legal nonsense".[20] It is little wonder that the ECJ in its first judgment concerning the interpretation of the directive was called on to clarify which of the two notions should be governing the assessment of infringement.

In that judgment – *SABEL/Puma*[21] – the ECJ firmly endorsed the more restrictive option, concluding that no regard should be had in the framework of Art. 5(1)(b) to a mere risk of association. However, this does not mean that protection against mere association is necessarily denied. Instead of invoking Art. 5(1)(b), such claims can be based on Art. 5(2), the provision granting protection for marks having a reputation against unfair advantage being taken,

---

[18] In the following discussion, only the provisions of the directive will be cited. The regulation typically contains parallel provisions.

[19] Account is given of the history of the provision by Anselm Kamperman-Sanders, *The Wagamama Decision: back to the Dark Ages of Trade Mark Law*, [1996] E.I.P.R. 3–5; Rolf Sack, *"Doppelidentität" und "gedankliches Inverbindungbringen" im neuen deutschen und europäischen Markenrecht* ("Double identity" and "association" in the new German and European trademark law), [1996] GRUR, 663, 668.

[20] Feer D.W. Verkade, *Angleichung des nationalen Markenrechts in der EWG: Benelux-Staaten* (Harmonisation of national trademark laws in the EEC: Benelux countries), [1992] GRUR Int., 92, 96; Rolf Sack*, Sonderschutz bekannter Marken* (Extended Protection for marks having a reputation) [1995] GRUR 81, 89.

[21] C-251/95, Judgment of 11/11/1997, *SABEL/Puma, Rudolf Dassler Sport*, [1997] E.C.R. I-6191.

or detriment being done to, their reputation or distinctive character. It is true that the provision only addresses use made of the mark for *dissimilar* goods,[22] thereby triggering doubts as to whether it provides sufficient legal ground for enjoining use taking advantage of a mark by using it for the *same or similar* products. The issue was resolved in the *Davidoff/Durffee*[23] and *Adidas/Fitnessworld*[24] decisions. In both cases, the national courts had found that the degree of similarity between the conflicting marks (which were protected and used for the same products) might not be sufficient to produce a likelihood of confusion, but that the younger signs nevertheless came close enough to their well-known counterparts to profit from their specific aura. The ECJ ruled that in those situations, Art. 5(2) is applicable in spite of its limited wording. *Cum grano salis*, this is old Benelux practice dressed in slightly different clothes.[25]

Even in *Puma/Sabèl* itself, where the "confusion only" principle was pronounced as a hard and fast rule, the exclusion of elements other than genuine origin confusion from the assessment was not as strict as it may appear at first glance. By expressly endorsing the principle that a wider scope of protection is granted to "strong" marks, i.e. marks that are either inherently highly distinctive or that are well-known to the interested public, the Court does assign weight to factors that would tend not, from an empirical point of view, to support the assumption of an enhanced risk of confusion. Instead, as has repeatedly been pointed out, the fact that the public is very familiar with a mark is likely to result in a more alert perception of differences, thereby even reducing the risk of actual confusion.[26]

---

[22] *Cf.* the wording of Art. 5(2): "Any Member State may also provide that the proprietor shall be entitled to prevent all third parties not having his consent from using in the course of trade any sign which is identical with, or similar to, the trade mark in relation to goods or services *which are not similar* to those for which the trade mark is registered, where the latter has a reputation in the Member State and where use of that sign without due cause takes unfair advantage of, or is detrimental to, the distinctive character or the repute of the trade mark" (emphasis added).

[23] C-292/00, Judgment of 9/1/2003, *Davidoff/Gofkid* (Durffee), [2003] E.C.R. I-389.

[24] C-408/01, Judgment of 23/10/2003, *Adidas/Fitnessworld Trading*, [2003] E.C.R. I-12537.

[25] It is true that contrary to previous Benelux law, Art. 5.2 requires that the mark has reputation in order to profit from extended protection. However, in Benelux law, the fact that a mark had to have a certain level of notoriety and goodwill resulted as a matter of course from the fact that it would not be plausible otherwise to assume that its position in the market had been tainted by someone causing non-origin association.

[26] *See e.g.*, *Baywatch Production Co. Inc.* v *The Home Video Channel*, High Court of Justice, Chancery Division, 31 July 1996 (Crystal J.), *citing BASF Plc v CEP (UK) Plc (Knox J.)*, 16 October 1995.

Nevertheless, the assertion endorsed by the ECJ that the risk of confusion expands in proportion to the goodwill acquired by a mark does have a sound basis. It is rooted in the empirical fact that it is much easier to catch the initial advertence of consumers by signs that resemble a well-known mark, than by imitating a weak, "anonymous" mark. The psychological phenomenon triggering that effect is exactly what would in general parlance be called an association: By emulating specific features that seem familiar to the targeted public, the second-comer "rings a bell" in the consumer's mind and attracts closer attention, which may be all it needs to be propelled into the set of principally eligible alternatives.[27] In other words, the second-comer uses an already established mark as an "entrance pass" into the consumer's brain, but once there, it moves onward under its own flag. Though similar in its economic results (if the purchase is actually made), the situation is markedly different from actual confusion in the strict sense, i.e. when consumers are and continue to be mistaken, even at the time of purchase, about the identity and/or the commercial origin of the goods they are buying.

If that analysis is accepted as basically sound, it follows that in order to obtain a clearer picture of what likelihood of confusion means in European trademark law, a distinction needs to be made between the different stages of the decision-making process. The notion endorsed by the ECJ in Puma/Sabèl and subsequent decisions appears plausible (only) on the basis of the presumption that the first stage, when the eligible set of alternatives is formed, is considered relevant.

Further investigation of that concept would appear useful not least with regard to establishing a clear dividing line between the meaning of likelihood of confusion in the trademark law sense, and the concept of commercial misrepresentation found in the regulation of unfair marketing practices or similar areas. Doing so might help to develop a satisfactory scheme for resolving situations when conflicting signs, for various reasons, need to coexist. Obviously, in that situation, likelihood of confusion in the sense of catching the consumer's attention by featuring distinctive elements of another mark must be tolerated, while safeguards must still exist in order to guarantee that the final decision process is not jeopardized, i.e. that a risk of consumer deception can be avoided.[28]

Until now, the ECJ has shown little inclination towards a more thorough

---

[27] The situation is similar, but not the same as has been labelled "initial interest confusion" in American case law, when the protected mark is actually shown in a situation preceding the decision process. *See Dr. Seuss Enters., L. P. v Penguin Books USA Inc..* 109 F. 3d 1394 (9th Cir. 1997); *Brookfield Communications, Inc. v West Coast Entertainment*, 174 F. 3d 1039 (9th Cir 1999).

[28] On that point, see Section IV *infra*.

elaboration of the issue. Rather than distinguishing the two concepts, the Court has repeatedly emphasized the congruencies between them. This concerns in particular the notion of the averagely circumspect and informed consumer, whose perspective is held to provide the relevant yardstick for the assessment of likelihood of confusion as well as of the deceptive and misleading nature of commercial speech.[29] While this does not preclude the distinction suggested above, it fails to encourage a better and more differentiated understanding of the two notions.

2. *Prerequisites for protection – distinctiveness, descriptive character, and the need to keep free*

a. The structure of the provision The language of the directive and the CTMR also leaves room for speculation as regards the conditions for protection. For example, the fundamental requirement of distinctiveness is mentioned twice in the directive (in Art. 2 and in Art. 3(1)(b)). In addition, Art. 3(1) enumerates two other, similar requirements – absence of descriptive and generic character – side by side with distinctiveness as criteria equally relevant to validity, thus inviting the question of how those three conditions relate to each other.

The riddle of the "double mention" of distinctiveness in Art. 2 and Art. 3(1)(b), respectively, can be solved relatively easily by observing that Art. 2 concerns distinctiveness in the abstract sense of whether specific forms of signs are principally eligible for trademark protection (i.e. whether they are generally capable of distinctiveness); whereas Art. 3(1)(b) addresses distinctiveness as a concrete concept, when a decision needs to be made as to whether one particular individual trademark is distinctive with a view to the goods or services it shall designate.[30]

Regarding the relationship between the three criteria listed in Art. 3(1)(b)–(d), things are more complicated.[31] As was stated above, the systematic order between them is such that, by contrast for example to American law, (lacking) distinctiveness is *not* considered as the overarching concept comprising the

---

[29] *See* C-342/97, Judgment of 22/06/1999, *Lloyd Schuhfabrik Meyer/Klijsen*, [1999] ECR, I-3819 (Lloyd/Loints).
[30] *See* C-299/99, Judgment of 18/06/2002 , *Philips/Remington*, [2002] I-5475 paras 37, 40 (ECJ).
[31] The difficulties originate from the fact that the structure of Art. 3(1)(b)–(d) as well as the wording have been adapted from Art. 6^{quinquies} B 2 of the Paris Convention. As Art. 6^{quinquies} reflects the outcome of political compromises rather than the result of thoroughly deliberated lawmaking, it is little wonder that it does not provide an optimal basis for legal practice. See also below, at the end of subsection a).

other two. Instead, all three aspects[32] must be considered separately, and must be allocated their specific place in the assessment.[33]

The interpretation of protection requirements was first addressed by the ECJ in the *Chiemsee* case,[34] which concerned the conditions for protecting a word referring to a lake in Bavaria as a trademark for clothing. In its reference to the ECJ, the national court (the "Landgericht" – district court – in Munich) had posed the question whether the manner in which account is taken under harmonized European law of the interests of actual and/or potential competitors to make unimpeded use of a sign, corresponds to what under previous German law had become known as the doctrine of the "need to keep free" (in German: "Freihaltebedürfnis").[35]

In response to that question, the ECJ declared that no further application of previous national doctrines should be encouraged.[36] Instead, an autonomous European approach was developed in *Chiemsee* and subsequent decisions.

---

[32] In practice, the issue is primarily relevant regarding the relationship between distinctiveness (Art. 3(1)(b)) and descriptive character (Art. 3(1)(c)), with genericness playing only a minor role. The presentation above is therefore concentrated on the two former requirements.

[33] It is noteworthy in this context that Art. 3(3), the proviso concerning the possibility of overcoming certain obstacles through use, only makes reference to distinctiveness, without mentioning the other two requirements. The reason for this somewhat inconsistent wording can be traced back to the legal history of the provision. In the first drafts, distinctiveness had been listed as the principal criterion, with descriptive or generic character being mentioned as main examples of signs being devoid of distinctive character. When the wording was subsequently changed so as to reflect the structure of Art. $6^{quinquies}$B 2 Paris Convention (see *supra*, note 31), it was forgotten to bring the third paragraph in line with the new wording.

[34] C-108/97 and 109/97, combined Judgments of 04/05/1999 *Windsurfing Chiemsee/Attenberger*, [1999] ECR I – 2779.

[35] As a historical footnote, it may be interesting to mention that for a certain period, still remembered with a shudder by practitioners as a kind of ice age, the "need to keep free" requirement was interpreted very strictly by German authorities, chilling the adoption of new suggestive marks. The fact that the afterlife of the criterion in the new European environment appeared precarious was therefore greeted with much relief in those circles.

[36] This concerned the way in which the "need to keep free" had been applied as an element in the assessment of descriptive character as well as its deployment as a tool for fashioning the threshold to be overcome in order to establish registrability through use. As a rule, it was held in previous German law that the burden in such cases increased in proportion with the weight to be placed on the need to keep free in a given case. The ECJ expressly distanced itself from that approach, stating that "Windsurfing Chiemsee and the Commission are therefore right to assert that Article 3(3) does not permit any differentiation as regards distinctiveness by reference to the perceived importance of keeping the geographical name available for use by other undertakings"; C-108/97, *supra* note 34 at para 48.

According to the established formula, "distinctiveness" and "descriptive character" must be assessed separately, [37] though a broad area of overlap exists between them.[38] It is sufficient for refusal of registration that one ground listed in Art. 3(1) applies.[39] Marks that are found to be descriptive will regularly also be devoid of distinctive character,[40] while non-descriptive marks do not necessarily meet the criterion of distinctiveness. It follows that distinctiveness is the broader concept of the two. However, in view of the systematic structure, this does not mean that descriptive character simply denotes a special case of lacking distinctiveness. Instead, a distinction between the two requirements is claimed to exist in so far as each one is based on its own, specific policy or "general interest", in the light of which the interpretation must be conducted.[41] According to that approach, the public interest of free competition, i.e. the need of competitors to keep a sign free for general use, is an aspect to be considered (only) in the appraisal of descriptive character,[42] whereas the general objective underlying the distinctiveness requirement concerns the interest of consumers in being able to recognize the products they want to buy.[43] In essence, this means that there is no possibility to take account of

---

[37] The formula is repeated in most ECJ judgments concerning protection requirements, see e.g. Joined Cases C-456/01 P and C-457/01 P, Judgment of 30/04/2004, *Henkel/OHIM*, [2004] ECR I-1725, at paras 45, 46; C-329/02 P, Judgment of 16/09/2004, *SAT.1/OHIM*, [2004] ECR, I-8317, at para 25; C-37/03 P, Judgment of 15/09/2005, *BioID AG/OHIM*, [2005] ECR I-7975, at para 59.

[38] C-517/99, Judgment of 04/10/2001, *Merz & Krell/DPMA*, [2001] ECR I-6959 at para 68; C-363/99, Judgment of 12/02/2004, *KPN&PTT Nederland NV/Benelux-Merkenbureau*, [2004] ECR I-1619, at para 67.

[39] C-104/00 P, Judgment of 19/09/2004, *DKV/OHIM*, [2002] ECR I-7561, at para 28.

[40] C-383/99 P, Judgment of 20/09/2002, *Procter & Gamble/OHIM* (BABY DRY), [2001] ECR I-6251, at para 37: "It is clear that ... the purpose of the prohibition of purely descriptive signs is ... to prevent registration of signs which ... could not fulfil the function of identifying the undertaking that markets them and are thus devoid of ...distinctive character." See also C-191/01, Judgment of 23/10/2003, *OHIM/Wm. Wrigley*, at para 19.

[41] According to the formula regularly repeated in ECJ judgments, "the general interest to be taken into account when examining each of those grounds for refusal may or even must reflect different considerations according to the ground for refusal in question"; see e.g. C-329/02, at para 25, C-37/03, at para 59; both judgments *supra* note 37.

[42] See already in C-108/97 and 109/9, *supra* note 34, at para 25, Joined cases C-53/01 to 55/01, Judgments of 08/04/200, *Linde, Winward, Rado/DPMA*, [2003] ECR I-3161, at para 73, C-191/01 P, Judgment of 23/10/2003, *OHIM/Wm. Wrigley*, [2003] ECR I-12447 at para 31.

[43] This is frequently clad in the formula that "the public interest underlying distinctiveness is manifestly indissociable from the essential function of a trademark", see e.g. C-329/02, *supra* note 37, at para 27.

competitors' interests when a mark's protectability is assessed solely under the aspect of distinctiveness.[44]

The problems ensuing from that scheme became obvious in *Libertel*,[45] the ECJ's landmark decision dealing with the conditions for protection of abstract colour marks. The contested application concerned the colour "orange" for telecommunication services. Quite obviously, the colour is not descriptive of the services, and hence, the case solely turned upon the question of distinctiveness. According to the scheme related above, this would have meant that the interests of competitors to keep the colour free for general use could not be taken into consideration. Sensing that such a consequence could not possibly be promoted as the result of a correct application of European trademark law, the ECJ based its reasoning *inter alia* on competition aspects,[46] without further commenting on the fact that only distinctiveness had been at stake.

The case might have served as a catalyst for the ECJ to acknowledge that the strict separation established in previous case law between the two main criteria for protection, and the ensuing ban against account being taken of competitors' interest in the assessment of distinctiveness, are not well founded. Unfortunately, however, no further move in that direction has been made by the Court. The legal situation therefore remains unchanged when it comes to forms of marks other than colours *per se*.

Admittedly, had the approach endorsed in *Libertel* been extended to all types of trademarks, this would have amounted to a *de facto* dereliction of the pertinent view that the individual criteria listed in Art. 7(1)(b)–(d) are separate from each other, and are distinguished not least by the different types of interests underlying each of them. However, to abandon that rather formal view, and to accept that no clear dividing line can be drawn between (in particular)

---

[44] See C-329/02 P, *supra* note 37, at para 36: "that criterion [i.e., the need to keep a sign free for use by others] is relevant in the context of Art. 7 (1) (c) of the regulation, but it is not the yardstick against which Art. 7 (1) (b) should be judged". In the same vein: C-37/03 P, *supra* note 41 at para 62; C-173/04, Judgment of 12/01/2006, *Deutsche SiSi-Werke/OHIM*, [2006] ECR I-551 at paras 55 and 63.

[45] C-104/01, Judgment of 06/05/2003, *Libertel Groep BV/Benelux Merkenbureau*, [2003] ECR I-3793.

[46] C-104/01, *supra* note 45, at para 54: "(a)s regards the registration as trade marks of colours *per se*, not spatially delimited, the fact that the number of colours actually available is limited means that a small number of trade mark registrations for certain services or goods could exhaust the entire range of the colours available. Such an extensive monopoly would be incompatible with a system of undistorted competition, in particular because it could have the effect of creating an unjustified competitive advantage for a single trader. Nor would it be conducive to economic development or the fostering of the spirit of enterprise for established traders to be able to register the entire range of colours that is in fact available for their own benefit, to the detriment of new traders."

distinctive character on the one hand and descriptiveness on the other, would be a relief rather than a loss. After all, the text from which the relevant provisions in the directive and the CTMR were adapted – Art. 6^{quinquies} B 2 of the Paris Convention – itself is not the result of thorough legislative considerations, but rather reflects the outcome of a political compromise, as is often found in international conventions. While that does not reduce its importance as a general guideline, it would be paying too much tribute to that provision to derive far-reaching conclusions from its somewhat clumsy structure.

b. How high to set the threshold? Apart from the structure of the provision regulating which marks can be protected, the crucial question to be posed with regard to protection requirements is that of the threshold to be observed. How easy should it be for a trademark to obtain protection? As was pointed out by the ECJ in *Postkantoor*,[47] this question must be answered uniformly for the whole European Union. Although the directive abstains from regulating the procedures through which Member States make this assessment, Member States are not free to pursue their own, possibly divergent policies in that regard, such as restricting the task of trademark offices to filter out the obvious cases in the registration procedure.[48]

The ECJ's early judgments concerning the protection requirements were generally perceived as marking a somewhat unstable course. To the amazement of many practitioners, the *BABY DRY* judgment[49] seemed to herald an age of extreme permissiveness. The following decision, *COMPANYLINE*,[50] was widely interpreted as suggesting a different policy, an interpretation which was finally confirmed in the *Postkantoor*[51] and *Biomild*[52] judgments. However, what seemed to be firm ground after the latter decisions was badly shaken again in the *SAT.2* judgement,[53] with an attempt at consolidation finally being made in the *BioID* case.[54] Irrespective of those twists and turns, it can be said quite safely by now that the standards propagated by the ECJ as well as by the CFI are rather generous, without being overly liberal. At least, this holds true for the protection of wordmarks.

---

[47] C-363/99, Judgment of 12/02/2004, *KPN&PTT/Benelux Merkenbureau*, [2004] ECR I-1619.
[48] C-363/99, *supra* note 47, at para 122.
[49] C-383/99 P, Judgment of 20/09/2001, *Procter & Gamble/OHIM*, [2002] ECR I-06251.
[50] C-104/00 P, Judgment of 19/09/2002, *DKV/OHIM*, ECR 2002 I-07561.
[51] C-363/99, *supra* note 47, at para 31.
[52] C-265/00, Judgment of 12/02/2004, *Campina melkunie /Benelux Merkenbureau*, [2004] ECR I-1699.
[53] C-329/02, *SAT.1 /OHIM*, [2004] ECR I-8317.
[54] C-37/03 P, Judgment of 15/09/2005, *BioID/OHIM* [2005] ECR I-7975.

164 *Trademark law and theory*

With regard to "non-traditional" marks, like colours, smells and three-dimensional objects, the Court has followed a slightly different and rather consistent policy. In principle, the ECJ is open to protection of any type of sign, with much emphasis being placed on the exact and durable quality of graphical representation.[55] However, in practice, access to the register is not easily granted to forms of signs other than those which consumers are used to recognizing immediately as marks. This is not a result of different standards being applied to different types of marks – an option the ECJ firmly rejects[56] – but rather is held to be a natural effect of the sign not being perceived by the relevant public as conveying a message about commercial origin.[57] In addition, it is justified as a tribute paid to the countervailing interests of those who might need the sign for their own use.

Indeed, the latter consideration probably plays a stronger role than is openly admitted in the ECJ's decisions. Until now, the ECJ's assertions concerning the way in which "unconventional" forms of signs are perceived by consumers have not been underpinned by empirical evidence. If studies were undertaken in that regard, they might well show that the relevant circles are more aware of the potential meaning of shapes and colours etc. than the Court assumes. In any case, a member of the German Federal Supreme Court commented in reaction to the ECJ's restrictive findings, this is an issue of consumer "education" – and with some effort on the part of interested business (and, as he suggests, with some help from the courts and authorities), it should be possible to amend, in the longer run, actual deficiencies in the public's capability to recognize all sorts of product properties as marks.[58]

---

[55] *See* C-273/00, Judgment of 12/12/2002, *Sieckmann/DPMA*, [2002] ECR I-11737 (smell marks); C-283/01, Judgment of 27/11/2003, *Shield mark, Kist/Benelux Merkenbureau*, [2003] ECR I-14313 (sound marks); C-104/01, Judgment of 6/5/2003, *Libertel/Benelux Merkenbureau*, [2003] ECR I-3793 (colour marks); C-49/02, Judgment of 24/06/2004, *Heidelberger Bauchemie/DPMA*, [2004] ECR I-6129 (colour combinations).

[56] *See* C-53/01–55/01, *infra* note 57, where the issue of applying different standards had been expressly raised by the referring court.

[57] See in particular *Libertel/Benelux Merkenbureau, supra* note 45 (colour marks); C-53/01-C-55/01, Judgments of 08/04/2003 – *Linde, Winward, Rado,* [2003], ECR I-3161; C-218/01, Judgment of 12/02/2004, *Henkel/DPMA,* [2004] ECR I-1725; C-456, 457/01 P etc., Judgments of 29/04/2004, *Henkel/OHIM,* [2004] ECR I-509; C-468/01-474/01, Judgments of 29/4/2004, *Procter & Gamble/OHIM,* [2004] ECR I-5741; C-136/02 P, Judgment of 07/10/2004, *Mag Instrument/OHMI,* [2004] ECR I-9165 (3D marks).

[58] Eike Ullmann, *The Shape of Goods as a Trade Mark – Illusion or Reality?* Oral presentation at the annual meeting of EC trademark judges in Alicante, available at OHIM's website, www.oami.eu.

Fundamental concerns in the harmonization of trademark law   165

While such a scenario is not at all unrealistic, it is not clear that its materialization would be desirable. Increasing the number of registered marks would inevitably lead to more litigation, with related costs and efforts. This would be a burden for the individual enterprises as well as for the economy as a whole, and it is at best doubtful whether those costs would be sufficiently balanced or even outweighed by creating an additional impulse for market development and/or a substantial improvement in information available to consumers

If the ECJ shared these or similar misgivings regarding the protection of non-traditional marks, the cautious attitude reflected to date in the relevant judgments ought to be maintained for reasons of sound policy, even in the face of potential changes in actual consumer perception. The only possible legal foundation for such an approach – if any – would be provided by the need to keep free. It would then have to be openly addressed and discussed, at last, whether that concept has a legitimate role to play as an independent, overarching evaluation criterion,[59] and how it can be ensured – if an independent role is generally accepted – that it does not mutate into an arbitrary blocking instrument.

3. Use as a mark   Whether "use as a mark" is a prerequisite to a finding of infringement is a third example of a rule of substantive EU trademark law that has been developed through the ongoing process of interpreting harmonization texts. Like the need to keep free, this requirement cannot be found anywhere in a legal text. However, it can be inferred from the fact that according to Art. 5 of the directive and Art. 9 CTMR, an infringement occurs (only) if the other sign is "used *for* (similar or dissimilar) goods", meaning that there must be a connection between the sign and the product or service to which it relates. In addition, and more importantly, Art. 5(5) of the directive allows Member States under certain conditions to maintain provisions prohibiting the use of marks for "other purposes than to distinguish goods or services". It follows logically that the preceding four paragraphs, in which the conditions for trademark infringement are spelled out, only apply to situations when the infringing sign is used exactly for that purpose, i.e. in order to distinguish.

The importance attributed to the unwritten criterion of use as a mark is directly proportional to that of the origin function as the concept on which trademark law is founded. If a crucial distinction is made between trademark

---

[59]   This can only be achieved if the ECJ gives up its present insistence that the need to keep free can only be considered as an element in the assessment of descriptive character; see *supra* (a). Further on the topic see Annette Kur, *Strategic Branding: Does Trade Mark Law Provide for Sufficient Self Help and Self Healing Forces?* in INGE GOVAERE & HANNS ULLRICH (EDS.), INTELLECTUAL PROPERTY, MARKET POWER, AND THE PUBLIC INTEREST, College of Europe Series, Bruxelles etc. (P.I.E. Lang), (forthcoming 2008).

law and other kinds of intellectual property, in the sense that by contrast to the other fields of IP, the legal protection of marks is strictly limited to, and defined by, their origin function, the determination of whether a sign was used as a mark is an obvious and indispensable part of assessing whether it has been infringed. Vice versa, the impact of the criterion may be small to negligible in a legal system that is built on the assumption that trademarks are basically the property of their owner just like any other intellectual property, and that they are therefore protected against any kind of unauthorized use.[60]

The approach taken by the ECJ in its judgments addressing the topic appears to lie between those two extremes. To give an exact account of the present situation is rendered difficult by the fact that some decisions have been unclear, and appear contradictory to some extent. The issue was first treated in the *BMW/Deenik* judgment.[61] The defendant, a dealer in used cars, who also offered repair services, had claimed in advertisements that he was a specialist for BMW. BMW argued that the mark had been used without authorization and was therefore infringed. The ECJ specified initially that in order for a conflict to be covered by trademark law, the allegedly infringed sign must be used as a mark. In the case at hand, use as a mark was found to lie in the fact that the mark "BMW" had been employed in order to identify the cars for which the defendant claimed to be a specialist, and to distinguish them from cars of a different commercial origin.[62] The defendant's advertisements were therefore held to fall under Art. 5(1)(a), the provision prohibiting use of identical marks for identical products.[63]

In subsequent decisions, the requirement of a mark being used as a mark was broken down into a two-tier assessment. In a first step, it is assessed whether the mark is used *for* goods and services – which is held to be the case when the mark is used *in connection* with the marketing of such goods, without necessarily indicating commercial origin.[64] Second, the use must be such

---

[60] As was stated above (Section I), these differences as to the basic concepts governing trademark law could be found in Europe prior to the CTMR and directive. It is remarkable, but also quite symptomatic of the process of harmonization, that those differences were hardly ever openly addressed and that the focus of negotiations was instead on the technical details of promulgating the new provisions.

[61] C-63/97, Judgment of 23/02/1999, *BMW/Deenik*, [1999] ECR I- 905.

[62] C-63/97, *supra* note 61, at paras 38, 39.

[63] The use could nevertheless be found admissible by the national court on the basis of Art. 6(1)(c), the provision allowing for use of marks to indicate the purpose of goods or services, provided that the actual mode in which the sign was used complies with honest business practice.

[64] C-48/05, Judgment of 25/01/07, *Opel AG/Autec*, at para 20; see also C-206/01, Judgment of 12/11/2002, *Arsenal Football Club/Reed*, [2002] ECR I-10273, at para 40, 41.

that it is "in conflict with the functions of a trademark, in particular its essential function of indicating commercial origin".[65]

In the decisions that have addressed the topic so far, three categories of cases can be distinguished: (1) use of a trade name (instead of a trademark) in connection with the commercialization of goods and services,[66] (2) decorative use in the wide sense, i.e. use which is primarily perceived as an element of the product's appearance,[67] and (3) referential use, i.e. use being made in order to refer, for one's own commercial purposes, to another person's goods or services, without confusion as to commercial origin being involved.[68]

The first category is least problematic.[69] It is clear that use as a mark will be found whenever the sign is viewed by the relevant public (also) as an indication of origin of the goods, i.e. not merely as indicating the name of an enterprise. The second category usually involves more problems. However, it seems to be settled at least as a matter of principle that in order to find for use as a mark in cases belonging to the second category, it is required that the sign is perceived as a badge of origin for the products on which it appears; i.e. it is not sufficient that it evokes a mark which is known as such to the public, without a connection being made between that mark and the goods on which the sign is used.[70]

Regarding the third category (referential use), the legal situation is somewhat doubtful. The first decision addressing the issue after *BMW – Hölterhoff/Freiesleben*[71] – concerned a reference made in oral sales negotiations to a competitor's trademark in order to identify and describe the specific cut of gem stones sold under the mark. Finding that no risk of confusion as to the true origin of the gem stones was involved, the ECJ declared that Art. 5(1)(a) could not be applied. A seemingly different approach was however

---

[65] C-48/05, *supra* note 64, at para 21, with further references.
[66] C-23/01, Judgment of 21/11/2002, *Robeco/Robelco*, [2002] ECR I-10913; C-245/02, Judgment of 16/11/2004, *Anheuser Busch/Budejovicky Budvar* [2004] ECR I-10989; C-17/06, Judgment of 11/09/2007, *Céline SARL/Céline SA*.
[67] C-206/01, *supra* note 64 (*Arsenal*); C-408/01, Judgment of 23/10/2003, *Adidas/Fitnessworld Trading*, [2003] ECR I-12537; C-48/05, *supra* note 64 (*Opel/Autec*).
[68] C-63/97, *supra* note 65 (*BMW*); C-2/2000, Judgment of 14/05/2002, *Hölterhoff/Freiesleben*, [2002] ECR I-4187; C-228/03, Judgment of 28/05/2005, *Gillette/LA Laboratories* [2005] ECR I-2337.
[69] At least this is true when it comes to use as a mark. However, the use of trade names as marks does imply problems with regard to the coexistence situation resulting from the ECJ's application of Art. 6(1)(a); see *infra*, Section III B.
[70] A different interpretation could have been endorsed on the basis of what the ECJ had held in *BMW*. However, the ECJ has clarified that point in *Opel/Autec* (C-48/05, *supra* note 64, at para 27 *et seq.*); *see also infra*, note 73.
[71] C-2/2000, *supra* note 68.

applied in *Gillette/LA Laboratories*.[72] The defendant produced and sold razor blades under his own, distinct trademark. On stickers affixed to the packages, he indicated that the blades also fit Gillette razors. The national court had submitted in the questions referred to the ECJ that the indication was not understood by the relevant public as indicating the origin of the defendant's blades. Nevertheless, the ECJ held that trademark law was applicable, without so much as arguing about the issue.[73]

So far, the decisions related above were based on Art. 5(1)(a), the provision on "double identity". The picture resulting therefrom needs to be completed by taking note of the fact that the ECJ in a recent decision[74] has highlighted the applicability of Art. 5(2), the provision on extended protection. The Court pointed out that if Art. 5(1)(a) cannot be applied because a sign is not perceived as an indication of origin, the use made of the sign might still be unfair or detrimental in the meaning of Art. 5(2). The case concerned the display of a car maker's picture mark ("Opel Blitz") on the hood of toy models. On the basis of the factual findings submitted by the referring court, it appeared most unlikely that the sign was actually used as a mark for the toys. Nevertheless, the national court was advised to examine whether unfair advantage had been taken of the car maker's reputation.[75]

All in all, and notwithstanding the remaining imponderabilities, the ECJ's case law endorses a rather broad interpretation of use as a mark. For all

---

[72] C-228/03, *supra* note 68.

[73] Doubts as to the validity of the *Gillette* approach could be raised after *Opel/Autec* (C-48/05, *supra* note 64) in view of the emphasis placed in that decision on the aspect that the use of a sign must lead to origin confusion in order to be encompassed by Art. 5(1)(a). Furthermore, in a dictum intended to rule out what the ECJ considered to be an overly broad interpretation of *BMW* (C-63/97, *supra* note 61), the Court declared that use made of a sign as a reference to *different* goods or services than those offered by the alleged infringer will be covered by Art. 5.1(a) only when it serves to identify the object of *services*; in all other cases, referential use will not be considered as satisfying the requirement of use as a mark in the meaning of the provision. However, this does not necessarily mean that *Gillette* has been overruled. The ECJ did not mention *Gillette*, and the situation at stake there is distinguished from that addressed in the Court's dictum by virtue of the fact that the reference in *Gillette* related to goods that were *identical* to those offered by the alleged infringer.

[74] C-48/05, *supra* note 64 (*Opel/Autec*)

[75] Regrettably, the ECJ refrained from providing any guidelines as to which aspects must be considered in assessing whether the advantage possibly taken of Opel's reputation was "unfair and without due cause." The pertinent questions posed by the national court – whether it was of relevance that the toy manufacturer had used Opel's mark only to the extent this was necessary to produce a toy model, and had clearly indicated his own mark on accessories such as remote control, product description and the package – remained unanswered.

Fundamental concerns in the harmonization of trademark law   169

practical matters, it barely stops short of rendering the criterion meaningless in practice, at least when it comes to marks having a reputation. Judicial practice in the member countries appears to have adopted a similar approach. For instance, in a recent judgment of the German Federal Supreme Court concerning a nonsense poem printed on a postcard bearing the same colour as the protected mark of a chocolate firm, it was held that use as a mark is established as soon as an association is created between a mark and the same or a similar feature appearing in any other context.[76] If that suffices to establish use as a mark,[77] the requirement might as well be skipped altogether.

After all, that might not be a bad solution either. It needs to be kept in mind that even in a very strict regime like former German trademark law, absence of use as a mark did not mean that the use was held admissible *per se*. It only meant that the issue had to be treated under a different legal regime than trademark law, most frequently under unfair competition law. For European law, this would mean that the issue would fall back into the separate and still quite diverse legal regimes existing in that area in individual member countries.[78] The situation would be particularly uncomfortable in the context of the CTM, where no uniform regime exists that could operate as a basis for adjudicating issues falling outside the ambit of trademark law proper. If the aim is to further a harmonized development of European practice in the field, a fairly broad interpretation is therefore the preferable approach.

However, an important caveat needs to be made here. To extend trademark law that far is a feasible route to take *only* if it is guaranteed that the ambit is broad enough to encompass all relevant aspects, including the countervailing interests of competitors and society at large. This does not pose a serious problem for claims that are based on the provision on extended protection, provided that the condition stipulated therein, that the use must be "unfair and without due cause", is given appropriate consideration. The situation is more hazardous when Art. 5(1)(a) is invoked as the sole basis for protection. The use of identical marks for identical products constitutes infringement *per se*, without further elements having to be established. Use falling under that provision can only be

---

[76] German Federal Supreme Court, Judgment of 3 February 2005 – I ZR 159/02, translated in 38 IIC, 119 (2007) (citing *Adidas/Fitnessworld* (C-408/01, *supra* note 67)).

[77] The Federal Supreme Court based its decision on Sec. 14.2 no. 3, the provision corresponding to Art. 5.2 directive; it is therefore in line with the ECJ's findings in *Opel/Autec*.

[78] The area of what is usually called unfair competition has remained largely outside harmonization efforts, as it was regarded as too difficult to reconcile the different national traditions in this field. Progress was made in that regard when the Unfair Commercial Practices Directive (29/2005/EC) was enacted in 2005. However, the directive only addresses "business to consumer" practices without attempting to achieve harmonization also regarding business to business relationships.

justified under the conditions set out in Art. 6, which contains, in accordance with continental European traditions, a closed catalogue of specifically defined limitations instead of providing for an open-ended fair use clause. The legislative technique employed makes it difficult or even impossible to address issues, such as free speech, parody and similar concerns, that do not fit into the closed list of actionable limitations. National courts have already reacted to the situation by invoking, in certain cases, provisions of constitutional law in order to declare certain modes of trademark use admissible. For instance, in the case concerning the poem printed on the coloured postcard,[79] the German Federal Supreme Court denied trademark infringement on the basis of the argument that this would clash with the principle of freedom of art.[80] A similar route was taken in the French decisions concerning critical commercial speech involving the trademarks of Esso and Danone.[81]

However, as reassuring as this may be, it is also unsatisfactory. It would be preferable if an appropriate solution in these cases could be found in trademark law proper, instead of having to refer to external grounds.

The matter therefore calls for regulatory action.[82] One solution might be to open the closed catalogue of limitations by turning it into an exemplary, non-conclusive list. If that should be considered as too "revolutionary" *vis-à-vis* cherished legal traditions, an express proviso might be added to Art. 6, such as "use in commercial speech relating to the mark, in particular in order to identify goods or services as that of the proprietor, or in order to make a statement relating to those goods or services" – provided, of course, that such use complies with honest business practices. It is remarkable that UK law, in Art. 10(6) TMA 1994 already holds a very similar rule.[83] When it was inserted, it did not have a proper basis in the directive. However, time and the development of legal practice have definitely proven it right.

---

[79] *Supra* note 76.

[80] The remarks above need to be qualified in so far as the decision was rendered on the basis of the provision on extended protection (i.e. the provision corresponding to Art. 5(2); *see supra*, note 77), which grants more room for considerations of equity and fairness, including constitutional aspects, than Art. 5(1)(a).

[81] English translation published in 35 IIC 342 (2004); *see also* Christophe Geiger, *Fundamental Rights, a Safeguard for the Coherence of Intellectual Property Law?*, 35 IIC 268 (2004).

[82] In the present situation, much depends on the willingness of courts to adopt a rather liberal approach to the interpretation of the limitation provisions. Unfortunately, however, the ECJ has sent the wrong signals in that regard in the *Opel/Autec* case (C-48/05, *supra*, note 64), by squarely rejecting the possibility that fairness of the use made of the sign as an element in the faithful reproduction of the car in the form of a toy model, with the manufacturer's trademark being clearly indicated, could be tested on the basis of Art. 6.1(b), the provision admitting use for descriptive purposes.

[83] *See also* Sec. 14(6), Irish TMA 1996.

III. Where to from here?

A. Procedures, sanctions and institutions

When the trademark directive came into existence, it was expected that this was just the first step in a continuous process of even closer harmonization – hence its denomination as "First" directive.[84] However, no more projects in the approximation of substantive law have been embarked upon. Instead, the only subsequent major step undertaken in the direction of European harmonization in trademark law has concerned procedures and sanctions, forming the object of enforcement directive 48/2004/EC.[85] Regulation of enforcement modalities as well the available remedies had heretofore been left nearly entirely to the Member States, which did create a conspicuous loophole in the otherwise harmonized body of law. It is therefore quite understandable that the European legislature took up the issue for consideration. On the other hand, the development of harmonized rules in such a sensitive field should have called for much more thorough research and consideration than that which the Commission (and those responsible in the Member States) were willing to invest. Instead, the political message was spread that the directive was a necessary step in combating counterfeiting and piracy, which infallibly proves an efficient way to boost legislative efforts and to freeze long and critical debates.[86]

In spring 2006, the enforcement directive, which deals with civil and administrative sanctions only, was complemented by a proposal for a directive on criminal remedies.[87] Again, the need to regulate was motivated by the undisputed need to combat piracy and counterfeiting, while the proposal would apply to all types of IP infringement.

---

[84] Full title: First Directive 89/104/EEC of the Council, of 21 December 1988, to Approximate the Laws of the Member States Relating to Trade Marks.

[85] Directive of the European Parliament and the Council of 29 April 2004 on Measures and Procedures to Ensure the Enforcement of Intellectual Property Rights, O.J. L 157/45, 30/04/2004; corrected version in O.J. L 195/16, 2/06/2004.

[86] The emphasis on piracy and counterfeiting was even more pronounced in the first proposal for a directive, *see* William Cornish, Josef Drexl, Reto Hilty & Annette Kur, *Procedures and Remedies for Enforcing IPRs: the European Commission's Proposed Directive*, [2003] E.I.P.R. 447–9 (critical opinion), supported by 31 law professors from 11 EU and EEA Member States. *See also* Drexl, Hilty & Kur, *Proposal for a Directive on Measures and Procedures to Ensure the Enforcement of Intellectual Property Rights – A First Statement*, 34 IIC 530–35 (2003).

[87] COM 2006/168, *see* Reto Hilty, Annette Kur & Alexander Peukert, *Statement of the Max Planck Institute for Intellectual Property, Competition and Tax Law on the Proposal for a Directive of the European Parliament and of the Council on Criminal Measures Aimed at Ensuring the Enforcement of Intellectual Property Rights*, 37 IIC 970–76 (2006).

With regard to trademark law, that approach is especially inappropriate. As was set out above (Section II.3), there is a tendency to interpret the ambit of trademark law rather broadly, with the consequence that virtually all modes of trademark use fall under its provisions. At least in countries which, like Germany, attribute much weight to the principle that in order to be punishable, an act must be clearly and exactly defined in a legal text (*nullum crimen sine lege*), the potential criminalization *en gros* of commercial speech involving protected marks gives rise to grave doubts as to its compatibility with constitutional principles. True, the problem already exists with regard to existing law, but its reinforcement by the proposed criminal law directive nevertheless needs to be taken seriously.

While the activities of the Community legislature with regard to procedures and sanctions therefore must be viewed with a certain scepticism, it has regrettably failed to take further steps with regard to completing the system of Community rights – CTM and Community design – in its procedural aspects. In particular, the present system does not comprise a common judiciary. Instead, specially designated courts in the Member States nominally act under the title of "Community Trademark Courts", while in fact remaining part of the national judicial system. At the time when the CTM system came into existence, this was the best solution one could have, as the Community lacked competence to establish a genuine court system at the Community level. Significant changes have occurred since then, however, with the option to establish a genuine Community judiciary in the field of industrial property having been anchored in Art. 229a of the EC (Nice) Treaty. Unfortunately, however, until now the discussions relating to that option have almost exclusively focused on the ill-fated Community Patent project.

As it is now clear that plans to establish the Community Patent have been abandoned for the near future,[88] the time may have come to direct thoughts and efforts to the already existing and thriving field of Community trademarks (and designs) instead. It is not unlikely that a success might be easier to achieve there, given that some issues that have created controversies in the patent field may be less ponderous or contentious when it comes to trademarks. And once a genuine CTM judiciary is successfully established, other fields may join – patents of course, but also IP at large, as well as, in the longer run, other commercial matters typically involving transborder issues.

---

[88] This position was reached after consultation between the Commission and interested circles showed that an overwhelming majority preferred to install the European Patent Litigation Protocol (EPLA) rather than to pursue the relevant proposal for a Community patent.

B. Towards new areas?

The recent trend to direct harmonization efforts away from substantive law issues and toward adjacent areas like procedures and sanctions instead will probably also be dominant in the foreseeable future. After all, at least in trademark law, all major issues of substantive law have been addressed in the harmonization directive, and practice is still busy filling the legal moulds with appropriate and generally accepted meaning.

Nevertheless, one cannot fail to notice that harmonization is far from complete with regard to the legal rules governing distinctive signs at large, in particular as regards the requirements and scope of protection of unregistered marks and trade names. As conflicts frequently arise from the use of such signs, which also constitute a typical ground for opposition or cancellation, the lack of harmonization is also felt within trademark law proper, most conspicuously in the CTM system.

Harmonization of the rules governing unregistered marks and trade names does however pose quite a challenge, as the present systems are very divergent. Some countries do not recognize unregistered marks at all, except for the mandatory base-line protection for well-known marks provided by Art. 6bis of the Paris Convention. In others, protection is granted on the basis of showing a certain amount of acquired goodwill, to be measured either by the time a sign has been used on the market or by the degree of public awareness. In Denmark, unregistered marks are even protected upon use, without further qualifications; the same result is attained on the basis of the "marchio di fatto" doctrine applying in Italy. As to trade names, many countries demand registration or, alternatively, showing of acquired goodwill or public awareness. In others – including countries applying stricter regimes when it comes to unregistered trade marks – use alone is sufficient of itself to establish a valid right.

In this situation, harmonization efforts would obviously have to face the dilemma that when the protection standard is set at the lowest level, the number of potentially conflicting rights within the EU would be catapulted to enormous heights. On the other hand, if the requirements for acquisition of such rights are tightened, the conditions for small and medium enterprises to conduct business in countries heretofore applying more generous standards might be considerably impaired.

Furthermore, an effort to harmonize the conditions and extent of protection for trade names and unregistered marks would have to respect binding norms of international law, in particular Art. 8 of the Paris Convention, according to which protection of (foreign) trade names must not be made dependent on registration. This invites the question whether it also means that use alone, without further qualifications, must be regarded as sufficient to obtain protection. In the context of questions referred to it by the Finnish Supreme Court concerning the conflict between Anheuser Busch and Budějovický Budvar over the Budweiser mark,[89] the ECJ has rejected that contention and declared that Member States are free to implement their own policies in that regard. The Court further ruled, however, that even if according to national law, a trade name has not acquired protection as such, its use – including use as a mark – must still be tolerated by the proprietor of a conflicting trademark on the basis of Art. 6(1)(a),[90] if it complies with honest business practices.[91]

The potential impact of the message conveyed by this ruling on established legal concepts should not be underestimated. If a trademark and a conflicting trade name can and must coexist in spite of the latter being used as a mark, there is hardly any reason why coexistence between two trademarks, under the precautions set out in Art. 6 of the directive – i.e. when this complies with honest business practices – should not also be the regular model to follow in certain situations, for example in a conflict between a registered mark and an earlier unregistered trademark that had been used before in *bona fide* trade without attaining the level of goodwill necessary to obtain legal protection on the basis of use alone. Obviously, this would amount to reintroducing the concept of honest concurrent use, which noone seems to be fond of. Nevertheless, after the BUDWEISER ruling, it needs to be given serious thought.

One crucial point in the scenario evoked by honest concurrent use concerns the establishment of an adequate dividing line between the likelihood of confusion that must be tolerated, and a situation when the interests of the public become preponderant to be protected against the risk of actually being misled as to the identity of products purchased, resulting in a misallocation of

---

[89] C-245/02, Judgment of 16/11/2004, *Anheuser Busch/Budejovicky Budvar* [2004] ECR I-10989.

[90] The result was surprising to some extent. In connection with the enactment of the trademark directive, the Commission and the Council had issued a joint declaration staing that "name" in the meaning of Art. 6(1)(a) had to be understood as "personal name", and did not include trade names. Without the issue having been raised in one of the questions referred to it, the ECJ ruled that the declaration was legally irrelevant, and that trade names did enjoy the privilege under Art. 6(1)(a). *See* C-245/02, *supra* note 89, at para 81: A third party may, in principle, rely on the exception provided for in Article 6(1)(a) of Directive 89/104 in order to be entitled to use a sign which is identical or similar to a trademark for the purpose of indicating his trade name, even if that constitutes a use falling within the scope of Article 5(1) of that directive which the trade mark proprietor may prohibit by virtue of the exclusive rights conferred on him by that provision.

[91] It is crucial in that situation to establish criteria for assessing when use of a conflicting (younger) trade name as a mark complies with honest business practices. Clarification on the point was sought in the Céline case (C-17/06, Judgment of 11/09/2007, *Céline SARL/Céline SA*). However, regrettably, the ECJ did not give a substantive answer to the question posed.

resources. It is suggested that the distinction set out above (Section II.A) with regard to the different phases in the decision-making process which are regarded as relevant for the assessment of likelihood of confusion and misrepresentation respectively might prove useful for the purpose.

Regardless of how the issue is solved, if it were possible to agree on a satisfactory solution, the approach might help to provide a feasible basis for European harmonization in the area of unregistered marks and trade names. In brief, a model might be developed which allows owners of prior rights that are protected on the basis of unqualified commercial use to continue the kind of use which was made of the sign at the time when a conflicting right came into *bona fide* existence, with neither of the two signs being in a position to claim exclusivity, and with both owners being under an obligation to take appropriate measures in order to avoid consumer deception. By contrast, honouring the concept that still is and ought to remain predominant in EU trademark law (exclusivity *vis-à-vis* signs of lesser priority) a fully exclusive right should as a rule be granted to unregistered marks and trade names which have attained a substantial level of goodwill and/or public awareness within the territory for which protection is claimed.[92]

Having said that, a caveat must be added. Even if it were accepted that such a model would be basically fair and sufficiently balanced, it would inevitably lead to new conundrums. Thorough deliberations are therefore needed before anything of that kind could be constructed and implemented. For the time being, neither the Community legislature nor the interested circles seem to be particularly keen to embark on such an exercise – "doing nothing" seems to be the preferred, and possibly also the most sensible, option.

IV. Conclusions

1. Trademark law in the EU can look back upon ten successful and dynamic years of harmonization. Nevertheless, some issues still remain unsolved.
2. More attention should be directed to the distinction of the concepts underlying "likelihood of confusion" within the meaning of trademark law and "misrepresentation" as applied in the context of unfair marketing practices.
3. Instead of focusing too much on the wording and systematic structure of the provisions regarding prerequisites for protection, the aspect of free competition – usually dressed in the concept of "need to keep free" – should be given due consideration in the assessment of all requirements for protection, instead of being confined to Art. 3(1)(c) of the directive (absence of descriptive character).

---

[92] Such a system would obviously come quite close to American law.

4. The general tendency to interpret use as a mark so broadly that it presents hardly any obstacle to treating virtually all modes of commercial speech involving a trademark as falling within the ambit of trademark law appears acceptable not least because it helps to further a harmonized development of European practice. However, as a corollary, it is mandatory then to take an equally broad approach towards limitations. Where this is not possible on the basis of the wording of limitations presently set out in the texts, courts must resort to external balancing instruments, for example constitutional law. However, taking legislative action to amend the present deficiencies would be a preferable option.
5. Harmonization in the field of sanctions and procedures risks compromising the checks and balances developed in Member States' legal traditions. A more cautious approach is advisable. In addition, steps should be taken to complement the CTM system by establishing a genuine Community judiciary.
6. No harmonization has been achieved with regard to unregistered marks and trade names. The legal regimes applying in the Member States differ widely. If harmonization is tackled at all in this situation, the solution can be neither a maximum nor a minimum approach. One possible model would involve features of honest concurrent use, which was to a certain extent reintroduced in European trademark law in the ECJ'S *Budweiser* decision. However, before that route can be safely taken, the concept of likelihood of confusion *vis-à-vis* commercial misrepresentation must be explored more thoroughly.

7 Substantive trademark law harmonization: on the emerging coherence between the jurisprudence of the WTO Appellate Body and the European Court of Justice

*Gail. E. Evans**

I. Introduction

The conclusion of the Agreement on Trade-Related Aspects of Intellectual Property Rights (TRIPS)[1] in 1994 presaged the advent of a global epoch in trademark rights. The TRIPS Agreement not only provides substantive standards for the eligibility and protection of trademarks, but also mandates that "effective" enforcement procedures are available under national legal systems. It does so by establishing a global network of "coordinate" national courts to enforce the substantive trademark provisions of the Agreement.[2] Without replacing the national, territorially-based trademarks of Member States, TRIPS is based on principles of territoriality requiring independent trademark applications and actions for the enforcement of rights in each Member State of the World Trade Organization (WTO).

Despite the fact that domestic trademark laws have been duly amended in accordance with the TRIPS Agreement throughout the 151 Member States of the WTO,[3] multi-jurisdictional actions for trademark infringement indicate that

---

* Reader in International Trade and Intellectual Property Law, Queen Mary, University of London. For an elaborated version of this chapter see *Substantive Trade Mark Law Harmonization by Means of the WTO Appellate Body and the European Court of Justice: The Case of Trade Name Protection*, JOURNAL OF WORLD TRADE LAW, Vol. 41, 6, 1127–62 (2007).

[1] Final Act Embodying the Results of the Uruguay Round of Multilateral Trade Negotiations, Marrakesh Agreement Establishing the World Trade Organization, signed at Marrakesh (Morocco), April 15, 1994 [hereinafter WTO Agreement]; Annex IC, Agreement on Trade-Related Aspects of Intellectual Property Rights [hereinafter TRIPS Agreement or TRIPS], *reprinted in* THE RESULTS OF THE URUGUAY ROUND OF MULTILATERAL TRADE NEGOTIATIONS – THE LEGAL TEXTS, 1–19, 365–403 (GATT Secretariat, Geneva 1994).

[2] *See* Part II, Sect. 2 of the TRIPS Agreement. Article 41 mandates WTO Members to ensure that "effective" procedures are available under domestic law.

[3] There were 151 members of the WTO as of 27 July 2007: http://www.wto.org/English/thewto_e/whatis_e/tif_e/org6_e.htm.

177

implementation of the TRIPS Agreement has not rendered the law more certain, nor the outcome of litigation significantly more predictable. The notoriety of multiple lawsuits in different countries between American brewer Anheuser-Busch and Czech rival Budějovický Budvar is illustrative. By Budvar's reckoning, the two rivals for world markets had engaged in 86 suits and administrative proceedings as of 2006. Although Budvar lays claim to victory in 69 countries including the United Kingdom, Japan, South Korea, Greece, Portugal and Finland, in a number of these jurisdictions the result is by no means a clearly defined division of the market. For example, in the featured case study, the Supreme Court of Finland ultimately upheld Budvar's right to use its trade name "Budweiser Budvar, N.C." when indicating the brewer of the beer on beer labels. However, the Court denied Budvar the use of the words "Bud" and "Budweiser" as trademarks on beer labels, marketing materials and invoices.[4] The problem is that in the absence of substantive harmonization, that is to say, without guidance from a supranational court as to an appropriate interpretation and application of the trademark provisions of the TRIPS Agreement, there is unlikely to be any measurable improvement in the predictability of decision-making by national courts worldwide.[5]

While the European Trademark Directive[6] is similarly intended to provide

---

[4] Following the reference to the ECJ, the Supreme Court of Finland delivered its ruling on December 29, 2005 (KKO 2005/143) in the prolonged trademark dispute between two breweries, Anheuser-Busch, Incorporated and Budéjovicky Budvar, národni podnik, over the words "Budweiser" and "Budvar": http://www.castren.fi/IPT_Newsletter06.pdf at pp 1–2. For a similar result see Anheuser Busch Inc. v Budějovický Budvar N.P. [2000] EWCA Civ 30 (February 7, 2000), where the U.K. Court of Appeal, in an action for passing off brought by Anheuser-Busch, found that neither the plaintiff nor defendant Budějovický Budvar was disentitled to use the name Budweiser, since both brewers enjoyed a dual reputation in the territory and neither had achieved their reputation improperly nor by misrepresentation. Further see Anheuser-Busch Inc v Budějovický Budvar NP [2006] Hogsta Domstolen (Sweden) E.T.M.R. 77 (prohibited Budvar from using marks containing the words 'Budweiser.'); but *see* Anheuser Busch Inc v Budějovický Budvar Narodni Podnik [2001] Bundesgericht (Switzerland) E.T.M.R. 7 (upheld Budějovický Budvar's use of "Budweiser" in Switzerland.)

[5] The World Trade Organization (WTO) Appellate Body functions as a public or inter-state, quasi-judicial tribunal as constituted by the Dispute Settlement Understanding (DSU). Article 17 of the DSU provides for the establishment of a Standing Appellate Body, composed of seven persons, three of whom shall serve on any one case to hear appeals from panel cases: http://www.wto.org/english/tratop_e/dispu_e/dsu_e.htm.

[6] *See* First Directive 89/104/EEC of the Council, of December 21, 1988, to Approximate the Laws of the Member States Relating to Trade Marks (OJ EC L 40 of 11.2.1989, p. 1); Article 249 EC ¶ 3; Case C-218/01 *Henkel* [2004] ECR I-0000, 60 [hereinafter Trademark Directive] *available at*: http://curia.europa.eu.

an approximation of national laws throughout the 27 Member States of the Union, there is a significant difference. When uncertain as to the interpretation of the Trademark Directive, the national courts of Member States may request a preliminary ruling from the European Court of Justice (ECJ), if they consider that a decision on the question is necessary to enable them to give judgment. The system of preliminary reference from national courts has allowed the ECJ to construct a formidable body of trademark jurisprudence since the introduction of the Trademark Directive in 1988. As a supranational court, the ECJ is able to utilize the European Community's membership of the WTO in order to interpret the TRIPS Agreement in a manner which will promote the substantive harmonization of trademark law throughout the European Union, particularly in those areas of law, such as unfair competition, where the Directive does not require an approximation of national laws.

It is therefore not unreasonable to consider the ECJ in the role of a coordinating court. Indeed, such an aspiration would be consistent not only with the Court's legal activism, as evident in the ensuing case study of trade name protection, but also with the European Community's regional trade policy and associated goal of promoting the global enforcement of intellectual property rights.[7] This chapter therefore argues that the trademark jurisprudence of the WTO Appellate Body and ECJ demonstrates a new coherence that may, in time, constitute a means of realizing the substantive harmonization of trademark law. In the exposition of this argument, the chapter begins by examining the respective capacities of the Appellate Body and ECJ to pursue substantive trademark law harmonization by deploying the rules of treaty interpretation. Thereafter, the core of the chapter analyzes in depth the respective roles of the two tribunals in such an enterprise, both as a matter of substantive trademark law and adjudicatory technique. The chapter concludes by offering an assessment of the character, legitimacy and potential costs of substantive trademark law harmonization.

---

[7] *See* Communication from the Commission to the Council, the European Parliament, the European Economic and Social Committee and the Committee of the Regions, "Global Europe: Competing In The World - A Contribution to the EU's Growth and Jobs Strategy", COM (2006) 567; *available at*: http://ec.europa.eu/prelex/detail_dossier_real.cfm?CL=en&DosID=194745. Based on this study, the European Commission compiled a short list of countries (including China, ASEAN, Korea, Mercosur, Chile, Russia, and Ukraine) that will be the subject of future enforcement efforts. *See* The European Commission (DG External Trade) survey on intellectual property enforcement in non-EU countries, EC Strategy (October, 2006), *available at* http://ec.europa.eu/trade/issues/sectoral/intell_property/pr051006_en.htm. Further regarding EC trade policy see preferential trade agreements notified under Article XXIV of the GATT or Article V of the GATS at http://ec.europa.eu/trade/issues/bilateral/index_en.htm.

II. Deploying the rules of interpretation as an instrument of substantive harmonization

As mediated by the ECJ, the relationship between the TRIPS Agreement and the European Trademark Directive is ambivalent. On the one hand, the Agreement does not have direct effect within the Community legal system; on the other hand our case study of trade name protection under Article 8 of the Paris Convention[8] will show how the Court invokes the authority of the TRIPS Agreement to pursue trademark law harmonization in areas where the Community has not yet legislated. The latter development prompts us to inquire as to where the ECJ derives its authority to interpret the substantive provisions of the TRIPS Agreement?

It is submitted that the ECJ, as an international court, is able to draw upon the European Community's membership of the WTO in order to interpret the TRIPS Agreement in a manner which will promote the substantive harmonization of trademark law beyond the current confines of the Europe Union. The European Community is a WTO member in its own right, and as such it is a party to the TRIPS Agreement. In accordance with Article 1, the EC is under an obligation to implement the provisions of the TRIPS Agreement within the Community "legal system and practice." Consequently, the Court's reference to the trademark jurisprudence of the Appellate Body is justified in accordance with the logic of Article 1 to the effect that the three levels of law, international, Community, and national law, should be implemented and interpreted with consistency. The Court is therefore able to assert its authority to interpret the TRIPS Agreement on behalf of Member States, who are, in their own right, also Members of the WTO and parties to the TRIPS Agreement. As the highest court in the Community legal order, the ECJ is in a unique position to interpret the trademark provisions of the Agreement in a manner which will promote their substantive harmonization throughout the courts of Member States.

A. *The jurisdiction of the ECJ to interpret the TRIPS Agreement*

According to its ruling in *Dior*[9] the ECJ has jurisdiction to interpret the provisions of the TRIPS Agreement when the courts of Member States are called upon to apply and interpret national law where the Community has legislated and the Agreement applies. In *Anheuser-Busch Inc. v Budějovický Budvar*, the Court affirmed that:

---

[8] Article 8 of the Paris Convention for the Protection of Industrial Property of March 20, 1883, as last revised at Stockholm on July 14, 1967, (United Nations Treaty Series, Vol. 828, No. 11847, p. 108) [hereinafter the Paris Convention].

[9] Parfums Christian Dior v Tuk Consultancy, [2000] European Court Reports I-11307.

the relevant provisions of the national trade-mark law must be applied and interpreted, as far as possible, in the light of the wording and purpose of the relevant provisions of both Directive 89/104 and the TRIPS Agreement. [10]

This ruling as to the hierarchy of trademark law begs the question as to how national courts are to approach the ordering of measures, in those cases where the Community has not legislated. This was precisely the novel question that arose in the case of *Anheuser-Busch Inc. v Budějovický Budvar* in respect of trade name protection. The trademark provisions of the TRIPS Agreement relate to a field in which the Community has adopted legislation and which therefore falls within the scope of Community law.[11] By contrast, the Community has not, as yet, adopted legislation relating to trade names. Consequently, in *Anheuser-Busch*, the Supreme Court of Finland asked the ECJ whether third-party use of an identical or similar trade name might be regarded as use of an unauthorized sign for the purposes of TRIPS Article 16. The Court drew upon its membership of the WTO to affirm the Community's obligation to interpret its trademark law in the light of the wording and purpose of the TRIPS Agreement.

The international rules concerning the interpretation of treaties and the way in which they are applied by the Appellate Body and the ECJ allow considerable flexibility in the interpretation of the TRIPS Agreement. Pursuant to TRIPS Article 64, adjudicators must interpret the Agreement in accordance with the Vienna Convention on the Law of Treaties 1969.[12] Consistently, Article 3.2 of the WTO Dispute Settlement Understanding directs Panels to interpret the TRIPS provisions "in accordance with customary rules of interpretation of public international law," as embodied in the Vienna Convention. Both tribunals have a common approach to the application of these rules, in so far as it embodies a teleological approach to the interpretation of the TRIPS Agreement. Such an approach involves two key assumptions that adjudicators rely upon to explain and justify their findings. The first is the assumption that meaning inheres in the legislative test and that, a good part of the time, such meaning is plain, clear, or unambiguous. This is consistent with Article 31 of

---

[10] Anheuser-Busch Inc. v Budějovický Budvar, národní podnik, Judgment of the Court in Case C-245/02 of November 16, 2004 at ¶ 57. Note: Cases of the European Court of Justice cited in this chapter are available at http://curia.europa.eu or; http://eur-lex.europa.eu/en/index.htm.

[11] *See* First Directive 89/104/EEC of the Council, of December 21, 1988, to Approximate the Laws of the Member States Relating to Trade Marks, Note 6; Article 249 EC ¶ 3; Case C218/01 *Henkel* [2004] ECR I0000, ¶ 60: http://curia.europa.eu.

[12] The Convention entered into force on January 27, 1980, in accordance with Article 84(1), United Nations Treaty Series, Vol. 1155, p. 331, [hereinafter Vienna Convention] *available at* http://fletcher.tufts.edu/multi/texts/BH538.txt.

the Vienna Convention, which provides that a treaty must be interpreted in "good faith in light of (i) the ordinary meaning of its terms, (ii) the context and (iii) its objects and purpose."

The second assumption is that the interpretation of the terms of the treaty should seek to follow its object and purpose. This assumes that negotiators have intentions when they draft treaties or directives and that these intentions are known by adjudicators when called on to interpret legislation. Article 32 of the Vienna Convention, entitled "Supplementary Means of Interpretation," defines what is meant by the "context of the treaty" and what other elements must be taken into account within the context, including the *travaux préparatoires*, any "subsequent practice in the application of the treaty establishing the understanding of the Parties as to its interpretation," and any relevant rules of international law.[13] The following analysis of case law will reveal the flexibility with which the rules of interpretation allow the Appellate Body and the ECJ to declare the law, and in so doing, to attain its supremacy.[14]

III. The protection of trade names in accordance with appellate body and ECJ jurisprudence

While trade names are a class of *trade indicia* that appear to have been overlooked as an element of brand management, transnational business is increasingly finding that the goodwill attaching to the company's name may constitute a decided competitive advantage. In practice, there is considerable overlap between trademarks and trade names, to the extent that the name under which a company trades will frequently qualify for trademark protection.[15] Independently of questions of trademark protection, however, the name of a

---

[13] In general, the Permanent Court of International Justice (PCIJ) and the International Court of Justice (ICJ) refused to resort to preparatory work if the text was sufficiently clear. Sometimes the Court has used preparatory work to confirm a conclusion reached by other means. *See* the dissenting opinion delivered by judge Schwebel in the Case Concerning Maritime Delimitation and Territorial Questions between Qatar and Bahrain (Qatar v Bahrain), ICJ, Judgment of February 15, 1995, Jurisdiction and Admissibility, available at: <www.icj-cij.org>. Brownlie cautions that "preparatory work is an aid to be employed with discretion, since its use may detract from the textual approach, and, particularly in the case of multilateral agreements, the records of conference proceedings, treaty drafts and so on may be confused or inconclusive." I. BROWNLIE, PRINCIPLES OF PUBLIC INTERNATIONAL LAW 630 (1990).

[14] KAREN J. ALTER, ESTABLISHING THE SUPREMACY OF EUROPEAN LAW: THE MAKING OF AN INTERNATIONAL RULE OF LAW IN EUROPE 2–3 (2001).

[15] *See* SIR DUNCAN KERLY, KERLY'S LAW OF TRADE MARKS AND TRADE NAMES (T.A. Blanco White & Robin Jacob, eds.) (11th ed. 1983) at p. 360.

company or trade name may possess a goodwill that the courts will protect by means of unfair competition law or passing off.[16]

In the case of *Anheuser-Busch Inc. v Budějovický Budvar* the defendant Budvar counterclaimed that it was entitled to use its trade names that had been duly registered in Czechoslovakia in 1967. Budvar submitted that the signs used in Finland to market its beer could not be confused with Anheuser-Busch's trademarks. It also submitted that, with respect to the sign "Budweiser Budvar," the registration of its trade name in Czech, English, and French conferred on it, pursuant to Article 8 of the Paris Convention, a right in Finland earlier than that conferred by Anheuser-Busch's trademarks. The earlier right was therefore protected under that Article.

If defendant Budějovický Budvar was to rely on trade name protection, the question was whether trade names were protected as a distinct category of intellectual property for the purposes of the TRIPS Agreement. As incorporated within that Agreement, Article 8 of the Paris Convention provides:

> A trade name shall be protected in all the countries of the Union without the obligation of filing or registration, whether or not it forms part of a trademark.[17]

The implementation of Article 8 requires State A not only to protect trade names registered or established by use in that state but also foreign trade names which have been registered in State B of the Paris Union, provided they are sufficiently well known in the relevant trade circles of State A.

Consistently, under the Finnish Law on trademarks, the *bona fide* use of a trade name may provide a defense to an action for trademark infringement:

> Any person may use, in the course of his trade, his name, address or trade name as a trade symbol for his products unless use of that symbol might give rise to confusion with the protected trade mark of a third party or with a name, address or trade name lawfully used by a third party in his trading activities.[18]

Nonetheless, in courts throughout the European Union, there remained some

---

[16] In the United Kingdom, for example, the complainant may bring an action for passing off whenever the defendant company's name is calculated to deceive, and so to divert business from the claimant, or to cause confusion between the two businesses: Office Cleaning v Westminster (1946) 63 R.P.C. 39 at 42, HL.

[17] Paris Convention for the Protection of Industrial Property, note 8 *supra*.

[18] The Tavaramerkkilaki (Law on Trademarks) (7/1964) of January 10, 1964 at ¶ 3.1 provides: "The right to use a sign for a product under Paragraphs 1 to 3 of this law means that no one other than its proprietor may use commercially as a sign for his products a sign liable to be confused therewith, on the product or its packaging, in advertising or business documents or otherwise, including also use by word of mouth."

184   *Trademark law and theory*

uncertainty as to whether the defense should apply not only in respect of the name of a natural person but also that of a company or business name. Thus, in *Scandecor Development AB v Scandecor Marketing*,[19] the House of Lords observed that the inclusion of company names in the ambit of the defense represented the "better view," nonetheless holding that the matter was not *acte clair* or free from doubt.[20]

Indeed, Article 6 of the EC Trademark Directive refers only to a trademark owner not having the right to prohibit a third party from using, in the course of trade, "his own name or address."[21] Moreover, at the time the Trademark Directive was adopted, the Council and the Commission issued a joint declaration, that the term "his own name" applied only in respect of natural persons' names.[22] Consequently, when Defendant Budvar sought to rely on the defence that it was doing no more than using its own name, the Supreme Court of Finland decided to refer the question to the ECJ.[23]

---

[19]   [2001] 2 C.M.L.R. 30. *See also* Asprey & Garrard v WRA (Guns) [2002] F.S.R. 310, 487 (CA); WebSphere Trade Mark [2004] EWHC 529 (Ch), [2004] F.S.R. 39, ¶¶ 37–8 In *Scandecor*, the House of Lords referred the question to the ECJ, but as the case subsequently settled, the matter remained unresolved.

[20]   The doctrine of *acte clair,* derived from French law, is accepted by the ECJ where (i) the question of Community law is irrelevant; (ii) the provision has already been interpreted by the ECJ; and (iii) the correct application is so obvious that it leaves no room for doubt: C283/81 Srl CILFIT and Lanificio di Gavardo SpA v Ministry of Health (1982) ECR 3415. The Council of the European Union and the Commission of the European Communities issued a joint declaration, which was recorded in the minutes of the Council when Directive 89/104 was adopted, that that provision covers only natural persons' names. Such a declaration is without prejudice to the interpretation of that text by the Court of Justice of the European Communities. Note that under the U.K. Trade Marks Act 1938, § 8, protection extended to the use by a company of its registered name. Parker-Knoll v Knoll Int'l [1961] R.P.C. 346 (CA); [1962] R.P.C. 265 (HL).

[21]   Article 6, First Council Directive 89/104/EEC of December 21, 1988 to approximate the laws of the Member States relating to trademarks (OJ 1989 L 40, p. 1). "Name" is not restricted in the text.

[22]   Compare the former position in U.K. and German trademark law regarding the breadth of the "own name" defense: Section 8 of the U.K. Trade Marks Act of 1938 provided: "No registration of a trade mark shall interfere with – (a) any bona fide use by a person of his own name or of the name of his place of business . . ." Similarly, the limitation clause in the previous German Trade Mark Act (§ 16 WZG) referred to trade names ("Firma") as well as to personal names. Over time, the German courts narrowed the scope of that limitation clause to the effect that only trade names including the personal name of the owner were held to be entitled to the privilege. *See* Annette Kur, *Trade names – a Class of Signs "more equal" than others?*, IPRinfo Magazine, 2004, *available at* http://www.iprinfo.fi/page.php?page_id=53&action=articleDetails&a_id=280&id=22.

[23]   In the case of a company, the use of its own "name" will include its full corpo-

A. The Appellate Body incorporates trade names within TRIPS

In *Havana Club*,[24] a curiously prescient claim by the European Communities concerning the protection of trade names presented the Appellate Body with the opportunity to rule upon the identification of new categories of intellectual property subject to the TRIPS Agreement. The EC argued that trade names are a category of intellectual property that should be protected under the trademark provisions of the TRIPS Agreement. The Panel however had declined to do so. The Panel interpreted the term "intellectual property" to refer to all categories of intellectual property that are the *subject* of Sections 1 through 7 of Part II, as if that phrase read "intellectual property means those categories of intellectual property appearing in the titles of Sections 1 through 7 of Part II." In absence of their specific reference, this interpretation would have excluded trade names from the TRIPS Agreement and from the ambit of its enforcement provisions.[25]

However, drawing upon the purposive approach to treaty interpretation, the Appellate Body took the view that intellectual property rights should not be limited in this way. It found that the Panel's interpretation ignored the plain meaning of Article 1.2, in so far as it failed to take into account that the phrase "the subject of Sections 1 through 7 of Part II" of the Agreement deals not only with the categories of intellectual property indicated in each section *title*, but also with other *subjects* as well. In order to justify the notion of including "other subjects of intellectual property," the Appellate Body looked first to evidence of the potential breadth of intellectual property rights in the TRIPS Agreement. It drew its justifications widely, seeking evidence in a reference to *sui generis* protection for plant inventions in Article 27(3)(b). In a second, more oblique purposive reference, the Appellate Body invokes the redundancy rule to argue consequentially that to adopt the Panel's approach would be to deprive Article 8 of the Paris Convention (1967), as it is incorporated in TRIPS Article 2.1, of meaning and effect.

Having rendered its own view of the negotiators' intention respecting the

---

rate name and the name by which it is known to its customers: that is to say, omitting such words at the end of the name as "Limited," "Corporation," "Incorporated," or other words or letters indicating corporate status. Reed Executive Plc v Reed Business Information Ltd. [2004] EWCA Civ 159 (March 3, 2004), [2004] R.P.C. 40 at ¶ 115; WebSphere Trade Mark, [2004] EWHC 529 (Ch), [2004] F.S.R. 39 at ¶ 39.

[24] United States – Section 211 Omnibus Appropriations Act of 1998 (*Havana Club*), Complainant: European Communities, WT/DS176/AB/R, Report of the Appellate Body, January 2002, ¶ 3: *available at* http://www.wto.org/english/tratop_e/dispu_e/cases_e/ds176_e.htm.

[25] Article 41.1 of TRIPS mandates that WTO Members make available the enforcement procedures listed in the Agreement "so as to permit effective action against any act of infringement of intellectual property rights" covered by the Agreement.

categories of intellectual property covered by the Agreement, the Appellate Body could do no more than reject reference to the negotiating history of Article 1.2 of the TRIPS Agreement. For the purposes of Article 32 of the Vienna Convention, the Appellate Body found that the negotiating history of the Agreement did not confirm the Panel's interpretation of Articles 1.2 and 2.1. The rejection was based on a lack of specific reference in the records as to the inclusion of trade names in the TRIPS Agreement. On this basis, the Appellate Body reversed the Panel's finding that trade names are not covered under the TRIPS Agreement[26] to conclude that WTO Members have an obligation to provide protection to trade names.

While the Appellate Body identified trade names as a category of intellectual property subject to TRIPS, the claims of the State Parties did not permit analysis of the substantive aspects of protection. The following analysis will show how the ECJ subsequently pursued the substantive elements of harmonization by undertaking the task of calibrating the scope of trademark rights in relation to trade names.

B. The ECJ interprets the scope of exclusive rights pursuant to TRIPS

The ECJ proceeded with the interpretation of TRIPS Article 16 by simultaneously invoking the trademark jurisprudence of both the Community and the WTO. Concerning the conditions under which the use of a trade name may be regarded as an infringing sign for the purposes of TRIPS Article 16(1), the court affirmed the approach taken traditionally by national courts. Its first step is to inquire whether the trade name was being used as a trademark, that is, to distinguish the goods or services of the defendant, or simply as the business name of the firm. For its part, Article 5(5) of the Trademark Directive reflects the absence of harmonization with respect to unfair competition law.[27] It provides:

> Paragraphs 1 to 4 shall not affect provisions in any Member State relating to the protection against the use of a sign other than for the purposes of distinguishing goods or services, where use of that sign without due cause takes unfair advantage of, or is detrimental to, the distinctive character or the repute of the trade mark.

Consequently, where the sign constitutes a trade name which is not used for

---

[26] United States – Section 211 Omnibus Appropriations Act of 1998 (*Havana Club*), Complaint by European Communities, WT/DS176/R, Report of the Panel, August 6, 2001 at ¶ 8.41.

[27] The sixth recital in the Preamble states that the Harmonization Directive 89/104 does not exclude the application of provisions of law of the Member States other than trademark law, such as laws relating to unfair competition, civil liability, or consumer protection. *See* http://oami.europa.eu/en/mark/aspects/direc/direc.htm.

the purposes of distinguishing goods or services, it is necessary to refer to national law to determine the extent and nature, if any, of the protection afforded to owners of trademarks who claim to be suffering damage as a result of use of that sign as a trade name or company name. An action under unfair competition law or for passing off will be available wherever the defendant company's name is calculated to deceive and so to divert business from plaintiff to defendant or to occasion confusion between the two businesses. Consistent with this position, the ECJ in *Robelco NV and Robeco Groep NV*[28] held that Article 5(5) of the Directive must be interpreted to mean that a Member State may protect a trademark against use of a sign other than for the purposes of distinguishing goods or services, where use of that sign without due cause takes unfair advantage of, or is detrimental to, the distinctive character or the repute of the trademark.

The *Anheuser-Busch* case gave the ECJ the opportunity to advance the Appellate Body's analysis with respect to the scope of trademark rights and their interrelationship with trade names. The ECJ began by asserting that the exercise of trademark rights is reserved to cases in which a third party's use of the sign affects or is liable to affect the functions of the trademark. It then invoked Community jurisprudence concerning the mark's "essential function." In *HAG II*, the Court held that to determine the effect of the *trademark* right, account must be taken of its essential function, which is "to give consumers a guarantee of the identity of origin of the marked products, thereby preventing confusion."

C. *The ECJ determines the interrelationship of trademarks and trade names*

The ECJ's definition of trademark use, as informed by the mark's essential function, considerably broadens the scope of trademark rights. In *Arsenal v Reed*,[29] the relevant question was not whether the use was a "trade mark use," but whether this was liable to jeopardize the guarantee of origin which constitutes

---

[28] Case C-23/01, November 21, 2002, ECJ (Sixth Chamber) (analyzing the interpretation of Article 5(5) of First Council Directive 89/104/EEC of December 21, 1988 to approximate the laws of the Member States relating to trademarks (OJ 1989 L 40, p. 1)): http://curia.europa.eu.

[29] Arsenal Football Club plc v Matthew Reed, Judgment of the Court, November 12, 2002 Case C-206/01: http://curia.europa.eu. Reference to the Court under Article 234 EC by the High Court of Justice of England and Wales, Chancery Division (referencing for a preliminary ruling in the proceedings pending before that court on the interpretation of Article 5(1)(a) of the First Council Directive 89/104/EEC of December 21, 1988, at ¶ 54).

the essential function of the mark.[30] The positive finding of the Court rested on the rationale that use of the defendant's sign would deprive the mark of its distinctive character, because it would no longer be capable of guaranteeing origin.[31] Subsequently, in *Anheuser-Busch Inc.* with respect to claims against the infringing use of trade names, the ECJ proceeded to incorporate Community jurisprudence regarding Article 5 of the Directive with the exclusive rights conferred on the trademark owner in TRIPS Article 16 as follows:

> A trade name may constitute a sign within the meaning of the first sentence of Article 16(1) of the Agreement on Trade-Related Aspects of Intellectual Property Rights (TRIPS Agreement). That provision is intended to confer on the proprietor of a trade mark the exclusive right to prevent a third party from using such a sign if the use in question prejudices or is liable to prejudice the functions of the trade mark, in particular its essential function of guaranteeing to consumers the origin of the goods.[32]

Prima facie plaintiff Anheuser-Busch could successfully sue for trademark infringement since Budvar's trade name was clearly being used as a distinguishing sign.[33] The fact that in this case the allegedly infringing sign was a trade name gave the ECJ the opportunity to calibrate the substantive scope of the trade name rights, including their priority in relation to those of the plaintiff trademark owner.

However, as trade name protection constitutes an area in which the Community has not legislated, in order to strengthen the legitimacy of the exercise, the ECJ invoked the authority of TRIPS and Appellate Body jurisprudence. Hence the Court provided the following advice to Member States concerning the nature of trade names as a distinct category of intellectual property, whose protection is mandated pursuant to the Agreement:

---

[30] Arsenal Football Club plc v Reed, [2003] EWCA Civ 696, at ¶ 27 (CA) (Aldous, L.J.).

[31] Arsenal Football Club plc v Matthew Reed, Judgment of the Court, November 12, 2002 Case C-206/01 at ¶ 36: http://curia.europa.eu.

[32] Anheuser-Busch Inc. v Budějovický Budvar, národní podnik, Judgment of the Court in Case C-245/02 of November 16, 2004 at ¶ 85.

[33] *See* Case C-292/00 *Davidoff* [2003] ECR I-389, ¶ 28; Case C-291/00 *LTJ Diffusion* [2003] ECR I799, ¶¶ 48–9. In the event of identity of the sign and the trademark and of the goods or services, the protection conferred by Article 5(1)(a) of Directive 89/104 is absolute, whereas, in the situation provided for in Article 5(1)(b), the plaintiff must also prove that there is a likelihood of confusion on the part of the public because the signs and trademarks and the designated goods or services are identical or similar. *See also* Article 16 TRIPS.

It should be observed that a trade name is a right falling within the scope of the term "intellectual property" within the meaning of Article 1(2) of the TRIPS Agreement. Moreover, it follows from Article 2(1) of the TRIPS Agreement that the protection of trade names, for which specific provision is made in Article 8 of the Paris Convention, is expressly incorporated into that agreement. Therefore, by virtue of the TRIPS Agreement, the members of the WTO are under an obligation to protect trade names (see also the Report of the WTO Appellate Body, United States – Section 211 of the Omnibus Appropriations Act, cited above, paragraphs 326 to 341).[34]

Since defendant Budvar had forfeited its Finnish trademark rights,[35] the first question was whether its trade name, used on its labeling for beer, could be considered an "existing prior right" within the meaning of Article 16(1) of the TRIPS Agreement.[36] To this end, the question was whether the basis for the trade-name right concerned had arisen at a time prior to the grant of the trademark with which it was alleged to conflict. In fact, Budvar registered its trade name in the Czechoslovakian commercial register on February 1, 1967. Registration of the trade name pre-dated the registration of Anheuser-Busch's trademarks in Finland.[37] As far as the first condition laid down in Article 16(1), defendant therefore possessed an existing right in the trade name falling within the temporal scope, and following the Appellate Body's decision, subject to the substantive provisions of the TRIPS Agreement.[38] Pursuant therefore to Article 8 of the Paris Convention, as incorporated, defendant's trade name was protected in Finland "without the obligation of filing or registration, whether or not it forms part of a trademark."[39]

Prima facie, the Court's ruling would result in plaintiff's trademarks having to co-exist with defendant's use of an identical or similar trade name in respect of the market for beer in Finland. Nor can such use be prohibited by

---

[34] Anheuser-Busch Inc. v Budějovický Budvar, národní podnik, Judgment of the Court in Case C-245/02 of November 16, 2004 at ¶ 91.

[35] Budvar was the proprietor in Finland of the trademarks BUDVAR and BUDWEISER BUDVAR, which designated beer and were registered on May 21, 1962 and November 13, 1972 respectively, but the Finnish courts declared that Budvar had forfeited those rights as a result of a failure to use the trademarks. Anheuser-Busch Inc. v Budějovický Budvar, národní podnik, Judgment of the Court in Case C-245/02 of November 16, 2004 at ¶ 25.

[36] With respect to the application of Article 8 as incorporated in TRIPS, there was no question that Budvar's trade name possessed a right falling within the substantive and temporal scope of that agreement: *ibid* at ¶ 57.

[37] Anheuser-Busch is the proprietor in Finland of the trademarks BUDWEISER, BUD, BUD LIGHT, and BUDWEISER KING OF BEERS, which designate beer and were registered between June 5, 1985 and August 5, 1992.

[38] Pursuant to TRIPS Article 70(2).

[39] Article 8, Paris Convention, note 8 *supra*.

virtue of plaintiff's earlier registered marks having priority over the trade name. In a reversal of the rule of territoriality, if the trade name is registered in its home state A, then it has priority in State B if the trade-name owner has established a minimum of sufficient goodwill and reputation in that territory. Nonetheless, undoubtedly concerned as to the degree its activism tended to privilege trade names, by way of limitation, the Court's reading of Article 8 does not preclude Member States laying down conditions relating to minimum use or minimum awareness of the trade name in their territory.

D. *The ECJ finds trade names an exception under TRIPS Article 17*

Having answered the questions on reference, the Court nevertheless pursued the entire scope of trade name rights, by examining the potential impact of Article 17 of the TRIPS Agreement, which allows the members of the WTO to provide for limited exceptions to the rights conferred by a trade mark as follows:

> Members may provide limited exceptions to the rights conferred by a trademark, such as fair use of descriptive terms, provided that such exceptions take account of the legitimate interests of the owner of the trademark and of third parties.

The ECJ began by posing a question of its own as to whether the "own name defense" may extend to corporate names. Our analysis will show the ECJ drawing upon the authority of Community trademark law and jurisprudence to conclude that the Directive similarly permits such an exception. In this respect, Article 6(1)(a) provides:

> The trade mark shall not entitle the proprietor to prohibit a third party from using, in the course of trade,
>
> (a) his own name or address; . . .
>
> provided he uses them in accordance with honest practices in industrial or commercial matters.

Invoking the canons of interpretation, the Court applied the *ejusdem generis* rule to the effect that, where general words follow an enumeration of specific items, the general words must be read as applying to items of the same kind.[40] Since company names are of the same class, the application of *ejusdem generis* permitted the limitation of trademark rights to prohibit the use of not only personal names but also trade names. The potential application of the

---

[40] BLACK'S LAW DICTIONARY 556 (8th ed. 2004).

exception was further broadened by reference to Community trademark jurisprudence concerning the interpretation of the proviso.

E. *Honest practice in industrial or commercial matters*

In the case of *Bayerische Motorenwerke* (BMW), the ECJ set out the test as to whether the use was in accordance with honest practice.[41] In that case, the Court held that the latter condition constitutes a duty to act fairly in relation to the legitimate interests of the trademark owner.[42] In assessing "honest practice," national courts must take into account first, the extent to which the use of the third party's trade name is understood by the relevant public as indicating a link between the third party's goods and the trademark owner; and, second, the extent to which the third party ought to have been aware of that link.[43] A third factor to be taken into account is whether the trademark concerned enjoys a certain reputation in the Member State in which it is registered and where its protection is sought – a reputation from which the third party might profit in marketing its goods. In the case of BMW, where defendant's business was the second-hand sale and repair of BMW cars, "honest practice" meant avoiding any suggestion that the business remained affiliated to the BMW dealer network. In retrospect, BMW appears to have been the thin end of the wedge. In *Gerolsteiner*,[44] the ECJ further broadened the scope of the derogation by ruling that third-party use of a sign is nevertheless "in accordance with honest practices," even if the use in question constitutes use as a trademark, as opposed to merely descriptive use, and it is likely to cause confusion.

---

[41] Bayerische Motorenwerke AG (BMW) and BMW Nederland BV v Ronald Karel Deenik, Judgment of the Court in Case C-63/97 of February 23, 1999 at ¶ 61. In respect of Article 6(1)(c) of the Directive, where it is necessary to indicate the intended purpose of a product or service, in particular as accessories or spare-parts use of a trademark to advertise to the public the repair and maintenance of products covered, such a use does not constitute further commercialization for the purposes of Article 7 of the Directive, but use indicating the intended purpose of the service within the meaning of Article 6(1)(c).

[42] Bayerische Motorenwerke AG (BMW) and BMW Nederland BV v Ronald Karel Deenik, Judgment of the Court in Case C-63/97 of February 23, 1999 at ¶ 61; Gerolsteiner Brunnen GmbH & Co. v Putsch GmbH, Judgment of the Court (Fifth Chamber) in Case C-100/02 of January 7, 2004, European Court Reports 2004 I-00691, at ¶ 24.

[43] Anheuser-Busch Inc. v Budějovický Budvar, národní podnik, Judgment of the Court in Case C-245/02 of November 16, 2004 at ¶ 83.

[44] Gerolsteiner Brunnen GmbH & Co. v Putsch GmbH, Judgment of the Court (Fifth Chamber) in Case C-100/02 of January 7, 2004 at ¶¶ 25 & 26.

F. Discounting consumer confusion in favor of free movement

Citing *Gerolsteiner*, the Court seamlessly incorporated the reading of "honest practice" for the purposes of Community Law with the injunction in Article 17 to consider the legitimate interests of the trademark owner as follows:

> The condition of "honest practice" is, in essence, an expression of the duty to act fairly in relation to the legitimate interests of the trade-mark proprietor . . . It is therefore essentially the same condition as that laid down by Article 17 of the TRIPS Agreement.[45]

Subsequently, the ECJ justified its interpretation of the limitation on the rights conferred by a trademark with reference to the fundamental principles of the EC treaty as follows:

> Article 6 seeks to reconcile the fundamental interests of trade mark protection with those of free movement of goods and freedom to provide services in the common market in such a way that trade mark rights are able to fulfil their essential role in the system of undistorted competition which the Treaty seeks to establish and maintain.[46]

The difficulty in so doing is that it risks conflating the general purpose of the regulatory intent and institutional background of TRIPS and the Trademark Directive. The Court's test resembles Article 17 in so far as it involves a consideration of the legitimate interests of the trademark owner. Article 17 contemplates a balancing of interests that is broader and in keeping with the decentralized institutional framework of the WTO. To incorporate the jurisprudence of Article 6 within a reading of Article 17 is to potentially remove the greater national discretion of WTO Members in respect of public policy goals. The Court's reading of Article 6 of the Directive is strongly informed by the imperative of the free movement of goods. As a matter of trademark theory, *Gerolsteiner* is again instructive, since the breadth of the derogation in that case is justified not with reference to the mark as an indicator of source or quality, but to that of the common market and the free movement of goods.[47] Taken to its limits such logic would no longer allow

---

[45] Anheuser-Busch Inc. v Budějovický Budvar, národní podnik, Judgment of the Court in Case C-245/02 of November 16, 2004 at ¶ 82.

[46] *See*, CNL-Sucal v Hag (Café Hag II) Judgment of the Court in Case C-10/89 of October 17, 1990 at ¶ 13; Bayerische Motorenwerke AG (BMW) and BMW Nederland BV v Ronald Karel Deenik, Judgment of the Court in Case C-63/97 of February 23 1999 at ¶ 62; Anheuser-Busch Inc. v Budějovický Budvar, národní podnik, Judgment of the Court in Case C-245/02 of November 16, 2004 at ¶ 16.

[47] This is an idea associated with the thinking of classical economists such as Adam Smith, who emphasized the advantages of free trade policies for the improvement of living standards and the promotion of economic growth. ADAM SMITH, THE WEALTH OF NATIONS (1776).

consumers to seek, or to avoid, particular sources of products or services. The question is how much confusion is needed to remove the defendant's use of its trade name from the sphere of honest practice. Presumably, as the UK Court of Appeal pointed out in *Reed Executive Plc*,[48] significant actual deception would be needed since the proviso is almost identical in wording to Article 10 *bis* (2) of the Paris Convention concerning unfair competition.

IV. Substantive trademark law harmonization and the legitimacy of the judicial activism

In our case study concerning the protection of trade names, we saw the WTO and the ECJ exercising some remarkable judicial activism. As the Appellate Body points out, the incorporation of trade names as a category of intellectual property subject to the TRIPS Agreement means that trade names are not only subject to the obligation in Article 41.1 requiring Members to make available the enforcement procedures listed in the Agreement, but also to the principles of non-discrimination contained in the obligations concerning national treatment and most favored nation treatment.[49]

The particularly marked activism of the ECJ is exemplified by the inclusion of trade names as a possible exception to the exclusive rights of the trademark owner. When we compare the approaches of the WTO Appellate Body and the ECJ, we find a noticeable contrast in the character of their justification for their "continuing the analysis" beyond what is strictly necessary in order to respond to the claims of litigants. Recall that the Appellate Body derives its power to review the national trademark laws of Members from Article 11 of the Dispute Settlement Understanding and the rule of international law that municipal laws are merely facts which express the will of the State. The authority of the Appellate Body in continuing its analysis is also derived from this rule.[50]

---

[48] Reed Executive Plc v Reed Business Information Ltd. [2004] EWCA Civ 159 (March. 3, 2004), [2004] R.P.C. 40 at ¶ 115.

[49] TRIPS Articles 3 and 4. *See also* G.E. Evans, *The Principle of National Treatment and the International Protection of Industrial Property*, 18(3) EUROPEAN INTELL. PROP. REV 149–60 (1996).

[50] The Appellate Body found that the Panel record contained a sufficient factual basis to proceed since (a) both trademark and trade names were subject to Section 211; (b) the Parties agreed that the TRIPS Agreement incorporated an obligation to protect trade names pursuant to the Paris Convention and; (c) both participants refer to protection of trade names as well as trademarks throughout their original submissions to the Panel. *See* Sections 211(a)(2) and (b); Article 2.1 of the TRIPS Agreement (in conjunction with Article 2(1) of the Paris Convention (1967)); Article 3.1 of the TRIPS Agreement; Article 4 of the TRIPS Agreement; Article 42 of the TRIPS Agreement; Article 2.1 of the TRIPS Agreement (in conjunction with Article 8 of the

In contrast, with greater confidence in the legitimacy of an action derived from the preliminary ruling mechanism, in the *Anheuser-Busch* case, the ECJ justified "completing the analysis" of trade-name protection by briefly referring to its responsibility to provide the national court with all the elements of interpretation of Community law which may be of assistance in adjudicating the case – significantly, whether or not that court specifically refers to them in its questions.[51] In particular, in cases where there might be some uncertainty or difference of opinion between the courts of Member States with respect to the question of whether company names are subject to the fair use or "own name" defense in cases of a *prima facie* trademark infringement.

The more cautious approach of the Appellate Body may be linked to greater concern for the foundations upon which it proceeds with an analysis of trade-name protection and the associated allocation of decision-making authority. Conversely, the comparative confidence of the ECJ in the authority of the preliminary ruling mechanism rests on the success with which the Court has deployed it to establish the supremacy of Community trademark law. The comparatively less certain foundation of the rule from which the Appellate Body derives its authority for the assessment of domestic law might prompt us to question the legitimacy of substantive harmonization.

In fact, the legitimacy of judicial activism has long tested the minds of jurists. Sir William Blackstone claimed that the judge's role is to determine the law "according to the known laws and customs of the land." The judge is "not delegated to pronounce a new law, but to maintain and expound the old one."[52] If judges merely find and apply authoritative law, and their interpretations are derived from the plain meaning of the legal text, their decisions presumptively carry the authority of the law they are applying. So it is that, in the instant the Appellate Body determines to be declaratory of the law, it calls upon the canon of interpretation that is known as the "plain meaning" rule. The claim that the meaning is clear serves to lend legitimacy to the rationale that the reading is determined by the fixed meaning of the text. Given the divergence of opinion between the Panel and Appellate Body, we see that there is no fixed meaning, and even if there were, the courts are not bound by it.

Paris Convention (1967)): United States – Section 211 Omnibus Appropriations Act of 1998 (*Havana Club*), Complainant: European Communities, WT/DS176/AB/R, Report of the Appellate Body, January 2002, ¶ 352: *available at* http://www.wto.org/english/tratop_e/dispu_e/cases_e/ds176_e.htm.

[51] *See* Case C-87/97 Consorzio per la tutela del formaggio Gorgonzola [1999] ECR I-1301, ¶ 16.

[52] WILLIAM BLACKSTONE, COMMENTARIES 69 (1765); *Cf.* Marbury v Madison, 5 U.S. (1 Cranch) 137, 177 (1803).

No less, in the respect of the activism of the Appellate Body and the ECJ, the case studies set out in Section II reveal that adjudicators' approach to the interpretation of the law, pursuant to the rules of the Vienna Convention, is critical both to the legitimacy and management of substantive harmonization. The following analysis therefore seeks to identify those interpretive techniques that may be considered common to their joint enterprise and characteristic of their new-found coherence.

A. Use of the "plain meaning" rule as declaratory of lawmaking

In the WTO case of the *Havana Club* trademark, it will be recalled that the EC claimed that Section 211[53] was discriminatory not only in respect of trademarks of Cuban origin, but also trade names. As trade names are not expressly protected in the TRIPS Agreement, this raised the question as to whether they were protected by means of the incorporation of Article 8 of the Paris Convention. When it reversed the Panel's decision regarding the incorporation of trade names within the TRIPS Agreement, the Appellate Body did so on the basis that the Panel's interpretation of the Agreement was contrary to the plain meaning of the words and was therefore not in accordance with the customary rules of interpretation prescribed in Article 31 of the Vienna Convention on the Law of Treaties. Employing this interpretative canon, the Appellate Body simply declared that it did "not believe" that the Panel's interpretation of Article 1.2 could be reconciled with the plain words of Article 2.1, since that Article "explicitly incorporates Article 8 of the Paris Convention (1967) into the TRIPS Agreement."[54]

Adjudicators may pair the plain-meaning rule with the redundancy rule to create the inference that the meaning was fixed once and for all at the moment law-makers drafted the treaty and that it cannot subsequently change. In the following extract, we can observe the Appellate Body doing so in order to lend greater legitimacy to the incorporation of trade names:

> If the intention of the negotiators had been to exclude trade names from protection, there would have been no purpose whatsoever in including Article 8 in the list of Paris Convention (1967) provisions that were specifically incorporated into the TRIPS Agreement. To adopt the Panel's approach would be to deprive Article 8 of the Paris Convention (1967), as incorporated into the TRIPS Agreement by virtue of Article 2.1 of that Agreement, of any and all meaning and effect.[55]

---

[53] United States – Section 211 Omnibus Appropriations Act of 1998 (*Havana Club*), Complainant: European Communities, WT/DS176/AB/R, Report of the Appellate Body, January 2002, ¶ 3: *available at* http://www.wto.org/english/tratop_e/dispu_e/cases_e/ds176_e.htm.
[54] *Id.* at ¶ 336.
[55] *Ibid* at ¶ 338.

Similarly, we can observe that the ECJ adopted the teleological approach to the interpretation of the TRIPS Agreement in *Anheuser-Busch Inc. v Budějovický Budvar*. In order to construe Article 16 in light of the purpose of the TRIPS Agreement, the Court referred to the leading paragraph of the Preamble. That paragraph expresses the purpose of the agreement as one that aims to "reduce distortions and impediments to international trade" by "taking into account the need to promote effective and adequate protection of intellectual property rights," while at the same time ensuring that "measures and procedures to enforce intellectual property rights do not themselves become barriers to legitimate trade."[56] The Court then characterized the intent of Article 16 in this light, holding that it provides registered trademark owners with a minimum international standard of exclusive rights which all members of the WTO "must guarantee in their domestic legislation."[57]

All the more significantly, proceeding to interpret Article 16 in light of the purpose of the TRIPS Agreement, the Court explained the text utilizing the terminology of Community trademark law as follows:

> [T]he exercise of the exclusive right conferred on the proprietor of the trade mark to prevent the use of the sign of which that mark consists or of a sign similar to that mark must be reserved to cases in which a third party's use of the sign prejudices or is liable to prejudice the functions of the trade mark, in particular its essential function of guaranteeing to consumers the origin of the goods.[58]

Of course, this process in itself might be simply considered analogous to the reception of international law by a national court, were it not for the fact that the position and function of the ECJ as an international tribunal give its findings far greater authority.

B. Use of the "supplementary material" rule to achieve supremacy

The reader will recall that Article 32 of the *Vienna Convention on the Law of*

---

[56] TRIPS: Agreement On Trade-Related Aspects Of Intellectual Property Rights, Preamble, ¶ 1 *available at*: http://www.wto.org/english/tratop_e/trips_e/t_agm1_e.htm.

[57] Anheuser-Busch Inc. v Budějovický Budvar, národní podnik, Judgment of the Court in Case C-245/02 of November 16, 2004 at ¶ 67. See, to the same effect, the Appellate Body: "Article 16 confers on the *owner* of a registered trademark an internationally agreed minimum level of 'exclusive rights' that all WTO Members must guarantee in their domestic legislation." United States – Section 211 Omnibus Appropriations Act of 1998 (*Havana Club*), Complainant: European Communities, WT/DS176/AB/R, Report of the Appellate Body, January 2002, ¶ 186: *available at* http://www.wto.org/english/tratop_e/dispu_e/cases_e/ds176_e.htm.

[58] Anheuser-Busch Inc. v Budějovický Budvar, národní podnik, Judgment of the Court in Case C-245/02 of November 16, 2004 at ¶ 71.

Treaties contains a "Supplementary means of interpretation." Our analysis of case law reveals that this rule may provide the Appellate Body or the ECJ with the technical means to set aside extraneous materials, where they are considered to be either ambiguous or lacking the necessary authority or specific reference to the subject matter at issue. Thus in the *Havana Club* trademark case, the Appellate Body found that the passages quoted by the Panel from the negotiating history of Article 1.2 were inconclusive for their lack of specific reference to trade names. In order to clear the ground for its interpretation, the Appellate Body dismissed the negotiating history as in no way decisive of the issue as to whether the TRIPS Agreement covers trade names. Similarly, in *Anheuser-Busch Inc.*, the ECJ deployed the rule to set aside a joint executive declaration of the European Commission and Council of the European Union as non-binding on the basis that no reference was made in its content to the specific wording of Article 6(1)(a) of the Directive. The Court concluded in favor of the inclusion of company names based on the "ordinary meaning" of "name," a term that includes company names as belonging to "the same kind, class, or nature." The Court's positive application of the "plain meaning rule" required no consideration of the reasons that might have prompted the joint declaration. Although trademarks and trade names differ with regard to the subjects they are intended to distinguish, there is often a close association of common elements between a company name and a trademark as the *Budweiser* case clearly demonstrates. These common characteristics are likely to be even more pronounced in the case of service marks where the difference between a trademark designating specific services and the trade name designating the company providing them may be hardly distinguishable for the average consumer.[59]

V. Evaluating the character and legitimacy of substantive trademark law harmonization

This chapter has posited that the trademark jurisprudence of the WTO Appellate Body and ECJ demonstrates a new coherence capable of realizing the substantive harmonization of trademark law. We have identified the elements of interpretive technique that are common to the Appellate Body and the ECJ as they each engage in construing the trademark provisions of the TRIPS Agreement. Nonetheless, the extent to which this new coherence is actually capable of realizing the substantive harmonization of trademark law

---

[59] For an analysis of the average consumer, see Lloyd Schuhfabrik Meyer & Co. GmbH v Klijsen Handel BV, Judgment of the Court in Case C-342/97 of June 22, 1999 at ¶ 26. ("... the average consumer of the category of products concerned is deemed to be reasonably well informed and reasonably observant and circumspect.")

will depend upon the standing of their jurisprudence before the network of national courts. We will therefore begin by considering the extent to which the courts of WTO Member States believe themselves bound to follow the rulings of the Appellate Body concerning the interpretation of the trademark provisions of TRIPS. Thereafter, we will inquire as to influence of the European Court's trademark jurisprudence beyond the immediate confines of the Community.

A. *The authority of Appellate Body and ECJ jurisprudence*

1. Appellate Body case law Article 19.2 of the Dispute Settlement Understanding states that Panels and Appellate Body "cannot add to or diminish the rights and obligations provided in the covered agreements." This direction as to the lack of law-making capacity on the part of WTO adjudicators is consistent with the sources of international law as they are enumerated in Article 38 of the Statute of the International Court of Justice. Judicial decisions are described in Article 38 as a subsidiary means for the determination of law. Thus, when a dispute arises between states with regard to a matter regulated by treaty, the parties' adjudicators should apply, in the first instance, the provisions of the treaty in question. In addition, Article 59 of the Statute states that decisions of the International Court of Justice have no binding force except between the parties to the case in question.[60]

While the international legal system is technically without the formal doctrine of binding precedent, as a matter of practice, the legal reality is otherwise. Treaty-making power may reside with Members' elected governments, but in practice "judicial activism" is as much a part of it, and is as necessary to the dialectic of legal interpretation at the level of international tribunals as it is at the national level. Reflecting this apparent inconsistency, Sir William Blackstone's famous declaratory theory of judging holds that judges "find" rather than "make" law. To conclude otherwise is to ignore the practical effect which a WTO Panel or Appellate Body decision may have on the development of trademark law. This is certainly borne out by the impact of Appellate Body jurisprudence in the *Havana Club* case on the protection of trade names in Europe.

2. ECJ case law As the judicial institution of the Community responsible for the definitive interpretation of trademark law, decisions of the Court of Justice must be followed throughout the common market. The enlargement of the Community has seen the authority of the Court's trademark law extend to an increasing number of European countries. Originally compris-

---

[60] H. LAUTERPACHT, COLLECTED PAPERS, Vol I, ed. E. Lauterpacht (1970) at 87.

ing six founding states in 1952, the European Union has grown over the duration of six successive enlargements to its current size of 27 Member States. Moreover, the authority of the Court's trademark jurisprudence extends to the process of candidature and accession, which, as exemplified by the case of Turkey, brings with it an intensification of cooperation between the EU Member States and a concomitant increase in authority of European legal institutions over those of the nation state.[61]

The influence of European trademark jurisprudence extends to the continents Africa, Asia, Europe, and the Americas by means of regional and bilateral agreements in the form of Partnership and Cooperation or Association Agreements.[62] The European Union is seeking the global projection of its legal institutions by concluding regional trade agreements and negotiating new Economic Partnership Agreements (EPAs). To this end it is, for example, implementing the Cotonou Agreement[63] with the African, Caribbean, and Pacific Group of States (ACP) and negotiating Economic Partnership Agreements (EPAs) with ACP regional groupings. The legal basis for the negotiation of external trade agreements, Article 133 of the European Community Treaty, indicates the significance with which the enforcement of intellectual property rights is regarded, in so far as paragraph 5 refers specifically to the conclusion of agreements concerning "the commercial aspects of intellectual property."[64] The States that have concluded EPAs are likely to

---

[61] The 2003 European Council summit in Thessaloniki set integration of the Western Balkans as a priority in the future expansion of the European Union. Between 2010 and 2015, the five Balkan states of Serbia, Montenegro, Bosnia-Herzegovina, Former Yugoslav Republic of Macedonia, and Albania may likely join the European Union depending on their satisfying the criteria for adhesion. In addition, candidate countries include Croatia, Moldova, Ukraine, and Turkey. In order to join the European Union, a state needs to fulfill the economic and political conditions generally known as the Copenhagen criteria (after the Copenhagen summit in June 1993).

[62] The European Union has a Common Commercial Policy whereby the Commission negotiates bilateral and regional trade agreements with countries outside the European Union on behalf of the Member States.

[63] *See* Partnership Agreement between the Members of the African, Caribbean and Pacific Group of States, of the One Part, and the European Community and its Member States, of the Other Part, Signed June 23, 2000 in Cotonou, Benin. This entered into force on April 1, 2003, The full text is available online. *See* Commission of the European Communities, *available at* http://europa.eu.int/comm/development/body/cotonou/agreement_en.htm.

[64] Chief among the trade policy initiatives of the European Union is the European Neighbourhood Policy (ENP). The ENP offers a deeper economic integration by means of bilateral Partnership Agreements and Action Plans. Originally, the ENP was intended to apply to Europe's neighbors of Algeria, Belarus, Egypt, Israel, Jordan, Lebanon, Libya, Moldova, Morocco, the Palestinian Authority, Syria, Tunisia, and Ukraine. In 2004, it was extended to also include the countries of the Southern

experience the impact of the ECJ's trademark jurisprudence most directly pursuant to provisions concerning the resolution of disputes between the parties. Most EC trade agreements employ a form of arbitration in which EC law enjoys a distinct advantage, given the political and economic asymmetry of the parties and the lack of formal procedure.

B. The constitutionalization of adjudication: a lasting legacy

This chapter's hypothesis concerning the new-found coherence of Appellate Body and ECJ jurisprudence is also consistent with the constitutionalization of adjudication. To the extent that the TRIPS enforcement regime created a supranational tribunal in the Appellate Body, it also set the stage for the allocation of decision-making between international and national trademark tribunals. It is possible to observe the Appellate Body creating a decision-making structure, retaining those issues foundational to the regulation of intellectual property to the international level, and allocating subsidiary or related issues to the national level. In the *Havana Club* case, for example, the Appellate Body ruled that questions pertaining to a mark's capacity to distinguish the product or the rights conferred on the trademark owner are matters to be determined at the international level, whereas questions pertaining to the ownership of the trademark are threshold matters to be decided by national courts.[65] In respect of the decision-making process, there can be little doubt that the adjudication of the Appellate Body will leave the network of national courts with a lasting legacy.

In keeping with its dual function, we can also observe the ECJ engaged in a similar but more elaborate process with respect to the allocation of decision-making between the Community and national courts. In the case of *Anheuser-Busch Inc. v Budějovický Budvar*, the Court issued the following directions: first, with respect to trademark use, the ECJ ruled that the national court has to confirm whether the use made is one that is "in the course of trade" and 'in relation to goods" within the meaning of Article 5(1) of the Directive.[66] The national court has to establish whether that is the case in the light of the specific circumstances of the use of the sign allegedly made by the defendant. Second, in cases of possible consumer confusion, it is for the national court to carry out an overall assessment of all the relevant circumstances, in order to

---

Caucasus, with whom Bulgaria, Romania, and Turkey share either a maritime or land border: Armenia, Azerbaijan, and Georgia. Significantly, in the implementation of the European Neighbourhood Policy, the benefit of European law and legal institutions is promoted as part of outreach and technical support programmes.

[65] Section 211 of Omnibus Appropriations Act of 1998 ("Havana Club").

[66] Directive 89/104. *See* Arsenal Football Club plc v Matthew Reed, Judgment of the ECJ in Case C-206/01 of November 12, 2002 at ¶ ¶ 40 & 41.

assess whether the producer of the product bearing the trade name can be regarded as unfairly competing with the owner of the trademark.

C. *Potential disadvantages of substantive trademark law harmonization*
In view of the increasing influence of the trademark jurisprudence of the Appellate Body and ECJ, this chapter concludes by considering the potential disadvantages to the adjudication of cases throughout the network of national courts. The Paris Convention allowed national courts considerable autonomy in decision-making. It provided the norms and the framework for adjudication without what the ECJ calls "the elements of interpretation." The latter were supplied principally by drawing on national trademark jurisprudence. This flexibility allowed the interpretation of national law to change in accordance with the nation's economic, social, and cultural development. Thus, Article 6 *quinquies* A(1) allowed the U.S. Court of Appeals for the Federal Circuit in *In re Rath*[67] the flexibility to affirm the USPTO's refusal to register the surname "Dr. Rath" on the principal register, on the ground that the mark was primarily merely a surname, absent proof of acquired distinctiveness.[68]

Conversely however, when the elements of the interpretation are supplied by a supranational tribunal, national courts have far less flexibility in the application of the law to the facts at hand. Thus, we have seen that in the matter of trade names, the Supreme Court of Finland was given little option but to privilege the trade name of the defendant in relation to the plaintiff's trademarks. Once the ECJ concluded that neither trademark use nor consumer confusion constituted elements capable of precluding the operation of the exception, little scope remained for the national court apart from deciding, based on evidence of local use, the extent to which the defendant's trade name enjoyed a reputation in Finland.[69]

---

[67] *See* In re Rath, 402 F.3d 1207, (Fed. Cir. 2005), in which the Federal Circuit affirmed a Trademark Trial and Appeal Board decision holding that "Dr. Rath" was primarily merely a surname.

[68] Relying on U.S. trademark law, the Court found that section 44 of the Lanham Act, which implements the Paris Convention, does not require registration of a mark that is primarily merely a surname. In re Establissements Darty et Fils, 759 F.2d 15, 225 USPQ 652 (Fed. Cir. 1985). The Lanham Act explicitly adopts the requirements of the Paris Convention, and the statutory bars to registration allowed by the Paris Convention are congruent with the bars to registration created by the Lanham Act. See also Stephen P. Ladas, 2 Patents, Trademarks and Related Rights, National and International Protection § 572 (1975) ("The reasons for which registration is denied on the principal register are those for which, under Article 6 *quinquies* of the Paris Convention, a contracting party may refuse a mark even though it is registered in the country of origin.") Compare the ECJ approach in Nichols plc v Registrar of Trade Marks, ECJ Judgment of September 16, 2004, Case C-404/02.

[69] Following a ruling by the Finnish Supreme Court on December 29, 2005,

The application of the ECJ's interpretive guidelines shows that there is, in practice, a fine line between interpreting the law and applying the facts of the case. The ECJ's decision in *Arsenal v Reed*,[70] for example, contained a number of references to the facts of the case; the Court went as far as to disagree with Mr. Justice Laddie's analysis of those facts. On return to the High Court of England, Mr. Justice Laddie again found in favor of the defendant, concluding that the ECJ's interpretation of the law did not change his original decision.[71] He maintained that as there was neither trademark use nor evidence of consumer confusion, there was no case for trademark infringement.[72] However, the Court of Appeals reversed, taking the view that the High Court should have followed the view of the European Court to the effect that the sale of unofficial merchandise was likely to damage the trademark or "jeopardize the guarantee of origin which constitutes the essential function of the mark."[73] Clearly therefore the substantive harmonization of trademark law involves national courts' having less flexibility to decide with reference to local socio-economic conditions.[74]

For the majority of developing countries and transitional economies, not having access to compensatory levels of financial support and technical assistance available to EC Members, the additional loss of sovereignty over their trademark law would constitute a decided disadvantage.[75] Equally, at the micro level, a small to medium size enterprise that plays such a decisive role in economic development will bear the cost of operating within a public domain that is increasingly eroded by new categories of intellectual property rights.[76] Likewise, as a matter of consumer protection, to entertain a greater

---

Budějovický Budvar cannot use the names Bud or Budweiser as trademarks in Finland. However, it will still be able to refer to its company as Budweiser Budvar, NC in small print on its beer labels, as well as on invoices and in marketing.

[70] Arsenal Football Club plc v Matthew Reed, Judgment of the Court, November 12, 2002, Case C-206/01.

[71] Arsenal Football Club Plc v Reed [2002] EWHC 2695 (Ch) (December 12, 2002) at ¶ 27.

[72] *Id.* at ¶ 24 & 25.

[73] Arsenal Football Club plc v Reed [2003] EWCA Civ 696, Court of Appeal, per Aldous LJ at ¶ 27.

[74] "It is in no one's interest, even Mr. Reed's, for there to be such a difference between the views expressed by the High Court and the ECJ. The courts of this country cannot challenge rulings of the ECJ within its areas of competence. There is no advantage to be gained by appearing to do so." Arsenal Football Club Plc v Reed [2002] EWHC 2695 (Ch) (December 12, 2002) per Laddie J. at ¶ 28.

[75] JOHN H. JACKSON, SOVEREIGNTY, THE WTO, AND CHANGING. FUNDAMENTALS OF. INTERNATIONAL LAW 76–8 (2006).

[76] *See* A Study For The European Commission On The Feasibility Of Possible Insurance Schemes Against Patent Litigation Risks, Final Report, prepared by CJA

likelihood of confusion between similar trademarks and identical or similar products is to increase the search costs on consumers who must either possess a more specialized knowledge or spend proportionately more time in searching for the desired quality.[77]

VI. Conclusion

We began our inquiry with the hypothesis that the trademark jurisprudence of the Appellate Body and ECJ demonstrates a new coherence, in time, capable of bringing about the substantive harmonization of trademark law. The foregoing analysis has shown that, as international trademark tribunals, they possess the distinct capacity to pursue such a project. The incorporation of trade names within the TRIPS Agreement attests to the new-found coherence or shared understanding between the Appellate Body and ECJ as international trademark tribunals. From the viewpoint of Community Law, the heightened protection accorded trade names suggests that the trademark jurisprudence of the Appellate Body permits the ECJ to pursue harmonization in those areas of law where the Community has not yet legislated. Therefore, in view of the capacity of the Appellate Body to allocate decision-making between international and national trademark tribunals, and in view of the authority with which the trademark jurisprudence of the ECJ is regarded both within the Community and beyond its borders,[78] the realization of substantive trademark law harmonization on a case-by-case basis begins to seem far less improbable.

Consultants for the European Commission, June 2006 at 9: available at: http://ec.europa.eu/internal_market/indprop/docs/patent/studies/pli_report_en.pdf.

[77] WILLIAM M. LANDES & RICHARD A. POSNER, THE ECONOMIC STRUCTURE OF INTELLECTUAL PROPERTY LAW 172–5 (2003).

[78] *See* Verimark (Pty) Ltd v BMW AG [2007] SCA 53 (RSA) where the Supreme Court of Appeal of South Africa defined the scope of the exclusive rights of the trademark owner in terms of Community jurisprudence concerning the mark's "essential function", at 5–6, available at: http://www.supremecourtofappeal.gov.za/judgments/sca_judg/judgem_sca_2007.htm.

8 The free movement (or not) of trademark protected goods in Europe
*Thomas Hays**

I. Community law of free movement

The Treaty of Rome[1] established a common market in Europe using the free movement of goods and services within that market as a primary means of achieving economic integration. EC Treaty Article 28 allows goods to enter one Member State of the European Union from another Member State (the front door of free movement) without governmental interference at the border. Article 29 allows goods to leave a Member State, again without national restrictions on exports. There are limited exceptions to these principles, mostly based on health and safety grounds, and now primarily exploited at customs in relation to specially taxed products, such as alcohol and tobacco, and regulated, potentially dangerous items, such as pharmaceuticals and explosives.[2]

---

* Ph.D. (Cambridge); Lewis Silkin LLP, London; CIER, the Molengraaff Institute, Utrecht.

[1] Treaty Establishing the European Economic Community, Rome, March 25, 1957, Ts.1 (1973) Cmnd 5179, 298 U.N.T.S. 11 (1958), as amended by the Single European Act, O.J. 1987, 169/1, [1987] 2 CMLR 741, as amended by the Treaty on European Union, Maastricht, February 7, 1992, O.J. 1992, C 224/1, [1994] 1 CMLR 719, as amended by the Treaty of Nice, March 10, 2001, O.J. 2001, C 80/1; as amended by the Treaty on European Union and the Treaty Establishing the European Community, December 24, 2002, O.J. 2002, C 325/5, 33 [hereinafter the EC Treaty].

[2] Art. 28 (ex 30) of the EC Treaty provides "[q]uantitative restrictions on imports and all measures having equivalent effect shall be prohibited between Member States." Art. 29 (ex 34) of the EC Treaty provides "[q]uantitative restrictions on exports, and all measures having equivalent effect, shall be prohibited between Member States." Art. 30 (ex 36) of the EC Treaty states:

> The provisions of Articles 28 and 29 shall not preclude prohibitions or restrictions on imports, exports or goods in transit justified on grounds of public morality, public policy or public security; the protection of health and life of humans, animals or plants; the protection of national treasures possessing artistic, historic or archaeological value; or the protection of industrial and commercial property. Such prohibitions or restrictions shall not, however, constitute a means of arbitrary discrimination or a disguised restriction on trade between Member States.

See G. Tritton, *Articles 30 to 36 and Intellectual Property: Is the Jurisprudence of the*

Parallel importation occurs when goods are purchased in one place and resold in another in competition with the distribution system preferred by the original source of the goods.³ The goals of the free-movement provisions would seem to be the natural beneficiaries of parallel trading. Many overtly restrictive national regulatory barriers to parallel trade have been eliminated.⁴ While Article 30 permits justifiable restrictions on the movements of some goods between Member States, any such impositions on intra-Community trade must be proportionate to the legitimate national interest being pursued through the restrictions.⁵ Less restrictive national provisions, such as those regulating litigation-related discovery requests, might, at least under the emerging construction used by the Community courts, pose barriers not so

---

ECJ now of an Ideal Standard?, 10 E.I.P.R. 422, 423 (1994); F. Beier, *Industrial Property and the Free Movement of Goods in the Internal European Market*, 2 I.I.C. 131 (1990).

³ The original source of parallel goods is the manufacturer of those goods, though the manufacturer may be no more than an otherwise disinterested licensee performing on behalf of an intellectual-property owner, the real party in interest. This is the origin of goods in a practical sense, rather than in a trademark-law sense, such as that applicable to a discussion of the specific subject matter or essential function of marks. See Case 3/78, *Centrafarm, BV v American Home Products*, [1978] ECR 1823, [1979] 1 CMLR 326, ¶¶ 10–12; Case 58/80, *Dansk Supermarked, A/S v Imerco, A/S*, [1981] ECR 181, [1981] 3 CMLR 590, ¶¶ 15–16. Throughout the discussion that follows, because it focuses on the influences exerted by intellectual-property rights, the origin of parallel goods should be understood as referring to the owner of the intellectual property in those goods, unless some other source, such as the manufacturer, is specified. The choice of terms is more than a problem of semantics. The terms take on the character of terms of art, subject to translational problems when being transferred among the languages of the Member States, as is shown by the originally supposed, though now recognized as vacuous, distinction between the specific subject matter and the specific object of intellectual-property rights. The source of parallel goods shall refer here to the licensee within a distribution system that supplied the goods to parallel traders, as the term is used in the line of decisions including Case C-244/00, *Van Doren + Q. GmbH v Lifestyle Sports +sportswear Handelsgesellschaft mbh and Michael Orth*, O.J. 2003, C-135/2, [2003] 2 CMLR 6, [2003] E.T.M.R. 44.

⁴ Case 302/86, *Commission v Denmark*, [1988] ECR 4607, where the European Commission (hereinafter "the Commission") successfully challenged a national-law requirement that had the effect of limiting the quantity of imported beverages that could be sold in unapproved containers. This case represented an example of the application of the proportionality principle. The ECJ held that while the purpose of protecting the Danish environment was a legitimate national interest, the means of achieving that interest, specifically the requirements that the containers in issue be approved, returnable, and the resulting restriction of intra-market trade, were not proportionate to that interest.

⁵ Case 120/78, *Rewe-Zentral, AG v Bundesmonopolverwaltung für Branntwein*, [1979] ECR 649, [1979] 3 CMLR 494, relating to national rules as to the sale and marketing of alcoholic beverages.

much to the movement of goods directly but to the mechanisms, like parallel importing, which promote that movement.[6] However, taken collectively, there are at present few internal barriers to the movement of parallel goods within the EEA.[7]

The situation becomes more complicated when the role of intellectual-property rights is considered in relation to parallel trading.[8] National intellectual-property rights, tied to the territories of the jurisdictions in which they are created, are immediately suspect as being in conflict with the goal of a common internal market, as well as the political usage of freely moving goods and unrestricted commerce as a tool of market integration. Marenco and Banks describe the suspicion with which national intellectual-property rights are viewed:

> According to the Court all national legislation in the field of intellectual property, insofar as it affects imported products, falls under the notion of measures having an effect equivalent to quantitative restrictions and is therefore technically in breach of Article [28]. From this point of departure the Court then proceeds to examine whether the measure under review can be justified under Article [30].[9]

This is to say, national-law-based intangible, movable property interests, while protected by EC Treaty Article 295,[10] are, by judicial definition, in

---

[6] See *Van Doren v Lifestyle Sports*, *supra* note 3 (expressing the ECJ's concern for protecting the sources of parallel goods from discovery by manufacturers).

[7] See G. Orlandini, *The Free Movement of Goods as a Possible "Community" Limitation on Industrial Conflict*, 4 EUR. L. J. 341 (2000); D. Rosenberg & M. Van Kerckhove, *Upjohn v Paranova: Utterly Exhausted by a Trip Too Far*, 5 E.I.P.R. 223 (1999); A. Geddes, *Free Movement of Pharmaceuticals within the Community: The Remaining Barriers*, 16 EUR. L. REV. 295 (1991).

[8] R Goebel, *The Interplay between Intellectual Property Rights and Free Movement of Goods in the European Community*, 55 FORDHAM INTELL. PROP. MEDIA & ENT. L.J. 125; V. Korah, *Dividing the Common Market through National Industrial Property Rights*, 35 M.L.R. 634 (1972). For an important discussion which is in conflict with the opinion expressed by Beier, *supra* note 2, see G. Marenco & K. Banks, *Intellectual Property and the Community Rules on Free Movement: Discrimination Unearthed*, 15 EUR. L. REV. 224 (1990). Beier's position was that national intellectual-property rights would, in time, organically grow toward uniformity when exercised in the context of a common market. F. Beier, *The Future of Intellectual Property in Europe: Thoughts on the Development of Patent, Utility Model and Industrial Design Law*, 2 I.I.C. 157 (1991).

[9] See Marenco & Banks, *supra* note 8 (referring to the ECJ's decision in Case 158/86, *Warner Bros., Inc. and Metronome Video, aps v Christiansen*, [1988] ECR 2625, [1990] 3 CMLR 684).

[10] EC Treaty Art. 295 (ex Art. 222) provides, "[t]his Treaty shall in no way prejudice the rules in Member States governing the system of property ownership." Thus,

violation of the free-movement requirements. To reconcile these incompatible aspects of the treaty, the Court of Justice constructed a dichotomy consisting of a difference between the protected existence of intellectual-property rights and their exercise,[11] the latter only being protected from legislative or judicial limitation if, in the particular instance, the exercise could be classified as falling within the specific subject matter of the particular right involved.[12] All other exercises of intellectual-property rights, even those not otherwise violating another aspect of Community law, could be held in contravention of the free-movement requirements. As the Court of Justice has explained:

> Articles [30], [295] and [307][13] of the Treaty . . . do not oppose every impact of Community law on the exercise of national industrial property rights . . . . The

---

national intellectual-property rights, as part of the national system of property ownership, may not, at least in form if not in substance, be prejudiced by Community legislation formulated under the authority of the EC Treaty.

[11] This dichotomy was first used in Cases 56, 58/64, *Etablissements Consten, SA and Grundig-Verkaufs-GmbH v E.E.C. Commission*, [1966] ECR 299, [1966] CMLR 418.

[12] The specific subject matters of trademarks and patents were defined in a pair of pharmaceutical parallel-importation cases as both giving right owners the opportunity to put protected goods on to the market for the first time and providing the owners with an active legal defence against infringers. *See* Case 16/74, *Centrafarm, BV and Adriaan de Peijper v Winthrop, BV*, [1974] ECR 1183, [1974] 2 CMLR 480, ¶ 8; Case 15/74, *Centrafarm, BV and Adriaan de Peijper v Sterling Drug, Inc.*, [1974] ECR 1147, [1974] 2 CMLR 480, ¶ 9. Also, in respect of patents, see Case 434/85, *Allen & Hanburys, Ltd v Generics (U.K.) Ltd*, [1988] ECR 1245, [1988] 1 CMLR 701, ¶¶ 11–13. Design rights received an identical definition in Case 144/81, *Keurkoop, BV v Nancy Keen Gifts, BV*, [1982] ECR 2853, [1983] 2 CMLR 47. The specific subject matter of copyrights is more complicated. It includes both an artistic integrity element and a commercial element. *See* Cases C-92, 326/92, *(Phil) Collins v Imtrat Handelsgesellschaft, mbH*, [1993] ECR I-5145, [1993] 3 CMLR 77, ¶ 20 (citing Cases 55, 57/80, *Musik-Vertrieb Membran, GmbH v GEMA*, [1981] ECR 147, [1981] 2 CMLR 44, ¶ 12, which pointed out that, while the commercial exploitation of copyright is done "particularly" through licenses, this does not lessen the weight of the court's statement that the occurrence of copyright protection "confers" on its owner a *prima facia* right to commercially exploit the underlying work, presumably limited by any applicable laws under which that commercial exploitation would be illegal). *See also* Case T-184/01 R, *IMS Health Inc. v Commission*, [2001] ECR II-3193, ¶ 144 (the Court of First Instance indicated that commercial exploitation of the specific subject matter of copyright was protected by a "clear public interest"). *See also* N. Traver, *Rental Rights and the Specific Subject-matter of Copyright in Community Law*, 24 EUR. L. REV. 280 (1999).

[13] EC Treaty, *supra* note 1, Art. 307 (ex Art. 234) (specifying, among other things, that "rights and obligations . . . between one or more Member States . . . and third countries . . . shall not be affected by the provision of [the] Treaty").

injunction [contained in the Commission's decision] not to use national law relating to trade marks to obstruct parallel imports, without touching the grant of those rights, limits their exercise to the extent necessary for the attainment of the prohibition deriving from Article [81(1)].[14]

The existence–exercise distinction took on its present form in *Deutsche Grammophon v Metro*,[15] but by merely fractionalizing national rights and dividing their existence from their exercise, it did not, in and of itself, eliminate those rights as hindrances to the free movement of goods and to market integration. In response, the Court of Justice adopted the doctrine of the first-sale exhaustion of rights, already in force in one form or another in most Member States.[16] Dyrberg and Pertursson succinctly describe the current legal effects of the doctrine:

> Once the trade marked good has been placed on the market within one Member State of the Community by the trade mark owner or with his consent, he cannot oppose its further commercialization in other States of the Community.[17]

Consensual sales of trademark-protected products within the EU, and by extension the EEA, eliminate the legal basis of the trademark owner's ability to object to the intra-market parallel importation of those products.

The doctrine was incorporated into the Trademarks Directive as part of the

---

[14] *Consten and Grundig, supra* note 11, at 476.

[15] Case 78/70, *Deutsche Grammophon, GmbH v Metro-SB-Grossmärkte, GmbH & Co. KG*, [1971] ECR 487, [1971] CMLR 631, ¶ 11.

[16] *Dansk Supermarked v Imerco, supra* note 3, ¶ 12. A prior expression of the doctrine is found in *Centrafarm v Winthrop, supra* note 12, and Decision 78/696/EEC, *The Community v Arthur Bell and Sons, Ltd*, O.J. 1978, L 235/15, [1978] 3 CMLR 298, ¶ 27. Other, pre-harmonization cases expressing the doctrine include: Case 35/83, *B.A.T. Cigaretten-Fabriken, GmbH v E.C. Commission*, [1985] ECR 363, [1985] 2 CMLR 470, ¶ 35; Case 16/83, *Prantl (Criminal Proceedings Against)*, [1984] ECR 1299, [1985] 2 CMLR 238; Case 7/82, *Gesellschaft zur Verwertung von Leistungsschutzrechten, mbH v E.C. Commission*, [1983] ECR 483, [1983] 3 CMLR 645, ¶ 39; Decision 87/406/EEC, *ISA France Sàrl and M. Visser's Industrie & Handelsonderneming- VIHO, BV v Tipp-EX Vertieb, GmbH & Co. KG*, O.J. 1987, L 222/1, [1989] 4 CMLR 425. See F. Beier & A. von Mühlendahl, *Der Grundsatz der internationalen Erschöpfung des Markenrechts in den Mitgliedstaaten der EG und ausgewählten Drittstaaten*, [1980] 6 MITTEILUNGEN DER DEUTSCHEN PATENTANWÄLTE 101.

[17] P. Dyrberg & G. Petursson, *What is Consent? A Note on Davidoff and Levi Strauss*, EUR. L. REV. 464 (2002). The differences between national, community, and international expressions of the exhaustion of rights are discussed in detail in J. Rasmussen, *The Principle of Exhaustion of Trade Mark Rights Pursuant to Directive 89/104 (and Regulation 40/94)*, 4 E.I.P.R. 174 (1995).

general effort to harmonize the disparate trademark laws of the Member States:[18]

> 1. The trade mark shall not entitle the proprietor to prohibit its use in relation to goods which have been put on the market in the Community under that trade mark by the proprietor or with his consent.
>
> 2. Paragraph 1 shall not apply where there exist legitimate reasons for the proprietor to oppose further commercialisation of the goods, especially where the condition of the goods is changed or impaired after they have been put on the market.[19]

Identical exhaustion provisions were made in respect of the Community trademark in the Trademark Regulation.[20] Similar statements on exhaustion are found in Community legislation on other forms of intellectual property,[21] with the exception of patents.[22]

Whether or not sales outside of the EEA would be effective to exhaust trademark rights within the EEA remained a question until the *Silhouette* case.[23] There, the Court of Justice held national rules allowing for the international exhaustion of trademark rights, because of the possible market-distorting effects

---

[18] First Council Directive (89/104 EEC) of December 21, 1988 [hereinafter the Trademarks Directive]. This was done to approximate the laws of the Member States relating to trademarks. *See* O.J. 1989, L 40/1, February 11, 1989, Art. 7.

[19] Trademark Directive, Art 7.

[20] Council Regulation (EC 40/94) of December 20, 1993, on the Community trade mark, O.J. 1994, L 11/1, January 14, 1994, Art. 13 [hereinafter the Trademark Regulation].

[21] *E.g.*, Directive 2001/29/EC of the European Parliament and of the Council of May 22, 2001 on the harmonization of certain aspects of copyright and related rights in the information society, O.J. 2001, L 167/10, 22 June 2001, Arts 3–4; Council Directive 92/100/EEC of November 19, 1992, on rental right and lending right and on certain rights related to copyright in the field of intellectual property, O.J. 1992, L 346/61, November 27, 1992, Arts 1, 2, 9; Directive 98/71/EC of the European Parliament and of the Council of October 13, 1998 on the legal protection of designs, O.J. 1998, L 289/28, October 28, 1998, Art 15; Council Regulation 6/2002/EC of December 12, 2001 on Community designs, O.J. 2002, L 3/1, January 5, 2002, Art. 21.

[22] While there is no Community legislation on patent exhaustion and national patent laws have not been harmonized, patent rights are exhausted by consensual sales in the Community. Case 35/87, *Thetford Corp. and another v Fiamma, SpA and others*, [1988] ECR 3785, [1988] 3 CMLR 549, ¶¶ 24–5.

[23] Case C-355/96, *Silhouette International Schmied GmbH & Co KG v Hartlauer Handelsgesellschaft mbH*, [1998] ECR I-4799, [1998] 2 CMLR 953, [1998] All E.R. (EC) 769, [1999] Ch. 77, [1998] 3 W.L.R. 1218, ECJ. The issues presented by international exhaustion in a Community context before *Silhouette* are discussed by H. Cohen Jehoram, *International Exhaustion versus Importation Right: A Murky Area of Intellectual Property Law*, 4 G.R.U.R. Int. 280 (1996).

of disparities in national laws on the subject, were incompatible with the harmonizing intention behind the Trademarks Directive.[24] The Court of Justice's decision was based on a concern for the possibility that variations in national exhaustion regimes could create situations in which goods imported from outside of the EEA into a Member State, where intellectual property rights in those goods were deemed to have been exhausted, would then be stopped at the common border of another Member State where the exhaustion regime was more territorially restrictive, defeating the free-movement requirements of the treaty. Goods from an extra-market source, even though physically present within the EEA, are not subject to the requirements of free movement.[25] The market-integration rationale that necessitates the internal exhaustion of rights and allows for parallel trade in otherwise protected goods does [not?] apply to extra-market goods.

In contrast, the competition-law provisions of the EC Treaty do apply extra-jurisdictionally, and to the extent intellectual-property owners seek to prevent parallel importation through actions or inactions that violate the competition-law provisions, their behavior, even that involving parallel goods of extra-market origins, is prohibited.[26] EC Treaty Article 81 (ex 85) prohibits agreements and concerted practices between undertakings that restrict or distort the development of competition within the market.[27] So anticompeti-

---

[24] The *Silhouette* case is discussed by the author in T. Hays & P. Hansen, Silhouette *is not the Proper Case Upon which to Decide the Parallel Importation Question*, E.I.P.R. 277 (1998). *See also* T. Hays, *The* Silhouette *Case: The European Union Moves to the Highest Common Denominator on the Gray Market Question*, 88 T.M.Rep'tr 234 (1998).

[25] Case 51/75, *EMI Records Ltd v CBS United Kingdom Ltd*, [1976] ECR 811, [1976] 2 CMLR 235.

[26] Case C-306/96, *Javico Int'l and Javico AG v Yves Saint Laurent Parfums, SA*, [1998] ECR I-1983, [1998] 5 CMLR 172. *But see, Hewlett-Packard Development Co. LP v Expansys UK, Ltd*, [2005] EWHC 1495 (Ch D, Laddie, J) (dismissing the parallel importer's defence based on the claimant brand owner's alleged Art. 82 (ex 86) EC dominance).

[27] Concerted practices were defined in Cases 89/85, etc., *Re Wood Pulp Cartel: A. Ahlström Oy and others v E.C. Commission*, [1993] 4 CMLR 407, ¶ 63. The Court stated:

> Co-ordination between undertakings which, without having been taken to the stage where an agreement properly so-called has been concluded, knowingly substitutes for the risks of competition practical co-operation between them.

A discussion of the complex operation of Art. 81 is beyond the scope of the present discussion. *See generally* S. Anderman, EC Competition Law and Intellectual Property Rights: The Regulation of Innovation 14.3–14.4 (1998). In regard to extra-market parallel goods, see T. Hays, *An Application of the European Rules on*

tive do the Community courts and the Commission consider efforts at frustrating intra-market parallel imports, those efforts are near-automatic violations of Article 81, even when carried out through otherwise exempt selective distribution systems.[28] However, the existence of an Article 81 violation requires an agreement, or its equivalent, between undertakings. In the absence of such an agreement, the use of intellectual-property rights to repel parallel goods from outside the market is a permissible exercise of those rights.[29]

Trademark Exhaustion to Extra-market Goods, 91 T.M.REP'TR 675 (2001), addressing the parallel distribution of extra-market perfumes in the Netherlands. In regard to intra-market goods, see V. Korah, *Dividing the Common Market through National Industrial Property Rights*, 35 MODERN L. REV. 634 (1972); V. Korah, *Recent Developments in European Competition and IP Law – A More Economic Orientation?*, Proceedings of the Fordham Ninth Annual Conference on International Intellectual Property Law & Policy, April 19–20, 2001.

[28] Case C-70/93, *Bayerische Motorenwerke AG v Ald Auto-Leasing D, GmbH*, [1995] ECR I-3439, [1996] 4 CMLR 478 (illustrating concept in the context of automobiles); Case C-279/87, *Tipp-ex, GmbH & Co. KG v E.C. Commission*, [1990] ECR I-261; Cases 100–103/80, *Musique Diffusion Française, SA, C. Melchers & Co., Pioneer Electronic (Europe) NV and Pioneer High Fidelity (GB) Ltd v E.C. Commission*, [1983] ECR 1825, [1983] 3 CMLR 221; Case 28/77, *Tepea BV v E.C. Commission*, [1978] ECR 1391, [1978] 3 CMLR 392. This is the position of the Commission. *See* Decision 87/409/EEC, *Community v Sandoz Prodotti Farmaceutici, Spa*, O.J. 1987, L 222/28, [1988] 4 CMLR 628; Decision 98/273/EC, *Community v Volkswagen, AG and others*, O.J. 1998, L 124/60, [1998] 5 CMLR 33. It is also the position of at least some national competition authorities. *See Importarzneimittel-Boykott*, Kart. 22/92, November 26, 1993, WuW 1994, 557; WuW/E O.L.G. 5241 (Berlin Court of Appeals); Commission Decision 781130, *Tanabe Seiyaku Co. v Bayer, AG*, November 30, 1978, [1979] 2 CMLR 80, ¶ 7. With the exception of cases involving new plant varieties, as in Case 258/78, *Nungesser (L.C.) KG and Kurt Eisele v E.C. Commission*, [1982] ECR 2015, [1983] 1 CMLR 278, there is no need to make a distinction between forms of intellectual-property protection. *Musik-Vertrieb Membran v GEMA*, *supra* note 12, ¶ 11–12. The now-dated work, V. KORAH & W. ROTHNIE, EXCLUSIVE DISTRIBUTION AND THE EEC COMPETITION RULES (2nd ed. 1992) describes the origins of the Community's position on intellectual-property-protected goods in selective distribution systems under the earlier versions of Regulation 17 and the relevant block exemptions. In respect of types of selectively distributed products not discussed here, see F. Murray & J. MacLennan, *The Future of Selective Distribution Systems: The CFI Judgments on Luxury Perfume and the Commission Green Paper on Vertical Restraints*, 4 EUR. COMP. L. REV. 230 (1997).

[29] *See, e.g.*, Case C-173/98, *Sebago, Inc. and Ancienne Maison Dubois et Fils, SA v G-B Unic, SA*, [1999] 2 CMLR 1317. Since goods from outside of the EEA market do not receive free-movement protection, unilateral actions to keep those goods out of the market by Community-based intellectual-property owners are permitted. See also, *Sportsware Co. SpA v Stonestyle Ltd.*, [2006] EWCA 380, CA (Civ. Div), where the Court of Appeals held that a defendant's allegation of a violation of Art. 81 by a trademark owner through the assertion of trademark rights could be both a claim and a defense to the infringement complaint, reversing a grant of summary judgment for the

An exception to the permissibility of unilateral activity in the enforcement of intellectual-property rights exists under Article 82 of the treaty, prohibiting the abuse of a dominant position by one or more undertakings. Such abuse can occur when the commercial strength of the legal monopoly created through intellectual-property rights is so great as to result in a near or complete commercial monopoly, as defined by the lack of available substitutes.[30] It is the effect of the lack of necessary precursors on subsequent, downstream markets that offends the competition rules.[31] Intellectual-property rights, giving their owners the exclusivity that creates the scarceness of substitutes that in turn supports the generally higher prices of protected goods, can create dominant positions.[32] The licensing of the intellectual property creating such dominance would alleviate the scarcity associated with exclusivity based on intellectual-property control, and while a refusal to license is not, in itself, an abuse of a dominant position,[33] a refusal to license combined with other anticompetitive behavior,[34] such as

---

trademark owner in *Sportsware Co. SpA v Sarbeet Ghattaura*, [2005] EWHC 2081 (Ch D, Warren J).

[30] *See, e.g.,* Joined Cases C-241–242/91, *Radio Telefis Eireann (RTE) and Independent Television Publications, Ltd v E.C. Commission*, [1995] ECR 808, [1995] 4 CMLR 718 (*Magill*). See also Case T-184/01 R, *IMS Health Inc. v Commission*, [2001] ECR II-3193, where copyright and database control over drug-prescription information was found not to create a dominant position. This is discussed in A. Narciso, *IMS Health or the Question whether Intellectual Property still Deserves a Specific Approach in a Free Market Economy*, 4 I.P.Q. 445–68 (2003).

[31] The existence of a dominant position is fundamental to the existence of an Article 82 violation. Whether such a position exists often turns on whether one product is an acceptable substitute for another. *See* Decision 22/78, *Hugin Kassaregister, AB and Hugin Cash Registers, Ltd v E.C. Commission*, O.J. 1978, L 22/23, [1978] 1 CMLR D19, [1979] ECR 1869, [1979] 3 CMLR 345 (discussing the determination of a substitution under Art. 82). *See also* Case T-83/91, *Tetra Pak International, SA v E.C. Commission*, [1994] ECR II-755; Commission Decision 88/501/EEC, *Elopak v Tetra Pak*, O.J. 1988, L 272/27, [1990] 4 CMLR 47; Commission Decision 94/19/EC, *Sea Containers v Stena Sealink: Interim Measures*, O.J. 1994, L 15/8, [1995] 4 CMLR 84. These cases can be traced to the Essential Facilities Doctrine, first formulated in the United States in *United States v Terminal R.R. Assoc.*, 224 U.S. 383 (1912), and incorporated into European Union law in Cases 6-7/73, *Commercial Solvents v E.C. Commission*, [1974] ECR 223, [1974] 1 CMLR 309, earning the line of reasoning presented by these decisions the alternative title: the Commercial Solvents Doctrine.

[32] Case T-30/89, *Hilti, AG v Commission*, [1991] ECR II-1439, [1992] 4 CMLR 16.

[33] Case 238/87, *Volvo, AB v Erik Veng (U.K.) Ltd*, [1988] ECR 6211, [1989] 4 CMLR 122, ¶ 8.

[34] See Case 226/84, *British Leyland, plc v Commission*, [1986] ECR 3263, [1987] 1 CMLR 185, where the failure to maintain road-worthiness certification for a variety of automobile that was subject to parallel importation, making the parallel-

price fixing, can be abusive.³⁵ In such circumstances, the competition laws imply a duty on a dominant undertaking to grant licenses on reasonable terms³⁶ where the failure to license would frustrate the development of secondary-market competition.³⁷

It would seem that cases involving patent protection, generating the greatest degree of technological exclusivity, would be the most likely venue for the application of Article 82 in the context of intellectual property,³⁸ and that cases involving trademark protection, possessing the least amount of exclusivity and not limiting substitution in any technological way, would not support a finding of dominance. However, brand appeal is so powerful, at least in the context of bananas, that trademark-based control over a popular brand can give rise to a dominant position where consumers would not consider a nearly identical product without the brand to be a substitute for the branded variety.³⁹

---

imported automobiles unmarketable, was held to be abusive on the part of the manufacturer. The manufacturer faired better in Denmark, where the Supreme Court held that while the manufacturer could not stop the parallel importation of spare parts through invoking its intellectual-property rights, it could stop the parallel importer from using its trademark in advertising where the public might be misled into believing the parallel importer was one of the manufacturer's authorized dealers. *Lindebjerg Car Parts v/Ib Lindebjerb Larsen v British Leyland Ltd and Domi A/S*, (September 13, 1983) (U1983.923 H).

35   *Volvo v Veng, supra* note 33, ¶ 9.

36   In *Intel Corp. (USA) v VIA Technologies and others* [2002] E.W.C.A. Civ. 1905, [2002] All ER (D) 346, ¶ 87, the court held a license, which was on terms that were so demanding the licensee could not reasonably be expected to accept them, was not an offer to license, to make the product available, for Art. 82 purposes.

37   For a case finding that a dominant position existed, see *Intel Corp. (USA) v VIA Technologies, supra.* note 36 (concerning protected topographies). For a case finding that a dominant position did not exist, see Case C-7/97, *Oscar Bronner, GmbH & Co., KG v Mediaprint Zeitungs-und Zeitschriftenverlag, GmbH & Co. KG*, [1998] ECR I-7791, [1999] 4 CMLR 112 (concerning access to a newspaper delivery network); Case T-504/93, *Tiercé Ladbroke v E.C. Commission*, [1997] ECR II-923, [1997] 5 CMLR 309 (concerning access to French horseracing broadcasts). It is difficult to draw definite rules from the case law. It well may be that the determination of the degree of dominance and the availability of substitutes is adjusted in each case to include or exclude anticompetitive behaviors.

38   To date, the majority of cases involving Art. 82 violations in regards to a refusal to license intellectual-property rights have been based on copyright.

39   Case 27/76, *United Brands Co. and United Brands Continental, BV v Commission*, [1978] ECR 207, [1978] 1 CMLR 429. In that case, the brand owner prevented the Danish wholesaler from purchasing the preferred bananas in Germany for parallel importing to Denmark; that was the anticompetitive act. See the discussion of the *United Brands* case in the larger context of inter-state trade in R. Burnley, *Interstate Trade Revisited – The Jurisdictional Criterion for Articles 81 and 82 EC*, 23 EUR. COMP. L. REV. 217, 220 (2002).

The implications of the application of Article 82 are significant, particularly in the case of pharmaceuticals, where patent protection may eliminate the substitutability of one drug for another, and consumer bias in favor of branded pharmaceuticals over generic varieties increases the ability of intellectual-property proprietors to regulate indirectly the trade in parallel-imported drugs. As is the case with Article 81, Article 82 applies to extra-market parallel imports.[40]

II. The nature of parallel trade

The commercial issues raised by parallel importation are those of both price and control. The differences in prices between markets allow for the arbitrage that makes parallel trading profitable. This trade is to be expected in the approximately free-market economy of the European Economic Area (EEA),[41] where the price-leveling effects of buying, transporting, and reselling are restricted for most goods only by the transactional costs – at some level dependent on the circumstances of individual parallel traders themselves – which make trading less profitable, and by government-imposed regulations intended, at least incidentally, to promote some greater public interest.

Distributors impose control over their products in several ways and at different levels in the commercial arrangements through which those products are traded as a means of protecting and promoting brand image, supporting higher prices, focusing distribution, and insuring pre- and post-sale technical support. The foremost mechanism of imposing control over the reselling of those sorts of goods susceptible to parallel trading is through the enforcement of intellectual-property rights. Because these government-granted rights are applicable in some form to nearly any product sold in a container,[42] they are the most widely used passive tools with which manufacturers regulate the reselling of their products.[43] The primary active means of exercising control is

---

[40] Case T-18/98, *Micro Leader Business v E.C. Commission*, [1999] ECR II-3989, [2000] 4 CMLR 886.

[41] The EEA is comprised of the 25 European Union countries plus Iceland, Norway, Lichtenstein, and Switzerland, forming the European Free Trade Association. It was created by the EEA Treaty, O.J. 1984, L 1/3, [1992] 1 CMLR 921.

[42] Even the most fungible products, such as sugar or potatoes, otherwise undifferentiated from ostensibly identical products originating from other sources, may benefit from intellectual property protection, such as that afforded by trademarks applied to packaging.

[43] In the context of parallel importation, intellectual property rights, while actively employed by their owners to the extent of licensing agreements, are passive in the sense that it is the general, passive threat of infringement suits that is used to deter unauthorized distribution and to further the commercialization of protected goods, rather than specific, current legal actions against particular parallel importers.

through selective or exclusive distribution systems. The purpose of these systems is to direct the distribution of goods, whether protected by intellectual property rights or not, to specific destinations under the circumstances and at the prices most favorable to manufacturers.

How these distribution systems operate depends on the types of goods they distribute. What is permissible selectivity within the context of the distribution of one product may not be permissible in relation to another.[44] Product characteristics also affect the occurrence of parallel trade. Small, easily transportable goods are more readily the subject of parallel trading than are large, bulky products, apart from those, like automobiles, that can transport themselves.[45]

Objective values[46] also influence the likelihood of parallel trade in particular

---

[44] See Case 75/84, *Metro-SB-Großmärkte, GmbH & Co. KG v E.C. Commission*, [1986] ECR 3201, [1987] 1 CMLR 118, and the line of cases following that decision. For cases before the European Court of Justice (ECJ), see e.g., Case 107/82, *Allgemeine Elektricitäts-Gesellschaft (AEG) Telefunken, AG v E.C. Commission* [1983] ECR 3151, [1984] 3 CMLR 325; Case 210/81, *Demo-Studio Schmidt v E.C. Commission*, [1983] ECR 3045, [1984] 1 CMLR 63; Case 126/80, *Salonia v Giorgio Poidonmani and Franca Baglieri*, [1981] ECR 1563, [1982] 1 CMLR 64; Case 31/80, *L'Oréal, NV and L'Oréal, SA v De Nieuwe A.M.C.K. Pvba*, [1980] ECR 3775, [1981] 2 CMLR 235. For cases before the Court of First Instance (CFI), see Case T-19, *Groupement d'Achat Édouard Leclerc v E.C. Commission*, [1996] ECR II-1851, [1997] 4 CMLR 995; Case T-19/91, *Société d'Hygiène Dermatologique de Vichy v E.C. Commission*, [1992] ECR II-415.

[45] Parallel trading in automobiles is of two parts: the distribution of new, complete automobiles and the distribution of new and reconditioned parts. Impediments to this parallel trade include several intellectual-property rights, both singularly and in combination, and, as is the case with most categories of parallel goods, national governmental regulations, which increase price differences between Member States. See e.g., Commission Reg. (EC) No. 2790/1999 of December 22, 1999 on the application of Art. 81(3) of the Treaty to categories of vertical agreements and concerted practices. O.J. 1999, L 336/21; *Lindebjerg Car Parts v/Ib Lindebjerb Larsen v British Leyland Ltd and Domi A/S*, supra note 34.

[46] The objective value of goods is the intrinsic money equivalent represented by the particular product, independent of any subjective enhancing factor, such as transitory consumer demand or supply shortages. The best estimate of the objective value of most goods is their replacement value. Gold, with a market value of, for example, 100 for a given quantity, has a replacement value and, by extension, an objective value of 100 for that quantity. Other products with market values of given amounts have various replacement values: a wrist watch with a market value of 100 could, perhaps, be replaced with a functional equivalent at the cost of 50. Most pharmaceuticals can be manufactured at a cost that is a small fraction of their market values. A musical recording has an objective value approximately equal to the value of the medium on which the recording is made. Replacement costs, as used here, do not include research and development costs or the enhanced value of a product due to the legal exclusivity of its

goods: gold bullion, with an absolute objective value, is not parallel traded; precision wrist watches, with some objective value, are subject to a low level of parallel trade; pharmaceuticals, digital recordings and perfumes, having relatively low objective values, are subject to the highest levels of parallel trade.[47] Objective values reflect the marginal cost of goods plus various price-enhancing factors, like those related to convenience and increased distribution, such as would be tolerated by a rational purchaser; minus subjective factors such as brand allure, perceived exclusivity, and the herd instinct in buyers. This estimation – and it is used here only as that, an estimation – relies more heavily on the assumption that consumers take a rational approach to purchasing than it does on behavioral analysis of why individuals make various choices. Certainly, individual behaviors, which are often irrational, influence purchases and prices,[48] but it is possible, at least at the level of the Community-wide market, to fuse both rationalist and behaviorist explanations of why people buy at various prices;[49] the greater macroeconomic numbers averaging out of significance individual microeconomic peculiarities, to produce a rough model of the market where individual irrationality is subsumed by the overall commercial context in which individuals operate.[50]

As a general rule, the lower the objective value of a product and the higher the portion of the retail-market value attributable to subjective consumer demand generated by the perceived allure and exclusivity of that product[51] – that allure and exclusivity being generated, to a degree, and enforced by intel-

---

manufacture resultant from intellectual-property protection, though Posner has questioned why this should be so. R. POSNER, ECONOMIC ANALYSIS OF LAW 38 (4th ed. 1992).

[47] See P. Kanavos, D. Gross, & D. Taylor, *Parallel Trading in Medicines: Europe's Experience and its Implications for Commercial Drug Importation in the United States* 6 Washington AARP (2005) (citing relevant authorities) [hereinafter *Parallel Trading in Medicines*]. Available at www.aarp.org/research/health/drugs/2005_07_trade.html (last viewed August 8, 2007).

[48] As described by R. HOGARTH & M REDER, (EDS) RATIONAL CHOICE: THE CONTRAST BETWEEN ECONOMICS AND PSYCHOLOGY vii (1987) [hereinafter HOGARTH & REDER, RATIONAL CHOICE].

[49] See V. Smith, *Rational Choice: The Contrast between Economics and Psychology*, 4 J. POLITICAL ECON. 877–97 (1991).

[50] See K. Arrow, *Rationality of Self and Others in an Economic System*, in HOGARTH & REDER RATIONAL CHOICE, *supra* note 48, p 201 ("Rationality is not a property of the individual alone . . . It gathers not only its force but also its very meaning from the social context in which it is imbedded.").

[51] This effect was described by and named for T. VEBLEN, THE THEORY OF THE LEISURE CLASS (1899). See also S. LEA, R. TARPY, & P. WEBLEY, THE INDIVIDUAL IN THE ECONOMY (1987).

lectual property protection – the more likely the product is to be the subject of parallel trading.[52]

III. The market for parallel goods

Parallel importing, the unauthorized movement of goods between national markets, is made possible by price differences between markets. For example, most (but not all) consumer goods are expensive in Denmark, and Denmark is, therefore, a target country for parallel trade.[53] The sources of parallel goods – apart from those semi-autonomous undertakings operating within the distribution networks of manufacturers in higher-priced markets, who sell goods into parallel trade in contravention of the manufacturer's instructions and their licensing agreements – are located in lower-priced markets. Different countries provide supplies of lower-priced goods, depending on the goods under consideration. For example, the Netherlands is a lower-priced market for automobiles than is the United Kingdom; the United Kingdom is a lower-priced market for pharmaceuticals than is the Netherlands.

The level of regional economic development and the restrictiveness of national governmental policies are the two factors that have the greatest influence over the prices for particular products in particular countries. Other factors influencing price differences within the EEA market include cultural tastes and preferences, geographical distances and the associated costs of transporting goods from the place of production, and technical requirements, such as electric current voltages and frequencies. Combinations of these factors relative to particular products determine whether a Member State is a source or a target country for parallel trading. The Iberian countries, because of relatively lower levels of economic development and governmental regulation, are source

---

[52] This interpretation of the relationship between objective values and parallel trading is supported by the findings contained in the NERA Report, discussed *infra* text accompanying notes 56–9. Those findings are not as helpful as one might wish, as the report is lacking a detailed statement of the methodology used for collecting and collating the statistic for the parallel trading that is the subject of the report. Also, the NERA Report was made for the inherently political purpose of studying the likely effects of a change in exhaustion of rights regimes, rather than for purely analytical purposes of quantifying the occurrence of existing parallel trade. Where the report is generally useful to support otherwise observable trends in the legal relationships affected by parallel trading, it is referred to here. Otherwise, the NERA Report falls outside the scope of the present discussion.

[53] *See Orifarm, A/S v Astra/Zeneca, AB* (January 4, 2002) (U2002.696 H); *Lancaster Group, GmbH v Parfume Discount Sjaelland, ApS* (June 18, 2001) (U2001.2105 S); *Pfizer Int'l, Inc. v Durascan Medical Products, A/S* (U1996.1309 H); *Glaxo, Plc v GEA* (U1993.859 H); *Den Kongelige Porcelænsfabrik A/S v Jytte Kondrup* (February 7, 1979) (U1979.593 SH).

countries for many parallel-imported products.[54] On the other hand, the Scandinavian countries, because of their higher levels of economic development and various governmental policies, generally are target countries for parallel imports. Higher consumer prices in northern Europe are a portion of the price differences within the overall EEA market that make intra-market parallel trading an ongoing, profitable industry.[55]

Qualitative considerations do not indicate the commercial importance of parallel importation within the market. Attempts at quantifying that importance have been only partially successful.[56] The drafters of the NERA Report found there was a large volume of parallel trade in musical recordings, cosmetics, and perfumes.[57] That same report indicated intermediate levels of parallel trade in the clothing and soft-drinks markets and only small levels of parallel trade in the other product sectors surveyed, including that for automobiles.[58] The NERA Report, inexplicably, did not survey the pharmaceuticals sector.[59]

---

[54] This includes products such as automobiles, Case 226/84, *British Leyland, plc v E.C. Commission*, [1986] ECR 3263, [1987] 1 CMLR 185, and pharmaceuticals, Case 187/80, *Merck & Co Inc v Stephar BV and Petrus Staphanus Exler*, [1981] ECR 2063, [1981] 3 CMLR 463; Joined Cases C-267 & 268/95, *Merck & Co., Inc. and others v Primecrown Ltd and others*, [1996] ECR I-6285, [1997] 1 CMLR 83.

[55] Unless otherwise specified, the market referred to in this discussion is the free-trade area created by the European Free Trade Association through the EEA Treaty. There are judicial reasons – particularly in the context of rights exhaustion, as described below – for differentiating between the European Union market and the larger EEA market. See the ongoing differences of opinion represented by Case E-2/97, *Mag Instrument Inc v California Trading Co Norway, Ulsteen*, [1997] Report of the EFTA Court 129, [1998] 1 CMLR 331; Case E-1/98, *Norwegian Government, represented by the Royal Ministry of Social Affairs and Health v Astra Narge, AS*, [1998] Report of the EFTA Court, [1999] 1 CMLR 860, described in detail by Rasmussen, *supra* note 17, noting the retained independence of the EFTA member countries in respect of international trade arrangements. *See also* Case E-3/02, *Paranova A/S v Merck & Co, Inc and others*, Judgment of the EFTA Court, July 8, 2003.

[56] *See* National Economic Research Associates and others, *The Economic Consequences of the Choice of a Regime of Exhaustion in the Area of Trade Marks: Final Report for DGXV of the European Commission*, (February 1999) [hereinafter the NERA Report], concluding that the Community should not adopt a policy of recognizing the global exhaustion of IP rights on the occurance of an authorized first sale anywhere in the world.

[57] *Id.* at Table 4.2, "Extent of Current Parallel Trade within the EU." The drafters of the NERA Report considered parallel trading of over 10% of total product sales to be a large level of parallel trading. Between 5% and 10% of total sales was considered an intermediate level, and less than 5% was considered a small level of parallel trading.

[58] *Id.*

[59] A now-dated report, "Impediments to Parallel Trade in Pharmaceuticals

IV. The effect of Community interpretations on national laws

The treatment of parallel importation under the provisions of Community law is made more complicated when it occurs in the context of national-court litigation. That treatment commonly has required only the reconciliation of one or two sets of Community law – such as free-movement principles or the competition prohibitions – with the laws of the jurisdictions in which such litigation has taken place. The impact of parallel importation disputes on national laws has been mostly superficial.

However, where parallel importation has raised more fundamental issues – like that of the giving or the withholding of consent for the further commercialization of protected products after a volitional first sale, an issue on which the laws of the Member States have differed and on which the EC Treaty and its subordinate legislation are silent – the resolution of the conflicts of laws has called for substantial jurisprudence from the Court of Justice. For example, the issue of consent for resale of once-protected products was addressed in the United Kingdom,[60] where, under national law of over 100-years standing, consent for resale in the form of an incidental license could be implied from the purchase of trademark-protected goods, unless that license was specifically withheld at the time of sale.[61] This is one approach in a spectrum of legal

---

within the European Community," prepared by REMIT Consultants for the European Commission, specifically considered the intra-market parallel importation of pharmaceuticals, but the report is unhelpful in quantifying parallel trade in some countries, such as Denmark, the first sales of parallel drugs in Denmark having occurred only a few months before the report was published. The levels of parallel pharmaceutical trading predicted in the REMIT Report were subsequently corroborated by other sources. See the figures in agreement given in J. Barker, *Parallel Importing Strategies*, Scrip Report (Richmond, Surrey: PJB Publications, 1998); J. Barker, *Parallel Pharmaceutical Distribution 2000: A Pan-European Perspective*, Scrip Report (Richmond, Surrey: PJB Publications, 2000); *Parallel Trading in Medicines*, *supra* note 47.

[60] *Zino Davidoff, SA v A&G Imports, Ltd*, [1999] 3 All E.R. 711, HC.

[61] *See Betts v Wilmott*, (1871) LR 6 Ch App 239, LC. The English construction is that consent for resale is implied. The doctrine of implied consent, while conceptually distinct from the Continental doctrine of the exhaustion of rights upon a first sale, yields approximately the same result. Under the English construction, the intellectual-property rights survive the first sale of protected goods but become subject to an implied license for resale that passes with the goods from one purchaser to the next, allowing each subsequent purchaser to freely commercialize the goods in question. Under the exhaustion-of-rights doctrine, the intellectual property rights in the subject goods are extinguished upon the conclusion of the first sale, allowing each subsequent purchaser to freely commercialize the goods.

The only practical difference is that, under English law, subsequent purchasers, perhaps far removed from the original seller/intellectual property owner, could still be subject to an infringement action, the intellectual-property rights in the goods in question

constructions in the national laws of the Member States concerning the relationship between a seller and a buyer of protected goods and the effects of a sale on the rights of the owner of the intellectual property incorporated in those goods.[62]

Another approach is represented by the national laws of Germany, where consent for resale of protected goods is deemed not to have been given at the time of the first sale of those goods unless the consent was expressed by the intellectual property owner.[63] The laws on consent for resale in the other Member States come somewhere between these two interpretations.

The issue of when and how consent for further commercialization could be implied, if at all, from a first sale of protected goods was decided by the Court of Justice in *Zino Davidoff v A&G Imports*.[64] The court held that consent, if not expressly given at the time of the first sale of protected goods, could only be implied if the seller's intention to give consent was "unequivocally demonstrated."[65] This holding could be perceived, and has been by some commentators, as the elevation of civilian law over the legal systems of common law in England and the Scandinavian countries. But the conflict was never joined. The German construction of how consent could be implied, the construction that most closely mirrors that adopted by the Court of Justice, was formulated in a legal environment that had previously acknowledged the global exhaustion of intellectual property rights after a volitional first sale.[66] German law

---

still being in existence and the implied-consent doctrine only giving subsequent purchaser-defendants an implied license as a defense. First-sale exhaustion is the stronger doctrine. Where the relevant intellectual-property rights are exhausted, no cause of action is possible. See the defendants' arguments in respect of their motions to dismiss the infringement actions against them in *Silhouette International Schmied GmbH & Co KG v Hartlauer Handelsgesellschaft mbH*, Supreme Court of Austria, September 28, 1998, [1999] 3 CMLR 267; *Parfums Christian Dior, SA v Etos, BV*, Case number 98/950, cause list number 97/1260, Appeals Court of the Hague, February 15, 2000; *Van Doren + Q v Lifestyle Sports*, supra note 3.

[62] The implied-consent doctrine is limited to the jurisdiction of the courts of England and Wales. It has now been replaced by the ECJ construction. See *Hewlett-Packard Development Co. LLP v Expansys UK, Ltd*, supra note 26; *Kabushiki Kaisha Sony Computer Ent. v Nuplayer Ltd*, [2005] EWHC 1522 (Ch D, Collins, J).

[63] See generally N. FOSTER & S. SULE, GERMAN LEGAL SYSTEM & LAWS 369–70, 383–90 (Oxford: OUP, 3rd ed. 2002); *Simmenthal v S. A. Import*, 1 ZR 291/91, 22 April 1994, Federal Court of Justice, Germany, [1994] G.R.U.R. 512.

[64] Joined Cases C-414–416/99, *Zino Davidoff, SA v A&G Imports, Ltd; Levi Strauss & Co. and Levi Strauss (UK) Ltd v Tesco Stores, Tesco plc, and Costco Wholesale UK Ltd*, [2001] ECR I-8691, [2002] 1 CMLR 1 [hereinafter *Davidoff*].

[65] *Id.*, ¶ 45.

[66] German law, prior to amendments intended to accommodate the Community-law concerns, considered a volitional sale of protected goods anywhere in the world to exhaust the relevant intellectual-property proprietor's ability to control the further commercialization of those goods. C. Heath, *Parallel Imports and International Trade*, 5 I.I.C. 623 (1997).

did not need a doctrine of implied consent to achieve the same freedom of alienability of protected goods as did English law. That freedom was achieved through the application of the exhaustion-of-rights doctrine.

Like the decision in *Silhouette*, the court's decision in *Davidoff* was based on an apprehension of the effects of differing national laws on the commercial mobility of goods within the market. Without an indigenous exhaustion-of-rights doctrine, the common-law system achieved the desired mobility by implying a license for resale through contract law – consent for resale being fundamentally an issue of the law of obligations. The holding in *Davidoff* did more than require one Member State to alter how a sale exhausts trademark rights: it forced a partial harmonization of contract law without a legislative mandate to do so. This sort of creeping harmonization can be expected to have significant consequences for the contract laws of the Member States, where those laws have been formulated over centuries as coherent bodies of commercial law. The forced reinterpretation of one part, as in the case of consent, has collateral effects on other interdependent aspects of the whole.

The issue of the proof of consent for the resale of extra-market parallel goods provides an example of this collateral destabilization of national substantive laws resultant from attempts at accommodating Community law. In most wholesale supply transactions, the relevant intellectual property owners and the eventual retailers of parallel goods are separated from each other by various commercial events. No dispute would be possible if the retailers involved in a particular case of parallel importation were the direct purchasers of protected goods from the owner of the intellectual property in those goods or the owner's licensee in the EEA market. If a sale takes place within the market, then the exhaustion doctrine would apply, as any economically related affiliate of an intellectual property right owner can give the consent for protected goods to be put into free circulation within the market.[67]

On the other hand, if a sale were to take place outside of the market, then the issue of whether consent for the resale of the goods within the market has been given could be decided on the terms of that sale, but the consent would have to be given by the owner of the applicable intellectual property rights in the Community, not by some economic affiliate, even a subsidiary of the rights owner, if operating outside of the market.[68] Thus, there are two rules for

---

[67] *Deutsche Grammophon v Metro*, *supra* note 15; *Doncaster Pharmaceuticals Group Ltd & others v Bolton Pharmaceuticals Co. 100 Ltd*, [2006] EWCA 661, CA (Civ Div) (dealing with pharmaceuticals from Spain).

[68] See *Roche Products Ltd & another v Kent Pharmaceuticals Ltd*, [2006] EWHC 335 (Ch D, Lewison, J) (pharmaceuticals from the Dominican Republic); *Sun Microsystems Inc v Amtec Computer Corp. Ltd*, [2006] EWHC 62 (Ch D, Warren, J) (computers from Israel); *Honda Motor Co. Ltd v Neesam and others*, [2006] EWHC

who can give consent sufficient to exhaust trademark rights and place products in free circulation within the EEA: (1) the lower standard, for goods already in the market, where any economic affiliate of the right owner can give consent, and (2) a much higher standard for goods to be imported into the market.

Clear relationships between plaintiffs and defendants are almost never the case in parallel-importation-based infringement litigation. In the vast majority of these cases, the defendant claims to have obtained the parallel goods within the EEA from sources at least indirectly related to the intellectual property owner's own distribution system. The plaintiff intellectual-property owner claims the goods were imported from outside the market and that no consent for their importation had ever been given.[69]

The question for the courts becomes that of who should bear the burden of proving the source of the parallel goods and along with it consent for further commercialization of the goods within the EEA. Under the procedural laws of the various Member States, a defendant to an infringement action bears the burden of proving an affirmative defense, such as the existence of exhaustion or consent. But, if the chain of selling and reselling from the manufacturer to the defendant is long, with many links in the chain of distribution hidden or lost entirely, the burden may be impossible to carry, even for products whose commercial histories can be surmised with a degree of accuracy but for which an admissible chain of documentary or testamentary evidence is unavailable. Furthermore, and of the most importance to the Community courts, a defendant's efforts in proving the history of particular batches of goods would reveal the disloyal link in an intellectual property owner's distribution system responsible for putting the goods into parallel circulation and arguably subjecting that source to retaliation by the intellectual-property owner. These facts and the concern for maintaining sources of supplies of parallel goods have given rise to the exotic construction of shifting burdens of proof in *Van Doren + Q*,[70] where a defendant can refuse to meet a legitimate discovery request, seeking to uncover a source of parallel goods, on the grounds of protecting that source from retaliation and maintaining the source of supply for the future.[71]

1051 (Ch D, Lewison, J) (motorcycles from Australia); *Mastercigars Direct Ltd v Hunters & Frankau Ltd*, [2006] EWHC 410 (Ch D, Judge Fysh, QC) (cigars from Cuba); *Kabushiki Kaisha Sony Computer Ent. v Nuplayer, supra* note 62 (game consoles from Japan).

[69] These were the arguments in Case C-173/98, *Sebago Inc. and Ancienne Maison Dubois et Fils SA v G-B Unic SA*, [1999] ECR I-4103, [1999] 2 CMLR 1317.

[70] *Van Doren + Q, supra* note 3.

[71] The shifting burdens of proof now in force in the Community and the *Van Doren + Q* case are discussed in detail in T. Hays, Parallel Importation under European Union Law (2003).

This demonstrates how parallel-importation disputes and the forced harmonization used by the Community courts to address those disputes move from primary questions of Community law, the EC Treaty Article 234 remit of the Court of Justice – such as the application of the free-movement requirements and the doctrine of right-exhaustion to the importation and resale of extra-market parallel imports – to secondary questions of substantive national law – such as how consent is given, implied, or withheld. The disputes then develop into tertiary questions of national procedural law – such as who, in an infringement action involving allegedly extra-market parallel goods, bears the burden of proof. The penetration of harmonization into national laws through questions concerning free movement and parallel importation referred to the Court of Justice under Article 234 appears to be unlimited, as does the amount of parallel importation litigation before the national courts.

This progression of harmonization is not limited to cases involving the reselling of extra-market goods. Cases of the parallel trade in entirely intra-market goods demonstrate a similar expansion of Community legal principles in what have previously been considered areas of exclusively national-law competence. The issues raised by the parallel trade in pharmaceuticals has been extended to allow for the unauthorized re-labeling of branded pharmaceuticals, and further, to unauthorized repackaging[72] and re-branding of pharmaceuticals where necessary to effectuate the free movement of the goods in question.[73]

These considerations are not limited to highly regulated products like medicines. They apply in only slightly modified form to automobile and film distribution, and to royalty-collecting societies and trade associations. The conflict between the rights of intellectual property proprietors – whether of trademarks, copyrights, designs, or patents – and parallel traders serves as a forum for the judicial implementation of remedies designed to meet the greater needs of market integration. This raises the more fundamental jurisprudential question: should the growth of national laws governing intellectual property

---

[72] Joined Cases C-427/93, 429/93 and 436/93, *Bristol-Myers Squibb and others v Paranova, AS*, [1996] ECR I-3457, [1997] 1 CMLR 1151.

[73] See the interpretations in *Bristol-Myers Squibb v Paranova, id.*; Case C-379/97, *Pharmacia & Upjohn, SA v Paranova, A/S*, [1999] ECR I-6927, [1999] All E.R. (EC) 880, [2000] 1 CMLR 51; Case 1/81, *Pfizer Inc. v Eurim-Pharm, GmbH*, [1981] ECR 2913, [1982] 1 CMLR 406; Case 107/76, *Hoffmann–La Roche, AG v Centrafarm Vertriebsgellschaft Pharmazeutischer Erzeugnisse, mbH*, [1977] ECR 957, [1977] 2 CMLR 334. These cases state the general rule that the unauthorized affixing of another's trademark to even authentic goods is an infringement of the proprietor's rights in the mark, but then give the three exceptions for re-labeling, repackaging, and re-branding where the use of another's mark is necessary to market the underlying product.

protection for such important products as prescription drugs, automobiles, films, and recorded music, along with the national laws of contract, which regulate commercial transactions in those products, and national procedural rules, which regulate the responsibilities of litigants, be made subordinate to the judicially interpreted needs of market integration in the absence of definitive Community legislation? That is, should parallel importation, a basic free-market exercise, be allowed to disrupt entire bodies of national laws through the fear it engenders of the negative ramifications for the free movement of goods resulting from the efforts of intellectual-property owners using national rights to protect themselves from parallel trade?

V. The parallel importation paradox

The problems, both commercial and legal, associated with parallel importation in the Community are effects rather than causes. The great number of disputes that have arisen in the Common Market over the past 40 years and within national legal systems over the past 150 years point to a lack of certainty as to how intellectual-property owners' rights are exhausted through use. Disputes between parallel traders and intellectual-property owners arise, are litigated, are adjudicated, but then metamorphose in the next instances of parallel trade into other varieties of the same or similar disputes requiring additional attention from the courts because both sides can make legally valid arguments about how, and in what instances, intellectual-property owners' rights end in respect of the underlying goods. The fact that the occurrence of the exhaustion of rights appears, superficially at least, to vary factually to such a wide degree indicates a lack of consistency in defining the reach of intellectual-property rights.

An example is given by *Class International v Colgate-Palmolive*.[74] It is settled law in all the Member States and under the Trademarks Directive that one of the exclusive rights of trademark ownership is the right to oppose the importation of goods bearing the mark without a license applicable in the country of importation.[75] Article 58 of the Community Customs Code[76] allows for the "imposition of prohibitions or restrictions justified on grounds of . . . the protection of industrial and commercial property,"[77] but when trade-

---

[74] Case C-405/03, *Class International BV v Colgate-Palmolive Co and others*, [2006] 1 CMLR 14 (ECJ), [2006] ETMR 12.

[75] The Trademarks Directive, *supra* note 18, Art. 5(1)(c). The Trademark Regulation, *supra* note 20, defines the exclusive rights of Community trademark ownership in the same way. *See* Art. 9(2)(c).

[76] Established by Council Regulation (EEC) No. 2913/92 of October 12, 1992, [1992] OJ L-302/1.

[77] *Class International v Colgate-Palmolive*, *supra* note 74, ¶ 11.

mark owners brought an enforcement action against a shipment of branded toothpaste in a customs warehouse, alleging the owner intended to put the goods onto the internal market, the parallel importer was able to defend on the point, recognized under Article 91(1) of the Customs Code, that the goods were only in a customs warehouse in Rotterdam and not yet on the market. The Court of Justice held "importing" to mean bringing into the Community market, and that, as the goods were under customs control and not within the market as such, the mere possibility of importing or evidence of the likelihood of doing so was not enough to establish infringement.[78] Goods in a Community customs office's control may be physically in the Community but are not necessarily on the market in the Community, regardless of the probable intentions of the importer: a fine point with many practical consequences for the border enforcement of intellectual-property rights.[79]

It confuses the issue to link the needs of market integration with the reach of exclusive rights. As a matter of policy, it may be necessary, in order to integrate the EEA market, that intellectual-property rights cease after a volitional first sale anywhere within that market, but this is a policy decision based on considerations other than determining the appropriate reach of exclusive rights.[80] It does not define that reach. In order to resolve in a definitive, generally applicable way the fundamental issues common to most parallel-importation disputes, it will be necessary to separate the determination of right exhaustion from its present dependency on considerations of the needs of internal-market integration.

The detrimental effects of reactive harmonization can be seen in the Court of Justice's judgment in *Davidoff* and the cases that have followed from it,[81] where commercial issues concerning parallel importation have become the means for overriding two articles of the Trademarks Directive (which declares itself not to have been intended as a complete harmonization of trademark

---

[78]   *Id,* ¶¶ 34, 44, 45, & 50.
[79]   O. VRINS & M. SCHNEIDER, ENFORCEMENT OF INTELLECTUAL PROPERTY RIGHTS THROUGH BORDER MEASURES (2006).
[80]   The market-integration policy considerations advanced here have been described alternatively as an undercurrent of judicial concern for discrimination against imports in national intellectual-property laws. G. Marenco & K. Banks, *Intellectual Property and the Community Rules on Free Movement,* 15 EUR. L. REV. 224, 254–5 (1990). The fact that policy considerations override the development of intellectual-property law is the same under either description, though the practical results of the Marenco and Banks interpretation are different in that it would allow for the partitioning of the internal market by non-discriminatory, national intellectual-property laws.
[81]   For the most recent cases, see *Hewlett-Packard v Expansys, supra* note 26; *Kabushiki Kaisha Sony Computer Ent. v Nuplayer, supra* note 62.

law[82]) and the basis for jurisprudential harmonization of the trademark rights in the Community.[83] This approach is driven by policy considerations other than determining the reach of trademark rights and, as such, represents a compromise between competing commercial interests rather than a methodical attempt to address the issues raised by parallel trading.

The harmonization of national intellectual property laws to counter restrictions on the free movement of goods generates additional, more extensive harmonization, not only of intellectual property laws but also of other national substantive and procedural laws. The effects of creeping harmonization affect differently the laws of individual Member States. Placing the burden of proof on defendant retailers to prove consent, as in *Davidoff*, appears harsh in the English legal system because of the financial and moral consequences of a finding of liability for infringement under that system. The effect is less onerous in some civilian systems, where liability for negligent or accidental infringement, while easily proven, such that the apportioning of the burden of proof is of less practical consequence than in the United Kingdom, is subject to adjustment by trial courts through judicial fine-tuning of damage awards and the general lack of opprobrium associated with defendants being found guilty of infringement at a non-criminal level.

From an intellectual property owner's point of view, the current state of the Community law appears equally inequitable. The holding in *Van Doren* allows parallel traders to refuse to answer prejudgment questions about their sources of supply when they fear retribution against those sources in violation of Article 81. Article 81 forms the basis of a defense to discovery, but Article 82, under the holding in *Hewlett-Packard v Expansys*,[84] forms a defense neither to discovery nor to infringement liability resultant from parallel trading in extra-market goods.[85] The Intellectual Property Enforcement Directive[86] is of little help before a judgment is given. While Article 8 of that directive requires infringers to reveal their sources for offending goods, the provision is phrased in the legal past tense: "infringement" requiring a holding of law to determine a defendant's status.

---

[82] The Trademarks Directive, *supra* note 18, Preamble, 3rd recital.
[83] *Davidoff*, *supra* note 60, ¶ 39.
[84] *Hewlett-Packard Development Co. LP v Expansys UK, Ltd*, [2005] EWHC 1495, ¶ 17–18 ("What is prohibited is the abuse, not the dominant position or the abuser's ability to continue in the relevant market and to exploit his various property rights.") (Ch D, Laddie, J).
[85] *But see contra Sportswear Co SpA v Stonestyle Ltd.*, *supra* note 29, where the Court of Appeals held the allegation of an Art. 81 violation on the part of the brand owner could be a defense to liability for trademark infringement.
[86] Directive 2004/48/EC of the European Parliament and of the Council of April 29, 2004 on the enforcement of intellectual property rights, O.J. 2004, L 195/16.

VI. The future of free movement and parallel trading

Parallel trade will continue in the Community as long as there are substantial, rather than superficial, differences between Member States, such as differences in *per capita* income, cultural preferences, governmental regulations, and transportation costs. So long as parallel trade exists, disputes between intellectual-property owners and parallel importers will continue to act as an engine for the generation of references to the Court of Justice. So long as the Court of Justice continues to address these references in terms of the political needs of market harmonization, rather than addressing them with a view to determining the appropriate reach of intellectual-property rights, the Court's efforts are likely to result in additional disruptions to national regimes of both substantive and procedural laws, which in turn will form the basis for further referred questions. The cycle of referral–solution–disruption–referral is endless. It would be better, from the point of view of judicial economy, for the Court of Justice to take a proactive approach to the overall issue of the reach of intellectual property rights, defining those rights in such a way as to minimize the friction between their exploitation and the goal of preserving the free movement of protected goods within the market.

The obvious place to start is with the reach of trademarks, which would require revisiting the issue of their function. Once that legal function is fulfilled in commerce, a trademark right in a product can comfortably end, the owner having gotten his value from his property and the rest of the market confident in having taken the relevant product free of trademark-based control. The established Community law is that trademarks function to designate the origin of branded goods,[87] but do they?[88] If they do have that function, is there more to it than designating the manufacturer of products?[89]

Until these fundamental questions are answered, the referrals will continue. The Court of Justice would be the appropriate forum to determine the reach of exclusive rights in the Community, though there may not be a sufficient legislative basis for the Court to take so proactive an approach, particularly in light of the protection given to national property systems under EC Treaty

---

[87] Case C-3/78, *Centrafarm v American Home Products*, *supra* note 3, ¶ 12. *See also* Case C-349/95, *Fritz Loendersloot, trading as F. Loenderloot Internationale Expedite v George Ballantine & Son, Ltd*, [1997] ECR I-6227, [1998] 1 CMLR 1015 ¶¶22–5.

[88] Joined Cases C-427/93, 429/93 and 436/93, *Bristol-Myers Squibb v Paranova, SA*, [1996] ECR I-3457, [1997] 1 CMLR 1151, ¶ 48 (noting a guarantor-of-quality function for marks).

[89] This is an old, but unanswered question. See F. Schechter, *The Rational Basis of Trademark Protection*, 40 HARV. L. REV. 813, 831 (1927), where the author concludes that the function of trademarks is to attract and hold product appeal, quantifiable to the brand owner as "selling power."

Article 295. The Court of Justice has known a dichotomy in the nature of marks for nearly 40 years.[90] Article 295 protects the existence of intellectual property rights, but not their exercise beyond their core function. The reach of trademarks – meaning the legal limits on their exploitation – is a hybrid. It is concerned with the core exercise of rights in a mark up to the point its protected existence ceases.

As with any boundary, there are two sides to Article 295: one protected under the treaty, one beyond that protection and subject to harmonization. At present, the Community courts are exploring this boundary, occasionally giving an indication of the limits on the function or functions of marks by determining what they are not. In the end, it may require the Community legislature to give a definitive accounting of the legal nature of trademarks and a solution to the problems raised by the free movement of branded goods.

---

[90] That is, since its decision in *Consten and Grundig, supra* note 11.

9 The trademark law provisions of bilateral free trade agreements
Burton Ong*

I. Trademarks and international trade

Trademarks are used by business enterprises to distinguish their goods and services from those offered by other traders in the marketplace. As badges of origin and guarantees of quality, trademarks are important devices which enable their owners to establish goodwill with their consumers and the public at large. Trademarks are also vital components of a trader's brand-building efforts when he has an established business in one jurisdiction and is seeking to penetrate new markets abroad. Where consumers in a foreign market are unfamiliar with the trademark of an enterprise with an established business in another country, the trademark owner needs to have some control over the usage of the trademark in that foreign market if he wants to extend the reach of his trademark by encouraging brand-recognition and developing brand-loyalty among these consumers. He needs to be able to prevent third parties from confusing or deceiving consumers through the use of identical or similar marks on goods or services which do not originate from, or are not connected to, his business. Only then will his trademark be able to perform its desired function – to establish an exclusive connection in the consumer's mind between the trademark owner and his wares. The trademark laws of other countries are therefore a matter of some concern to the trademark-owning enterprises venturing into overseas territories – these laws will determine the nature and extent of their ability to exercise control over their established registered trademarks, and marks similar to their registered trademarks, in these foreign markets.

Bilateral free trade agreements (FTAs) are international agreements reached between two sovereign states to promote trading activity between business enterprises operating from within their respective territories. These agreements seek to make the domestic markets of one party accessible to business enterprises operating from the other by eliminating or reducing barriers to trade – import taxes, quotas, subsidies and various other regulatory mechanisms which

---

* Faculty of Law, National University of Singapore.

may impede the flow of goods or services between the two states. Among the contents commonly included in free trade agreements are provisions relating to the intellectual property laws of the signatory states because the inadequate protection of intellectual property rights may serve as a non-tariff barrier to free trade.[1] Since intellectual property rights are essentially territorial in nature, the availability and scope of legal protection available to the rights holder in one jurisdiction may not be available in another state unless the latter has enacted a similar legal framework. The intellectual property law provisions found in free trade agreements oblige the parties to ensure that their domestic intellectual property laws meet stipulated minimum standards of protection and are intended to encourage trade flows between these states. Traders in one state may not be prepared to enter the market in another state unless they have some assurance that their intellectual property rights are adequately respected overseas. These traders may be hesitant to release their products or services in a foreign market with lower standards of intellectual property protection, if any, only to have their competitors in these markets misappropriating their innovations, designs or other valuable intangibles without adequate legal recourse. Some businesses – especially the members of the media, pharmaceutical and high-technology industries – are particularly keen on the availability of robust copyright and patent protection abroad because modern technology has made it very easy to produce pirated copies of their products which may deprive them of part of the economic rewards which flow from intellectual property ownership. Considerable efforts have therefore been made by some states negotiating their free trade agreements to include copyright and patent law-related provisions in their treaties, which require the parties to strengthen the positions of copyright owners and patent holders in their respective jurisdictions.

Similarly, trademark law provisions which have found their way into bilateral free trade agreements are also intended to fortify and, in most cases, expand the domestic legal framework from which trademark owners derive their exclusive rights. Traders with valuable trademarks which are accustomed to higher levels of trademark protection in one state may have greater confidence in expanding their businesses into the foreign markets of another state, which have been opened up to them as a result of the free trade agreement between these states, if the latter adopts similar trademark laws. This would

---

[1] *See* Marshall A. Leaffer, *Protecting United States Intellectual Property Abroad: Towards a New Multilateralism*, 76 IOWA L. REV. 273, 277 (1991), where the author explains how inadequate intellectual property protection may undermine the goal of free trade because it leads to trade distortions, and Lori M. Berg, *The North American Free Trade Agreement & Protection of Intellectual Property: A Converging View*, 5 J. TRANSNAT'L L. & POL'Y 99, 105–11 (1995).

facilitate one of the principal goals of the free trade agreement: to increase the volume of trading activity between the two states by making it more attractive for businesses operating from one party to enter the markets of the other. With similar trademark laws in both states, traders from one signatory state get some assurance that the "rules of the game" which they have to play by in the overseas market, when dealing with competitors who use identical or similar marks in their businesses, are familiar to them. Inadequate intellectual property protection raises a slightly different set of concerns for trademark owners from those shared by copyright owners and patent holders: except in cases involving well-known trademarks, the trademark owner is concerned less with the unfair misappropriation of the products of his intellect, but rather with the damage to his goodwill if third parties were able to engage in misleading conduct in the marketplace through the use of marks identical or similar to the registered trademark, thereby interfering with his ability to use the trademark as a device to distinguish his goods and services from those offered by his competitors.[2]

The spirit of trademark law provisions of free trade agreements lies very near to one of the core objectives of such agreements: to make the domestic markets of each party more accessible to traders operating out of the other. Trademarks are relied upon by consumers as indicators of origin or guarantees of quality, allowing trademark owners to use these devices as instruments of communication with their customers through which the former may cultivate the goodwill and loyalty of the latter. A third party's conduct involving the use of an identical or similar sign on his own goods or services, in circumstances which may cause some confusion among consumers or otherwise weaken the strength of the trademark, will damage this connection which the trademark owner has tried to establish with his customers. Such conduct, if left unchecked, will operate as a barrier to market entry to other firms with concerns about preserving the value of their trademarks. Markets with well-developed trademark laws are more accessible to the new market entrant because, upon the registration of his trademark within the jurisdiction, this

---

[2] It should be noted that excessively generous trademark laws may be just as detrimental to free trade as inadequate levels of trademark protection. For example, states with trademark regimes which permit the registered trademark owner to prevent third parties from making parallel imports of "gray goods" bearing the trademark could restrict the flow of foreign-made genuine goods into their domestic markets, thereby restricting the product choices available to domestic consumers. *See generally* Ng-Loy Wee Loon, *Exhaustion of Rights in Trademark Law: The English and Singapore Models Compared*, [2000] European Intellectual Property Review 320; Daniel R. Bereskin, *The Canada-United States Free Trade Agreement: Are Trademarks a Barrier to Free Trade?*, 80 TRADEMARK REP. 272 (1990).

foreign trader can focus on the task of winning over new customers and goodwill-generation without being too distracted by third parties disrupting their efforts through the unauthorized use of marks, identical or similar to a registered trademark, on goods or services which have nothing to do with the registered trademark owner.

II. Setting intellectual property standards through free trade agreements

The linkage between intellectual property protection and international trade is a well-established one. Governments have placed intellectual property issues on the agendas of their various bilateral, regional and multilateral trade negotiations since the 1980s. Recognizing the efficacy of trade-based approaches as a means of coercing its trading partners to adopt adequate standards of intellectual property protection, the United States of America has employed threats of unilateral trade sanctions on more than one occasion against several of its trading partners which were placed on intellectual property piracy "Section 301 watch lists" since enacting its *Omnibus Trade and Competitiveness Act* of 1988.[3] By placing pressure on those trading partners with significant levels of intellectual property piracy taking place within their respective jurisdictions to step up their levels of enforcement activity, or lose the right to export their goods to the United States, such trade-based measures were seen as effective short-term strategies for dealing with the problem of counterfeit goods in overseas markets.[4]

Between 1986 and 1994, the members of the General Agreement of Tariffs and Trade (GATT) integrated intellectual property protection issues as one of the key aspects of their multilateral free trade negotiations, culminating in the conclusion of the *Agreement on Trade Related Aspects of Intellectual Property Rights* (TRIPS)[5] as one of the several Uruguay Round Agreements. This landmark multilateral agreement between the members of the World Trade Organization (WTO) introduced minimum standards of intellectual property protection which had to be implemented into the domestic legal frameworks of each member state. Under the TRIPS Agreement, the standards which countries seeking membership of the WTO are obliged to adopt in their respective domestic trademark laws include the following:

---

[3] Pub. L. 100–418, title I, § 1101, August 23, 1988, 102 Stat. 1121, which amended the Trade Act of 1974, codified as 19 U.S.C. §§ 2411–19 (1988).

[4] See generally Myles Getlan, *TRIPS and the future of Section 301: A Comparative Study in Trade Dispute Resolution*, 34 COLUM. J. TRANSNAT'L L. 173 (1995).

[5] 33 I.L.M. 81.

The trademark law provisions of bilateral free trade agreements 233

- Any sign capable of distinguishing the goods and services of one undertaking from those of other undertakings should be capable of constituting a trademark, though members "may require, as a condition of registration, that signs be *visually perceptible*."[6]
- Registered trademark owners must have the exclusive right to prevent third parties from making unauthorized use, in the course of trade, of "identical or similar signs for goods or services which are identical or similar to those in respect of which the trademark is registered where such use would result in a *likelihood of confusion*. Where the third party uses an identical sign for identical goods or services, a *likelihood of confusion* shall be presumed."[7]
- Article 6*bis* of the Paris Convention (1967),[8] which offers additional protection to well-known trademarks, must apply to "goods and services which are *not similar* to those in respect of which a trademark is registered, provided that use of that trademark in relation to those goods or services would indicate a *connection* between those goods or services and the owner of the registered trademark and provided that the *interests of the owner of the registered trademark are likely to be damaged* by such use."[9]
- "Limited exceptions" to the rights conferred on trademark owners are permissible, "such as fair use of descriptive terms, provided that such exceptions take into account the *legitimate interests* of the owner of the trademark and of third parties."[10]

In setting legal benchmarks like these, the TRIPS Agreement has been an important driving force behind the global harmonization of domestic intellectual property law regimes around the world. With the passage of more than a decade since this international legal instrument came into force, repeated calls

---

[6] Article 15(1) (emphasis added).
[7] Article 16(1) (emphasis added).
[8] Article 6*bis* of *The Paris Convention for the Protection of Industrial Property* (1883), last amended in 1979, which is administered by the World Intellectual Property Organization (WIPO), provides that member countries are "to refuse or cancel the registration, and to prohibit the use, of a trademark which constitutes a reproduction, an imitation, or a translation, *liable to create confusion*, of a mark considered by the competent authority of the country of registration or use to be *well known* in that country as being already the mark of a person entitled to the benefits of this Convention and used for identical or similar goods. These provisions shall also apply when the essential part of the mark constitutes a reproduction of any such well-known mark or an imitation liable to create *confusion* therewith" (emphasis added).
[9] Article 16(3) (emphasis added).
[10] Article 17 (emphasis added).

have been made by many governments of developed nations, acting on behalf of their intellectual property-owning corporate constituents, to review and strengthen its provisions while developing countries, arguing that the property rights need to be rebalanced to better take into account other public interests, have called for the opposite.[11] As the debates continue as to whether the legal standards which have been set in the TRIPS Agreement are too stringent or not demanding enough, most of the international intellectual property community's attention has been focused on issues relating to pharmaceutical patents and public health, copyright and technological protection measures, and other politically contentious debates which have been given extensive coverage by the international media. Trademark law has not attracted the same level of public interest, or controversy, because the stakeholders who are most directly affected by changes to these laws are corporate entities and business enterprises, rather than the average man-on-the-street.

Given the practical difficulties in reaching an international consensus in the TRIPS Agreement review process, and the unlikelihood of an expeditious resolution any time soon, some states have chosen to place greater reliance on regional and bilateral trade agreements as intellectual property standard-setting mechanisms instead. With fewer states involved, and with fewer political, cultural, ideological and socio-economic interests, and sensitivities to take into consideration, the process of reaching a consensual compromise is far less time-consuming. Negotiations for such agreements can take place entirely in private and away from the intense media scrutiny which typically arises from large-scale multilateral meetings. Even before the conclusion of the TRIPS Agreement, regional trading blocs have emerged from regional free trade agreements – such as the North American Free Trade Agreement (NAFTA)[12] between the United States, Canada, and Mexico – through which intellectual property standards have been introduced into the domestic laws of member countries. While NAFTA entered into force before the TRIPS Agreement, it had paid close attention to the TRIPS negotiations, which had been in progress for five years before the commencement of NAFTA negotiations, and had built upon the legal standards which were eventually incorporated into the TRIPS Agreement. The result was a broader scope of protection for intellectual property rights under NAFTA than in any other multilateral intellectual property agreement.[13]

---

[11] See generally L. Danielle Tully, *Prospects for Progress: The TRIPS Agreement and Developing Countries after the Doha Conference*, 26 B.C. INT'L & COMP. L. REV. 129 (2003).

[12] 32 I.L.M. 612, signed on December 17, 1992. Chapter 17 contains the intellectual property-related provisions of the regional free trade agreement.

[13] For example, the definition in Article 15(1) of the TRIPS Agreement of a

The inclusion of intellectual property provisions in bilateral free trade agreements which set standards higher than those specified by the TRIPS Agreement – 'TRIPS-plus' provisions – has become an increasingly common strategy for many states which have entered into such agreements in the last decade. Countries which are dissatisfied with the slow progress made through multilateral negotiations in raising intellectual property standards since the conclusion of the TRIPS Agreement, or who are skeptical about the likelihood of any real international consensus being reached in the near future on the appropriate standards which ought to be adopted in every intellectual property regime, have resorted to bargaining for higher levels of protection for intellectual property owners through their bilateral free trade agreements. Greater access to markets in one jurisdiction is traded in exchange for granting a broader bundle of rights to intellectual property owners in another jurisdiction. Countries with large and affluent domestic markets which rely on such strategies are therefore in a strong position to influence the intellectual property systems found in their trading partners through their bilateral trade agreements. Bilateral trade agreements can thus be used as an important standard-setting mechanism, through which similar intellectual property standards may potentially be replicated across a spread of bilateral agreements reached between an economically dominant country and its numerous trading partners. This eventually results in common intellectual property standards, strongly in favor of intellectual property owners, being imposed upon a broad spectrum of countries without the need for all of them to, mutually and simultaneously, agree that such standards should be adopted by each of them. Legal academics have noted, with some consternation, that this phenomenon of "forum-shifting" in the intellectual property standard-setting process, from multilateralism to bilateralism, has resulted in a "ratcheting process" through which legal standards moved progressively only in one direction – upwards.[14] The United

---

trademark refers to signs which are "capable of distinguishing the goods and services of one undertaking from those of other undertakings . . . in particular personal names, letters, numerals, figurative elements and combinations of colours as well as combinations of such signs." The definition given to a protectable trademark in NAFTA is significantly wider – Article 1708(1) provides that a "trademark consists of any sign, or any combination of signs, capable of distinguishing the goods or services of one person from those of another, including personal names, *designs*, letters, numerals, colors, figurative elements, or the *shape of goods or of their packaging*. Trademarks shall include *service marks* and *collective marks*, and may include *certification marks*." (emphasis added). *See* Laurinda L. Hicks and James R. Holbein, *Convergence of National Intellectual Property Norms in International Trading Agreements*, 12 AM. U. J. INT'L L. & POL'Y 769, 791–800 (1997).

[14] *See* Peter Drahos, "Developing Countries and International Intellectual Property Standard-Setting", 5 J. WORLD INTELLECTUAL PROPERTY 756, 769–70 (2002); Peter Drahos, *Intellectual Property Engineering: The Role of the Chemical,*

States has been singled out as having had considerable success in executing such a strategy. A brief examination of some of the trademark law provisions it has included in the bilateral free trade agreements it has recently concluded reveal this quite clearly.

III. "TRIPS-plus" trademark law provisions found in bilateral free trade agreements

The intellectual property chapters of the bilateral free trade agreements which the United States has entered into since the year 2000 clearly demonstrate how these international legal instruments have been used to harmonize the trademark law regimes of its various trading partners and to expand the scope of trademark protection in these jurisdictions. The trademark law provisions which have found their way into these agreements fall within three broad categories – some provisions merely reiterate the legal standards articulated in the TRIPS Agreement, some relate to the legal framework regulating the procedural aspects of the trademark registration system which are not dealt with directly in the TRIPS Agreement, while other provisions require member states to introduce legal standards that go beyond what is required of them under the TRIPS Agreement.

A. Provisions reiterating the legal standards relating to trademarks found in the TRIPS Agreement ("TRIPS-based" provisions)

These are not 'TRIPS-plus' provisions because they simply re-state the legal norms articulated by the TRIPS Agreement in the Intellectual Property Chapters of the various bilateral free trade agreements which the United States has concluded. The specific inclusion of these provisions emphasizes the perceived importance of these legal standards to the contracting parties and their significance to the trademark-owning businesses which they represent. In particular, three particular trademark law provisions found in the TRIPS Agreement are echoed consistently in these bilateral agreements. Firstly, trademark proprietors must be entitled to prevent third parties from using identical or similar signs on identical or similar goods where such use would result in a likelihood of confusion (the "likelihood of confusion" provision).[15] Secondly, proprietors of well-known trademarks must be entitled to prevent third parties from applying their marks to goods or services which are not similar to those goods or services in respect of which their trademark has been registered, where such use would indicate a connection between those goods

---

Pharmaceutical and Biotechnology Industries, in INTELLECTUAL PROPERTY AND BIOLOGICAL RESOURCES (Burton Ong ed., 2004); JOHN BRAITHWAITE & PETER DRAHOS, GLOBAL BUSINESS REGULATION 564 (Cambridge University Press, 2000).

[15] *See supra* note 7 and accompanying text.

or services and the proprietors of the well-known trademark, provided that the interests of these proprietors are likely to be damaged by such use (the "Article 6*bis* Paris Convention extension" provision).[16] Thirdly, the exclusive rights conferred on trademark proprietors should only be subjected to "limited exceptions", such as fair use of descriptive terms, which take into account "the legitimate interests of the owner of the trademark and of third parties" (the "limited exceptions" provision).[17] Table 9.1 identifies the relevant "TRIPS-based" trademark law provisions of the various bilateral agreements which oblige contracting parties to abide by the legal standards articulated by the TRIPS Agreement.

It is readily apparent that these trademark law provisions have practically become "boilerplate" provisions in the Intellectual Property Chapters of the bilateral free trade agreements made by the United States. These provisions create separate international obligations which require each trading partner to implement the legal norms of the TRIPS Agreement in their respective domestic laws, in addition to their international obligations – arising from their membership of the World Trade Organization – under the TRIPS Agreement itself. Should a dispute arise as to whether a contracting party has met its obligations to implement one of these legal standards into its domestic trademark system, it may be settled privately at the election of the parties outside of the World Trade Organization's Dispute Settlement mechanisms, where negotiations can be carried out in confidence between the government officials of the contracting parties.[18] If, for example, the trademark owners in one contracting party believe that the trademark laws of the other contracting party provide third parties with overly-generous defenses to trademark infringement, they could lobby their government to raise the issue directly with the government of the other contracting party as a matter of non-compliance with the "limited exceptions" provision found in the free trade agreement between the two countries, thereby placing pressure directly on the government of the other contracting party to amend its trademark laws to confer stronger rights on trademark owners within its jurisdiction.

---

[16] *See supra* note 9 and accompanying text.
[17] *See supra* note 10 and accompanying text.
[18] For example, in the Dispute Settlement Chapter of the US-Singapore FTA, Article 20.4(3)(a) provides that "where a dispute regarding any matter . . . arises under this Agreement and under the WTO Agreement, or any other agreement to which both Parties are party, the complaining Party may select the forum in which to settle the dispute", while Article 20.4(3)(c) explains that "Once the complaining Party has selected a particular forum, the forum selected shall be used to the exclusion of other possible fora."

Table 9.1 Trademark law provisions reiterating legal standards articulated by the TRIPS Agreement

TRIPS Provisions	US-Jordan FTA 2000	US-Singapore FTA 2003	US-Chile FTA 2003	US-Australia FTA 2004	US-Morocco FTA 2004	US-Bahrain FTA 2004	US-Oman FTA 2004	US-Peru TPA 2006	US-Colombia TPA 2006	US-Panama TPA 2007	US-Korea TPA 2007
"Likelihood of confusion" (TRIPS Art. 16(1))	Art. 4(7)	Art. 16.2(2)	Art. 17.2(4)	Art. 17.2(4)	Art. 15.2(4)	Art. 14.2(4)	Art. 15.2(4)	Art. 15.2(4)	Art. 16.2(4)	Art. 15.2(3)	Art. 18.2(4)
"Article 6bis Paris Convention extension" (TRIPS Art. 16(3))	Art. 4(8)	Art. 16.2(4)	Art. 17.2(6)	Art. 17.2(6)	Art. 15.2(6)	Art. 14.2(6)	Art. 15.2(6)	Art. 15.2(6)	Art. 16.2(6)	Art. 15.2(5)	Art. 18.2(7)
"Limited exceptions" provision (TRIPS Art. 17)	–	Art. 16.2(3)	Art. 17.2(5)	Art. 17.2(5)	Art. 15.2(5)	Art. 14.2(5)	Art. 15.2(5)	Art. 15.2(5)	Art. 16.2(5)	Art. 15.2(4)	Art. 18.2(5)

B. *Provisions relating to the legal framework regulating the procedural aspects of the trademark registration system not dealt with in the TRIPS Agreement*

These provisions require signatory states to give effect to, or ratify or accede to, or make best efforts to ratify or accede to, the various treaties administered by WIPO that deal with the procedures which member states should adopt in their respective trademark registration regimes. In the intellectual property chapters of the bilateral free trade agreements which the United States has concluded thus far, these WIPO-administered treaties include the Trademark Law Treaty[19] and the Protocol Relating to the Madrid Agreement Concerning the International Registration of Marks ("Madrid Protocol").[20] The Trademark Law Treaty aims to harmonize the procedural aspects of national and regional trademark registration systems, making the process for acquiring a registered trademark more user-friendly, setting out an exhaustive list of formal requirements for effecting changes in ownership or a trademark owner's details, and standardizing the duration of the initial period of registration and the duration of each renewal to ten years each. The Madrid Protocol supplements the Madrid Agreement Concerning the International Registration of Marks[21] by creating a system of international trademark registrations through which trademark protection may be secured in multiple contracting parties by filing a single international registration with the WIPO International Bureau using a contracting party's competent domestic agency as an intermediary. Under the system created by the Madrid Protocol, the formalities relating to applications for international registrations of a trademark are examined by the WIPO International Bureau, which then transmits valid applications to the competent authorities of those contracting parties designated by the applicant to examine substantive matters relating to the application – whether the mark qualifies for protection, whether it conflicts with earlier registered marks, and so forth.

Countries which undertake in their bilateral free trade agreements to accede to or ratify these treaties are required to implement procedural reforms in their respective trademark systems in accordance with the details prescribed by

---

[19] The full text of the Trademark Law Treaty, adopted on October 27, 1994, is available online from the WIPO website at http://www.wipo.int/treaties/en/ip/tlt.

[20] The full text of the Madrid Protocol, signed on June 28, 1989, is available online from the WIPO website at http://www.wipo.int/treaties/en/registration/madrid_protocol.

[21] The full text of the Madrid Agreement Concerning the International Registration of Marks of April 14, 1891, as revised in Brussels (1900), Washington (1911), The Hague (1925), London (1934), Nice (1957) and Stockholm (1967), and as amended in 1979, is available online from the WIPO website at http://www.wipo.int/treaties/en/registration/madrid.

these treaties. Specific provisions referring to these two treaties can be found in the United States' bilateral free trade agreements with Jordan,[22] Singapore,[23] Chile,[24] Australia,[25] Morocco,[26] Bahrain,[27] Oman,[28] Peru,[29] Colombia,[30] Panama[31] and South Korea.[32]

C. *Provisions introducing legal standards which go beyond the minimum legal standards set out in the TRIPS Agreement ("TRIPS-plus" provisions)*

A survey of the trademark law provisions in the bilateral free trade agreements which the United States of America has concluded since 2000 reveals two obvious species of true "TRIPS-plus" provisions which clearly exceed the legal standards agreed upon multilaterally by the members of the World Trade Organization via the TRIPS Agreement.

1. Non-visually perceptible trademarks Firstly, while Article 15(1) of the TRIPS Agreement permits member states to require visual perceptibility of a criterion for signs to be registrable as trademarks, the majority of these bilateral free trade agreements have removed this discretion completely. Parties to these agreements cannot restrict their respective registered trademark regimes to visually perceptible marks alone: scent marks, sound marks and even taste and tactile marks must not be disqualified as protectable subject matter simply because they are detected by the sensory organs other than the eyes. The language used in these trademark law provisions from one of the earlier free trade agreements reads as follows:

> Neither Party shall require, as a condition of registration, that signs be visually perceptible, but each Party shall make best efforts to register scent marks . . .[33]

---

[22] Signed on October 24, 2000. *See* Article 4(2). The full text of all the FTAs which the United States of America has entered into can be found online at the Office of US Trade Representative's website: http://www.ustr.gov/Trade_Agreements/Section_Index.html.
[23] Signed on May 6, 2003. *See* Articles 16.1(2)(b)(ii) and (c)(ii).
[24] Signed on June 6, 2003. *See* Articles 17.1(3)(b) and 17.1(4)(c).
[25] Signed on May 18, 2004. *See* Articles 17.1(2)(c) and (f).
[26] Signed on June 15, 2004. *See* Articles 15.1(2)(c) and (f).
[27] Signed on September 14, 2004. *See* Articles 14.1(2)(c) and (f).
[28] Signed on January 19, 2006. *See* Articles 15.1(2)(c) and (f).
[29] Signed on April 12, 2006. *See* Articles 16.1(3)(b) and (c).
[30] Signed on November 22, 2006. *See* Articles 16.1(3)(b) and 16.1(4)(c).
[31] Signed on June 28, 2007. *See* Articles 15.1(3)(b) and 15.1(4)(c).
[32] Signed on June 30, 2007. *See* Articles 18.1(3)(e) and (h).
[33] *See* Article 16.2(1) of the 2003 US-Singapore FTA. A provision requiring trademark protection to be made available to scent marks can be found in Article

This expansion of the scope of registrable trademarks to include non-visually perceptible subject matter has important consequences on the boundaries of trademark law and how scents, sounds, tastes and textures are used in the marketplace as devices by traders to differentiate their goods or services from those offered by their rivals. Parties who stand to gain the most from the trademark law provisions in these bilateral free trade agreements are those large corporations which have the resources to include these non-visual elements in their marketing campaigns so that they acquire the necessary degree of distinctiveness to qualify for trademark protection.

Examples of sound marks which have been successfully registered at the United States Patent and Trademark Office include Intel Corporation's "five tone audio progression of the notes D-Flat, D-Flat, G, D-Flat and A-Flat", Microsoft Corporation's "music sequence in the key of D major in 4/4 time" and Twentieth Century Fox Film Corporation's "8 to 10 second musical phrase . . . with a forte fanfare-like 6 note brass motive."[34] In the emerging area of scent or smell marks, trailblazing corporations like Manhattan Oil from California have secured registrations over cherry, grape and strawberry scents as trademarks for its engine lubricants and motor oils,[35] while The Smead Manufacturing Company from Minnesota have registered the scents of grapefruit, lavender, peach, peppermint, apple cider and vanilla as trademarks for their office supplies, paper files and expandable folders.[36]

The trademark registries of those states which have entered into FTAs with the United States would have had to amend their legal and procedural frameworks to accommodate applications to register such non-conventional trademarks.[37] The American registered proprietors of these sound and scent marks

---

17.2(1) of the 2003 US-Chile FTA. Both sound and scent marks are specifically identified as registrable subject matter in Article 17.2(2) of the 2004 US-Australia FTA, Article 15.2(1) of the 2004 US-Morocco FTA, Article 14.2(1) of the 2004 US-Bahrain FTA, Article 15.2(1) of the 2006 US-Oman FTA, Article 16.2(1) of the 2006 US-Peru Trade Promotion Agreement, Article 16.2(1) of the 2006 US-Colombia TPA and Article 18.2(1) of the 2007 US-Korea FTA.

[34] *See* USPTO Trademark Registration Numbers 2315261 (Intel), 2870456 (Microsoft) and 3141398 (Twentieth Century Fox Film Corporation).

[35] *See* USPTO Trademark Registration Numbers 2463044, 2568512 and 2596156 which relate to the scent marks used by the company in relation to its high-octane fuels – "Power Plus Cherry", "Liquid Power Groovy Grape" and "Supercharged Strawberry".

[36] *See* USPTO Trademark Registration Numbers 3140692, 3140693, 3140694, 3140700, 3140701 and 3143735.

[37] An international administrative framework for the registration of non-traditional marks was adopted by the WIPO Diplomatic Conference through the Singapore Treaty on the Law of Trademarks on March 27, 2006. The full text of the Singapore Treaty, which has not yet entered into force at the time of writing, is available online from the WIPO website at http://www.wipo.int/treaties/en/ip/singapore.

will therefore be able to obtain trademark monopolies over the use of their non-conventional marks in all these jurisdictions without having to wait around for a global multilateral agreement to be reached on the registrability of non-visually perceptible signs.

2. *Additional protection for well-known trademarks*   Secondly, the intellectual property chapters of some of these bilateral free trade agreements contain trademark law provisions which require contracting states to give higher levels of protection for well-known trademarks than what is required of them under the TRIPS Agreement. Articles 16(2) and 16(3) of the TRIPS Agreement already require member states to extend the scope of application of Article 6*bis* of the Paris Convention[38] to services and to

> goods and services which are not similar to those in respect of which the trademark is registered, provided that use of that trademark in relation to those goods or services would indicate a connection between those goods or services and the owner of the registered trademark and provided that the interests of the owner of the registered trademark are likely to be damaged by such use.

Article 6*bis* of the Paris Convention requires a likelihood of confusion to be established by a third party's use of a mark identical or similar to the well-known registered trademark before there is trademark infringement. Some of the trademark law provisions of the bilateral free trade agreements which the United States has entered into require signatory states to offer higher levels of protection to well-known trademarks even in the absence of confusion in the marketplace.

In the both the US-Jordan FTA and the US-Singapore FTA, the signatory states are required to give effect to Articles 1 to 6 of the Joint Recommendation Concerning Provisions of the Protection of Well-Known Marks (1999), adopted by the Assembly of the Paris Union for the Protection of Industrial Property and the General Assembly of the World Intellectual Property Organization ("the WIPO Joint Recommendation").[39] The WIPO Joint Recommendation was adopted at the Thirty-Fourth Series of Meetings of the Assemblies of the Member States of WIPO in September 1999 and encour-

---

[38]   Under which member states are "to refuse or cancel the registration, and to prohibit the use, of a trademark which constitutes a reproduction, an imitation, or a translation, *liable to create confusion*, of a mark considered by the competent authority of the country of registration or use to be *well known* in that country as being already the mark of a person entitled to the benefits of this Convention and *used for identical or similar goods* . . . " (emphasis added).

[39]   *See* Article 4(1)(a) of the US-Jordan FTA and Article 16.1(2)(b)(i) of the US-Singapore FTA.

ages Member States to "protect a well-known mark against conflicting marks, business identifiers and domain names, at least with effect from the time when the mark has become well known in the Member State."[40] A mark "shall be deemed to be in conflict with a well-known mark":

- [Article 4(1)(a)] . . . where that mark, or an essential part thereof, constitutes a reproduction, an imitation, or a transliteration, *liable to create confusion*, of the well-known mark, if the mark . . . is used, is the subject of an application for registration, or is registered, in respect of goods and/or services which are *identical or similar to the goods and/or services* to which the well-known mark applies;[41]

  and

- [Article 4(1)(b)] *Irrespective of the goods and/or services for which a mark is used*, is the subject of an application for registration, or is registered . . . where the mark . . . constitutes a reproduction, an imitation, a translation, or a transliteration of the well-known mark, and at least one of the following conditions is fulfilled:
  (i) The use of the mark would indicate a *connection* between the goods and/or services . . . and the owner of the well-known mark, and would be *likely to damage his interests*;
  (ii) The use of the mark is likely to *impair or dilute in an unfair manner* the distinctive character of the well-known mark;
  (iii) The use of that mark would *take unfair advantage of the distinctive character* of the well-known mark[42]

Article 4(1)(b) of the WIPO Joint Recommendation clearly envisages a broader scope of protection for well-known trademarks which is *not* dependent on a likelihood of confusion arising from the unauthorized use of the mark and *irrespective* of whether such use is made in relation to goods or services which are identical, similar or dissimilar to the goods or services in respect of which the well-known trademark has been registered. These additional layers of protection clearly reflect legal standards which are "TRIPS-plus" in character, conferring extra exclusive rights on those trademark

---

[40] *See* Article 3(1) of the WIPO Joint Recommendation.

[41] (Emphasis added). The scope of protection for well-known marks articulated in this Article is no different from the legal standards enshrined in Article 6*bis* of the Paris Convention, which also deals with the unauthorized use of the mark on "identical or similar goods and/or services" and which also requires such use to be "liable to create confusion" before the trademark proprietor's exclusive rights are infringed upon.

[42] (Emphasis added). Article 4(1)(c) of the WIPO Joint Recommendation also provides that the extended scope of protection in paragraphs (b)(ii) and b(iii) may be confined to those trademarks which are "well known by the public at large."

proprietors whose trademarks have acquired a "well known" status. Under this enhanced regime made available only to well-known trademarks, the proprietor of a well-known trademark is able to stop third parties from making use of the same or a similar mark in a wider range of situations, even if there is no likelihood of confusion in the marketplace as to the source or origin of the goods or services to which it has been applied – so long as the unauthorized use tarnishes the reputation of the well-known trademark, erodes the distinctiveness of the well-known trademark or misappropriates the goodwill generated by the well-known trademark.

Pursuant to its treaty obligations to confer stronger protection on the proprietors of well-known trademarks under the US-Singapore FTA, Singapore amended its trademark legislation, the *Trademarks Act 1998*, in 2004 to strengthen the position of such proprietors in trademark registration, invalidation and infringement proceedings.[43] Similarly, in response to the Supreme Court's decision in *Moseley v V Secret Catalogue*,[44] the United States amended the Lanham Act in 2006 to empower proprietors of famous marks to prevent unauthorized uses of the mark which are "likely to cause dilution by blurring or dilution by tarnishment of the famous mark, regardless of the presence or absence of actual or likely confusion, of competition, or of actual economic injury."[45] However, from the divergence in the statutory language used in the trademark laws of both these countries, it appears that Singapore has adopted a more stringent test requiring proof of *actual* dilution of a well-known trademark before its proprietor can take action under the trademark statute, whereas the amendments made to the laws of the United States adopt a less demanding approach under which injunctive relief is available so long as the proprietor of a famous mark is able to establish a mere *likelihood* of dilution.[46]

---

[43] *See* sections 8(4) and 55(3) of the Singapore *Trademarks Act 1998* (as amended in 2004).

[44] 537 U.S. 418 (2003).

[45] *See* section 2(1) of H.R. 683 (The Trademark Dilution Revision Act of 2006) which amends section 43 of the Trademark Act of 1946 (15 U.S.C. 1125). This amendment is an improvement on the previous version of the federal anti-dilution provisions in the Act insofar as it clearly identifies two distinct forms of harm: dilution by blurring and dilution by tarnishment. For a further discussion of the uncertainty surrounding the objectives behind the federal anti-dilution provisions when they were first introduced in 1995, see Graeme B. Dinwoodie, *Trademarks and Territory: Detaching Trademark Law from the Nation-State*, 41 HOUS. L. REV. 885, 923 (2004).

[46] *See* sections 8(4)(b)(ii)(A) and 55(4)(b)(i) of the Singapore *Trademarks Act 1998* ("would cause dilution in an unfair manner of the distinctive character of the proprietor's trademark") in contrast with Section 43(c) of the United States *Lanham Act* ("likely to cause dilution by blurring or dilution by tarnishment of the famous

The trademark law provisions of the US-Jordan FTA and the US-Singapore FTA which specifically introduce additional levels of protection for well-known trademarks set these treaties apart from the clutch of other bilateral free trade agreements which the United States has recently concluded. Apart from the US-Chile, US-Oman and US-Korea FTAs, the other bilateral treaties do not contain any specific references in their trademark law provisions which deal with the higher standards of protection which should be conferred on well-known trademarks. The US-Chile FTA makes a passing reference to the WIPO Joint Recommendation and declares that the parties recognize "the importance of the *Joint Recommendation Concerning Provisions on the Protection of Well-Known Marks* (1999) . . . and shall be guided by the principles contained in this Recommendation", and only requires measures to be put in place to:

> prohibit or cancel the registration of a trademark identical or similar to a well-known trademark, if the use of that trademark by the registration applicant is likely to cause confusion, or to cause mistake, or to deceive or risk associating the trademark with the owner of the well-known trademark, or constitutes unfair exploitation of the reputation of the trademark.[47]

No specific reference is made in the text of the US-Chile FTA to the dilution of well-known trademarks or a prohibition against unauthorized *use* by third parties of a mark identical or similar to the well-known trademark in circumstances where there is no confusion, mistake or deception arising from such unauthorized conduct.

The US-Oman FTA does not make any reference to the WIPO Joint Recommendation in any of its trademark law provisions, but requires the signatory states to confer additional protection upon proprietors of well-known trademarks through the following provision:

> Each Party shall provide for appropriate measures to *refuse or cancel the registration* and *prohibit the use* of a trademark or geographical indication that is identical or similar to a well-known trademark, for *related goods or services*, if the use. . . is *likely to cause confusion, or to cause mistake, or to deceive* or risk associating the

---

mark"). The amendments made to the United States' trademark legislation were catalyzed by the negative reaction which owners of famous marks had towards the Supreme Court's decision in *Moseley v V Secret Catalogue*, 537 U.S. 418 (2003), which took a literal reading of the then-unamended anti-dilution statutory provisions and required the proprietor of the famous trademark to prove that *actual* dilution had taken place. For a comparison between the trademark laws of these two jurisdictions in respect of the protection offered to well-known and famous trademarks, *see* Burton Ong, *Protecting Well-Known Trademarks: Perspectives from Singapore*, 95 TRADEMARK REP. 1221 (2005) at 1251–4.

[47] *See* Articles 17.2(7), (8) and (9) of the US-Chile FTA (emphasis added).

trademark or geographical indication with the owner of the well-known trademark, or constitutes unfair exploitation of the reputation of the trademark.[48]

As with the US-Chile FTA, this trademark law provision also does not explicitly require signatory states to protect well-known trademarks from unauthorized acts which may dilute their distinctiveness. This provision in the US-Oman FTA, which can also be found in the US-Korea FTA,[49] is essentially a watered-down version of the contents of the WIPO Joint Recommendation, with its scope of application limited to "related goods or services", as opposed to the much broader Article 4(1)(b) of the WIPO Joint Recommendation, which is intended to apply irrespective of whether the unauthorized use of the well-known trademark has taken place in relation to identical, similar or dissimilar goods or services. The phrase "likely to cause confusion, or to cause mistake, or to deceive" – which is also found in the US-Chile FTA – appears to have been taken from the language found in the trademark legislation of the United States,[50] while the references to "associating the trademark . . . with the owner of the well-known trademark" and "constitutes unfair exploitation of the reputation of the trademark" appear to be condensed approximations of the provisions found in Article 4(1)(b)(i) and Article 4(1)(b)(iii) of the WIPO Joint Recommendation. Such an expansively-worded trademark law provision introduces legal standards which clearly exceed the minimum requirements articulated by the TRIPS Agreement, extending the scope of the well-known trademark proprietor's monopoly beyond situations where there is a likelihood of customer confusion relating to the source or origin of a trader's goods or services.

The obvious beneficiaries of these higher standards of legal protection are the proprietors of well-known trademarks – archetypically large business enterprises with deep advertising budgets and omnipresent consumer product and service portfolios. Many of these trademark proprietors are multinational corporations based in the United States which have expanded their operations and sales into a number of different foreign markets. Special interest groups representing these trademark proprietors would naturally have lobbied the United States government to include such trademark law provisions in its bilateral free trade agreements. It would be manifestly advantageous to American proprietors of well-known trademarks who export their brands to foreign markets, which are more accessible to them as a result of these FTAs, to operate within domestic trademarks regimes which enable them to prohibit unauthorized conduct by third parties which may jeopardize the value of their

---

[48] *See* Article 15.2(7) of the US-Oman FTA (emphasis added).
[49] *See* Article 18.2(8) of the US-Korea FTA.
[50] *See* 15 U.S.C. § 1114(1), § 1125(a)(1)(A).

well-known trademarks. Why is it that trademark law provisions which provide additional legal protection to proprietors of well-known trademarks have found their way into the United States' FTAs with Jordan, Singapore, Chile, Oman and South Korea, but not into its FTAs or TPAs with Australia, Morocco, Bahrain, Peru, Colombia or Panama?

Without access to further details relating to the confidential negotiations which lead to the conclusion of these bilateral agreements, one can only speculate as to the precise reasons for these provisions concerning well-known trademarks being successfully incorporated into only some of these FTAs – unlike the almost-uniform inclusion of the "TRIPS-plus" trademark law provisions concerning non-visually perceptible trademarks in all these FTAs. One explanation may simply rest with the unequal bargaining positions of the signatory states and the relative importance of these trademark law provisions when trade-offs were made in the course of negotiations between the officials representing the United States and these states. The additional protection given to proprietors of well-known trademarks was probably a more controversial issue given its far-reaching impact on other traders in the market, including traders who are not even remotely in competition with the proprietor of the well-known trademark, and its potentially chilling effect on their commercial freedom to use marks or signs which are similar to the well-known trademark. In addition, the commercial significance of having these additional layers of trademark protection for the American proprietor of a well-known trademark probably varies from foreign market to foreign market. These stronger rights are probably more valuable to it in a country – such as Singapore – where English is the principal language of commerce and is widely understood by consumers in the marketplace, and where American brands are popular among local and expatriate consumers. Conversely, in countries where Arabic or some other non-romanized language is used as the *lingua franca* of the marketplace, the importance of having stronger protection for well-known trademarks is, from the perspective of corporations which own well-known English-language word marks, correspondingly diminished.

The advantages of an FTA with trademark law provisions compelling the introduction of additional layers of protection for well-known trademarks into the domestic trademark regimes of the signatory states are probably more real to American trademark proprietors than their non-American counterparts. Given the vast disparity in the population sizes[51] of the United States and those countries which have agreed to extra protection for well-known trade-

---

[51] The US Census Bureau's International Data Base offers the following estimates for the population sizes of the following countries in 2007: United States of America (301.1 million), Jordan (6 million), Singapore (4.5 million), Chile (16.3 million), Oman (3.2 million), South Korea (49 million). *See* http://www.census.gov/ipc/www/idb/summaries.html.

marks under their FTAs, it will be significantly less of a challenge for an American trademark proprietor to elevate the status of his trademark into a "well-known" trademark in Jordan, Singapore, Chile, Oman or South Korea than it would be for the Jordanian, Singaporean, Chilean, Omani or South Korean trademark proprietor to attain the status of a "famous" mark in the United States of America. Vast amounts of resources would have to be expended by the non-American trademark proprietor to raise the level of public recognition of the trademark across the United States before it qualifies as a "famous" mark. In contrast, in a small island nation like Singapore, a relatively modest advertising campaign promoting public awareness of the trademark would enable the American trademark proprietor to enjoy the enhanced levels of statutory protection conferred on well-known trademarks.

Table 9.2 below identifies the "TRIPS-plus" trademark law provisions discussed above and their corresponding locations in various bilateral free trade agreements.

IV. Trademark law provisions across an international web of bilateral free trade agreements

The discussion above has focused on the trademark provisions found in those bilateral free trade agreements which have been concluded by the United States with its various trading partners. The picture painted thus far situates the United States at the centre of a hub-and-spoke system of bilateral treaties with Jordan, Singapore, Chile, Australia, Morocco, Bahrain, Oman, Peru, Colombia, Panama and South Korea (see Figure 9.1 below). Further spokes will be added down the road if and when the United States should conclude its free trade agreements with Malaysia, Thailand, the United Arab Emirates and the countries of the South African Customs Union. Bilateral free trade agreements have also been concluded between these countries and their respective non-US trading partners as well. A more appropriate metaphor which captures the range of bilateral treaties which have been concluded in recent years would be that of a "web" of free trade agreements between individual states and their trading partners, between these trading partners and with other states which are *their* respective trading partners. The United States has FTAs with Singapore and Jordan, while Singapore and Jordan have an FTA between themselves and their own FTAs with their other trading partners as well.

An examination of the some of the key trademark law provisions found in the bilateral FTAs which the United States has concluded – as captured in Tables 9.1 and 9.2 – reveals a very significant degree of consistency in the contents of these provisions. Substantially similar, if not identically-worded, "TRIPS-based" and "TRIPS-plus" provisions can be found in all these FTAs. There is thus a clear factual basis for those who have criticized the use of bilateral FTAs

Table 9.2 *Trademark law provisions in bilateral FTAs which require signatory states to implement "TRIPS-plus" legal standards in the domestic trademark law regimes*

TRIPS Provisions	US-Jordan FTA 2000	US-Singapore FTA 2003	US-Chile FTA 2003	US-Australia FTA 2004	US-Morocco FTA 2004	US-Bahrain FTA 2004	US-Oman FTA 2004	US-Peru TPA 2006	US-Colombia TPA 2006	US-Panama TPA 2007	US-Korea TPA 2007
Visual Perceptibility not to be a condition of trademark registration	N.A.	Art. 16.2(1)	N.A.	Art. 17.2(2)	Art. 15.2(1)	Art. 14.2(1)	Art. 15.2(1)	Art. 15.2(1)	Art. 16.2(1)	N.A.	Art. 18.2(1)
Specific reference to scent marks and/or sound marks as protectable subject matter	N.A.	Art. 16.2(1) (scents)	Art. 17.2(1) (scents and sounds)	Art. 17.2(2) (scents and sounds)	Art. 15.2(1) (scents and sounds)	Art. 14.2(1) (scents and sounds)	Art. 15.2(1) (scents and sounds)	Art. 15.2(1) (scents and sounds)	Art. 16.2(1) (scents and sounds)	Art. 15.2(1) (scents)	Art. 18.2(1) (scents and sounds)
Additional protection for well-known trademarks	Art. 4( )(a)	Art. 16.1(2)(b)(i)	Art. 17.2(5)–(9)	N.A.	N.A.	N.A.	Art. 15.2(7)	N.A.	N.A.	N.A.	Art. 18.2(8)

250   *Trademark law and theory*

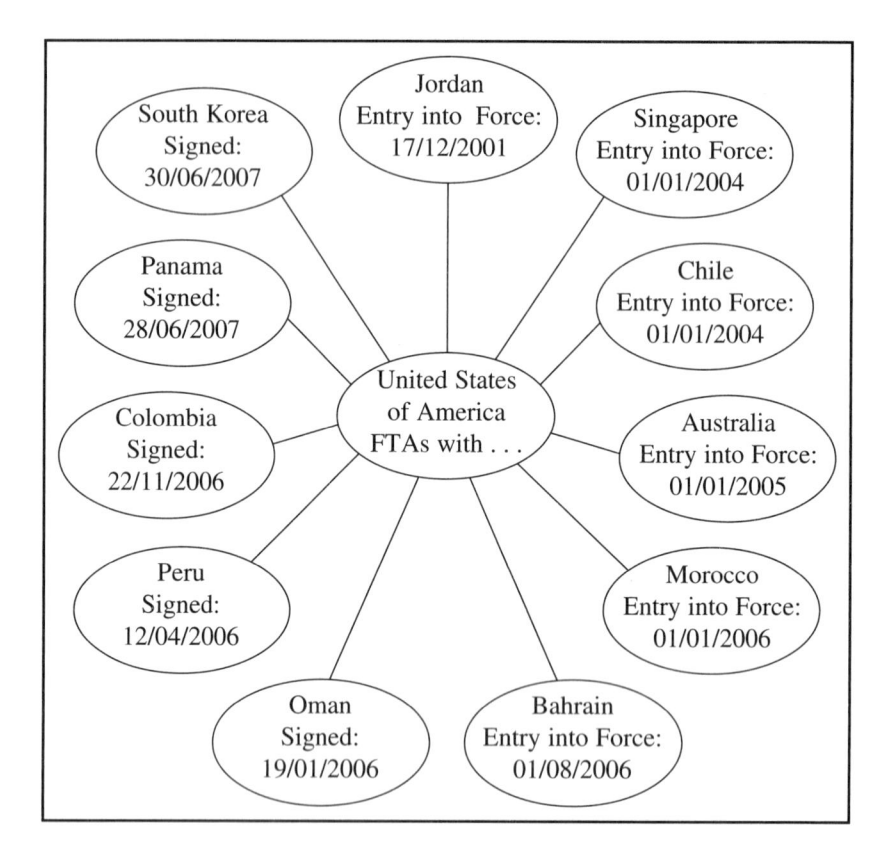

```
                    Jordan
  South Korea    Entry into Force:      Singapore
    Signed:        17/12/2001        Entry into Force:
   30/06/2007                           01/01/2004

    Panama                                Chile
    Signed:                           Entry into Force:
   28/06/2007                            01/01/2004
                   United States
    Colombia       of America           Australia
    Signed:         FTAs with...     Entry into Force:
   22/11/2006                            01/01/2005

      Peru                               Morocco
    Signed:                          Entry into Force:
   12/04/2006                            01/01/2006

              Oman              Bahrain
            Signed:          Entry into Force:
           19/01/2006           01/08/2006
```

Figure 9.1   The "wheel" of bilateral FTAs between the United States of America and its trading partners

as a "forum-shifting" device of sorts to set higher intellectual property standards outside of multilateral regimes such as the TRIPS Agreement.[52] If enough spokes are added to the "wheel" of bilateral free trade agreements concluded by the United States, with each FTA demanding the same stronger

---

[52]   *See supra* note 14 and accompanying text. It is worth noting that the European Union appears to be moving in the same direction as the United States in seeking the inclusion of substantive "TRIPS-plus" intellectual property provisions in its bilateral free trade agreements. As the author of one report has noted, in the existing trade agreements which the EU has entered into, "the IP chapters in the agreements are quite homogenous, with relatively few variations between them" and "with very few exceptions, the provisions of the EU agreements do not incorporate substantive provisions dealing, for instance, with exclusive rights, exceptions to rights, terms of protection . . . instead they are built, basically, on commitments to adhere to the TRIPS Agreement

levels of protection for intellectual property as are required under the TRIPS Agreement, and if signatory states each fulfil their respective obligations under these FTAs and implement these standards in their respective domestic intellectual property laws, a new set of international intellectual property standards will eventually emerge.

Is this strategy of using bilateral trade agreements as an intellectual property standard-setting process reinforced by the other FTAs that comprise the remainder of the "web" of trading agreements between countries other than the United States? Looking at just the trademark law provisions of a few of these other FTAs, to which the United States is *not* a party, the current position requires this question to be answered in the negative. For example, while the trademark law provisions of the United States' bilateral free trade agreements with Jordan, Australia, Singapore, Chile and South Korea contain the "TRIPS-plus" elements discussed above, these trademark law provisions are *not* found in any of the bilateral FTAs which Singapore has concluded with Jordan, Australia, Chile or South Korea (see Figures 9.2 and 9.3 on pp 252–3). Instead, the FTAs which Singapore has concluded merely reiterate the legal standards found in the TRIPS Agreement which signatory states are already obliged to implement as members of the World Trade Organization.

What does the non-inclusion of "TRIPS-plus" legal standards in the trademark law provisions of these FTAs, to which the United States is not a party, suggest about the importance attached by the signatory states to such developments in the law of trademarks? One might reasonably conclude that the governments of Singapore, Australia, Jordan, Chile and South Korea have not prioritized trademark law issues in the same way as the government of the United States when conducting their trade negotiations, and that trademark owners based in these jurisdictions were not as concerned with securing higher standards of trademark protection as their American counterparts.

It would thus be fair to say that the government of the United States, acting

---

and to multilateral IP agreements negotiated within the framework of WIPO . . .". In the EU's bilateral trade agreements, particular emphasis has been placed on compliance with the Geographical Indications provisions of the TRIPS Agreement. However, the author goes on to point out that the "EU is shifting towards a more comprehensive approach" in its more recent trade negotiations, with proposed IP provisions "going beyond the TRIPS Agreement in various aspects" – one such comprehensive proposal was made by the EU to the Caribbean Forum of the African, Caribbean and Pacific States (CARIFORUM) in which it was proposed, *inter alia*, that the CARIFORUM states accepted the *WIPO Joint Recommendation Concerning Provisions on the Protection of Well-Known Marks*. See Maximiliano Santa-Cruz S. (2007), INTELLECTUAL PROPERTY PROVISIONS IN EUROPEAN UNION TRADE AGREEMENTS: IMPLICATIONS FOR DEVELOPING COUNTRIES, ICTSD IPRs and Sustainable Development Issue Paper No. 20, International Centre for Trade and Sustainable Development, Geneva, Switzerland, at pp. 10, 18 and 23.

252 *Trademark law and theory*

```
"TRIPS-based"
Trademark Law
Provisions:
A. Article 16(1)
B. Article 16(3)
C. Article 17
(See Table 9.1 above)
```

Jordan — Entry into Force: Dec. 17, 2001 — **A, B, E**

Chile — Entry into Force: Jan. 1, 2004 — **A, B, C, D, E**

United States of America FTAs with . . .

Singapore — Entry into Force: Jan. 1, 2004 — **A, B, C, D, E**

South Korea — Signed: Jun. 30, 2007 — **A, B, C, D**

Australia — Entry into Force: Jan. 1, 2005 — **A, B, C, D, E**

```
"TRIPS-plus"
Trademark Law
Provisions:
D. Registrability of non-visual
   trademarks (especially
   scents and sounds)
E. Additional protection for
   well-known trade marks
(See Table 9.2 above)
```

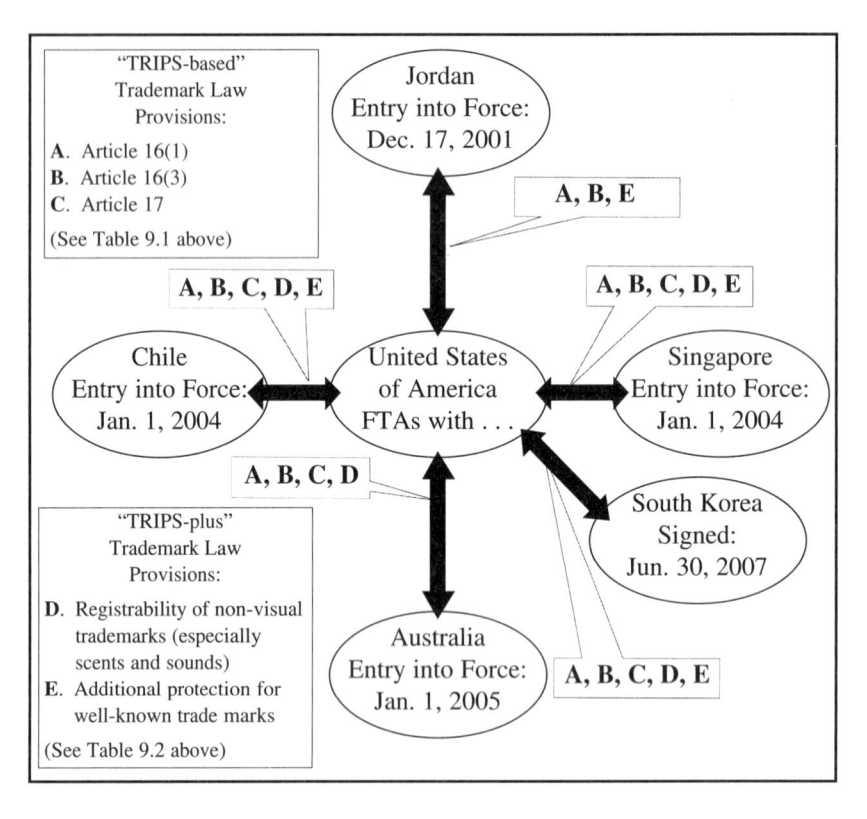

Figure 9.2   The trademark law provisions found in five selected FTAs concluded by the United States of America

in the interests of the trademark-owning corporate constituents it represents, has played a pivotal role in steering the course of global trademark jurisprudence by securing bilateral treaty commitments from its various trading partners to expand their respective domestic trademark law regimes and implement "TRIPS-plus" legal standards. In the medium to long term, if this strategy continues to be successfully employed by the United States (and perhaps the European Union in its future trade agreements)[53] and trademark statutes around the world are amended to reflect these new standards, a new set of international legal norms will eventually emerge in the law of trademarks without the need for a multilateral consensus among the global community. Given that bilateral free trade agreements are negotiated privately between governments, the

---

53   *See supra* note 52.

```
                    ┌─────────────────┐
                    │     Jordan      │
                    │ Entry into Force:│
                    │  Aug. 22, 2005  │
                    └─────────────────┘
```

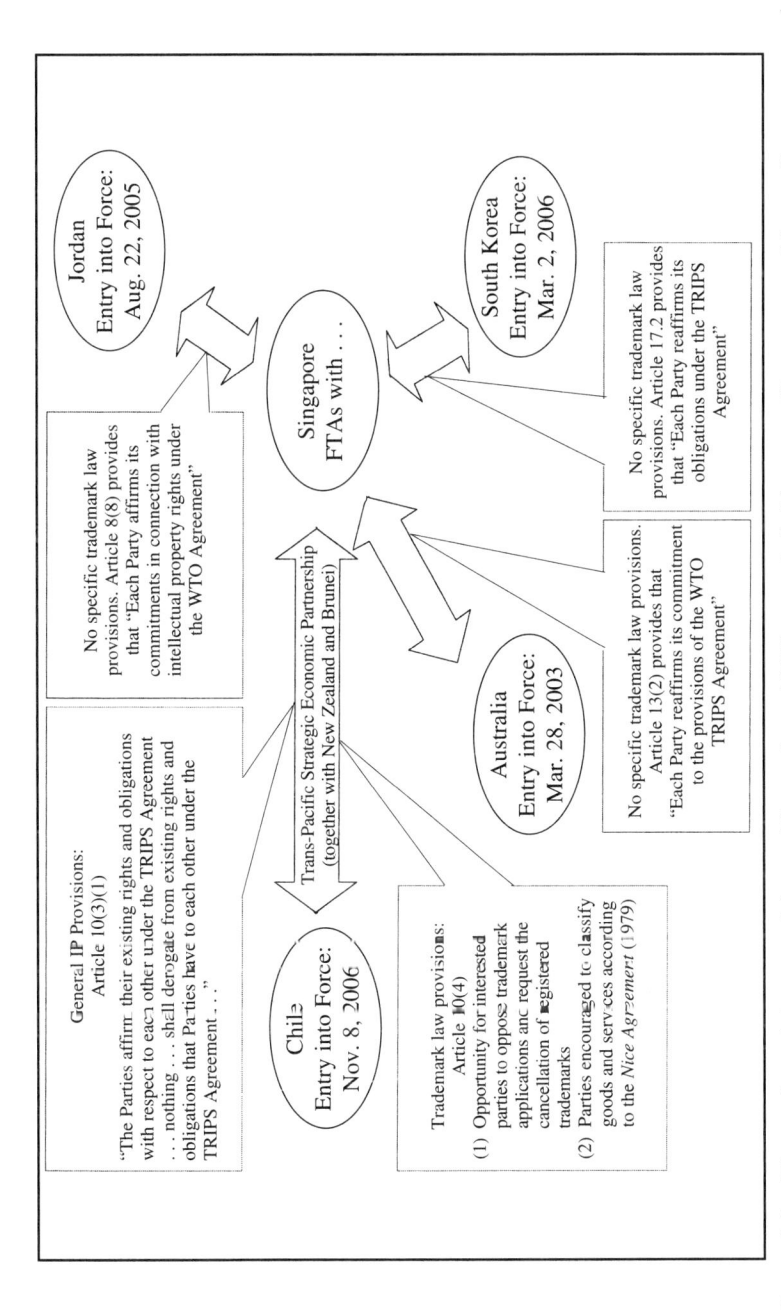

General IP Provisions: Article 10(3)(1)

"The Parties affirm their existing rights and obligations with respect to each other under the TRIPS Agreement ... nothing ... shall derogate from existing rights and obligations that Parties have to each other under the TRIPS Agreement ..."

No specific trademark law provisions. Article 8(8) provides that "Each Party affirms its commitments in connection with intellectual property rights under the WTO Agreement"

Singapore FTAs with ...

South Korea — Entry into Force: Mar. 2, 2006

No specific trademark law provisions. Article 17.2 provides that "Each Party reaffirms its obligations under the TRIPS Agreement"

Australia — Entry into Force: Mar. 28, 2003

No specific trademark law provisions. Article 13(2) provides that "Each Party reaffirms its commitment to the provisions of the WTO TRIPS Agreement"

Trans-Pacific Strategic Economic Partnership (together with New Zealand and Brunei)

Chile — Entry into Force: Nov. 8, 2006

Trademark law provisions: Article 10(4)

(1) Opportunity for interested parties to oppose trademark applications and request the cancellation of registered trademarks
(2) Parties encouraged to classify goods and services according to the *Nice Agreement* (1979)

Figure 9.3 The trademark law provisions of four selected FTAs concluded between Singapore and its trading partners that have also entered into FTAs with the United States of America

253

254 *Trademark law and theory*

downside to this approach towards standard-setting in the intellectual property world is that there are few, if any, opportunities for public debate on the desirability of adopting these new standards before the signatory states contractually commit themselves to these changes.

V. Pushing the frontiers of trademark law in a globalized economy

As with the other areas of intellectual property, the pressures to expand the scope of legal protection conferred by trademarks originate from the intellectual property owners themselves. Resource-rich trademark proprietors, and the lobbyists who represent them, are the real driving force behind the inclusion of trademark law provisions amongst the package of trade-related issues that governments address when negotiating bilateral free trade agreements. Not content with just influencing the domestic laws of the country in which they are based, these trademark owners have very successfully persuaded their government representatives to export similar legal standards into the trademark law frameworks of other countries through the network of bilateral free trade agreements which they have entered into with these trading partners.

This trend towards harmonizing – "upwards" – the trademark law standards adopted by different legal systems is driven by the increasingly globalized character of the business environment in which trademark-owning corporations operate. Having spent substantial resources cultivating the goodwill associated with their trademarks, developing a distinctive brand identity, and investing in marketing and promotional activities, often on a global scale, successful trademark proprietors are very likely to eye overseas markets as potential avenues for expanding their businesses. Venturing beyond the shores of their home market will often involve utilizing these trademarks on goods and services offered to customers abroad. Some degree of uniformity in the trademark laws of these foreign markets, to the extent that they are similar to the laws which the trademark proprietor is already familiar with, would facilitate the extension of their trading activities into these markets.

But at what cost? Expanding the scope of registrable subject matter to include non-visually perceptible marks as trademarks creates an entirely new set of practical and conceptual difficulties[54] in applying classic principles of trademark law to smells, sounds, tastes and textures. This would include trying

---

[54] For an idea of the difficulties which the European Courts have had with non-visual trademarks, *see* Sieckmann v Deutsches Patent Und Markenamt (Case C-273/00), [2003] R.P.C. 38 ("balsamically fruity with a slight hint of cinnamon" olfactory mark); *cf.* Vennootschap Onder Firma Senta Aromatic Marketing's Application (Case R 156/1998-2), [1999] E.T.M.R. 429 ("smell of fresh cut grass" for tennis balls). In the context of sound marks, *see* Shield Mark BV v Joost Kist H.O.D.N. Memex (Case C-283/01), [2004] R.P.C. 17 ("first nine notes of Beethoven's 'Für Elise'. . ." and "an onomatopoeia imitating a cockcrow").

to determine if a smell or sound is *a part of* a product or service, or whether it is a trademark which has been *applied* to a product or a service. Legal concepts such as "inherent distinctiveness", "secondary meaning", and "trademark use" – which have an established place in current trademark jurisprudence – may not make as much sense in the world of non-visual trademarks, thereby creating additional uncertainty among traders in the marketplace. Expanding the scope of trademark protection given to well-known trademarks to situations where there is no risk of public confusion is certainly an attractive proposition to the proprietor of the well-known trademark, but it may have an unintended chilling effect on the commercial freedom of other traders, parodists and other interested members of the public to use the same or a similar mark on any goods or services.

In a globalized economy, the international trade agenda of states with highly sought-after consumer markets will continue to play a highly significant role in shaping the frontiers of trademark law for so long as intellectual property issues remain an integral part of the bargains struck between states in reaching their bilateral free trade agreements. The political realities of the present-day international economic landscape make it possible for countries such as the United States to utilize bilateral free trade agreements as an effective tool to initiate changes in the domestic trademark regimes of its trading partners. The bilateral free trade agreements which have been concluded thus far indicate that this has been a fairly successful strategy towards setting new legal standards which may, over time, evolve into international legal norms without the need for a multilateral consensus. That this approach towards standard-setting may eventually result in a global convergence towards "TRIPS-plus" standards of protection for trademarks is cause for some concern, particularly since the process does not give other stakeholders adequate opportunities to air their concerns. But while individual states may introduce the same intellectual property standards into their respective legislative regimes, it is ultimately left to the courts of each territory to interpret and apply these legal standards to the cases which are argued before them, thereby creating interesting opportunities for divergence in the trademark jurisprudence of each territory. Judicial experience with intellectual property statutes suggests that there is no guarantee that similarly worded laws will lead to similar legal outcomes given that judges have demonstrated varying degrees of skepticism towards the monopoly-creating propensities of these legislative instruments.[55]

---

[55] *See supra* note 46 and accompanying text (referring to the debate concerning the scope of the anti-dilution right for well-known or famous trademarks).

PART III

CRITICAL ISSUES

Section A

Trademarks and Speech

10 Reconciling trademark rights and expressive values: how to stop worrying and learn to love ambiguity

*Rochelle Cooper Dreyfuss**

> *I'm a Barbie girl, in my Barbie world*
> *Life is plastic, it's fantastic . . .*[1]

2

When I campaign alone, I'm approachable. Women talk to me, complain, but when I'm with Ted I'm a Barbie doll.[3]

---

[*] Pauline Newman Professor of Law, New York University School of Law. I would like to thank Jesse Dyer, NYU Class of 2008, for his superb research assistance and the Filomen and D'Agostino and Max E. Greenberg Research Fund for its financial support. This chapter was shaped, in part, by the national responses I received in my capacity as Trademark Reporter for the Association Littéraire et Artistique Internationale (ALAI) Study Session on Copyright & Freedom of Expression (Barcelona 2006).

[1] AQUA, *Barbie Girl, on* AQUARIUM (MCA Records 1997).
[2] The Distorted Barbie: X-files Barbie, http://www.detritus.net/projects/barbie/ ("What about all those aspects of our society that are not represented by Barbie? Let's open up the closet doors and let out the repressed real-world Barbies; Barbie's extended family of disowned and inbred rejects; politically correct Barbies that celebrate the ignored and disenfranchised.").
[3] MARCIA CHELLIS, THE JOAN KENNEDY STORY: LIVING WITH THE KENNEDYS

The waitress rallies quickly. "I'm Barbie. No last name . . . I sign it like this, with a little trademark sign after it." She picks up Alice's ballpoint pen and writes a carefully looped, upward slanting "Barbie TM."[4]

Trademarks and free expression are on a collision course. In the early 1990s, I wrote two articles examining the expansion of trademark law from its core focus on confusion about marketing signals, to cover such matters as dilution, implications of sponsorship, and rights of publicity. I suggested that these expansions were putting increasing pressure on speech interests.[5] It seemed to me that signifiers drawn from mythology, history, and literature were losing their potency in a globalized environment in which the populace lacks a shared vocabulary or much interest in the classics. I posited that well-known marks were taking the place of these references.[6] Used as metaphors, similes, and metonyms, trademarks were becoming the *lingua franca* of the communicative sphere. I was concerned, however, at the extent to which these "allusive uses"[7] were coming under private control: judges were jumping ever more quickly from recognizing the value in a mark, to allowing the mark's proprietor to capture that value. I thought that, in fact, the significance of a mark was in large part generated by its audience, through the way in which it was recoded and recontextualized. Accordingly, it was incumbent upon courts to understand how signals functioned and to recognize the dual provenance of their value. While it was appropriate to give proprietors marketing control—rights over signaling value—other aspects—expressive value—belonged to the public. I admitted that separating these two dimensions would sometimes be difficult, but suggested techniques to make that division workable.

---

191 (Jove ed. 1986) (quoting Joan Kennedy's account of her life with Senator Ted Kennedy); *see also* Rochelle Cooper Dreyfuss, *Expressive Genericity: Trademarks as Language in the Pepsi Generation*, 65 NOTRE DAME L. REV. 397 (1990) (citing Chellis's book).

[4] BARBARA KINGSOLVER, PIGS IN HEAVEN 139 (1993); *see also* Rochelle Cooper Dreyfuss, *We Are Symbols and Inhabit Symbols, So Should We Be Paying Rent? Deconstructing the Lanham Act and Rights of Publicity*, 20 COLUM. VLA J.L. & ARTS 123 (1996) [hereinafter *We Are Symbols*] (citing Kingsolver's book).

[5] *See Expressive Genericity, supra* note 3; *We Are Symbols, supra* note 4.

[6] I use the terms "mark" and "trademark" to denote trademarks as well as service, certification, and collective marks, and use the terms "goods" and "products" to encompass services. Much of what I say here applies equally to celebrity images. *See, e.g.*, Alain A. Levasseur, *The Boundaries of Property Rights: La Notion de Biens*, 54 AM. J. COMP. L. 145 (2006); Diane Leenheer Zimmerman, *Who Put the Right in the Right of Publicity?*, 9 DEPAUL-LCA J. ART. & ENT. L. 35 (1998).

[7] I owe this term to Michael Spence, *The Mark as Expression/The Mark as Property*, 58 CURRENT LEGAL PROBS. 491 (2005).

Over the last decade, a solution based on separating the spheres in which symbols operate has become increasingly less tractable. On the trademark holders' side, interest in and power over marks have expanded considerably. Proprietors use trademarks to maintain exclusivity after patents and copyrights have expired and trade secrets have been exposed; they also use them to leverage reputation across product categories.[8] They engage in "lifestyle marketing"—offering goods across a range of sectors.[9] In some cases, trademarks take on a life of their own: merchandising a mark through various licensing ventures can sometimes earn as much as the sales of the underlying product.[10]

Trademark holders have had remarkable success developing law responsive to these concerns: a range of new concepts, such as initial-interest[11] and post-sale confusion;[12] a new focus on trade dress protection;[13] and new and improved rights of action, including federal dilution protection (in the European Community as well as in the United States[14]) and cybersquatting prohibitions (emanating both from law and from contractual obligation).[15] Parallel developments are unfolding at the international level: it is now

---

[8] See, e.g., Gideon Parchomovsky & Peter Siegelman, *Towards an Integrated Theory of Intellectual Property*, 88 VA. L. REV. 1455 (2002).

[9] See, e.g., Jennifer Steinhauer, *That's Not a Skim Latte. It's a Way of Life*, NEW YORK TIMES, March 21, 1999, at Sec. 4, p. 5, col. 1 ("Once people get to know a brand's most famous product, the thinking goes, they will trust that brand to deliver any number of items, even if the original product has no relationship to the subsequent stuff the company hawks.").

[10] See, e.g., Arsenal Football Club plc v Reed, [2002] ECR I-10273, ¶ 83, [2003] All ER (EC) 1 (opinion of the Advocate General) (sale of objects depicting the mark).

[11] See, e.g., Brookfield Commc'ns. Inc. v West Coast Entm't. Corp., 174 F.3d 1036, 1062–5 (9th Cir. 1999).

[12] See, e.g., Ferrari S.P.A. Esercizio v Roberts, 944 F.2d 1235 (6th Cir. 1991).

[13] See generally Margreth Barrett, *Consolidating the Diffuse Paths to Trade Dress Functionality: Encountering TrafFix on the Way to Sears*, 61 WASH & LEE L. REV. 79 (2004). Although trademark holders' interest in protecting trade dress is growing, this may be one area where the courts have been less than sympathetic. Indeed, trade dress has occupied an unusual amount of the U.S. Supreme Court's attention. See TrafFix Devices, Inc. v Mktg. Displays, Inc., 532 U.S. 23 (2001); Wal-Mart Stores, Inc. v Samara Bros., Inc., 529 U.S. 205 (2000); Qualitex Co. v Jacobson Prods. Co., Inc., 514 U.S. 159, 163–4 (1995); Two Pesos, Inc. v Taco Cabana, Inc., 505 U.S. 763 (1992).

[14] See, e.g., 15 U.S.C. § 1125(c) (1996, amended 2006); Council Regulation 40/94, 1994 O.J. (L 11), art. 9(1)(c) [hereinafter Regulation on the Community Trademark]; EC Trademark Directive, 89/104/EEC, 21 December 1988, art. 5(2) [hereinafter EC Trademark Directive] (permitting each State to enact dilution law and some have. See, e.g., UK Trade Marks Act of 1994 § 10(3)).

[15] See, e.g., 15 U.S.C. § 1125(d); Domain Name Dispute Resolution Policies, available at http://www.icann.org/udrp.

mandatory for the members of the World Trade Organization to recognize geographical indications and to offer enhanced protection to marks that are well known;[16] accumulating soft law suggests the scope of this protection is quite broad and may encompass protection against dilution.[17] Through a combination of soft law, multilateralism, bilateralism, and old-fashioned industry pressure, less conventional signs, such as scents, sounds, and color, are also becoming the subject matter of trademark protection.[18] And moves are afoot to create new rights to control traditional knowledge, including tribal symbols.[19]

Public use of trademarks has also multiplied. Fans have always put marks on tee shirts, sports caps, bumper stickers, buttons, mugs, posters—even birthday cakes—to express their affiliation with schools, teams, social organizations, and products. Some of these usages have become less complimentary. As one South African judge put it, tee shirts decorated with trademarks are now a focus for "young irreverent people who enjoy the idea of being gadflies."[20] Nor is "gadflying" as limited as was once the case. Digitization reduces the cost of using trademarks in traditional media while the Internet offers fresh opportunities—the chance to create widely available websites to sell marked products or to use trademarks artistically, politically,

---

[16] Agreement on Trade-Related Aspects of Intellectual Property Rights, April 15, 1994, Marrakesh Agreement Establishing the World Trade Organization, Annex 1C, Results of the Uruguay Round vol. 3, 33 I.L.M. 1125, arts. 22 and 16(2) (1994) [hereinafter TRIPS Agreement] (incorporating art. 6bis of the Paris Convention for the Protection of Industrial Property, March 20, 1883, as revised at the Stockholm Conference, July 14, 1967, 21 U.S.T. 1538, 828 U.N.T.S. 305 [hereinafter Paris Convention]).

[17] *See* 1999 WIPO Joint Resolution Concerning Provisions on the Protection of Well-Known Marks, General Report of the Assemblies of the Member States of WIPO, 34th Annual Meeting, Doc. A/34/16 ¶¶ 171–83 (September 1999); *see also* TRIPS Agreement art. 16(3); Frederick W. Mostert, *Well-Known and Famous Marks: Is Harmony Possible in the Global Village?*, 86 TRADEMARK REP. 103, 130 (1996) (suggesting dilution is a requirement); Paul J. Heald, *Trademarks and Geographic Indications: Exploring the Contours of the TRIPS Agreement*, 29 VAND. J. TRANSNAT'L L. 635, 642–3, 654–5 (1996) (suggesting it is not).

[18] *See, e.g.*, David Vaver, *Unconventional and Well-Known Trade Marks*, 2005 SING. J. LEGAL STUD. 1 (2005).

[19] *See, e.g.*, Stephen D. Osborne, *Protecting Tribal Stories: The Perils of Propertization*, 28 AM. INDIAN L. REV. 203 (2003/2004) (citing Rebecca Lopez, *Tribes Seek Trademark Protection for Sacred Symbols* (July 9, 1999), *available at* www.onlineathens.com/stories/070999/new_tribe.shtml; *cf.* Rick Mofina, *Culture "Confiscated" for High Fashion: Inuit Women Want to Trademark Tradition to Fend Off Fashion Industry's "Exploitation,"* OTTAWA CITIZEN, November 16, 1999, at A1).

[20] Laugh It Off Promotions CC v SAB Int'l (Finance) BV, 2005 (8) BCLR 743 (CC) (May 27, 2005), ¶ 87 (Sachs, J., concurring).

and humorously, or to critique the trademark holder's activities, politics, or products.²¹

Most important, the dichotomy between the marketing and expressive spheres, which was always somewhat indistinct, has collapsed entirely. In the absence of a means for communicating directly with customers, trademark holders use their marks to send not only traditional messages about the attributes of their products (source, quality and the like), but also a range of other, more expressive (and, as Jessica Litman says, "atmospheric"²²) kinds of information. "Life style marketing," after all, requires transmission of lifestyle information—information about social values, ideals, and world-view.²³ Other trademark usages are likewise becoming highly complex. Comparative ads, a staple of U.S. marketing, have spread to other countries.²⁴ Trade dress and trademarks are particularly useful in such ads because they can create forceful images and sound bites, calling one product to mind while marketing its rival.

Trademarks have also taken on a wholly new role: on the Internet, they are navigation tools, used by consumers to find merchants and by merchants to find consumers. Some shoppers look for goods on the Internet by using the trademark as a domain name. If they enter it correctly, they will likely find the trademark holder's website, but they may also discover that the same mark is used by merchants in remote locations,²⁵ or incorporated into several Internet addresses.²⁶ Even if they reach the right trademark holder's website, they may

---

[21] *See, e.g.*, Bridgestone Firestone, Inc. v Myers, WIPO Arbitration and Mediation Center, Case No. D2000-0190 (July 6, 2000), *available at* http://arbiter.wipo.int/domains/decisions/html/2000/d2000-0190.html (concerning the domain names <ihatebridgestone.com>, <ihatefirestone.com> and <bridgestonesucks.com>); The Distorted Barbie, *supra* note 2; http://www.somethingawful.com/ (offering a range of gadflying services).

[22] Jessica Litman, *Breakfast with Batman: The Public Interest in the Advertising Age*, 108 YALE L.J. 1717 (1999).

[23] *See generally* Vincent Chiappetta, *Trademarks: More Than Meets the Eye*, 2003 U. ILL. J.L. TECH. & POL'Y 35.

[24] European law is an example. *See, e.g.*, Council Directive 97/55/EC, 1997 O.J. (L 290) 18, amending Council Directive 84/450/EEC of September 10, 1984 on misleading and comparative advertising (1984 O.J. (L 250) 17) to permit nonmisleading comparative ads.

[25] An example is the clash between American Budweiser beer and Czech Budvar beer. *See, e.g.*, Richard M. Terpstra, *Which Bud's For You? An Examination of the Trademark Dispute Between Anheuser-Busch and Budejovicky Budvar in the English Courts*, 18 TEMP. INT'L & COMP. L.J. 479 (2004).

[26] *See, e.g.*, Columbia University v Columbia/HCA Healthcare Corp., 964 F. Supp. 733 (S.D.N.Y. 1997) (raising questions about whether columbia.net, the defendant's domain name, could be confused with the plaintiff's columbia.edu.)

be treated to a competitor's ad, set to pop-up when the site is accessed.[27] And, of course, if the mark is typed incorrectly, the consumer may encounter a "typosquatter"—the site of a rival, perhaps, or a griper.[28] Another strategy is to "google" the trademark (enter it into a search engine); such key-word searches will present the consumer with a list of sites, some of which may hawk alternative products—a rival may be gaming the algorithm of the search engine[29] or the listing-cum-ad may be keyed to appear whenever a search on the mark is conducted.[30]

The result is a highly complicated picture. Images and trade symbols are increasing in cultural significance at exactly the time when protection is expanding. The exigencies of a global, on-line marketplace make stronger protection for trademarks necessary just when technology makes their widespread expressive use more feasible. Internet shopping requires *both* exclusivity *and* unrestricted availability—the former, to keep search costs down by ensuring that consumers find the right site; the latter to allow markets to work efficiently by ensuring that consumers receive information about comparable products. As the commercial/expressive duality of marks' meanings become salient, so too does the expressive/commercial duality of their use: many of those tee shirts, mugs, posters, and art works are sources of profits—profits that derive from the trademark but which are channeled back into efforts to destabilize its meaning.

It is not as though courts are unaware of these problems. In fact, cases with expressive claims to trademark usage have arisen in jurisdictions around the world and adjudicators have developed a variety of responses. In some places, judges exploit statutory language and the facts of the case to limit the ambit of trademark protection and preserve space for free (or free-er) speech; other jurisdictions recognize very strong trademark claims, but courts will balance these rights against constitutive norms. Each approach has advantages and limitations. However, it is not always clear that the courts considering these issues have fully grappled with the reality of the problem. To many judges, the

---

[27] *See, e.g.*, 1-800 Contacts, Inc. v WhenU.Com, Inc., 414 F.3d 400 (2d Cir. 2005).
[28] *See, e.g.*, Google Inc. v Sergey Gridasov, Claim Number: FA0505000474816, *available at* http://www.arb-forum.com/domains/decisions/474816.htm (denying respondent in a domain name dispute rights over <googkle.com>, <ghoogle.com>, <gfoogle.com> and <gooigle.com>).
[29] At one time, this was done by using the trademark as a metatag. *See, e.g.*, Playboy Enters., Inc. v Welles, 279 F.3d 796 (9th Cir. 2002).
[30] *See, e.g.*, Google France v Louis Vuitton Malletier, Cour d'appel de Paris (June 28, 2006) (key word advertising). For a review of searching strategies involving trademarks, see Eric Goldman, *Deregulating Relevancy in Internet Trademark Law*, 54 EMORY L.J. 507 (2005).

goal of trademark law is to safeguard the ability of a mark to "guarantee the identity ... of marked products ... without any possibility of confusion"[31] (or tarnishment, or blurring, or on-line interference). In today's markets, however, that goal may be unattainable. Even if the problems noted above did not exist, cheap airline tickets and a taste for foreign food and culture expose consumers to familiar trademarks that signify unfamiliar merchants. Converging product functionalities (such as computers that play music) can similarly confer multiple meanings on a single mark.[32] In short, conflicting uses of trademarks cannot be avoided.

If preventing confusion, dilution, and cyberconflicts is not feasible, the best a legal system can do is adopt rules that help consumers accurately resolve the inevitable tension. This chapter begins with an examination of the doctrinal approaches taken thus far and the limits on what such analyses can achieve. After an assessment of the normative commitments underlying these approaches, the chapter closes with an argument for paying closer attention to the strategies people employ when confronted with ambiguity. Lessons drawn from cognitive and behavioral research may provide better protection for the interests of trademark holders and expressive users alike.

I. Doctrinal approaches

As noted above, two kinds of legal systems can be distinguished. In one, the trademark statute is interpreted to delegate authority to courts to protect expressive interests by taking a hard look at the individual facts of individual cases. A second approach is to adopt highly protective legislation, but to ameliorate harsh results by weighing the outcomes against constitutionally-based user interests. Each approach has important limitations.

A. Statute-based factual solutions

In theory, trademark law is crafted with the goal of balancing the interests of trademark holders against the interests of expressive users—or at least, with the goal of giving judges the tools to achieve that balance in individual cases.[33] Statutes interpreted this way include several mechanisms that can be used to allocate rights. For all three kinds of trademark violations (traditional infringement, dilution, and cyberpiracy), these include (broadly speaking) the

---

[31] S.M. Maniatis, *Whither European Trade Mark Law? Arsenal and Davidoff: The Creative Disorder Stage*, 7 MARQ. INTELL. PROP. L. REV. 99, 132 (2003) (discussing Arsenal Football Club Plc v Reed, 2002 ECR I-10273, Case C-206/01).

[32] *See, e.g.*, Apple Corps Ltd v Apple Computer, Inc., [2006] EWHC 996 (Ch) Ch D (the so-called Beatles v iTunes case over rights to the mark "Apple" for music).

[33] *See generally* Pierre N. Leval, *Trademark: Champion of Free Speech*, 27 COLUM. J.L. & ARTS 187 (2004).

requirements of distinctiveness, actionable use, a showing of harm, as well as the absence of a recognized defense.

1. Distinctiveness Cases involving any of the three trademark violations begin with the assertion that the plaintiff holds a valid mark.[34] Thus, the primary safeguard for speech interests is that marks are unprotectable if they are understood to explain what the product is, or on the trade dress side, to be needed for the product to function properly.[35]

Classical trademark law takes an essentially all-or-nothing approach to distinctiveness: if a mark is not intrinsically distinctive or has failed to acquire secondary meaning, then it cannot be protected at all. As such, the requirement is not capable of carving out expressive access to marks that operate in both the marketing and expressive spheres. In my earlier work, I had high hopes that a middle ground could nonetheless be found, that this requirement could be redefined to allocate interests in marks that were, at least in some applications, not "merely" expressive and thus, could function as trademarks within those realms.[36] I argued that courts should analyze how even valid trademarks were being utilized. If, in a given case, the defendant was using the mark expressively, then I thought it incumbent upon the court to assess the need for that particular expression by looking at how the term functioned in the general vocabulary. If a trademark had been recoded in a way that made it particularly (or uniquely) meaningful, then the mark should be considered "expressively generic," and available for expressive use. I gave the example of the prefix "Mc," which had been analyzed by linguists and shown to denote a class of services that are standardized, basic, consistent, and convenient—a cluster of qualities that had no other designation. I suggested that cases preventing the use of "Mc" to identify these characteristics were wrongly decided.[37]

Since these articles were written, concepts akin to the genericity idea have developed. In response to the Internet, free trade, and consumers' increasing interest in foreign goods, decision makers place greater emphasis on the doctrine of foreign equivalents, denying protection to words that are generic in any language, no matter what language is spoken locally.[38] And, as

---

[34] *See, e.g.*, 15 U.S.C. § 1051 (2006); EC Trademark Directive art. 2; EC Regulation on the Community Trademark art. 4; *see also* TRIPS Agreement art. 15(1).

[35] *See, e.g.*, TrafFix Devices, Inc. v Mktg. Displays, Inc., 532 U.S. 23 (2001); Wal-Mart Stores, Inc. v Samara Bros., Inc., 529 U.S. 205 (2000).

[36] *See* Dreyfuss, *supra* note 3.

[37] *See, e.g.*, Quality Inns Int'l v McDonald's Corp., 695 F. Supp. 198, 215–16 (D. Md. 1988) (describing testimony by a linguist on the meaning of "Mc").

[38] *See, e.g.*, Otokoyama Co. Ltd. v Wine of Japan Import, Inc., 175 F.3d 266 (2d Cir. 1999) (holding that if a term for sake is generic in Japanese, then it is unprotectable in the United States).

discussed below in connection with defenses, there is both a statutory fair use defense and (in U.S. law) an emerging concept of "nominative use," both of which turn on the linguistic function that a trademark plays in the defendant's speech.[39] In addition, various commentators have suggested other types of expression that could be safeguarded with this general approach.[40]

This idea has, however, proved to have a fairly limited range. For example, international agreements require acceptance of marks registered in the trademark holder's country of origin "as is."[41] This so-called "telle quelle" provision may require a country to provide comprehensive protection for marks that, from a domestic perspective, have important expressive dimensions.[42] The defenses that turn on the defendant's use have a tightly specified range. Nominative use, for example, deals only with the defendant's use of the trademark to discuss the trademark holder; it cannot be invoked to defend other expression. More significantly, the concept of expressive genericity cannot reach all of the problems of today's complex linguistic marketplace, where trademark holders and consumers all use marks in their core denotation, to indicate the trademark holder, discuss the characteristics (and character) of products, and find one another in cyberspace.

2. *Actionable use* To many observers, a better way to distinguish between marks functioning in their signaling capacity from marks used expressively is to refine what is meant by a wrongful use.[43] The use requirement is variously articulated in national trademark statutes as "using in the course of trade,"[44] "used in association with wares,"[45] "use in commerce,"[46] or "commercial use in commerce."[47] Each of these phrases can be interpreted as the use of a mark

---

[39] *See, e.g.*, New Kids on the Block v News America Pub., Inc., 971 F.2d 302 (9th Cir. 1992). Nominative fair use has been mentioned in over 50 opinions in the Second, Third, Sixth, and Ninth Circuits.

[40] *See, e.g.*, Jeremy Philips & Ilanah Simon, *No Marks for Hitler: A Radical Reappraisal of Trade Mark Use and Political Sensitivity*, 26(8) E.I.P.R. 327 (2004). For a theoretical treatment of distinctiveness, see Barton Beebe, *The Semiotic Analysis of Trademark Law*, 51 UCLA L. REV. 621 (2004).

[41] Paris Convention, art. 6^{quinquies}.

[42] *But see In re* Rath, 402 F.3d 1207 (Fed. Cir. 2005) (refusing to register a foreign mark constituting a surname).

[43] *See generally* Margreth Barrett, *Internet Trademark Suits and the Demise of "Trademark Use"*, 39 U.C. DAVIS L. REV. 371 (2006).

[44] EC Trademark Directive art. 5.1; Regulation on the Community Trademark art. 9.1.

[45] Canada Trade-marks Act, R.S.C., c. T-13 § 4.

[46] 15 U.S.C. § 1114(1) (2006).

[47] *Id.*, § 1125(c)(1).

on a seller's goods for the purpose of telling consumers about the attributes of the goods in order to sell them.

Under this proposal, "use" would be parsed into categories: use to inform for purposes of sale (that is, use to identify source and quality) would be actionable because unauthorized use to inform interferes with a mark's signaling function, increases consumer search costs, and undermines the efficiency of the marketplace. However, use to persuade (through, for example, comparative ads and gripe sites), use to entertain and affiliate, or use to navigate would not be considered the type of use with which trademark law is concerned.[48] For example, affiliation products and "gadfly" products (such as marked tee shirts) use the trademark, but not to transmit information about the qualities of the goods (the source and origin of the wearing apparel). Thus, both would escape infringement liability. Such an approach would be especially welcome on the Internet because it would permit competitors to draw a consumer's attention to alternatives to the product he or she is using the trademark to find. Indeed, cybertheorists have proposed an even more intricate taxonomy of use for the on-line environment.[49]

In fact, there are expressive-use cases that are decided in this way. *Michelin*

---

[48] *See, e.g.*, Litman, *supra* note 22 (describing the approach suggested in Ralph S. Brown, *Advertising and the Public Interest: Legal Protection for Trade Symbols*, 57 YALE L.J. 1165, 1177–8 (1999)). Several lower courts have held that navigation uses are not trademark uses. *See, e.g.*, U-Haul Int'l, Inc. v WhenU.com, Inc., 279 F. Supp. 2d 723, 727 (E.D. Va. 2003) (machine-linking function); Wells Fargo & Co. v WhenU.com, Inc., 293 F. Supp. 2d 734, 762 (E.D. Mich. 2003); Lockheed Martin Corp. v Network Solutions, Inc., 985 F. Supp. 949, 960 (C.D. Cal. 1997) ("The fact that NSI makes a profit from the technical function of domain names does not convert NSI's activity to trademark use."); Academy of Motion Picture Arts & Sciences v Network Solutions, Inc., 989 F. Supp. 1276, 1279 (C.D. Cal. 1997); *see also* Blue Bell, Inc. v Farah Mfg. Inc., 508 F.2d 1260, 1267 (5th Cir. 1975); *In re* Universal Oil Prods. Co., 476 F.2d 653, 655 (C.C.P.A. 1973) (holding uses not directly associated with the sale of goods are not uses in commerce); *cf.* Interactive Products Corp. v a2z Mobile Office Sol'ns, 326 F.3d 687, 695–8 (6th Cir. 2003) (distinguishing between a trademark in the domain name (which the court considered a trademark use) from the appearance of a trademark in the post-domain path of a URL (a purely technical use)).

[49] *See* Goldman, *supra* note 30; *see also* Holiday Inns, Inc. v 800 Reservation, Inc., 86 F.3d 619 (6th Cir. 1996). The case furnishes a non-Internet example of this approach. In that case, the defendants maintained a typical misdialing of the Holiday Inn mark (the "O" in holiday was replaced by a zero), but the court denied relief, reasoning that the defendants were not "using" the trademark in the sense of advertising or publicizing it, even though they were diverting customers. *Id.* at 623–5. Use has received a similarly nuanced interpretation in Australia, apparently as the way to reconcile competing values. *See, e.g.*, Fender Australia Pty Ltd. v Strauss and Co., (1994) 28 IPR 193 (use on second-hand goods); ROCQUE REYNOLDS AND NATALIE STOIANOFF, INTELLECTUAL PROPERTY: TEXT AND ESSENTIAL CASES 513, 515–16 (2d ed. 2005).

& Cie v C.A.W.-Canada is a good example.[50] In that Canadian case, pamphlets utilizing the Michelin marks, including its tire man logo, Bibendum, were circulated in Canada as part of an attempt to unionize Michelin's workers. Michelin sued for infringement, claiming that, among other things, use of the term, "Michelin" and an image of Bibendum trying to crush a worker underfoot were confusing. The court admitted that use of the marks was in a sense commercial because the defendants stood to gain over a million dollars a year from unionizing the workers. However, it interpreted the use requirement narrowly, holding that a plaintiff in a trademark infringement action must show (1) that the defendant associated its wares with the mark in the ordinary course of trade and (2) that the use was as a trademark—that is, for "the *purpose* of distinguishing or identifying the Defendants' services in connection with the Plaintiff's wares or services."[51] As to the first (association) test, the court held that: "Handing out leaflets and pamphlets to recruit members into a trade union does not qualify under that test as commercial activity. Wares is defined to include 'printed publications,' but the Defendants are not in the business of printing leaflets."[52]

As to the second (trademark use), the court stated: "The Defendants did not use the 'Bibendum' design as a trademark but as a campaign tool to attract the attention of Michelin employees as they entered the factory gates . . . [T]he Defendant CAW was not using the 'Bibendum' to identify with . . . Michelin's wares and services."[53] Indeed, in another part of the case, Michelin claimed the union was diluting its marks and the court held that only a showing of associative use (and not trademark use) was required. Still, it found for the union, holding that "CAW is competing for the hearts and minds of . . . Michelin's employees, not its customers."[54]

Because U.S. dilution law explicitly makes "noncommercial use" a defense, a similar distinction has been drawn in that context. Thus, *Mattel, Inc. v MCA Records, Inc.*[55] was a challenge to Aqua's use of the trademark "Barbie

---

[50] (1996) 71 CPR 3d 348.
[51] *Michelin*, 71 CPR 3d at 360 (citing Clairol International Corporation v Thomas Supply & Equipment Co. Ltd. (1968), 38 Fox Pat. C. 176).
[52] *Id.* at 367.
[53] *Id.* at 368. In addition, the court held that use was not confusing. *See id.* ("There could be no mistake that the Defendant CAW was the originator of the pamphlets and leaflets. Their origin was amply indicated by the use of the CAW logo in the top right-hand corner and the appeal in bold print on the bottom of the leaflets to act 'before too late' by calling the CAW telephone number provided."); *see also id.* at 370–1.
[54] *Michelin*, 71 CPR 3d at 371. It may, however, be significant that in the end the union lost, albeit on a copyright theory.
[55] 296 F.3d 894 (9th Cir. 2002).

Girl" in a song. Because the song was on the album *Aquarium*, it was clearly sold in commerce. However, Judge Kozinski reasoned that mere sale cannot be dispositive of the availability of the noncommercial use defense because the affirmative case for dilution also requires a showing that the mark was used in commerce: "If a use has to be commercial in order to be dilutive, how then can it also be noncommercial so as to satisfy the exception . . . ?"[56] To solve the "conundrum," the court limited the concept of commercial speech for the purpose of utilizing the statutory defense to speech that "does no more than propose a commercial transaction."[57] Since Aqua used Barbie to lampoon the image of the ideal woman, and not to induce the purchase of dolls, the court held that the noncommercial use defense was applicable.[58]

But despite case like *Michelin* and *Mattel*, the weight of worldwide authority runs counter to this approach. One reason may be practical: it is too difficult to parse the many classifications that courts and commentators have identified. As discussed below, the rejection of this approach may also betray a normative error in which trademark law is assumed to be aimed at preventing free-riding.[59] In any case, many courts equate "use in commerce" (i.e. use to conduct commerce; to "propose a commercial transaction") with "commercial use" (i.e. use intended to earn a profit). They would likely reject the Canadian view that it is irrelevant that the defendant stood to benefit financially from unionizing Michelin workers.

Arsenal Football Club Plc v Reed,[60] an English dispute involving the sale of apparel decorated with the Arsenal football team trademarks, is an example. The Arsenal marks were not affixed to describe the quality or source of the products, but rather to make them appealing to fans. Nonetheless, the European Court of Justice (ECJ) found the use actionable. According to the court, a use that "takes place in the context of commercial activity with a view to economic advantage" is "indeed use in the course of trade."[61] There are increasing numbers of Internet cases decided along the same lines: the sale of

---

[56] *Id.* at 904
[57] *Id.* at 906 (quoting Hoffman v Capital Cities/ABC, Inc., 255 F.3d 1180, 1184 (9th Cir. 2001)).
[58] There are also occasional dilution cases that decide for the defendant on the ground that it was not using the mark in commerce (in other words, on the theory that the plaintiff had not made out the affirmative case). *See, e.g.*, Avery Dennison Corp. v Sumpton, 189 F.3d 868, 879–80 (9th Cir. 1999).
[59] *See* notes 128–33 *infra* and accompanying text.
[60] For a full account of this complex litigation, see Arsenal Football Club Plc v Reed (No. 2), [2003] RPC 696.
[61] 2002 ECR I-10273 ¶ 40.

trademarks as key words for Internet advertising is regarded as a commercial use even though neither the seller nor the buyer is using the marks to sell the goods for which the trademarks are protected.[62]

U.S. courts are adopting this approach in off-line cases as well, holding, for example, that when a trademark is associated with the sale of a product, it is a commercial use and therefore "in commerce."[63] Indeed, the Lanham Act may be particularly susceptible to that interpretation. The definition of "use in commerce" includes placement of a trademark on "documents associated with the goods" and use of service marks "displayed in the sale or advertising of services."[64]

3. *Harm* In the classic trademark tort, harm is defined as the likelihood of consumer confusion and in the United States in particular, this definition has traditionally provided robust protection for parodic, humorous, and political uses of trademarks. Indeed, the more thoroughly expressive the use—the more the mark has been recoded or distorted—the harder it has been to convincingly argue that consumers will likely be confused. Furthermore, because the typical multi-factored test for confusion takes into account the "proximity of the products" and the "likelihood of plaintiff's bridging the gap" between them, many expressive products will escape infringement on the ground that they are outside the range of the trademark holder's market.[65] If the user adds enough

---

[62] *See, e.g.*, Société Viaticum et Société Luteciel v Société Google France, T.G.I. Nanterre, 2ième chambre, 13 octobre 2003, *available at* http://www.legalis.net/jnet/decisions/marques/jug_tgi_nanterre_080304.htm. *See generally*, Brett August, *Plus Ça Change . . . How a French Court May Have Changed Internet Advertising Forever: Google France Fined For Selling Trademarked Keywords*, 2 NW. J.TECH. & INTELL. PROP. 5 (2004).

[63] *Cf.* San Francisco Arts & Athletics, Inc. v U.S. Olympic Committee, 483 U.S. 522 (1987) (sale of items bearing the term "Gay Olympics" was actionable under a special statute protecting the Olympic marks, even though the Gay Olympics was politically motivated).

[64] 15 U.S.C. § 1127 (2006). Margreth Barrett notes that the Restatement of Unfair Competition also supports the view that use in advertising is a use in commerce, Barrett, *supra* note 43, at 384 n. 38. Commentators have, however, offered cogent reasons to reject the symmetry between the requirements for establishing rights to a trademark and the elements needed to enforce those rights. *See* Graeme B. Dinwoodie & Mark D. Janis, *Confusion Over Use: Contextualism in Trademark Law*, 92 IOWA L. REV. 1597 (2007).

[65] Polaroid Corp. v Polarad Electronics Corp., 287 F.2d 492, 495 (2d Cir. 1961). For an assessment of how these factors play out in the case law, see Barton Beebe, *An Empirical Study of the Multifactor Tests for Trademark Infringement*, 94 CAL. L. REV. 1581 (2006).

new "atmospherics" to the mark, even a court intent on preventing free riding may think there is enough added value to escape infringement liability.[66]

Hormel Foods Corp. v Jim Henson Productions, Inc.[67] is illustrative. Thanks to Monty Python's Flying Circus, Hormel's Spam mark for luncheon meat has become synonymous with unwanted e-mail. The Python group also used the mark for the title of its Broadway play, *Spamalot*. The case, however, concerned a different usage: a Muppet that Jim Henson named Spa'am. The court declined to find consumer confusion, reasoning that:

> Henson's use of the name "Spa'am" is simply another in a long line of Muppet lampoons. Moreover, this Muppet brand of humor is widely recognized and enjoyed. Thus, consumers of Henson's merchandise, all of which will display the words "Muppet Treasure Island," are likely to see the name "Spa'am" as the joke it was intended to be.[68]

A few Internet navigation cases have also been decided on this ground. For example, attempts by trademark holders to prevent use of their marks on gripe sites (of the trademarkholdersucks.com or ihatetrademarkholder.com variety) have sometimes been rejected.[69] Decision makers reason that these sites are not likely to strike the viewer as related to the trademark holder and therefore they will not likely generate consumer confusion.[70]

---

[66] For example, cases permitting artistic uses of trademarks (*see, e.g.*, ETW Corp. v Jireh Pub., Inc., 332 F.3d 915 (6th Cir. 2003)) may be influenced by the proportion of the ultimate value added by the expressive user.

[67] 73 F.3d 497 (2d Cir. 1996).

[68] *Id.* at 503; *see also, e.g.*, Elvis Presley Enters., Inc. v Capece, 141 F.3d 188, 199 (5th Cir. 1998) ("A successful parody of the original mark weighs against a likelihood of confusion because, even though it portrays the original, it also sends the message that it is not the original and is a parody, thereby lessening any potential confusion."); Jordache Enters. v Hogg Wyld, Ltd., 828 F.2d 1482, 1486 (10th Cir. 1987) ("An intent to parody is not an intent to confuse."). For a case involving political commentary, see Lucasfilm Ltd. v High Frontier, 622 F. Supp. 931 (D.D.C. 1985).

[69] *See, e.g.*, Northland Ins. Cos. v Blaylock, 115 F. Supp. 2d 1108 (D. Minn. 2000) (noting no "reasonable Internet user" would think gripe site northlandinsurance.com was affiliated with plaintiff because, among other things, one of the first lines on the site states: "If you feel you have been ABUSED at the hands of Northland Insurance please click the link above. You're not alone."); *cf.* Hasbro, Inc. v Clue Computing, Inc., 66 F. Supp. 2d 117, 122 (D. Mass. 1999) (holding very low likelihood of confusion between Clue Computing's clue.com and the Clue board game); Juno Online Servs., L.P. v Juno Lighting, 979 F. Supp. 684, 692 (N.D. Ill. 1997) (indicating mere registration of a domain does not create a likelihood of confusion).

[70] *Cf., e.g.*, Wal-Mart Stores, Inc. v wallmartcanadasucks.com, WIPO Arbitration and Mediation Center, Administrative Panel Decision, Case No. D2000-1104, *available at* http://arbiter.wipo.int/domains/decisions/html/2000/d2000-1104.html. *See generally* Sarah J. Givan, *Using Trademarks as Location Tools on the Internet: Use in Commerce?*, 2005 UCLA J. L. & TECH. 4.

But as powerful as the confusion tool can be, it cannot safeguard all expressive uses. Indeed, it appears that over time, it is safeguarding fewer and fewer. First, the concept of confusion is broadening. It has proved relatively easy to demonstrate confusion as to association or sponsorship, in part because some courts accept the idea that consumers will assume that permission to use a mark is required and will therefore infer sponsorship from use.[71] Many courts have also concluded that dissipating confusion at the point of sale is not the only goal. If consumers are likely to start off confused, that is regarded as sufficient harm, even if the confusion is dispelled by the time a product is purchased. On the Internet, this claim of "initial interest confusion" is based on the notion that being drawn to a rival website is like getting off at the wrong exit from a highway, finding the rival's store, and deciding it isn't "worth the trouble to continue searching."[72] Courts have not, apparently, noticed that clicking on a second website is nothing like getting back into a car, starting it up, locating the highway entrance, finding the new exit, searching for the "right" store, stopping the car, and getting out. Similarly, courts will consider the impact of a product after it is sold.[73] This move is especially curious, as it is difficult to understand why "post-sale confusion" regarding a rival product is any more dangerous than the "post-sale" bad impression an observer might get from viewing an authentic product that has been mistreated.

Second, courts have grown skeptical of attempts by expressive users to avoid confusion. Experts hired by trademark holders have been very successful at convincing courts that disclaimers are ineffective.[74] The globalization of the marketplace has brought consumers into contact with foreign goods and websites, raising the possibility that foreign speakers will take the trademark at face value, even when the provenance is clear to those who understand the

---

[71] *See generally* Jacob Jacoby & Maureen Morrin, *"Not Manufactured or Authorized by . . . ": Recent Federal Cases Involving Trademark Disclaimers*, 17(1) J. PUBLIC POLICY AND MARKETING 97 (1998) (giving the example of Pebble Beach Co. v Tour 18 I Ltd., 155 F.3d 526 (5th Cir. 1998), where consumers playing golf on a Texas course modeled after the holes of famous courses that were not in Texas were thought likely to be confused about whether permission to use the layout was required).

[72] Brookfield Commc'ns, Inc. v West Coast Entm't Corp., 174 F.3d 1036, 1064 (9th Cir. 1999) (similar domain names); *see also* Playboy Enters., Inc. v Netscape Commc'ns Corp., 354 F.3d 1020, 1024 (9th Cir. 2004) (banner ads); Paccar, Inc. v Telescan Techs., L.L.C., 319 F.3d 243, 253 (6th Cir. 2003); OBH, Inc. v Spotlight Magazine, Inc., 86 F. Supp. 2d 176, 190 (W.D.N.Y. 2000); Planned Parenthood Fed'n of Am., Inc. v Bucci, 42 U.S.P.Q. 2d (BNA) 1430, 1441 (S.D.N.Y. 1997).

[73] *See, e.g.*, Ferrari S.P.A. Esercizio v Roberts, 944 F.2d 1235, 1244–45 (6th Cir. 1991).

[74] *See* Jacoby & Morrin, *supra* note 71; Jacob Jacoby & George J. Szybillo, *Why Disclaimers Fail*, 84 TRADEMARK REP. 224 (1994).

surrounding text.[75] As U.S. copyright law's (arguable) distinction between satire and parody migrates to trademark law,[76] courts are also beginning to believe that only parody—which is designed to make fun of the trademark—is capable of dissipating confusion and that consumers will think that satire—which aims at broader commentary—is sending a message of sponsorship.[77]

Third, unlike the American test for confusion, which uses the similarity of the products and the similarity of the marks as factors for deciding whether there is a likelihood of confusion, some modern trademark statutes explicitly create an irrebutable presumption of confusion whenever the defendant sells similar goods under similar trademarks.[78] Arguably, this presumption can be overcome, but *Arsenal* demonstrates how difficult rebuttal can be. In that case, the national court (presumably, the forum responsible for factual findings) explicitly held that consumers saw the goods only as expressions of affiliations, and thus were (presumably) not confused about their source: the seller had been in business for a long time without complaints and had a sign disclaiming association with the team. When the case was sent back down after the ECJ enunciated the standards for infringement, the national judge reiterated his views about the consumers' perceptions, but that finding was reversed by the national appellate court.[79]

Finally, even if a use is considered unlikely to confuse, the expressive user may still be faced with claims for cybersquatting or dilution, which have different standards for harm. Thus, both U.S. law and the Uniform Domain Name Dispute Resolution Policy initially were aimed at preventing "bad faith"—opportunistic registration of a domain name encompassing a trademark with the intent of, essentially, ransoming it back to the trademark holder.[80] Accordingly, they both appear to lend themselves to factual limitation. Nonetheless, trademark holders have managed to gain control over many

---

[75] Société Accor v M. Philippe Hartmann Dossier, WIPO Arbitration and Mediation Center, Administrative Panel Decision, Case No. D2001-0007 (to a non-Anglophone public, "la formule 'accorsucks' ne signifie rien de plus que l'adjonction à la marque connue "accor" d'un suffixe dénué de sens"), *available at* http://arbiter.wipo.int/domains/decisions/html/2001/d2001-0007.html.

[76] Campbell v Acuff-Rose Music, Inc., 510 U.S. 569 (1994). For migration into trademark law, *see, e.g.,* the arguments in MasterCard Int'l Inc. v Nader 2000 Primary Comm., Inc., 70 U.S.P.Q. 2d 1046 (S.D.N.Y. 2004).

[77] *See, e.g.*, Anheuser-Busch, Inc. v Balducci Publ'ns, 28 F.3d 769, 776 (8th Cir. 1994).

[78] *See, e.g.*, EC Trademark Directive art. 5.1; South Africa Trade Marks Act 194 of 1993 § 34(1)(c).

[79] Arsenal Football Club v Reed, [2003] All E.R. 865 (Eng. C.A.).

[80] *See* 15 U.S.C. § 1125(d)(1); http://www.icann.org/udrp/udrp-policy-24oct99.htm.

rather benign uses of trademark-related Internet addresses (in actions that should properly have been characterized as "reverse domain name hijacking").[81] "Bad faith," like "commercial use," is in the eye of the beholder.

Dilution is intended to protect the "whittling away of the value of a trademark" and a weakening of its "commercial magnetism."[82] Although the bar on dilution is limited to famous marks,[83] that limitation is not an effective safeguard of free speech. After all, famous marks are the ones that expressive users are most interested in utilizing. Accordingly, this right of action can pose great danger to expressive interests. At the normative level, it shifts the focus from the pure signaling capacity of the mark (its ability to denote source and quality) to other functions (such as instilling cachet in the brand). Because it suggests that *all* of the value in a mark belongs to the trademark holder, this shift reinforces the notion that every free ride is actionable. More prosaically, making a case for dilution does not require a showing of a likelihood of confusion. As a result, it removes from the judicial toolbox one of the major factual devices for resolving the tension between proprietary and expressive interests.

Courts have, however, proved remarkably adept at cabining the ambit of these claims—at least in the United States, and at least for now. In the decade after the Federal Trademark Dilution Act of 1995 (FTDA) came into force, Clarisa Long conducted an empirical study of the federal cases litigating dilution claims.[84] That work demonstrated that after a slow start in which judges rather routinely found for plaintiffs in dilution cases,[85] courts became skeptical of the reach of the claim and evolved an arsenal of weapons to avoid it in

---

[81] *See, e.g.*, Keith Blackman, *The Uniform Domain Name Dispute Resolution Policy: A Cheaper Way to Hijack Domain Names and Suppress Critics*, 15 HARV. J. LAW & TECN. 211, 233–6 (2001) (finding UDRP arbitration panels, contrary to the Policy, routinely transfer domain names that were not registered in bad faith to trademark holders); Wal-Mart Stores, Inc. v Wallsucks, WIPO Case No. D2000-0477 (July 20, 2000), *available at* http://arbiter.wipo.int/domains/decisions/html/2000/d2000-0477.html. *See generally* http://www.chillingeffects.org/acpa (exhibiting "cease and desist" letters threatening suits under § 1125(d) unless owners relinquish domain names). The U.S. now recognizes a right of action for reverse domain name hijacking. *See* 15 U.S.C. § 1114(2)(D)(iv)-(v) (injunctive relief and damages when reverse domain name hijacking shown); Sallen v Corinthians Licenciamentos LTDA, 273 F.3d 14 (1st Cir. 2001).

[82] *See, e.g.*, Frank I. Schechter, *The Rational Basis of Trademark Protection*, 40 HARV. L. REV. 813 (1927).

[83] *See, e.g.*, 15 U.S.C. § 1125(c)(1) (factors for determining when a mark is famous).

[84] Clarisa Long, *Dilution*, 106 COLUM. L. REV. 1029 (2006).

[85] Nabisco, Inc. v PF Brands, Inc., 191 F.3d 208 (2d Cir. 1999) provides a particularly egregious example of early receptivity to dilution law: the court protected the fish shape of a cracker by barring a competitor's sale of crackers in various animal shapes.

circumstances that are social-welfare reducing. First, they looked at the question of what the term actually means. It has long been recognized that there are potentially two types of dilution, dilution by blurring and dilution by tarnishment. Tarnishment, which reflects the concern that a mark will be harmed by unsavory associations, is arguably a problem of the know-it-when-I-see it variety, making it relatively easy to establish.[86] However, the post-1995 FTDA courts thought it was unclear whether the federal legislation was meant to cover this harm.[87] That left blurring as the only federally actionable form. But the concept of blurring proved notoriously difficult to define and measure.[88] Second, the Supreme Court held that the plaintiff must prove *actual* as opposed to *a likelihood of* dilution.[89] Third, some courts protected only marks that were inherently distinctive, and thus not as susceptible to descriptive usages.[90] The combination of these factors—that is, the need to show actual blurring of an inherently distinctive mark—created a strong safeguard for expressive interests.

But even here, there is reason for caution. The limitations that, according to Long, judges were relying on do not exist in all dilution laws—U.S. state laws and foreign laws do not generally reject dilution by tarnishment or require a demonstration of actual dilution.[91] Furthermore, recent legislation in the United

---

[86] For example, consider the facts of *Dallas Cowboys Cheerleaders, Inc. v Pussycat Cinema, Ltd.*, 604 F.2d 200 (2d Cir. 1979), which involved "'Debbie Does Dallas,' a gross and revolting sex film whose plot, to the extent that there is one, involves a cheerleader [Debbie] at a fictional high school, who has been selected to become a 'Texas Cowgirl.'" *Id.* at 202 (decided on a straight trademark infringement theory).

[87] Moseley v V Secret Catalogue, Inc., 537 U.S. 418, 432 (2003) ("Whether [tarnishment] is actually embraced by the statutory text, however, is another matter. Indeed, the contrast between the state statutes, which expressly refer to both 'injury to business reputation' and to 'dilution of the distinctive quality of a trade name or trademark,' and the federal statute which refers only to the latter, arguably supports a narrower reading of the FTDA.").

[88] *See, e.g.*, J. Thomas McCarthy, *Dilution of a Trademark: European and United States Law Compared*, 94 TRADEMARK REP. 1163, 1180 (2004); Jonathan Moskin, *Victoria's Big Secret: Wither Dilution under the Federal Dilution Act?*, 93 TRADEMARK REP. 842, 843 (2003).

[89] *Moseley*, 537 U.S. at 433.

[90] *See, e.g.*, TCPIP Holding Co., Inc. v Haar Commc'ns, Inc., 244 F.3d 88 (2d Cir. 2001); I.P. Lund Trading ApS v Kohler Co, 163 F.3d 27, 50 (1st Cir. 1998). *See generally* Anne E. Kennedy, *From Delusion to Dilutions: Proposals to Improve Problematic Aspects of the Federal Trademark Dilution Act*, 9 N.Y.U. J. LEGIS. & PUB. POL'Y 399 (2005–6).

[91] Canadian law, for example, refers to "depreciation of goodwill," Canada Trade-marks Act § 22. Nonetheless, there are Canadian cases declining to find dilution. *See, e.g.*, Veuve Clicquot Ponsardin v Les Boutiques Cliquot Ltée (Veuve Clicquot),

States reversed many of these limitations. Under the new Act,[92] tarnishment is expressly covered;[93] the standard for finding dilution was changed from "actual" to "likelihood of;"[94] and even marks with "acquired distinctiveness" are now protectable.[95] To be sure, the statute also adds very carefully delineated defenses, including a "nominative use" defense.[96] Ironically, however, the detail with which the dilution defenses are written could negatively affect the breadth given to the defenses to infringement by confusion.

4 Defenses Clearly, the most straightforward protection for expression lies in the defenses to trademark infringement. The various rights of action (and, of course, national laws) differ as to the defenses provided, but they generally fall into two classes. Some are uses that are exempt because of their high social value. For example, in U.S. federal law, the statutory defenses to dilution include news reporting and commentary.[97] These defenses are safeguards for extremely important speech interests, but they clearly apply only in particularized circumstances.

As suggested earlier, other defenses turn on the unique role that the mark plays in the defendant's speech. Comparative advertising is one example— without the capacity to use a rival's mark, trademark holders could not convey the comparative message. In addition, a proprietor can make "fair use" of the mark to describe her own goods or to denote her own surname.[98] There are also cases permitting the use of a mark on goods that have been resold or repackaged,[99] and on replacement parts or accessories for trademarked products.[100] Finally, in the United States, fair use has been extended to include nominative uses.[101] As a judge in one of the many Barbie cases explained:

2006 SCC 23 and Mattel, Inc. v 3894207 Canada Inc. (Mattel), 2006 SCC 22 (Can.) (permitting a woman's clothing store to be named "Cliquot" and a restaurant chain to call itself "Barbie"). European law similarly avoids the term dilution, but has similar protection. *See, e.g.*, Regulation on the Community Trademark art. 9(1). *See generally* Arthur Schwartz & David Morfesi, *Dilution Comes of Age: The United States, Europe, and South Africa*, 87 TRADEMARK REP. 436 (1997).

[92] 15 U.S.C. § 1125(c) (2006).
[93] § 1125(c)(1); tarnishment is further defined in subsection (c)(2)(C).
[94] § 1125(c)(1).
[95] *Id.*
[96] § 1125(c)(3)(A).
[97] 15 U.S.C. § 1125(c)(4) (2006).
[98] 15 U.S.C. § 1115(b)(4); *see also* EC Trademark Directive art. 6.1(a).
[99] Some of the resale cases go off on an exhaustion theory. *See, e.g.*, Champion Spark Plug Co. v Sanders, 331 U.S. 125, 128–30 (1947).
[100] Toro Co. v R & R Products Co., 787 F.2d 1208 (8th Cir. 1986); *see also, e.g.*, EC Trademark Directive art. 6.1(c).
[101] *See* New Kids on the Block v News America Pub., Inc., 971 F.2d 302, 308 (9th Cir. 1992).

[A] defendant's use of a plaintiff's mark is *nominative* where he or she "used the plaintiff's mark to describe the plaintiff's product, *even if the defendant's ultimate goal is to describe his own product.*" The goal of a nominative use is generally for the "purposes of comparison, criticism[or] point of reference."[102]

Once again, however, these permitted uses are highly circumscribed and usually require the user to persuade the court that the use is "fair" or "in good faith."[103] Although the Supreme Court has recently cautioned that this requirement does not impose a burden on the user to negate the possibility of confusion,[104] "good faith" remains ill-defined.[105] Courts have held that the defendant must lack any intent to "trade on the good will of the trademark owner by creating confusion."[106] Since expressive users (parodists for example) do, in fact, intend to exploit the audience's understanding of the mark (and may even hope to cause a frisson of confusion) this standard could be somewhat limiting.[107]

B.   Constitution-based solutions

In jurisdictions that offer expansive trademark protection (for example, jurisdictions where use of similar marks on similar products raises a near-irrebuttable presumption, or jurisdictions where a likelihood of dilution is actionable) and with respect to rights of action that are not statutorily grounded (such as some U.S. right of publicity cases) constitutional norms can play a significant role in protecting free speech concerns. That is, although a court may fail to

---

[102]   Mattel, Inc. v Walking Mountain Productions, 353 F.3d 792, 809 (9th Cir. 2003) (citations omitted); *see also* ETW Corp. v Jireh Pub., Inc. 332 F.3d 915 (6th Cir. 2003) (artistic use of the registered mark "Tiger Woods"); Playboy Enters., Inc. v Welles, 279 F.3d 796 (9th Cir. 2002) (website correctly identified the defendant as an ex-Playboy playmate).

[103]   *See, e.g.*, 15 U.S.C. § 1115(b)(4). The term in the EC Trademark Directive is "honest practices."

[104]   KP Permanent Make-Up, Inc. v Lasting Impression I, Inc., 543 U.S. 111 (2004).

[105]   *See, e.g.*, Int'l Stamp Art, Inc. v U.S. Postal Service, 456 F.3d 1270, 1271 (11th Cir. 2006) ("The appropriate legal standard for good faith with respect to a fair-use defense in [a trademark infringement action is] an issue of first impression for us.").

[106]   *Id.* at 1274-5 (citing Inst. for Scientific Info., Inc. v Gordon & Breach, Science Publishers, Inc., 931 F.2d 1002, 1009-10 (3d Cir. 1991)); Packman v Chicago Tribune Co., 267 F.3d 628, 642 (7th Cir. 2001); Sierra On-Line, Inc. v Phoenix Software, Inc., 739 F.2d 1415, 1423 (9th Cir. 1984); Zatarains, Inc. v Oak Grove Smokehouse, Inc., 698 F.2d 786, 796 (5th Cir. 1983).

[107]   A further complication is that the courts that have considered the standard of good faith also require the absence of a non-infringing commercially viable alternative. *See Int'l Stamp Art, Inc.*, 456 F.3d at 1276.

see its law as incorporating expressive values directly, it may understand the statute through "the prism" of constitutional values.[108]

This approach can reach results similar to those obtained through more nuanced statutory construction. For example, in *Laugh It Off Promotions CC v SAB Int'l (Finance) BV*,[109] the Constitutional Court of South Africa was faced with a tee shirt parody of the Carling Beer mark, in which the producer's name was replaced with "White Guilt" and the term "Black Label," with "Black Labour." Laugh It Off is in the business of selling such parodic items, so the case presented a stark example of a user turning a profit off the sale of marked goods. Furthermore, the nature of the parody created an especially strong possibility that the mark would be permanently tarnished (indeed, the parody could be understood as accusing Carling of racist practices), and the claim was based on an open-ended statute that prohibited unauthorized use "likely to take unfair advantage of, or be detrimental to, the distinctive character or the repute of the registered trade mark."[110] Nonetheless, the Court decided for the expressive user, holding that the terms of the statute—"detriment," "unfair advantage"—are to be interpreted in light of a constitutional commitment to expressive interests.[111] According to the Court, the "onus to demonstrate the likelihood of substantial harm or detriment" must remain on the plaintiff and it must be proved with "established facts and not bald allegations."[112] Inferences of substantial economic detriment could be drawn, but only from proven facts and not a "conjecture" that the expression on the shirt would be discomforting. The Court, in short, wanted to see numbers: how many shirts were sold; how many beer sales were lost.[113]

If *Laugh It Off* is any indication, the constitutional approach has much to recommend it: it is inherently flexible and avoids the normative pitfalls of

---

[108] Laugh It Off Promotions CC v SAB Int'l (Finance) BV, 2005 (8) BCLR 743 (CC) ¶ 43 (May 27, 2005).
[109] *Id.*
[110] South Africa Trade Marks Act No. 194 of 1993, § 34(1)(c).
[111] *Laugh It Off*, (8) BCLR 743 (CC) ¶44
[112] *Id.* at ¶ 51, ¶ 54.
[113] European courts take a similar approach. *See, e.g.*, Lila Postkarte I ZR 159/02, February 3, 2005; BGH GRUR 2005, 583 (The Bundesgerichtshof held that a play on the Suchard trademark, Milka, was not infringement on a principle of "freedom of art"); Decisions Paris Court of Appeals 14th Chamber, Section A February 26, 2003 (1. Assoc. Greenpeace France v SA Sté Esso; 2. SA SPCEA v Assoc. Greenpeace et al., April 30, 2003; 3. Assoc. Le Réseau Voltaire pour la liberté d´expression v Sté Gervais Danone), IIC 2004 Heft 3 (permitting political use of the Esso and Danone marks). New Zealand cases are analyzed in a similar fashion, see PC Direct v Best Buys [1997] 2 NZLR 723 (HC); SUSY FRANKEL & GEOFF MCLAY, INTELLECTUAL PROPERTY IN NEW ZEALAND 27, 606–07 (2002).

assuming that the goal is to prevent all confusion and all unauthorized commercial exploitation.[114] There is, however, reason to be wary. Balancing tests are notoriously unpredictable, making it risky for anyone who is contemplating an investment in expressive use. Thus, although there are not many U.S. cases that reach the constitutional issue, the few cases decided on that ground are difficult to reconcile. For instance, while *L.L. Bean v Drake Publishers, Inc.*,[115] which involved the publication of "L.L. Beam's Back-to-School-Sex Catalogue," a parody of the famous L.L. Bean camping catalogue, found in favor of an expressive user on free speech grounds, *Anheuser-Busch, Inc. v Balducci Publications*,[116] which involved a play on a Michelob ad, rejected a constitution-based defense. Similarly, where *Winter v DC Comics*[117] held that constitutional interests in free speech outweigh a claim based on the right of publicity, *Comedy III Productions, Inc. v Gary Saderup*[118] rejected a free speech defense in a publicity case. Similar unpredictability can be found in cases from other jurisdictions. For example, the facts of *Miss World Ltd. v Channel 4 Television Corp*,[119] an English case, are quite analogous to *Laugh It Off*: the defendant planned to broadcast a transvestite beauty pageant under the name "Mr. Miss World"—a parodic reference to the Miss World mark which is registered for (more conventional) female beauty pageants. The issue in the two cases was, essentially, the same in that the constitutional norm to be balanced against the trademark interests was similar. And the English judge was well aware of the South African decision.[120] Nonetheless, he came to the opposite result and enjoined the program.[121]

Nor is it clear that courts will always see exclusivity as raising constitutional problems. Thus, there are structural similarities between using intellectual property (a trademark) without authorization in order to deliver a message effectively and trespassing on real property in order to speak effectively. But

---

[114] This analysis also allows courts to incorporate other constitutional norms. *See, e.g.*, Cases 56, 58/64 Etablissements Consten SARL and Grundig Verkaufs-GmbH v Commission [1966] ECR 299 (free movement of goods within the EC); Piazza's Seafood World, LLC v Odom, 448 F.3d 744 (5th Cir. 2006) (free commerce within the United States).
[115] 811 F.2d 26 (1st Cir. 1987).
[116] 28 F.3d 769, 776 (8th Cir. 1994).
[117] 69 P.3d 473 (Ca. 2003).
[118] 21 P.3d 797 (Ca. 2001).
[119] [2007] EWHC 982 (Pat).
[120] *Id.* at ¶ 29.
[121] See especially *id.* at ¶ 41 ("The scope of the intervention of [free expression interests] in matters concerning registered trade marks is far from well worked out. Indeed, I think it is fair to say that it is almost completely unworked out.")

although the Supreme Court has countenanced the latter (in, for example, *Robins v Pruneyard Shopping Center*[122]), courts have yet to fully appreciate the free speech implications of barring the use of trademarks in information space.[123]

II. A normative assessment

To sum up the previous discussion, a variety of doctrinal mechanisms have been developed to safeguard speech. None of these devices protects all expressive interests and less speech is likely to be shielded as trademark rights generally, and dilution rights specifically, continue to expand. Communication on the Internet appears to be particularly threatened. Marks are often used as search terms to navigate.[124] When trademark holders gain control over such uses, they can prevent the Internet from fulfilling its promise as a global forum for the interchange of ideas. Even commerce is affected. When consumers browse in real space, they find the product they begin looking for shelved side-by-side with alternatives that they may then consider. The Internet can mimic this real-space behavior only if searches, search results, sponsored links, and advertisements can be freely keyed to trademarks. Given these rather obvious problems, it is something of a mystery why trademark law has become so suspicious of all unauthorized usages. Yet, without a theory for what is underlying these suspicions, it is difficult to devise a way to cabin the trend. Before moving on to the question of finding new ways to mitigate the dysfunctional aspects of expansionism, this section explores the reasons why highly protectionist regimes are emerging.

Interest group politics is, of course, one obvious culprit. Trademark holders are better heeled and better organized than expressive users and are thus better positioned to present a persuasive case to national and international lawmakers. But standard public choice theory cannot fully explain this phenomenon. First, not all unauthorized users lack voice—for example, googlers' interests are well represented by Google. Second, to some extent, conflicting uses are a wash—the consumer who searched on merchant A's mark but decided to buy merchant B's product, is cancelled by the consumer who searched on merchant B's mark but bought from merchant A. Indeed, learning of other (bad) alternatives can sometimes prod consumers into purchasing. The moment of indecision is, apparently, overcome by providing

---

[122] 447 U.S. 74 (1980).
[123] *See* Dawn C. Nunziato, *The Death of the Public Forum in Cyberspace*, 20 BERKELEY TECH. L.J. 1115 (2005).
[124] *See generally* RONALD E. RICE, MAUREEN MCCREADIE & SHAN-JU L. CHANG, ACCESSING AND BROWSING INFORMATION AND COMMUNICATION (2001).

a new justification for making a particular purchase.[125] Thus, in addition to the public regarding reasons for favoring open interchange, trademark holders have private reasons to permit at least some unauthorized use.

A variant cause of high protectionism focuses on governmental, rather than private, interests. In this view, the concern may be about cultural dominance. Thus, it is interesting to note how many of the Internet cases that reach results antithetical to free-speech values are adjudicated in French courts and involve the activities of Americans (or companies controlled by Americans).[126] The problem of cultural hegemony is a longstanding concern of the French,[127] and it may be particularly resonant in the context of the Internet where so much pop culture is disseminated. However, trademark law seems entirely unsuited to dealing with this issue effectively. None of the definitions of harm captures the cultural problem adequately. Moreover, on the Internet, one court's decision can affect usage worldwide. These extraterritorial consequences may be entirely out of proportion to the domestic problem.

But whatever the explanatory power of public choice theory and its variants, they represent structural problems that are not confined to trademark law and that are not susceptible to modification through trademark law. However, two explanations merit careful consideration.

One is the possibility of normative error. To some, any attempt to free ride on another's asset is objectionable. For example, Jacob Jacoby, who designs many of the surveys used in trademark cases,[128] writes:

---

[125] *See* Eldar Shafir, Itamar Simonson & Amos Tversky, *Reason Based Choice*, 49 COGNITION 11, 23 (1993).

[126] *See, e.g.*, Google France v Louis Vuitton Malletier, Cour d'appel de Paris (June 28, 2006) (barring key word advertising); Société Accor v M. Philippe Hartmann Dossier, WIPO Arbitration and Mediation Center, Administrative Panel Decision, Case No. D2001-0007 (Anglo website confusing to non-Anglophones), *available at* http://arbiter.wipo.int/domains/decisions/html/2001/d2001-0007.html; Société Viaticum et Société Luteciel v Société Google France, T.G.I. Nanterre, 2ième chambre, October 13, 2003, *available at* http://www.legalis.net/jnet/decisions/marques/jug_tgi_nanterre_080304.htm; *cf.* Yahoo! Inc. v La Ligue Contre Le Racisme Et L'Antisemitisme, 433 F.3d 1199 (9th Cir. 2006) (refusing to enforce a French judgment barring the sale of Nazi memorabilia on the Internet). In contrast, French courts appear to have fewer problems with French nationals using American marks expressively. *See* note 109, *supra*.

[127] *See, e.g.*, Thomas Bishop, *France and the Need for Cultural Exception*, 29 N.Y.U. J. INT'L L. & POLITICS 187 (1997); Judith Beth Prowda, *U.S. Dominance in the "Marketplace of Culture" and the French "Cultural Exception"*, 29 N.Y.U. J. INT'L L. & POLITICS 193 (1997).

[128] A search on "Jacoby w/20 [report or survey]" in the fip-cs database in Westlaw brought up 58 citations; in the jlr base, a search on "Jacob w/2 Jacoby" brought up 125 citations.

[A]ttempts to capitalize on the goodwill or favorable set of associations established by the original user of the mark are referred to by legal scholars as "free rides." If brand names are, in fact, valuable corporate assets, they should be accorded protection in a manner similar to that of real property rights. That is why the courts generally have enjoined the second user from such activity.[129]

If this is the theory that undergirds the survey evidence presented to trademark courts, it is easy to understand why the cases come out as they do—why courts disregard the value contributed by the audience; why they conflate "use in commerce" (use to propose a transaction) with "commercial use" (use that earns money); why they are so quick to find harm; and why they are developing such a narrow conception of "good faith."

Intellectual property law is not, however, about preventing free rides.[130] If free riding were always actionable, we could not, for example, enjoy a neighbor's garden or learn from a colleague's teaching technique. One merchant could not benefit from the interest a rival generates for a product category. Intellectual property law is aimed at preventing more particularized kinds of harm. Thus, evidence that does no more than demonstrate that an economic benefit was derived from a use, such as a parodic use, of a mark should not suffice to establish trademark infringement. As the concurring justice in the *Laugh It Off* case put it, even if it earns money, a parody may just be a "take-off, not a rip off."[131] In other words, one way to cabin the protectionist trend is to recognize that a trademark holder who is—essentially—trying to control the language is asking for more than trademark law provides.[132] In the marketing context, this means that courts must be alert to the possibility that the trademark holder is trying to eliminate the search rather than reduce its cost.[133]

Expanding trademark protection may also arise out of an aspirational error. Courts appear eager to eliminate all sources of confusion and dilution, and all opportunities for unauthorized navigation. As the *Arsenal* court put it:

---

[129] *See, e.g.*, Jacoby & Morrin, *supra* note 71, at 99 (citations omitted).

[130] Feist Publications, Inc. v Rural Telephone Service Co., Inc., 499 U.S. 340 (1991); Bonito Boats, Inc. v Thunder Craft Boats, Inc., 489 U.S. 141, 156 (1989) (noting that the base line is free competition); Compco Corp. v Day-Brite Lighting, Inc., 376 U.S. 234, 237 (1964).

[131] *Laugh It Off*, (8) BCLR 743 (CC), at ¶ 102 (Sachs, J.).

[132] As has been noted in a different context (namely, the perennial discussion of why democrats have been so ineffectual in the "values" debate): "capture the field of language and the political field will be yours because the words everyone responds to will have the meanings you have conferred on them." Stanley Fish, *They Write the Songs*, a review of GEOFFREY NUNBERG, TALKING RIGHT, *in* THE NEW YORK TIMES BOOK REVIEW, July 16, 2006, at 20.

[133] *See generally* Stacy L. Dogan & Mark A. Lemley, *Trademarks and Consumer Search Costs on the Internet*, 41 HOUSTON L. REV. 777 (2004).

> For a trade mark to be able to fulfill its essential role in the system of undistorted competition . . . , it must offer a *guarantee* that *all* of the goods or services bearing it have been manufactured or supplied under the control of a single undertaking which is responsible for their quality.[134]

And yet it is clear that this goal is unattainable. Because trademarks are territorial, there will sometimes be different trademark holders using the same mark on similar goods in different trading regions. As consumers travel, use the Internet, read foreign books and magazines, they will inevitably encounter these potentially confusing and dilutive marks. There is also functionality convergence: telephones now take pictures, computers play music, and mobile devices download radio programs. As a result, the same mark may be used in connection with goods that were once different, but have, over time, become similar. Further, there are the various trademark doctrines discussed above: some uses that might be confusing or dilutive will not be regarded as commercial enough to trigger a trademark violation; some uses will fit within one of the statutorily or judicially created defenses; a few will be considered so expressive they will be constitutionally safeguarded, no matter what their effect on the trademark. Finally, some people will forever be confused.[135] As the Supreme Court noted in *KP Permanent Make-Up, Inc. v Lasting Impression I, Inc.*, "[T]he common law [tolerates] a certain degree of confusion on the part of consumer . . . . The Lanham Act adopts a similar leniency."[136]

Given that there will always be some residual confusion, and given the increasingly important role that trademarks play in speech and in cyberspace, the time has clearly come to learn more about ambiguity—how it is caused, how it affects consumers' activities, and—most important—how it is alleviated.

---

[134] Arsenal Football Club Plc v Reed, 2002 ECR I-10273 ¶ 48 (emphasis added). The ECJ went on to say: "Once it has been found that . . . the use of the sign in question by the third party is liable to affect the guarantee of origin of the goods and that the trade mark proprietor must be able to prevent this, it is immaterial that in the context of that use the sign is perceived as a badge of support or loyalty or affiliation to the proprietor of the mark." *Id.* at ¶ 61.

[135] *See, e.g.*, Ellen R. Foxman, Phil W. Berger & Joseph A. Cote, *Consumer Brand Confusion: A Conceptual Framework*, 9 PSYCHOLOGY & MARKETING 123 (1992) (giving the example of customers who drank Sunlight dishwashing liquid because they thought it was lemon juice); *see also* Jacob Jacoby & Wayne Hoyer, *Viewer Miscomprehension of Televised Communication: Selected Findings*, 46 J. MARKETING 12 (1982) ("The vast majority (96.5%) of the 2700 respondents . . . miscomprehend at least some portion of the 60 seconds' worth of televised communications that they viewed. [I]t would appear that no communication is immune from being miscomprehended. Every test communication was miscomprehended at least some of the time by some of the viewers.").

[136] 543 U.S. 111, 122 (2004).

III. Cognitive and behavioral approaches

Trademarks are not, after all, the only place where conflicting signals create confusion and misunderstanding. I have a brother and a son-in-law named David, two friends called Graeme, acquaintances at Washington University, the University of Washington, George Washington University, and American University's Washington College of Law. I live in Greenwich Village, shop in Greenwich, Connecticut, and visit friends on Greenwich Avenue (or do they live on Greenwich Street?). Somehow, I manage to sort all this out. In recent years, cognitive and behavioral scientists have begun to study how that happens—the impact of these conflicts and the strategies used to resolve them. While this is not the place to delve into the details of cognitive science (even were I equipped to do so), the work to date suggests that there is room for considerable improvement in the way trademark law is structured.

Admittedly, cognitive research appears to support many of the concerns of trademark holders. Under the prevailing "activation theory" of cognition, information is stored in cognitive units called nodes, which are hierarchically arranged in a series of links. When a stimulus calls for the retrieval of information, it excites one node, and that "activation" spreads from node to node, through the established linkages, until the node carrying the information sought is activated, and the information is recalled. The stronger each node, and the stronger degree of association between nodes, the better information is retained and the quicker it is retrieved. The strength of each node depends on repeated exposure to facts involving the concept stored in the node.[137]

Since trademarks function as nodes, heavy advertising can create strong nodes and links, permitting information about a mark to be recalled quickly.[138] Indeed, some trademarks can become so engrained in memory, they are said to dominate—a mark can come to stand for the entire product category (instance dominance); alternatively, naming a product category can immediately summon recall of a particular mark (category dominance).[139] Instance dominance likely accounts for the tendency of consumers to use a trademark to look for a product category on the Internet. But category dominance is

---

[137] This theory was developed by John Anderson and is widely cited in the literature. For a review of the extensive experiments supporting it, see John A. Anderson, *A Spreading Activation Theory of Memory*, 22 J. VERBAL LEARNING AND VERBAL BEHAV. 261 (1983).

[138] *See* Paul M. Herr, Peter H. Farquhar & Russell H. Fazio, *The Impact of Dominance and Relatedness on Brand Extensions*, 5(2) J. CONSUMER PSYCHOL. 145 (1996).

[139] *Id.* at 138. Nike may be an example of instance dominance because it invokes the category "athletic shoe." It would also exemplify category dominance if it is the case that any mention of athletic shoes invokes the concept "Nike."

particularly prized because a consumer looking for a product will often stop shopping once the category-dominant brand is encountered. This may be because the mark preempts the choice (as the literature puts it, the trademark holder "owns" the product category as a cognitive matter[140]). But cognitive research also suggests that consumers display "satisficing" behavior: their ability to process information is bounded, and so they adopt a strategy of ending an inquiry once they find a choice that fits their purpose, even if it is not the choice that would optimize their preferences.[141] The bottom line is that trademark holders are right to think of their strong marks as extraordinarily powerful marketing tools.

They are also right to worry that this power can be diminished. Activation theory suggests that when consumers are presented with extraneous information, a "fan effect" is produced—each association activates chains of nodes and information retrieval slows.[142] In situations where a consumer is confronted with many choices, information overload or confusion can lead to a decision to forgo purchase—at least until the ambiguity is resolved (for example, the consumer finds a reason to choose one product over another).[143] Worse, consumers could encode, and then rely on, information about a trademark that is incorrect.[144]

Before rushing to safeguard trademark holders' interests, there are, however, countervailing considerations. Take, for example, the concept of the dominant mark. The examples cited in the cognition literature include Crayolas for crayons, Band-Aids for adhesive strips, Jell-O for gelatin, and Vaseline for petroleum jelly[145]—all marks that are arguably generic. Of course, regarding all dominant marks as unprotectable would not be a good idea—they contribute to the efficiency of decision making and thus lower search costs. Nonetheless, a strong argument can be made that trademark holders should be charged with the consequences of advertising marks to the point where they become dominant. As the *KP Permanent Make-Up* Court noted in

---

[140] *Id.* at 136; *see also id.* at 153.

[141] *See* Herbert A. Simon, *Rational Decision Making in Business Organizations*, 69 AM. ECON. REV. 493, 503 (1979) (Nobel Prize address). For the application of this theory to Internet navigation, see, e.g., Denise E. Agosto, *Bounded Rationality and Satisficing in Young People's Web-Based Decision Making*, 53 J. AM. SOC'Y FOR INFO. SCI. AND TECH. 16, 17 (2002).

[142] Anderson, *supra* note 137, at 272.

[143] *See, e.g.*, Foxman et al., *supra* note 135, at 133–4; Shafir et al., *supra* note 125, at 22.

[144] Vincent-Wayne Mitchell, Gianfranco Walsh & Mo Yamin, *Toward a Conceptual Model of Consumer Confusion*, 32 ADVANCES IN CONSUMER RES. 143, 147 (2005).

[145] Herr et al., *supra* note 138.

the context of descriptive marks, "If any confusion results, that is a risk the plaintiff accepted when it decided to identify its product with a mark that uses a well known descriptive phrase."[146] Similarly, those who decide to give their marks dominance should be deemed to accept the risk that their marks will be used for expressive and navigational purposes.[147]

In fact, a little less dominance could be in trademark holders' own interest: cognitive research also shows that marks that become too associated with product categories do not lend themselves to brand extension and life-style marketing.[148] To put this another way, Frank Schechter may have been exactly wrong. There is little need for dilution law to protect trademark holders from the possibilities of "Dupont shoes, Buick aspirin, Schlitz varnish, Kodak pianos, and Bulova gowns"[149] because there is little value destroyed by these associations: category-dominant marks are understood only in relation to the categories they dominate. Dilution may, in short, be more of a theoretical problem than a real one, which may be why it has proved so difficult to establish.

Even with confusion, we may well be asking the wrong question: not how to eliminate it, but rather how to deal with it. For that, we need to understand what consumers do when they are confused. Not as much is known about this side of things. As one observer noted, "almost all conceptual and empirical work examining consumer confusion has disregarded how consumers cope with confusion and the idea that they employ confusion reduction strategies."[150] But a few observations can be made.

---

[146] KP Permanent Make-Up, Inc. v Lasting Impression I, Inc., 543 U.S. 111, 122 (2004) (citing Cosmetically Sealed Industries, Inc. v Chesebrough-Pond's USA Co., 125 F.3d 28, 30 (2nd Cir., 1997)). This mirrors the philosophy underlying the genericity doctrine: the penalty for failing to establish a name for a new product is that the public adopts the mark as the name, and the mark becomes generic.

[147] *See* Sara Stadler Nelson, *The Wages of Ubiquity in Trademark Law*, 88 IOWA L. REV. 731 (2003).

[148] *See* Herr et al., *supra* note 138, at 153; *see also* Kevin Lane Keller & David A. Aaker, *The Effect of Sequential Introduction of Brand Extensions*, 29 J. MARKETING RES. 35 (1992).

[149] *See* Beebe, *supra* note 40, at 684–5 (describing Schechter's testimony before Congress on a dilution bill).

[150] Mitchell et al., *supra* note 144, at 143. That this should be the case is not entirely surprising. A significant amount of the work on consumers' reaction to conflicting signals seems to have been conducted by the same people who design the consumer confusion and dilution surveys that are used in litigation. For example, according to the CV of Jacob Jacoby, a key designer of consumer surveys, see *supra*. note 128, he has authored more than 135 chapters and articles as well as ten monographs, *available at* http://pages.stern.nyu.edu/~jjacoby/.

First, unfamiliar associations do not always give rise to consumer confusion. Cognitive research shows that individuals monitor the activation process as it unfolds. When an individual encounters an unknown association, activation begins, but as successive nodes fail to recall the source of the association, the individual eventually concludes that the association is unknown.[151] In other words, consumers generally recognize when they are in situations of information deficit. To quote Donald Rumsfeld, "There are things we know we know. We also know there are known unknowns. That is to say we know there are some things we do not know." [152] While it is true that when in an information deficit, a consumer may forgo purchase (and a trademark holder may lose a sale),[153] that moment of uncertainty is, arguably, as important to the smooth operation of the marketplace as reducing search costs. After all, it is at that point that consumers seek out more information and learn about other considerations that influence purchasing decisions, such as the existence and characteristics of other products or, in the purely expressive context, information about the trademark holder's reputation and politics. An approach that cuts off learning imperils competition, blocks the effective interchange of ideas, and even undercuts the benefits of trademark law. If a dominant trademark cannot be used to explore a product category, the dominant trademark holder has little need to further maintain goodwill.

Second, consumers have a variety of techniques for reducing confusion. Of course, cognitive styles differ, but the research largely bears out the intuitions of the courts that are receptive to expressive interests. When confronted with ambiguity, people will rely on their priors,[154] just as the *Henson* court assumed when it found that consumers' experience with the Muppets would resolve their confusion about whether Spa'am was sponsored by Hormel. Context and contextual clues are extremely important,[155] as the *Mattel* court reasoned when it decided that people hearing a song about Barbie would understand it as entertainment, and not an offer to sell a doll. People use the gestalt of the experience—the totality of the circumstances in which the mark

---

[151] *See* Anderson, *supra* note 137, at 273.
[152] Hart Seely, The Poetry of D.H. Rumsfeld, Slate, posted April 2, 2003, *available at* http://www.slate.com/id/2081042/ (based on a Department of Defense news briefing, February 12, 2002. To be sure, Rumsfeld also said, "there are also unknown unknowns, the ones we don't know we don't know." But my claim is not that consumers are never confused, just that they do not remain as confused as courts assume.
[153] *See* Mitchell, *supra* note 144, at 148; Shafir et al., *supra* note 125.
[154] *See, e.g.*, Foxman et al., *supra* note 128, at 137.
[155] *See, e.g.*, Anderson, *supra* note 137.

is encountered,[156] just as the *Michelin* court imagined when it held that employees who were handed union pamphlets depicting Bibendum would not think about tires.

But much remains to be learned. One issue that cognitive research could usefully explore is the effect of disclaimers. As *Arsenal* demonstrates, courts hearing trademark cases often discount the value of disclaimers[157]—a skepticism that is clearly supported by the many surveys showing their inadequacy.[158] Yet in other contexts, information is conveyed through similar devices: warning labels, washing instructions, and warranties are, in fact, often required by law. Clearly, there are circumstances when such transmissions are regarded as effective.[159] One reason for the difference in approach may go back to the framework under which trademark courts operate. If the goal is to avoid *all* free riding and *all* confusion, then disclaimers are sure to be rejected. The harm is committed as soon as the unauthorized mark is confronted (hence, the notion of initial interest confusion). Under a more realistic approach, it would be useful to know more about how visual information is integrated, what sorts of messages attract attention, and what can easily be recalled.[160] In the Internet context, it would be especially helpful to learn more about how to

---

[156] See Dan Simon, Cadwick J. Snow & Stephen Read, *The Redux of Cognitive Consistency Theories: Evidence Judgments by Constraint Satisfaction*, 86(6) J. PERSONALITY AND SOC. PSYCHOL. 814 (2004) (exploring various styles, such as gestalt and Baysian reasoning).

[157] *See, e.g.*, 1-800 Contacts, Inc. v WhenU.com, 309 F. Supp. 2d 467, 504 (S.D.N.Y. 2003). For the contrary view, see Consumers Union of U.S., Inc. v Gen. Signal Corp., 724 F.2d 1044, 1053 (2d Cir. 1983); Playboy Enters., Inc. v Welles, 78 F. Supp. 2d 1066, 1080 & n. 9 (S.D. Cal. 1999). For a general assessment of the use of disclaimers as remedies in trademark litigation, see Weight Watchers Int'l, Inc. v Stouffer Corp., 744 F. Supp. 1259, 1276 (S.D.N.Y. 1990). *See also* Int'l Stamp Art, Inc. v U.S. Postal Service, 456 F.3d 1270, 1275 (11th Cir. 2006) (use of self-identification information to establish good faith on the part of a defendant relying on a fair use defense).

[158] *See* note 74, *supra*.

[159] To be sure, there is also a literature on why these devices are not understood. *See, e.g.*, G. Ray Funkhouser, *An Empirical Study of Consumers' Sensitivity to the Wording of Affirmative Disclosure Messages*, 3 J. OF PUB. POL'Y AND MARKETING 26 (1984) (health warnings); Jacob Jacoby, Robert W. Chestnut & William Silberman, *Consumer Use and Comprehension of Nutrition Information*, 4 J. OF CONSUMER RES. 119 (1977).

[160] For a flavor of this literature, *see, e.g.*, MICHAEL W. EYSENCK, PRINCIPLES OF COGNITIVE PSYCHOLOGY 17–18 (perception), 126–30 (integration); Rijo Savolainen & Jarkko Kari, *Facing and Bridging Gaps in Web Searching*, 42 INFO. PROCESSING AND MGMT. 519 (2005); Kirk G. Thompson, Narcisse P. Bichot, & Jeffrey Schall, *From Attention to Action in Frontal Cortex*, in VISUAL ATTENTION AND CORTICAL CIRCUITS (Jochen Braun, Christof Koch, & Joel L. Davis eds. 2001).

unambiguously signal the provenance of a site and help consumers locate other holders of the same mark.[161]

Because of the rise in interjurisdictional cases, it would also be useful to learn more about the language issue. As suggested above, decisions considering foreign websites may have more to do with fears of cultural hegemony than with consumer confusion, dilution, or cyberpiracy. If those concerns are, as I have argued, disregarded, then it would help to know more about how people react when they encounter a mark embedded in text they do not understand. Are courts right to worry that they will be confused? Or will consumers unacquainted with the language of a site realize that they are missing information and simply move on to sites they do understand or find ways to translate the site they are viewing?

But in the final analysis, what trademark law especially needs is a better account of the reasonable consumer. As noted earlier, cognitive styles differ. Some individuals are cognitive levelers—they simplify their environments by ignoring detail—others are sharpeners—they actively look for cues that eliminate ambiguity; some have a wide equivalence range—they classify stimuli into broad categories, others attend to detail; some individuals are impulsive and others, reflective; some are field dependent and are easily thrown by complex environments, others are better at handling multiple stimuli.[162] The law could attempt to protect individuals at the far (less discerning) end of each of these cognitive categories; the question is whether it makes sense to do so. If there is mobility within these categories (and only cognitive research can tell us where that mobility lies and how far it extends), then designing the law to protect the reasonable consumer would encourage individuals to develop their facilities. Not all ambiguity will be eliminated in any event; creating incentives to deal with it will, in the long run, provide trademark holders with surer protection and give greater freedom to those who would use their marks expressively.

IV. Conclusion

Slightly less than two decades ago, I began to explore the clash between the proprietary interests of trademark holders and those who sought to use their marks expressively. Since that time, expressive uses have soared, but lawmakers have come no closer to protecting expressive interests. Indeed, for the most part, trademark holders have gained the upper hand, reducing the opportunity for creative usages of their marks, particularly on the Internet.

---

[161] *See generally* Patricia W. Cheng & Keith J. Holyoak, *Pragmatic Reasoning Schemas*, 17 COGNITIVE PSYCHOL. 391 (1985).
[162] *See* Foxman et al., *supra* note 135, at 131–3.

In some ways, the response of the judiciary is surprising. Courts have a variety of mechanisms for allocating rights in trademarks: the genericity approach I (and others) suggested, narrowing the meaning of commercial; taking a hard look at what is confusing, dilutive, or opportunistic; applying defenses, including constitutional defenses, designed to shelter socially important uses. But to an alarming extent, these approaches have been rejected. Perhaps the parsing required is too difficult to perform. More likely, the problem lies in the goals that courts are pursuing—avoiding all confusion and preventing all free riding. Thus, it may be that a more realistic understanding of possible outcomes is required. In an economy in which consumers have immediate access to products and services everywhere on the globe, in a legal environment in which symbols are protected in multiple ways, in a culture in which trademarks constitute a significant medium of expression, freedom from all sources of confusion or dilution is simply not achievable.

What can be achieved is a marketplace in which consumers understand what they are experiencing. Interpreting trademark legislation in a manner that is attentive to how encounters with multiple meanings are deciphered could lead to law that is protective of both trade and creativity. To be sure, there may be some expressive situations where confusion, dilution, or free-riding is so rampantly likely and destructive, trademark holders should win—the affiliation products at issue in *Arsenal* may present such a case. But a fuller understanding of how perception is shaped is likely to provide more durable protection for our shared expressive vocabulary.

My examination of the current crop of cases disclosed another revealing factor. Judges who are attracted to arguments grounded in expressive concerns tend to be colorful writers. They characterize disputes as fights between Davids and Goliaths;[163] they make reference to Umberto Eco,[164] Samuel Johnson,[165] Chaucer, Shakespeare, Pope, Voltaire, Fielding, Hemingway, and Faulkner.[166] No one ever accused Alex Kozinski—the self-styled judge of the "Court of Appeals for the Hollywood Circuit"[167]—of writing turgid prose. In contrast, it is clear from the way certain judges write that they just don't get it—that they are not gripped by language and remain unworried by trademark holders' assault on the arsenal guarding "the vibrancy of our culture."[168] I wonder, too, about their senses of humor.

---

[163] Laugh It Off Promotions CC v SAB Int'l (Finance) BV, 2005 (8) BCLR 743 (CC) (May 27, 2005), ¶ 81 (Sachs, J., concurring).
[164] *Id.* at ¶ 106, n. 102.
[165] Campbell v Acuff-Rose Music, Inc., 510 U.S. 569, 583 (1994).
[166] L.L. Bean, Inc. v Drake Publishers, Inc., 811 F.2d 26, 28 (1st Cir. 1987).
[167] White v Samsung Elec's Am., Inc., 989 F.2d 1512, 1521 (9th Cir. 1993).
[168] *Id.*

11 Truth and advertising: the Lanham Act and commercial speech doctrine
Rebecca Tushnet

Commercial speech, defined roughly as speech that proposes a marketplace transaction, has been easier for the government to regulate than noncommercial speech throughout the development of the modern First Amendment. The commercial/noncommercial divide has long been controversial, and several current Supreme Court Justices have suggested their willingness to abandon the distinction, given the importance of commercial speech to modern social, economic and political life.[1] Distinguishing between commercial and noncommercial speech creates definitional problems.[2] Yet the alternative of treating all falsifiable claims alike might be far less palatable, especially when we consider the range of commercial speech that is currently regulated to protect consumers against false or misleading claims.[3]

In particular, the Lanham Act and its state counterparts in trademark and unfair competition law could be profoundly affected if courts were to equate commercial speech with political speech. The difficulties could only be resolved by invalidating a large amount of modern trademark and advertising law or by recalibrating First Amendment standards in some core areas. But even if the Supreme Court preserves the commercial/noncommercial distinction, we need a better account of how to deal with informational speech that helps some people but deceives others. As it stands, there are significant mismatches between the approaches of free speech law and unfair competition law.

In the past, courts have denied First Amendment protections to advertisers in trademark and false advertising cases, reasoning that trademark and false

---

[1] *See, e.g.*, 44 Liquormart, Inc. v Rhode Island, 517 U.S. 484, 501, 510–14 (1996) (joint opinion of Stevens, Kennedy and Ginsburg, JJ.); *id.* at 517 (Scalia, J., concurring in part and concurring in the judgment); *id.* at 518 (Thomas, J., concurring in part and concurring in the judgment).

[2] Even for those who accept that commercial speech deserves less First Amendment protection than political speech, line-drawing can be problematic: What is an ad for an abortion clinic? What is an ad for McDonnell-Douglas praising the company's contribution to our nation's defense?

[3] *See generally* Frederick Schauer, *Commercial Speech and the Architecture of the First Amendment*, 56 U. CIN. L. REV. 1181 (1988).

advertising law pose no constitutional problems because they only regulate false and misleading commercial speech, which the Supreme Court has said can simply be banned.[4] The expansion of trademark law to include protection against dilution, which operates even when consumers are not confused or deceived, puts obvious pressure on this reasoning. First Amendment concerns have also arisen in trademark infringement claims against classic expressive media such as movies, which are not commercial speech for First Amendment purposes even when they are disseminated for profit. Most First Amendment analysis of the Lanham Act focuses on attempts – both successful and not – to extend trademark law beyond protecting against confusion in sales of ordinary goods and services.[5]

This chapter goes further, exploring concepts in First Amendment law that, if applied to the Lanham Act, would cast doubt on several of its significant elements. The lines between confusing and informative and between true and false are difficult to draw, in ways that in other contexts – particularly libel doctrine – have led courts to impose increasing burdens on those entities, whether private or governmental, who would penalize defendants for speech that is deemed harmful because it is deemed false. I will discuss the First Amendment implications of distinguishing truth from falsity in commercial speech, applied to trademark infringement and to other types of false advertising.

In addition, on a somewhat different note, I will consider an increasingly popular theory that justifies trademark dilution law as a benefit to consumers, not just to producers, because it decreases search costs just as trademark infringement law does. One important corollary is that dilution law serves a substantial government interest and thus does not violate the First Amendment even though it bans truthful, nonmisleading commercial speech. Largely because the new search costs theory of dilution cannot distinguish between commercial and noncommercial speech, however, I conclude that it is ultimately unpersuasive in answering First Amendment objections to dilution law.

---

[4] *See* Central Hudson Gas & Electric Corp. v Public Service Comm'n, 447 U.S. 557 (1980).

[5] *See, e.g.*, Mark A. Lemley, *The Modern Lanham Act and the Death of Common Sense*, 108 YALE L.J. 1687, 1687–8, 1693–7, 1710–15 (1999). For an interesting exception, see Lisa P. Ramsey, *Descriptive Trademarks and the First Amendment*, 70 TENN. L. REV. 1095 (2003) (arguing that current protections for descriptive marks with secondary meaning conflict with First Amendment rights).

I. False advertising

A. Background: Supreme Court discussions of truth versus falsity[6]

In *Virginia State Board of Pharmacy v Virginia Citizens Consumer Council, Inc.*,[7] the Supreme Court held that the First Amendment offers some protection to commercial speech because such speech has value to people trying to make decisions about how to live, including political decisions.[8] The Court later elaborated on the standard for permissible regulation of commercial speech. The resulting *Central Hudson* test has four parts: (1) truthful, nonmisleading speech may be regulated when (2) the regulation serves a substantial government interest, (3) the regulation directly advances that government interest, and (4) the regulation is no more extensive than necessary. The government bears the burden of proof,[9] which cannot be satisfied "by mere speculation or conjecture; rather, a governmental body seeking to sustain a restriction on commercial speech must demonstrate that the harms it recites are real and that its restriction will in fact alleviate them to a material degree."[10]

One very odd thing about the *Central Hudson* test is that a regulation will be sustained if it meets all four prongs of the test, *or* if it fails the first prong, that is, if it deals with false or misleading commercial speech. In the latter case, the speech may be banned outright.[11] Commercial speech that is "not

---

[6] Sections A & B are adapted from Rebecca Tushnet, *Trademark Law as Commercial Speech Regulation*, 58 S. CAR. L. REV. 737 (2007).

[7] 425 U.S. 748 (1976).

[8] *See id.* at 763 ("As to the particular consumer's interest in the free flow of commercial information, that interest may be as keen, if not keener by far, than his interest in the day's most urgent political debate."). Increasingly, the Court has justified protection for commercial speech with reference to the speaker's interests, but I will focus here on the value of the speech to the recipient. Recipient-focused theories allow more regulation of speech than speaker-focused theories, given that they do not consider the commercial speaker to have a distinct autonomy interest in speaking about its products. *See, e.g.*, Robert Post, *Transparent and Efficient Markets: Compelled Commercial Speech and Coerced Commercial Association in* United Foods, Zauderer, *and* Abood, 40 VAL. U. L. REV. 555, 559 (2006).

[9] *See, e.g.*, Rubin v Coors Brewing Co., 514 U.S. 476, 487 (1995) ("[T]he Government carries the burden of showing that the challenged regulation advances the Government's interest 'in a direct and material way'."); Bolger v Youngs Drug Prods. Corp., 463 U.S. 60, 71 n. 20 (1983) ("The party seeking to uphold a restriction on commercial speech carries the burden of justifying it.").

[10] Edenfield v Fane, 507 U.S. 761, 770–71 (1993).

[11] As Robert Post points out, misleading speech might be commercial speech that can be regulated, or it might instead be excluded from the category "commercial speech" and entirely outside the First Amendment's coverage, much like contract law and warranties presently are. *See* Robert Post, *The Constitutional Status of Commercial Speech*, 48 UCLA L. REV. 1, 22 (2000); Schauer, *supra* note 3.

provably false, or even wholly false, but only deceptive or misleading" may be regulated by the state to keep "the stream of commercial information flow[ing] cleanly as well as freely."[12]

For years, courts and commentators have assailed the Supreme Court's commercial speech jurisprudence as incoherent at best. The controversy, however, has focused on the line between commercial and noncommercial speech and on the test for regulating truthful, nonmisleading commercial speech. On the threshold issue of how one determines truth for constitutional purposes, the Supreme Court has been all but silent, and the academic literature generally little better.[13]

The Supreme Court has been most attentive to the line between true speech and false or misleading speech in the context of regulations of advertising for professional services, a field in which it probably feels more comfortable assessing likelihood of deception than in other areas.[14] For example, in *Ibañez v Florida Department of Business & Professional Regulation*,[15] the Court stated that the government may not assert that commercial speech is "potentially" misleading in order to ban it; rather, it must prove that the speech is actually or inherently misleading.[16]

---

[12] *Virginia Pharmacy*, 425 U.S. at 771–2.

[13] *See, e.g.*, Daniel E. Troy, *Advertising: Not "Low Value" Speech*, 16 YALE J. ON REG. 85, 130 (1999) ("In most applications of *Central Hudson*, the first and second prongs of the test are not at issue. The first prong, concerning whether the speech involves a lawful activity and is not misleading, is generally uncontroversial."). There are a few exceptions in the literature of false advertising law, but essentially nothing in the literature of trademark. *See* Lillian BeVier, *Competitor Suits for False Advertising Under §43(a) of the Lanham Act: A Puzzle in the Law of Deception*, 89 VA. L. REV. 1 (1992); Martin H. Redish, *Product Health Claims and the First Amendment: Scientific Expression and the Twilight Zone of Commercial Speech*, 43 VAND. L. REV. 433 (1990); Troy, *supra*, at 130 (suggesting that the breadth of "misleading" is troubling to those who support more rigorous First Amendment protections for commercial speech).

[14] *See, e.g.*, In re R.M.J., 455 U.S. 191, 202 (1982) ("[T]he public's comparative lack of knowledge, the limited ability of the professions to police themselves, and the absence of any standardization in the 'product' renders advertising for professional services especially susceptible to abuses that the States have a legitimate interest in controlling."); *see also* Alex Kozinski & Stuart Banner, *Who's Afraid of Commercial Speech?*, 76 VA. L. REV. 627, 630 (1990) ("Lawyer advertising, initially an area covered by mainstream commercial speech jurisprudence, became the subject of so many cases that it developed into its own distinct area of common law. . . . At present, the law of attorney advertising has grown to such an extent that it has been able to seal itself off from its roots in first amendment theory. . . . ").

[15] 512 U.S. 136 (1994).

[16] *See id.* at 146. *See also In re R.M.J.*, 455 U.S. at 203 (holding that regulators could ban commercial speech "when the particular content or method of the advertising suggests that it is inherently misleading or when experience has proved that in fact such advertising is subject to abuse").

The Court left itself much room for maneuver by indicating that some speech is "inherently" misleading but not explaining how that category should be defined. Sometimes the Court has approved broad prophylactic rules against whole categories of commercial speech, such as in-person solicitation by a lawyer that is "inherently" likely to involve deception or other misconduct.[17] By contrast, *Peel v Attorney Registration and Disciplinary Commission*[18] held that, when lawyers' statements about their certifications and specializations could confuse clients, the state could require a disclaimer or could screen certifying organizations, but could not "completely ban statements that are not actually or inherently misleading,"[19] again without explaining how misleadingness was to be determined.

The most we know is that, unsurprisingly, the lawyers on the Court favor more words rather than fewer – the Court's preferred cure for incomplete or unqualified claims is more disclosure, not less.[20] In another lawyer advertising case, the Court held that government "may not place an absolute prohibition on certain types of potentially misleading information . . . if the information also may be presented in a way that is not deceptive."[21] Yet even that knowledge is uncertain; the Court has also said that "there is no First Amendment rule . . . requiring a state to allow deceptive or misleading commercial speech whenever the publication of additional information can clarify or offset the effects of spurious communication."[22]

B. Trademark infringement

1. First Amendment precedents   The Supreme Court has confronted the First Amendment implications of trademarks only in unusual factual and legal situations, which has not helped it go beyond its inconsistent and shallow treatment of deception in commercial speech cases. In *Friedman v Rogers*,[23] a case that predates *Central Hudson*, the Court upheld a ban on the practice of optometry under a trade name. The ban furthered the state's interest in protect-

---

[17] Ohralik v Ohio State Bar Ass'n, 436 U.S. 447, 464 (1978).
[18] 496 U.S. 91 (1990).
[19] *Id.* at 110.
[20] *Bates v State Bar of Arizona*, 433 U.S. at 376.
[21] *In re R.M.J.*, 455 U.S. at 203.
[22] Friedman v Rogers, 440 U.S. 1, 15–16 (1979); *see also Ohralik*, 436 U.S. at 449, 466 (in-person solicitation for profit "under circumstances likely to pose dangers that the State has the right to prevent" could be banned without showing actual harm to a particular client; a broad rule was acceptable because the dangers would materialize often, perhaps more often than not).
[23] 440 U.S. 1 (1979).

ing the public from "deceptive and misleading" practices.[24] The Court distinguished trade names from the commercial speech it had recently held deserved First Amendment protection. Statements about products or services and their prices are "self-contained and self-explanatory," but trade names "have no intrinsic meaning."[25] They convey no information about price or services until they acquire meaning over time. The Court's distinction is hard to understand. All words, at least the non-onomatopoeic ones, lack inherent meaning. If a trade name or other mark can convey misleading information – the premise of the regulation – it can also convey truthful information, depending on the circumstances.

Nonetheless, the Court was certain that the factual (as opposed to emotional or potentially misleading) information associated with a trade name could be communicated directly by advertising price, available services, or the fact of a joint practice.[26] By contrast, the Court feared that trademark associations with price and quality remain ill-defined and can be manipulated by trademark owners, creating a significant possibility that trade names will be used to mislead, for example by keeping the name the same when the staff changes.[27]

Thus, the Court credited lower courts' findings that Rogers had used a trade name "to convey the impression of standardized optometrical care" even though he did not exercise supervision or control of the services rendered at the various offices using the trade name.[28] Trademark law is usually thought to promote quality control, except in cases of naked licensing. Notably, trademark law would find Rogers's mark invalid for abandonment, though that in itself wouldn't stop the offices from using it. Instead of banning trade names, a more limited and speech-protective remedy would be a ban on naked licensing of a trade name, at least in health care-related fields. But the Court didn't consider that alternative, because it was skeptical of the benefits of trade names generally. A shady optometrist can use a new trade name if negligence or misconduct tarnishes the old one, or can use different trade names for multiple shops to "give the public the false impression of competition among the shops."[29] Even if use of a trade name wasn't misleading, it would still "facilitate the large-scale commercialization which enhances the opportunity for misleading practices."[30]

---

[24] *Id.* at 15.
[25] *Id.* at 12.
[26] *See id.* at 16.
[27] *See id.* at 12–13.
[28] *Id.* at 14.
[29] *Id.* at 13.
[30] *Id.* at 15.

Though the Court purported to be relying on Texas's specific judgments about optometry, similar manipulation to detach actual producers from specific identifiers is possible in any market. Nike shoes come from hundreds of subcontractors. In the other direction, corporations such as Procter & Gamble make multiple national brands of the same product type, and house brands in the supermarket are often produced by generic companies that serve both the Safeway and the Food Lion across the street from it,[31] producing the "false impression of competition" the Court feared. Indeed, the separation of trademark's source-identifying function from actual production is characteristic of modern marketing.[32]

Friedman's apparent opposition to modern industrial practices is part of its pervasive conflict with trademark's rationale. The Court's factual presumptions are inconsistent with subsequent commercial speech doctrine and with the dominant theory of efficiency that justifies trademark protection generally, which the Court later endorsed.[33] By treating short-term opportunities to deceive through changes in quality as more important than long-term incentives to provide a consistent product, the Court missed the informational efficiency of trademarks, the ability to encapsulate in a word or image a constellation of qualities. By serving as shorthand, trademarks make it easier for consumers to recognize the goods and services they want. The rule in *Friedman* required longhand, and the result was (at least according to standard trademark theory) information that was more difficult to process, meaning that consumers had more difficulty satisfying their preferences. Under *Virginia Pharmacy*, this is a harm to free circulation of relevant information in the marketplace – here the information that optometric services *can* be standardized and provided at consistent quality across offices.

---

[31] *See, e.g.*, McNeil Nutritionals, LLC v Heartland Sweeteners LLC, 2007 WL 1520101 (E.D. Pa. May 21, 2007) (involving a defendant that made identical house-branded artificial sweeteners for Giant, Stop & Shop, Tops, Food Lion, and Safeway, among others).

[32] *See* Barton Beebe, *The Semiotic Analysis of Trademark Law*, 51 UCLA L. REV. 621 (2004).

[33] *See* Qualitex Co. v Jacobson Products Co., 514 U.S. 159, 163–4 (1995) ("In principle, trademark law, by preventing others from copying a source-identifying mark, 'reduce[s] the customer's costs of shopping and making purchasing decisions,' for it quickly and easily assures a potential customer that *this* item – the item with this mark – is made by the same producer as other similarly marked items that he or she liked (or disliked) in the past. At the same time, the law helps assure a producer that it (and not an imitating competitor) will reap the financial, reputation-related rewards associated with a desirable product. The law thereby 'encourage[s] the production of quality products,' and simultaneously discourages those who hope to sell inferior products by capitalizing on a consumer's inability quickly to evaluate the quality of an item offered for sale.") (citations omitted).

The best defense of the Court's reasoning might be that personal services like optometry *cannot* be provided consistently by a large company. A more zealous partisan for commercial speech than I might claim that consumers are capable of figuring out whether personal services can be provided as consistently as McDonald's hamburgers, and of balancing that consideration against other possible advantages of industrial organization, such as centralized recordkeeping and lower prices. Trademark law, regardless, does not make a distinction between standardizable and nonstandardizable goods and services; accepting this logic would still mean *Friedman* had no bearing on First Amendment claims involving trademarks in mass-market goods or services, like Starbucks coffee.

In its only return to analyzing the relationship between trademark law and free speech, *San Francisco Arts & Athletics Inc. v United States Olympic Committee*,[34] the Court stated that trademark laws that "regulat[e] confusing uses" of marks are constitutional because the government "may regulate 'deceptive or misleading' commercial speech."[35] That reasoning, combined with the idea that trademarks are valuable property, ended the inquiry. There is no free speech right to use another's property, at least when there are adequate alternative channels for the defendant-speaker to use to convey its message. Lower courts have explicitly applied similar property reasoning to ordinary trademarks, though the Supreme Court addressed itself only to the special laws protecting the Olympic marks. For example, the Second Circuit found that a pornographic film didn't need to use the Dallas Cowboys cheerleaders' trademarks when it could have depicted a fictional team instead.[36]

The property argument is entirely unimpressive with respect to noncommercial, expressive uses. It is dangerous to let legislatures or common law

---

[34] 483 U.S. 522 (1987).
[35] *Id.* at 535 n. 12. The law at issue in *SFAA* was not an ordinary trademark law, but banned any unauthorized use of the term "Olympic" for, among other things, nonprofit sports competitions. The Court found that "Congress reasonably could conclude that most commercial uses of the Olympic words and symbols are likely to be confusing. It also could determine that unauthorized uses, even if not confusing, nevertheless may harm the USOC by lessening the distinctiveness and thus the commercial value of the marks." *Id.* at 539. With respect to the specific use of the term to promote the Gay Olympics, the court found the possibility of confusion "obvious." *Id.* The Court, nonetheless, didn't directly engage the first prong of *Central Hudson*, and thus didn't say that *possible* confusion satisfies the "false or misleading" test. Instead, the Court applied the *United States v O'Brien*, 391 U.S. 367 (1968), test for evaluating content-neutral regulations. *See SFAA*, 483 U.S. at 535, 536 n. 16.
[36] *See, e.g.*, Mutual of Omaha Insurance Co. v Novak, 836 F.2d 397, 402 (8th Cir. 1987); Dallas Cowboys Cheerleaders, Inc. v Pussycat Cinema, Ltd., 604 F.2d 200, 206 (2d Cir. 1979).

define intangibles as property in order to fend off First Amendment challenges. A reputation can be called property as easily as a trademark – indeed, they are much the same thing – and yet libel law is pervasively constrained by the First Amendment. Property concepts are perhaps more persuasive with respect to commercial uses which seek to use a term to attract consumers in the same way as the trademark owner does. The adequate alternative channels concept has echoes within trademark doctrine, which looks to whether a term is necessary for competition to see whether it should be regarded as generic (and thus unprotectable as a trademark), descriptive (and thus protectable only to the extent that consumers learn to see it as an indicator of source), suggestive, arbitrary, or fanciful.[37] Even so, the label "property" does not solve boundary problems, for example, whether trademark rights should bar a defendant's use of a mark on noncompeting goods. In the past, courts using property rhetoric for trademarks limited that property right to actual sales diversion, but now trademark rights extend whenever consumers are likely to perceive an association between producers, even without competition.[38]

Friedman and *SFAA*, as others have noted, are out of line with the Court's more recent treatment of commercial speech as having substantial value.[39] As the Court held in *Edenfield v Fane*,[40] to sustain a regulation of nonmisleading speech, the government "must demonstrate that the harms it recites are real."[41] If the government can avoid that requirement by simply asserting that the harm is that the speech is misleading, hardly any protection for commercial speech will be left. It is easy to recast a concern about the effects of speech as a concern that the speech misleads consumers by obscuring the relevant facts – for example, that optometric services cannot be standardized. Despite that, the Court accepted blanket legislative judgments in both *Friedman* and *SFAA*. Lower courts have consistently followed the same cursory analysis with respect to traditional trademark infringement: confusing uses are misleading and therefore may be enjoined without consideration of First Amendment interests.[42] The only exceptions involve creative works such as music and

---

[37] In addition, the functionality doctrine performs the same competition-reinforcing function for trade dress as genericity does for terms, and the defenses of nominative and descriptive fair use often appeal to expressive or competitive efficiency. See Rebecca Tushnet, *Why the Customer Isn't Always Right: Producer-Based Limits on Rights Accretion in Trademark*, 116 YALE L.J. POCKET PART 352 (2007).

[38] See Mark P. McKenna, *The Normative Foundations of Trademark Law*, 82 Notre Dame L. Rev. 1839 (2007)

[39] See, e.g., Robert N. Kravitz, *Trademarks, Speech, and the Gay Olympics Case*, 69 B.U. L. REV. 131 (1989).

[40] 507 U.S. 761 (1993).

[41] *Id.* at 770–71.

[42] See, e.g., E. & J. Gallo Winery v Gallo Cattle Co., 967 F.2d 1280, 1297 (9th

movies, whose uses of marks sometimes lead courts to invoke free speech concerns.[43]

2. *Application in more conventional trademark cases*

a. The problem of partially useful information: Even conceding that protecting consumers against deception as to source is a compelling government interest,[44] many of trademark law's core presumptions would disappear if the field were subject to the same analysis as other kinds of commercial speech regulations. In *Zauderer*, for example, the Supreme Court suggested that the First Amendment requires that government interventions into the commercial speech market be minimal – disclaimers and disclosures are preferred alternatives to suppressing speech. Although the Second Circuit briefly flirted with using disclaimers to avoid consumer confusion through similar trademarks, disclaimers are not the default remedy in infringement cases, as they would be if courts applied commercial speech doctrine.

The deeper conflict between trademark and the modern First Amendment is that information is rarely completely helpful or completely misleading. The idea that prohibitions on fraud improve the information environment depends on truth and falsity being pure binaries. Many trademark (and false advertising) cases, however, are more complicated. A mark may convey useful information to some while misleading others; eliminating a use that misleads 15 percent of consumers while helping 30 percent may make the market less efficient overall.[45] The problem isn't limited to descriptive terms that have acquired

---

Cir. 1992); Transgo, Inc. v Ajac Transmission Parts Corp., 768 F.2d 1001, 1022 (9th Cir. 1985); Kelley Blue Book v Car-Smarts, Inc., 802 F. Supp. 278, 291 (C.D. Cal. 1992); *see also, e.g.*, Robert C. Denicola, *Trademarks as Speech: Constitutional Implications of the Emerging Rationales for the Protection of the Trade Symbols*, 1982 WIS. L. REV. 158, 165–6, 169; Mark A. Lemley & Eugene Volokh, *Freedom of Speech and Injunctions in Intellectual Property Cases*, 48 DUKE L.J. 147, 221 (1998).

[43] *See, e.g.*, Mattel, Inc. v MCA Records, Inc., 296 F.3d 894 (9th Cir. 2002); Rogers v Grimaldi, 875 F.2d 994 (2d Cir. 1989); Cliffs Notes, Inc. v Bantam Doubleday Dell Publ'g. Group, Inc., 886 F.2d 490, 495 (2d Cir. 1989).

[44] Though it may not be, if the goods or services are of equal quality. Judge Kozinski, who supports full constitutional protection for commercial speech, nonetheless describes trademark infringement as "essentially a fraud on the consuming public" and thus enjoinable without concern for the First Amendment, Mattel v Universal Music Int'l, 296 F.3d 894, 905 (9th Cir. 2002). But others have argued that there is no public interest in prohibiting misrepresentations that don't affect the physical quality of a product or service, since consumers suffer no material loss. *See infra* Section I.C.

[45] *See generally* BeVier, *supra* note 13 (making this point about false advertising cases, though she believes that trademark protection is generally more justified).

secondary meaning. It can occur with resale of used goods, or new products which advertise truthfully that they incorporate other trademarked goods, in which case some consumers may believe that the trademark owner endorses the new product. It can occur with comparative advertising or claims that "If you like X®, you'll love Y."[46]

The problem of suppressing partially useful information exists independent of whether there is any chilling effect from the existence of government regulation and competitor lawsuits. But, of course, chilling effects do exist. A reseller's fear of being sued by the original manufacturer, a competitor's fear that *Health Selections* frozen dinners will bring a lawsuit by *Healthy Choice*, and so on are likely to deter the adoption and use of marks in contexts where they would inform some consumers. Trademark owners have also objected to resales of genuine goods through unapproved channels such as eBay. This chilling effect is increased because a defendant's good-faith belief that its marks (or its uses of another's marks) are not confusing, founded in a study of the relevant market and a trademark search, is insufficient to avoid liability if a court disagrees with the defendant's evaluation.

A trademark owner's ability to deter competitors' truthful, useful commercial speech is not the same thing as the ability to suppress political speech. But if it is true that commercial speech is as relevant and vital to modern citizens as political speech, then suppressing competition is analogous to silencing political opponents, and certainly merits skeptical scrutiny. Like partisan officials deciding which political speech to pursue, trademark owners may see harm where there is only competition. The paradoxical consequence of this private incentive to overlitigate is that infringement law is most dangerous, from the perspective of First Amendment doctrine, at its core – as applied between competitors. That is, a plaintiff's motives are most likely to include the illegitimate desire to suppress even truthful speech when it sues a competitor.[47]

---

[46] In cases in which the defendant's use of a mark conveyed information to some consumers, the First Amendment argument for required disclaimers is strongest. In such cases, a simple injunction against use deprives the nonconfused market participants, who may well be the majority of consumers, of valuable information about the goods. Commercial speech doctrine requires the government to try a more moderate solution than total suppression. *See Zauderer v. Office of Disciplinary Counsel*, 471 U.S. 626, 651 (1985) ("warning[s] or disclaimer[s] might be appropriately required . . . in order to dissipate the possibility of consumer confusion or deception.").

[47] In the modern, trademark-friendly environment, courts have been most likely to recognize anticompetitive motives in trademark cases dealing with trade dress. *See, e.g.*, Wal-Mart Stores, Inc. v Samara Brothers, Inc., 529 U.S. 205, 213–14 (2000) (invoking anticompetitive harassment suits as a reason to require secondary meaning before protecting product design trade dress); I.P. Lund Trading ApS v Kohler Co., 163 F.3d 27, 48 (1st Cir. 1998) (expressing skepticism about dilution claims brought by

b. Problems in determining deception: Separately, the consequences of rigorous commercial speech protection for federal trademark registration, which is a governmentally conferred benefit that provides many advantages in enforcement, could be dramatic.[48] Registration of deceptive marks is barred by the Lanham Act along with scandalous or disparaging marks. But the Patent and Trademark Office (PTO) uses limited evidence to make a deceptiveness determination and has no particular expertise in assessing consumer behavior or understanding. A recent case, *Piazza's Seafood World, LLC v Odom*,[49] suggests the potential effects of robust commercial speech production on the overall trademark system. The plaintiff sold Chinese-farmed catfish under the trade names "Cajun Boy" and "Cajun Delight." Ninety-nine percent of its products were imported from overseas. Louisiana's "Cajun Statute" provided that "No person shall advertise, sell, offer or expose for sale, or distribute food or food products as 'Cajun', 'Louisiana Creole', or any derivative thereof unless the food or food product [was] produced, processed, or manufactured in Louisiana . . . ."[50]

The court of appeals agreed with the district court that Piazza's use of the "Cajun Boy" and "Cajun Delight" trade names was only potentially misleading, not actually or inherently misleading, because Piazza largely sells its products to (presumably sophisticated) wholesalers and it labels its products with their country of origin. Though the state's interest in preventing deception was substantial, the statute went further than necessary to serve that interest because there was no actual deception in this case. As a result, the law, as applied to plaintiff, flunked the test set forth in *Central Hudson*.

The reason this case deserves attention from trademark scholars is that the Lanham Act, and coordinate state laws, do not distinguish between potentially and inherently misleading commercial speech. Imagine what would happen if

---

competitors who cannot show confusion). But because trade dress is far removed from ordinary First Amendment topics – words and images – the correspondence between anticompetitive motives and the broader category of censorious motives has not drawn attention.

[48] The current statutory provision for refusing registration on grounds of scandalousness or disparagement, see 15 U.S.C. § 1052(a), is particularly hard to reconcile with *Central Hudson*'s protection for truthful, nonmisleading commercial speech. See, e.g., Theodore H. Davis, Jr., *Registration of Scandalous, Immoral, and Disparaging Matter Under Section 2(a) of the Lanham Act: Can One Man's Vulgarity Be Another's Registered Trademark?*, 54 OHIO ST. L.J. 331, 345–7 (1993); Llewellyn Joseph Gibbons, *Semiotics of the Scandalous and the Immoral and the Disparaging: section 2(a) Trademark Law After* Lawrence v Texas, 9 MARQ. INTELL. PROP. L. REV. 187, 231 (2005); Jeffrey Lefstin, Note, *Does the First Amendment Bar Cancellation of REDSKINS?*, 52 STAN. L. REV. 665, 677–9 (2000).

[49] 448 F.3d 744 (5th Cir. 2006).

[50] La. Rev. Stat. Ann. § 3:4617(D).

the plaintiff sought to register its "Cajun Boy" mark and was denied using the PTO's test for deceptiveness, which does not require the examiner to show actual deception.[51] Because the PTO has the burden of proof in rejecting a mark on deceptiveness grounds, and limited resources with which to investigate the hundreds of thousands of applications it receives, it routinely relies on common-sense inferences about the effects of facially false or intuitively misleading claims. Given the important evidentiary and procedural benefits of registration, robust application of commercial speech doctrine would require more from the PTO before it could deny those benefits. Under the Fifth Circuit's reasoning, absent specific proof of actual or inherent deceptiveness, the applicant would have a First Amendment right to the benefits of federal registration.

Moreover, the commercial speech concepts of potentially and actually misleading do not map onto trademark infringement in any coherent way. One could argue that "actually" misleading speech is that shown by a consumer survey or anecdotal evidence from confused consumers. Even that would require a serious disruption of the test for infringement, which is whether confusion is "likely" and which currently does not require evidence of actual confusion for a plaintiff to prevail. Nor does commercial speech doctrine have anything like trademark's numerical threshold, in which confusion among a minority of consumers (15–20 percent, in many cases) is enough to enjoin a defendant's use even if the majority of consumers get relevant information from the use.

One possibility suggested by the lawyer regulation cases is that the difference between inherently and potentially misleading speech in First Amendment doctrine is whether further disclosures can correct the misleading implications of the challenged speech on its own. If that is the distinction, however, then consumer surveys aren't useful to show "actual" misleadingness unless they also show that a disclaimer fails to correct the problem. Most surveys don't show "inherent" deception because they don't test disclaimers.

c. A final note on intent: Another big problem with trademark law from the perspective of mainstream First Amendment doctrine involves the role of intent. Historically, "passing off" involved deliberate deception by a competitor, though intent to deceive could be inferred from circumstances.[52] While

---

[51] An actual deception requirement would be difficult to administer, especially in the context of intent-to-use applications. Even with marks used in commerce, the Patent and Trademark Office (PTO) lacks the resources to conduct a survey on consumer perceptions of a mark.

[52] *See, e.g.*, Robert G. Bone, *Hunting Goodwill: A History of the Concept of Goodwill in Trademark Law*, 86 B.U. L. REV. 547, 565–6 (2006). Trademark historically also used a property theory, granting exclusive rights in arbitrary or fanciful

this requirement disappeared relatively early in the history of trademark law, the trend in First Amendment-governed doctrines such as libel (including trade libel and product disparagement) has been the opposite. Some degree of fault, at least negligence, is generally required before liability can be imposed.[53] Intent requirements help decrease the chilling effects of speech prohibitions, because they allow speakers to speak with confidence after a reasonable investigation. The price of freeing speech is that there is no liability even if the speakers are actually mistaken and their mistakes do harm.

Currently, trademark law imposes liability for honest mistakes, creating great uncertainty among businesses. This uncertainty may be worth the information costs it exacts, but courts have yet to perform that balancing. No-fault liability combines with the other features of trademark law noted above to make trademark unusually indifferent to the costs of error, costs which are elsewhere considered to be constitutionally problematic when they affect truthful speech.

C. Non-trademark false advertising

False advertising law may be particularly vulnerable to First Amendment challenges because it, unlike copyright and trademark, has no well-recognized property interest to which it can appeal as a counterweight to a free speech claim.[54] *Eldred v Ashcroft*,[55] which upheld a retrospective twenty-year extension of the copyright term against a First Amendment challenge, shows the potential of defining an intangible interest as a property right – it moves from part of the marketplace of ideas to the actual marketplace, where it's all

---

marks (known as technical trademarks) that had no relevance to the product before a seller adopted them. Infringement of technical trademarks didn't require proof of fraudulent intent because it was a violation of property rights, like a trespass, but courts still linked deception with infringement because use of an arbitrary mark on a particular product was likely to confuse consumers, and wasn't likely to be done accidentally or in good faith. *See id.* at 560–61, 564–5, 567–8.

[53] This is an application of the narrow tailoring requirement that restrictions on speech be no greater than necessary to avoid the harm. Essentially, the judgment (rarely fully articulated) is that the gain in harm-prevention from banning mistaken but non-malicious, or non-negligent, speech is less than the cost of deterring speech that the speaker cannot verify with perfect certainty. One could balance the costs and benefits of deterring mistaken but good-faith speech differently – a good-faith but wrong belief that a drug cures cancer, for example, could do much more harm than its suppression would – but many trademark cases won't involve that kind of risk from allowing the speech to continue.

[54] *See* College Savings Bank v Florida Prepaid Postsecondary Ed. Expense Bd., 527 U.S. 666 (1999) (protection against false advertising is not a property interest protected by the Due Process Clause).

[55] 537 U.S. 186 (2003).

308   *Trademark law and theory*

right to deny access to those who can't pay. Trademark law has self-consciously moved in the direction of property right, instead of consumer protection device, for decades. That may save it from criticisms such as those set forth in the previous section. But other types of false advertising law have similar weaknesses without the shield of property.

In *Nike v Kasky*,[56] the Supreme Court initially agreed to decide whether a consumer could maintain a class action suit over Nike's statements about the conditions under which its contractors in foreign countries produced shoes. In a series of letters to university presidents and athletic directors, advertorials (purchased space on newspaper editorial pages), press releases, and the like, Nike claimed that workers making its shoes were not generally underpaid, underfed, or otherwise abused. Kasky sued for false advertising. Though much of the legal argument was about whether Nike's statements constituted commercial speech, Nike and its amici made a number of arguments that would apply even to commercial speech, arguments some on the Supreme Court found persuasive even though the Court ultimately dismissed certiorari as improvidently granted.

Specifically, Nike attacked California's strict liability regime, which made it responsible for good-faith but factually erroneous claims about conditions of production, as inconsistent with numerous precedents dealing with libel, disparagement, and related claims. In this, California law was far from unique. Whether in private lawsuits under the Lanham Act, consumer suits under laws in all 50 states, or FTC enforcement actions, liability attaches to false or misleading statements regardless of the advertiser's intent or good-faith belief. To take a recent example, a federal court agreed with the FTC that an advertiser who sincerely believes that its metal bracelet relieves pain, based on discussions with thousands of satisfied customers, can still be fined millions of dollars because there is no adequate scientific evidence that the bracelet relieves pain.[57] The decision in that case, *FTC v QT, Inc.*, poses all the problems of chilling speech and of oversuppression of truthful but not provable claims that libel law would scrutinize using a higher standard of culpability.

The legal treatment of the placebo effect in *QT* also illustrates a deeper tension in false advertising law.[58] The placebo effect of the metal bracelet was

---

[56]   539 U.S. 654 (2003).
[57]   *See* Federal Trade Commission v QT, Inc., 448 F.Supp. 2d 908 (N.D. Ill. 2006).
[58]   It is well established in advertising law that advertisers cannot rely on the placebo effect. *See* Federal Trade Comm'n v Pantron I Corp., 33 F.3d 1088, 1100 (9th Cir. 1994) ("[A]llowing advertisers to rely on the placebo effect would not only harm those individuals who were deceived; it would create a substantial economic cost as well, by allowing sellers to fleece large numbers of consumers who, unable

generated simply by telling customers they would experience less pain, but the court held that its existence did not make the claim true, even though it strongly resembles the ways in which trademarks "create" value by convincing consumers they will experience more utility by wearing a shirt with a Nike swoosh on it than by wearing a plain shirt. The fact that a product works for the wrong reasons – that it has value because its advertising creates that value – can only justify suppression of the advertising under *Central Hudson* if we define "misleading" very broadly, in ways likely incompatible with the main line of commercial speech precedents.

A separate argument in *Nike* was that consumers have no legitimate interest in conditions of production that don't affect the physical composition of a product.[59] Nike argued that it could not be liable for misstatements about how its subcontractors' workers were treated. Prohibitions on false or misleading statements, that is, are justified because they protect consumers' legitimate interests in getting the products they paid for. But whether a worker made five cents an hour or five dollars, the resulting shoe is the same, so there's no consumer protection interest in liability for false statements about intangible conditions of production. Not getting what you want while still getting the (objectively defined) benefit of your bargain can be seen as a psychic harm that cannot count in a First Amendment analysis.

This argument, if accepted, would invalidate a wide range of consumer protection measures, from regulation of claims to "dolphin-safe" tuna to "Made in the U.S.A."[60] It also rejects any consumer interest in living in a

---

to evaluate the efficacy of an inherently useless product, make repeat purchases of that product."); United States v An Article ... Acu-Dot ..., 483 F. Supp. 1311, 1315 (N.D. Ohio 1980) (claims of efficacy from placebo effect are "'misleading' because the [product] is not inherently effective, its results being attributable to the psychosomatic effect produced by the advertising and marketing of the [product]"); Bristol-Myers Co., 102 F.T.C. 21, 336 (1983) ("The Commission cannot accept as proof of a product's efficacy a psychological reaction stemming from a belief which, to a substantial degree, was caused by respondent's deceptions. Indeed, were we to hold otherwise, advertisers would be encouraged to foist unsubstantiated claims on an unsuspecting public in the hope that consumers would believe the ads and the claims would be self-fulfilling."); *cf.* American Home Prods. Corp. v Johnson & Johnson, 436 F.Supp. 785, 799 n. 9 (S.D.N.Y. 1977) ("A claim concerning a drug's effect made in lay advertising to consumers must be understood as representing that the effect will be experienced in humans and thus that it has some significance in a clinical context.").

59   *See, e.g.*, Kasky v Nike, Inc., 45 P.3d 243, 280 (Cal. 2002) (Brown, J., dissenting).

60   *See* International Dairy Foods Ass'n v Amestoy, 92 F.3d 67 (2d Cir. 1996) ("consumer curiosity" was insufficient justification to require retailers to label milk from cows given certain bovine hormones when there was no evidence that the hormones affected the milk, though they may have affected the health of the cows to

certain type of world, or in refusing to accede to immoral business conduct.[61] Consumers make purchasing decisions based on their values as well as their desires for particular product characteristics. Failure to protect against false claims about production would allow false advertisers to drive out producers whose claims were true and whose products were therefore more expensive. But if consumer preferences for conflict-free diamonds, cruelty-free cosmetics, and T-shirts made by people paid a living wage are worth honoring, then the harm of false advertising is not just or essentially that it exposes consumers to inferior products. Rather, the harm of false advertising is that it disrespects consumers' autonomy. Yet, if one accepts this justification, it is relatively easy to construct arguments for many speech regulations that help consumer-citizens realize their true preferences. The inseparability of consumers from the market that surrounds them makes claims about real or true preferences inherently difficult to evaluate.

In trademark, for example, it has long been a matter of dispute among courts and theorists how to conceive of the psychic value of a brand. Is a two-dollar shirt with an authorized Nike logo worth $20? What about the same shirt with an unauthorized logo? How, if at all, is a consumer who buys the second shirt for $15 harmed, and does that harm differ if she believes the shirt was authorized by Nike but doesn't actually care one way or the other, as long as she can wear a shirt with a Nike logo? Consumer understandings alone cannot serve as a justification for regulation. Some normative idea of what understandings deserve legal protection is required.

Courts have been willing to protect consumers from potential confusion over sponsorship or authorization even without evidence that consumers care about those business relationships. Outside trademark, the story is different; some cases have retreated to a concept of misleadingness that bars government intervention except in the most blatant cases of fraud. In *Pearson v Shalala*,[62] for example, a regulation-skeptical panel of the D.C. Circuit affirmed a district court ruling invalidating certain FDA regulations for dietary supplement claims. The FDA wanted to ban claims unless there was significant scientific agreement as to the ultimate conclusion: "this product reduces the risk of heart disease." The court was concerned that the FDA therefore banned some truth-

---

whom they were given and may also have made it more difficult for small milk producers to compete with big producers). *Amestoy* qualifies *Zauderer*'s statement that a commercial speaker's "constitutionally protected interest in not providing any particular factual information in his advertising is minimal," Zauderer v Office of Disciplinary Counsel, 471 U.S. 626, 651 (1985), by holding that the state must nonetheless have some defined reason, supported by evidence, to outweigh that minimal interest.

[61] *See* Douglas A. Kysar, *Preferences for Processes: The Process/Product Distinction and the Regulation of Consumer Choice*, 118 HARV. L. REV. 525 (2004).

[62] Pearson v Shalala, 164 F.3d 650 (D.C. Cir. 1999).

ful claims: "there is inconclusive evidence that this product may reduce the risk of heart disease" or "this product may improve heart health, but there is no significant scientific agreement that this is true." *Pearson* rejected as "almost frivolous" the FDA's argument that such second-order claims were inherently misleading, because health claims lacked "such an awesome impact on consumers as to make it virtually impossible for them to exercise any judgment . . . as if the consumers were asked to buy something while hypnotized."[63] This is itself a misleading and irrelevant comparison; even *false* claims don't hypnotize. Instead, what they do is encourage purchase based on mistaken beliefs.

After *Pearson*, the FDA was required to allow claims in most circumstances as long as the claims included a disclaimer.[64] The court suggested "The evidence in support of this claim is inconclusive" or "The FDA does not approve this claim."[65] Though the court of appeals was confident that disclaimers could prevent consumers from being deceived by claims with limited scientific backing, marketing research demonstrates that effective disclaimers are difficult in principle and extremely rare in practice.[66] A recent study evaluating the judicially mandated disclaimer in *Pearson* shows that its presence on a supplement label has no significant effect on consumer reactions. The disclaimer doesn't affect the level of consumers' belief in the health claim, and it doesn't even affect whether or not they think the FDA has evaluated the claim.[67]

---

[63] *Id.* at 655.

[64] The *Pearson* court rejected the FDA's defense, based on *Friedman v Rogers*, 440 U.S. 1 (1979), that the government could outright ban misleading speech even if adding a disclaimer was an alternative. The court read *Friedman*'s statement that the state is not "requir[ed] to allow deceptive or misleading commercial speech whenever the publication of additional information can clarify or offset [its] effects," *id.* at 15–16, as applying only to the special case of deceptive trade names. While this limit lacks any logical validity, it is true that the Supreme Court has not applied *Friedman* broadly either. The court did agree that the FDA could bar certain claims as inherently misleading if the evidence for the *express* claim (that is, the basic efficacy claim, not the second-order claims about evidence) was outweighed by or qualitatively weaker than the evidence against it, or if empirical evidence indicated that disclaimers would "bewilder" consumers. *Pearson*, 164 F.3d at 659–60.

[65] *Pearson*, 164 F.3d at 659.

[66] *See, e.g.*, David W. Stewart & Ingrid M. Martin, *Intended and Unintended Consequences of Warning Messages: A Review and Synthesis of Empirical Research*, 13 J. PUB. POL'Y & MARKETING 15 (1994) (even when consumers notice disclaimers, they are unlikely to use them).

[67] *See* Paula Fitzgerald Bone & Karen Russell France, *West Virginia University Research Presentation*, Transcript of Public Meeting: Assessing Consumer Perceptions of Health Claims, Nov. 17, 2005, http://www.cfsan.fda.gov/~dms/qhctran.html#wvu.

Anti-regulatory positions presume a careful and competent consumer. Arguably, when political speech is at issue we *must* presume a fully rational citizen, given the risks of letting the government ban any political speech. But consumer behavior in the market is so plainly inconsistent with the behavior of idealized speech-evaluators that painful compromises are required. The question is who will bear the burden of imperfection: the real consumer, or the (equally real, but perhaps not equally rights-bearing) commercial speaker?

II. Trademark dilution

Dilution, which is not a form of false advertising but a right peculiar to trademark, poses special First Amendment challenges. Dilution law can be construed to apply to works of art, news reporting, and other noncommercial uses. When it does, it is in substantial tension with First Amendment values,[68] and courts that have noticed this have been quick to limit the application of the law to core commercial speech. Likewise, the recent amendments to the federal dilution law were careful to carve out exceptions for news reporting, parody, and other types of noncommercial speech.[69]

The problem with this easy solution is that it is far from sufficient to insulate dilution from constitutional infirmity, despite assumptions to the contrary.[70] Dilution law that prohibits a nonconfusing use of a famous trademark to sell another product prohibits truthful, nonmisleading commercial speech. As such, dilution claims should be subject to analysis under *Central Hudson*, requiring courts to evaluate the strength of the government's interest

---

On a more global level, in a context of pervasive, hard-to-comprehend disclaimers, consumers may be so inundated with claims not worth believing that they discount the few verifiable claims, to their detriment. Ellen Goodman has explored this variant of the market for lemons problem, *see* George A. Akerlof, *The Market for "Lemons": Quality Uncertainty and the Market Mechanism*, 84 Q. J. ECON. 488 (1970), as a justification for government regulation of advertising. *See* Ellen Goodman, *Stealth Marketing and Editorial Integrity*, 85 Tex. L. Rev. 83 (2006).

[68] *See, e.g.*, Pratheepan Gulasekaram, *Policing the Border Between Trademarks and Free Speech: Protecting Unauthorized Trademark Use in Expressive Works*, 80 WASH. L. REV. 887 (2005); Sarah Mayhew Schlosser, *The High Price of (Criticizing) Coffee: The Chilling Effect of the Federal Trademark Dilution Act on Corporate Parody*, 43 ARIZ. L. REV. 931 (2001); Hannibal Travis, *The Battle For Mindshare: The Emerging Consensus That the First Amendment Protects Corporate Criticism and Parody on the Internet*, 10 VA. J. L. & TECH. 3 (2005).

[69] *See* Trademark Dilution Revision Act of 2006, Pub. L. No. 109-312, § 2, 120 Stat. 1730 (codified at 15 U.S.C. § 1125(c)(3)).

[70] *See* H.R. Rep. No. 104-374, at 4 (1995), *reprinted in* 1995 U.S.C.C.A.N. 1029, 1031 (the noncommercial use exception "adequately addresses legitimate First Amendment concerns espoused by the broadcasting industry and the media").

and the extent to which the regulation serves that interest without encroaching too much on free commercial speech.[71]

One possible response is that dilutive use, while not false or misleading, is also not truthful. In what sense is it possible to say that the name Dogiva for dog biscuits, or Buick for soap, is a truthful description of them? Dogiva evokes an association with Godiva, but it has no inherent meaning. Dilution thus presents U.S. law with a situation previously only encountered in theory: a prohibition on the emotional meaning of commercial speech.

One of the clearest indictments of the special status of commercial speech came from Judge Kozinski and Stuart Banner. They argued that, just as much political speech contains verifiable factual representations, much commercial speech is neither true nor false. Current commercials are often long on story and entertainment value but short on falsifiable representations of fact.[72] Yet speech cannot ordinarily be banned because it is non-falsifiable. Their conclusion was that commercial speech is just like other speech and deserves as much constitutional protection. One response to this critique was to point out that regulation of commercial speech has not targeted the stories or entertainment values of commercial speech, but only their falsifiable representations. Since no regulator is about to come after the image-based aspects of ads, their existence has no bearing on the justifications for regulation.[73]

Dilution changes all that. Now Porsche can sue when its cars appear in humorous ads for a competitor's SUV,[74] even though there are no factual

---

[71] *See, e.g.*, Brian A. Jacobs, *Trademark Dilution on the Constitutional Edge*, 104 COLUM. L. REV. 161, 175 (2004) (stating that "[u]nless courts find the FTDA [Federal Trademark Dilution Act] narrowly tailored in service of a substantial government interest, the Act should be deemed an unconstitutionally broad regulation of commercial speech under the First Amendment"); Mary LaFrance, *No Reason to Live: Dilution Laws as Unconstitutional Restrictions on Commercial Speech*, 58 S.C. L. REV. 709 (2007); Lemley & Volokh, *supra* note 43, at 221 n. 325 (the usual justification for trademark infringement law "offers no [constitutional] support for dilution statutes"); *cf.* Denicola, *supra* note 43, at 194–7 (concluding that bans on dilutive uses of a distinctive mark to identify a defendant's goods or services are sustainable under *Central Hudson*, while uses to identify and criticize the trademark owner are constitutionally protected). Denicola's position seems self-contradictory: He concludes that, under the rule of *Friedman v Rogers*, trademarks have no inherent meaning and thus suppressing their unauthorized commercial use inflicts no constitutional harm. But the justification for dilution law is precisely that distinctive trademarks distill meanings in powerful ways for which there are no substitutes. It is hard to maintain both that trademarks are meaningless and that protecting their current meaning is a substantial government interest.

[72] *See* Kozinski & Banner, *supra* note 14, at 627, 635, 639–41, 645–6.

[73] *See* Nat Stern, *In Defense of the Imprecise Definition of Commercial Speech*, 58 MD. L. REV. 55, 120 nn. 442–4 (1999).

[74] *See* Dr. ING H.C.F. Porsche AG v Daimlerchrysler AG, No. 1:02-cv-00483-JTC (N.D. Ga. filed 2/20/2002).

representations in the ad. By targeting the non-factual elements of advertising, dilution departs from what Justice Stevens has characterized as the only legitimate reason to treat commercial speech differently from noncommercial speech: the preservation of a fair bargaining process.[75] Under that analysis, dilution is a content-based speech restriction. And, while trademarks are big business, it seems unlikely that protecting their selling power against the mere possibility of diminution – a harm that will only occur if dilution of a particular mark becomes widespread – is a substantial state interest.

A. *A new basis for dilution*[76]

Recently, courts and commentators have begun offering a theory of dilution that seems to answer both general and First Amendment-based objections: Dilution as harm to consumers' cognitive processing. In *Ty, Inc. v Perryman*,[77] a case about a website that sold Beanie Babies and other stuffed bean-bag animals, Judge Posner set forth the standard search costs model that justifies protecting trademarks against infringement. He then contrasted infringement to dilution, which deals with internal search costs – difficulties not in figuring out whether two products or services are from the same source, but in retrieving the mark from memory in the first place.

In the cognitive model, blurring takes place when a single term activates multiple, non-confusing associations in a consumer's mind. Meanings or concepts, including sounds, images, and other sensory impressions, are linked by mental networks. Words or concepts are activated through links in the network, triggering related meanings or concepts, as when late-afternoon thoughts of home lead to thoughts of dinner.[78] Blurring involves relatively extended activation of two different meanings for a mark, until the consumer sorts out the proper referent. The basic theory is that an unrelated, nonconfusing mark similar to a famous mark adds new associations to a pre-existing network, which slows processing time, especially if the junior mark has a very different meaning than the senior mark.[79] Like several pebbles thrown into a

---

[75] *See* 44 Liquormart, Inc. v Rhode Island, 517 U.S. 484, 501 (1996) (joined by Kennedy, J., and Ginsburg, J.).

[76] The following sections are adapted from Parts III and V of Rebecca Tushnet, *Gone in 60 Milliseconds: Trademark Law and Cognitive Science*, 86 TEXAS L. REV. 507 (2008).

[77] 306 F.3d 509 (7th Cir. 2002).

[78] *See, e.g.*, JOHN R. ANDERSON, COGNITIVE PSYCHOLOGY AND ITS IMPLICATIONS 148 (2d ed. 1985) (spreading activation causes "a good many associated concepts [to] become active" whenever an individual concept is explicitly invoked).

[79] *See* Maureen Morrin & Jacob Jacoby, *Trademark Dilution: Empirical Measures for an Elusive Concept*, 19 J. PUB. POL'Y & MARKETING 265, 267 (2000).

pond at once, activation of different meanings causes interference with each one.

Posner gave the example of a high-end restaurant called Tiffany's, which would interfere with a consumer's immediate recognition of the jewelry store Tiffany's. "Consumers will have to think harder – incur as it were a higher imagination cost – to recognize the name as the name of the store."[80] When they see "Tiffany's," they will have to stop and ask themselves, "Which Tiffany's"? A number of legal scholars have agreed with Judge Posner and explicitly identified the harm of dilution as increased mental search costs for consumers.[81]

In Posner's model, dilution by tarnishment also involves interference with cognitive processing, but of a different kind. Perception of words or images, including trademarks, activates a web or tree of concepts linked to them. Posner posited a strip joint named Tiffany's, and assumed that reasonable consumers do not think it has any connection with the jewelry store. Nevertheless, "because of the inveterate tendency of the human mind to proceed by association, every time [people who know about the strip joint] think of the word 'Tiffany' their image of the fancy jewelry store will be

---

[80] *Ty*, 306 F.3d at 511. *See also* Richard A. Posner, *When is Parody Fair Use?*, 21 J. LEGAL STUD. 67, 75 (1992) ("A trademark seeks to economize on information costs by providing a compact, memorable, and unambiguous identifier of a product or service. The economy is less when, because the trademark has other associations, a person seeing it must think for a moment before recognizing it as the mark of the product or service.").

[81] *See, e.g.*, Stacey L. Dogan & Mark A. Lemley, *What the Right of Publicity Can Learn from Trademark Law*, 58 STAN. L. REV. 1161, 1197 (2006) ("[L]ike traditional trademark law, dilution properly understood is targeted at reducing consumer search costs."); Daniel Klerman, *Trademark Dilution, Search Costs, and Naked Licensing*, 74 FORDHAM L. REV. 1759 (2006); J. Thomas McCarthy, *Proving a Trademark Has Been Diluted: Theories or Facts?*, 41 HOUS. L. REV. 713, 727–8 (2004) ("[T]here is potential harm to both consumers and mark owners if a once-unique designation loses its uniqueness. The argument is that this makes it harder for consumers to link that designation with a single source – the hallmark of a strong trademark. Under this theory, dilution increases the consumer's search costs by diffusing the identification power of that designation."); Maureen A. O'Rourke, *Defining the Limits of Free-Riding in Cyberspace: Trademark Liability for Metatagging*, 33 GONZ. L. REV. 277, 306–07 n. 114 (1998) ("Dilution by blurring is concerned with preventing the erosion of the distinctiveness of the mark because of its use on non-related products. The 'noise' that this creates around the mark may increase consumer search costs."); Brian A. Jacobs, Note, *Trademark Dilution on the Constitutional Edge*, 104 COLUM L. REV. 161, 188 (2004) ("The mark holder surely benefits from the FTDA's preservation of her mark's uniqueness, but consumers also benefit, as they experience a more efficient market.").

tarnished by the association of the word with the strip joint."[82] As with blurring, this inveterate tendency can be equated to the psychological concept of activation.[83]

Tarnishment is probably a more intuitively obvious concept than blurring, as evidenced by the considerable debate in the literature over what blurring is, with substantially less attention paid to tarnishment. Emotion is key to cognition,[84] meaning that negative associations may do real, even measurable harm, even though it's not rational to think less of Tiffany's-the-jeweler because of the existence of the strip club Tiffany's (or, more likely, Stiffany's). No matter what people consciously believe, Tiffany's-the-strip-joint will become a branch on the tree of associations connected to Tiffany's-the-jeweler, and it will bear poison flowers.

Finally, Posner offers a third possible meaning of dilution, which is simply free riding. The example is a Tiffany's restaurant in Kuala Lumpur, which grabs some of the luster of Tiffany's-the-jeweler because of the same tendency to make associations. People in Kuala Lumpur know about the jewelry store but would never patronize it, so no jewelry store customers have their mental models of Tiffany's distorted in any way.[85] This definition focuses on the mental processes of the junior user's customers, not the senior user's, but is otherwise quite similar to Posner's definition of blurring.

If dilution is about preserving the efficient dissemination of information in the marketplace, then it is subject to the same criticisms set forth above: Other areas of First Amendment doctrine require courts to consider whether information helps some consumers even if it harms others, and concerns for erroneous suppression of speech throw no-fault and other features of trademark law into question. Nonetheless, some have argued that the search costs model of dilution, by identifying harm to consumers, bolsters dilution against the numerous First Amendment attacks to which it has been subjected.[86] As the following sections show, the matter is not so simple.

---

[82] *Ty*, 306 F.3d at 511.
[83] *See supra* note 82 and accompanying text.
[84] *See, e.g.*, DANIEL J. SIEGEL, THE DEVELOPING MIND: HOW RELATIONSHIPS AND THE BRAIN INTERACT TO SHAPE WHO WE ARE 159 (1999).
[85] *See Ty*, 306 F.3d at 512.
[86] *See* Dogan & Lemley, *Publicity*, *supra* note 82, at 1218 n. 269 ("One benefit of understanding dilution law as we have explained it elsewhere – as directed at reducing consumer search costs – is that our approach may reduce the tension between dilution law and the First Amendment.") (citation omitted); *see also* Jacobs, *supra* note 72, at 188–90 (treating dilution as based on search costs and efficiency considerations satisfies the substantial interest and tailoring prongs of *Central Hudson*). I have criticized the empirical basis of the cognitive model elsewhere, *see* Tushnet, *supra* note 77, Part IV. Here, I proceed under the assumption that it is a descriptively accurate account of dilution.

B. The cognitive model of dilution and noncommercial uses

A not inconsiderable advantage of the search costs explanation of dilution is that it converts dilution into a protection for consumers as well as for producers.[87] After all, we believe that external search costs are inefficient and therefore welfare-diminishing for consumers, and it seems natural that internal search costs would also decrease efficiency.[88] Thus, a focus on the workings of the consumer's diluted mind produces a response to Judge Kozinski's more skeptical take on dilution, in which he found dilution less important than infringement law because it served only trademark owners' interests and did not protect consumers.[89] The Supreme Court, for the moment, has sided with Judge Kozinski, but it has not had the occasion to address the search costs argument directly.[90]

One could argue that the new vision of dilution is as paternalistic as other commercial speech regulations the Court has criticized: Dilution rests on the conclusion that consumers will react irrationally to information that does not deceive them, but merely changes their preferences, the way ads for alcohol or tobacco or soda may change preferences. The diluting junior user may not have a good reason for changing consumers' preferences for the senior mark, but First Amendment law rarely asks whether a speaker has a legitimate interest in saying nondeceptive things. It is for the audience to take up or reject the

---

[87] *See* Graeme W. Austin, *Trademarks and the Burdened Imagination*, 69 BROOKLYN L. REV. 827, 891 n. 276 (2004) ("Certainly, dilution doctrine seems more palatable from a policy perspective if it does something positive for consumers rather than just protecting the property interests of proprietors of famous trademarks."); Jerre B. Swann, Sr., *Dilution Redefined for the Year 2002*, 92 TRADEMARK REP. 585, 603–04 (2002) (because consumers' lives are so hectic, they need help from strong, unique signals that simplify messages, which dilution law protects); *cf.* Clarisa Long, *Dilution*, 106 COLUM. L. REV. 1029, 1035 (2006) (discussing change in judicial explanations of dilution towards a consumer focus).

[88] *See, e.g.*, Mark Lemley, *The Modern Lanham Act and the Death of Common Sense*, 108 YALE L.J. 1687, 1704 n. 90 (1999) ("The information consumers can obtain and process is in part a function of how clear the association between mark and product remains in their minds; 'clutter' therefore imposes real costs on consumers."); *Id.* at 1705 n. 91 ("Properly conceived, however, I think dilution law is protecting consumers against a real harm: the loss of the informational value of a famous trademark through crowding.").

[89] *See* Mattel, Inc. v MCA Records, Inc., 296 F.3d 894, 905 (9th Cir. 2002) ("[D]ilution law protects only the distinctiveness of the mark, which is inherently less weighty than the dual interest of protecting trademark owners and avoiding harm to consumers that is at the heart of every trademark claim.").

[90] *See* Moseley v V Secret Catalogue, Inc., 537 U.S. 418, 429 (2003) ("Unlike traditional infringement law, the prohibitions against trademark dilution are not the product of common-law development, and are not motivated by an interest in protecting consumers.").

junior user's competing message. The cognitive model provides a partial answer to this critique. A ban on tarnishment is rank paternalism, but a ban on blurring is closer to an anti-fraud law. It seeks to prevent not *irrational* changes in preferences, but *inefficient* ones produced by increased search costs. This is something a nightwatchman state could do while remaining indifferent to the rightness or wrongness of consumer preferences and agnostic on the merits of changes in such preferences.[91]

Yet the strength of the cognitive model is also a major weakness. Internal search costs cannot explain why dilution should be limited to "commercial uses in commerce."[92] As Laura Heymann puts it

> A dilution action essentially argues . . . "We have spent a lot of money and effort on telling consumers what they should think about our brand, and the defendant's activities have caused them to think something different." . . . The brand owner, in other words, is claiming a right to the exclusive mental association with the brand in the minds of the public.[93]

Unfortunately for trademark owners, market conditions preclude trademark owners from controlling associations in the way this theory assumes. In fact, the things that we can be most confident affect mental models of brands are noncommercial, casual uses: what our friends think of the Gap, or Old Navy.[94] The problem isn't generally competitors, but all the other people who have opinions about the product and the trademark, promiscuously creating associations. Yochai Benkler's discussion of Google's search engine results for the term "Barbie" illustrates both blurring and tarnishment from noncommercial uses.

---

[91] *See* Kathleen M. Sullivan, *Cheap Spirits, Cigarettes, and Free Speech: The Implications of* 44 Liquormart, 1996 SUP. CT. REV. 123, 127–8 (arguing that the Supreme Court's recent commercial speech jurisprudence distinguishes between regulations based on an ad's communicative message and regulations based on an ad's associated material harms, invalidating only the former).

[92] Search cost explanations may offer an incomplete account of the interests served by trademark law more generally. My point here is that, regardless of whether one generally finds such explanations satisfactory, the search costs justification for dilution can't explain why commercial dilution increases mental clutter more or differently than noncommercial dilution. I thank Graeme Dinwoodie for pressing me on this point.

[93] Laura A. Heymann, *Metabranding and Intermediation: A Response to Prof. Fleischer*, 12 HARV. NEGOT. L. REV. 201, 218 (2007).

[94] *See, e.g.*, ALEX WIPPERFÜRTH, BRAND HIJACK: MARKETING WITHOUT MARKETING (2005) (marketers must recognize that consumers decide on the meaning of brands and promote those meanings to other consumers); Chris Gaither, *Where Everyone is a Critic*, L.A. TIMES, Aug. 25, 2006, http://www.latimes.com/business/la-fi-yelp25aug25,0,3179102,full.story?coll=la-home-headlines (discussing a consumer review site with a powerful effect on businesses' success or failure).

The top results on Google, in order, were Mattel's official site; the official collector's site; AdiosBarbie.com (critical of Barbie); a Barbie collectible magazine; a quiz, *If You Were a Barbie, Which Messed Up Version Would You Be?*; the Visible Barbie Project (Barbies sliced through as if vivisected); *Barbie: The Image of Us All* (undergraduate paper on the cultural history of Barbie); a Barbie and Ken sex animation; a Barbie dressed as a suicide bomber; and Barbies dressed and painted as countercultural images.[95] As Benkler explains:

> [I]n an environment where relevance is measured in non-market action – placing a link to a Web site because you deem it relevant to whatever you are doing with your Web site – as opposed to in dollars, Barbie has become a more transparent cultural object. It is easier for the little girl to see that the doll is not only a toy, not only a symbol of beauty and glamour, but also a symbol of how norms of female beauty in our society can be oppressive to women and girls. . . . [The search results] render transparent that Barbie can have multiple meanings . . .[96]

These critical and parodic uses dilute.[97]

Another example of dilutive use to which dilution law does not currently apply comes from the multiple uses in news reporting and other noncommercial speech of the suffix "Mc" to indicate convenience, cheapness, uniformity, and other qualities associated with McDonald's – McJob, McPaper, McArt, McLawyers.[98] Even if McDonald's can get McSleep Inns enjoined, the pervasive communicative uses of "Mc" as shorthand for a set of qualities keeps the mark's meanings from being locked down.[99]

Repurposing and cultural commentary aside, standard uses of marks as marks can dilute. Comparative advertising that names the comparison product is designed to create new associations between a brand and its competitor. Reviews also affect perceptions of quality. It is possible to convince people

---

[95] *See* YOCHAI BENKLER, THE WEALTH OF NETWORKS 286 tbl. 8.1 (2006).

[96] BENKLER, *supra* note 96, at 287. *See also* Julie Bosman, *Agencies Are Watching as Ads Go Online*, N.Y. TIMES, Aug. 15, 2006 (discussing spoof ads that attack products or offer inconsistent meanings for the brand, and quoting a creative director who describes such spoofs as "brand terrorism," while acknowledging that there's little companies can do to control them).

[97] *See, e.g.*, Mattel, Inc. v MCA Records, Inc., 296 F.3d 894, 903–04 (9th Cir. 2002) ("MCA's use of the [Barbie] mark [for the song title *Barbie Girl*] is dilutive. . . . [A]fter the song's popular success, some consumers hearing Barbie's name will think of both the doll and the song, or perhaps of the song only. This is a classic blurring injury . . .") (footnote omitted); *cf.* Heymann, *supra* note 94, at 214–15, 220–22 (discussing ways in which intermediaries such as reporters can distort brand messages).

[98] *See also, e.g.*, The Ronald McHummer Sign-O-Matic, http://ronaldmchummer.com/ (visited Aug. 19, 2006) (allowing users to design their own digital images of McDonald's signs, often critical of the company).

[99] *See* ROGER SHUY, LINGUISTIC BATTLES IN TRADEMARK DISPUTES 4–5 (2002).

that they liked a product that they specifically said they disliked by showing them positive reviews (or vice versa, turning positive opinions negative); not only will their evaluations become more positive, they will insist that their initial opinions were also positive.[100] If that's so, then dilution law should be especially concerned about negative reviews and comparative advertising. But comparative advertising and reviews as noncommercial speech are explicitly excepted from the federal dilution law, and no court is likely to apply state dilution law to cover them either.

New associations from nonapproved sources are constant and inevitable. Proust's madeleines conjured up not just memories of their maker but a whole web of references – hundreds of pages of interference with hypothetically efficient cognitive processing. In the blooming, buzzing confusion of the modern marketplace, trademarks are constantly thrown at us, jostling shoulders in ways that ensure multiple associations, whether it's the hundreds of marks visible side by side in Times Square or the dozens that obscure the uniforms and cars of NASCAR drivers.[101] The same pervasive branding of everyday life that supposedly requires legal protection for the ability of a unique mark to cut through ad clutter itself drowns marks in multiple uncontrollable contexts.

C. First Amendment implications

Largely for the reasons that convinced Congress to enact a noncommercial speech exception to dilution law in the first place, it is extremely unlikely that dilution law can constitutionally expand to cover reviews, casual references, and other expressive uses. The result is a law that cannot give trademark owners control over their marks' images, regardless of its rhetoric.

But that is not the end of the interaction between free speech and dilution law. The enormous disconnect between cognitive processing explanations of dilution and the scope of dilution law offers a simple analogy: *City of*

---

[100] *See* GERALD ZALTMAN, HOW CUSTOMERS THINK: ESSENTIAL INSIGHTS INTO THE MIND OF THE MARKET 182–83; *see also id.* at 12–13, 166–7, 180–81 (describing various successful experiments in manipulating memories about products or services); Kathryn A. Braun et al., *Make My Memory: How Advertising Can Change Our Memories of the Past*, 19 PSYCHOL. & MARKETING 1 (2002); Kathryn A. Braun, *Post-Experience Effects on Consumer Memory*, 25 J. CONSUMER RES. 319 (1999).

[101] One might argue that trademark owners can control side-by-side exposures through contract. But in most cases, they lack the ability to do so. A McDonald's might discover that the Gap next door lost its lease and is now a Hooter's. Eric Goldman has written about the pervasive constraints faced by most manufacturers, giving retailers substantial control over how a particular brand will be categorized and displayed to consumers. Eric Goldman, *Brand Spillovers* (Aug. 6, 2006) (draft manuscript, *available at* http://www.law.berkeley.edu/institutes/bclt/ipsc/papers2/goldman.pdf).

Cincinnati v Discovery Network.[102] In that case, the Supreme Court ruled that the city could not target commercial speech by banning newsracks containing commercial handbills but permitting newsracks containing traditional newspapers. The city's rationale was that newsracks interfered with the safety and beauty of the public streets. While the city conceded that it could not ban newsracks containing fully protected speech like that of the *New York Times*, it argued that it could ban commercial speech, which is less valuable.

The problem with that argument was that the nature of the speech conveyed by the newsracks, commercial or not, had nothing to do with their effects on safety and aesthetics. There were 62 commercial newsracks that the city wished removed, but between 1500 and 2000 newsracks selling conventional newspapers would remain. This complete absence of fit between the harm and the targeted speech invalidated the law. The similarities between *Discovery Network* and dilution law, understood as a measure against mental clutter, indicate that dilution also irrationally targets commercial speech for a harm done by a much larger set of speech acts.[103]

The response to a *Discovery Network*-type First Amendment challenge would plainly be to identify the harm of dilution as that caused by free riding. Not the mental effects, but the commercial advantage to the junior user, justify distinguishing commercial diluting uses from noncommercial diluting uses.[104] A strong believer in protecting commercial speech under the First Amendment might see this response simply as a restatement of the claim that commercial speech gets less First Amendment solicitude than noncommercial speech: it is an argument that advertisers are doing something that is less valuable than parodists and reporters. In *Discovery Network*, this commercial-speech discount was insufficient to justify special regulation.[105]

---

[102] 507 US 410 (1993).

[103] Eugene Volokh has drawn on *Discovery Network* to argue that the FTDA's exclusion of noncommercial speech is content-based, but to my knowledge no one has yet made this direct analogy. *See* Eugene Volokh, *Freedom of Speech and Intellectual Property: Some Thoughts After* Eldred, 44 Liquormart, *and* Bartnicki, 40 HOUS. L. REV. 697, 706–07 (2003).

[104] One could argue that trademark owners need to be able to appropriate all the commercial gains from their marks in order to give them incentives to develop famous marks, but that seems quite unlikely, given the other incentives to make one's mark famous; and again, it does not address why a commercial/noncommercial divide sets the incentives at the appropriate level.

[105] *See* Sullivan, *supra* note 92, at 124 ("[C]ommercial speech may not be given an automatic discount in the scale of First Amendment values.") (citing *Discovery Network*, 507 US at 428 ("In the absence of some basis for distinguishing between

Even though I accept the commercial/noncommercial divide, I find the free riding explanation for dilution unpersuasive, mainly because free riding is endemic to a functioning economy. Moreover, a noncompetitor's free riding doesn't damage a trademark owner (as opposed to the junior user's competitors, like Joe's Diner forced to compete against the classy-sounding Tiffany's Restaurant) unless and until the trademark owner's customers experience the mental effects discussed above, so the harm of free riding is elusive. Still, even someone who thinks that there's no reason to allow free riding on *trademarks*, as opposed to business models, expired patents, and the like, should consider that the cognition-based harms of dilution are largely inflicted by noncommercial uses.

If free riding on a mark is really what we're targeting, much of current dilution law makes very little sense, from the federal statutory test for whether dilution is likely to the exception for comparative advertising. If dilution is wrong because it is just not fair, we should say so – though "just not fair" might well be insufficient to survive *Central Hudson* scrutiny.

III. Conclusion

Taking modern First Amendment doctrine seriously would have significant effects on the Lanham Act, from everything from the standard of proof to the definition of what counts as misleading. Trademark's property-like features could insulate it better than false advertising, but the constitutional constraints on libel law – which also protects property-like interests in reputation – show that property concepts are not a panacea. First Amendment protection for commercial speech is increasing simultaneously with trademark's expansion to new areas, from dilution to geographic indications, and the two fields will inevitably overlap more often. Courts adopting First Amendment principles to cabin expansive trademark claims may then find that the same free-speech reasoning reaches trademark's core commercial functions.

Critics of the Supreme Court's commercial speech jurisprudence who would remove the commercial/noncommercial distinction often assert that applying the First Amendment to commercial speech would be relatively easy and wouldn't require major doctrinal restructuring. They treat modern unfair competition law as not much more than fraud law. But that is a misdescription of the field, perhaps understandable from the outside; both practically and on a rule-by-rule level, the consequences of full political speech treatment for the Lanham Act and related laws would be enormous.

'newspapers' and 'commercial handbills' that is relevant to an interest asserted by the city, we are unwilling to recognize Cincinnati's bare assertion that the 'low value' of commercial speech is a sufficient justification for its selective and categorical ban on newsracks dispensing 'commercial handbills.'")).

On the other hand, rather than treating ads like campaign speech, we could use unfair competition law – and the reasons why the jurisprudence of the last hundred years has generally moved away from a pure fraud law – as a basis for evaluating and reforming First Amendment doctrine. In particular, First Amendment cases have rarely grappled with the problem of speech that affirmatively harms some people (e.g., through deception) and benefits others (e.g., through providing useful information). A more honest approach to the variations among consumers, or other audience groups, would require us to decide what magnitude of harm, or harm-to-benefit ratio, justifies banning speech, and on whom the burden of showing benefits and harms will rest.

Even if, as is likely, courts prove reluctant to invalidate modern unfair competition law, allowing consumer protection to trump freedom of commercial speech requires more than simply declaring false and misleading commercial speech to be outside the boundaries of the First Amendment. Rather, we must pay attention to substance and to form, asking both how much deception is enough to suppress a competitor's speech and what presumptions and burdens of proof should be allowed or required. Moreover, the persistent appeal of concepts such as dilution and the ban on using the placebo effect as the only support for a product's efficacy indicate that some level of commercial morality, over and above truthfulness, retains its grasp on many assessments of what commercial speech is worthy of protection. There are insights to be had from a hard look at the First Amendment from an unfair competition perspective, as well as from a hard look at unfair competition law from a First Amendment perspective.

12 Restricting allusion to trade marks: a new justification
*Michael Spence**

I. Introduction

The scope of an intellectual property right should reflect its justification: the assistance of state power ought only to be available if those subject to that power can be offered a reasoned account for its exercise. This principle is a vital check on arbitrary government and means that the intellectual property systems, even if in fact they are the product of historical contingency, must be explained and developed in ways that reflect consistent and coherent purposes.

In the context of trade mark, protection of a trader against the use of signs that might be confused with her trade mark is relatively easy to justify. First, to persist in using a potentially confusing sign is to engage in a type of deliberate deception. The circumstances in which deliberate deception is wrong are something about which moral philosophers are apt to disagree. But none would condone deception for the purpose of profit at the expense of another person, and it is of this that trade mark infringement involving likely consumer confusion is exemplary. Second, causing consumer confusion has undesirable economic consequences. An important function of trade marks is to reduce consumer search costs, and to maintain the incentive that a producer has both to invest in product quality and to supply goods at the lowest possible price. This is especially the case with "experience" goods, those which a consumer must try in order to determine whether they meet her needs or tastes. Once a consumer has tried and liked a particular product, an identifiable trade mark enables her to find it again easily. This encourages the producer to make sure that her goods maintain the quality that they had on first sampling and to lower the price of her goods to attract repeat purchases. Consumer confusion about the identity of goods undermines this process by muddying the channel of communication between producer and consumer.

More difficult to justify, however, is protection of a trader against the use

---

* This chapter draws extensively on work published as, 'An Alternative Approach to Dilution Protection: A Response to Scott, Oliver and Ley Pineda', in L. Bently, J. Davis and J. Ginsburg (eds), *Trade Marks and Brands: An Interdisciplinary Critique*, Cambridge: Cambridge University Press, 2008).

of signs that involve, not confusion with a registered trade mark, but rather allusion to the registered mark. Most trade mark systems include at least some protection against two types of allusion to a trade mark not involving consumer confusion: allusions to a mark that take unfair advantage of its distinctive character or reputation and allusions to a mark that cause unfair detriment to its distinctive character or reputation. Such allusion can occur by the use of a sign identical, or similar, to a trade mark in circumstances in which it is clear that the goods or services to which it is attached are those of neither the trade mark owner, nor an undertaking authorised by her. Of the two types of protection against allusion often available, it is protection against detriment by allusion that is most commonly sought. This is not surprising. In almost all circumstances in which an allusion to a mark takes unfair advantage of the mark, it will also cause detriment to its distinctive character and such detriment is usually easier to establish.

The detriment by allusion against which protection is commonly available is likewise of two types. The first is the detriment entailed in what has been called "loss of distinctiveness." This involves detriment to the distinctive character of the mark. The example often given is drawn from classic American cases in which the jeweller Tiffany was able to prevent the use of that name by a motion picture company,[1] a bar in Boston,[2] and a perfume company.[3] The damage entailed in the loss of distinctiveness is that the mark gradually loses its ability to identify the activities of the registered owner. In the language of Peircean semiotics, the danger is that a mark such as "Tiffany" ceases to operate primarily as a symbol with the activities of the jeweller as its object and begins to operate primarily as an index for quality, luxury and prestige.[4] The second type of detriment against which protection is normally available is that entailed in what has, somewhat ungrammatically, been called "tarnishment." It involves detriment to the reputation of the mark. The example often given is again from the facts of a classic American case. In that case, the cheerleaders of the Dallas Cowboys were able to prevent the use of a uniform similar to their own in a pornographic film.[5] The damage entailed in tarnishment is that the mark is unable to be used free of the damaging associations that its allusive use has created. These two types of detriment are commonly referred to

---

[1]   Tiffany & Co. v Tiffany Productions, Inc., 188 N.E. 30 (N.Y. 1933).
[2]   Tiffany & Co. v Boston Club, Inc., 231 F. Supp. 836 (D.C. Mass., 1964).
[3]   Tiffany & Co. v L'Argene Products Co., 324 N.Y.S. 2d 326 (N.Y. App. Div. 1971).
[4]   2 C.S. PEIRCE, COLLECTED PAPERS OF CHARLES SANDERS PEIRCE 156–73 (C. Hartshorne and P. Wiess, eds., 1960).
[5]   Dallas Cowboy Cheerleaders, Inc. v Pussycat Cinema Ltd., 604 F.2d 200 (2d Cir. 1979).

as the "dilution" of marks, though that term is here avoided because it is used by legal writers in many different ways.

This chapter offers a new justification for protection against allusion to a trade mark.[6] This argument is built upon the expressive autonomy of the trade mark owner. It justifies protection against allusion, but only in circumstances in which due regard is also paid to the expressive autonomy of the party who would allude to a trade mark. In broad terms, the expressive autonomy of that other party becomes a consideration where the use of the mark is necessary to achieve an expressive purpose not otherwise practically achievable. Before turning to this argument, however, existing alternative justifications for this type of protection should briefly be explored.

II. Common justifications for protection against allusion

Existing arguments for protection against allusion to a trade mark are, on the whole, unsatisfactory. These arguments have mostly fallen into three groups.

A. *Protection against allusion as protection against confusion*

Arguments in the first group involve the claim that protection against allusion, whatever it might appear, is really protection against confusion. These arguments rely on two possible expanded understandings of confusion.

The first of these is post-sale confusion. While a consumer purchasing a product may be under no illusion as to its trade origins, those who subsequently come into contact with the goods that she has purchased may well be. The European Court of Justice recently relied upon this argument in a case concerning the use of trade marks owned by the English soccer club "Arsenal" on unauthorised souvenirs. As a result of the complex litigation in *Arsenal Football Club Plc v Reed* the use of the trade marks was prevented, even though it was clear at the point of sale that the souvenirs were not "official" merchandise. The European Court of Justice was concerned that "some consumers . . . if they come across the goods [bearing the Arsenal mark] after they have been sold by Mr. Reed and taken away from the stall . . . may interpret the sign as designating Arsenal FC as the undertaking of origin of the goods."[7]

---

[6] The chapter builds upon work that I began with *Intellectual Property and the Problem of Parody*, 114 L. Q. REV. 594 (1998), and continued in *The Mark as Expression/The Mark as Property* 58 CURRENT LEGAL PROBLEMS 491 (2005) and, with L. Treiger-Bar-Am, in *Private Control/Public Speech* in HUMAN RIGHTS AND PRIVATE LAW: PRIVACY AS AUTONOMY (2007) (K. Ziegler ed.). For a similar argument based on an individual's interest in preventing implied endorsement and the "destabilization of meaning," *see* Mark P. McKenna, *The Right of Autonomy and Autonomous Self-Definition* 67 U. PITT. L. REV. 225 (2005).

[7] Arsenal Football Club Plc. v Reed (C-206/01) [2003] R.P.C. 144 at 172.

Protection against this type of confusion is not difficult to justify. Landes and Posner make an argument based on the so-called "complementary view" of advertising, the view that brands can be regarded by consumers as themselves complementary goods for which they are willing to pay.[8] Their argument is that protection against post-sale confusion facilitates the creation of markets in what they call reputation capital, the prestige that comes from association with particular goods. But, in fact, this problematic argument is unnecessary. Protection against post-sale confusion can be justified on a similar basis to confusion at the point of sale. It can be just as deceptive to persist in the use of a sign likely to cause post-sale confusion as to persist in the use of a sign likely to cause confusion at the point of sale. Moreover, the ability of the trade mark system to create incentives for investment in product quality and price must depend upon a consumer's ability to identify the goods of a particular producer in whatever context she encounters them. However, though justified, protection against post-sale confusion does not require that the law prohibit allusive uses of a mark. Some such uses may give rise to post-sale confusion, but there is no reason to suggest that all, or even most, will do so. The likelihood of post-sale confusion should be assessed in exactly the same way as confusion at the point of sale.[9] If it is, then the possibility of post-sale confusion provides no justification for protection against allusive uses that do not cause confusion.

An alternative expanded concept of confusion thus also makes its way into the decision of the European Court of Justice in the *Arsenal* decision. This is the notion that use can sometimes damage the ability of a mark to signal the origin of goods, even if that use does not entail confusion of the type traditionally required for trade mark infringement. The only way in which this could happen, it is submitted, is if a consumer, either at the point of sale or afterwards, subconsciously associates goods bearing the potentially infringing sign with the trade mark owner, even though, when asked a direct question as to their trade origin, she can identify that this association is mistaken. This must clearly be a possible scenario. We often make hasty subconscious assessments which we, even unawares, correct when focusing our minds more clearly. This subconscious confusion is the expanded concept of confusion upon which protection against allusion is sometimes said to be built. However, this concept cannot be a satisfactory basis for such protection. The law cannot

---

[8] William M. Landes and Richard A. Posner, *The Economics of Trademark Law*, 78 TRADEMARK REP. 267, 305 (1987).

[9] Though in fact this has not been the approach of the European Court of Justice which has regarded post-sale confusion as irrelevant for the assessment of infringement on the basis of causing confusion. Ruiz-Picasso v Office for Harmonisation in the Internal Market (C-361/04 P) [2006] ECR I-643 at [42]–[48].

remedy the chaos of our subconscious minds. We will see later on that there may be good reasons for using a sign that is very similar to an existing brand. If someone who is not the trade mark owner does so in a way that will not confuse the average consumer, it is difficult to know how much responsibility she should bear for the disorder of the notional consumer's unconscious.

B. *Protection against allusion and trade marks as property*

Another common approach to the justification of protection against allusion treats such protection as the logical implication of the categorisation of trade marks as "intellectual property." The assumption often made by trade mark owners is that if a trade mark is "property," then as "property" its owner ought presumptively to be able to control all its uses and to protect it against unwarranted harm. An analogy is often drawn with protection against other forms of intellectual property, the infringement of which does not depend upon the likelihood of consumer confusion.

However, this approach is built upon a misunderstanding of the object of the intellectual property rights generally. The object of an intellectual property right is not the subject matter that the right protects (the copyright work, the patented invention or the protected mark). It is rather the legal right to control particular uses of that subject matter. For example, that which a copyright or patent owner can assign or devise is not the protected work or invention, but the copyright or patent. It was long ago recognised that an intellectual property right is in this way analogous to, though distinct from, a chose in action.[10] There is no presumption that all potential uses of the protected subject matter should be reserved to the holder of the right or that it should be protected against all harm. Each new use to which the holder of an intellectual property right lays claim, each new type of harm that she seeks to rely upon her intellectual property right to prevent, requires separate justification. And the rights entailed in each intellectual property regime must carefully reflect its purpose. The analogy implied in the common categorisation of these rights as intellectual property—a term of relatively recent American coinage[11] and long difficult to render in languages other than English—does not mean that the scope of those rights should necessarily be similar. Indeed, the arguments of this chapter might suggest that to think of

---

[10] H.W. Elphinstone, *What is a Chose in Action?*, 9 LQR 311 (1893); C. Sweet, *Choses in Action*, 10 LQR 303 (1894); F. Pollock, *What is a Thing?*, 10 LQR 318 (1894); S. Brodhurst, *Is Copyright a Chose in Action?*, 11 LQR 64 (1895); C. Sweet, *Choses in Action*, 11 LQR 238 (1895).

[11] The first use in a U.S. case appears to be Davoll v Brown, 7 F. Cas. 197, 199 (C.C.D. Mass. 1845).

trade mark as law regulating speech is at least as helpful as to think of it as property law.[12]

C. *Protection against allusion and the justification of the other intellectual property regimes*

A third group of arguments for protecting trade marks against allusion focuses on common justifications for the other intellectual property regimes. Indeed, the argument advanced in this chapter is one that might equally be used to justify aspects of the protection afforded by the law of copyright and moral rights. Nevertheless, the analogies between trade mark and the other intellectual property regimes implied in many arguments falling in this third group are often false, and the process of translating arguments suited to the justification of copyright or patent protection into arguments for the justification of trade mark protection is one that must be undertaken with some care.[13]

An example might be drawn from the work of Richardson, who suggests that an argument for the protection of trade marks against allusion might be built upon the need for incentives to encourage the creation, dissemination and efficient exploitation of works and inventions, given their categorisation as "public goods." Richardson argues for protection of trade marks against allusion on the basis that "[i]f there is any policy justification for protecting copyright works as the products of intellectual and innovative activity . . . it extends to . . . expressive trade marks," and that the law ought to encourage their creation by affording such protection.[14] However, the extent to which investment in branding is desirable is debated by welfare economists: to some it simply distorts consumer preferences (the so-called "persuasive view" of advertising);[15] to others it signals important information to consumers beyond product origin such as a producer's concern for product quality (the so-called "informative view' of advertising);[16] and, as we have already seen, to still

---

[12]   *See* M. Spence, *The Mark as Expression/The Mark as Property*, 58 CURRENT LEGAL PROBLEMS 491 (2005).

[13]   *See* M. SPENCE, INTELLECTUAL PROPERTY 41–2 (2007).

[14]   Megan Richardson, *Copyright in Trade Marks? On Understanding Trade Mark Dilution*, IPQ 66, 80 & n.13 (2000).

[15]   *See, e.g.*, D. Braithwaite, *The Economic Effects of Advertisement*, 38 ECON. J. 16 (1928); E. CHAMBERLIN, THE THEORY OF MONOPOLISTIC COMPETITION (1933); N.V. Kaldor, *The Economic Aspects of Advertising*, 18 REV. OF ECON. STUD. 1 (1950); A. Dixit & V. Norman, *Advertising and Welfare*, 9 BELL J. OF ECON. 1 (1978).

[16]   *See* P. Nelson, *Advertising as Information Once More*, *in* ADVERTISING: THE ECONOMICS OF PERSUASION 133 (D.G. Tuerck ed., 1978); P. Nelson, *The Economic Value of Advertising*, *in* ADVERTISING AND SOCIETY 43 (Y. Brozen ed., 1974); P. Nelson, *Information and Consumer Behaviour*, 78 J. OF POL. ECON. 311 (1970); P. Nelson, *Advertising as Information*, 82 J. OF POL. ECON. 729 (1974); P. Nelson, *The Economic Consequences of Advertising*, 48 J. OF BUS. 213 (1975).

others it creates secondary markets in which the brand has itself become the product.[17] Even if such investment is desirable, it is unlikely to require the incentive of the protection of trade marks against allusion. Landes and Posner are right that "we do not need trade mark protection [let alone protection against allusive use] just to be sure of having enough words, though we may need patent protection to be sure of having enough inventions, or copyright protection to be sure of having enough books, movies and musical compositions."[18]

Two further arguments in this third group focus upon justifications for the intellectual property regimes grounded in notions of unjust enrichment and desert: protection against allusion remedies the unjust enrichment of those who allude to trade marks, or recognises the desert of those who create brand reputations. It has often been shown that these justifications for the intellectual property law regimes are problematic. They are even more so as justifications for trade mark protection. As for the unjust enrichment argument, we are all regularly enriched by the innovative and creative activities of others. The claim that we stand on the shoulders of giants is platitudinous because it rings true. But if we are all regularly enriched by the activities of others, the question is when that enrichment will be unjust. This is the question that those who speak of "reaping without sowing," a phrase that draws its rhetorical power from a New Testament source in which the behaviour is neither lauded nor condemned,[19] have been unable to answer. To do so would surely involve invoking some other argument for intellectual property. If that is right, then the argument from unjust enrichment does not itself add any weight to the trade mark owner's claim. As for the desert arguments, there is no clear reason why someone who has built a successful brand reputation is particularly deserving. As Advocate General de Lamonthe pointed out in *Sirena SRL v Eda SRL (C-40/70)*[20] in a passage later taken up by the European Court of Justice:[21] "From the point of view of humanity, certainly the debt that society owes to the 'inventor' of the name 'Prep Good Morning' is not of the same order (this is the least that may be said) as that which humanity has contracted with the 'inventor' of penicillin." Moreover, it has never been made clear why the creator of any intangible asset deserves control over its use and not some

---

[17] See, e.g., G.J. Stigler & G.S. Becker, *De Gustibus Non Est Disputandum*, 67 AM. ECON. REV. 76 (1977); L.M. Nichols, *Advertising and Economic Welfare*, 75 AM. ECON. REV. 213 (1985); G.S. Becker & K.M. Murphy, *A Simple Theory of Advertising as a Good or Bad*, Q. J. OF ECON. 942 (1993).
[18] Landes & Posner, *supra* note 8, at 275.
[19] *Luke* 19:22.
[20] [1971] C.M.L.R. 260 at 264–5.
[21] SA Cnl-Sucal NV v Hag CF AG (Case C-10/89) [1990] 3 C.M.L.R. 571.

other form of reward, particularly in contexts such as that of a successful brand when reward may already have come in the form of a market advantage.

It cannot be assumed, then, that arguments for the justification of copyright or patent, even if they are coherent, can simply be applied to the justification of trade mark protection.

III. Protection against allusion to a trade mark and the expressive autonomy of the trade mark owner

Having rejected, therefore, some of the most commonly advanced justifications for protection against allusion to a trade mark, we turn to an argument built upon the expressive autonomy of the trade mark owner. This argument falls into the third category outlined above: it also has power to explain some features of other intellectual property and related regimes, such as copyright, moral rights and personality rights. Our discussion here, however, is restricted to the justification of protection against allusion to a trade mark.

A. The argument from expressive autonomy

The right to expressive autonomy arguably entails at least four claims, though the strength of those claims depends upon how the right is justified. In this section a justification grounded in speaker autonomy is assumed. First, freedom of speech entails freedom from unjustified speech restraint. Second, freedom of speech may entail a right to be heard, although the extent to which it does is highly contentious. Third, freedom of speech may entail freedom from compulsion to express a message not of the speaker's choosing. Fourth, freedom of speech may entail freedom from compulsion to subsidise a message with which the person from whom the subsidy is sought chooses not to be associated. It is upon the third and fourth of these claims that the argument of this section is built.

The third and fourth of these claims have been given expression in the free speech jurisprudence of the United States, though they have not long been carefully distinguished. In *Pacific Gas and Electric Company v Public Utilities Commission of California*,[22] the right to expressive autonomy was relied upon to prevent the compelled distribution with utility bills of a newsletter expressing views which the utility company did not endorse. In *Hurley v Irish-American Gay, Lesbian and Bisexual Group of Boston*,[23] it was relied upon to prevent the compelled inclusion of a gay rights group in a St. Patrick's Day parade organized by a war veterans group. In *Boy Scouts of America v Dale*,[24] it was used to justify the dismissal of a Boy Scout leader who was

---

[22] 475 U.S. 1 (1986).
[23] 515 U.S. 557 (1995).
[24] 530 U.S. 640 (2000).

openly gay on the basis that his retention would "force the organization to send a message, both to its young members and the world, that the Boy Scouts accepts homosexual conduct as a legitimate form of behavior."[25] Finally, in *United States v United Foods Inc.*,[26] it was used to prohibit compelled contributions by growers to a mushroom advertising fund.

The principle that underpins each of these cases must be that expressive autonomy entails the ability to choose not only which messages a speaker will herself convey or be taken to have conveyed, but also in the expression of which messages she will participate (in the sense that she facilitates their communication). A concern to protect a person's expressive autonomy is not merely a concern that she should be free to determine how she is presented to others, but also a concern that she should be free to choose those messages that she wishes to promote. Participation in, and the promotion of, speech may consist in its financial subsidy. This is because choices about how to use our money are, in our culture, important autonomy-constituting choices (particularly as regards so personally important an issue as the meanings with which we are associated, whether by others or only by ourselves).[27] Participation in, and the promotion of, speech may also consist in the use of words with which we are associated, whether or not the use of those words gives rise to any suggestion that we have endorsed, or are even connected with, the message of which they become a part. This is because choices about the words we use are also, in our culture, important autonomy-constituting choices, as our commitment to expressive autonomy demonstrates. This may be what Michael Madison means when, in relation to the fair use exceptions in copyright, he claims that allowing access to a work can be forcing its author to "subsidize, with raw material, the speech of [the] ... second user."[28] Of course, there is a difference between these two types of subsidy because one has a general claim to control the use of one's money that one may not have in relation to one's words, but the analogy does not seem too strained.

Quite so broadly expressed, this principle is potentially problematic, both as regards compelled speech and as regards the compelled subsidy of speech. As regards compelled speech, it is important to remember that communication is almost always difficult. There are many situations in which a speaker may be represented to have expressed a particular point of view, been misquoted or poorly paraphrased, and legal redress ought not to be available. We would

---

[25] *Id.* at 653.
[26] 533 U.S. 405 (2001).
[27] *See also* Howard M. Wasserman, *Compelled Expression and the Public Forum Doctrine*, 77 TUL. L. REV. 163 (2002).
[28] Michael J. Madison, *Complexity and Copyright in Contradiction*, 18 CARDOZO ARTS & ENT. L.J. 125, 166 (2000).

need to be very cautious, for example, in affording relief for non-defamatory misquotation. The chilling effect of such regulation would weigh against preventing the compulsion of speech to so great an extent: the usual remedy for misunderstanding is more speech. But that a principle ought not in many circumstances to be given legal expression does not mean that it ought never to be. If that were the case, then even protection against the restraint of speech would be difficult to justify. At least some level of protection against compelled speech is arguably a corollary of a commitment to protecting expressive autonomy.

Similarly, as regards the compelled subsidy of speech, the case of government speech exemplifies a situation in which an overbroad protection of expressive autonomy gives rise to particular difficulties. In the most recent U.S. Supreme Court case on the issue, *Johanns v Livestock Marketing Association* (*Johanns*), the Court was faced with the dilemma that allowing claimants to invoke the right to expressive autonomy whenever the subsidy of speech was compelled could effectively silence government: a complaint could be brought any time that tax revenues were used to propagate a message with which any individual taxpayer disagreed.[29] This position was clearly unsustainable. The Supreme Court dealt with the problem by emphasising the distinction between compelled speech and the compelled subsidy of speech, and by creating a further distinction between the compelled subsidy of government speech and the compelled subsidy of private speech. The majority in *Johanns* wrote:

> The principal dissent conflates the two concepts [of compelled speech and compelled subsidy] into something it describes as citizens' "presumptive autonomy as speakers to decide what to say and what to pay for others to say" . . . [T]here might be a valid objection if "those singled out to pay the tax are closely linked with the expression" . . . in a way that makes them appear to endorse the government message. But this compelled-speech argument . . . differs substantively from the compelled-subsidy analysis. The latter invalidates an exaction not because being forced to pay for speech that is unattributed violates personal autonomy, but because being forced to fund someone else's private speech unconnected to any legitimate government purpose violates personal autonomy . . . Such a violation does not occur when the exaction funds government speech.[30]

The Supreme Court's judgment has been rightly criticised.[31] But the distinction between the compelled subsidy of government speech and the compelled

---

[29] 544 U.S. 550 (2005).
[30] *Id.* at 565 n. 8.
[31] *See, e.g.*, Robert Post, *Compelled Subsidization of Speech:* Johanns v Livestock Marketing Association, 2005 SUP. CT. REV. 195 (2005).

subsidy of private speech does have some merit. It is not that the compelled subsidy of government speech does not raise expressive autonomy concerns, but rather that the compelled subsidy of government speech through general taxation is not a compelled subsidy of a type for which legal redress ought to be available. This is on a number of bases: government would otherwise be impossible; the sense in which a taxpayer "participates" in government speech is clearly far more attenuated than the sense in which a member of a private organisation "participates" in the speech that she is compelled to subsidise; and participation in government activities is in any case moderated through the whole framework of representative democracy. Once again the problem seems to be not with the general principle, but with the extent to which it might conceivably be given legal expression, a problem that marks every aspect of the law of free speech.

For our purposes, it is important that even when it was shown to create real difficulties and even in situations in which no implication of endorsement was raised, the Supreme Court in *Johanns* did not abandon the intuition that the subsidisation of at least private speech raises issues of expressive autonomy. The basis of that intuition must be that subsidising speech is participating in speech, even if the recipient of the speech does not identify it with all the subsidising parties. Even though they distinguished between the two, the Supreme Court continued to affirm that protection against the compelled subsidy of speech ought to be afforded alongside protection against compelled speech.

If all this is right, then the implications for protection against allusion to a trade mark should be clear. When someone uses a sign that alludes to a mark, she may be involved either in compelling speech, or in an activity analogous to compelling a subsidy of speech. This consists either: in altering the meaning of a mark so that it subsequently bears a meaning with which the owner of the mark will be associated each time it is used, but from which she would wish to be disassociated; or in forcing the owner of the mark to participate in, or promote, speech with which she would disagree by providing the material upon which that speech is built.

Each of these possible wrongs is exemplified by the facts of the well-known American trade mark case *Girl Scouts of the United States of America v Personality Posters Manufacturing Co.*[32] This case concerned a poster with a picture of a pregnant Girl Scout wearing the uniform of the organisation and marked with its trade mark. Her hands were clasped above her abdomen and

---

[32] 304 F. Supp. 1228 (D.C.N.Y. 1969). Note, however, that in the case itself the dilution claim of the Girl Scouts was unsuccessful on the basis that New York law was said then to require a showing of confusion for a successful dilution claim.

next to her hands was the Girl Scouts' motto "Be Prepared." This use of the trade mark may have involved a type of compelled speech. Were this poster widely distributed, the Girl Scouts would have been forced either to abandon the use of their motto, a type of silencing, or to contend with the fact that they no longer controlled the message that it conveyed. It would be difficult, having seen the poster, ever to hear the motto again, or to receive the Girl Scouts' use of it, in quite the same way. If forcing the Boy Scouts to retain a gay Scout Leader constituted forcing them to express a message with which they might disagree, it must be at least conceivable that this use of the motto of the Girl Scouts also entailed a type of compelled speech.[33] Second, this use of the trade mark might have involved an activity analogous to the compelled subsidy of speech. The Girl Scouts were effectively conscripted to express a message about sexual activity with which they might have disagreed. Even if their use of the motto remained unaffected by the distribution of the poster, the Girl Scouts might have argued that the use of the motto forced them to participate in the expression of a message from which they would have wished to be disassociated. The claim to protect trade marks against allusive use then becomes a claim grounded in preserving autonomy of expression.

B. Objections to the argument from expressive autonomy

Before considering important qualifications to protection against allusion to a trade mark implied in this argument from expressive autonomy, we should briefly address the three most obvious objections to it.

The first of these objections is that in each of the free speech cases discussed in the preceding section it is the government that is responsible for compelling either speech or the subsidy of private speech. In the situation of allusion to a trade mark, it is a private party who has allegedly compelled either speech or its subsidy. As a theoretical matter, it is hard to see why this distinction is of any importance. A government that is committed to expressive autonomy bears a responsibility to uphold it both in its own actions and in regulating the actions of private parties.

The second objection is that a trade mark is commercial speech and, in the usual course of events, the trade mark owner will be a corporation. The American cases dealing with compelled speech, and with corporate speech

---

[33] Of course it could be argued that it would be open to the Girl Scouts simply to correct any misunderstanding with more speech. However: (i) such a claim would not rebut the argument that the Girl Scouts had a free speech claim on the compelled speech ground, but rather constitute a potential reason for not giving that claim legal force, and (ii) it would only constitute a reason for not giving that claim legal force if effectively forcing the abandonment of a long-cherished motto were thought proportionate to the protection of the free speech claim of the parodist.

more generally, have been the subject of powerful criticism on this basis.[34] However, the fact that speech is commercial is not a reason for it to be denied protection altogether, although it may affect the level of protection that the speech is given.[35] Protection of the expressive autonomy of a speaker must surely entail protecting the way in which a person chooses to be presented in inviting commercial transactions at least to some extent, given the importance of commercial transactions to our community life. But this reasoning, though it may justify the protection of commercial speech, highlights the difficulty regarding the corporate identity of most trade mark owners. It makes sense to protect the personal autonomy of natural persons, but does it make sense to protect the personal autonomy of legal persons? This is an important question for many areas of the law, a full consideration of which is outside the scope of this chapter. However, a robust defence of the attribution of rights to corporations, including rights grounded in autonomy, can be made. For example, Finnis mounts a defence of the attribution of rights to corporations based on the rights of the individuals who use a corporate vehicle to achieve their collective aims.[36] In doing so, he builds upon classic arguments made by Hohfeld.[37]

The third objection to my argument is that infringement of a trade mark, whether infringement by causing confusion or by allusion, can in most trade mark systems only be constituted by the use of a sign in the course of trade. If protection against allusion is best understood as protection against a type of compelled speech or the compelled subsidy of speech, why ought that protection only be available in these particular circumstances?[38] Few marks, and certainly not those iconic marks to which allusion is most likely to be made, represent the unaltered speech of their owners. The meaning of a mark can be altered in a variety of ways, and in a variety of expressive acts from which its owner would wish to be disassociated, only some of such situations giving rise

---

[34] *See, e.g.*, C. Edwin Baker, *Paternalism, Politics, and Citizen Freedom: The Commercial Speech Quandary in Nike*, 54 CASE W. RES. L. REV. 1161 (2004); Randall P. Bezanson, *Institutional Speech*, 80 IOWA L. REV. 735 (1994–5); Alan Hirsch & Ralph Nader, *"The Corporate Conscience" and Other First Amendment Follies in Pacific Gas & Electric*, 41 SAN DIEGO L. REV. 483 (2004). *But see* Martin H. Redish & Howard M. Wasserman, *What's Good for General Motors: Corporate Speech and the Theory of Free Expression*, 66 GEO. WASH. L. REV. 235 (1997–8).
[35] Cent. Hudson Gas & Elec. Corporation v Pub. Serv. Comm'n of N.Y., 447 U.S. 557 (1980).
[36] John Finnis, *The Priority of Persons, in* OXFORD ESSAYS IN JURISPRUDENCE (FOURTH SERIES) 9, 11 (Jeremy Horder ed., 2000).
[37] Wesley Newcomb Hohfeld, *Nature of Stockholders' Individual Liability for Corporation Debts*, 9 COLUM. L. REV. 285 (1909).
[38] Professor Tushnet has spoken to this point. *See supra* Ch. 11.

to the possibility of an infringement action because they constitute use in the course of trade. Moreover, it is appropriate that this should be the case. The law cannot, and should not, try to control all the ways in which vehicles of expression such as trade marks are used and acquire new meanings. Respect for the expressive autonomy of the trade mark owner does not require that the law give her so complete control over her mark. However, it may well be an appropriate way of evincing that respect to remove a powerful incentive for using and altering the meaning of speech, the incentive of potential economic advantage. It is the contention of this chapter that, subject to the qualifications outlined below, this is an appropriate alternative to offering the trade mark owner either no control, or complete control, over the meaning of her mark. If that is right, then the function of the requirement that an infringement occur in the course of trade is evident.

C. *Limiting protection against allusion*

On the basis of her right to expressive autonomy, then, there seems to be good reason for permitting the trade mark owner to control some allusions to her mark. The question that now arises is how that control ought to be limited. It is at this point that the expressive autonomy of the party who, free from legal restraint, would use the mark for an expressive purpose becomes relevant. The expressive autonomy claim of that other party is perhaps the most important way of limiting the availability of relief against allusion to a trade mark. It is, of course, not the only potential limitation to such a claim, but the history of intellectual property law shows that it is likely to be particularly powerful, stemming as it does from the same principles that underpin the claim itself. There are at least two situations in which allusion to the mark ought to be permitted despite the expressive autonomy claims of the trade mark owner.

The first of these is the situation in which it is necessary to allude to the mark in order adequately to comment upon, or even identify, the mark, its owner or her goods or services. It is reasonable to allow allusion to the mark for this purpose because there may be no other effective way in which to make such comments than to use, and sometimes to alter the meaning of, the mark. Moreover, using a mark for this purpose does not undermine, but recognises the nexus between the mark and its owner. A speaker cannot object to compelled participation in an argument about her own activities, and trade mark law sometimes acknowledges this in its treatment of nominative uses.[39]

Most trade mark systems include partial provision for this problem. However, I would argue that many systems have been insufficiently willing to

---

[39] *See, e.g.,* New Kids on the Block v News Am. Publ'g Inc., 971 F.2d 302 (9th Cir. 1992) (setting forth a test for nominative fair use).

allow allusive uses of the mark for this purpose. In particular, some courts seem suspicious of allowing allusive uses of a mark for one of the most commercially important purposes, that of signalling the substitutability of a product to consumers. The *Arsenal* decision is instructive here. There is undoubtedly a market for Arsenal souvenirs. That market is defined by a very low cross-price elasticity of demand. Arsenal souvenirs would need to become very expensive indeed in order for Arsenal fans to buy Chelsea souvenirs. Within that market, the decision of the European Court of Justice in *Arsenal* potentially gives a powerful monopoly to the football club. It does so by effectively preventing the use of the word "Arsenal" to signal the substitutability of unauthorised souvenirs, even unauthorised souvenirs where no possibility of post-sale confusion arises. If branding is not to become the powerful barrier to entry that persuasive advertising theorists claim, new entrants must be allowed to allude to trade marks to signal the substitutability of their products for those of the market leaders. This argument becomes particularly pertinent in fields such as "me-too" marketing, allusion to the trade marks of market leaders by new entrants, often store-brand products, for the purpose of signalling substitutability. Of course, some substitutability claims might constitute truthful comparative advertising and thus be permissible under most current trademark regimes, but not all regimes are equally permissive even in relation to comparative advertising.[40]

The second situation in which it might be necessary to limit the expressive autonomy claim of a trade mark owner to prevent allusive uses of her mark is more problematic. We have already seen that protection against allusion can help in preventing a mark from losing its primary value as a symbol and operating as an index of some broader set of associations. However, if a mark has already acquired an important indexical function, it may be essential that it be available to other speakers. "Barbie" as an index for a particular understanding of womanhood is an example much discussed in the literature. In the United States it has been the subject not only of the litigation in *Mattel v Walking Mountain Productions*[41] but also of the case *Mattel v MCA Records Inc*[42] concerning the song "Barbie Girl" by the Danish group "Aqua." Indeed, Mattel themselves recognise the indexical status of Barbie. When Barbie turned thirty-five, the company supported the production of one hundred images of the doll, most of which exploited its indexical function in some

---

[40] *See, e.g.*, the rather strict requirements for comparative advertising contained in Directive 2006/114/EC of the European Parliament and of the Council of 12 December 2006 concerning misleading and comparative advertising, [2006] O.J. L. 376.
[41] 353 F.3d 792 (9th Cir. 2003).
[42] 296 F.3d 894 (9th Cir. 2002).

way.⁴³ Many did so in ways not too dissimilar from those over which Mattel took action in *Mattel v Walking Mountain Productions*. If there genuinely exists no satisfactory alternative index for an idea or set of ideas—as there may not be in the case of Barbie—then the mark itself should be available for use. To put it another way, the mark may have become a kind of public forum. It may have become a space for debate rather than a contribution to debate. This type of thinking seems to underpin the law of trade mark genericide, although that law is arguably inadequate to protect the relevant free speech interest.⁴⁴ In particular, genericide happens when a trade mark shifts from being a symbol with one particular referential function (that of identifying the supplier of goods or services) to being a symbol with a different referential function (that of signifying a whole type of goods or services). However, if a mark has already acquired an important indexical function in the way that the "Barbie" mark has, there may be just as good a reason for protecting it less strongly as there is for denying protection to a mark that has become generic altogether. In particular, there may be good reason for only protecting these marks against confusion and not dilution. In the case of a limited range of marks which have become important cultural indices, such a response seems justified by a commitment to protecting the expressive autonomy of not only the owner of the mark, but also those who would allude to it.

Significantly, these two categories of cases reflect the two categories of parody recognised in American copyright commentary, so-called "target" and "weapon" parody,⁴⁵ though situations of parody do not exhaust those in which the party who would allude to a trade mark has a claim of one or other of these two kinds. Indeed, the intuition of copyright law that weapon parody is usually more difficult to justify than target parody also seems sound on the arguments of this section. Framing contests between the trade mark owner and those who would allude to her mark as contests between competing claims to expressive autonomy seems far more analytically fruitful than the more usual approach of framing them as contests between a "property" right and a right to freedom of

---

⁴³ THE ART OF BARBIE 72 (Craig Yoe ed., 1994)
⁴⁴ For more on this topic, see Professor Dreyfuss' work, *supra* Chapter 10.
⁴⁵ The distinction between parodies that use a text to comment on the text itself or its author and parodies that use the text as vehicles for commenting on something else was drawn in *Campbell v Acuff-Rose Music, Inc.*, 510 U.S. 569, 580–81 (1994), though the labels "target" and "weapon" parody were not actually used in the case. The Court instead used the terms "parody" and "satire". Although terminology in this field is extremely unsettled, few would exclude "target parody" from the scope of the term "satire" and so the terms "target" and "weapon" parody are preferred. The distinction between the two has been widely criticised, but may find some justification in the reasoning of this section, see Michael Spence, *Intellectual Property and the Problem of Parody*, 114 L. Q. REV. 594, 608–15 (1998).

expression. These are effectively arguments about who can be compelled to say, or subsidise the saying of what, and who can be silenced by whom.

IV. Conclusion

Before concluding, an argument potentially complementary to that made in this short chapter should briefly be outlined. The arguments of this chapter have been grounded in the rights-based claims of the trade mark owner. Bosland has recently mounted a parallel justification for the protection of trade marks against allusion of a more instrumental kind. He argues that, in order to facilitate speech, it is necessary to "preserve the expressive capacity of trade marks and protect their status as effective instruments of cultural dialogue."[46] This is because:

> In order to facilitate the exchange of information in the public sphere, trade marks need to retain a relatively stable denotative structure upon which their expressive potential is built. The "trade dilution" of the denotative aspect of a trade mark through dual signification—namely, where one trade mark (signifier) is used to more than one trader (signified)—would usurp the ability of a trade mark to become and remain a distinctive part of our expressive dialogue . . . Using the same mark (or even aspects of the same mark) to denote two or more traders would potentially lead to conflicting associations with the trade mark, effectively resulting in an inability to use the trade mark as an expressive and communicative resource.[47]

The merits of this argument are not easy to assess. It might be assumed that the "denotative aspect" of a trade mark is sufficiently protected by the prohibition of use creating consuming confusion. The extent to which protecting the "connotative aspect" of a trade mark is necessary to "facilitate the exchange of information in the public sphere" is an empirical question, the answer to which is not obvious. It is true that a trade mark might acquire many different connotations if it is again and again recoded by allusion to it, whether that recoding is intended to take advantage of the reputation of the mark or to do it damage. But even if the "connotative aspect" of a particular mark is blurred or tarnished in this way, there will always be new marks with similar connotations. If the mark "Rolls Royce" ceases to evoke a particular sense of luxury and prestige, some new mark will inevitably take its place. The "public sphere" is remarkably fertile ground for creating, as well as for destroying, powerful vehicles of meaning. The assumption underpinning Bosland's argument seems to be that our "public sphere" is in danger of descending into a morass of indistinct signifiers. This is a strong claim and may not be verifi-

---

[46] Jason Bosland, *The Culture of Trade Marks: An Alternative Cultural Theory Perspective*, 10 Media & Arts L. Rev. 99, 110 (2005).
[47] *Id.* at 111–12.

able. If it were, however, Bosland's more instrumental argument might complement the rights-based arguments of this chapter.

A commitment to expressive autonomy seems to require the recognition of rights against compelled speech and the compelled subsidy of speech. Those rights, as we have seen, can themselves be used to justify the protection of trade marks against at least some allusive uses. Perhaps equally importantly, an argument for protection against allusion to a trade mark grounded in expressive autonomy implies its own limitation, one built upon respect for the expressive autonomy of the party who would make the allusion. It therefore provides an approach able to reconcile the rights of both the trade mark owner and individuals in the broader community of which she is a part, and it is this reconciliation that makes the argument particularly attractive.

Section B

Limiting the Scope of Trademark Rights

13 Protecting the common: delineating a public domain in trade mark law
Jennifer Davis

I. Introduction

From the early twentieth century, the House of David (an unincorporated religious and business association) maintained a baseball team, which toured the United States, "playing several hundred games a year," and earning a substantial income. According to Judge Woolsey,[1] the team played "a sound game of baseball." However, the most "notable characteristic" of the team was that its players wore beards and had "House of David" printed across their uniforms. In 1929, an individual named Murphy also formed a baseball team whose players wore beards and whose uniforms carried the words, "House of David." It was Murphy's strategy to book games for his teams in towns a few days before those dates set for the original House of David, and in so doing according to Judge Woolsey, "diluted the neighborhood's interest in seeing a bearded baseball team play ball." Furthermore, the House of David claimed that Murphy's team played an "inferior game of baseball," so injuring the House of David's reputation and, as a result, its gate receipts. The House of David sued for unfair competition.[2] It was successful. The use of the plaintiff's name and appearance together with Murphy's stratagem of booking in his team ahead of the plaintiff established mens rea. However the court made a particular point about the beards. "From time immemorial," the judge stated,

> The wearing of beards has been in the public domain. In respect of matters within that domain all men have rights in common. Any man, therefore, if so minded, may—without being subject to any challenge, legal or equitable—not only grow such beard as he can, but purposely imitate another's facial shrubbery—even to the extent of following such topiary modification thereof as may have caught his fancy.

This article is concerned with the idea of a common as it relates to the law of registered trade marks. The idea of a common as a metaphor for a category of

---

[1] Israelite House of David v Murphy, 6 F. Supp. 914 (D.C.N.Y. 1934).
[2] It is perhaps worth noting that the original team was itself "exposed" for "hiring professionals and dressing them in wigs and fake beards." V.S. Engel, *This Issue's Samson* (1998), *available at* http://the-light.com/mens/samson/4/samson.html.

signs which should remain free for others to use is a peculiarly British one. Part of the interest of the "House of David" judgment is that it is perhaps unique among U.S. trade mark cases[3] in referring to the idea of a "common." But it is also significant that for Judge Woolsey, at least, the idea of a common as a repository for unprotected signs could co-exist happily with that of the public domain. In fact, it will be argued here that the two are not synonymous, and indeed just as the common metaphor is rare in U.S. trade mark law, so the public domain is largely absent from trade mark law in the U.K.[4]

The fact that, for a least a century, the U.K. courts employed the idea of a "trade mark common" as a repository for signs which should remain free for others to use, derives from a number of related ideas they held, about both trade marks and the common itself. In particular, these ideas concerned how the meaning and therefore the value of trade marks are produced and to whom that value belongs, the correct balance between competing interests in the market, including those of trade mark proprietors, other traders, and the public at large, and finally, the nature of the common. However, after operating as a dominant metaphor in U.K. trade mark law for much of the twentieth century, the idea of a trade mark common lost its relevance with the advent of a harmonized law of registered trade marks across the European Union.[5] Certainly, E.U. trade mark law identifies various categories of signs which should be left free for others to use: most notably non-distinctive, descriptive and generic signs. However, the extent of the protection given to such signs is markedly less than that afforded under a regime which recognized the existence of a "trade mark common."[6] Indeed, it is precisely those assumptions which underlie the relevance of the common metaphor, particularly about the nature of the market, which have been displaced under the

---

[3] The case was decided before the 1946 Lanham Act, which offered federal protection for unregistered trade marks (§ 43(a)). In the U.K., the facts of the *House of David* case would fall squarely within the tort of passing off, which offers protection to unregistered trade marks.

[4] The idea of a public domain is used in the U.K. almost exclusively in relation to confidential information. *See, e.g.*, HRH Prince of Wales v Associated Newspapers Ltd. [2006] E.C.D.R. 20; McKennit v Ash [2006] E.M.L.R. 10.

[5] Harmonization was the result of the implementation of the First Council Directive 89/104/EC of 21 December 1988 to approximate the laws of the Member States relating to trade marks [hereinafter Trade Mark Directive] OJ L 040/1. The Directive was implemented in the UK by the 1994 Trade Marks Act.

[6] The German doctrine of "Freihaltebedürfnis" had much in common with the idea of a trade mark common developed by the English courts. *See infra* nn. 44–7 and accompanying text, discussing Windsurfing Chiemsee Productions- und Vertriebs GmbH v Boots- und Segelzubehör Walter Huber and Franz Attenberger, Joined Cases C-108/97 [1999] E.T.M.R. 585.

E.U. Trade Mark Directive. It is notable, however, that while the trade mark common has disappeared from U.K. trade mark law, the tradition of identifying a public domain of unprotected marks in the U.S. remains strong. The possible reasons for the relative longevity of the public domain will be discussed later in this chapter. However, it is certainly the case that before its enclosure by the E.U. Trade Mark Directive, the common of U.K. trade mark law offered a protected repository for certain signs, including some which were functioning as an indication of origin, which, under the present European trade mark regime, would be registrable and hence no longer left free for others to use.

This chapter will begin by examining how the idea of a trade mark common was developed by U.K. courts and how it was deployed in setting the parameters of trade mark protection over the course of the twentieth century. It will then go on to examine the impact of the E.U. Trade Mark Directive on the idea of a trade mark common. It will show that the Directive, as interpreted by the European Court of Justice (ECJ), no longer allows for the possibility of a trade mark common. Finally, by identifying both the similarities and the differences which underlie the ideas of a trade mark common and a public domain, this chapter will offer suggestions as to why the former has continued to carry resonance in U.S. trade mark law while the latter has all but disappeared from the U.K. The chapter will conclude by suggesting that it was the very richness of the trade mark common which made it, unlike the public domain, vulnerable to enclosure.

II. The delineation of a trade mark common

Registered trade marks were introduced into the U.K. by the 1875 Trade Marks Registration Act. The first U.K. trade mark case to introduce the idea of a trade mark common was the "Fruit Salt"[7] case fourteen years later.[8] In this case, the plaintiff, J. C. Eno was the owner of the marks "Eno's Fruit Salt" and "Fruit Salt" for fruit-flavoured effervescing drinks. Eno sought to prevent the respondent W. G. Dunn from registering the mark, "Dunn's Fruit Salt Baking Powder," as a trade mark and in addition claimed that the use of the latter was infringing. In the course of the proceedings, Lord Justice Fry in the Court of

---

[7] *In re* Dunn's Trade Marks (1889) Ch.D. 439 (Fruit Salt).
[8] In the intervening years, there had been significant extensions of trade mark protection. The 1883 Patents, Designs and Trade Marks Act allowed for the registration of trade marks which had not been in use before 1875 and also added to the marks allowed by the 1875 Act, marks which were "a distinctive device, mark, brand, heading, label or ticket," and by the 1888 Patents, Designs and Trade Marks Act, "fancy words or words not in common use." Section 64.

Appeal queried whether J. C. Eno's own mark was too descriptive to be registered as a trade mark.[9] He stated:[10]

> I cannot help regarding Mr. Eno's attempt [to register the mark] as an instance of a perpetual struggle which it seems to me is going on, to enclose and to appropriate as private property certain little strips of the great open common of the English language. That is a kind of trespass against which the courts ought to set their faces.

In the House of Lords, Lord Watson for the majority disagreed.[11] He took the view that the registration of the descriptive words "Fruit Salt" would not enable Eno "to appropriate to his own property, words in common use." On the contrary, according to Lord Watson:

> The argument appears to me to underrate the resources of the English language, which are in my opinion quite sufficient to enable any one honestly desirous of distinguishing his own goods to use these words in a trade mark in such a manner as to prevent any possibility of their being connected with the appellant's fruit salt.

In 1894, Lord MacNaghten returned to the idea of a common in the "Solio" case.[12] This judgment was concerned with an expansion to the categories of registrable marks, namely under § 10(1) of the 1888 Patents, Designs and Trade Marks Act, which allowed for the registration of invented words. The issue in "Solio," which concerned the registration of the word "Solio" for photographic equipment, was whether, under the 1888 Act, all invented words might be registered or whether those with a descriptive element could not. In this case, the Spanish word "Solio" contained a reference to the sun. After quoting Lord Justice Fry's words approvingly, Lord McNaghten in the House of Lords held that "Solio" was registerable. He noted that if "the object of putting a restriction on words capable of being registered as trade marks was, of course, to prevent persons appropriating to themselves that which ought to be open to all," this should not prevent the registration of invented words, because, "[a]fter all, invention is not so very common."[13] In the same judgment, Lord Herschell said[14] that it was wrong to allow the registration of

---

[9] The CA decided by a majority that Dunn's use of the mark for baking soda did not infringe Eno's use for fruit drinks, a decision which was reversed by a majority in the House of Lords. James Eno v William George Dunn (1890) LR 15 App. Cas. 250.
[10] In Re *Dunn*, Ch.D. at 455.
[11] *Eno v Dunn*, 15 App. Cas. at 259.
[12] Eastman Photographic Materials Company v Comptroller General of Patents, Designs and Trade Marks, (1898) H.L. (E.) 571.
[13] *Eastman Photographic*, H.L. (E.) at 583.
[14] *Eastman Photographic*, H.L. (E.) at 580.

descriptive marks because: "The vocabulary of the English language is common property: It belongs alike to all; and no one ought to be permitted to prevent the other members of the community from using for such purposes of description a word which has reference to the character or quality of goods."

The 1905 Trade Marks Act introduced other categories of marks capable of registration. In particular, it became possible to register descriptive marks which had acquired distinctiveness. Four years later, an application was sought for the registration of the mark "Perfection" for soap. The application was denied. In the Court of Appeal,[15] Sir Herbert Cozens-Hardy M.R. explained this refusal in words that have come to be seen as the authoritative statement of the common's approach to trade mark registration, and have been frequently quoted since.[16] According to Cozens-Hardy,[17] "[w]ealthy traders are habitually eager to enclose part of the great common of the English language and to exclude the general public of the present day and of the future from access to the enclosure."

Cozens-Hardy believed that laudatory words "ought to be open to all the world" and should not be registered. Fletcher-Moulton L.J. concurred.[18] He could not see "how words which are simply a direct statement of quality, for example, 'good' or 'perfect' can ever lose their primary meaning and come to mean not good or best but articles made by A.B. [the plaintiff]." He added[19] that the present application "was a bold attempt by a wealthy firm to deprive their competitors, great and small, of the use of a laudatory term common to all." Farwell L.J. believed that if such words were registered,[20] "large and wealthy firms with whom smaller folk are unwilling to litigate, could divide amongst themselves all the ordinary words of description and laudation in the English language."

The courts, in trade mark cases, imported the idea of common, and indeed the terminology surrounding it, from its use in relation to real property. Metaphors are not, of course, chosen randomly. Or if they are, they do not acquire the longevity accorded to the metaphor of the common in U.K. trade mark law. We have seen how, in its early years, the idea of a trade mark common had been employed by the courts following changes to the law which

---

[15] *In re* Joseph Crosfield & Sons Ltd. to Register a Trade Mark, (1909) 26 R.P.C. 387.
[16] Perhaps most notably in the first major case which was decided under the 1994 Trade Marks Act, British Sugar Plc v James Robertson & Sons Ltd., [1996] R.P.C. 284 (Jacob, J.).
[17] In re *Joseph Crosfield*, 26 R.P.C. at 854.
[18] *Id.* at 862. John Fletcher-Moulton had helped to draft the 1905 Act.
[19] In re *Joseph Crosfield*, 26 R.P.C. at 858.
[20] *Id.* at 861.

had expanded the category of registrable marks. It will be suggested here that, in the U.K., the land common carried a variety of meanings, both legal and historical, which for some judges at least made it a fitting metaphor when used in relation to trade mark protection. It is therefore worth briefly examining those aspects of the law and history relating to the land common which suggested it as an apt metaphor for courts engaged in mapping the boundaries of trade mark protection.

It should first be noted that the land common, as it was legally understood, had some characteristics which made it an uneasy fit with the law as it was applied to trade mark registration. As I have noted elsewhere, both historically and in contemporary law, common land is not land that is owned in common, but rather land that must be owned by some legal person.[21] Commoners have a right to take from common land "some portion of that which another man's soil naturally produces."[22] Traditionally, commoners did not denote the general public. A right to the fruits of the common generally annexed to property owned by the commoner. However, such a right might also arise through custom or payment. In effect, this would mean that in some villages, before the enclosure movement of the late eighteenth and early nineteenth century, a majority of inhabitants would have acquired access to the common either as commoners or by other means.[23] Thus, although the legal definition of common land in the U.K. featured neither the common ownership of the land nor universal access to its fruits, in practice, before enclosure, large numbers of the public did indeed have access to it.[24] One notable commonality, then, between the land common and the trade mark common, as described by the U.K. courts, resides in the fact that in both cases the public were held to have a positive right of access, whether in the case of land to partake of its natural produce or in the case of trade marks to use the English language. This understanding is reflected in the comment of Lord Herschell in the "Solio" case:

> If then, the use of every word of the language was to be permitted as a trade mark, it was surely essential to prevent its use as a trade mark where such use would deprive the rest of the community of the right which they possessed to employ the word for the purposes of describing the character or quality of the goods.[25]

---

[21] See J. Davis, *European Trade Mark Law and the Enclosure of the Commons*, IPQ, No. 4, 342, 347 (2002) [hereinafter Davis, *Enclosure of the Commons*]. See generally IAN CAMPBELL, A GUIDE TO THE LAW OF THE COMMONS (2d ed. 1976) (1971); G. D. GADSEN, THE LAW OF THE COMMONS (1988).
[22] Campbell, *supra*, note 21 at 7.
[23] Davis, *supra* note 21, at 347.
[24] *Id.*
[25] Eastman Photographic Materials Company v Comptroller General of Patents, Designs and Trade Marks, (1898) H.L. (E.) at 580–81.

Lord Herschell's comment also highlights a second, crucial commonality between how the courts understood a trade mark common and a land common. They viewed both as an arena for a variety of often competing rights. In the case of the land common, those with access to the natural fruits of the land might include the land owner, the commoner and even the landless labourer whose claim was based on custom. In the case of the trade mark common, the courts frequently made clear their view that there were a number of sometimes competing interests that must be considered in defining its boundaries. In "Perfection," the court identified these as trade mark proprietors or, in the words of Cozens-Hardy, "wealthy traders," their "competitors great and small," of both today and of the future, and the general public. Perhaps the leading trade mark judgment, before the implementation of the Directive, which illustrates the courts' recognition that trade mark law, like the law of the common, must negotiate between different, often competing interests, was the House of Lords decision, *W. and G. du Cros Ltd.'s Application (W & G)*.[26] In *W & G*, the applicant, who operated a taxicab service, sought to register the mark *W & G* for motor vehicles. The application was rejected by the Trade Mark Registrar on the basis that the mark lacked distinctiveness, a decision that the House of Lords upheld. In a widely quoted judgment, Lord Parker stated:[27]

> The applicant's chance of success must depend upon whether other traders are likely, in the ordinary course of their business and without any improper motive, to desire to use the same mark, or some mark nearly resembling it, upon or in connection with their own goods. It is apparent from the history of Trade Marks in this country that both the Legislature and the Courts have always shown a natural disinclination to allow any persons to obtain by registration under the Trade Marks Act a monopoly in what others may desire to use.

As characterized by the U.K. courts, the trade mark common, like the land common, was an arena of positive rights and of potentially conflicting interests. The clearest illustration of the courts' recognition of these two fundamental principles in relation to trade mark protection was their refusal, until

---

[26] W. and G. du Cros Ltd.'s Application, (1913) 30 R.P.C. 660. For a further discussion of this case see J. Davis, *The Need to Leave Free for Others to Use and the Trade Mark Common*, in TRADE MARK USE 29–30 [hereinafter *Need to Leave*] (J. Phillips & I. Simon eds., 2005). The judgment has been frequently cited as authority for the view that the law must deny registration to marks which other traders may legitimately desire to use, including in a number of House of Lords judgments. *See, e.g.*, Smith, Kline & French Laboratories Ltd. v Sterling Winthrop Ltd. [1976] R.P.C. 511, 538 (Lord Diplock); YORK Trade Mark, [1984] R.P.C. 231, 253 (Lord Wilberforce).
[27] *W. and G. du Cros Ltd.'s Application*, 30 R.P.C. at 671.

the implementation of the Trade Mark Directive, to allow the registration of certain signs, even though they were recognized as a badge of origin by consumers, in order to ensure that the public had a continuing right of access to them. The legal basis for the refusal to register these distinctive signs was to be found in sections 9 and 10 of the 1938 Trade Marks Act, which related to the registration of descriptive and non-distinctive signs.[28] Put briefly, these sections purported to allow the registration of such signs if they had acquired distinctiveness through use. In interpreting these sections, however, the courts drew a distinction between trade marks which were capable in fact of acting as a badge of origin,[29] and those which, while they were distinctive in fact, were incapable of being distinctive in law and could not be registered. The U.K. courts chose to place in this latter category factually distinctive marks which they believed other traders and the general public should have a continuing right to use. In the leading case, "Yorkshire Copper",[30] the House of Lords once again employed the metaphor of the common to justify this approach.

The "Yorkshire Copper" case concerned an application to register the word "Yorkshire" for copper "solid-drawn tubes and capillary fittings." It was accepted by all parties that "to everyone concerned with the trade in these goods the word 'Yorkshire' had lost its primary geographical significance and become 100 per cent distinctive of the Applicants." The application was refused by the Registrar and the appeal eventually reached the House of Lords.[31] The House of Lords upheld the decision of the Registrar. In his leading judgment, Lord Simonds L.C. cited the *W & G* decision as authority[32] for the proposition that courts had discretion to deny registration to factually

---

[28] These sections were pre-figured by section 9 of the 1905 Trade Marks Act as amended by the Trade Marks Act 1919.

[29] Either because they were initially distinctive or, if they were descriptive, had acquired distinctiveness through use. For a fuller discussion of these sections, see Davis, *supra* note 21, at 352.

[30] Yorkshire Copper Works Ltd.'s Application for a Trade Mark, (1954) 71 R.P.C. 150.

[31] For the Court of Appeal decision, see Yorkshire Copper Works Ltd. v Registrar of Trade Marks, (1952) 70 R.P.C. 1 (CA).

[32] A further authority, cited by Lord Simonds, was the Liverpool Electric Cable Coy. Ltd's Application, (1929) 45 R.P.C. 99 (holding that the courts had discretion to refuse registration of the mark LIVERPOOL). In that case, Lord Hanworth stated that, ". . . When you come to regard the rights of the public at large, the traders at Liverpool and the like, it appears to me that the Registrar would be quite right in holding that a word of that importance and significance ought not to be treated as a word capable of distinguishing, because it has not merely to be capable in fact, but it must be capable in law." *Id.* at 118 (Lord Hanworth, J.).

distinctive marks if other traders might wish to use them. He noted that "a geographical name can only be inherently adapted to distinguish the goods of A. when you can predicate of it that it is such a name as it would never occur to B. to use in respect of his similar goods." He went on:

> Just as a manufacturer is not entitled to a monopoly of a laudatory or descriptive epithet, so he is not to claim for his own territory, whether country, county or town, which may be in the future, if it is not now, the seat of manufacture of goods similar to his own.
> There will probably be border-line cases, but there is, in my opinion, no doubt on which side of the border lies Yorkshire, a county not only of broad acres but of great manufacturing cities.[33]

In his assenting judgment, Lord Cohen paid homage, as had the Master of the Rolls in the Court of Appeal, to the words of both Cozens-Hardy M.R. and Farwell L.J. in *Perfection*, thus explicitly linking the Yorkshire Copper decision to the metaphor of the trade mark common. Indeed, as late as the 1980s, the courts continued to cite the line of authority from *Perfection* to *W & G* to *Yorkshire Copper* when refusing registration to distinctive marks which others might wish to use. Thus, once again, in *York Trailer* in 1981, Lord Wilberforce refused registration for *York*, although this time in relation to freight containers and trailers, despite its factual distinctiveness on the grounds that, as he put it:[34]

> In relation to certain words, of which laudatory epithets and some geographical names were established examples, traders could not obtain a monopoly in the use of such words (however distinctive) to the detriment of members of the public who, in the future, and in connection with other goods, might desire to use them.

During this same period, the U.K. courts also took a similar approach to factually distinctive shape marks. The most prominent case in this regard was *Coca Cola Trade Marks*. In refusing Coca Cola's application to register the shape of the distinctive Coca Cola bottle, Lord Templeman stated that the application was an "attempt to expand the boundaries of intellectual property and to convert a protective law into a source of monopoly."[35]

---

[33] Interestingly, in his description of Yorkshire as both a sign but also a distinct geographical area, Lord Simonds seems to be conflating the trade mark common with common land.
[34] York Trade Mark, [1984] R.P.C. 231, 254.
[35] Coca Cola Trade Marks, [1986] R.P.C. 421 (H.L.); *see* Davis, *supra* note 21, at 353.

III. The Trade Mark Directive and the enclosure of the common

The struggle over land enclosure was a lengthy one, beginning in the fifteenth century and ending with a decisive victory for land owners in the 1840s.[36] The demise of the trade mark common has been far swifter, and is a result of the implementation of the E.U. Trade Mark Directive in 1994. Superficially, it would appear that E.U. trade mark law, like the U.K. courts before the 1994 Trade Marks Act, recognizes a number of parties as having an interest in trade mark registration. Thus, according to the ECJ in *Arsenal v Reed*:[37]

> Trade mark rights constitute an essential element in the system of undistorted competition which the Treaty is intended to establish and maintain. In such a system, undertakings must be able to attract and retain customers by the quality of their goods or services, which is made possible only by distinctive signs allowing them to be identified.
>
> In that context, the essential function of a trade mark is to guarantee the identity of origin of the marked goods or services to the consumer or end user by enabling him, without any possibility of confusion, to distinguish the goods or services from others which have another origin. . . . For that guarantee of origin, which constitutes the essential function of a trade mark, to be ensured, the proprietor must be protected against competitors wishing to take unfair advantage of the status and reputation of the trade mark by selling products illegally bearing it.

Thus, in interpreting the Trade Mark Directive, the ECJ has recognized that the interests of the proprietor, its competitors and consumers all play a role. However, the important difference is, to quote one historian commenting on the arguments in favour of land enclosure, that the Directive shifts "the terms of analysis from a language of rights to a language of markets."[38]

According to the Trade Mark Directive's preamble, trade mark harmonization was necessary because disparities between trade mark protection granted in Member States might "impede the free movement of goods and freedom to provide services and may distort competition within the common market . . . ." The Trade Mark Directive therefore was designed to remove these impediments to the free functioning of the market. Implicit in this approach is the assumption that unimpeded competition best serves the interests of all market

---

[36] Although the enclosure movement began in the fifteenth century, a majority of common land was still open in the eighteenth century. Most of it had been enclosed by 1840, largely through an accretion of Private Acts. *See* J. M. NEESON, COMMONERS: COMMON RIGHT, ENCLOSURE AND SOCIAL CHANGE IN ENGLAND, 1700–1820 at 5 (1993).

[37] Arsenal Football Club plc v Reed, [2003] R.P.C. 144, ¶ 47, 48 & 50; *see also* Case C-10/89 HAG GF, [1990] E.C.R. I-3711, ¶ 13; Case 102/77 Hoffman-La Roche, [1978] E.C.R. 1139, ¶ 7; Case C-349/95 Loendersloot, [1997] ECR I-6227, ¶ 22.

[38] E. P. THOMPSON, CUSTOMS IN COMMON 162 (1991) (referring to the achievement of Adam Smith in justifying the enclosure movement).

actors, including traders and consumers.³⁹ By contrast, the UK courts had assumed that trade mark registration might impact upon a number of different, and at times, irreconcilable interests. One indication of the different approach taken by the Directive is to be found in the contrasting language of the Directive and of the trade mark common. The former speaks of traders and of consumers, who are of course defined by their role in the market. The latter was defined in relation not only to traders but also to the general public whose interests were at times defined as being opposed to those of the market.⁴⁰

The primacy which the Directive gives to the market in determining the limits of trade mark protection can also be seen in the articles dealing with the registration of non-distinctive, descriptive and generic marks. As we have seen, the U.K. courts sought to protect the diverse interests, frequently described as "rights," of proprietors, other traders and the general public, by delineating a protected common of trade marks which stood outside the market mechanism. In a number of cases, the courts determined that certain marks which had acquired distinctiveness on the market should nonetheless be left free for others to use. By contrast, under the Directive, all marks which are deemed to be distinctive in the market will be registered. Thus, according to Art. 2 of the Directive, to be registered, a trade mark must be capable of acting as a badge of origin.⁴¹ Article 3 of the Trade Mark Directive then identifies marks which may not be registered. This category includes marks which do not satisfy Art. 2 (Art. 3(1)(a)). It also includes marks which are devoid of distinctive character (Art. 3(1)(b)), descriptive marks (Art. 3(1)(c)) and generic marks (Art. 3(1)(c)). However, the category of marks identified by Art. 3(1)(b–d) may be registered provided that before the date of registration and following the use made of them, they have acquired a distinctive character through use (Art. 3(3)).⁴² The obvious implication of Art. 3 of the Directive is that the boundary of the domain of marks which should be left free for others to use will now be determined not by courts acting to protect the interests of disparate groups, but by the market itself.⁴³ This understanding of Art. 3 has

---

³⁹ See J. Davis, *A European Constitution for IPRs? Competition, Trade Marks and Culturally Significant Signs*, 41 COMMON MARKET L.R., August 2004, at 1005.

⁴⁰ Thus, it may be argued that in the *Yorkshire Copper* case, the House of Lords was not merely concerned that other traders should be free to use the word "Yorkshire" as an indication of origin for their own goods, but that Yorkshire's other meaning as a place rather an indication of origin would remain available to the general public.

⁴¹ It must also be capable of graphic representation.

⁴² The equivalent in the 1994 Trade Marks Act is § 3.

⁴³ Thus, a Department of Trade and Industry Report which preceded the 1994 Act stated that "if a sign functions in the market place as a trade mark, it is to be recognised as trade mark." Dep't of Trade and Industry, Reform of Trade Marks Law D.T.I. C.M. 1203 (1990), at 301. *See also*, Davis, *supra* note 21, at 356–9.

been confirmed in a number of decisions from the ECJ which followed the implementation of the Trade Mark Directive by Member States. However, it is possible to identify two key judgments, decided over a three-year period, whose effect was to enclose the trade mark common. These two cases are *Windsurfing*[44] and *Philips*.[45]

In *Windsurfing*, the mark at issue was the name "Chiemsee," which is a Bavarian lake popular with tourists. Windsurfing had a registration for the word "Chiemsee," combined with other graphic elements, for clothing which it produced locally. In Germany, the word "Chiemsee" on its own had been refused registration because it was regarded as an indication of geographical origin and under German trade mark law, before the implementation of the Directive, geographical names were refused registration if there was a perceived and present need to leave them free for others to use.[46] Among the questions addressed to the ECJ was first whether Art. 3 recognized a public interest in allowing descriptive signs, including geographical names, to be left free for others to use and second, whether the factual distinctiveness of a sign should be judged differently depending upon the degree of need to leave free. The ECJ confirmed that the public interest behind Art. 3(1)(c) was that descriptive signs should be freely available for others to use. Indeed, it held that included amongst such signs would be not only geographical designations which were already associated with the goods concerned, but also signs for which it was reasonable to assume such an association might arise in the future. Such a finding would appear to be compatible with the U.K. approach to geographical names and the trade mark common. However, it was in answer to the second question that the ECJ diverged from the common approach. It held that, in judging the factual distinctiveness of a mark which should be left free for others to use, no different standards should be applied to geographic terms than in judging marks in general for the purposes of registration. In other words, once such marks had acquired distinctiveness in the market, then under Art. 3(3) they could be registered, whatever the initial public interest in leaving them free.[47]

---

[44] Windsurfing Chiemsee Produktions- und Vertriebs GmbH v Boots- und Segelzubehor Walter Huber and Franz Attenberger, Joined Cases C-108/97 and C-109/97, [1999] E.T.M.R. 585.

[45] Koninklijke Philips Elecs. NV v Remington Consumer Prods. Ltd., Case C-299/99, [2002] E.T.M.R. 955.

[46] Under the doctrine of "Freihaltebedürfnis". *See* A. Fox, *Does the Harmonisation Directive Recognise a Public Interest in Keeping Non-distinctive Signs Free for others to Use?*, EIPR 4 (2002).

[47] For a more detailed discussion, see Davis, *supra* note 21, at 359–60 and *Need to Leave*, *supra* note 26, at 36.

The decision in *Windsurfing* appeared to preclude the U.K. courts from continuing to defend a trade mark common, characterized by a category of marks which should be left free in the public interest despite their factual distinctiveness. Three years later the question of whether the distinction between marks which were distinctive in fact but not in law had survived the Directive was addressed directly to the ECJ in the *Philips* case. Philips had a U.K. registration for the graphic representation of the shape and configuration of the head of a three-headed rotary electric shaver. Remington began to market its own three-headed rotary shaver and Philips sued for trade mark infringement. In turn, Remington argued, inter alia, that the Philips mark lacked distinctiveness and was descriptive and should be revoked. The High Court agreed[48] and Philips appealed. Among the questions addressed to the ECJ by the Court of Appeal[49] was the following: is there a category of marks that is not excluded by Art. 3(1)(b), (c) and (d) of the Directive, but which is nonetheless excluded from registration as being incapable of distinguishing the goods of the proprietor from those of other undertakings (Art. 3(1)(a) of the Directive).

Philips argued that following *Windsurfing* it was no longer possible to identify a category of marks which were distinctive in fact, but yet were incapable of distinguishing in law. In response Remington contended that there were signs which would be caught by Art. 3(1)(a)[50] of the Directive and which would never be capable of acting as a badge of origin. In its judgment, the ECJ pointed out Art. 3(1)(a) of the Directive excluded the registration of signs which were incapable of distinguishing the goods and services of one undertaking from those of other undertakings, while Art. 3(1)(b), (c) and (d) precluded the registration of signs which were devoid of distinctive character, descriptive or generic. However, citing *Windsurfing*, it noted that Art. 3(3) "adds a significant qualification to the rule laid down by Art. 3(1)(b), (c) and (d) in that it provides that a sign may, through use, acquire a distinctive character which it initially lacked and thus be registered as a trade mark." It went on to hold that Art. 3(1)(a) of the Directive, like the rule laid down by Art. 3(1)(b), (c) and (d), precludes the registration of signs or indications which do not meet the condition of being capable of distinguishing.[51] However, all signs which were capable of distinguishing through "nature" or had acquired distinctiveness through "nurture" would be registrable. It concluded: "It follows that there is no class of marks having a distinctive character by their

---

[48] Philips Elecs. BV v Remington Consumer Prods., [1998] R.P.C. 283.
[49] Philips Elecs. BV v Remington Consumer Prods., [1999] R.P.C. 890.
[50] Koninklijke Philips Electronics NV v Remington Consumer Products Ltd., Case C-299/99, [2002] E.T.M.R. at para. 34 (E.C.J.).
[51] *Id.* at ¶ 38.

nature or the use made of them which is not capable of distinguishing goods or services within the meaning of Art. 2 of the Directive."[52]

Philips thus made clear that the distinction, which was fundamental to the maintenance of a trade mark common, between marks which were capable in fact of being registered but were incapable in law, had not survived the Directive. There then followed a number of judgments by the ECJ which affirmed that whatever the initial public interest in leaving signs free for others to use (either because the signs were non-distinctive or descriptive), such signs could be registered if they had acquired distinctiveness. Most notable were two cases involving shape marks and colour marks, respectively. Thus, in *Linde*,[53] the marks at issue were three-dimensional shapes of goods marks, including a three-dimensional shape of a vehicle for motorized trucks. We have seen that before the Directive, the U.K. courts had refused to register factually distinctive shape marks. One of the questions put to the ECJ in *Linde* was whether, when assessing the distinctiveness of a three-dimensional shape of goods mark, a more stringent test be applied than for other types of trade mark, whether because it was devoid of distinctive character or was descriptive. In answer, the ECJ reiterated their finding in *Philips*, that any sign may constitute a trade mark provided it satisfies Art. 2 of the Directive and is capable of distinguishing the goods of one trader from those of any other. In the case of marks which are devoid of distinctive character, there was a public interest in not allowing the registration of non-distinctive marks. However, in judging whether such marks had acquired distinctiveness the ECJ held that no "stricter criteria than used for other categories of trade mark ought to be applied."[54] In relation to the issue of descriptiveness, the ECJ cited *Windsurfing* to the effect that the Directive pursues the public interest in denying registration to descriptive signs, which should be freely used by all. But it also noted that the relevant registering authority must apply the "same concrete examination" in relation to descriptive marks as it would for other marks.[55] Thus, while under Art. 3(c), a purely descriptive mark (such as a shape of goods mark) should not be registered ab initio, once it had acquired distinctiveness on the market it could be registered.[56]

---

[52] *Id.* at ¶ 39.
[53] Linde AG v Deutsches Patent- und Markenamt, Joined Cases C-53/01 to C-55/01, [2003] R.P.C. 45.
[54] *Id.* at ¶ 46. Although the ECJ acknowledged that in the case of signs which the public is not used to perceiving as trade marks, establishing distinctiveness may prove more difficult. *Id.* at ¶ 48.
[55] *Id.* at ¶ 75.
[56] *Id.* at ¶ 77.

The second case, *Libertel*,[57] concerned the registration of the colour orange for telecommunications goods and services. Among the questions addressed to the ECJ was whether it was possible for a single specific colour to acquire distinctive character and, if so, in what circumstances would the relevant authority accept that it had acquired such character. The ECJ was also asked whether, in assessing whether the colour had acquired distinctive character, account should be taken of a "general public interest in availability, such as can exist in respect of signs which denote a geographical origin."[58] In answer, the ECJ first held that while a colour per se cannot be "presumed" to constitute a sign, depending upon the context in which it is used, it is capable of doing so.[59] The ECJ noted:[60]

> [I]t must be borne in mind that, whilst colours are capable of conveying certain associations of ideas, and of arousing feelings, they possess little inherent capacity for communicating specific ideas, especially since they are commonly and widely used, because of their appeal, in order to advertise and market goods or services, without any specific message.
>
> However that factual finding would not justify the conclusion that colours per se cannot, as a matter of principle, be considered to be capable of distinguishing the goods of one undertaking from those of other undertakings.

The ECJ then turned to the relationship between colours and the public interest. It agreed that because the number of colours is limited, to allow a single trader a monopoly of a colour would be to undermine the aim of the Directive, which was to underwrite a competitive market in the EU. It also noted that the purpose behind Art. 3 of the Directive was to prevent the registration of non-distinctive signs in the public interest. It concluded:[61]

> As regards registration as trade marks of colours per se, not spatially delimited, the fact that the number of colours actually available is limited means that a small number of trade mark registrations for certain services or goods could exhaust the entire range of colours available. Such an extensive monopoly would be incompatible with a system of undistorted competition, in particular because it would have the effect of creating an unjustified competitive advantage for a single trader

For this reason, there was a public interest in not allowing the registration of

---

[57] Libertel Groep BV v Benelux-Merkenbureau, Case C-104/01, [2003] E.T.M.R. 63.
[58] *Id.* at ¶ 20.
[59] *Id.* at ¶ 27.
[60] *Id.* at ¶ 41 & 42.
[61] *Id.* at ¶ 54.

colours without evidence of acquired distinctiveness through use. However, when addressing the question of whether there was, therefore, a different (and more difficult) test for assessing the factual distinctiveness of a colour for the purposes of registration, it followed *Linde* and *Windsurfing* in finding there was not.[62]

In the years following *Windsurfing*, the ECJ has sought to define that category of signs which might be considered non-distinctive or descriptive in the first instance, and so be caught by Art. 3, more broadly. Thus, in *Wrigley*, the ECJ held that a descriptive term does not have to be in current use by other traders to preclude it from initial registration.[63] More recently, in *Campina v Benelux–Merkenbureau*, it found that a neologism made up of two descriptive words (in this case "Biomild" for yogurt) would still fall foul of Art. 3(1)(c) and would not be registered without acquired distinctiveness.[64] But these cases do not detract from the fact that following *Windsurfing* and *Philips*, the trade mark common as it had been demarcated by the UK courts had been enclosed. Nor was this an unintended consequence of the Directive. Before its passage, the U.K. Government had characterized the Directive as an opportunity to escape from the position that some trade marks were distinctive in fact and not in law: a situation which it described as "unattractive," but to which the courts were bound through "a long history of case law, much of it dating from a period in which trading conditions were very different from today."[65] This sentiment was echoed early after the Directive was adopted, by the Advocate General in *Windsurfing*. Advocate General Cosmas described the distinction made by the U.K. courts between marks distinctive in fact and in law, as exemplified by the *York Trailer Holdings* decision, as a "rigid" and "misconceived" approach which was inconsistent with the Directive.[66]

---

[62] *Id.* at ¶ 76.

[63] OHIM v Wrigley Jr. Co., [2004] R.P.C. 18. The mark at issue was "Doublemint" for chewing gum. This was a Community Trade Mark application, and so the relevant law precluding the registration of descriptive signs was Art. 7 of the Community Trade Mark Regulations (Council Regulation (E.C.) No. 40/94 on the Community trade mark). Art. 7 of the Regulations is equivalent to Art. 3 of the Trade Mark Directive, and the judgment was relevant to both. For further discussion, see *Need to Leave*, *supra* note 26, at 36–57.

[64] Campina Melkunie BV v Benelux-Merkenbureau (Case C-265/000) [2004] E.T.M.R. 58.

[65] U.K. Government White Paper, Reform of Trade Mark Law Cm. 1203 [1990] ¶ 3.08.

[66] Windsurfing Chiemsee Produktions- und Vertriebs GmbH v Boots- und Segelzubehör Walter Huber and Franz Attenberger, [2000] Ch. 523 at ¶ 49–54 (Advocate General Cosmas). For a discussion of *Windsurfing* see A. Fox, *Does the Trade Mark Harmonisation Directive Recognise a Public Interest in Keeping Non-distinctive Signs Free for Use?*, EIPR 4 (2000).

IV. The commons and the public domain compared

The concepts of the "public domain" and the "common" have a long history in intellectual property law in the U.S. and the U.K., respectively. In the case of the U.S., it is generally accepted that the Copyright Clause of the U.S. Constitution, by granting a limited span of protection to copyright works and patents, implicitly demarcated a public domain.[67] Indeed, there is extensive U.S. case law which has recognized the public domain. Interestingly, it has been argued that it was a trade mark case. *Singer Mfg. Co. v June Mfg. Co. No. 6*, decided in 1896,[68] which was the first to explicitly recognize a public domain in relation to intellectual property.[69] Similarly, we have seen that around this same period, the U.K. courts were describing a trade mark common.

For the most part, the public domain has been defined very broadly. It has been characterized as the realm of intellectual production, which is "thought of as unowned, unownable or commonly owned."[70] Or, alternatively, "an invention, creative work, commercial symbol, or any other creation that is not protected by any form of intellectual property."[71] In fact, it may be argued that the public domain has most often been defined in the "negative," containing intellectual property which is "unclaimed," is outside the scope of existing intellectual property protection or whose term of protection has expired.[72] There have also been a number of attempts to define a public domain more positively. Thus, in relation to copyright, Jessica Litman has defined the public domain as a "commons that includes those aspects of copyright works which copyright does not protect."[73] According to James Boyle in his essay, 'The Second Enclosure Movement and the Construction of the Public Domain', it is possible to identify two kinds of public domain. The first would be a negative

---

[67] *See, e.g.*, Jessica Litman, *The Public Domain*, 39 EMORY L.J. 978 (1990). For a recent restatement of this argument, see Edward Lee, *The Public's Domain: The Evolution of Legal Restraints on the Government's Power to Control Public Access Through Secrecy or Intellectual Property*, 55 HASTINGS L.J. 91, 103 (2003–4).
[68] Singer Mfg. Co v June Mfg. Co., 163 U.S. 169 (1896); *see also* Star Brewery Co. v Val. Blatz Brewing Co., 36 App. D.C. 534, 537 (C.A.D.C. 1911).
[69] Lee, *supra* note 67, at 105.
[70] Keith Aoki, *Authors, Inventors and Trade Mark Owners: Private Intellectual Property and the Public Domain*, 18 COLUM.-VLA J.L. & ARTS 1, 2 (1993–4).
[71] J. THOMAS MCCARTHY, MCCARTHY ON TRADEMARKS AND UNFAIR COMPETITION 1:2 (4th Ed. 2003).
[72] W. Van Caenegem, *The Public Domain: Scientia Nullius?*, EIPR 324 (2002); *see also* Lee, *supra* note 67, at 102. In the *Singer* case, for example, the Supreme Court held that a patent, once it had expired, fell "into the domain of things public" as did "the generic designation of the thing." *Id.* at 106.
[73] Litman, *supra* note 67, at 1023.

public domain, "to be made up of works that are completely free for appropriation, transfer, redistribution, copying, performance, and even rebundling into a new creation, itself covered by intellectual property."[74] He then contrasts this "bundle of rights" public domain against one characterized by a "bundle of privileges," and gives as an example of the latter fair use in copyright law.[75]

The commons has also been variously described in relation to intellectual property law. In some instances, the commons and the public domain are used interchangeably.[76] However, it has also been argued, most notably by Boyle, that the two are not the same. Thus, he notes that whereas the public domain is commonly characterized as "a realm of vaguely defined 'freedom,' the commons may be defined as a 'realm of collective, and sometimes informal controls . . . without the need for single party ownership.'"[77] Peter Drahos, in his book, *A Philosophy of Intellectual Property*,[78] identifies four types of commons. These are: an inclusive, positive community where the intellectual commons is a global resource whose ownership is shared by all, but where it is possible to have private property in goods produced using resources from it; an inclusive negative community, where the commons does not belong to anyone but anyone may take ownership of it; an exclusive negative community, where ownership in things in the commons is open only to a group; and an exclusive positive community, where ownership of "things in the commons" is by a specific group, therefore excluding those who are not members of the group.[79] It is notable that while the commons described by Boyle and Drahos do not necessarily coincide with the public domain,[80] neither do they fit with the trade mark common as defined by the U.K. courts. Indeed, quite the opposite. The trade mark common was a creature of positive law. It was not viewed as a global resource or a realm of collective controls;

---

[74] James Boyle, *The Second Enclosure Movement and the Construction of the Public Domain*, 66 LAW AND CONTEMP. PROBS. 33, 68 (2003), [hereinafter *Second Enclosure Movement*]; *see also*, James Boyle, *Foreword: The Opposite of Property?*, 66 LAW AND CONTEMP. PROBS. 1, 2–29 (2003) [hereinafter *Opposite of Property*]. *See generally* WILLIAM M. LANDES AND RICHARD A POSNER, THE ECONOMIC STRUCTURE OF INTELLECTUAL PROPERTY 12–13 (2003) (making the distinction between the commons and the public domain).
[75] *Second Enclosure Movement*, *supra* note 74, at 68.
[76] *See, e.g.*, Litman, *supra* note 67, at 1023; *see also* LAWRENCE LESSIG, THE FUTURE OF IDEAS: THE FATE OF THE COMMONS IN A CONNECTED WORLD (2001).
[77] *Opposite of Property*, *supra* note 74, at 8.
[78] PETER DRAHOS, A PHILOSOPHY OF INTELLECTUAL PROPERTY (1996).
[79] *Id.*, at 57–8.
[80] Although, Drahos's inclusive, positive community ironically appears to have most in common with a negative public domain.

instead it was defined by the courts as an arena of conflicting interests and positive rights. While it was the law, most notably successive Trade Mark Acts, which protected the rights of traders to register non-distinctive or descriptive marks which had acquired distinctiveness, that same law, as interpreted by the courts, ensured that in certain cases, these marks should remain available for use by other traders and the public at large. In other words, in certain instances the right of the minority ("the wealthy trader") to register a trade mark was trumped by the right of the majority to have continuing access to it.

The question remains as to why the public domain remains a vital concept in U.S. intellectual property law, including trade mark law, despite the fact that many commentators believe that it also now subject to unprecedented attack, while the trade mark common was so easily enclosed.[81] It is submitted here the public domain has survived and adapted to judicial and statutory inroads precisely because the public domain was initially defined in a largely negative fashion. Thus, in the early case, *Singer*, which concerned the genericization of the name "Singer" for sewing machines, the Supreme Court compared the expiration of a patent, which then enters the public domain, to the genericization of a trade mark. It noted: "It is elementary that there is a right of property in a name which the courts will protect. But this right, like the right to an arbitrary mark or any other, may become public property by dedication or abandonment."[82]

In the case of the word, "Singer," it was held that it

> had become public property, and the defendant had a right to use it. Clearly, as the word 'Singer' was dedicated to the public, it could not be taken by the Singer Company out of the public domain by the mere fact of using that name as one of the constituent elements of a trade-mark.[83]

In later trade mark cases, this negative definition of the public domain continued.[84] In *Coca-Cola v Nehi*, Coca-Cola failed to prevent a competitor from

---

[81] An apt example would be Eldred v Ashcroft, 537 U.S. 186 (2003), which retrospectively increased the copyright term, but where a great deal of the argument was directed to the effect of this extension on the public domain. Another case which considered the effect of copyright extension on the public domain was Dastar Corp. v Twentieth Century Fox Film Corp., 539 U.S. 23 (2003). In this case, the Supreme Court refused to extend unregistered trade mark protection to videotapes, for which the copyright had expired. In both case, it is fair to say that the public domain at issue was a negative one.

[82] Singer Mfg. Co. v June Mfg. Co., 163 U.S. 169, 186 (1896).

[83] *Singer*, 163 U.S. at 203.

[84] *See, e.g.*, Shredded Wheat Co. v Humphrey Cornell Co., 250 F. 960 (2d Cir. 1918).

using the word "cola" for its drinks, despite the fact that "Coca-Cola" was a registered trade mark. According to the Court, the word "cola" is "in the public domain, incapable of exclusive appropriation, and apart from special circumstances, may be freely used denominatively, provided that the name as a whole is not deceptively similar to 'Coca-Cola'."[85]

More recently, in *Wal-Mart Stores Inc. v Samara Bros*,[86] the U.S. Supreme Court held that § 43(a) of the Lanham Act will not protect unregistered trade dress, in that case product design, without proof that it has acquired secondary meaning. However, this case, while recognizing the need to ensure that certain signs remain in the public domain ab initio, takes a similar approach to the protection of marks with acquired distinctiveness as has been taken by the ECJ following the implementation of the Directive. In other words, it does not allow, as had the U.K. courts before the Directive, for a category of signs which will not be protected even with acquired distinctiveness.

V. Conclusion

At roughly the same period that the U.K. courts were defining a trade mark common, the U.S. courts introduced the concept of the public domain into trade mark law.[87] It is submitted here that it is precisely because the public domain was defined negatively as a respository of signs which could be freely appropriated (provided that is they were either distinctive or had acquired distinctiveness), that it has been able to maintain its relevance in trade mark law.[88] Indeed, it is possible to argue that the manner in which the ECJ has interpreted Art. 3 of the Trade Mark Directive resulted in the creation of a public domain which, in all but name, closely mirrors that which exists in the

---

[85] Coca-Cola Co. v Nehi Corp., 36 A.2d 156, 161 (Del. 1944). This was also a case of unfair competition, equivalent to the U.K. law of unregistered trade marks or passing off, as was of course the *House of David* case which began this article.

[86] Wal-Mart Stores Inc. v Samara Bros., 529 U.S. 205 (2002). For comment, see W. S. Hunt, *The Supreme Court's Mixed Messages on the Public Domain: Cases Interpreting Section 43 of the Lanham Act*, 93 KY. L.J. 787, 797 (2004–5). The Supreme Court took a similar approach to *Libertel* in relation to colours, although it was concerned with unregistered marks, in Qualitex Co. v Jacobson Prods. Co., 514 U.S. 159 (1995). It held that colours could function as trademarks provided they had acquired distinctiveness through use.

[87] The concept of the public domain also arose in U.S. trade mark law in relation to 'abandonment', i.e. non-use of a registered trade mark. *See, e.g.*, Dupont Cellophane Co. Inc. v Waxed Products Co. Inc., 6 F. Supp. 859 (D.C.N.Y. 1934). For a recent case, see ITC Ltd. v Punchgini Inc., 482 F.3d. 135 (2d Cir. 2007).

[88] This would be as true for signs which had once had distinctiveness but had entered the public domain because they were no longer distinctive, such as "Singer," as it would for signs which had a descriptive meaning.

U.S. in relation to trade marks. By contrast, as we have seen, the U.K. trade mark common was understood by the courts not as a negative domain but rather as an arena of positive rights. However, just as the land common was undone by statute, so the trade mark common was similarly vulnerable, once the prevailing discourse had changed to one which privileged the market over collective rights. Furthermore, when the U.K. courts adopted the metaphor of the common, they did so with the land common in mind. Their adoption of the common metaphor in trade mark law was thus rooted in a particular, historical reality which could not be altered to accommodate changing views of the role of the trade mark in the market place. Indeed, it is perhaps illuminating to recognize that the concept of the public domain in intellectual property law also draws in some measure from the law of real property. As we have seen, in the U.K., common land was traditionally privately owned but there was a class of people, often very broadly defined, who had positive, but differing, rights to its fruits. In the United States, by contrast, land in the public domain is regulated under the "public trust doctrine," where the legal title is held by the state and *all citizens have an equitable interest* in it.[89]

It is a cliché, but nonetheless true, that it is the victor who writes history. Following the enclosure of the land common, in the early nineteenth century, the United Kingdom entered upon a period characterized by unprecedented industrial and agricultural output. For many academics and social commentators, the enclosure movement was a necessary precondition for the country's increasing prosperity.[90] More recently, historians have questioned whether common land was in truth an impediment to the efficient exploitation of land—certainly many would argue that land held in common ensured a more

---

[89] L. L. Butler, *The Commons Concept: An Historical Concept with Modern Relevance*, 23 WM. & MARY L.R. 855 (1982) (emphasis added); *see also* Carol Rose, *The Comedy of the Commons: Custom, Commerce, and Inherently Public Property*, 53 U. CHI. L. REV. 711, 711–23, 739–49 (1986). It has been suggested that the public domain concept in U.S. intellectual property law derived not from its use in the U.S. to describe public land, but rather from the French "domaine public." *See Second Enclosure Movement, supra* note 74, at 58. Indeed, the *Singer* case makes numerous references to French law. However, Lee, *supra* note 67, convincingly argues that the court has a more land-based metaphor in mind because it specifies that the public domain "contains—things public," and he notes, "'Public things' are things owned by the public to which they have unrestricted rights," a notion which has more in common with the U.S. concept of *publici juris* than with the French "domaine public." *Id.* at 106–07.

[90] The orthodox view is to be found in J. D. CHAMBERS & G. E. MINGAY, THE AGRICULTURAL REVOLUTION, 1750–1880 (1986) and J. D. Chambers, *Enclosure and Labour Supply in the Industrial Revolution*, ECON. HIST. REV. 391–443, 2nd Series, 5 (1953). NEESON, *supra* note 36, at 46–8.

equal distribution of its products.[91] However, the idea that without enclosure, there would have been a "tragedy of the commons," has found its way out of history and into other academic disciplines,[92] including law. Thus, William Landes and Richard Posner argue in favour of property rights in intellectual production, because the alternative would be "overgrazing." Adopting the common metaphor, they write: "The enclosure movement in England transformed common pastures into private property. Although much criticized on grounds of distributive (in)justice, the movement increased agricultural productivity enormously, though less by eliminating crowding of pastures than by reducing transaction costs."[93]

It follows, according to Landes and Posner, that intellectual property rights have the same positive effects. As I have argued elsewhere, the U.K. judiciary was not a notable opponent of land enclosure.[94] Nonetheless, it is submitted that in considering trade mark law, the judges recognized that enclosure of the trade mark common, like that of the land common, would have at least one inevitable result. It would cede greater power to the "wealthy trader" to monopolize the resources of the common, whether it be the fruits of the soil in relation to land or the English language in relation to trade marks.[95] In seek-

---

[91] *See, e.g.*, C. J. DAHLMAN, THE OPEN FIELD SYSTEM AND BEYOND (1980). This point has also been made by Boyle, *supra* note 74, at 36.

[92] Most notably, it was introduced by Garrett Hardin into environmental studies in his seminal article, *The Tragedy of the Commons*, 162 SCIENCE 1243 (1968). He wrote that all things being equal, "where a number of users have access to a common-pool resource, the total resource units will be greater than the optimal economic level of withdrawal." *Id.* Hardin's pessimism was questioned by E. Olstrom in GOVERNING THE COMMONS: THE EVOLUTION OF INSTITUTIONS FOR COLLECTIVE ACTION 3 (1990). Later, Hardin himself amended his views by arguing that the tragedy of the commons occurs only when scarce resources are unmanaged. *See* G. Hardin, *The Tragedy of the Unmanaged Commons: Population and the Disguises of Providence*, in COMMONS WITHOUT TRAGEDY: PROTECTING THE ENVIRONMENT—A NEW APPROACH 162 (R. V. Andelson ed., 1991).

[93] LANDES & POSNER, *supra* note 74, at 12. In fact, Landes and Posner misunderstand the nature of the English land common. They assume that it was uncultivated, when much of it was highly cultivated and they also assume that it was privately owned. Indeed, in the view of the courts, the "English language common" was itself highly cultivated.

[94] Davis, *Enclosure of the Commons*, *supra* note 21, at 349.

[95] Thus, in Nichols Plc's Trade Mark Application [2003] R.P.C. 16, Mr. J. Jacob, at ¶ 13 (citing Cozens-Hardy in *In re* Joseph Crosfield & Sons Ltd. to Register a Trade Mark, (1909) 26 R.P.C. 387), questioned whether use of a mark descriptively was an adequate defence to trade mark infringement, given that "in the practical world powerful traders will naturally assert their rights even in marginal cases. By granting registration of a semi-descriptive or indeed a nearly-but-not-quite-completely descriptive mark one is placing a powerful weapon in powerful hands. Registration will

ing to prevent the enclosure of the English language common for almost a century, it was this latter result that the courts set out to avoid. With the benefit of hindsight, it can be argued that in both cases it was a losing battle.

---

require the public to look to its defences." The case concerned the registration of a common surname, which was held to be non-distinctive. In the ECJ, it was held that common surnames could be registered provided they had acquired distinctiveness. It was also held that the criteria for judging acquired distinctiveness should be no stricter than those for other marks.

14 Tolerating confusion about confusion: trademark policies and fair use
*Graeme W. Austin**

I. Introduction

A straightforward explanation of trademark law might go something like this: trademark law prohibits unauthorized uses of trademarks to protect against the likelihood[1] that "ordinarily prudent" consumers will be confused about the source of products and services by misleading uses of others' trademarks.[2] Consequently, trademark law protects firms against the misappropriation of the goodwill that their trademarks represent.[3] Protection of trademarks encour-

---

* J. Byron McCormick Professor of Law, James E. Rogers College of Law, University of Arizona. © Graeme Austin 2006. Thanks to Graeme Dinwoodie, Mark Janis, Bryan Patchett, Susy Frankel, Ellen Bublick, Robert Burrell and Paul Myburgh for their insightful comments on an earlier draft of this chapter. A version of this chapter also appears as an essay in 50 ARIZONA L. REV. (2008).

[1] *See, e.g.,* Lois Sportswear, U.S.A., Inc. v Levi Strauss & Co., 799 F.2d 867, 875 (2d Cir. 1986) (actual confusion need not be shown).

[2] As Professor Robert Bone explains, moral arguments provide another set of explanations for protecting trademark rights, including prohibiting "lying or intentional deception" and "unjust enrichment," and protecting "consumer autonomy." Robert G. Bone, *Enforcement Costs and Trademark Puzzles*, 90 VA. L. REV 2099, 2105–08 (2004) [hereinafter Bone, *Enforcement Costs*] (discussing the "standard policy arguments" supporting protecting trademark rights). Whereas moral concerns once featured more prominently in Anglo-American trademark and unfair competition doctrine (*see, e.g.,* Thomson v Winchester, 36 Mass. 214, 217 (1837) (showing of "fraud" required in trademark infringement actions)), economic rationales now tend to dominate in U.S. trademark law. *See, e.g.,* Qualitex Co. v Jacobson Prods. Co., Inc., 514 U.S. 159, 163–4 (1995); Ty Inc. v Perryman, 306 F.3d 509, 510 (7th Cir. 2002). *See also infra* Section II.

[3] This rationale has a long history. *See* McLean v Fleming, 96 U.S. 245, 252 (1877):

> [T]he court proceeds on the ground that the complainant has a valuable interest in the goodwill of his trade or business, and, having adopted a particular label, sign, or trade-mark, indicating to his customers that the article bearing it is made or sold by him or by his authority, or that he carries on business at a particular place, he is entitled to protection against one who attempts to deprive him of his trade or customers by using such labels, signs, or trade-mark without his knowledge or consent.

Justice Story once characterized the harm in trademark infringement case as follows:

ages firms to maintain, and preferably enhance, their goodwill.[4] This provides firms with an incentive to compete, and, as a result, consumers get better products and services.[5]

Anti-dilution statutes[6] protect trademark owners against changes to consumers' impressions of trademarks that trademark owners don't want to see happen: in particular, these laws protect against other firms' marks coming to mind when consumers think about the senior user's mark in ways that alter consumers' impressions of the senior mark. A consumer protection rationale has also been advanced for anti-dilution laws: these laws protect consumers against incurring "imagination costs."[7] Without prohibitions against dilution, consumers would incur the "cost" of having to filter from their minds a wide variety of different uses of the same trademark. Apparently, this is a problem.[8]

"designed infringement of the rights of the plaintiffs, for the purpose of defrauding the public and taking from the plaintiffs the fair earnings of their skill, labor and enterprise." Taylor v Carpenter, 23 F.Cas. 742, 744 (C.C.D. Mass. 1844). On the historical development of trademark law, *see* Mark P. McKenna, *The Normative Foundations of Trademark Law*, 82 NOTRE DAME L. REV. 1839 (2007).

[4] *See, e.g.*, WILLIAM M. LANDES & RICHARD POSNER, THE ECONOMIC STRUCTURE OF INTELLECTUAL PROPERTY LAW 168 (2003).

[5] Referring to the federal trademark system, for example, the Supreme Court has observed: "The Lanham Act provides national protection of trademarks in order to secure to the owner of the mark the goodwill of his business and to protect the ability of consumers to distinguish among competing producers. National protection of trademarks is desirable, Congress concluded, because trademarks foster competition and the maintenance of quality by securing to the producer the benefits of good reputation." Park 'N Fly, Inc. v Dollar Park and Fly, Inc. 469 U.S. 189, 198 (1985) (citations omitted).

[6] The federal anti-dilution statute is codified at: 15 U.S.C. § 1125(c) (stipulating that injunctive relief is available against another whose conduct is likely to cause dilution "regardless of the presence or absence of actual or likely confusion."). *See also* RESTATEMENT (THIRD) OF UNFAIR COMPETITION § 25(1) (1995) (dilution provides a cause of action for use of a trademark "without proof of a likelihood of confusion").

[7] *Ty Inc. v Perryman*, 306 F.3d at 511.

[8] Some commentators liken the imagination costs that anti-dilution protections apparently spare consumers with the consumer search costs rationale underlying traditional trademark infringement. *See* Stacey L. Dogan & Mark A. Lemley, *The Merchandising Right: Fragile Theory or Fait Accompli?*, 54 EMORY L.J. 461, 493 (2005) [hereinafter Dogan & Lemley, *Merchandising Right*] ("[P]roperly understood, dilution is targeted at reducing consumer search costs, just as traditional trademark law is."). On the consumer search costs rationale, *see* Section II, *infra*. For a contrasting perspective, *see* Graeme W. Austin, *Trademarks and the Burdened Imagination*, 69 BROOK. L. REV. 827, 895 (2004) [hereinafter Austin, *Burdened Imagination*] (questioning whether, even assuming consumers incur imagination costs from dilutive uses of trademarks, these costs should be considered harmful). *See also* Welkowitz, *Reexamining Dilution*, *supra* note 8 (questioning whether *firms* suffer as a result of dilutive uses of their marks); Rebecca Tushnet, *Gone in 60 Milliseconds: Trademark*

If this were all there was to it, trademark law—or, more specifically, the law of trademark infringement[9]—would be quite simple indeed. Primarily "fact based,"[10] it would involve courts determining whether a junior use of a mark was likely to confuse consumers—or, in the dilution context, whether the junior use of the mark would likely[11] change consumers' impressions of the senior user's mark in prohibited ways. But beyond the most obvious case of trademark piracy, or, in the dilution context, flagrant unauthorized use of famous marks, this is an incomplete description of trademark infringement principles. "Likelihood of consumer confusion" and "changed impressions of trademarks" provide analytical starting points. However, the straightforward explanation fails to capture the role that other principles and policies play, and ought to play, in determining the scope of trademark rights.

Recourse to these additional policies and principles is needed because the key concepts governing trademark infringement, "likelihood of consumer confusion" and "dilution," do not provide sufficiently coherent controls on parties' rights and obligations.[12] One reason for this is that a finding of likelihood of confusion is not an unassailable empirical truth. Courts invariably ascertain likely consumer responses to the defendant's unauthorized use of a mark through the filter of a legal test that involves application of a number of

---

Law and Cognitive Science 86 TEX. L. REV. (forthcoming, 2008) (questioning whether assumed and claimed harms of dilution are consistent with insights about human mental processes provided by cognitive science).

[9] "Trademark law" of course concerns many more issues than "infringement."

[10] To the extent that trademark infringement cases are regarded as primarily fact-based, summary judgment is disfavored. *See, e.g.*, KP Permanent Make-Up, Inc. v Lasting Impression I, Inc., 408 F.3d 596, 608 (9th Cir. 2005) (*citing* Clicks Billiards, Inc. v Sixshooters, Inc., 251 F.3d 1252, 1265 (9th Cir. 2001)). Summary judgment may be appropriate, however, where the evidence is clear and tilts heavily in favor of a likelihood of confusion. Nissan Motor Co. v Nissan Computer Corp., 378 F.3d 1002, 1009 (9th Cir. 2004) (affirming summary judgment where the marks were "legally identical," the goods at issue were related, and the marketing channels overlapped). And the Supreme Court has emphasized the importance of the availability of summary judgment in an analogous context. *See* Wal-Mart Stores, Inc. v Samara Bros., Inc., 529 U.S. 205, 213–14 (rejecting the applicability of the test articulated in Seabrook Foods, Inc. v Bar-Well Foods, Ltd., 568 F.2d 1342 (C.C.P.A. 1977) for determining whether product design is inherently distinctive, partly on the ground that the test would reduce the opportunities for summary disposition).

[11] *See* Section III.A. *infra* for discussion of the Trademark Dilution Revision Act of 2006 (TDRA), which provides that "likelihood" is actionable. In this aspect, the TDRA overturns the Supreme Court's judgment in Moseley v V Secret Catalogue, Inc., 537 U.S. 418 (2003) (holding that only *actual* dilution, not *likelihood* of dilution, is actionable under the Lanham Act).

[12] *See generally*, Barton Beebe, *Search and Persuasion in Trademark Law*, 103 MICH. L. REV. 2020 (2005) [hereinafter Beebe, *Search and Persuasion*].

"likelihood of confusion factors."[13] There is considerable uncertainty about some of the key questions that are germane to the factual inquiry at the heart of the likelihood of confusion analysis. Often courts don't get close to ascertaining the actual responses of real consumers. Sometimes this is due to the quality of the evidence. And, when a plaintiff seeks a preliminary injunction, there may be insufficient time. As a result, empiricism in trademark law can only ever be "inchoate." Similar, perhaps more acute, problems arise in the trademark dilution context.[14]

A second reason why trademark rights cannot simply be determined by "factual analyses" of the likelihood of consumer confusion or the dilution of famous trademarks is that the worldview of consumers seems to be vulnerable to manipulation. We usually call this "marketing." The efforts of marketing experts enable firms to "grow" their marks, thereby changing consumer expectations associated with the marks.[15] This is good for firms: their trademarks come to occupy more market space and, as a result, their bundles of property rights get bigger. Whatever the benefits that accrue to firms, however, even the most enthusiastic member of the invisible hand club would be unlikely to think that absolutely everything that is good for business is good for society.[16] A purely fact-based analysis of the likelihood of consumer confusion or of changed impressions of trademarks would not provide sturdy impediments against the trespass of trademark rights on other important legal and social policies—policies that, in some circumstances, might outweigh the interests firms have in protection of their goodwill. Accordingly, rights in a trademark do not, and should not, protect firms against everything other firms might do that would be likely to cause confusion or change consumers' impressions of their trademarks.

In this chapter, I suggest that courts might look a little harder at the role played by the "ordinarily prudent consumer" in trademark law. Protecting consumers from confusion or dilution of trademarks may be a *necessary* component in trademark law, but it may not necessarily be *sufficient*: The law of trademark infringement must also contend with a range of different policies that do, and should, supplement the straightforward story. Once this is acknowledged, such policies may achieve a more secure place in the development of trademark doctrine. Additionally, acknowledging the inchoate quality of the empiricism of the likelihood of confusion and dilution analyses may

---

[13] *See* Barton Beebe, *An Empirical Study of the Multifactor Tests for Trademark Infringement*, 94 CAL. L. REV. 1581 (2007) [hereinafter Beebe, *Empirical Study*].
[14] *See infra* Section III.B.
[15] *See* McKenna, *supra* note 3, at 1899.
[16] *See infra* Section III.

lead to a greater preparedness to weigh countervailing policies and principles more heavily in the scale.

The Supreme Court's most recent foray into trademark infringement doctrine, *KP Permanent Make-Up, Inc. v Lasting Impressions I, Inc.*,[17] provides a useful context in which to explore these ideas. *KP Permanent* concerned trademark fair use, a defense to trademark infringement that applies when a party makes descriptive use of another's trademark. While the Court held that a defendant did not bear the burden of showing that no likelihood of confusion would follow from its descriptive use, it reasoned nevertheless that the degree of likely confusion may be relevant to whether the defendant's actions were "fair," and thus protected by the defense.[18] The Court's approach to fair use tolerates some consumer confusion where the defendant has used the mark fairly to describe its products or services, but it also risks valorizing consumer confusion in a context in which it should be downplayed; moreover, the Court's holding risks constraining the analytical space available in trademark law for expression and development of policy concerns other than those that underlie trademark infringement's straightforward story.

II. Consumers are necessary ...

We usually try to find utilitarian rationales for property rights.[19] We don't like free-riding very much,[20] but we also recognize that "preventing free-riding" is

---

[17] 543 U.S. 111 (2004). In 2007, the Supreme Court handed down a decision on antitrust law that had important consequences for trademark law. Leegan Creative Leather Prods., Ltd. v PSKS, Inc., 127 S. Ct. 2705 (holding that application of per se rule is unwarranted as to vertical agreements to fix minimum resale prices).

[18] 543 U.S. at 123.

[19] As Professor Carol Rose explains, "[a]t the root of ... economic analyses [of property entitlements] lies the perception that it costs something to establish clear entitlements to things, and we won't bother to undertake the task of removing goods from an ownerless 'commons' unless it is worth it to us to do so." Carol M. Rose, *Crystals and Mud in Property Law*, 40 STAN. L. REV. 577, 578 (1988). For a detailed examination of this point in the context of trademark law, see William P. Kratzke, *Normative Economic Analysis of Trademark Law*, 21 MEMPHIS ST. U. L. REV. 199 (1991) [hereinafter Kratzke, *Normative Economic Analysis*]. *See also* Pope Automatic Merch. Co. v McCrum-Howell Co., 191 F. 979, 981–2 (noting dangers of allowing unfair competition suits to protect new products unless a patent right is secured); U.S. Shoe Co. v Brown Group, Inc., 740 F.Supp. 196, 198 (S.D.N.Y. 1990), *aff'd*, 923 F.2d 844 (2d Cir. 1990) ("In general, the law disfavors the grant of exclusive monopoly rights. Exceptions exist, however, where the grant of monopoly rights results in substantial benefits to society.").

[20] David J. Franklyn, *Debunking Dilution Doctrine: Toward a Coherent Theory of the Anti-Free-Rider Principle in American Trademark Law*, 56 HASTINGS L. J. 117, 118 (2004) [hereinafter Franklyn, *Debunking Dilution Doctrine*]. *See also* Austin, *Burdened Imagination*, *supra* note 8, at 845 (exploring ways that concerns about "commercial morality" influence the scope of trademark rights).

usually an insufficiently robust concept to justify creating and enforcing property rights.[21] Indeed, quite a lot of free-riding is necessary for society to function. Much of our culture is, of course, passed on for "free."[22] In commercial contexts, "free-riding" is often just another term for "competition." As a result, copying is the rule, and intellectual property is the exception.[23] Consequently, we tend to require appropriate *justifications* for the creation of property rights whose enforcement inhibits firms from competing with each other on price.

The consumer is central to the utilitarian rationales for trademark law that dominate today.[24] A more elaborate version of the "straightforward story" might be as follows: Assume trademark x symbolizes the goodwill of firm x in certain goods. Absent protections for x's rights in the x mark, firms y, z, a and b could also use trademark x for *their* goods in a manner that confused consumers into thinking that their goods also came from firm x. Providing trademark protections lowers consumers' search costs, by helping consumers to find firm x's goods more easily than would be the case if other firms could use the x mark.[25] It also stops firm x from losing sales to firms y, z, a and b. Everyone wins[26] (except, of course, firms y, z, a and b). To be sure, consumers might pay more for the information trademarks provide—through the premium above marginal cost of goods and services that can be charged by

---

[21] *See generally* Mark A. Lemley, *Property, Intellectual Property and Free Riding*, 83 TEX. L. REV. 1031 (2005).

[22] Wendy J. Gordon, *On Owning Information: Intellectual Property and the Restitutionary Impulse*, 78 VA. L. REV. 149, 167, (1992) (characterizing a "stand-alone prohibition on free riding" as "drastically overbroad," and observing that "[a] culture could not exist if all free riding were prohibited within it").

[23] The Supreme Court has recently explained: "In general, unless an intellectual property right such as a patent or copyright protects an item, it will be subject to copying." TrafFix Devices, Inc. v Marketing Displays, Inc., 532 U.S. 23, 29 (2001).

[24] "Consumers rather than producers are the object of the law's solicitude." Bretford Mf'g, Inc. v Smith Sys. Mfg. Corp., 419 F.3d 576, 581 (7th Cir. 2005). *See* Bone, *Enforcement Costs*, supra note 2. Daniel M. McClure, *Trademarks and Competition: The Recent History*, 59 LAW & CONTEMP. PROBS. 13 (1996).

[25] The Supreme Court appeared to endorse the search costs rationale for trademark protection in *Qualitex*, 514 U.S. at 163–4: "In principle, trademark law, by preventing others from copying a source-identifying mark, 'reduce[s] the customer's costs of shopping and making purchasing decisions,' for it quickly and easily assures a potential customer that *this* item—the item with this mark—is made by the same producer as other similarly marked items that he or she liked (or disliked) in the past." (citation omitted). It also appeared to do so in its 1942 decision in Mishawaka Rubber & Woolen Mfg. Co. v S.S. Kresge Co. 316 U.S. 203, 205 (1942) ("A trade-mark is a merchandising short-cut which induces a purchaser to select what he wants, or what he has been led to believe he wants.").

[26] *See generally* Alex Kozinski, *Trademarks Unplugged*, 68 N.Y.U. L. REV. 960 (1993).

firms with reliable trademarks—but the increased price seems to be good value for money. For consumers, the premium paid for the mark is presumably considered to be cheaper (on average) than searches would otherwise be. The protections firms get for their marks encourage them to produce goods or services of a sufficient quality so that consumers *want* to find them—for trademarks can, of course, also help consumers to avoid goods and services they don't like. But without trademark rights, other firms could brand their goods "*x*," and firm *x* would be unable to sufficiently internalize its investment in the quality of its *x* branded goods.[27] Guarantees of consistent—or, better still, enhanced—quality of goods and services are also good for consumers. Protection of trademarks is thus "win/win."[28]

For a trademark to come to symbolize a firm's goodwill in goods or services, it is usually necessary for the mark to have impacted on consumers' minds.[29] Through use in commerce,[30] the mark needs to have come to designate the source of a firm's goods or services. What goes on in consumers'

---

[27] The Supreme Court has made similar observations on a number of occasions. *See, e.g.*:

> Equity gives relief in such a case, upon the ground that one man is not allowed to offer his goods for sale, representing them to be the manufacture of another trader in the same commodity. Suppose the latter has obtained celebrity in his manufacture, he is entitled to all the advantages of that celebrity, whether resulting from the greater demand for his goods or from the higher price the public are willing to give for the article, rather than for the goods of the other manufacturer, whose reputation is not so high as a manufacturer. (McLean v Fleming, 96 U.S. 245, 251 (24 L.Ed. 828)).

> The law helps assure a producer that it (and not an imitating competitor) will reap the financial, reputation-related rewards associated with a desirable product. The law thereby "encourage[s] the production of quality products," and simultaneously discourages those who hope to sell inferior products by capitalizing on a consumer's inability quickly to evaluate the quality of an item offered for sale. (*Qualitex*, 514 U.S. at 164 (citations omitted)).

[28] It might even be "win/win/win" if we take account of the additional income streams licensing opportunities provide firms that own valuable trademarks.

[29] Kratzke, *Normative Economic Analysis, supra* note 19, at 205 ("Until a word, name, symbol or device plays some informational or identificatory role with respect to a product it has no value.").

[30] The Trademark Law Revision Act of 1988, Pub. L. No. 100-667, 102 Stat. 3935 (1988), amended the Lanham Act to allow priority of trademark rights to be achieved through filing documentation establishing a bona fide *intention* to use a mark. The rights in the trademark are perfected on actual use, however. 15 U.S.C. § 1051(a)(2) (2006).

minds is crucial to both the creation of trademarks, and, in the infringement context, to the scope of trademark rights. Before consumers can be confused about the source of goods or services as a result of a defendant's use of a trademark, we need to be able to say that consumers *recognize* the mark as a symbol for the source of the goods or services. In a crowded marketplace, branding messages sometimes need to be quite strong to achieve this kind of recognition, particularly if a firm selects a trademark that is not particularly distinctive.[31] Likewise, before a defendant's use of a mark can be dilutive, and change consumers' impressions of the plaintiff's mark, the plaintiff's mark needs to have already conveyed a message[32] to consumers about the connection between the mark and the plaintiff's goodwill.

If protecting consumers' interests provides the principal rationale for trademark rights, we might expect to see the scope of those rights limited[33] by that purpose.[34] A number of dicta and some key parts of trademark doctrine suggest that there does exist an important connection between the scope of rights in trademark and the policy of protecting consumer welfare. We see this most clearly when courts refer to the "limited" nature of the property in a trademark.[35] "A trade-mark confers no monopoly whatever in a proper sense," announced the Supreme Court in 1916; "[it] is merely a convenient means for facilitating the protection of one's good-will in trade by placing a distinguishing mark or symbol—a commercial signature—upon the merchandise or the package in

---

[31] *See, e.g.*, Nabisco v Warner-Lambert Co., 32 F. Supp.2d 690 (1999) (identifying the vulnerability of a weak, but suggestive, mark to being "out shouted" by other similar marks already in the marketplace).

[32] Federal trademark dilution law protects only nationally 'famous' trademarks. 15 U.S.C. § 1125(c)(1).

[33] *But see* Beebe, *Search and Persuasion, supra* note 12 (noting the absence of limits in trademark law). *Compare* Graeme B. Dinwoodie, *The Rational Limits of Trademark Law, in* U.S. INTELLECTUAL PROPERTY LAW AND POLICY (H. Hansen ed., 2002) [hereinafter Dinwoodie, *Rational Limits*] (advancing a normative argument in support of affirming "the classic avoidance of consumer confusion rationale" as a key organizing principle for trademark law).

[34] *See, e.g.*, New Kids on the Block v News Am. Publ'n, Inc., 971 F.2d 302, 308 (9th Cir. 1992), where Judge Kozinski characterized trademark use that "does not implicate the source-identification function that is the purpose of trademark" as "not constitut[ing] unfair competition." *Compare* Peaceable Planet, Inc. v Ty, Inc., 362 F.3d 986 (7th Cir. 2004), revealing that the Court of Appeals for the Seventh Circuit, in a case involving a contest over trademarks used in the soft toy market, loosened former limitations on trademark rights by overturning the district court's application of the traditional rule that names are descriptive and require secondary meaning to function as trademarks.

[35] *But cf.* Avery Dennison Corp. v Sumpton, 189 F.3d 868, 875 (9th Cir. 1999), where the Ninth Circuit characterized prohibitions against trademark dilution as coming "very close to granting rights in gross in a trademark" (citations omitted).

which it is sold."[36] Thus, there is no "property" in the trademark except to the extent that the mark symbolizes a firm's goodwill in particular types of goods and/or services.[37]

An important doctrinal corollary of all of this is that the same word or device—let's say the word mark—SPARROW—can, when used as a trademark, mean different things in different marketing contexts. SPARROW used in the marketing of breakfast cereal is a different trademark from SPARROW when used in the marketing of electronic goods. Assuming the SPARROW mark is not sufficiently famous to benefit from anti-dilution prohibitions, the scope of the property rights in the mark is determined by what consumers consider "SPARROW" to mean in the relevant market or markets. Because consumers would presumably not consider a firm that sells SPARROW breakfast cereal also to market SPARROW electronic goods, the rights of the former firm in the SPARROW mark do not extend into the electronic goods market. Put another way, even if SPARROW had first been used for breakfast cereal, consumers would not be confused by seeing the same word subsequently used for totally different kinds of goods. A consumer's "search" for the right breakfast food is not made any more costly by the use of the SPARROW mark by a different trader in the electronic goods market. The two SPARROW trademarks are thus different property rights. One firm's initial adoption and use of SPARROW in the breakfast cereal market does not necessarily give that firm any rights in the SPARROW mark that extend into other consumer markets.

It is not quite so easy to rationalize dilution doctrine by reference to consumer welfare, but some leading theorists have tried quite hard to do so, notwithstanding the Supreme Court's acknowledgement that anti-dilution statutes are not animated by a consumer protection rationale.[38] Dilution protects the potency of branding messages in contexts where confusion-based liability theories cannot be relied upon to provide all the protections of the mark that firms desire. So, if the SPARROW mark for breakfast cereal were sufficiently famous, legal prohibitions against dilution may give its owner a remedy against a junior user that used the SPARROW mark in a remote marketing context, even if there was no likelihood that any consumers would be confused into thinking that, say, SPARROW brand electronic goods were from the same source as SPARROW brand breakfast cereal. Dilution doctrine protects the potency of the mark, and can be invoked to stop trademarks

---

[36] United Drug Co. v Theodore Rectanus Co. 248 U.S. 90, 98 (1916).
[37] Id.
[38] Moseley v V Secret Catalogue, Inc., 537 U.S. 418, 430 (2003).

becoming weaker as a result of use by other firms in remote market contexts that alter consumers' mental impressions of the mark.

Commentators' suspicion of dilution doctrine largely comes down to one question: what's in it for consumers?[39] Why should state and federal governments enlarge the bundle of property rights in trademarks if the protections consumers need against confusion are already provided by the traditional "likelihood of confusion" form of liability? One answer has been essayed by Judge Posner in the Seventh Circuit: according to Judge Posner, dilution doctrine might spare consumers the imagination costs they would otherwise incur if diluting conduct were permitted.[40] Consumers would have to think harder, for example, if, when they were confronted by SPARROW branded breakfast cereal, another firm's SPARROW branded electronic goods also came to mind. When shopping for breakfast cereal, a consumer need not expend cognitive resources banishing other SPARROW branded goods from his or her consciousness. Legal prohibitions against dilution ensure that our passage down supermarket aisles is not impeded by consumers who pause to think, or perhaps worse, exclaim, "Get thee behind me, SPARROW branded electronic goods!," as they struggle to keep the original branding messages in the cereal context clear in their minds. And, presumably, consumers make productive use of the time, energy, and cognitive resources that anti-dilution statutes save them, the cumulative effect of which must be a significant boon to any economy with lawmakers wise enough to enact such laws.

The attempt to answer the "what's in it for consumers?" question in terms of consumer welfare—an attempt, no less, by one of the nation's leading jurists—does seem to underscore the current importance of rationalizing trademark rights

---

[39] *See generally*, Clarisa Long, *Dilution*, 106 COLUM. L. REV. 1029, 1035 (2006) ("The harm of dilution is . . . elusive because it is not clear from the face of the statute whom the law is trying to protect."). Much criticism of dilution doctrine has suggested that it may be harmful to consumer and societal welfare. Wendy J. Gordon, *Introduction, Symposium, Ralph Sharp Brown, Intellectual Property, and the Public Interest*, 108 YALE L.J. 1611, 1614–15 (1999) (discussing in the context of dilution doctrine the problem of identifying any increase in the net social product); Franklyn, *Debunking Dilution Doctrine*, *supra* note 20, at 118 (noting that dilution doctrine marks a shift in trademark law toward a property regime, but supporting dilution principles on the basis of preventing certain forms of free-riding); Paul Heald, Sunbeam Products, Inc. v The West Bend Co.: *Exposing the Malign Application of the Federal Dilution Statute to Product Configurations*, 5 J. INTELL. PROP. L. 415, 416–17 (1998) (noting that, in the product configuration context, anti-dilution statutes cut across the checks and balances of federal patent law).

[40] *Ty Inc. v Perryman*, 306 F.3d at 511. *See also* Dogan & Lemley, *Merchandising Right*, *supra* note 8.

in terms of consumer welfare.[41] The centrality of consumer welfare to rationales for trademark rights is also suggested by asking what trademark law would be like if consumer welfare did not provide the principal rationale for the existence of trademark rights. If consumer welfare were not necessary to trademark rights, a firm's rights in its marks would come close to being a right simply to *reproduce* the mark.[42] One might limit the contexts in which the right might be enforced, perhaps with reference to constitutional concepts (perhaps: all uses "in commerce" are infringing), or more narrowly (perhaps: all uses "on or in conjunction with goods and/or services" are infringing). However, without some consumer-focused limitation, such as preventing consumers from being confused or incurring imagination costs, rights in a trademark might come close to being simply a reproduction right, albeit perhaps a narrowly tailored one.[43] In addition, even if it were possible to adopt arbitrary rules as to when rights in trademarks come into existence without reference to consumers, by, for example, only protecting marks on registration, accurate assessment of the strength of the mark in any dispute would be difficult without some reference to consumers' impressions. Assessing the strength of a mark necessarily involves some kind of

---

[41] Much of the controversy that surrounds more exotic versions of trademark infringement—such as initial interest confusion, and post-sale confusion—may be provoked by skepticism as to whether these forms of liability do very much to enhance consumer welfare. Indeed, initial interest confusion, which needs to be invoked only because no likelihood of actual point of purchase confusion exists, might *harm* consumers. In a case of initial interest confusion the defendants often, albeit perhaps in the context of free-riding on the senior users' goodwill, add to the information consumers have prior to purchase. Initially, the consumer may be confused: but by the time the consumer makes the purchase, she will have information about at least one other firm's goods or services. The doctrine of initial interest confusion therefore risks amplifying the rights firms have in their brands, without offering any obvious enhancement to consumer welfare. If preventing free-riding were a sufficient justification for trademark rights, little of this would be a problem.

[42] Copyright Office regulations provide that a claim to copyright cannot be registered in a print or label consisting "solely of trademark subject matter and lacking copyrightable matter" (37 C.F.R. § 202.10(b)); the regulations also characterize "words and short phrases such as names, titles, slogans, familiar symbols, and designs" as "works not subject to copyright." 37 C.F.R. § 202.1. The Court of Appeals for the Seventh Circuit in *Ty v Perryman* rejected a theory of federal dilution law that would extend the concept of dilution to allow trademark proprietors to bring a dilution claim against a party that used a trademark in a dictionary in a non-trademark sense. *Ty, Inc. v Perryman*, 306 F.3d at 514.

[43] *But see* San Francisco Arts & Athletics, Inc. v U.S. Olympic Comm., 483 U.S. 522, 537–9 (1987) (suggesting that Congress may, consistent with the Constitution, rationally conclude that a statutory grant of exclusive rights in the word "Olympic" appropriately rewards the efforts of a particular entity, even if such rights can be enforced absent any showing of likely confusion).

inquiry into how consumers respond to the messages about the trademark that its proprietor has conveyed, mostly through branding and promotion. Similarly, a firm achieves sufficient "fame" for the purposes of dilution doctrine when the trademark has sufficiently penetrated consumers' consciousness. Proxies are sometimes used in the course of this inquiry: courts might focus on how long the mark has been used in a particular marketing sector, or how many promotion and advertising dollars have been spent on it.[44] Generally, though, these more objective factors are used to assess how much of an impact the mark has made on consumers' minds.

Support for the centrality of consumer welfare to trademark rights, particularly the *federal* law on the topic, may perhaps also be grounded in constitutional principles. The Supreme Court's narrow ruling in *The Trade-mark Cases*[45] of 1879 was that the scope of the Commerce clause, as it was then understood, did not empower criminal prohibitions against unauthorized intrastate trademark use. But the Court also held that Congress was not empowered to enact trademark laws under the Patent and Copyright Clauses. The adoption and use of a trademark, the Court reasoned, did not manifest the inventiveness required for a patented invention; nor were trademarks original works of authorship of the kind that Congress is empowered to protect under the Copyright Clause. This perhaps suggests that there is a negative proscription in *The Trade-mark Cases*: without *invention* or *original authorship* Congress is simply not empowered to create property rights in what we might call "expressive material." Some other justification is thus required. "Consumer welfare" may provide a more politically attractive rationale for empowering a federal law of trademarks (and perhaps also to limit the scope of federal intervention) than the claim that protecting established trademark proprietors' goodwill for its own sake is sufficiently related to interstate commerce to be constitutional under the Commerce Clause.

Preemption[46] in the intellectual property context is an increasingly complex

---

[44] *See, e.g.*, Zatarain's, Inc. v Oak Grove Smokehouse, Inc., 698 F.2d 786 (5th Cir. 1983).

[45] 100 U.S. 82 (1979).

[46] "Preemption" here is a marker for a broader inquiry into the structural relationship between the Commerce Clause and the Copyright and Patents Clauses and any limitations on Congressional power that that relationship might impose. *See generally* Thomas Nachbar, *Intellectual Property and Constitutional Norms*, 104 COLUM. L. REV. 272 (2004). As the Supreme Court noted in *Eldred v Ashcroft*, preemption, strictly understood, and the scope of congressional choices under the articles of the Constitution that provide Congress with its repository of power raise different issues. Referring to Sears, Roebuck & Co. v Stiffel Co., 376 U.S. 225 (1964), the *Eldred* Court said: "A decision . . . rooted in the Supremacy Clause cannot be turned around to shrink congressional choices." Eldred v Ashcroft, 537 U.S. 186, 202 n. 8 (2003).

subject,[47] and the precise delineation between the Copyright and Patent Clause and federal or state trademark law is still emerging.[48] Nonetheless, it is arguable that protecting consumers against confusion (or, perhaps, imagination burdens) is what enables legislatures to avoid thwarting the policies inherent in the prerequisites for granting patents and copyrights.[49]

III. ... But are they sufficient?

Consumer welfare may provide a *necessary* rationale for trademark rights, as well as a set of arguments about the appropriate scope of trademark rights. The role of trademark rights in protecting consumer welfare may also support the case for federal intervention in this field. But do preventing confusion and saving consumers from incurring imagination costs provide *sufficient* bases for delineating trademark rights? For at least two reasons, the answer should be "no." The first has to do with how the legal system apprehends the consumer worldview. Second, consumers' worldviews change over time.

---

[47] *See, e.g.,* U.S. v Martignon, 492 F.3d 140 (2d Cir. 2007) (Commerce Clause does not empower enactment of criminal statute prohibiting sale of bootlegged recordings where the statute violates the Copyright Clause); United States v Moghadam, 175 F.3d 1269, 1277 (11th Cir. 1999); Kiss Catalog v Passport Int'l Products, 350 F. Supp.2d 823 (C.D. Cal. 2004) (upholding civil prohibitions against sale of bootlegged recordings, and rejecting defendant's theory that the Commerce Clause cannot empower legislation that is inconsistent with the Copyright Clause).

[48] In TrafFix Devices, Inc. v Marketing Displays, Inc., 532 U.S. 23 (2001), the Court declined to engage with the issue whether the Patent Clause "of its own force, prohibits the holder of an expired utility patent from claiming trade dress protection." *TrafFix Devices, Inc.*, 532 U.S. at 35. *But see* Vornado Air Circulation Sys. Inc. v Duracraft Corp., 58 F.3d 1498 (10th Cir. 1995), *cert. denied*, 516 U.S. 1067 (1996), a case decided before *TrafFix*, where the relationship between the Commerce and Patent Clauses appeared to influence the Tenth Circuit's holding that trade dress protection should be withheld from a product configuration that is a "described, significant inventive aspect of [a patented] invention." *Vornado Air Circulation Sys.*, 53 F.3d at 1510. At least one court has, however, relied on *The Trade-mark Cases*, 100 U.S. 82 (1879) as authority for the proposition that "legislation which would not be permitted under the Copyright Clause could nonetheless be permitted under the Commerce Clause, provided that the independent requirements of the latter are met." United States v Moghadam, 175 F.3d 1269, 1277 (11th Cir. 1999).

[49] The division between copyright law and trademark law is occasionally policed quite vigorously. *See, e.g.,* Comedy III Prods., Inc. v New Line Cinema, 200 F.3d 593 (9th Cir. 2000), in which the Ninth Circuit declined to entertain a trademark claim based on unauthorized use of a public domain movie depicting the comedy group known as the Three Stooges partly on the ground that the court would not "entertain this expedition of trademark protection squarely into the dominion of copyright law". *Id.* at 596. *Compare* Frederick Warne & Co. v Book Sales, Inc., 481 F.Supp. 1191 (S.D.N.Y. 1979) (trademark and copyright protection complementary).

A. Knowing consumers

The "ordinarily prudent consumer," whom trademark law protects against the likelihood of confusion and against changes to mental impressions of famous brands, is not a real person. She is both a legal construct and a conglomeration of judicial impressions and theories about how actual consumers behave. Sometimes, courts do find out about the mental impressions of real people—through consumer surveys and the like. This can provide valuable information that may, in some circumstances, provide a counterweight to some of the assumptions courts sometimes make about consumer responses.[50] Even so, while the likelihood of confusion inquiry is invariably characterized as principally consumer-focused and context-dependent,[51] it is usually quite difficult for courts to really "know" consumers; that is, to know very much about their vulnerability to harm as a result of defendants' allegedly unauthorized uses of trademarks.

Courts give detail and depth to the picture by analyzing a number of "factors"—such as the strength of the plaintiff's mark, and its similarity to the mark used by the defendant. The list of factors applied by the Court of Appeals for the Third Circuit is typical. Courts within the Third Circuit are instructed to consider: (1) the degree of similarity between the owner's mark and the alleged infringing mark; (2) the strength of the owner's mark; (3) the price of the goods and other factors indicative of the care and attention expected of consumers when making a purchase; (4) the length of time the defendant has used the mark without evidence of actual confusion; (5) intent of the defendant in adopting the mark; (6) evidence of actual confusion; (7) whether the goods, though not competing, are marketed through the same channels of trade and advertised through the same media; (8) the extent to which the targets of the parties' sales efforts are the same; (9) the relationship of the goods in the minds of consumers because of the similarity of function; and (10) other facts suggesting that the consuming public might expect the prior owner to manufacture a product in the defendant's market or that he is likely to expand into that market.[52]

Testing for likelihood of confusion is hardly a model of analytical rigor. Not all factors are necessarily relevant in every case; and, in some contexts, particular factors may be given more weight than others. Courts may also consider other factors. As the Ninth Circuit put the point: "The list of factors is not a score-card—whether a party wins a majority of the factors is not the

---

[50] See generally, Austin, *Burdened Imagination*, supra note 8, at 917.
[51] Long, *supra* note 39, at 1034.
[52] In the Third Circuit, these are known as the "Lapp" factors, after *Interpace Corp. v Lapp, Inc.*, 721 F.2d 460, 463 (3d Cir.1983).

point. Nor should the factors be rigidly weighed; we do not count beans."[53] There is also an incommensurability issue. How, for example, does one assess the likelihood of confusion where the plaintiff's mark is strong, but there is little similarity between it and the defendant's mark? Or where the plaintiff's mark is weak, and the defendant's mark is quite similar to it, but the goods and services are sold in quite different marketing contexts, with only a little crossover in a few instances? The test itself doesn't tell legal actors which should matter more. In addition, many of the underlying premises in the analysis are often matters of judicial discretion. How many consumers are we talking about? About what exactly need they be confused? How likely need the confusion be? How confused need they be? And how smart are the consumers to begin with—that is, how reasonable and prudent *are* they?[54]

As Professor Barton Beebe has demonstrated in an exhaustive analysis of the thirteen circuits' application of the "likelihood of confusion factors,"[55] it is possible to discern patterns in the way that different courts apply the factors, enabling some factors to be characterized as "core" and others as "non-core."[56] It may thus be possible, following the kind of detailed empirical analyses of judicial practice exemplified by Professor Beebe's recent work, to achieve greater predictability in application of the test. That said, the very need for the kind of path-breaking analysis undertaken by Professor Beebe is itself revealing: a significant amount of analysis and effort is required to render the test more predictable. Moreover, even with more information about how the test has been applied historically, there remains an information gap as to the connection between each factor and likely consumer responses. For instance, knowing that courts accord particular weight to the similarity of plaintiff's and defendant's marks in the likelihood of confusion analysis provides important, if not crucial, information for litigants; but weighing similarities between the marks more heavily in the scale doesn't tell us how to determine real consumers' responses to such similarities. "Likelihood of confusion" is not something "out there"—a matter of fact that we necessarily

---

[53] Thane Int'l Inc. v Trek Bicycle Corp., 305 F.3d 894, 901 (9th Cir. 2002).
[54] With respect to this last question, one leading U.S. commentator on law has suggested that if a court wishes to find infringement, consumers will be characterized as susceptible to being confused; but if a court wishes to find no infringement, consumers will be characterized as careful and discriminating 4 J. THOMAS MCCARTHY, MCCARTHY ON TRADEMARKS AND UNFAIR COMPETITION § 24:94 (4th ed. Supp. 2004) [hereinafter MCCARTHY] (footnotes omitted).
[55] Beebe, *Empirical Study*, *supra* note 13.
[56] Professor Beebe's data show, for instance, that the similarity of the marks is "by far" the most important factor. *Id.* at 1600 (discussing the relative importance of the different likelihood of confusion factors).

get closer to through analysis of the circumstantial evidence that is scrutinized via the factors.

All of this accounts for the inchoate quality of the empiricism of the likelihood of confusion test. To be sure, analysis of likelihood of confusion can involve *some* empirical analysis of consumers' likely responses, particularly when evidence is made available through consumer surveys. But analysis of the likelihood of consumer confusion is also a *theory* or collection of theories about the likelihood that consumer confusion will result from the presence or absence of certain factors, given the particular circumstances of the dispute. Of course, the idea of an "ordinarily prudent consumer" is itself a theory about consumer behavior, one that is often belied by some consumers' impassioned, irrational, and imprudent responses to brands, the kinds of responses that are so important to "brand capital."[57]

Prior to the Trademark Dilution Revision Act (TDRA) of 2006,[58] the Supreme Court's holding in *Moseley v V Secret Catalogue Inc.*,[59] that federal dilution law requires a showing of "actual" dilution rather than a "likelihood" of dilution, appeared to avoid such issues in the dilution context. The *Mosley* holding indicated that courts must ascertain whether dilution really has occurred.[60] Because the Court's holding emphasized ascertainable fact, rather than speculation about the likelihood of the occurrence of a fact, the holding seemed, at least at first blush, to require trial courts in dilution cases to get closer to the minds of real consumers than may be required when ascertaining "likelihood" of confusion. But the *Moseley* Court also stated that empirical evidence will not always be needed to establish dilution, observing that circumstantial evidence may reliably prove dilution in some instances: "the obvious case is one where the junior and senior marks are identical."[61] Given the difficulties with ascertaining whether dilution has or has not actually occurred, it is not surprising that some lower courts welcomed the suggestion that use of a trademark that is identical to the plaintiff's mark may provide a critical piece of circumstantial

---

[57] Not necessarily all, however. *See* Austin, *Burdened Imagination*, *supra* note 8, at 904–920 (exploring the significance for trademark doctrine of marketing strategies that rely on consumers' discriminating and intelligent responses to branding signals).

[58] The Trademark Dilution Revision Act (TDRA) of 2006 (TDRA) is codified at 15 U.S.C. § 1125(c) (2006).

[59] 537 U.S. 418 (2003).

[60] The TDRA overturns this aspect of *Moseley*, and provides that likelihood of dilution is actionable. *See* 15 U.S.C. § 1125(c).

[61] *Moseley*, 537 U.S. at 434.

evidence[62]—or may even support a *per se* presumption[63]—relevant to determining if dilution has actually occurred.

Before the 2006 amendments, the Lanham Act defined dilution as "the lessening of the *capacity* of a famous mark to identify and distinguish goods or services. . . ."[64] Thus, after *Moseley*, *likelihood* of the lessening of the *capacity* to distinguish was out, and *actual* lessening of the capacity to distinguish was in. Moreover, as Justice Kennedy noted in his *Moseley* concurrence, injunctions to prevent future harms remained available in dilution cases, notwithstanding the Court's holding about actual dilution.[65] Trademark proprietors who feared that another's actions would cause dilution did not need to wait until dilution actually occurred before seeking an injunction.[66] Accordingly, *Moseley* might only have served to replace "*fear* of *likelihood* of the lessening of the *capacity* to distinguish" with "*fear* of *actual* lessening of the *capacity* to distinguish" as the test for dilution—hardly a momentous contribution to doctrinal clarification.

As Professor McCarthy points out, even after *Moseley*, dilution was understood to mean the *gradual* diminution or whittling away of the value of a famous mark by blurring uses by others: "Like being stung by a hundred bees, significant injury is caused by the cumulative effect, not by just one."[67] The passage of the TDRA, making "likelihood of dilution" the test, may simply have made explicit that the harm in a dilution case almost invariably involves a "likely" future occurrence: the collective harm of the "swarm."

This opaque doctrine rendered it extraordinarily difficult to substantiate the

---

[62] GMC v Autovation Techs., 317 F. Supp.2d 756, 764 (E.D. Mich. 2004) ("GM's evidence establishes actual dilution that Defendant has used marks that are identical to the world famous GM Trademarks.").

[63] *See, e.g.*, Savin Corp. v Savin Group, 391 F.3d 439, 452 (2d Cir. 2004) (surveying case law on this point, and concluding that defendant's use of an identical trademark provides *per se* evidence of actual dilution). *Id.* at n. 4. It may be useful to compare this observation with the discussion above of the problems associated with characterizing trademark rights as encompassing a right to "reproduce" the mark. *See* text at note 42, *supra*. A *per se* presumption in favor of liability grounded in the identity of the defendant's mark to the plaintiff's mark would seem to come quite close to a right of reproduction.

[64] Federal Trademark Dilution Act of 1995, Pub. L. No. 104-98, 109 Stat. 985 (codified as amended at 15 U.S.C. §§ 1125, 1127 (2000)).

[65] 537 U.S. at 436 (Kennedy, J., concurring) ("A holder of a famous mark threatened with diminishment of the mark's capacity to serve its purpose should not be forced to wait until the damage is done and the distinctiveness of the mark has been eroded.").

[66] *Id.*

[67] 4 MCCARTHY, *supra* note 54, at § 24:94 (footnotes omitted). *Accord* General Motors Corp. v Autovation Techs., Inc., 317 F. Supp.2d 756, 764 (E.D. Mich. 2004).

claim that a realistic consumer protection rationale animates dilution doctrine. Perhaps the group of consumers who know both the SPARROW branded electronic goods and the SPARROW branded breakfast cereal might *eventually* need protection against changes to their collective worldview, but this will be because of the actions of other firms that might use the trademark in diverse contexts. Until the mark is used in such ways, it is difficult to know what, as an empirical matter, dilution means for any group of consumers at any particular time, if liability can be based on the risk that the capacity of the brand to "distinguish" will diminish *if such behavior becomes widespread*. If we wanted to inquire into the worldview of consumers who are *currently* exposed to SPARROW brand electronic goods, what would we ask? The concept of "likely dilution" doesn't tell us if there are any limits to the number of hypothetical "stings" that consumers of products marketed under a famous brand might eventually endure. Presumably, though, the inquiry is meant to go something like this: "we understand that you don't currently think differently of SPARROW brand breakfast cereal because of your exposure to SPARROW brand electronic goods, but *would* you, do you suppose, if you were also exposed to SPARROW brand bicycles, SPARROW brand garden hoses, SPARROW brand bath salts, and SPARROW brand cement mix?" If we focus on *this* group of consumers, currently subjected to *this* defendant's use of the trademark, the empirical inquiry begins to look decidedly abstract.

Added to this, the TDRA provides that dilution by "blurring" is to be tested by a "factored" analysis.[68] The new dilution statute provides that:

> In determining whether a mark or trade name is likely to cause dilution by blurring, the court may consider all relevant factors, including the following: (i) The degree of similarity between the mark or trade name and the famous mark; (ii) The degree of inherent or acquired distinctiveness of the famous mark; (iii) The extent to which the owner of the famous mark is engaging in substantially exclusive use of the mark; (iv) The degree of recognition of the famous mark; (v) Whether the user of the mark or trade name intended to create an association with the famous mark; (vi) Any actual association between the mark or trade name and the famous mark.[69]

The TDRA confirms that the focus will (mostly) be on circumstantial evidence. As with the approach to "likelihood of confusion," testing for dilution by these kinds of "factors" may loosen the inquiry from the worldview of actual consumers even more.

---

[68] The TDRA defines dilution by "tarnishment" as "association arising from the similarity between a mark or trade name and a famous mark that harms the reputation of the famous mark." 15 U.S.C. § 1125(c)(2)(C). The statute does not explain how reputational harm is to be assessed or analyzed.

[69] 15 U.S.C. § 1125(c)(2)(B).

B. Growing brands

For now, however, let's assume that the law of trademark infringement is much more interested in, and successful at, finding out what happens in the minds of real consumers than it probably is, or ever can be. Assuming courts can, and want to, understand what goes on in consumers' minds, does the concept of "harm" to consumers (whether through confusion or dilution) provide a coherent basis for delimiting rights in trademarks?

One problem with that proposition is that the consumer worldview no doubt changes as a result of marketers' efforts and firms' investments in growing their brands.[70] If rights in marks depend on what consumers think of them, trademark proprietors have every motivation to enhance the power of brands through advertising and promotion.[71] Of course, other things can change consumers' impressions of brands,[72] but marketers typically want to control the branding message as much as they can. The overall marketing context may be relevant to the extent of consumer confusion, as appears to be recognized, for example, by factor (10) in the Third Circuit's iteration of the likelihood of confusion factors, which references "other factors" impacting on consumers' impressions.[73] Through innovative and persistent branding strategies, marketers amplify consumers' expectations about the meaning and scope of trademarks. As a result, trademarks come to occupy more societal and cognitive "space." The space a brand occupies is not limited to geographical space:[74] achieving greater conceptual and marketplace "space" means that

---

[70] In the likelihood of confusion analysis, there is ample scope for taking account of the overall marketing context. For example, of the ten factors applied by the Third Circuit, the final one, "other facts suggesting that the consumer public might expect the prior owner to manufacture a product in the defendant's market," recognizes that the marketing context may affect consumer responses to brands. *See supra* note 52 and accompanying text.

[71] *See generally* Barton Beebe, *The Semiotic Analysis of Trademark Law*, 51 UCLA L. Rev. 621 (2004) [hereinafter Beebe, *Semiotic Analysis*] (discussing how trademark rights come to occupy increasing amounts of conceptual and marketplace space).

[72] *See, e.g.*, JULIET B. SCHOR, THE OVERSPENT AMERICAN: UPSCALING, DOWNSHIFTING, AND THE NEW CONSUMER 69 (noting that goods friends and family have purchased provide powerful stimulators of consumer desires) (citing Susan Fournier & Michael Guiry, *A Look into the World of Consumption, Dreams, Fantasies, and Aspirations* (Research Report, University of Florida, Dec. 1991)).

[73] "(10) other facts suggesting that the consuming public might expect the prior owner to manufacture a product in the defendant's market or that he is likely to expand into that market." *See supra* note 52 and accompanying text.

[74] An early and important discussion of geographical space occupied by a trademark appears in *Hanover Star Milling v Metcalf*, 248 U.S. 90 (1918).

more things get to be sponsored or endorsed.[75] When trademarks are "used" in many more different ways, consumers may more easily be assumed to expect such uses to be authorized. The logical corollary seems to be that consumers will be confused if they are not. If consumer impressions were fully delineating of the rights in a trademark, the metes and bounds of trademark rights could be largely determined by the genius of marketers and the resources firms have available to promote their brands.

For the most part, trademark law has increased the repertoire of legally cognizable things about which consumers can be confused.[76] Doctrines such as post-sale confusion, initial interest confusion, and the new, legally-relevant phenomena that the Lanham Act says consumers can get confused about, such as sponsorship and endorsement, all bolster the rights of trademark proprietors and encourage the efforts of marketers. We have a typical chicken-and-egg problem here: do brands expand as a result of the efforts of marketers, or do

---

[75] See generally NAOMI KLEIN, NO LOGO: NO SPACE, NO CHOICE, NO JOBS (2002).

[76] In *Two Pesos, Inc. v Taco Cabana, Inc.*, 505 U.S. 763, 779 (1992), *reh'g denied*, 505 U.S. 1244 (1992), Justice Stevens explained: "Over time, the Circuits have expanded the categories of 'false designation of origin' and 'false description or representation'." *Id*. Justice Stevens cited with approval the following observation by the Sixth Circuit, in *L'Aiglon Apparel, Inc. v Lana Lobell, Inc.*, 214 F.2d 649, 651 (3d. Cir. 1954): "We find nothing in the legislative history of the Lanham Act to justify the view that [§ 43(a)] is merely declarative of existing law. . . . It seems to us that Congress has defined a statutory civil wrong of false representation of goods in commerce and has given a broad class of suitors injured or likely to be injured by such wrong the right to relief in the federal courts." Justice Stevens concluded that this expansion is "consistent with the general purposes of the Lanham Act." *Two Pesos*, 505 U.S. at 781.

Amendments to § 43(a) have expanded the repertoire of legally cognizable things about which consumers can be confused. The statute now makes actionable likelihood of confusion as to "any word, term, name, symbol, or device, or any combination thereof" that is "likely to cause confusion, or to cause mistake, or to deceive as to the affiliation, connection, or association of such person with another person, or as to the origin, sponsorship, or approval of his or her goods, services, or commercial activities by another person." 15 U.S.C. § 1125(a). *See also* Wal-Mart Stores, Inc. v Samara Bros., 529 U.S. 205, 209 (2002) (noting "[t]he breadth of the . . . confusion-producing elements actionable under § 43(a)"). The breadth of the types of legally cognizable confusion can be dispositive, as is illustrated by the following dictum in *Star Industries, Inc. v Bacardi & Co., Ltd*, 412 F.3d 373, 390 (2d Cir. 2005), where the plaintiff alleged that defendant's use on an orange flavored rum product of a mark that was similar to that used by the plaintiff on its orange flavored vodka product infringed plaintiff's trade dress. The Second Circuit responded to defendant's argument that consumers are sufficiently astute to distinguish between rum and vodka as follows: "As we noted above, [plaintiff] asserts associational confusion, not direct confusion, and so it is irrelevant whether consumers are capable of distinguishing rum from vodka." *Id*. at 390.

changes in the law encourage marketers to think of new ways of expanding brands? And there is also an important normative aspect to all of this: *should the law fall into step with marketers' innovations, and bolster their activities with legal rights to match?* Professor Graeme Dinwoodie captures part of what is at stake very well when he asks: "Should trademark law be structured *reactively* to protect whatever consumer understandings or producer goodwill develops, or should it *proactively* seek to shape the ways in which consumers shop and producers sell or seek to acquire rights, thus ordering how the economy functions?"[77] To the extent that trademark law bolsters branding and marketing strategies implicated in consumerism, any normative inquiry into trademark law must surely also engage with the new economics of "happiness,"[78] and with commentary that is skeptical about connections between consumerism and societal welfare.[79]

Even without engaging with these broader normative concerns, concerns that strike at the heart of some forms of market capitalism, it is clear that once trademark rights expand past a certain point they have the potential to trespass on important legal policies, such as preserving scope for other firms' legitimate commercial activities and protecting citizens' expressive freedoms. Accordingly, as a legal policy matter, equating trademark rights with what consumers might become confused about cannot be sufficient. Trademark rights need to be shaped by other legal principles, values, and agendas. Of course, there's nothing very special about trademarks here. Similar things occur with other property rights. Landowners usually can't make more land, but they can certainly enhance the value of what's on the land—constructing tall buildings, factories, condos, running businesses, and so on. Eventually, these activities might impact others' rights and interests, and legal doctrines such as nuisance and other environmental laws can be invoked to curb exorbitant assertions of property rights.

"Fair use" provides a potentially very useful vehicle for shaping trademark rights according to the demands of other legal policies and economic agenda. Fair use preserves other firms' ability to use others' trademarks descriptively.[80] Fair use can also protect the development of some after-markets.[81] These are important economic and social polices that are, in some respects,

---

[77] Graeme B. Dinwoodie, *Trademarks and Territory: Detaching Trademark Law From the Nation-State*, 41 HOUS. L. REV. 885, 889–90 (2004). *See also* Graeme B. Dinwoodie, *Trademarks and Social Norms* (unpublished paper on file with author).

[78] *See, e.g.*, RICHARD LAYARD, HAPPINESS: LESSONS FROM A NEW SCIENCE (2005).

[79] *See, e.g.*, TIM KASSER, THE HIGH PRICE OF MATERIALISM (2002).

[80] *See* text at Section IV, *infra*.

[81] *Id.*

external to trademark law's dominant concern with protecting firms against misappropriation of their goodwill, and protecting consumers against whatever harms confusion and dilution cause. Unfortunately, in *KP Permanent* the Court ducked an opportunity to provide much needed guidance on the relationship between protecting consumers and other policy agenda that need to contribute to the shape of trademark law. The following section suggests that the Supreme Court's analysis in *KP Permanent* leans too heavily on "likelihood of confusion" and, in so doing, accords insufficient weight to the policies that the fair use defense was meant to further. More generally, the Court's approach to fair use illustrates a broader problem of courts providing insufficient analytical space for policies *other than* the consumer welfare ends served by the "straightforward" explanation for trademark infringement doctrine to shape the development of trademark jurisprudence.

IV. Tolerating confusion: fair use

Fair use is one of a number of trademark doctrines that further policies that are different from policies that provide the basis for trademark law's "straightforward story."[82] If functional aspects of products have achieved secondary meaning, for example, courts may withhold protection from such badges of origin, even if there exists some likelihood of consumer confusion.[83] Similarly, in cases involving generic terms that have achieved some "de facto secondary meaning," courts may deny all protection of the term,[84] or may sometimes engage in a more searching inquiry into the cause of any consumer confusion before providing injunctive relief.[85] In the first instance, some confusion may be tolerated to further the legal policies of allowing firms to

---

[82] Doctrines of this kind do not, of course, exhaust the opportunities for courts to tailor trademark analysis to further broader societal policies. The emerging doctrine on trademark use, which can immunize from liability some uses of marks that are not "trademark" uses, provides another important example. *See* Graeme B. Dinwoodie & Mark D. Janis, *Confusion Over Use: Contextualism in Trademark Law*, 92 IOWA L. REV. 1597 (2007).

[83] *See, e.g.,* Wallace Int'l Silversmiths, Inc. v Godinger Silver Art Co., Inc., 916 F.2d 76, 81 (2d Cir. 1990), *cert denied*, 499 U.S. 976 (1991) (stating that plaintiff may not exclude competitors from using functional design elements necessary to compete in the market, "whatever secondary meaning [plaintiff's design] may have acquired").

[84] *See, e.g.,* Abercrombie & Fitch Co. v Hunting World, Inc., 537 F.2d 4, 9 (2d Cir. 1976) ("[N]o matter how much money and effort the user of a generic term has poured into promoting the sale of its merchandise and what success it has achieved in securing public identification, it cannot deprive competing manufacturers of the product the right to call an article by its name.").

[85] *See* Blinded Veterans Ass'n. v Blinded Am. Veterans Found., 872 F.2d 1035 (D.C. Cir. 1989) (drawing on the analysis of the Supreme Court in *Kellogg Co. v Nat'l Biscuit Co.*, 305 U.S. 111 (1938)).

compete on price in functional goods markets unless the product is protected by some other intellectual property right. The second set of doctrines aims at ensuring that firms do not gain proprietary rights in words that name the relevant goods or services. Both policies aim at avoiding anti-competitive effects. As the Supreme Court confirmed in *KP Permanent*, the Lanham Act's statutory fair use defense also requires consumer confusion sometimes to be tolerated to allow firms to make descriptive uses of otherwise-protected marks. Curtailing the trademark monopoly on descriptive words facilitates competition; it may also protect after-markets for such things as second hand goods, sundries, and repairs services. Nominative fair use, a doctrine first described as such by the Ninth Circuit,[86] may serve to protect First Amendment values by enabling firms to use others' trademarks in certain expressive contexts.

A key reason for tolerating consumer confusion as a matter of formal doctrine is that even "fair descriptive uses" could be quite easily found to be infringing on a traditional likelihood of confusion analysis. Assume that the defendant uses descriptively an identical mark to that owned by the plaintiff in the same or, at least, a very similar, context in which the plaintiff uses the mark.[87] Assume also that the plaintiff's mark was "strong;" that consumers typically purchase the relevant category of goods casually, rather than carefully; that the channels of trade are identical and both plaintiff and defendant target their goods to the same market segments; and that the goods have the same function. Under the Third Circuit's test for likelihood of confusion as summarized above, factors (1), (2), (3), (6), (7) and (9) would likely weigh in the plaintiff's favor, with the result that other firms might be denied the opportunity to use the trademark in descriptive contexts. It may not be possible always to rely on the likelihood of confusion test as a means to limit the scope of trademark rights to further the important legal policies that animate fair use doctrine.

The susceptibility of consumer perceptions to be altered by changes in the marketing context provides another reason in support of having a separate defense for fair use. Some uses that were once non-confusing could become

---

[86] New Kids on the Block v News Am. Publ'g Inc., 971 F.2d 302 (9th Cir. 1992). "Nominative fair use" now has statutory recognition in the Trademark Dilution Act of 2006, H.R. 683, which includes in its exclusion section, "Any fair use, including a nominative or descriptive fair use, or facilitation of such fair use. . . ." 15 U.S.C. § 1125(c)(3)(A) (2006).

[87] *See, e.g.*, Century 21 Real Estate Corp. v Lendingtree, Inc., 425 F.3d 211, 224 (3d Cir. 2005). The Third Circuit recently acknowledged that unthinking application of the factors could lead to a finding for the plaintiff where no confusion exists. The Third Circuit attempted to solve this problem by amending the factor analysis in nominative fair use cases. *Id.* at 224–6.

so as a result of changes in the marketing context. In a case from the 1960s, *Volkswagenwerk Aktiengesellschaft v Church*,[88] the Ninth Circuit upheld a finding of non-infringement in favor of a firm that styled itself as an "independent" Volkswagen repair shop. The defendant used only the Volkswagen name in its business, not the characteristic VW logo. Two key findings supported this holding. First: "The evidence is clear that there is a widespread practice, at least in southern California, among businesses that service Volkswagen vehicles, to identify those that are part of the plaintiff's organization, by the use of the word 'Authorized,' and also by liberal use of the encircled VW emblem; and to identify those that are not part of plaintiff's organization, by use of the word 'Independent.'"[89] Second: "Plaintiff requires a remarkable degree of uniformity from its dealers, with regard to the construction and layout of their facilities, size, location and colors of their signs, and the style of lettering for their signs and printed advertising of all kinds. This makes it easier to distinguish plaintiff's dealers from those not connected with the plaintiff."[90] The outcome thus depended on the court's perception of what consumers understood already about the use of the VOLKSWAGEN mark in the repair shop market in southern California at the relevant time.

But what if there had not been an established practice of denoting the plaintiff's own shops as "authorized," or if there had been greater diversity in the layout and trade dress of the "authorized" repair shops? The use of the VOLKSWAGEN mark might then have meant something different for consumers in the relevant market, and it might have been easier for a court to have reached the opposite conclusion—that prominent use of the VOLKSWAGEN mark in the advertising of the services of a repair shop might have indeed suggested sponsorship or endorsement. Here, the changed marketing context might lead to a weighing of the factors in favor of the plaintiff. As a result, competition in an important after-market could have been significantly curtailed.

A third reason supporting the need for a fair use defense is that without formal doctrinal or statutory protections of fair use, the assertion of trademark rights could curtail expressive freedoms.[91] This is particularly important for

---

[88] Volkswagenwerk Aktiengesellschaft, 411 F.2d 350 (9th Cir. 1969), upholding the district court's analysis (256 F.Supp 626 (D.C. Cal. 1966)) applying a "not clearly erroneous" standard.
[89] 256 F.Supp at 630.
[90] *Id.* at 630–31.
[91] The Supreme Court acknowledged the relationship between the statutory fair use defense and expressive freedoms in *San Francisco Arts & Athletics, Inc. v U.S. Olympic Committee*, 483 U.S. 522, 565 (1987) ("The fair-use defense also prevents the award of a trademark from regulating a substantial amount of noncommercial speech.") (citation omitted).

nominative fair use, which treats as non-infringing some uses of a trademark simply as a "name". In a nominative fair use case, the trademark is being used because it is the most efficient way to identify some other firm or party, even if the defendant's ultimate aim is to describe its own goods or services. *New Kids on the Block v News America Publishing, Inc.*,[92] the leading Ninth Circuit decision on nominative fair use, illustrates the lengths to which some courts can go to preserve expressive freedoms, even where the factual context might plausibly have supported a finding of likely confusion, or, at least, raised a factual issue requiring the matter to go to trial. *New Kids* was a suit brought by the eponymous "boy band' from the 1990s against two newspapers that both solicited calls to 0900 numbers in response to newspaper "polls" that assessed the popularity with their readers of individual members of the band. Defendants' readers were invited to telephone these numbers to answer questions such as; "Who is the most popular" New Kid?; "Which of the five is your fave? Or are they a turn off?;" and "Which kid is the sexiest?" The essence of the New Kids' complaint was that the use by the newspaper of the "New Kids" trademark "implied that the New Kids were sponsoring the polls."[93]

On the newspaper defendants' summary judgment motion, neither the district court nor the Court of Appeals for the Ninth Circuit considered that "implied" endorsement was a sufficient basis for trademark infringement. The district court had reasoned that the newspapers' First Amendment rights outweighed whatever damage might have been done to the trademark by an implication of endorsement.[94] The Ninth Circuit approached the question in a different way, holding that in a nominative fair use case such as this, where the most efficient way to refer to this particular boy band was to use its name, even if the name was also a trademark, a new three-step test should replace the likelihood of confusion analysis. According to the Ninth Circuit, to successfully assert the nominative fair use defense, the alleged infringer must show that: (1) the product in question is not readily identifiable without use of the trademark; (2) only so much of the mark is used as reasonably necessary to identify the product; and (3) the user of the mark did nothing that would suggest sponsorship by the trademark holder.[95] On its face, the third factor would seem to invite some empirical inquiry into whether the defendants' actions did, in fact, "suggest" sponsorship. After all, likely confusion as to sponsorship is one of the specific bases upon which a party may be liable for

---

[92] 971 F.2d 302 (9th Cir. 1992).
[93] *Id.* at 308 (footnote omitted).
[94] New Kids on the Block v News Am. Publ'g Inc., 745 F.Supp. 1540, 1545 (C.D. Cal. 1990).
[95] *New Kids on the Block*, 971 F.2d at 308.

trademark infringement and unfair competition under the Lanham Act.[96] The Ninth Circuit held, however, that in *New Kids* there had not even been implied endorsement, relying on one of the newspaper's questions as to whether the band members were "a turn off;" but even the other newspaper, which had been more effusive had, in the Court of Appeals' view, said "nothing that expressly *or by fair implication* connotes endorsement or joint sponsorship on the part of the New Kids."[97] Also supporting this holding were the connections that the newspapers made between the 0900 "survey" and other editorial material, such as a review of a New Kid's televised concert.

From a purely doctrinal perspective, the holding in *New Kids* that there existed no material issue of fact on the question of consumer confusion is problematic. By the time of the litigation, New Kids had used its mark on some 500 products and services, and two authorized 0900 "hotlines" were being marketed under the "New Kids" trademark. Given that the likely target audience for the defendants' 0900 surveys might include at least some teenage fans of boy bands (a group hardly renowned for its careful reading of newspapers) the conclusion that there was no material issue of fact as to consumers' beliefs about endorsement seems like quite a close call. It is precisely because factual questions of this kind are so difficult to answer that courts generally consider trademark infringement cases to be ill-suited to summary disposition.[98]

Detailed consideration of the likely apprehension of the defendants' use of the "New Kids" mark was conspicuously absent from the Ninth Circuit's analysis. No consideration, for instance, was given to the possibility that, given that there had already been substantial authorized uses of the mark in a wide variety of contexts, including the use of 0900 numbers, the defendants' use of the "New Kids" was *in itself* sufficient to signal a connection—of at least the sponsorship or endorsement variety—between the defendants and the trademark owner. Had the owner of the New Kids trademark, through its prior marketing practices, "taught" the relevant group of consumers that such uses are typically authorized—indeed, had *other* owners of trademarks for popular entertainment groups taught consumers of popular music the same lesson—this may have created an expectation that other like uses would also be authorized.

This is not to suggest that the New Kids' use of the mark in conjunction with 500 different products and services and its own hotlines was necessarily enough to generate this kind of assumption; even so, whether it might have

---

[96] 15 U.S.C. § 1125(a).
[97] *New Kids on the Block*, 971 F.2d at 309 (emphasis added).
[98] *See supra* note 10.

done so surely warranted further discussion. Judge Kozinski's conclusions on the trademark and unfair competition claims do seem decidedly truncated: "Summary judgment was proper," the court reasoned, because "all [claims] hinge on a theory of implied endorsement; there was none here as the uses in question were purely nominative."[99] The court avoided engaging with an alternative possibility: uses that are "nominative" might nevertheless imply endorsement. Instead, it seems, if a use is characterized as nominative, any implication of endorsement can be assumed away.

While the *New Kids* court specifically eschewed reliance on the First Amendment (the principal basis for the district court's analysis), its holding and parts of its reasoning are certainly *consistent* with the policy of carving out from trademark rights sufficient "space" for communication using another's trademark. The following passage warrants quoting at length:

> While the New Kids have a limited property right in their name, that right does not entitle them to control their fans' use of their own money. Where, as here, the use does not imply sponsorship or endorsement, the fact that it is carried on for profit and in competition with the trademark holder's business is beside the point. See, e.g., Universal City Studios, Inc. v Ideal Publishing Corp., 195 U.S.P.Q. 761 (S.D.N.Y. 1977) (magazine's use of TV program's trademark "Hardy Boys" in connection with photographs of show's stars not infringing). Voting for their favorite New Kid may be, as plaintiffs point out, a way for fans to articulate their loyalty to the group, and this may diminish the resources available for products and services they sponsor. But the trademark laws do not give the New Kids the right to channel their fans' enthusiasm (and dollars) only into items licensed or authorized by them. See International Order of Job's Daughters v Lindeburg & Co., 633 F.2d 912 (9th Cir. 1990) (no infringement where unauthorized jewelry maker produced rings and pins bearing fraternal organization's trademark). The New Kids could not use the trademark laws to prevent the publication of an unauthorized group biography or to censor all parodies or satires which use their name. We fail to see a material difference between these examples and the use here.[100]

Two of these protected uses—magazine copy and an unauthorized biography—are "expressive." A further example cited in a footnote to this passage—satirical use—also involves a type of expressive use of a trademark.[101]

---

[99] *New Kids on the Block*, 971 F.2d at 309.
[100] *Id.*
[101] The footnote reads: "Consider, for example, a cartoon which appeared in a recent edition of a humour magazine: The top panel depicts a man in medieval garb hanging a poster announcing a performance of "The New Kids on the Block" to an excited group of onlookers. The lower panel shows the five New Kids, drawn in caricature, hands tied behind their backs, kneeling before "The Chopping Block" awaiting execution. *Cracked* # 17 (inside back cover) (Aug. 1992). Cruel? No doubt—but easily within the realm of satire and parody." *Id.* (reference omitted).

Likewise, the *Job's Daughters* court considered that the depiction of a fraternal organization's trademark in the form of pins and rings was not use of the trademark to denote the goodwill in the products themselves; instead, the defendant was selling the mark "in itself."[102] The holding of no infringement for unauthorized rings and pins protected their wearers' ability to express their affiliation with a particular organization without having to pay the (presumably higher) prices that would be charged if the trademark proprietor's rights extended into this market.[103]

With this kind of analysis, consumers seem to drop out of the picture—that is to say, consumers as they are predominantly understood by trademark law: marketplace actors who are vulnerable to confusion (or incurring imagination costs) in the course of their purchasing decisions. In cases such as *New Kids* and *Volkswagenwerk*, courts try to, and often can, have it both ways. Consumers are *not* confused—in *New Kids* because the defendant's use was "nominative," and in *Volkswagenwerk*, because of the prior practice of designating repair shops as "authorized" and controlling the trade dress—*and* the holdings can achieve consistency with other values and agenda, such as protecting after-markets and freedom of expression. A more realistic take on these decisions is that the courts are creating "space" to give expression to other important policies, such as protection of after-markets and First Amendment values.[104]

But what about cases where the tension between "trademark" policies and other legal policies cannot be so easily avoided—where, for example, there *is* a likelihood of consumer confusion, yet a decision for the trademark proprietor would thwart other important policies or values? This was the issue that engaged the Supreme Court in *KP Permanent Make-Up, Inc. v Lasting Impressions*.[105]

A. KP Permanent *and the continued relevance of consumer confusion to fair use*

KP Permanent involved two competitors in the permanent make-up market.

---

[102] *International Order of Job's Daughters v Lindeburg & Co.*, 633 F.2d 912 (9th Cir. 1990).

[103] For an alternative analysis, upholding trademark rights in merchandising material, see Boston Prof. Hockey Ass'n, Inc. v Dallas Cap & Emblem Mfg., Inc., 510 F.2d 1004 (5th Cir. 1975). *See also* Au-Tomotive Gold, Inc. v Volkswagen of America, Inc. 457 F.3d 1062, (9th Cir. 2006).

[104] For discussion of other issues that may have been at stake in the *New Kids* decision, *see* Graeme B. Dinwoodie and Mark D. Janis, *Confusion Over Use: Contexualism in Trademark Law*, 92 IOWA L. REV. 1597, 1620–21 (2007).

[105] 543 U.S. 111 (2004).

Lasting Impression I, Inc. held a federal registration for MICRO COLORS that became incontestable in 1999. KP Permanent, which claimed to have used the term "microcolor" in its advertising materials since the early 1990s, initially sought a declaratory judgment that its use of the term did not infringe Lasting's trademark. On Lasting's counterclaim for trademark infringement, the District Court for the Central District of California held for KP Permanent on its summary judgment motion, on the ground that KP Permanent's descriptive use of the term enabled it to rely on the statutory fair use defense.[106] The Ninth Circuit reversed and remanded.[107] Resolving a circuit split,[108] the Supreme Court held that a party relying on the affirmative statutory defense of fair use in section 33(b)(4) of the Lanham Act[109] was not required to disprove the likelihood of confusion as a prerequisite for relying on the defense.[110]

"Starting from ... textual fixed points,"[111] the Court first analyzed the relationship between the wording of the fair use defense in the Lanham Act and the sections describing liability for various forms of trademark infringement. It reasoned that Congress was unlikely to have meant the same thing when it used the phrase "likely to cause confusion, or to cause mistake, or to deceive," in the section describing trademark infringement[112] and "used fairly"[113] in the section providing for the fair use defense.[114] Additionally, the Court pointed out that it was illogical to require the party asserting the defense to disprove

---

[106] 15 U.S.C. § 1115(b)(4).
[107] 303 F.3d 1061 (9th Cir. 2003).
[108] *See, e.g.*, PACCAR Inc. v TelScan Technologies, L.L.C., 319 F.3d 243, 256 (6th Cir. 2003); Zatarains, Inc. v Oak Grove Smokehouse Inc., 698 F.2d 786, 796 (5th Cir. 1983) (stating that fair use defense enables use of words contained in a trademark "in their ordinary, descriptive sense, so long as such use [did] not tend to confuse customers as to the source of goods"); Lindy Pen Co. v Bic Pen Corp., 725 F.2d 1240, 1248 (9th Cir. 1984) (fair use defense unavailable if likelihood of confusion has been shown). *But compare* Cosmetically Sealed Indus., Inc. v Chesebrough-Pond's USA Co., 125 F.3d 28, 30–31 (2d Cir. 1997) (fair use defense may succeed even if there is likelihood of confusion); Shakespeare Co. v Silstar Corp. of Am., 110 F.3d 234, 243 (4th Cir. 1997) ("[A] determination of likely confusion [does not] preclud[e] considering the fairness of use."); and Sunmark, Inc. v Ocean Spray Cranberries, Inc., 64 F.3d 1055, 1059 (7th Cir. 1995) (likelihood of confusion does not preclude the fair use defense).
[109] 15 U.S.C. § 1115(b)(4).
[110] Specifically, the Ninth Circuit considered that as there were material questions of fact relating to the likelihood of confusion, the district court erred in its holding on fair use grounds in favor of the counterclaim defendant's motion for summary judgment.
[111] *KP Permanent*, 543 U.S. at 118.
[112] 15 U.S.C. § 1114.
[113] *KP Permanent*, 543 U.S. at 118.
[114] 15 U.S.C. § 1115(b)(4).

confusion, where a showing of likelihood of confusion is part of the trademark owner's case: "[I]t defies logic to argue that a defense may not be asserted in the only situation where it even becomes relevant."[115] The Court then engaged with the broader policy issues implicated by the statutory fair use defense: "The common law's tolerance of a certain degree of confusion on the part of consumers followed from the very fact that in cases like this one an originally descriptive term was selected to be used as a mark, not to mention the undesirability of allowing anyone to obtain a complete monopoly on use of a descriptive term simply by grabbing it first. . . ."[116]

In these passages, the Court comes very close to articulating a policy agenda in favor of competitive use of descriptive terms in a non-trademark sense that "trumps" the policy concerns described at the beginning of this chapter as providing the bases for the "straightforward" explanation for trademark infringement.[117] Indeed, immediately following these passages, the Court cited a Second Circuit opinion for the proposition that, "If *any* confusion results, that is a risk the plaintiff accepted when it decided to identify its product with a mark that uses a well known descriptive phrase,"[118] implying that the law must "tolerat[e] some degree of confusion from a descriptive use of words contained in another person's trademark."[119] While some ambiguity is created by the juxtaposition of "any" and "some," in this there does seem to be a fairly strong endorsement of the importance of policies *other* than protecting consumers from confusion.

But the Supreme Court ultimately shied away from trumping the putatively empirical issue of confusion with the policies underlying the fair use defense. The Court's endorsement of the Second Circuit's analysis underscored the

---

[115] *KP Permanent*, 543 U.S. at 120 (*quoting* Shakespeare Co. v Silstar Corp., 110 F.3d 234, 243 (4th Cir. 1997). On remand, the Court of Appeals for the Ninth Circuit took the hint: "KP's motion raises essentially issues that are defenses to an infringement action." KP Permanent Make-Up, Inc. v Lasting Impression I, Inc., 408 F.3d 596, 602 (9th Cir. 2005). "The fair use defense only comes into play once the party alleging infringement has shown by a preponderance." *Id.* at 608 (citation omitted).

[116] *KP Permanent*, 543 U.S. at 122 (internal citation omitted).

[117] Leading U.S. trademark commentator, Professor J. Thomas McCarthy has adopted the opposite view, using similar terminology. "Because the paramount goal of the law of trademarks is to prevent likely confusion, a showing of likely confusion should trump a 'fair use.'" 4 MCCARTHY, *supra* note 54, at § 11.47 (*cited with approval in* Paccar Inc. v Telescan Technologies, L.L.C., 319 F.3d 243, 256 (6th Cir. 2003)).

[118] *KP Permanent*, 543 U.S. at 122 (*quoting* Cosmetically Sealed Industries, Inc. v Chesebrough-Pond's USA Co., 125 F.3d 28, 30 (2d Cir. 1997) (emphasis added)).

[119] "[T]he common law of unfair competition also tolerated some degree of confusion from a descriptive use of words contained in another person's trademark." *KP Permanent*, 543 U.S. at 119 (*citing* William R. Warner & Co. v Eli Lilly & Co., 265 U.S. 526, 528 (1924)).

importance of the fair use defense, but the Court *also* reasoned that it would be "improvident" to go further than recognizing that mere risk of consumer confusion will not rule out fair use,[120] and then specified that its holding "does not foreclose the relevance of the extent of any likely consumer confusion in assessing whether a defendant's use is objectively fair."[121]

Some key implications of the Court's analysis are suggested by the approach of the Ninth Circuit on remand. Denying the counterclaim defendant's summary judgment motion on the fair use issue, the Ninth Circuit reasoned:

> Summary judgment on the defense of fair use is also improper. There are genuine issues of fact that are appropriate for the fact finder to determine in order to find that the defense of fair use has been established. Among the relevant factors for consideration by the jury in determining the fairness of the use are the degree of likely confusion, the strength of the trademark, the descriptive nature of the term for the product or service being offered by KP and the availability of alternate descriptive terms, the extent of the use of the term prior to the registration of the trademark, and any differences among the times and contexts in which KP has used the term.[122]

In other words, a party relying on the fair use defense not only has to satisfy the requirements of the statute; it may also be required to marshal evidence about the likelihood of confusion, with the possible result that summary judgment on the fair use issue may be much less easily secured by defendants confronting infringement allegations, even when their use of the trademark is descriptive. The risk for defendants, as the Ninth Circuit's approach attests, is that "fair use" will become one of those questions considered to be "intensely factual." While summary judgment is to be generally disfavored in trademark

---

[120] *KP Permanent*, 543 U.S. at 123.

[121] *Id.* Here, the Court's analysis seemed to echo an exchange between Justice O'Connor and Petitioner's counsel in oral argument: "JUSTICE O'CONNOR: In this case, did the plaintiff offer any evidence of confusion, consumer confusion? MR. MACHAT: This was a motion for summary judgement (*sic*). JUSTICE O'CONNOR: And was there anything in the affidavits or attachments that have to do with consumer confusion on behalf of the plaintiff? MR. MACHAT: Yeah, actually, the record does contain some references to confusion. The—in this case, the respondent, they were claiming that they did have some people that actually were confused. And when that happens, you need to look at what is causing the confusion. And essentially— JUSTICE O'CONNOR: Well, it might make it necessary for a defendant in such a situation, in order to avoid some kind of summary judgement, (*sic*) to also offer evidence on consumer confusion to try to show there wasn't any." Official Transcript of Oral Argument at *3. KP Permanent Make-Up, Inc. v Lasting Impression Inc., 2004 WL 2340185 [hereinafter KP Permanent Transcript].

[122] *KP Permanent Make-Up*, 408 F.3d, at 609.

infringement actions,[123] the Supreme Court has nevertheless emphasized the importance of summary disposition in trademark infringement cases.[124] In the terms used earlier in this chapter, there is a risk that likelihood of confusion will become pretty much all there is to it. As the following subsection discusses, this may poorly serve the policies underlying the fair use defense; and it may also serve to make litigation more complex and expensive.

B. *The wrong way to develop trademark law*
Even on the statutory interpretation grounds with which the Supreme Court began its analysis, where the Court carefully *distinguished* the concept of "fair use" from "likelihood of confusion," it seems strange, to say the least, to read back into the fair use statute a requirement that the defendant make a showing on the "extent" of confusion. In section 33(b)(4), the concept of likelihood of confusion is conspicuously absent. The Court's analysis also masks a substantive shift: insisting on the continued relevance of likelihood of confusion may limit opportunities for summary adjudication where the fair use defense is raised, a result likely to favor proprietors of trademarks that are susceptible to descriptive use by others. Substantively, this approach risks weighing the policies underlying trademark protection more heavily than those that would permit competitors to use descriptive marks. There is no clue in the Lanham Act that this was intended.

More generally, *KP Permanent* illustrates the wrong way to develop trademark law. The holding tells us almost nothing about how much confusion is tolerable, other than to say that the fair use defense will not be defeated by a "mere risk" of consumer confusion. And the Court doesn't explain how to balance or negotiate between the different policy concerns that underlie the likelihood of confusion and the fair use questions. By folding the fair use question back into the analysis of "likelihood of confusion," the *KP Permanent* Court forces the latter concept to do too much. Likelihood of confusion risks becoming the single yardstick by which the facts of any case implicating the fair use defense will be assessed. And this is to occur in a legal environment

---

[123] *See supra* note 10.
[124] Albeit in the slightly different context of determining whether trade dress is inherently distinctive. *See* Wal-Mart Stores, Inc. v Samara Bros., Inc., 529 U.S. 205, 213–14; *see supra* n. 10. Other aspects of the Ninth Circuit's analysis also appear questionable. Whereas 15 U.S.C. § 1115(b)(4) requires the party relying on it to establish that the term is used "fairly," "in good faith," and "otherwise than as a mark," the Ninth Circuit's analysis appears to import a requirement, or, at least, to make relevant, that the mark was the only, or one among a few, descriptive terms available. Facially, the subsection requires merely that the term be used in its "descriptive" sense, "only to describe the [defendant's] goods or services."

in which the Court has provided almost no guidance on the relative importance of avoiding consumer confusion, on the one hand, and permitting firms to use trademarks descriptively, on the other. One step toward achieving greater coherence in the development of trademark law and policy would be for appellate courts to look harder at how findings of the presence or absence of likelihood of confusion really come about, and to acknowledge inchoate quality of the empiricism of the analysis. Where relevant, the uncertainties associated with testing for dilution should provoke a similar type of inquiry.

Some Circuit Courts of Appeal have provided some much-needed guidance as to how best to shape the likelihood of confusion analysis where other important policies are at issue. The Ninth Circuit did some of this in *New Kids*—even if it meant slipping quickly over important factual questions. Other courts have adapted the likelihood of confusion analysis to tailor it better to fair use cases.[125] However, trademark law continues to exist in a legal environment where different forms of legally cognizable confusion keep being added to the legal repertoire. Moreover, in the current marketing environment, brands constantly compete to occupy increasing amounts of social and cognitive space. As a result, the increasing range of things about which consumers might likely be confused may lead to an accompanying reduction in the scope for the fair use defense. For our highest appellate court to offer no guidance on whether or not this is a good thing bespeaks, at the very least, a lack of engagement with this important area of unfair competition and economic policy.

In this aspect, *KP Permanent* recalls a position adopted by the Court in *San Francisco Arts & Athletics, Inc. v U.S. Olympic Committee*,[126] a case involving assertions of First Amendment protections against special rights in the "Olympic" mark. There, the Court observed: "the danger of substantial regulation of noncommercial speech is diminished by denying enforcement of a trademark against uses of words that are not likely 'to cause confusion, to cause mistake, or to deceive.'"[127] In other words, we need be less concerned than we might otherwise be about property rights existing in expressive material because it will be only those trademarks that are likely to cause "confusion" or "mistake" or which will "deceive" that will be enjoined; moreover, marks will be privatized only to the extent that the property rights in marks protect consumers against such things. But to imply that the First Amendment is safe from trademark law because trademark law prohibits only those uses of

---

[125] Century 21 Real Estate Corp. v Lendingtree, Inc. 425 F.3d 211 (3d Cir. 2005).
[126] 483 U.S. 522 (1987).
[127] *Id.* at 564.

marks that are likely to cause confusion puts enormous faith in tests for trademark infringement, faith that might not always be warranted.[128] It takes no account of the reality that changes in marketing practices and in the scope of legal rights can affect the amount of speech that can be privatized. Nor does this analysis contend with the problem of determining whether, as the scope of trademark rights changes, the current law provides an appropriate trade-off between expressive freedoms and trademark rights.[129] And, most seriously, the analysis does not acknowledge that the method by which likelihood of consumer confusion is ascertained will often fail to produce a durable division between uses of marks that will or won't cause legally cognizable consumer harms.

Perhaps if the *KP Permanent* Court had been more cognizant of the character of the "likelihood of confusion" analysis, it would not so readily have concluded that tolerating "some" confusion does not foreclose the relevance of the extent of consumer confusion to a finding of fair use, a conclusion that subsequently allowed the Ninth Circuit to withhold summary judgment on the ground that there existed a material issue of fact as to the degree of consumer confusion likely to be caused by the KP Permanent's use of "micro colors" in its promotional material.

Cognizance of the uncertainties and contingencies associated with testing for infringement in U.S. trademark support an acknowledgement that "likelihood of confusion" and "dilution" are not, or at least not entirely, pre-legal phenomena. Once this is recognized, appellate courts might engage with the kind of question that the *KP Permanent* Court side-stepped. Which matters more—avoiding whatever it is that is established by tests for trademark infringement, on the one hand, or allowing firms' descriptive use of words that happen also to be trademarks owned by other firms, on the other? Recognizing that these are potentially competing *policy* concerns may lead to a more orderly development of trademark doctrine, and more rigorous judicial engagement with the wide variety of policy questions that trademark law distills. Certainly, trademark doctrine should not weigh something less heavily in the policy balance because something else is traditionally understood as involving matters of "fact."

---

[128] A number of distinguished commentators have urged that more attention should be given to keeping expressive freedoms safe from trademark law. For one of the leading discussions of these issues, *see* Rochelle Cooper Dreyfuss, *Expressive Genericity: Trademarks as Language in the Pepsi Generation*, 65 NOTRE DAME L. REV. 397 (1990).

[129] For a recent exploration of the relationship between intellectual property rights and expressive freedoms, *see* Sonia K. Katyal, *Semiotic Disobedience*, 84 WASH. U. L. REV. 489 (2006).

If the absence or presence of confusion is to remain relevant to fair use, it would be more useful to see courts engaging in the same kind of analysis that sometimes occurs in analogous contexts. For example, in what is still one of the leading opinions on the functionality doctrine, the Court of Customs and Patent Appeals in *In re Morton-Norwich Prods., Inc.*[130] characterized the required judicial analysis as follows: "Given, then, that we must strike a balance between the 'right to copy' and the right to protect one's method of trade identification, what weights do we set upon each side of the scale? That is ... what facts do we look to in determining whether the 'consuming public' has an interest in making use of [one's design], superior to [one's] interest in being [its] sole vendor?"[131] This kind of approach engages more directly with what is at stake in those parts of trademark law in which "likelihood of confusion" cannot be the sole determinant of parties' rights and obligations. The public still has an interest in not being confused, but it also has an interest in firms being able to copy non-patented functional aspects of products. Consumers have an interest, in other words, in a thriving marketplace in which firms can compete freely on price for aspects of products that are unpatented and "non-reputation-related."[132] In *Morton-Norwich*, the countervailing principles at stake in the functionality context[133] prompted a detailed and searching analysis of the kinds of factors that might be analyzed and weighed to determine whether an aspect of a product genuinely is to be characterized as "functional."

This approach provides a helpful analytical starting point, because it articulates the policy concerns at stake, and attempts to shape the doctrine in the light of those concerns. To some extent, the *KP Permanent* Court was cognizant of the policies animating the fair use defense, particularly with its references to the reasons for the common law's tolerance of confusion caused by descriptive uses of trademarks. But in *all* contexts where countervailing principles require consumer confusion or other consumer harms to be tolerated, it would also be helpful for courts to recognize that there are risks accompanying according too much weight to the consumer harms caused by trademark infringement (and those apparently caused by dilution). Given the uncertainties and contingencies

---

[130] *In re* Morton-Norwich Prods., Inc., 671 F.2d 1332 (C.C.P.A. 1982).
[131] *Id.* at 1340.
[132] *See Qualitex*, 514 U.S. at 165 ("This Court ... has explained that, '[i]n general terms, a product feature is functional,' and cannot serve as a trademark, 'if it is essential to the use or purpose of the article or if it affects the cost or quality of the article,' that is, if exclusive use of the feature would put competitors at a significant non-reputation-related disadvantage." (*quoting* Inwood Labs., Inc. v Ives Labs., Inc., 456 U.S. 844, 850 n. 10 (1982))).
[133] *See generally* Graeme B. Dinwoodie, *The Death of Ontology: A Teleological Approach to Trademark Law,* 84 IOWA L. REV. 611 (1999) (providing an exhaustive analysis of the countervailing principles at stake in functionality doctrine).

associated with establishing whether likelihood of confusion exists, and the increasing array of things about which consumers can be confused, it is not at all clear that consumers will always get a good deal when firms are prevented from making descriptive use of others' trademarks. Protection of trademark rights helps protect the integrity of the valuable information trademarks provide to consumers, but there is also value in facilitating accurate descriptions of other firms' goods and services. Consumers benefit when the law ensures that the privatization of terms that can be used descriptively does not impede competition. Put another way, consumers may not get such a good deal when they are protected against everything that trademark law considers harmful. In the fair use context, and in other parts of trademark doctrine, it is time for courts to start engaging with that possibility.

V. Conclusion

The *KP Permanent* Court's approach to fair use risks valorizing likelihood of confusion, and perceptions of consumer harm generally, at the expense of other important social values and economic policies. To be sure, *KP Permanent* helpfully confirmed that toleration of some consumer confusion is required by the fair use defense. However, other parts of the Court's analysis, specifically its conviction that likelihood of confusion was nevertheless *relevant* to whether the fair use grounds are established and its refusal to engage with the issue of how much confusion is tolerable, add little to the coherence of this part of trademark doctrine.

KP Permanent perpetuates a problem that permeates so much trademark law: the idea that likelihood of consumer confusion is a pre-legal phenomenon, something "out there" able to be ascertained as a matter of unassailable empirical fact.[134] As a result, in a number of contexts apparent empiricism continues to trump policy. Given the problems that exist with ascertaining "facts" about consumers in trademark law, *and* the vulnerability of consumers' worldviews to manipulation, the Court's apparent faith in empirical analysis of likelihood of confusion may not always be warranted. At the risk of putting the point too epigrammatically, *KP Permanent* seems mostly to tolerate confusion about confusion.

---

[134] Of course, this problem is not confined to trademark law, but is endemic to legal analysis, as the Legal Realists (amongst others) emphasized. *See, e.g.,* Felix S. Cohen, *Transcendental Nonsense and the Functional Approach*, 35 COLUM. L. REV. 809 (1935). In *KP Permanent*, this mindset was also apparent in the oral argument in the course of which Justice O'Connor commented: "[I]t might make it necessary for a defendant in such a situation, in order to avoid some kind of summary judgment, to also offer evidence on consumer confusion to try to show there wasn't any." KP Permanent Transcript, *supra* note 121.

15 Online word of mouth and its implications for trademark law
*Eric Goldman**

I. Introduction

It is already well-understood that the Internet is a major new medium for human communication.[1] It is less well understood how this new medium should affect trademark law. Trademark law is wrestling with cybersquatting/domainers,[2] the sale of keyword-triggered ads and other high-profile Internet trademark disputes, but I believe that "online word of mouth" poses the most important challenge to Internet trademark law.

"Word of mouth" describes the process of transmitting information from person to person. In commercial contexts, word of mouth involves consumers sharing their opinions about marketplace offerings with each other, often through everyday conversations.

Offline, consumer word of mouth plays a major role in the marketplace by disciplining some brands and rewarding others, but a person's views typically reach only a limited number of people. In contrast, the Internet helps create new word of mouth content (otherwise foreclosed by higher offline communication costs) and disseminate word of mouth to new and previously unreachable audiences.

The broad reach of online word of mouth gives consumers tremendous

---

* Eric Goldman, Assistant Professor of Law and Director, High Tech Law Institute, Santa Clara University School of Law. Email: egoldman@gmail.com. Website: http://www.ericgoldman.org. I was General Counsel of Epinions.com from 2000 to 2002. Thanks to Graeme Dinwoodie, Mark Janis, Mark Lemley, Michael Risch, Rebecca Tushnet, Fred von Lohmann, Tal Zarsky and the participants at the October 2006 Works in Progress Intellectual Property (WIPIP) Colloquium at the University of Pittsburgh School of Law for their helpful comments.

[1] "The Internet is 'a unique and wholly new medium of worldwide human communication.'" Reno v Am. Civil Liberties Union, 521 U.S. 844, 850 (1997) (quoting Am. Civil Liberties Union v Reno, 929 F. Supp. 824, 844 (E.D. Pa. 1996)).

[2] Domainers "make their living buying and selling domain names and turning their Web traffic into cash." Paul Sloan, *Masters of their Domains*, BUSINESS 2.0, Dec. 1, 2005, http://money.cnn.com/magazines/business2/business2_archive/2005/12/01/8364591/index.htm.

power to influence brand perceptions,³ and this has put doctrinal pressure on trademark law. Trademark law distinguishes between commercial and non-commercial activity, but online word of mouth often does not neatly fit into either category.⁴ As a result, courts are applying trademark law to online word of mouth inconsistently, and the developing jurisprudence puts online word of mouth at legal risk.

Trademark law's inhibition of online word of mouth has adverse implications. Most importantly, trademark owners may be able to suppress or excise negative word of mouth, allowing trademark owners to escape accountability for their choices. Counterproductively, then, trademark law could hinder consumers' ability to make informed decisions that are critical to the operation of marketplace mechanisms.

This chapter proceeds in three parts. Section II discusses online word of mouth and its implications for consumer formation of brand perceptions. Section III considers the implications of online word of mouth for trademark law. The Conclusion reiterates why it is important for trademark law to foster, not squelch, online word of mouth.

II. The rise of online word of mouth, and the decline of trademark owner control over consumer brand perceptions

Offline, trademark owners have a fair amount of control over consumer perceptions of their brands. Online word of mouth undermines that control.

A. *Offline factors that shape brand perceptions*

Consumer brand perceptions are created by multiple sources, and no trademark owner can completely control how consumers perceive its brand. Nevertheless, trademark owners have significant control over some of the offline influences:

Product experiences Consumers' past experiences with a trademark owner's products affect consumer expectations about future interactions with the product.⁵ Generally, trademark owners can affect consumer perceptions through the quality of their goods/services.

---

[3] *See* GLEN URBAN, DON'T JUST RELATE—ADVOCATE: A BLUEPRINT FOR PROFIT IN THE ERA OF CUSTOMER POWER (2005); *cf.* GLENN REYNOLDS, AN ARMY OF DAVIDS: HOW MARKETS AND TECHNOLOGY EMPOWER ORDINARY PEOPLE TO BEAT BIG MEDIA, BIG GOVERNMENT, AND OTHER GOLIATHS (2006).

[4] *Cf.* Ellen P. Goodman, *Peer Promotions and False Advertising Law*, 58 S.C. L. REV. 682 (2007) (discussing how false advertising doctrines do not neatly apply to consumer-generated promotions).

[5] This is a key basis of the "goodwill" doctrine. *See* 1 J. THOMAS MCCARTHY,

Trademark owner's advertising A trademark owner can advertise via many media, ranging from broadcast/print advertising to marketing collateral to event sponsorships. By specifying the ads' content and placement, trademark owners generally control the brand perceptions created by these ads.

Third party advertising Third party advertising can affect consumer perceptions of a trademark owner's brand in a couple of ways. First, a competitor's ad may affect the trademark owner's brand by expressly referencing/denigrating the trademark owner's brand or through implicit associations/comparisons. Second, third party advertising can affect consumer demand for the entire product class; those effects can be positive, such as when a manufacturer's ad stimulates demand for the product, or negative, such as the anti-tobacco public service advertising.

Third party advertising is generally beyond the trademark owner's control. However, it is subject to some significant limitations, including false advertising laws and a major advertiser's threat to withhold future advertising as retaliation for running demand-reducing third party ads.[6] Further, because advertising is costly, typically advertising is undertaken only by profit-maximizing commercial players, not by consumers or other non-profit actors. (Public service ads like the anti-tobacco ads are a conspicuous anomaly.)

Retail interactions Consumer brand perceptions are influenced by interactions in the retail context. Retailers, not upstream trademark owners, typically control these interactions (except when the trademark owner sells direct-to-consumer),[7] but trademark owners nevertheless can influence the retail experience.

- *Pricing.* Price can signal quality to consumers,[8] and pricing can deter-

---

MCCARTHY ON TRADEMARKS AND UNFAIR COMPETITION §2:18 (4th ed. 2003) (explaining that "goodwill" means, among other things, "the lure to return," "buyer momentum" and the "expectancy of continued patronage").

[6] *See* Eric Goldman, *My First Three Months in an Internet Start-Up*, E-COMMERCE L. REP., Sept. 2000 (broadcasters refused to run an Epinions television ad that criticized Chrysler for fear of damaging the broadcasters' relationships with Chrysler, a major advertiser).

[7] *See generally* Eric Goldman, *Brand Spillovers* (forthcoming), *available at* http://web.si.umich.edu/tprc/papers/2007/774/brandspilloversv19.pdf) [hereinafter Goldman, *Brand Spillovers*].

[8] *See, e.g.*, David J. Curry & Peter C. Riesz, *Prices and Price/Quality Relationships: A Longitudinal Analysis*, J. MARKETING, Jan. 1998, at 36; Paul Milgrom & John Roberts, *Price and Advertising Signals of Product Quality*, 94 J. POL. ECON. 796 (1986).

mine post-purchase satisfaction[9] and perceptions of brand exclusivity.[10] Retailers set prices paid by consumers, but trademark owners can exercise indirect control over these prices through wholesale pricing and by restricting sales to discount retailers.[11]

- *Placement.* Retailers choose where to place products within stores,[12] and these decisions can lead consumers to make various inferences and associations that can affect brand perceptions.[13] While retailers make the final in-store placement decisions, trademark owners can influence placement decisions through a variety of incentives and restrictions.[14]
- *Advertising.* Retailers generally may advertise the products they sell under the trademark exhaustion/first sale doctrine.[15] Trademark owners can get oversight of some retailer choices through co-op advertising programs.[16]
- *Salesperson–Consumer Interactions.* Retail salespeople's statements and conduct can affect consumer brand perceptions.[17] Trademark owners can conform the behavior of retail salespeople to some degree through financial incentives and salesperson training (if permitted by the retailer), and trademark owners can control some retail messaging through product packaging or by providing retailers with marketing collateral.

---

[9] *See, e.g.*, Glenn B. Voss et al., *The Roles of Price, Performance, and Expectations in Determining Satisfaction in Service Exchanges*, J. MARKETING, Oct. 1998, at 46.

[10] This principle animated states' Fair Trade Acts before the Consumer Goods Pricing Act of 1975 largely mooted them. *See* Note, *Fair Trade Laws and Discount Selling*, 64 HARV. L. REV. 1327 (1951); Consumer Goods Pricing Act of 1975, Pub. L. No. 94-145, 89 Stat. 801.

[11] Trademark owners also can exercise some limited control over prices directly through vertical price restrictions to the extent such restrictions are permissible.

[12] *See* Goldman, *Brand Spillovers*, *supra* note 7.

[13] *See id.*

[14] *See generally* Marianne M. Jennings et al., *The Economics, Ethics and Legalities of Slotting Fees and Other Allowances in Retail Markets*, 21 J.L. & COM. 1 (2001).

[15] *See* MCCARTHY, *supra* note 5, §25:43.

[16] With co-op advertising programs, trademark owners subsidize retailer advertising or make other resources available to retailers (such as licenses to copyrighted material). *See Co-op Advertising*, ENTREPRENEUR.COM, http://www.entrepreneur.com/encyclopedia/printthis/82096.html.

[17] *See, e.g.*, Brent Goff et al., *The Influence of Salesperson Selling Behaviors on Customer Satisfaction with Products*, 73 J. RETAILING 171 (1997).

Editorial content   Editorial content about goods and services, such as product reviews, plays a crucial role in shaping consumer brand perceptions. For example, good product reviews can boost sales, while bad reviews can sink them.[18]

By definition, trademark owners are not supposed to be able to control editorial content. Editorial content is expected to be free from outside influences, and many publishers voluntarily adopt policies limiting advertisers' ability to influence editorial decisions.[19] Nevertheless, trademark owners can influence editorial content written about them:

- Marketers routinely "pay-to-play"[20] despite legal doctrines (like anti-payola laws) designed to restrict their ability to do so.
- Even when trademark owners do not directly pay-to-play, they can stimulate and steer media coverage through public relations campaigns. In extreme cases, media outlets will republish brand owner-supplied content (such as video news releases) verbatim as "editorial" content.[21]
- Despite publisher/broadcaster policies separating "church and state," trademark owners can influence editorial decisions by threatening to withhold advertising.[22]

---

[18]   *See* Neil Terry et al., *The Determinants of Domestic Box Office Performance in the Motion Picture Industry*, 43 Sw. Econ. Rev. 137 (2005) (recapping the literature). *But see* Alan T. Sorensen & Scott J. Rasmussen, *Is any Publicity Good Publicity? A Note on the Impact of Book Reviews*, Apr. 2004, http://www.stanford.edu/~asorense/papers/bookreviews.pdf (showing that even negative New York Times book reviews increase sales).

[19]   *See* C. Edwin Baker, Advertising and a Democratic Press (1994).

[20]   *See* Press Release, Manning Selvage & Lee, Almost 50% of Senior Marketing Executives Said they have Paid for an Editorial or Broadcast Placement (June 13, 2006), http://www.mslpr.com/buzz/press_releases/pdf/Ethicspressrelease_062606.pdf. For example, although payola is illegal, it still appears to occur in the radio industry. *See* Chuck Phillips, *Logs Link Payments with Radio Airplay*, L.A. Times, May 29, 2001, at A1; Erin McClam, *Sony Agrees to $10M "Payola" Settlement*, Associated Press, July 25, 2005; Jeff Leeds, *2nd Music Settlement by Spitzer*, N.Y. Times, Nov. 23, 2005, at C1.

[21]   *See* Diane Farsetta & Daniel Price, *Fake TV News: Widespread and Undisclosed*, Center for Media and Democracy, Apr. 8, 2006, http://www.prwatch.org/fakenews/execsummary; David Barstow & Robin Stein, *The MESSAGE MACHINE: How the Government Makes News; Under Bush, a New Age of Prepackaged TV News*, N.Y. Times, Mar. 13, 2005, at A1 (discussing U.S. government-produced and -distributed video news releases). *See generally* Baker, *supra* note 19, at 104–07 (criticizing television stations for accepting content produced by marketers).

[22]   *See* Baker, *supra* note 19; Blake Fleetwood, *The Broken Wall; Newspaper Coverage of its Advertisers*, Wash. Monthly, Sept. 1999.

Therefore, while much editorial content remains truly independent of trademark owner influence, sometimes trademark owners can control or at least guide editorial content.

Further, offline editorial content is expensive to produce and publish, which limits the number of speakers who can afford to speak about the trademark owner.[23] This economic barrier to entry systematically blocks a lot of brand-influencing content from being produced in the first place.

Consumer word of mouth Consumer word of mouth is another important factor in shaping consumer brand perceptions.[24] For some industries, such as media products (i.e., books/movies/music)[25] and restaurants,[26] word of mouth can make or break businesses.

People routinely discuss brands with each other as part of their normal interactions; according to one study, "people discuss about a dozen brands each day."[27] Due to their sociability or expertise, some consumers (sometimes called "brand advocates")[28] are more influential than other consumers. But

---

[23] *See* Larry Ribstein, *From Bricks to Pajamas: The Law and Economics of Amateur Journalism*, 48 WM. & MARY L. REV. 185 (2006).

[24] *See* Michael R. Solomon, *Consumer Behavior: Buying, having and being 379* (6th ed, 2004) (estimated that word of mouth influences 2/3 of consumer-good sales). Yahoo.com, *Long & Winding Road: The Route to the Cash Register* (Apr. 2006), http://us.i1.yimg.com/us.yimg.com/i/adv/lwr_06/long_and_winding_road.pdf ("Word of mouth remains the most important factor in purchase decision making (particularly in building awareness of specific brands or products).") [hereinafter Yahoo.com, *Long & Winding*]; *The Rising Roar of Word-of-Mouth*, EMARKETER, June 29, 2007, http://www.emarketer.com/Article.aspx?id=1005072&src=article1_newsltr.

[25] Word of mouth repeatedly has been shown to affect consumers' purchases of books, movies and music. *See* Judith Chevalier & Dina Mayzlin, *The Effect of Word of Mouth on Sales: Online Book Reviews*, J. MARKETING RES., Aug. 2006; Charles C. Moul, *Measuring Word of Mouth's Impact on Theatrical Movie Admissions*, Mar. 2006, http://www.artsci.wustl.edu/~moul/pdf_drafts/wordofmouth.pdf; Yong Liu, *Word of Mouth for Movies: Its Dynamics and Impact on Box Office Revenue*, J. MARKETING, July 2006, at 74 (indicating that high quantity of word of mouth, regardless of whether it is positive or negative, increases movie box office receipts).

[26] *See* Amy Hoak, *Bill of Fare Game*, MARKETWATCH, May 4, 2007, http://www.marketwatch.com/news/story/more-diners-dish-online-eateries/ story. aspx?guid=%7B0D5DBF3E-17E6-4C21-B242-5AB03BD57E99%7D&dist= hplatest.

[27] Louise Story, *What We Talk About When We Talk About Brands*, N.Y. TIMES, Nov. 24, 2006.

[28] *See* Press Release, Yahoo.com, *Yahoo! and comScore Networks Reveals Influential Consumers Can Be Reached Through Search, Social Media and Communication Tools* (Dec. 13, 2006), http://yhoo.client.shareholder.com/press/ReleaseDetail.cfm?ReleaseID=222291 [hereinafter Yahoo.com, *Influential Consumers*]; *see also* MALCOLM GLADWELL, THE TIPPING POINT (2000) (discussing "mavens" who play a vital role in helping other consumers make marketplace decisions).

even the most influential brand advocates typically directly influence only the few dozen people in their social network,[29] often in time-consuming seriatim conversations with one or a few people at a time.

Like editorial content, trademark owners cannot directly control word of mouth very well.[30] Indeed, this implicit independence—that word of mouth reflects peers' bona fide opinions, not a marketer's economically motivated views—gives extra credibility to word of mouth, which in turn makes it highly influential to other consumers.[31] Marketers can try to take advantage of word of mouth's extra credibility through techniques such as "buzz marketing," but these efforts often do not succeed.[32]

Conclusion This discussion can be summarized by Table 15.1

Table 15.1 Relationship between trademark owner control and brand perception

Brand perception influences	Effect on brand perceptions	Trademark owner control
Product experiences	Significant	High
Trademark owner's advertising	Potentially significant	High
Third party advertising	Often indirect	Low
Retail interactions	Significant	Shared between retailers and trademark owners
Editorial publication	Significant	Low in theory, non-trivial in practice
Consumer word of mouth	Significant in aggregate, but each person's influence may be low	Low

[29] See GLADWELL, *supra* note 28, at 179 (estimating that a social network rarely exceeds 150 people). Solomon, *supra.* note 24 at 382 (an average disgruntled consumer will share his/her negative opinions with nine people, only 13% of disgruntled consumers will tell over 30 people).
[30] See PlayMakers, LLC v ESPN, Inc., 297 F. Supp. 2d 1277, 1283–4 (W.D. Wash. 2003) (word of mouth is not trademark owner-controlled "marketing").
[31] See, e.g., Bob Tedeschi, *Help for the Merchant in Navigating a Sea of Shopper Opinions*, N.Y. TIMES, Sept. 4, 2006; Story, *supra* note 27.
[32] See Gerry Khermouch, *Buzz Marketing*, BUS. WK., July 30, 2001, at 54.

B. The Internet and online word of mouth

1. Amplification of word of mouth Online word of mouth differs from offline word of mouth in several important ways. First, the Internet reduces consumers' costs to share their views. For example, a consumer can easily disseminate an email or blog post to the consumer's entire social network,[33] which makes it easier (in terms of time and money) to share the consumer's views with more people. The ease of online communication also may encourage consumers to produce and share their brand perceptions more freely than would have taken place offline, especially when such a communication would be inhibited by geographic separation or social norms.

Second, through Internet dissemination, a consumer's opinions can reach people outside the consumer's social network. Members of a consumer's social network can easily forward the message to *their* social network, quickly expanding the reach of a single communication.[34] If the consumer publishes opinions to the web (via a blog or other online tool), the consumer can build a readership that includes people who would not have been in the consumer's social network in physical space. Further, offline word of mouth is typically ephemeral, but content published to the web can remain available indefinitely, thus potentially influencing generations of future consumers.[35]

Third, new online intermediaries have emerged to systematically capture and republish consumer opinions, such as merchant ratings in eBay's feedback forum[36] and product reviews at Amazon.com, Epinions or Yelp. Intermediaries may spur the creation of new incremental brand commentary by soliciting consumer opinions (in some cases paying for those opinions),[37] and intermediaries can provide useful metadata (such as identity/geography authentication or ranking credentials) that helps readers assess the credibility of those opinions. Intermediaries can also make online word of mouth easier

---

[33] *See* Yahoo.com, *Influential Consumers*, *supra* note 28 (brand advocates are much more likely to use IM, Podcasts and email to disseminate their views than non-advocates).

[34] *See* CASS SUNSTEIN, REPUBLIC.COM (2001) (using the unflattering term "cyber-cascades" to describe the phenomenon).

[35] *See* Posting of Carlo Longino to Techdirt, *Online Criticism Isn't Just Easy, It Sticks Around Too*, Aug. 6, 2007, http://www.techdirt.com/articles/20070803/123409.shtml.

[36] *See* Chrysanthos Dellarocas, *The Digitization of Word of Mouth: Promise and Challenges of Online Feedback Mechanisms*, 49 MGMT. SCI. 1407 (2003) (discussing eBay's feedback forum as a case study).

[37] For example, Epinions pays a nominal amount of cash to reviewers. *See Earnings on Epinions.com*, Epinions.com, http://www.epinions.com/help/faq/show_~faq_earnings.

to use and compare by "summarizing" multiple consumers' opinions into a collective wisdom, such as a star rating.

2. Search engines and the competition for attention Search engines also enhance the impact of online word of mouth. Typically, a search results page has several "zones" of ads and content. For example, Google presents paid advertising at the top and along the right side of a search results page and presents "organic" search results along the left side. Both editorial[38] and ad[39] zones are sorted by proprietary algorithms. Search engines typically only present ten organic results and up to ten ads per page. Typically, consumers examine only the first page of search results.[40] Thus, even if a keyword search yields thousands or even millions of responsive results, consumers likely will consider no more than the top twenty.[41] With so much consumer attention and cash at stake,[42] competition for these top spots can be intense.

The competition-for-placement is exacerbated by players who traditionally do not compete with the trademark owner for attention in the offline world. For example, offline advertising by members of a trademark owner's distribution channel (such as retailers and marketing affiliates) typically complements the trademark owner's efforts. However, in search engines, trademark owners may compete against their distribution channel members for the top twenty spots. Trademark owners also compete with other commercial actors

---

[38] *See* Eric Goldman, *Deregulating Relevancy in Internet Trademark Law*, 54 EMORY L.J. 507, 534–7 (2005) [hereinafter Goldman, *Deregulating Relevancy*].

[39] For example, Google uses an "Ad Rank" that considers the advertiser's willingness to pay and a proprietary "quality score" that considers a variety of relevancy factors. *See How Are Ads Ranked?*, Google.com, http://adwords.google.com/support/bin/answer.py?answer=6111&query=ad%20rank&topic=&type=f.

[40] *See, e.g.*, Leslie Marable, *False Oracles: Consumer Reaction to Learning the Truth About How Search Engines Work*, CONSUMER REPORTS WEBWATCH, June 30, 2003, at 21, http://www.consumerwebwatch.org/pdfs/false-oracles.pdf (in ethnographic study, 88% of search results links were made from the first page of search results).

[41] Even within the first page, placement matters. The first editorial search result may get ten times the number of clicks as the tenth search result. *See* Nico Brooks, *The Atlas Rank Report: How Search Engine Rank Impacts Traffic*, ATLAS INSTITUTE DIGITAL MARKETING INSIGHTS (June 2004), http://app.atlasonepoint.com/pdf/AtlasRankReport.pdf.

[42] *See* JOHN BATTELLE, THE SEARCH 153–7 (2005) (describing the adverse business consequences suffered by Neil Moncrief, operator of 2bigfeet.com, after being kicked out of Google's search index right before the holiday shopping season); Michael Totty & Mylene Mangalindan, *Web Sites Try Everything To Climb Google Rankings*, WALL ST. J., Feb. 26, 2003, at A1 (discussing how a retailer's sales dropped 80% after its Google ranking was reduced).

who are not normally directly competitive for offline advertising, such as vendors of complementary goods; vendors catering to common consumer interests; vendors of used goods; and publishers producing content about the trademark owner.

More importantly for our purposes, trademark owners face competition for search engine placement from consumers, gripers, critics and other speakers who publish their views about the trademark owner but lack any profit motive for doing so. These views, along with word of mouth distillations from intermediaries like product review sites, can make their way into the top ten organic search results (or, in some cases, may appear in the search ads). Some searchers exposed to these search results will investigate further, in which case this word of mouth content may shape the consumer's brand perceptions.[43] Indeed, searcher perceptions may be influenced merely by seeing word of mouth content displayed in the search results itself, even if searchers do not click on the link to investigate it further.[44]

Thus, in contrast to trademark owners' relatively high level of control over brand perceptions in the offline world, the Internet and online word of mouth substantially degrade trademark owners' control over consumers' brand perceptions. Indeed, a single consumer, through favorable search engine placement, might influence thousands or even millions of potential consumers, and because online word of mouth can survive indefinitely, the Internet "remembers" a trademark owner's historical choices and practices.

As a result, online word of mouth creates unprecedented accountability on trademark owners for their decisions. Unfortunately, these effects are not uniformly beneficial; online word of mouth can be inaccurate or unfair. Consumers will need to develop mechanisms to distinguish trustworthy from untrustworthy information. But even as consumers (and intermediaries) develop these mechanisms, many consumers will use online word of mouth to sharpen their marketplace decisions. In turn, the entire marketplace benefits as online word of mouth improves trademark owner accountability.

---

[43] *See* Goldman, *Brand Spillovers, supra* note 7; *see also* Promatek Indus., Ltd. v Equitrac Corp., 300 F.3d 808 (7th Cir. 2002).
[44] *See* Maughan v Google Tech., Inc., 143 Cal. App. 4th 1242 (Cal. App. Ct. 2006) (an accountant complained that the text of Google's search result was harming his business); Posting of Chris Bennett to 97th Floor Blog, *29 Fortune 100's Are Letting Google Tarnish Their Reputation*, Mar. 29, 2007, http://www.97thfloor.com/ blog/29-fortune-100s-are-letting-google-tarnish-their-reputation/ (showing that many prominent companies' trademarks will prominently display negative search results when searched); *cf. Online Banner Advertising Raises Brand Awareness By 6% On Average*, DYNAMIC LOGIC: BEHIND THE CLICK®, June 2000, http://www.dynamic logic.com/na/research/btc/beyond_the_click_0600.html (claiming that banner ads raise brand awareness by 6% even if consumers do not click on the ads to investigate further).

III. Trademark consequences of online word of mouth

This section explores the trademark law implications of online word of mouth. To focus the discussion, this section only considers trademark infringement, not trademark dilution, the Anti-Cybersquatting Consumer Protection Act or other trademark laws.

To establish a *prima facie* case of trademark infringement under the Lanham Act, a trademark owner must establish (1) ownership of a valid trademark, (2) priority of use, (3) the defendant used the trademark in commerce in connection with the sale of goods or services, and (4) a likelihood that the use will cause consumer confusion about the product's source. After the trademark owner establishes a *prima facie* case, the defendant can assert affirmative defenses, including fair use. The Internet does not change the ownership or priority analyses, but it raises important new issues about the other two elements of a trademark infringement claim.

A. Use in commerce

1. Defined The Lanham Act's trademark infringement provisions reference "use in commerce" three separate times: §32(a) (infringement of registered marks); §43(a) (infringement of unregistered marks) and §45 (definitions). §45 defines "use in commerce" as:

> the bona fide use of a mark in the ordinary course of trade, and not made merely to reserve a right in a mark. For purposes of this chapter, a mark shall be deemed to be in use in commerce—
> (1) on goods when—
> (A) it is placed in any manner on the goods or their containers or the displays associated therewith or on the tags or labels affixed thereto, or if the nature of the goods makes such placement impracticable, then on documents associated with the goods or their sale, and
> (B) the goods are sold or transported in commerce, and
> (2) on services when it is used or displayed in the sale or advertising of services and the services are rendered in commerce, or the services are rendered in more than one State or in the United States and a foreign country and the person rendering the services is engaged in commerce in connection with the services.[45]

This definition has plenty of ambiguity, especially the somewhat tautological definition of services ("use in commerce" means "used . . . in the sale or advertising of services"). However, it requires that the use take place in the "ordinary course of trade," and it implies that the use should be visible to consumers either on the product packaging or in marketing collateral.

---

[45] 15 U.S.C. §1127.

From a purely textualist perspective, this definition should govern all references to "use in commerce" in the statute. After all, §45's preamble says that the definitions apply "[i]n the construction of this chapter [Chapter 22, which governs trademarks], unless the contrary is plainly apparent from the context...." Where the statute uses the phrase "use in commerce," the §45 definition should apply by its terms.

Prof. McCarthy rejects the textualist approach, calling it a "robotic statutory reading divorced from the history and meaning" of trademark law.[46] He views the §45 definition as a "quaint" "anachronism" that, when applied to the §32(a) and §43(a) "use in commerce" references, leads to an "awkward and inept" result.[47] Instead, Prof. McCarthy believes the plaintiff's *prima facie* infringement case does not contain a separate "use in commerce" element.[48] Profs. Dinwoodie and Janis agree with Prof. McCarthy about the lack of a "use in commerce" element and the merit to rejecting the textualist approach,[49] arguing that such an approach would make language in §33(b)(4) (the trademark fair use provision) superfluous and, as a result, would be inconsistent with the Supreme Court's interpretation of that language in the recent Supreme Court *KP Permanent* ruling.[50]

Similarly rejecting a textualist approach, some courts have ignored the §45 "use in commerce" definition entirely,[51] instead construing the §32 and §43 references to "use in commerce" to be coextensive with Congress' power under the Commerce Clause.[52] This expansive argument proceeds as follows:

- Congress needs Constitutional authorization to enact the Lanham Act.
- The Intellectual Property Clause[53] does not provide that authorization; it only authorizes Congress to enact patent and copyright protection.[54]
- Instead, Congress enacts the Lanham Act under the Commerce Clause.
- Congress' references to "use in commerce" are designed to keep the statute within its Commerce Clause authority.

---

[46] MCCARTHY, *supra* note 5, §23:11.50.
[47] *Id.*
[48] *Id.*
[49] *See* Graeme B. Dinwoodie & Mark D. Janis, *Confusion Over Use: Contextualism in Trademark Law*, 92 IOWA L. REV. 1597 (2007).
[50] K.P. Permanent Make-Up, Inc. v Lasting Impression, Inc., 543 U.S. 111 (2004).
[51] *See, e.g.*, Bosley Med. Inst., Inc. v Kremer, 403 F.3d 672 (9th Cir. 2005); Planned Parenthood Fed'n of Am., Inc. v Bucci, 1997 WL 133313 (S.D.N.Y. 1997); SMJ Group, Inc. v 417 Lafayette Rest. LLC, 439 F. Supp. 2d 281 (S.D.N.Y. 2006).
[52] U.S. CONST. art. I, §8, cl. 3.
[53] *Id.*, §8, cl. 8.
[54] *See* Trade-Mark Cases, 100 U.S. 82 (1879).

- As a result, the courts interpret the "use in commerce" language as extending the statute to the maximum extent of Congress' authority under the Commerce Clause.

In support of this argument, some courts[55] have cited the §45 definition of "commerce," defined as "all commerce which may lawfully be regulated by Congress."[56] This expansive reading relies on an odd method of statutory construction. To reach this result, the courts read the "use in commerce" language in §32 and §43 as "use in *commerce*" where only the word *commerce* is defined in §45 even though §45 also contains a definition of the entire phrase "*use in commerce*." If Congress had intended for §32 and §43 to use only the §45 definition of "commerce" instead of the "use in commerce" definition from the same section, it certainly did not make this intent very clear.

As this discussion illustrates, there is no ideal reading of the statute;[57] any reading of the statute exposes drafting anomalies or creates statutory conflicts. Accordingly, it is not surprising that courts cannot agree on the definition, and their efforts are likely to be irresolute. It is likely that definitive resolution will come only from the Supreme Court or Congressional action.

Even if courts read the "use in commerce" definition expansively, the statute requires that the trademark be used "in connection with a sale of goods or services." At minimum, this language contemplates that some set of non-commercial activity would be outside the reach of trademark infringement. However, some courts have taken an expansive view of this phrase as well. For example, in *PETA v Doughney*,[58] Doughney created a parody website entitled "People Eating Tasty Animals" at peta.org. Doughney did not derive revenues from the website, but the court found a connection to the sale of goods/services because (1) the peta.org website "prevented users from obtaining or using PETA's goods or services," and (2) the website had uncompensated, editorially selected links to thirty third-party commercial websites.

Thus, by combining two expansive statutory interpretations, the Lanham Act can reach unambiguously non-commercial activity—such as the *Doughney* case, involving a parody website that was not making money, advertising third parties, or interfering with the trademark owner's ability to make money.

---

[55] *See, e.g.*, Bosley Med. Inst., Inc. v Kremer, 403 F.3d 672 (9th Cir. 2005).
[56] 15 U.S.C. §1127.
[57] *See* Graeme B. Dinwoodie & Mark D. Janis, *Lessons from the Trademark Use Debate*, 92 IOWA L. REV. 1703, 1713 (2007) ("no one can settle on what 'trademark use' means").
[58] People for the Ethical Treatment of Animals v Doughney, 263 F.3d 359 (4th Cir. 2001).

2. *"Use in commerce" gone awry* The result of a double-expansive interpretation of trademark "use in commerce" creates significant legal risks for online word of mouth for at least two reasons. First, in some cases, consumers may legitimately generate revenues from online word of mouth. Individual consumers self-publishing their content can easily sign up to advertising programs, such as Google's AdSense program,[59] that pay them to display third party ads on their websites. These ad programs can help consumers defray their web hosting costs and, in some cases, provide some modest compensation for their time. In this respect, consumer-publishers are just like newspaper reporters who are paid a salary or royalty for writing a story about a trademark owner. Yet, unlike these journalists, under an expansive/double-expansive reading of the "use in commerce" requirement, consumers who disseminate their brand-related opinions via an ad-supported website could satisfy the trademark use in commerce standard.[60]

Second, courts have found a trademark use in commerce even when a consumer engaged in no commercial activity at all. This was illustrated by *Doughney* (discussed above) and emphasized by *Planned Parenthood v Bucci*.[61] In that case, an anti-abortion griper operated a website at plannedparenthood.com. On the site, he called visitors' attention to an anti-abortion book by a third party author. This "plug" was uncompensated, but it nevertheless satisfied the court's double-expansive interpretation of use in commerce. In other words, the single word of mouth reference to a commercial product pushed Bucci's entire gripe site into the Lanham Act's ambit.

The *Bucci* case may represent the zenith (nadir?) of use in commerce overreaching. Two recent online griper appellate decisions—*Bosley*[62] and *Lamparello*[63]—have diverged from *Bucci* and *Doughney* and excused online griping. Yet, amidst the good news for gripers, there remain troubling signs about the applicability of the use in commerce doctrine to online word of mouth.

In *Bosley*, Kremer (a dissatisfied customer of the plaintiff) set up a gripe site at bosleymedical.com. Kremer did not try to generate revenues, and the

---

[59] https://www.google.com/adsense/. Another example is the Amazon Affiliates program. See http://affiliate-program.amazon.com/gp/associates/join.

[60] The fact that these editorial references should not create a likelihood of consumer confusion will be addressed in Section III(B).

[61] Planned Parenthood Fed'n of Am. v Bucci, 42 U.S.P.Q. 2d (BNA) 1430 (S.D.N.Y. 1997), *aff'd*, 1998 U.S. App. LEXIS 22179 (2d Cir.), *cert. denied*, 525 U.S. 834 (1998).

[62] Bosley Med. Inst., Inc. v Kremer, 403 F.3d 672 (9th Cir. 2005).

[63] Lamparello v Falwell, 420 F.3d 309 (4th Cir. 2005), *cert. denied*, 547 U.S. 1069 (2006).

site's only outlinks were to Kremer's lawyers and to a sister site operated by Kremer, which in turn had links to a newsgroup that displayed ads for the plaintiff's competitors. On these facts, the court could have simply concluded that this was a non-commercial gripe site which was categorically outside the Lanham Act's express terms. Instead, the court evaluated the nature of the outlinks and, only after the court was satisfied that Kremer had made the "right" type of links, determined that there was no use in commerce.

In *Lamparello*, Lamparello set up a gripe site at fallwell.com to critique Rev. Jerry Falwell's attitude towards gays. The parties stipulated that "Lamparello has never sold goods or services on his website."[64] However, at one point, Lamparello had an apparently uncompensated outbound link to an Amazon.com web page where visitors could purchase a book recommended by Lamparello. On these facts, Lamparello easily should have qualified as a non-commercial actor. Yet, the court punted on the use in commerce issue, calling it a "difficult question,"[65] and instead found for the griper on likelihood of confusion grounds. In other words, the defendant's recommendation of a commercial product through a single outbound link, even if uncompensated and for a limited period of time, made the use in commerce question a difficult one.

3. A normative view of "use in commerce" Although the *Bosley* and *Lamparello* cases ultimately reached the right outcome on trademark infringement, those cases (and others)[66] have turned the use in commerce element into a bizarre link-counting witchhunt where a "wrong" link may flip on Lanham Act coverage like a light switch. Not only does this discourage websites from providing links that are beneficial to users, but it is significantly overinclusive, leading to substantial risk of bona fide non-commercial activity being deemed a use in commerce.[67]

Instead, a use in commerce should occur only when the defendant uses the plaintiff's trademark to designate the source of the defendant's goods or services.[68] This source-designation requirement is explicit in the definition of

---

[64] *Id.* at 311.

[65] *Id.* at 314.

[66] *See, e.g.*, Utah Lighthouse Ministry, Inc. v Discovery Computing, Inc., 2007 U.S. Dist. LEXIS 21978 (D. Utah 2007) (another griper case where the court engaged in link-counting).

[67] *Cf.* Nissan Motor Co. v Nissan Computer Corp., 378 F.3d 1002 (9th Cir. 2004) (outlinks to critical commentary are not "commercial," and restrictions against such outlinks violated the First Amendment).

[68] *See* Stacey L. Dogan & Mark A. Lemley, *Grounding Trademark Law Through Trademark Use*, 92 IOWA L. REV. 1669, 1681 (2007).

a "trademark," defined in §45 as a word (or other symbol) used "to identify and distinguish his or her goods, including a unique product, from those manufactured or sold by others and to indicate the source of the goods."[69] This definition constitutes a predicate requirement for protectable rights, but it also is a constituent requirement of an infringement. Section 45's definition of "use in commerce" references the definition of "trademark," thus implicitly requiring that the defendant cannot infringe unless the defendant makes a source-designating use of the third party trademark.

Admittedly, the source-designation requirement for a "use in commerce" creates some problems even as it solves others. First, as Dinwoodie and Janis have noted, this statutory interpretation would make some language in the descriptive fair use provisions of §33(b)(4) superfluous (specifically, the exclusion for when the defendant is using the trademark "otherwise than as a mark").[70] However, other statutory interpretations create other conflicts as well. Until Congress fixes its drafting mistakes, something has to give.

Second, Dinwoodie and Janis have also noted that a source-designation requirement creates the risk that defendants could confuse consumers but categorically avoid trademark liability.[71]

Third, consumers routinely do not understand the "source" of goods or services they are buying—even when no one is trying to cloud the issue—because trademarks rarely designate a specific manufacturing plant or the work of specific personnel, and trademark owners make source determinations difficult through trademark licensing, co-branding, merchandising and brand ownership by low-profile conglomerates. Further, it is not clear how much consumers even care about a product's "source" when making marketplace choices. So predicating the trademark use in commerce doctrine on source designation may be, at best, somewhat anachronistic.

Nevertheless, descriptively, the source-designation approach is consistent with the statute, and normatively, the approach provides an efficient way to analyze some socially beneficial behavior involving trademarks that has been vexing courts. Specifically, to the extent that the Lanham Act requires a defendant to designate the source of its products using the plaintiff's trademark, some types of activities do not qualify as uses in commerce:

a. No goods/services If a defendant does not offer any of its own goods or services in the marketplace, its actions should be outside the use in commerce standard by definition. Many consumers disseminating online word of mouth

---

[69] 15 U.S.C. §1127.
[70] 15 U.S.C. §1115(b)(4).
[71] See Dinwoodie & Janis, *supra* note 49.

should qualify under this standard, including gripers such as Bucci, Doughney, Kremer and Lamparello. In these cases, the consumers are espousing their opinions, not offering goods or services.[72] As a result, any trademark references contained in their online word of mouth cannot designate source of the consumer's (non-existent) goods/services.[73]

b. *Referential uses* Even when a word of mouth disseminator is offering its own goods and services, it is not making a trademark use in commerce when it uses the third party trademark for its referential meaning of describing/identifying the trademark owner's goods or services.[74]

An offline example illustrates this point. Newspapers offer their goods in the marketplace. In editorial stories they publish (and sell), such as product reviews, newspapers use third party trademarks for their referential value. These trademark references do not designate the newspaper's source and thus do not qualify as a use in commerce of those trademarks they editorially reference—even if the trademark is prominently displayed in a first page headline, which might prompt some new incremental customers to buy single copies of the newspaper to learn more about the trademark owner; and even if the newspaper places ads adjacent to the story.

As this example illustrates, a publication's commerciality does not dictate the trademark law characterization of trademark references made in the publication. So long as references to third party trademarks are not designed to designate the *publication's* goods or services, they do not qualify as a use in commerce.

This is true in the online context as well. Even if online word of mouth is published as part of a commercial endeavor (such as an ad-supported website),

---

[72] Admittedly, some judges might circularly characterize the dissemination of word of mouth as a service of disseminating word of mouth. *See* SMJ Group, Inc. v 417 Lafayette Rest. LLC, 439 F. Supp. 2d 281 (S.D.N.Y. 2006). However, in effect this tautology eliminates the element. *Compare* The Freecycle Network, Inc. v Oey 505 F.3d 898 (9th Cir. 2007) (disparaging a trademark owner did not constitute a trademark use in commerce).

[73] In contrast, word-of-mouth marketing can constitute a trademark use in commerce when it is part of a trademark owner's marketing campaign to sell its goods and services. *See* Allard Enters., Inc. v Advanced Programming Res., Inc., 146 F.3d 350, 359 (6th Cir. 1998).

[74] *See* Universal Commc'n Sys., Inc. v Lycos, Inc., 478 F.3d 413, 425 (1st Cir. 2007) ("Lycos is not using the 'UCSY' trade name 'on' a product (or business) at all, but is simply referring to the existing company that has adopted that trade name.").

The exception is when the defendant's reference to a third party trademark is part of the defendant's source designation of its own products/services, in which case the reference may qualify as a nominative use. *See infra* Section III(C).

referential trademark uses should still be excused.[75] Thus, there is no reason to engage in link-counting exercises; even a for-profit website with hundreds of compensated links does not make a use in commerce when it uses third party trademarks referentially.

c. Imperceptible uses   Online, web publishers can reference trademarks in a manner that consumers cannot perceive. For example, web publishers can include trademarks in their "keyword metatags," which are index terms readable by a search engine's robots but generally not visible to web visitors.[76]

Judicial scrutiny of these "imperceptible uses" typically has been unfavorable. For example, courts often have treated inclusion of third party trademarks in the keyword metatags as a per se infringement[77]—in many cases ignoring the use in commerce requirement entirely.

However, if consumers do not "perceive" the trademark's inclusion in the keyword metatags, then the metatags do not act as a source designator and the metatag usage should be irrelevant to the trademark analysis. Further, to the extent that search engines ignore keyword metatags—the case with Google's and Microsoft's search engines, among others[78]—the keyword metatags do not have any functional consequence at all, and therefore they are incapable of acting as source designators. As a result, the inclusion of a third party trademark as a keyword metatag, without more, should not constitute a use in commerce.[79]

---

[75] See Universal Commc'n Sys., Inc. v Lycos, Inc., 478 F.3d 413, 424 (1st Cir. 2007). See generally Posting of Eric Goldman to Technology & Marketing Law Blog, *Commercial Referential Trademark Uses (Rescuecom v Google Amicus Brief Outtakes)*, June 28, 2007, http://blog.ericgoldman.org/archives/2007/06/ commercial_refe.htm.

[76] See Goldman, *Deregulating Relevancy*, supra note 38, at 529–30. Description metatags are another metatag type that has created some confusion in the courts. In some cases, search engines may display description metatags verbatim as part of search results, see id., in which case the description metatags act like ad copy. In other cases, search engines ignore description metatags, see id., in which case they are imperceptible like keyword metatags.

[77] See, e.g., Tdata Inc. v Aircraft Technical Publishers, 411 F. Supp. 2d 901 (S.D. Ohio 2006).

[78] See Posting of Danny Sullivan to Search Engine Land, *Meta Keywords Tag 101: How to "Legally" Hide Words On Your Pages For Search Engines*, Sept. 5, 2007, http://searchengineland.com/070905-194221.php.

[79] See Site Pro-1 v Better Metal, 2007 WL 1385730 (E.D.N.Y. 2007); Posting of Eric Goldman to Technology & Marketing Law Blog, *Outdated Metatags Don't Infringe—Pop Warner v NH Youth Football & Spirit Conference*, Sept. 25, 2006, http://blog.ericgoldman.org/archives/2006/09/outdated_metata.htm.

4. Procedural considerations Even if a court improperly characterizes the defendant's behavior as a use in commerce, the defendant's use often will not create a likelihood of consumer confusion or may qualify for the trademark fair use defense. Assuming these defendants will prevail in any case, does it matter what doctrinal factor is used to resolve the case?

With respect to trademark infringement and online word of mouth, the answer is yes. First, there is the matter of judicial economy. Trademark law lacks many bright-line rules, but a clear rule delimiting its boundaries would save some wasted resources. For example, the multi-factor likelihood of consumer confusion test is a poor substitute for screening out non-trademark uses because consumer confusion is typically a fact question that is not easily resolved on summary judgment.[80] Thus, litigating consumer confusion in these cases increases defendants' costs, requires more adjudicative resources, and reduces predictability. Also, as discussed below, some courts have misused judicial heuristics (such as the initial interest confusion doctrine) to eviscerate the consumer confusion requirement, making the use in commerce doctrine a better safeguard against overexpansive cases.

Second, plaintiffs have the burden to establish the *prima facie* elements of a trademark infringement, but defendants have the burden to establish any defenses such as trademark fair use. This burden-shifting further puts defendants at risk of losing meritorious defenses. Further, as discussed below, some defenses (such as the nominative use doctrine) are not universally recognized, so these defenses may not be doctrinally robust enough to provide adequate coverage for non-use circumstances.

Therefore, other trademark doctrines are not an adequate substitute for rigorous scrutiny of the trademark use in commerce requirement. If the defendant is not making a trademark use, courts should resolve the case on that basis.

5. Source designation and intermediaries So far, this subsection has considered trademark references by consumers themselves. The use in commerce doctrine is also important to the liability of online intermediaries that disseminate online word of mouth, including product review sites and search engines.

a. Product review websites Product review websites, such as Epinions or Yelp, allow their users to opine on marketplace offerings. Typically, a product review site builds a catalog ("taxonomy") of products and services and allows consumers to post opinions (the site may also contain product reviews

---

[80] *See* Dogan & Lemley, *supra* note 68, at 1695–6.

from other sources). To build this taxonomy, product review sites necessarily must reference third party trademarks, which can result in these trademarks appearing in the site's URLs, page titles, metatags and site text. Consumer-supplied product reviews can create revenue for the websites by helping the website get good placement in the search engines, which can increase advertising revenue and, if (as Amazon does) the site sells products as a retailer, by improving conversion-to-sale.[81]

A product review website's trademark uses might be excused by trademark exhaustion or nominative use doctrines. Either way, like other referential uses, taxonomical references should not constitute trademark uses in commerce because they do not attempt to designate the source of the product review sites' services (irrespective of the product review site's commerciality).[82] This narrow construction of trademark use in commerce allows product review sites to build and organize useful databases of online word of mouth.

b. Search engines   Search engines often sell and display advertising in response to users' search keywords. Courts have irreconcilably split about whether selling or buying ads triggered by trademarked keywords constitutes a trademark use in commerce,[83] which is not surprising given the statutory ambiguity discussed above.

Descriptively, keyword triggering should not constitute a use in commerce because neither search engines nor advertisers use keywords as source designators of their goods/services. Instead, keywords are the functional equivalent of product review websites' taxonomical structures. Like other types of referential uses, keywords act as the lingua franca for interested consumers to match with relevant content. Also, because consumers do not "see" the triggering, it lacks the perceivability to designate source.[84]

Normatively, keyword triggering creates a new and important way for consumers to obtain helpful content not controlled by the trademark owner.

---

[81] See Chevalier & Mayzlin, *supra* note 25.

[82] *See* Universal Commc'n Sys., Inc. v Lycos, Inc., 478 F.3d 413, 424 (1st Cir. 2007) ("Lycos might profit by encouraging others to talk about UCS under the UCSY name, but neither that speech nor Lycos's providing a forum for that speech is the type of use that is subject to trademark liability.").

[83] *See* Eric Goldman, Keyword Law, http://www.ericgoldman.org/Resources/keywordlaw.pdf.

[84] *See* 1-800 Contacts, Inc. v WhenU.com, Inc., 414 F.3d 400 (2d Cir. 2005); Merck & Co. v Mediplan Health Consulting, 2006 WL 800756 (S.D.N.Y. 2006); Rescuecom Corp. v Google, Inc., 2006 WL 2811711 (N.D.N.Y. 2006). A trademark reference in ad copy could constitute a use in commerce, Hamzik v Zale Corp./Delaware, 2007 WL 1174863 (N.D.N.Y. 2007), but each specific ad must be independently evaluated.

Like other examples of online word of mouth, this material can increase competitive pressures on trademark owners, hold them accountable for their choices, and allow marketplace mechanisms to work.

Although selling keywords should not be a use in commerce, search engines might be contributorily liable if advertisers commit trademark infringement.[85] Advertisers do not make a use in commerce solely by purchasing keywords (due to the lack of perceivability), but an advertiser's overall activities (keyword purchase + ad display + product sales) collectively could infringe. Even so, search engines generally should not be contributorily liable because they only provide ad space and thus do not control the instrumentalities advertisers use to infringe.[86] In the rare situations where search engines may have sufficient control over such instrumentalities, they should get the benefit of the printer/publisher remedy exclusion,[87] which limits remedies to a prospective injunction (no damages).

B. Likelihood of consumer confusion

Assessing consumer confusion about product source is an inherently inexact process. Factfinders try to create a hypothetical person ("the reasonable consumer") and speculate how that person would perceive the litigants' marketing. Then, factfinders may find infringement when a small minority of hypothetical consumers are likely to be confused,[88] and even if (1) no consumer is actually confused, and (2) many consumers completely understand the relationship between the litigants. Collectively, these factors increase the risk that factfinders will erroneously find a likelihood of consumer confusion.

Online, likelihood of confusion determinations are even more likely to skew towards finding infringement. First, consumers vary their search methodologies depending on their search objectives,[89] and different consumers seeking to accomplish the same objective may choose different

---

[85] *See* Dogan & Lemley, *supra* note 68.
[86] *See* Lockheed Martin Corp. v Network Solutions, Inc., 194 F.3d 980 (9th Cir. 1999).
[87] *See* 15 U.S.C. §1114(2)(B).
[88] *See* MCCARTHY, *supra* note 5, §23:2.
[89] *See* Andrei Broder, *A Taxonomy of Web Search*, http://www.acm.org/sigs/sigir/forum/F2002/broder.pdf#search=%22navigational%20informational%20search%22 (describing navigational, informational and transactional search objectives); LOUIS ROSENFELD & PETER MORVILLE, INFORMATION ARCHITECTURE FOR THE WORLD WIDE WEB §6.2 (1st ed. 1998) (describing search methodologies such as known-item searching, existence searching, exploratory searching and comprehensive searching/research).

search methodologies.[90] Search methodology heterogeneity makes it difficult to establish a reasonable consumer baseline.

Second, factfinders try to infer an online consumer's search objectives with minimal data from the searcher. Offline, many consumer searches take place within a context, such as a retail environment, that adds crucial data about the searcher's possible intent.[91] Online, in general-purpose search engines such as Google, searchers manifest their objectives through a single decontextualized search term—which does not provide enough data to support reliable inferences about those objectives.

In response to the dearth of reliable data about consumer intent, courts sometimes bypass the traditional multi-factor likelihood of consumer confusion test and instead use the "initial interest confusion" ("IIC") doctrine as a heuristic. In 1999, the Ninth Circuit defined IIC as "the use of another's trademark in a manner reasonably calculated to capture initial consumer attention, even though no actual sale is finally completed as a result of the confusion,"[92] but courts cannot agree on a single definition of IIC,[93] making the doctrine unusually plastic.

In some cases, IIC has subtly changed the basic thrust of the court's consumer confusion inquiry. Instead of examining consumer confusion about *product source*, courts applying IIC may focus on consumer confusion about *content source*.[94] Content source confusion occurs when consumers experience confusion about why they are seeing the content presented to them, even though this content does not cause consumers to make any errors in their marketplace choices. Content source confusion cannot be cured by subsequent clarification (as the *Promatek* court said, the defendant "cannot unring the bell"),[95] so disclaimers or subsequent corrective information may not adequately dispel the confusion.

Content source confusion is problematic for numerous reasons, including the fact that consumers are routinely confused about why they see any particular

---

[90] *See* Yahoo.com, *Long & Winding, supra* note 24 (a consumer's search methodology reflects his/her values and personalities).
[91] *See* Goldman, *Deregulating Relevancy, supra* note 38, at 527–8.
[92] Brookfield Commc'ns, Inc. v West Coast Entm't Corp., 174 F.3d 1036, 1062 (9th Cir. 1999) (quotations and citations omitted).
[93] At various times, courts have characterized IIC as (1) a subset of sponsorship confusion, (2) diversion of consumer attention, (3) deceptive diversion, or (4) competitive diversion. *See* Goldman, *Deregulating Relevancy, supra* note 38, at 563.
[94] *See, e.g.*, Brookfield Commc'ns, Inc. v West Coast Entm't Corp., 174 F.3d 1036 (9th Cir. 1999); Playboy Enters., Inc. v Netscape Commc'ns Corp., 354 F.3d 1020 (9th Cir. 2004); Promatek Indus. v Equitrac Corp., 300 F.3d 808 (7th Cir. 2002).
[95] *Promatek*, 300 F.3d, at 808.

content[96] and because there is little social science support for the proposition that content source confusion harms trademark owners.

Further, the content source confusion doctrine can adversely affect online word of mouth. Because online word of mouth competes with trademark owners' content for consumer attention, consumers may not immediately understand the source of online word of mouth, even if subsequent consumer investigation clears this up. As a result, some courts have, in fact, found that online word of mouth (or analogous content) creates IIC.[97]

For reasons I have explained elsewhere,[98] courts should ditch any heuristics, such as IIC, for evaluating consumer confusion and instead continue to apply the venerable multi-factor likelihood of consumer confusion test. Thus, courts evaluating consumer confusion should carefully consider the totality of the circumstances, including consumer expectations and all of a defendant's behavior (not just single actions, such as a keyword purchase).

C. Fair use defenses

Descriptive fair use occurs when the defendant describes its product using a descriptive trademark for its dictionary meaning.[99] For example, the trademarked phrase "sealed with a kiss" for lip gloss does not prevent other companies from informing their consumers that they can "seal it with a kiss" when that phrase describes exactly what consumers should do.[100]

Nominative use occurs when the defendant designates its product source using a third party trademark for its referential meaning. According to the Ninth Circuit, nominative use occurs when:

---

[96] For example, consumers do not understand how print publishers make their editorial judgments. *See* Posting of Eric Goldman to Technology & Marketing Law Blog, *Bracha Responds re. Search Engine Regulation*, Aug. 11, 2007, http://blog.ericgoldman.org/archives/2007/08/bracha_responds.htm. Similarly, consumers have no idea how search engines work. *See* Marable, *supra* note 40.

[97] *See, e.g.*, J.K. Harris & Co. v Kassel, 2002 WL 1303124 (N.D. Cal. 2002), *rev'd* 253 F. Supp. 2d 1120 (N.D. Cal. 2003) (disgruntled customer site); PACCAR Inc. v TeleScan Techs., L.L.C., 319 F.3d 243 (6th Cir. 2003) (information about accessories and dealers); Key3Media Events, Inc. v Convention Connection, Inc., 2002 U.S. Dist. LEXIS 4043 (D. Nev. 2002) (travel information tailored to conference attendees); *see also* SMJ Group, Inc. v 417 Lafayette Rest. L.L.C., 439 F. Supp. 2d 281 (S.D.N.Y. 2006) (physical-space distribution of gripe leaflet).

[98] *See* Goldman, *Deregulating Relevancy*, *supra* note 38, at 575–95.

[99] It is a defense to infringement to use "a term or device which is descriptive of and used fairly and in good faith only to describe the goods or services of such party, or their geographic origin." 15 U.S.C. §1115(b)(4).

[100] *See* Cosmetically Sealed Indus., Inc. v Chesebrough-Pond's USA Co., 125 F.3d 28 (2d Cir. 1997).

- The defendant cannot readily identify its offering without referencing the trademark;
- The reference uses only as much of the trademark as is reasonably necessary to identify the offering; and
- The reference does not suggest the trademark owner's sponsorship or endorsement.[101]

Nominative use cases often involve media products where the media content relates to third party trademarks. For example, a book entitled "The Unofficial Guide to Maximizing Sales on the eBay Website" should qualify as nominative use.

However, the nominative use doctrine is not universally accepted. Although it is recognized in the Ninth Circuit,[102] the Sixth Circuit declined to adopt the doctrine in 2003.[103] As a result, defendants cannot universally rely on its availability, especially given the unsettled nature of Internet jurisdiction.

Because both trademark fair use doctrines are narrow in scope, some legitimate activities, such as parody or comparative advertising, may fall outside their boundaries. Further, defendants must carry the burden of fair use as an affirmative defense. As a result, fair use is often unhelpful for trademark defendants.

Online word of mouth activities can directly implicate trademark fair use (especially nominative use) because consumers must refer to trademarks to opine about them. Typically, these references should not constitute a "use in commerce" because they do not designate the source of the consumer's offerings. When courts mischaracterize online word of mouth as a trademark use in commerce, they put a lot of doctrinal pressure on the narrow nominative use doctrine, and this increases the risks of erroneous outcomes. The use in commerce doctrine is better suited to do this heavy lifting.

In limited cases, online word of mouth does constitute a trademark use in commerce. For example, a recent case[104] involved *Acomplia Report*,[105] an ad-supported online publication of news and commentary about Sanofi-Aventis'

---

[101] *See* New Kids on the Block v News Am. Publ'g, Inc., 971 F.2d 302 (9th Cir. 1992).
[102] *See, e.g., id.*; Playboy Enters., Inc. v Welles, 279 F.3d 796 (9th Cir. 2002).
[103] *See* PACCAR Inc. v TeleScan Techs. L.L.C., 319 F.3d 243 (6th Cir. 2003).
[104] Med. Week News, Inc. v Sanofi-Aventis Group (N.D. Cal. complaint filed June 27, 2005), *available at* http://www.eff.org/legal/cases/medweek_v_sanofi/acomplia_initial_complaint.pdf. The case ultimately settled. *See News Website Can Keep Domain Name After Trademark Fight*, EFF.org, Nov. 9, 2005, http://www.eff.org/news/archives/2005_11.php#004143.
[105] http://www.acompliareport.com/.

anti-obesity drug (rimonabant) marketed as Acomplia.[106] The *Acomplia Report* actively promotes its business using a source designator that includes a third party trademark, so it may be using the trademark "Acomplia" in commerce. Nevertheless, the publication title should qualify as a nominative use. The publication title accurately explains its editorial focus to consumers, in ways that alternative titles without the brand name would not do. Further, the *Acomplia Report* generates and disseminates online word of mouth about the drug that acts as a valuable marketplace resource, and the publication title increases the chances that consumers can find this word of mouth information. As this example illustrates, trademark fair use doctrines have an important role to play in preserving online word of mouth, but only as a narrow complement to a rigorous application of the use in commerce doctrine.

IV. Conclusion

In theory, trademark law helps consumers make good choices in the marketplace. In practice, misapplication of trademark law can *hinder* consumer decision-making, and this chapter illustrates those risks. Online word of mouth can play an essential marketplace-disciplining/rewarding function for brands (rewarding the good; punishing the bad),[107] but trademark law can interfere with that mechanism, acting as a tool to curb the production and dissemination of online word of mouth.

With these tools, trademark owners can selectively excise content from the Internet—favorable word of mouth can stay, but unfavorable word of mouth must go.[108] The resulting content purge can produce "lopsided" brand perceptions of trademark owners where consumers do not learn about negative aspects of brands.[109] This allows trademark owners to mitigate marketplace

---

[106] http://en.sanofi-aventis.com/events/event1/en/about.asp.

[107] See URBAN, *supra* note 3; Shmuel I. Becher & Tal Zarsky, *E-Contract Doctrine 2.0: Standard Form Contracting in the Age of Online User Participation*, http://papers.ssrn.com/sol3/papers.cfm?abstract_id=984765.

[108] See Dogan & Lemley, *supra* note 68, at 1700–01; Bob Sullivan, *Companies' Online Reputation Scrubbed Clean*, MSNBC, Sept. 11, 2007. In fact, negative word of mouth has a disproportionately higher impact on consumer perceptions, *Solomon*, *supra* note 24, at 381–2, making it even more compelling for trademark owners to suppress.

[109] There are countless examples of trademark owners' efforts to use trademark law to suppress unwanted criticism, as the numerous lawsuits and UDRP actions over [trademarkowner]sucks.com attest. A more poignant example may be *BidZirk v Smith*, where a trademark owner sued a disgruntled customer for blogging about his negative experiences with the company. BidZirk, L.L.C. v Smith, 2006 WL 3242333 (D.S.C. 2006) *aff'd*, 2007 WL 664302 (4th cir. 2007) dismissed 2007 WL 3119445 (D.S.C. 2007). Fortunately, the district and appellate courts in the *BidZirk* case have realized the importance of Smith's blog post, but these risks will continue to arise frequently.

recourse for their poor choices. Taken to an extreme, the depletion of negative online word of mouth reduces the utility of the Internet as a credible information resource, forcing consumers to seek other information sources that may have higher search costs.

This result could turn trademark law on its head—instead of reducing consumer search costs, trademark law could increase those costs. Fortunately, courts sensitive to the value of online word of mouth can find ways to avoid this undesirable outcome.

Section C

Trademarks and Traditional Knowledge

16 Trademarks and traditional knowledge and cultural intellectual property
Susy Frankel*

I. Introduction

The substantive law of trademarks is in the wings rather than on center stage of the international intellectual property debate. Similarly, traditional knowledge and cultural property concerns of indigenous peoples in relation to trademarks have not taken the center stage of the debate regarding indigenous peoples' intellectual property rights.[1] Much of the international intellectual property discourse concerning indigenous peoples' rights is focused on patent law and copyright. Patent law, in particular, has drawn attention to indigenous peoples' rights in their traditional knowledge because of the role patent law plays in the relationship between indigenous peoples and bio-prospecting. Patent law's direct nexus with development, technology transfer, and subject-specific matters, such as pharmaceuticals, places it at the epicenter of international intellectual property tensions. This tension is played out in debate where two apparent sides emerge: the developed and developing world.[2] The intellectual property rights of indigenous peoples have, in part, evolved as a concern primarily of developing countries that are looking for their comparative advantage in intellectual property at times when their disadvantage under

---

* Professor of Law, Victoria University of Wellington, New Zealand, susy.frankel@vuw.ac.nz. Thanks to Graeme Dinwoodie and Mark Janis for their constructive comments on drafts.

[1] There are a number of forums where the ambit of international intellectual property protection and traditional knowledge is on the agenda. The main arenas of this discussion are: the Convention on Biological Diversity, *see* http://www.biodiv.org/programmes/socio-eco/traditional/default.aspx; the World Intellectual Property Organization ("WIPO"), *see* www.wipo.org/tk/en/; and the TRIPS Council of the World Trade Organization ("WTO"), *see* http://192.91.247.23/ english/tratop_e/trips_e/art27_3b_e.htm. The WTO discussions are in their early stages. *See* WTO, *The Protection of Traditional Knowledge and Folklore Summary of Issues Raised and Points Made* IP/C/W/370/Rev.1, Mar. 9, 2006.

[2] *See generally* KEITH E. MASKUS AND JEROME H. REICHMAN, INTERNATIONAL PUBLIC GOODS AND TRANSFER OF TECHNOLOGY (Cambridge Univ. Press, 2005).

the current TRIPS Agreement[3] regime is so apparent.[4] That said, the calls for recognition of indigenous intellectual property rights are not limited to the developing world. Many developed countries with indigenous peoples are faced with examining how, if at all, to recognize indigenous peoples' intellectual property rights. The United States, Canada, Australia and New Zealand are examples of such developed nations.[5]

Trademark law has been used to both protect and undermine indigenous peoples' claims of protection for their traditional knowledge and cultural property. Indigenous peoples have recognized that in some circumstances existing trademark regimes may be a means by which to protect their cultural icons, signs, and symbols.[6] At the same time, third parties have utilized trademark registrations as a means of harnessing indigenous peoples' culture in pursuit of their own commercial ends. This can work against indigenous peoples because they lose control of their signs and symbols to the trademark owner, at least in respect of uses covered by the trademark registration.[7]

The appropriate role for trademarks in protecting indigenous peoples' traditional knowledge and cultural property is not easily determined. Indigenous

---

[3] Agreement on Trade Related Aspects of Intellectual Property, April 15, 1994, 1869 U.N.T.S. 299, 33 I.L.M. 1197 [hereinafter TRIPS Agreement].

[4] It is often stated that developing countries agreed to the TRIPS Agreement because of the other benefits of WTO membership. *See* J.H. Reichman & David Lange, *Bargaining Around the TRIPS Agreement: The Case for Ongoing Public-Private Initiatives to Facilitate World Intellectual Property Transactions*, 9 DUKE J. COMP. & INT'L L. 11, 17 (1998) (describing the TRIPS Agreement as "a non-cooperative game").

[5] For a discussion of indigenous peoples and cultural intellectual property generally in the United States, see, R. Guest, *Intellectual Property Rights and Native American Tribes*, 20 AM. INDIAN L. REV. 111 (1995–6) and Rachael Grad, *Indigenous Rights and Intellectual Property Law: A Comparison of the United States and Australia*, 13 DUKE J. COMP. AND INT'L L. 203 (2003). In Australia, see Brad Sherman & Leanne Wiseman, *Towards an Indigenous Public Domain?* in LUCIE GUIBAULT AND P. BERNT HUGENHOLTZ (eds) *The Future of the Public Domain*, 259 (Kluwer Law Int'l, 2006). For Māori and intellectual property in New Zealand, see SUSY FRANKEL AND GEOFF MCLAY, INTELLECTUAL PROPERTY IN NEW ZEALAND, ch. 3 (Butterworths, LexisNexis, 2002) [hereinafter FRANKEL & MCLAY].

[6] The TRIPS Agreement, *supra* note 3, art. 15, uses "sign" as the term that catches all potential trademark subject matter including words. "Signs and symbols" is used in this chapter to encompass the subject matter of indigenous peoples' icons, signs, and symbols.

[7] The scope of the registration is primarily governed by what is on the register – the description of the registration in relation to a class of goods or services. Infringement can occur by use of a sign similar to the registration and so the scope must be construed broadly.

peoples sometimes seek the exclusivity that arises from trademark registration as protection for signs and symbols, and thus registration is potentially a valuable legal protection. At the same time trademarks are tools that lend only a small amount of assistance in protecting limited aspects of indigenous peoples' cultural intellectual property claims.[8]

The trademark right, like all intellectual property rights, and indeed property rights more generally, is not a right to own or to control all uses, but a right to exclude others from certain uses.[9] The right to exclude will often practically result in the right to use. However, trademark registration does not give a positive right to use the trademark in all situations. It is limited to certain uses in relation to the class of goods or services in which it is registered. And third parties may make legitimate fair use of trademarks.[10]

It would be incorrect, therefore, to view existing trademark systems as providing a mechanism through which indigenous peoples can claim exclusive rights to all signs and symbols relating to their culture. The use of trademarks to protect signs and symbols of indigenous cultures is, at the most, happenstance. Trademarks only protect such signs and symbols if those signs and symbols are used in a way that invokes the possibility of trademark protection. In most, if not all, common and civil law systems, this requires the use of the trademark in trade or commerce of some kind.[11] If indigenous signs and symbols are protected by trademarks this is not the result of any overarching policy of protecting of indigenous peoples' culture.

It is not possible in this chapter to address all aspects of all trademark systems relevant to the protection of indigenous peoples' cultural property.[12] Where details of national systems are relevant they will be referred to. Otherwise the fundamental tenets of trademark law referred to are those derived from recognized international substantive law agreements in the field,

---

[8] *See* Darrel Posey & Graham Dutfield, *Beyond Intellectual Property*, 84–7 (International Development Research Center, Canada, 1996) (outlining how indigenous peoples can use trademarks).

[9] TRIPS Agreement, *supra* note 3, art. 16.

[10] TRIPS Agreement, *supra* note 3, art. 17 ("Members may provide limited exceptions to the rights conferred by a trademark, such as fair use of descriptive terms, provided that such exceptions take account of the legitimate interests of the owners of the trademark and of third parties."). In national systems, this "fair use" translates to statutory defenses such as allowing comparative advertising or honest and fair practices. *See also* Graeme Austin, *Tolerating Confusion*, Ch. 14 of this volume.

[11] TRIPS Agreement, *supra* note 3, art. 15 (incorporating the notion of distinguishing "goods and services").

[12] The chapter is primarily concerned with trademark law, particularly registered rights. Unregistered rights arising from unfair competition and passing off are also included in discussion where relevant.

particularly the TRIPS Agreement and its incorporation of the Paris Convention.[13]

Section II addresses the question of what indigenous peoples seek. Section III examines the various ways in which trademark registration supports the protection of indigenous peoples' rights and the ways in which such systems are not useful for such protection. Section IV discusses objection and revocation procedures available for indigenous peoples to object to third-party registrations of the culturally inappropriate or offensive. In that section, the United States' disparaging and scandalous mark provision is compared with New Zealand's system, which gives a greater right to objection and revocation. In New Zealand, signs may not be registered as trademarks if they are offensive or likely to be offensive to Māori.[14]

Section V discusses the relationship between indigenous peoples' use of trademarks and geographical indications.[15] Section VI discusses the justifications and rationales for trademark protection and their compatibility with protecting indigenous peoples' signs and symbols. Section VII discusses issues relating to the public domain and freedom of expression. The chapter concludes, in Section VIII, that indigenous peoples' signs and symbols should receive greater protection, most probably in the form of a *sui generis* system related to trademarks, but that the existing trademark-registration systems should have robust objection procedures for registration of culturally inappropriate or offensive marks so that they can co-exist with, rather than clash with, a *sui generis* system.

---

[13] Paris Convention for the Protection of Industrial Property, July 14, 1967, 21 U.S.T. 1583, 828 U.N.T.S. 305 [hereinafter Paris Convention].

[14] Throughout this chapter, I use illustrative examples from Māori, the indigenous people of Aotearoa (New Zealand).

[15] Intellectual property rights are grouped into three broad categories: patents, copyright and trademarks. All of these categories have related rights. The term "neighbouring rights" has also been used, particularly by European countries. The rights that could be described as trademark-related rights include geographical indications. Protection of geographical indications is included in the TRIPS Agreement, *supra* note 3, arts. 22–4. Geographical names are often excluded from trademark protection because they do not meet the test of distinctiveness, primarily because all traders associated with the geographical name have a right to use the geographical name as an identification of the origin of goods or services. *See* Lanham Act, 15 U.S.C. § 1227(2)(e), Trade Marks Act 2002 (NZ), § 18(1)(c). Geographical names have often found protection as unregistered trademarks in passing-off actions. For example, in the United Kingdom, regarding the use of SWISS, see *Chocosuisse Union des Fabricants Suisses de Chocolat v Cadbury, Ltd.* [1998] 41 IPR 1 (EWHC) and [1999] RPC 826 (EWCA). In New Zealand regarding the use of CHAMPAGNE, see *Wineworths Group, Ltd. v Comité Interprofessionel du vin de Champagne* [1992] 2 NZLR 327 (CA).

II. What do indigenous peoples seek?

To pose the question "what do indigenous peoples seek," in the context of trademark law, is to ask something which is not easily summarized in a short answer. In part, this is because trademark law is just one aspect of intellectual property. But perhaps more importantly, it is because trademark law is a tool that indigenous peoples may harness to achieve some goals, but not all. Most aspects of trademark law are not designed with the protection of indigenous interests as an underlying policy goal. Therefore the utility of trademark law as a tool for indigenous peoples to use to protect their signs is largely a matter of coincidence.[16]

Indigenous peoples seek recognition and protection of their signs and symbols. Often indigenous peoples will have their own system that regulates the use of signs and symbols.[17] Indigenous people may also seek protection and acknowledgement of those systems from the state in which they reside. This may include protection from third parties using such signs and symbols as intellectual property.

While intellectual property law is fundamentally based on drawing distinctions between the tangible property rights in intellectual property products and the intangible rights of intellectual property, indigenous peoples often regard the intangible and tangible as inextricably linked.[18] So, for the Māori people, for example, a carving or weaving is not just a piece of art using cultural symbols, but a *tāonga* (treasure) embodying *whakapapa* (genealogy), which carries with it the spirituality and *Mauri* (life force) of that *whakapapa* and culture.[19] To a certain extent a similar theme is arguably behind moral rights claims in copyright law.[20] Moral rights are rights which are designed to

---

[16] It has only been relatively recently that cultural offensiveness and similar concepts have been used to oppose trademark registration. *See infra* section IV.

[17] Such systems are often described as customary law. For a general discussion of Māori and customary law, see RICHARD BOAST, ANDREW ERUETI, DOUG MCPHAIL, & NORMAN SMITH, MAORI LAND LAW (2d ed., LexisNexis, 2002). In the Canadian context, see JOHN BORROWS, RECOVERING CANADA: THE RESURGENCE OF INDIGENOUS LAW (Univ. of Toronto Press, 2002).

[18] For a discussion of the elements of traditional knowledge, including the tangible and intangible, see Daniel Gervais, *Spiritual but not Intellectual? The Protection of Sacred Intangible Traditional Knowledge*, 11 CARDOZO J. INT'L & COMP. L. 467 (2003).

[19] In Māori culture, *whakapapa*, translated as genealogy, includes the family history of an *iwi* or *hapu* or *whanau* (different parts of tribe or family group). As people have *whakapapa*, so does all flora and fauna, and their *Mauri* (life force) and *whakapapa* are connected. *See* FRANKEL & MCLAY, *supra* note 5, ¶ 3.2.4.

[20] See art. 6*bis* of the Berne Convention for the Protection of Literary and Artistic Works, Sept. 9, 1886, revised July 24, 1971, 1161 U.N.T.S. 30 [hereinafter Berne Convention].

protect the personality and integrity of the author who is a creator of a copyright work and are often juxtaposed to the economic exploitation rights of copyright law. If moral rights are to be used to protect indigenous peoples' interests they would need to be developed considerably to achieve that goal.[21]

In addition, there is no one goal of indigenous peoples. The goals that such peoples seek are as diverse as the range of peoples around the world that may be called indigenous. Even so, some commonalities can be found, particularly in relation to the protection of signs and symbols. This section outlines those commonalities.

A. *Recognition, preservation, use, control and development*

As a starting point, indigenous peoples seek to have rights to their cultural heritage and traditional knowledge recognized by the legal systems of the states in which they reside.[22] From this basic recognition indigenous peoples seek to preserve, control, use, and develop signs and symbols that have a traditional or special significance to them.[23] Indigenous peoples may seek to revive their traditional and cultural signs and symbols where their traditions have been destroyed. They may also seek to preserve what remains of their culture and revive the parts that have been erased or put into disuse. These aspirations go well beyond trademark law, but trademark law may potentially play a valuable role in enhancing the ability of indigenous peoples to fulfill these goals. Indigenous peoples may, for example, harness registered trademark systems to prevent others from registering signs and symbols if they can utilize a ground for opposition to registration.[24]

---

[21] For a discussion of using moral rights to protect Māori interests, see Susy Frankel, *Towards a Sound New Zealand Intellectual Property Law*, 32 VICTORIA U. WELLINGTON L. REV., 47, 68–71 (2001).

[22] *See* United Nations Draft Declaration on the Rights of Indigenous Peoples, *available at* http://www.ohchr.org/english/issues/indigenous/docs/declaration.doc. For a general discussion of indigenous peoples' rights, see S.J. ANAYA, INDIGENOUS PEOPLES IN INTERNATIONAL LAW (2d ed., Oxford Univ. Press, 2004).

[23] For example, see the claim brought by Māori against the Crown in New Zealand; see Statement of Issues, Part One: Intellectual Property Aspects of Taonga Works, [hereinafter WAI 262], *available at* http://www.waitangi-tribunal.govt.nz/doclibrary/public/Inquiries/Wai262SOI26217July2006.pdf. The Waitangi Tribunal is a tribunal of inquiry established under the Treaty of Waitangi Act 1975, that makes recommendations to the government on claims that the Treaty of Waitangi (Te Tiriti o Waitangi) has been breached. Hearings relating to the WAI 262 claim were completed in June 2007. At the time of writing the report of the Tribunal is pending. For a discussion of the Treaty of Waitangi, see CLAUDIA ORANGE, THE TREATY OF WAITANGI (Allen & Unwin, 1987).

[24] Such a ground may be specifically directed to indigenous peoples, see *infra* Section IV, or other grounds of opposition may coincidentally be available.

Signs and symbols of indigenous peoples are often mechanisms through which traditional knowledge is communicated and passed on.[25] If signs and symbols are inappropriately used, the traditional knowledge that they communicate is distorted by an association with an inappropriate context.

An example, in the context of trademark law, is instructive. The world-renowned Lego company used certain Māori names to identify its BIONICLE toys. The characters included Toa, Whenua and the evil beast Makuta, who inhabit the imaginary island of Mata Nui. Some of the names Lego used had, and continue to have, a particular cultural and religious significance.[26] Some Māori complained to Lego about its use of the names, stating that the uses trivialized and inappropriately used Māori culture. Those Māori emphasized that had Lego consulted them, some names could have been used that were not culturally inappropriate and would have been just as effective in evoking the imagery that Lego sought.[27] Initially Lego was unresponsive to the request to cease using the names. Perhaps this initial reluctance was based on legal advice that there was no internationally recognized legal basis to support the Māori objection.[28] It would seem that after some negotiation Lego undertook to cease using some Māori words.

Notably, the major concern of Māori was the inappropriate use of *Te Reo* (Māori language). The Māori objection is unlike that often found in trademark oppositions based on prior use of the names on the same type of goods or in a similar area of trade. Although indigenous peoples might well claim a prior use in trade, the main concern in the Lego example was the absence of consultation to obtain consent for appropriate use of *Te Reo* and the consequent inappropriate use.

This sort of claim about appropriate use reflects a concern that the signs and symbols of indigenous peoples' culture be used in ways that are consistent and respectful of that culture. It does not mean that the culture cannot

---

[25] The function of passing knowledge through cultural intellectual property is not limited to trademark law. It is part of all cultural property interests. In this chapter, however, the context is trademark law.

[26] One example is the word "Tohunga" (Māori for priest). *See* Kim Griggs, *Lego Site Irks Māori Sympathiser*, http://www.wired.com/news/culture (quoting Maui Solomon, Barrister).

[27] *See* Susy Frankel, *Third Party Trade Marks as a Violation of Indigenous Cultural Property: A New Statutory Safeguard*, 8 J. WORLD INTELL. PROP. 83, 88 (2005).

[28] The incident apparently led to Lego setting a code of conduct for the use of indigenous people's knowledge in the manufacture of toys. *See* Kim Griggs *Māori Take on Hi-Tech Lego Toys*, BBC News, http://news.bbc.co.uk/1/hi/world/asia-pacific/1619406.stm.

be used, but that certain uses might require consultation and some kind of prior consent.[29]

Another example of possible inappropriate use concerns the Māori haka[30] known as "Kamate Kamate". This haka is often performed by New Zealand's international rugby team the All Blacks. The haka was, without the consent of Māori or of the All Blacks, "adapted" to sell Fiat cars.[31]

One view of the Fiat advertisement usage is that it should be regarded as great publicity. But did Māori want this sort of publicity? The answer is "no" because of the inappropriate use of the haka that is either offensive or destroys the meaning and traditional knowledge components of the haka. It was "completely inappropriate to misuse cultural icons or symbolism in the manner that Fiat have. They had the opportunity to engage on a culturally appropriate level but chose to ignore this."[32]

An important consequence of indigenous peoples being in a position to control the use of culturally significant signs and symbols is the opportunities that may afford indigenous peoples to prosper from their own cultures.

B. *Authenticity and source identification*

Indigenous peoples are quite legitimately concerned that counterfeiters purport to be making genuine indigenous peoples' cultural products. This might be done to exploit the tourist market or simply to commercialize the unknown and therefore apparently create a new and exotic product. Some indigenous peoples have developed and designed collective or certification

---

[29] How such consent might be sought will vary according to the traditions of the indigenous communities. Systems for handling requests for use from persons outside of the community may need to be developed.

[30] "Haka" is the Māori word which encompasses many forms of song and dance or performance, for a variety of purposes, including ceremonial, entertainment, and battle-related. For definitions of "Haka", see www.maori.org.nz; www.teara.govt.nz/1966/H/Haka/Haka/en; WIRA GARDINER, HAKA: A LIVING TRADITION (2003). *See also* Megan Richardson, *The Haka, Vintage Cheese and Buzzy Bee: Trade Mark Law the New Zealand Way*, 23 E.I.P.R. 207–10 (2001).

[31] *See Italian haka ad labeled culturally insensitive*, Stuff headlines, July 4, 2006, originally available at http://www.stuff.co.nz/stuff/0,2106,3720117a10,00.html. Also see *The Italian haka*, http://stuffucanuse.com/italian_haka/fiat_haka.htm. The Italian version of the haka was performed by women, seemingly to parody an incident involving an All Black and a handbag. Although haka can be written for women to perform, "Kamate Kamate" was not. Whatever view is taken of this Italian usage, it clearly shows that indigenous traditions often have great marketability. The difficulty is of course who has the right to exploit that market demand.

[32] *No time for Maori input into haka ad*, New Zealand Herald, July 9, 2006, http://www.nzherald.co.nz/location/story.cfm?l_id=55&ObjectID=10390436.

trademarks to assist in ensuring authenticity.[33] For example, in Aotearoa (New Zealand) the main Māori product quality mark *Toi Iho* was developed to indicate not only authenticity but also a high-quality product.[34] Users of the *Toi Iho* mark must be licensed.[35]

Certification trademarks, although valuable, have their limitations. Such marks do provide trademark protection against use of the certification mark, but they do not stop third parties from making counterfeit cultural products without applying the certification mark. Moreover, registration of certification marks and maintenance of their integrity requires resources. If cultural signs and symbols are primarily used as part of cultural identity, rather than in trade or commerce, indigenous peoples may not have those resources.

C. *Existing intellectual property law should not define what is protectable traditional knowledge or cultural intellectual property interests*

Indigenous peoples seek recognition of and control of their culture. For the most part, they do not seek to have their cultural intellectual property squeezed into or accommodated within another culture's intellectual property system.[36]

In the international debate surrounding traditional knowledge and protection of cultural heritage, several definitions of what traditional knowledge might mean in connection with intellectual property have emerged.[37] In relation to trademarks, definitions of relevance include:

> "traditional knowledge" refers to tradition based . . . designs, marks, names and symbols . . . "[T]radition based" refers to knowledge systems creations, innovations and cultural expressions which: have generally been transmitted from generation to generation; are generally regarded as pertaining to a particular people or its territory; and, are constantly evolving in response to a changing environment.

---

[33] For a discussion of authenticity marks in Australia see Leanne Wiseman, *The Protection of Indigenous Art and Culture in Australia: The Labels of Authenticity*, 23(1) E.I.P.R. 14 (2001). *See also* Indian Arts and Crafts Act, 25 U.S.C. § 305(a)(3) (1990).

[34] *See* Creative New Zealand – Arts Council of New Zealand Toi Aotearoa http://www.creativenz.govt.nz/funding/other/toi_iho.html.

[35] This is true although some Māori have informally expressed the view that one *iwi* (tribe) or *hapu* (family group) should not make a decision of quality over another *iwi* or *hapu*.

[36] *See generally* Graham Dutfield, *TRIPS-Related Aspects of Traditional Knowledge*, 33 CASE W. RES. J. INT'L L. 233 (2001).

[37] WIPO Intergovernmental Committee on Intellectual Property and Genetic Resources, Traditional Knowledge and Folklore, *Traditional Knowledge – Operational Terms and Definitions*, 20 May 2002 WIPO/GRTKF/IC/3/9. *See also* Graham Dutfield, *Legal and Economic Aspects of Traditional Knowledge*, in Maskus & Reichman, *supra* note 2, at 495.

> Categories of traditional knowledge could include . . . "expressions of folklore" in the form of . . . designs [and] elements of languages such as names, geographical indications and symbols. . . ."[38]
>
> The heritage of indigenous peoples includes . . . all kinds of literary and artistic creations such as . . . symbols and designs. . . .[39]

Definitions, although of guidance, fail to encapsulate the scope of what indigenous peoples seek. In this chapter I use "traditional knowledge" to refer to the knowledge that has led to the creation of signs and symbols, but also the spiritual and other cultural values that may be regarded as being part of such signs and symbols. I utilise the phrase "cultural intellectual property" to indicate that the intellectual property claimed by indigenous communities may be based on those communities' systems of knowledge and custom, which is a kind of intellectual property system.[40] So, for example, a system of knowledge that recognizes and protects the use of certain signs and symbols might be described as a customary intellectual property system of an indigenous community.

III. The utility and limitations of registered trademarks to protect indigenous peoples' signs and symbols

International trademark law requires that signatory countries operate a system of registration.[41] In addition, many nations also retain various forms of protection for unregistered signs.[42] Because trademark registration is not a system that was designed with any policy to protect indigenous signs and symbols,

---

[38] *Traditional Knowledge – Operational Terms and Definitions*, supra note 37, ¶ 25.

[39] Irene-Erica Daes, "Principles and Guidelines for the Protection of the Heritage of Indigenous Peoples," United Nations Sub-Commission on the Prevention of Discrimination and Heritage of Indigenous Peoples, UN Sub-Commission on Prevention of Discrimination and Protection of Minorities, E/CN.4/Sub.w/1995/26 revised in E/CN.4/Sub.2/2000./26, ¶ 13.

[40] I am using "intellectual property" expansively, rather than referring only to existing law. As such, in this context it is a nomenclature of convenience.

[41] *See* TRIPS Agreement, *supra* note 3, art. 15. While there are many contests between states as to the details of registration systems, the process of application, examination and acceptance, or otherwise, are, in broad principle, common to all systems.

[42] A number of international agreements exist in relation to trademark registration. *See generally* Paris Convention, *supra* note 13; Madrid Agreement Concerning the International Registration of Marks, (June 28 1989), *available at* http://www.wipo.int/madrid/en/legal_texts/trtdocs_wo016.html; Singapore Trade Mark Treaty 2006, *available at* http://www.wipo.int/meetings/en/doc_details.jsp?doc_id=58393.

indigenous peoples sometimes utilize the system where advantageous, but generally remain of the view that the system is problematic and fails to provide the protection that indigenous peoples seek.

A. *The utility of trademark registration*

In many ways, of all the intellectual property rights, trademarks are uniquely suited to indigenous peoples as a way of using intellectual property regimes, beyond their own customary law, to obtain protection.[43] Indefinite protection accords with the reality that traditional knowledge and associated cultural intellectual property interests are not finite, but are rather passed from generation to generation.[44] The potential indefinite duration of trademarks avoids the difficulties that the finite terms of patent and copyright pose for indigenous peoples of traditional knowledge falling into the public domain. The recognition of an association between a sign and a particular source, rather than novelty or originality, accords more with the goals of protection of some traditional knowledge and cultural intellectual property interests.

A trademark must be a sign.[45] The TRIPS Agreement does not give an exhaustive definition of what is a sign, but it includes "personal names, letters, numerals, figurative elements and combinations of colours as well as any combinations of such signs."[46] Where indigenous peoples' symbols are in their traditional form or have been developed, either in a traditional or non-traditional manner, they will most likely fall into the concept of a sign at domestic law. Many jurisdictions recognize sounds, smells, and even tastes as types of signs.[47] This expansion of what a sign includes is recognition of the

---

[43] Graeme Dinwoodie in his proposal for an international framework indicated that he draws primary inspiration from models of trademark law and geographical indications because trademark law has already created a number of exceptions to territoriality that are likely to be important in an international framework for the protection of traditional knowledge. *See* Graeme B. Dinwoodie, *Towards an International Framework for the Protection of Traditional Knowledge* in ELEMENTS OF NATIONAL SUI GENERIS SYSTEMS FOR THE PRESERVATION, PROTECTION AND PROMOTION OF TRADITIONAL KNOWLEDGE: INNOVATIONS AND PRACTICES AND OPTIONS FOR AN INTERNATIONAL FRAMEWORK, (Twarog & Turner, eds., U.N. Conference on Trade & Development, 2005), *available at* http://ssrn.com/abstract=707002 [hereinafter Dinwoodie, *Traditional Knowledge*].

[44] TRIPS Agreement, *supra* note 3, art. 18 provides that the registration of a trademark shall be renewable indefinitely.

[45] TRIPS Agreement, *supra* note 3, art. 15.1.

[46] *Id.*

[47] "Tastes" are included in the definition of sign in Trade Marks Act 2002 (NZ), § 2. These are also accepted by the Benelux Trade Mark Office. *See* JEREMY PHILLIPS, TRADE MARK LAW: A PRACTICAL ANATOMY 5.143 (2003). The TRIPS Agreement,

role that senses other than sight play in the associations people make between signs and source.[48] The ever expanding role of the "sign" potentially lends itself to being even more useful for indigenous peoples.

While trademarks need not be original in the copyright sense[49] or novel and non-obvious in the patent sense[50] they do need to be distinctive[51] or of "distinctive character."[52] The problems of applying novelty and originality to indigenous peoples' traditional knowledge and cultural property interests are that, while such knowledge or property may pass the subject-matter test of copyright or patent protection, it will ordinarily fail to reach the novelty or originality threshold. This is primarily because of the age of the traditional knowledge and its mode of transmission from generation to generation.[53] Distinctiveness in trademark law is less demanding than copyright originality and patent law novelty, and indigenous peoples' signs and symbols may more readily pass the trademark distinctiveness test.

Indigenous peoples' signs and symbols may often involve a number of similar uses. For example, a weaving pattern may have variants all of which are common to one group or tribe and which collectively are identifiable as belonging to that group, but which may individually not be demonstrably distinctive from each other. This does not mean that such signs are incapable of meeting trademark distinctiveness standards. It means, rather, that in this respect, indigenous peoples' signs may be similar to series marks or related registered trademarks.[54]

---

supra note 3, does not mention sounds, smell, and tastes in what is a sign, but the definition is inclusive rather than restrictive. In addition, members may offer greater protection than that set out in the agreement. *See id.*, at art. 1.1.

[48] The associations that sounds and smells can create have, not without some controversy, led to their inclusion in the scope of what is a sign. See discussion in Jacey McGrath, *The New Breed of Trade Marks: Sounds, Smells and Tastes*, 32 VICTORIA U. WELLINGTON L REV. 277 (2001).

[49] Copyright only vests in works of authorship. *See* Berne Convention, *supra* note 20; TRIPS Agreement, *supra* note 3, art. 9 (incorporating Berne Convention). Differences are found in national laws as to what amount to originality. *See* SAM RICKETSON & JANE C. GINSBURG, INTERNATIONAL COPYRIGHT AND NEIGHBOURING RIGHTS: THE BERNE CONVENTION AND BEYOND 404 (2d ed., 2006).

[50] TRIPS Agreement, *supra* note 3, art. 27.1.

[51] This concept is discussed above in relation to the definition of trademark. The grounds for not registering a trademark are discussed here although the concepts are closely related.

[52] *See* Trade Marks Act 2002 (NZ), § 18; Trade Marks Act 1994 (UK), § 3.

[53] Although there may be instances where this does not result in an absence of novelty or originality. *See* Dutfield, *supra* note 36, 498.

[54] A series trademark registration usually involves variations on the one core mark registered as a series.

Although these aspects of trademark registration appear to coincide with what indigenous peoples seek, there are many inadequacies of trademark law for such protection.

B. The limitations of trade mark registration

As noted above, the use of trademarks to protect indigenous peoples' interests is largely coincidental rather than a recognized policy of trademark law. In addition, indigenous peoples' use of trademark protection is often dependent on the ability, frequently economic, for them to engage with the system. Most problematically a number of substantive requirements for trademark protection may be barriers to indigenous peoples using trademark registration.

The most disadvantageous aspects of using trademarks to protect indigenous peoples' signs and symbols are the limits of that protection relating to use in trade, as a requirement for registration and the benefits that flow from that exclusive-rights regime. First, the indefinite protection of registered trademarks has the significant limitation that use in trade must be maintained or there is the possibility of removal from the trademark register for non-use.[55] Second, the TRIPS Agreement requires that signs may be registered as trademarks if they are "capable of distinguishing the goods or services of one undertaking from those of other undertakings."[56] Many signs and symbols of indigenous peoples' cultures, although meeting the definition of sign, will not meet the requirements of "trademark" because the sign is not applied to goods and services or not used to distinguish goods and services in a trade context. Therefore, using existing trademark registration procedures to protect indigenous peoples' interests requires squeezing indigenous interests into a system designed for interests in trade and commerce. Moreover, use "in trade" may also be a requirement for systems that protect unregistered trademarks, making such systems also of only limited value to indigenous peoples unless they use culturally significant signs and symbols in trade.[57]

Trademark protection is fundamentally about protecting the sign or symbol and does not necessarily protect the knowledge and values that are incorporated in that expression of cultural intellectual property, although where there is a trademark registration that may, as an indirect consequence, protect the knowledge from misrepresentation by prohibiting others from misusing the

---

[55] TRIPS Agreement, *supra* note 3, art. 19. Applications for such removal are usually made by traders who wish to use the sign in question.
[56] TRIPS Agreement, *supra* note 3, art. 15.1.
[57] Passing off in the United Kingdom, Australia and New Zealand protects reputation and goodwill obtained through use in trade of a mark. *See generally* LIONEL BENTLEY & BRAD SHERMAN, INTELLECTUAL PROPERTY LAW 673–9 (2001); FRANKEL & MCLAY, *supra* note 5, at 476–80.

sign or symbol. However, for the most part third-party uses of indigenous signs and symbols are not prevented by trademark law.

Third parties may decide to adopt cultural symbols and use them in trade. By such means the third parties become the user of the signs in trade and thus are prima facie entitled to register the trademark. Such registrations may exclude indigenous peoples from certain uses of their cultural intellectual property.

An application to register the "Kamate Kamate" haka[58] as a trademark provides an example of how an indigenous people's attempt to use the expanding concept of sign may be defeated by third party use.[59] That haka has for a number of years been used by and consequently become associated with the national rugby team of New Zealand, the All Blacks.[60] Arguably the association the public makes between the haka and the All Blacks is an association with the All Blacks "in trade" and an association with Māori in a "non-trade" context.[61] The haka is not a registered trademark of the All Blacks or any organization that runs rugby in New Zealand. However, Māori attempts to register the "Kamate Kamate" haka as a trademark have not, so far, met with success.[62] Primarily this is because the Intellectual Property Office of New Zealand[63] has taken the view that it is not associated with one particular trader, but with New Zealand.[64] The Māori, descendants of Te Rauparaha of Ngati Toa, who filed the application for registration, have given the All Blacks, and other New Zealanders, permission to use the haka but believe that when it comes to any issues of trade or commercialization they ought to have the right to consent or otherwise on the appropriateness of such activity.[65]

Many trademarks systems require the graphic representation of signs.[66] While it might be possible to graphically represent indigenous symbols, the requirement to register variations may be cumbersome and in some circumstances even inappropriate, if contrary to some aspect of traditional knowledge

---

[58] *See supra* note 30.

[59] P. Crewdson, *Iwi claim to All Black haka turned down will be disputed*, NEW ZEALAND HERALD, July 2, 2006, *available at* http://www.nzherald.co.nz/section/print.cfm?c_id=1&objectid=10389347.

[60] The All Blacks more recently have commissioned a new "haka."

[61] The All Blacks website sells items, including cell phone rings, of the haka. *See* http://www.allblacks.com/, visited December 27, 2006.

[62] *See*, Crewdson, *supra* note 59.

[63] Known as IPONZ, a branch of the Ministry of Economic Development that includes the Trade Mark Office and the Patent Office.

[64] Crewdson, *supra* note 59.

[65] *Id.*

[66] This is an optional requirement of the TRIPS Agreement, *supra* note 3, art. 15.

and custom. In patent and copyright law, for example, fixation can cause indigenous peoples difficulties because, in some circumstances, it requires an oral tradition to be recorded in some way. The traditional knowledge users may not wish to record that knowledge because the reasons for its status as oral knowledge relate to the ways in which traditional knowledge is retained within a community and passed from generation to generation. Although by their nature many indigenous signs and symbols will be able to be fixed for registration purposes, fixation may be alien to indigenous peoples and may also require that the sign is recorded in a manner that fails to recognize indigenous peoples' concerns regarding knowledge, spiritual, and other values that the sign or symbol embodies.

Within indigenous peoples' communities, identifying the "owner" of traditional knowledge and cultural intellectual property rights is often not a requirement for the use of the traditional knowledge. This is because the knowledge is governed by rules and regulations about how and who can use it rather than notions of exclusive ownership.[67] Trademark law is not wholly divorced from notions of joint ownership, but registration requires an identifiable owner rather than a community.[68] Thus, indigenous peoples may have to nominate an owner to use trademark registration to protect signs and symbols, and this raises issues of whether the registered owner is the true owner.

The exclusive rights that arise from trademark registration, in relation to what is recorded on the register, do not take into account the traditional knowledge and cultural processes that may lead to variation and development of culturally significant signs and symbols. Some may be used in traditional ways or may even be modern adaptations of traditional symbols made with permission and in accordance with the cultural expectations that are associated with the sign or symbol. Other variations may simply be inappropriate and without permission. Variations of known symbols that create distinctiveness in trade can qualify for registration. It is debatable whether permission should be sought for every use of a known symbol or whether uses that are not culturally

---

[67] See Dutfield, *supra* note 37, at 501; Sherman & Wiseman, *supra* note 5, at 269 (discussing the ways in which knowledge is organized in Australian aboriginal communities). *See also* Paul Kuruk, *Protecting Folklore Under Modern Intellectual Property Regimes: A Reappraisal of the Tensions Between Individual and Communal Rights in Africa and the United States*, 48 AM. U. L. REV. 769, 781–3 (1999) (discussing the ways in which folklore is regulated in African customary law).

[68] Some form of collective or communal ownership is the norm for cultural intellectual property rights. *See* Gervais, *supra* note 18, at 481–5; Terence Dougherty, *Group Rights to Cultural Survival Intellectual Property Rights in Native American Cultural Symbols*, 29 COL. HUM. RIGHTS L. REV. 355, 386 (1997–8). Ownership could, however, be held on trust for a group of beneficiaries. *See also* Gervais, *supra* note 18, at 481 (comparing such collective ownership to collecting societies).

inappropriate can take place in any event. The difficulty for a third-party user is obtaining the knowledge of what may or may not be appropriate. Without an assurance of protection, indigenous peoples are and will be reluctant to part with such knowledge. There will be some instances where no non-indigenous person's use is appropriate.[69] Arguably the playing field for these disputes, within the trademark system, is the opposition and revocation procedures.

IV. Trademark opposition and revocation

During the process of trademark registration trademark offices may refuse to register trademarks because they do not meet the criteria for registration or are unregistrable because they fall afoul of an affirmative prohibition on registration. Third parties may also oppose the registration of trademarks. National laws frequently provide that trademarks which are immoral or contain scandalous matter are not registrable. In this section I compare the opposition grounds of disparaging and scandalous matter, which have been and are used by indigenous peoples in the United States, with that available to indigenous people in New Zealand. Under New Zealand law, a trademark may not be registered if it is "offensive to a significant section of the community, including Māori."[70] At the outset it should be noted that neither the United States nor New Zealand offers anything greater than a right to oppose registration and in that sense it is a negative right rather than a positive endowment of rights to ownership and control over indigenous signs and symbols, which, as discussed above, is what indigenous peoples seek. Inability to register does mean that a sign or symbol cannot be used. The ability to oppose registration in some instances amounts to a sort of control over some aspects of inappropriate use, which is a step towards what indigenous peoples seek. The control is somewhat limited for two reasons. First, because the control lies primarily in the hands of the registration system rather than the indigenous peoples and, second, because it does not extend as far as the aspiration of having third party users seek indigenous peoples' consent to all uses of indigenous signs and symbols.

A. Scandalous or disparaging marks and the Lanham Act

In the "normal" process of examination of trademarks, examiners may refuse registration of applications, without the application being published, if an application does not meet the criteria for registration. In relation to objections

---

[69] If the regulation in an indigenous community is that only certain persons may designate an item as an item of cultural significance, then that right is unlikely to be delegable to a non-qualified person. *See also* Gervais, *supra* note 18, at 478.

[70] Trade Marks Act 2002 (NZ), § 17.

to disparaging and scandalous marks, a policy exists to publish the mark so that the party "disparaged" or "scandalized" can bring the objection rather than the examiner imposing his or her judgment.[71] This places a significant burden on indigenous peoples to monitor trademark registers and to expend the resources to challenge applications.

In the United States, cases involving indigenous peoples' attempts to remove the registrations relating to "Redskins"[72] have established a framework for understanding what may amount to scandalous or disparaging marks in the context of indigenous peoples' objection to trademark registration.[73] The Trademark Trial and Appeal Board held that the "Redskins" trademarks were disparaging, but not scandalous, on the basis that the mark was disparaging to a substantial number of Native Americans, and that for it to be scandalous, it must be so to "a substantial composite of the general public."[74] The finding of disparagement was reversed on appeal because it was not supported by substantial evidence. The decision, however, left open the possibility that it could be supported by substantial evidence in the future, even if brought by different claimants.[75] The burden, however, lies entirely on the indigenous people to establish that the trademark is disparaging or scandalous; there is no

---

[71] Lynda J. Oswald, *Challenging the Registration of Scandalous and Disparaging Marks Under the Lanham Act: Who has Standing to Sue?* 41 AM. BUS. L.J. 251, 264 (2004).

[72] *See* Harjo v Pro-Football, Inc., 30 U.S.P.Q. 2d 1828 (T.T.A.B. 1994); Harjo v Pro-Football, Inc., 50 U.S.P.Q. 2d 1705, 1748 (1999). The case was reversed and suit was barred by laches. Pro-Football, Inc. v Harjo, 284 F. Supp. 2d 96 (D.C. Cir. 2003). It was then appealed and sent back to the District Court to reconsider laches. Pro-Football, Inc. v Harjo, 2006 WL 2092637 (D.C. Cir. 2006).

[73] The Lanham Act provides:

> No trademark by which the goods of the applicant may be distinguished from the goods of others shall be refused registration on the principal register on account of its nature unless it (a) consists of or comprises immoral, deceptive or scandalous matter; or matter which may disparage or falsely suggest a connection with persons, living or dead, institutions, beliefs, or national symbols, or bring them into contempt or disrepute.

Lanham Act, 15 U.S.C. § 1052(a).

[74] Harjo v Pro-Football, Inc. 50 U.S.P.Q. 2d 1705, 1736 (1999).

[75] Pro-Football, Inc. v Harjo, 284 F. Supp.2d 96, 131 (D.C. Cir. 2003). For a full discussion of each step in the case see Rachel Clark Hughey, *The Impact of Pro-Football Inc. v Harjo on Trademark Protection of Other Marks*, 14 FORDHAM INTELL. PROP. MEDIA & ENT. L.J. 327 (2004). New petitioners Amanda Blackhorse, Marcus Briggs, Philip Gover, Shquanebin Lone-Bentley, Jullian Pappan and Courtney Tsotigh have filed an applications for cancellation of various "Redskins" trademarks under matter number 191158, before the Trademark Trial and Appeal Board, August 11, 2006.

responsibility placed on the Registrar of Trademarks not to register that which is scandalous or disparaging of indigenous peoples.

The Lanham Act style of provisions is not unique and similar forms are found in a number of trademark statutes worldwide.[76] Provisions that rely on judgments of what is scandalous or immoral to oppose registration or apply for revocation of trademarks are inherently difficult to use in practice. The vagueness or subjectivity of terms such as "scandalous," "disparaging" or "immoral" has resulted in a different law to protect indigenous peoples' interest in New Zealand.

B. Offensive trademarks in New Zealand

In New Zealand, a greater level of objection is available to Māori than is available to indigenous peoples under the Lanham Act. The Commissioner of Trade Marks must not register a sign that is offensive to Māori.[77] If an application for a trademark contains a sign that is offensive to Māori then there is an obligation not to register it. This obligation is not discretionary and since 2002 is an "absolute ground for not registering a trademark."[78] This provision replaced the previous system for objecting to immoral or scandalous applications for registration.[79] There is, however, some degree of limited discretion over whether the Commissioner will find such a sign to be offensive. The Commissioner, or authorized person acting as a trademark examiner or Hearing Officer, is not able to substitute his or her view of what is offensive to M?ori. The Commissioner's decision is based on advice from a specially created M?ori Advisory Committee. The Committee's function is to advise the Commissioner whether "the proposed use or registration of a trademark, that is, or appears to be, derivative of a Māori sign, including text and imagery, is, or is likely to be, offensive to Māori."[80] The Committee has examined several trademark appplications, and many have been withdrawn by the applicants from the registration process based on the Committee's advice.[81] To date the Commissioner has not differed from the Committee's advice, but the wording of the Act theoretically makes that possible. Such a situation is possible,

---

[76] See, e.g., Trade Marks Act (UK), § 3(3); Trade Marks Act 1995 (Aus.), § 42.

[77] Trade Marks Act 2002 (NZ), § 17(b)(ii). For a discussion of this section, see Frankel, *supra* note 27; Owen Morgan, *Protecting Indigenous Signs and Trademarks – The New Zealand Experiment*, [2004] INTELL. PROP. QUARTERLY 58.

[78] Trade Marks Act 2002 (NZ). Sub-part 2 of the Act contains absolute grounds for not registering a mark, including if the mark is not distinctive.

[79] Trade Marks Act 1953 (NZ repealed), § 16(1).

[80] Trade Marks Act 2002 (NZ), § 177.

[81] See Maori Trade Marks Advisory Committee Report, *available at* http://www.iponz.govt.nz/pls/web/dbssiten.main.

particularly if the applicant submits contrary advice from a different group of Māori.

The entire orientation of the New Zealand system is to recognize that culturally offensive marks should not be registered and therefore the system places a burden on the Registration Office to not register such marks. Opposition and revocation procedures are still available should a trademark be registered. Interestingly, the statute uses the phrase "culturally aggrieved" in relation to revocation.[82] The practical effect of the difference in meaning (if any) between offensive and culturally aggrieved has not yet been tested.

It is tempting for those outside of New Zealand to think that such a system is only possible in New Zealand because of its geographical isolation and the Treaty of Waitangi.[83] One possible difficulty that some might perceive is that the system appears to adopt a race-based solution and that such a system is discriminatory. It is not. First, the ground for not registering a mark on the basis of offensiveness is available to everyone. The Advisory Committee is established only for Māori.[84] Second, this does not preclude any trademark registering authority from taking a more proactive approach in monitoring marks that are misappropriated from a culture. If a trademark office cannot identify a particular culture, in the way the New Zealand law has created a Māori Advisory Committee, because this is somehow discriminatory, then it may be incumbent on the office to take a proactive approach to prevent offensive registrations in relation to all cultures.

V. Related systems – geographical indications

Geographical indications are a relative of the trademark that has received significant attention since the formation of the TRIPS Agreement.[85] Much of the debate has centered on the dispute between the European Union and United States over the scope of the European registration system for geographic indications.[86] As many traditional-knowledge claimants identify their knowledge through geographical indicators, the use of geographical indications as a potential weapon in the armoury of traditional knowledge has emerged.

---

[82] Trade Marks Act 2002 (NZ), § 73(1).
[83] *See id.*
[84] See *supra* note 81 and accompanying text. Prof. Paul McHugh has argued that the Treaty of Waitangi is not a race-based treaty. Paul McHugh, *Treaty Principles: Constitutional Relations Inside a Conservative Jurisprudence, Special Issue in Honour of Lord Cooke*, VICTORIA U. WELLINGTON L. REV. (forthcoming 2008).
[85] Negotiations about the extent of geographical indications protection are ongoing in the TRIPS Council. *See* http://www.wto.org/english/tratop_e/trips_e/gi_e.htm.
[86] *See* WTO Panel Report, *Protection of Trademarks and Geographical Indications for Agricultural Products and Foodstuffs* (WT/DS174/R, WT/DS290/R). This dispute is arguably a sideshow in the overall debate over geographical indications.

Indigenous peoples seek to protect their geographically significant names for use by those indigenous peoples and to prevent third parties from misappropriating those names.[87] Geographical indications registration systems such as the European Union's system can give a particular community the right over a geographical indication. This gives rise to an "unusual" allegiance between indigenous peoples outside of the European Union and members of the European Union over the expansion of geographical indications protection beyond what is recognized internationally.[88]

One major objection to the expansion of geographical indications is the scope of the rights that, unlike trademarks, potentially detract from the public domain of generic words which are free for use by all.[89] The proponents of geographical indications dispute the appropriateness of the indications being used by anyone, primarily on the basis that such geographical indications should only be used in an appropriate context. That context would be use by a person who meets certain criteria, predominantly that they are located in the relevant geographical area or the product that the person makes is in some way fundamentally connected to the geographical area. Some claims to geographical exclusivity of geographical use precede the use of geographical-indications registration systems. The worldwide pursuit of exclusive use of "champagne" provides such an example.[90]

Some commentators have advocated that geographical indications provide a model for a *sui generis* system for the protection of cultural intellectual property because they recognize collective rights and underlying values.[91] I look at the relationship between indigenous peoples' traditional knowledge and cultural property rights and geographical indications from another angle.

Geographical location often gives rise to a cultural identity associated with a geographical area, but cultural identity is not always a question of geography. There is no objective intellectual property law justification that can support geographical cultural identity as more important than any other cultural identity. Viewed that way, geographical indications and cultural intel-

---

[87] An example of this includes basmati rice. *See Traditional Knowledge and Geographical Indications, in* INTEGRATING PROPERTY RIGHTS AND DEVELOPMENT POLICY 73, at 89, *available at* http://www.iprcommission.org/papers/pdfs/final_report/Ch4final.pdf#search=%22%22traditional%20knowledge%20and%20geographical%20indications522%22.

[88] See TRIPS Agreement, *supra* note 3, arts. 22–4 (describing the current minimum legal standards required multilaterally).

[89] See *infra* Section VIII for the discussion of the public domain and protection of indigenous rights.

[90] The champagne dispute has involved trademark and passing-off claims.

[91] See, e.g., Sherman & Wiseman, *supra* note 5; LIONEL BENTLEY & BRAD SHERMAN, INTELLECTUAL PROPERTY LAW 962–89 (2d. ed. 2004).

lectual property claims are similar. Geographical indications may have other functions such as consumer protection in receiving "authentic" products.[92] One possible view is that neither is meritorious of legal protection. However, I argue that, at the very least, geographical indications do not have more credibility than indigenous cultural property claims. The European claim to repatriate many of its geographical indications is, in many ways, simply a claim to its traditional heritage. In this respect it is essentially a claim to traditional knowledge dressed up in non-indigenous peoples' clothing. Although Europeans could be said to be indigenous to Europe,[93] being "indigenous" is not the articulated basis for requiring geographical indications. Rather the claim is of tradition associated with a geographic locality. The legitimacy of European repatriation of geographical indications can be questioned because the Europeans distributed their culture to the "public domain,"[94] whereas, by and large, indigenous peoples have been colonized rather than having willingly donated their culture to the same public domain.

The use of geographical indications to develop agricultural communities away from subsidized farming may be forward looking from the viewpoint of reducing subsidies.[95] However, from an intellectual property perspective, indigenous trademark claims might be more forward-looking because many indigenous peoples are seeking to protect their culture so as to enhance their development aspirations and this encourages the creativity and innovation of indigenous culture.

VI. Indigenous peoples' rights and consistency with trademark justifications and theory

There is no internationally consistent theory of trademark law. Common themes emerge between jurisdictions, but differences in approach tend to suggest that the underlying philosophical bases on which trademark law has developed are not the same.[96] While avoiding consumer confusion is the principal justification of Lanham Act protection, it is not so clear that it is such a

---

[92] Opponents of geographical indications would argue that no consumer confusion arises where the origin of a product is clearly indicated.

[93] A point that I might leave to the anthropologists. A key unifying factor of peoples who adopt the label "indigenous peoples" is that they are not the majority population in the state in which they reside.

[94] One perspective is that the European Union's approach to geographical considerations raises issues of whether they are concerned about intellectual property or agriculture. See http://www.uwcc.wisc.edu/farmercoops05/cotton%5Ccotton.ppt.

[95] *See id.*

[96] For a general discussion on trademark theory in the United Kingdom, see C.D.G. PICKERING, TRADE MARKS IN THEORY & PRACTICE (Hart Publishing, 1998).

principal justification in the United Kingdom, Australia or New Zealand.[97] Avoiding consumer confusion is an important part of the law, but the development of case law in both trademarks and passing off is riddled with pronouncements that the owner's goodwill is the basis for trademark protection.[98] Although the Lanham Act recognizes the trademark owner's investment as a policy supporting trademark law,[99] United Kingdom law is more obviously tilted towards protecting goodwill as a rationale for protection. Demonstrated goodwill is a fundamental requirement in passing off because, without registration as proof of ownership, the plaintiff must prove some kind of rights to the unregistered mark. Those rights, while they rely on evidence of use, are often articulated as being based on the acquired goodwill of the plaintiff in the mark.[100] In registered trademarks the goodwill language is also often at the forefront. What this means is that although international commonalities are found in trademark laws, and those commonalities are articulated in international agreements, looking for a universally applicable rationale and justification proves difficult. It is then difficult for "new" applicants entering the system, such as indigenous peoples, to philosophically ally themselves with disparate underlying philosophies. However, that may mean that strategically it is easier to introduce protection of indigenous signs and symbols into the trademark system than it is to acknowledge indigenous peoples' rights in other areas of intellectual property. This section discusses some of those common themes which are at the core of trademark law even if there is some dispute over the extent of their application. By examining the underlying principles of the trademark systems, this section illustrates commonalities with cultural intellectual property and consequently demonstrates core themes that can link such systems, rather than keeping them in opposition.[101]

---

[97] This is illustrated in the way that commentaries in those jurisdictions describe justifications. *See*, e.g., BENTLEY & SHERMAN, *supra* note 57, at 661–5; J. Phillips, TRADEMARK LAW: A PRACTICAL ANATOMY 21–33 (Oxford Univ. Press, 2003).

[98] For examples in 2006, see *Bouverie No. 1 Limited v. De Vere Hotels & Leisure Limited* [2006] EWHC 2242, [69] (Ch), which discusses the value and goodwill in the trademarks, and *Ellerman Investments Limited, The Ritz Hotel Casino Limited v. Elizabeth C- Vanci*, 2006 EWHC 1442 (Ch), [14] (stating "the Ritz Club Online website has been very successful and a significant reputation and substantial goodwill has accrued in relation to the Ritz trade marks").

[99] *See* Graeme B. Dinwoodie, *Trademark Law and Social Norms* 6 (draft September 5, 2006).

[100] *See* BENTLEY & SHERMAN, *supra* note 57, at 673–89.

[101] An important link between such systems will be the ability within the trademark system to oppose registration of signs and symbols that should not be registered if they are otherwise protected in the system that recognizes indigenous peoples' cultural intellectual property.

A. Minimizing consumer confusion

An important function of trademarks and their justification for legal protection is the avoidance of consumer confusion.[102] The scope of confusion is somewhat difficult to define and some confusion may be tolerated or be important to ensure concurrent rights or competing social objectives.[103] Core principles of trademark law provide that it is an infringement of a trademark for a person, without a licence, to use identical or similar signs on the same or similar goods,[104] or falsely to suggest that there is implied sponsorship or an endorsement.[105]

The goals of indigenous peoples in using trademark protection or in seeking to create a greater level of protection are consistent with the goal of minimizing consumer confusion. Indigenous peoples' reasons for wanting protection of signs and symbols include the desire to avoid consumers thinking products are made by an indigenous community, sourced from an indigenous community, or made according to indigenous communities' traditional knowledge, if such products are in fact not. In addition, an inappropriate use of traditional knowledge can create confusion over what that traditional knowledge in fact is.

B. Enhancing competition and reducing search costs

The economic rationale for trademarks protection is that trademarks reduce consumer search costs because consumers are able to rely on trademarks as indicators of product quality, and that this reduction in search costs is good for competition. Those advocating economic bases of trademark law have promoted these rationales as justifications for trademark law in various ways.[106]

At first blush, the goals and aspirations of indigenous peoples in seeking to protect their signs and symbols neither offend these rationales, nor draw particular support from them. Where indigenous peoples have commercialized their signs and symbols by applying them to goods and services in trade, then search costs may well be reduced and competition enhanced. Perhaps the more important point is that the goals of indigenous peoples are another indication

---

[102] Such views of trademark law have been described as "altruistic" and "not really a substantial objective of trade mark law." Pickering, *supra* note 96, at 106.
[103] See Graeme Austin, *Tolerated Confusion*, Ch. 14 of this volume; Rochelle Cooper Dreyfuss, *Reconciling Trademark Rights and Expressive Values: How to Stop Worrying and Learn to Love Ambiguity*, Ch. 10 of this volume.
[104] Trade Mark Act 2002 (NZ), § 89; Trade Marks Act 1994 (UK), § 10.
[105] 15 U.S.C. 1125(a) (1988).
[106] WILLIAM LANDES & RICHARD POSNER, THE ECONOMIC STRUCTURE OF INTELLECTUAL PROPERTY LAW 166–8 (2003).

of the limitations of these rationales, which are an incidental benefit of registration for some trademark protection, but not a fundamental rationale or justification underlying all trademark law. Such rationales, grounded in law and economics, are incomplete explanations of trademark rights and as such should not be used to inhibit the development of trademark law in ways that protect indigenous peoples' signs and symbols.

C. Trademark law and the perseveration of the public domain

Maintenance of the public domain is not a core function of trademark law. Although there is some disagreement about the function of the public domain in patent and copyright law,[107] these parts of intellectual property law are also directly motivated by the encouragement of innovation and creativity. Some trademarks may indeed be innovative or creative; but encouraging such activity is not a core goal or rationale of trademark protection. That said, as the subject matter of trademark law expands, as discussed above, to encompass more than words but also expressive values, the public domain has a closer relationship with trademark law than it did in the past. A major concern with trademarks that relate to colour, get-up, shape, and packaging is that giving these expressive values trademark protection gives too much monopoly power, effectively removing too much from the public domain, potentially giving backdoor protection to subject matter more appropriately dealt with in copyright or patent. That said, trademark registrations always exclude the sign or symbol that is registered from the public domain.[108]

D. Distinctiveness and other reasons for protecting trademarks

At present trademarks are registered on the basis of a recognized form of ownership based on distinctiveness. Distinctiveness in trademark law arises primarily in two ways: by creating a fanciful or inherently distinctive trademark, or through creating a secondary meaning as a result of use of suggestive or descriptive terms. The justification for this is because one or more persons have obtained a proprietary right over use of that sign and symbol. Trademark law may presently only recognize one predominant kind of proprietary right, arising from distinctiveness in trade, but on a principled basis it is questionable if this is the only sort of proprietary right in signs and symbols that a legal system can recognize. Such a suggestion might require a radical rethink of

---

[107] See, e.g., Ch. 13 of this volume.
[108] Some trademarks incorporate a number of signs and symbols and the combination of these gives rise to the registration, even though each part could not be registered separately. Those separate parts would be available for others in the development of new signs and symbols. In that regard such parts may be viewed as in the public domain.

trademark law. Evolving social norms can inspire different approaches to trademark infringement.[109] Changes in society, such as greater recognition of indigenous peoples' rights, may require a different consideration of what merits proprietorship of trademarks in the first place.

Trademark law and its related rights recognize that there are other ways that signs and symbols can become distinctive. Flags and emblems distinguish one nation from another. Tartans may distinguish one Scottish clan from another. Indigenous peoples are often able to distinguish between uses of one sign or symbol as belonging to a particular group or sub-group within their communities. All of these are forms of cultural distinctiveness of signs and symbols flowing from cultural heritage. Trademark registration systems do not recognize distinctiveness arising from cultural heritage alone as meriting registration. Trademarks protect signs and symbols that are applied to goods and services and distinguish one trader from others. This disjunction between the protection of the sacred and trademark registration has led to protection independent of, but related to, trademark registration for flags and emblems.[110] These are protected independent from the need for distinctiveness in relation to goods and services of one trader from other traders. This protection of the sacred is limited to state emblems, official hall-marks, and emblems of inter-governmental organizations.[111] To indigenous peoples, this is arguably simply the recognition of one culture over another.

The protection of flags and emblems is well established in international intellectual property law.[112] Protecting these sorts of things reflects international recognition of the protection of the sacred and consequently such things are removed from the public domain. The protection of Olympic insignia is another example.[113] Such extensive and non-trade-related protection of signs and symbols is not more justifiable from a legal viewpoint than the protection of "emblems" of indigenous peoples.

In addition, many national laws may provide specific protections for named entities. In New Zealand, Te Papa Tongarewa, The Museum of New Zealand, has its own statute to protect the names, signs and symbols associated with it.[114]

Indigenous peoples sometimes also wish to commercialize their signs and symbols, resulting in the "accusation," usually informally made, that indigenous peoples want "to have their cake and eat it too." The real issue here is

---

[109] See generally Dinwoodie, *supra* note 99.
[110] See Paris Convention, *supra* note 13, art. 6*ter*.
[111] *Id.*
[112] See id.
[113] For a general discussion, *see* FRANKEL & McLAY, *supra* note 5, at 9.2.3(d).
[114] Museum of New Zealand Te Papa Tongarewa Act 1992 (NZ).

whether the "first in, first served" principle should apply when one culture has dominated another. In part, this is a question of self-determination and goes well beyond trademark or indeed intellectual property law.[115]

Moreover, the desire to commercialize one's own culture is not materially different from the operation of some aspects of territoriality in trademark law. Trademark law, in various ways, will prevent a trader from appropriating a mark from another jurisdiction. The first of these is the protection afforded to famous or well-known marks.[116] While the reward given to the success of multinational companies may be justified, it is an impoverished international culture that protects only this and not the diversity of cultures within the global community. Second is the concept of international spill-over reputation that applies in some jurisdictions to marks whether well-known or not. In some instances a very small amount of use of a mark, which originates from foreign parts, will allow the overseas trademark owner to oppose registration in a new jurisdiction.[117] Indeed, the whole notion of opposing proprietorship is built on the idea that misappropriation of someone else's mark can result in successful opposition to registration or revocation of a wrongly registered mark. Although the protection of indigenous peoples' intellectual property in signs and symbols is analytically distinct from these examples, they show that the aspirations of indigenous peoples are not conceptually alien to trademark law.

As discussed above, many indigenous peoples do not want any of their culture inappropriately commercialized and therefore aspire to have a system that requires their consent so that if there is commercialization, it is culturally appropriate. This does not mean that indigenous peoples have greater rights than others, but that in relation to what is primarily associated with indigenous communities, there is a proprietary right in the same way that a primary association with a business gives a proprietary right in trademark law to that business.[118]

---

[115] *See* Draft Declaration of Indigenous Peoples E/CN.4/Sub.2/1994/2/Add.1 (1994); Maatatua Declaration on Cultural and Intellectual Property Rights of Indigenous Peoples, June 1993, *available at* http://aotearoa.wellington.net.nz/imp/mata.htm.

[116] Paris Convention, *supra* note 13, art. 6*bis*; TRIPS Agreement, *supra* note 3, arts. 16.2 & 16.3.

[117] See FRANKEL & MCLAY, *supra* note 5, at 517–18.

[118] Whether the law requires that indigenous peoples are consulted on the use of their culture is an issue of political will to protect indigenous peoples' rights and the relative power of indigenous peoples to demand such protection.

VII. Public domain and freedom of expression issues

A. *The scope of the public domain*

When the suggestion is made that indigenous peoples ought to have protection of their signs and symbols, a perceived incursion into the public domain or limitation on freedom of expression is raised as a barrier to indigenous peoples' goals and aspirations. The concern is that restricting the use of or access to any subject matter diminishes the platform on which new works can be created.[119] This view implicitly casts indigenous peoples, who are seeking to protect their cultural intellectual property rights, as holding back the rest of society by aspiring to benefit directly from their own cultural heritage ahead of people from different cultures.

However, indigenous peoples' wish to benefit directly from their own culture is in part motivated by the desire to *support* cultural survival (admittedly in an attempt to close the socio-economic gap between the indigenous people and the dominant culture). One might also ask "whose public domain is it anyway?"[120] The protection of indigenous cultural property does not need to be regarded as undermining the value of the public domain. In any case, cultural appropriation is not the ideal way to claim that something is in the public domain and consequently available for any use by anyone regardless of its origin.[121] If indigenous rights are to be absorbed into the so-called public domain, then advocates of such an approach need to establish that the cultural intellectual property and heritage of indigenous peoples has been "donated" or "appropriated" fair and square. But perhaps a more useful approach comes from examining more closely what we mean by the public domain.[122] A possible result of this analysis is that there is more than one conception of the public domain, resulting in multiple public domains with differing boundaries.

---

[119] See WIPO/GRTKF/IC/5/3, 6 para 23(b) (stating that "public domain status of cultural heritage is also tied to its role as a source of creativity and innovation"); WIPO /GRTKF/IC/5/3, 6 annex 2, para 30 (citing WIPO/GRTKF/IC/3/11) (suggesting that protecting traditional knowledge means "the public domain diminishes"). *See also* Graeme Austin, *Re-Treating Intellectual Property? The WAI 262 Proceeding and the Heuristics of Intellectual Property Law*, 11 CARDOZO J. INT'L & COMP. L. 333, 360 (2003) (describing the inclusion of the opposition ground of offensive to Māori, in New Zealand's trademark law, as "retreating of intellectual property" as it "reduce[s] the signs available to be registered as trademarks"); Steve Franks, Speech in the New Zealand Parliament, August 1, 2001, (quoted in Frankel, *supra* note 27, at 84).

[120] This is my adaptation of "Whose Knowledge is it Anyway?," from Dutfield, *supra* note 36, at 244.

[121] For a view that appropriated use of indigenous peoples' culture is stealing, see generally Angela Riley, *"Straight Stealing": Towards an Indigenous System of Cultural Property Protection*, 80 WASH. L. REV. 69 (2005).

[122] *See generally* Guibault & Hugenholtz, *supra* note 5.

Broadly, in Western intellectual property, something is regarded as in the public domain if it is not protected by intellectual property, because either it does not meet the criteria for protection or, in the case of rights of finite duration, those rights have expired.[123] The possibility of breaking secrecy and benefiting society with acquired innovation or creativity is precisely the rationale on which the reward of a patent is granted. The major exception to this model is where a potentially patentable invention is kept secret and that secrecy is protected by some kind of trade-secret law.[124]

Indigenous peoples often do not consider the public domain in this way.[125] Indigenous peoples' customary systems of cultural intellectual property are often highly regulated so that not everyone is able to make certain creations and once they are made they must be used in a particular way. Also such creations often are representative of something else, beyond their physical form, and therefore must be treated in a way that respects that something else. For example, in Māori culture only certain members of tribes may use particular features in their carving or weaving. As a carving is created it embodies the *whakapapa* (genealogy) of ancestors and must be respected and used in ways that honour that *whakapapa*.[126] So, for example, a McDonald's disposable placemat purporting to depict the New Zealand icon of a *heitiki* (a carving) would not be an appropriate use of such a symbol.[127] The view that such symbols are in the public domain is not broadly accepted by Māori.[128]

That said, there are times when indigenous knowledge is in the public domain. Any protection of cultural intellectual property in signs and symbols

---

[123] This is probably truer for patent law than for copyright, where there is considerable dispute over what aspects of copyright are in the public domain, such as whether or not information obtained through fair use is in the public domain. *See* Pamela Samuelson, *Challenges in Mapping the Public Domain,* in GUIBALT & HUGENHOLTZ, *supra* note 5, at 7. Dreyfuss and Dinwoodie identify the "need to make this distinction" as "almost incomprehensible" for patent lawyers. See Graeme B. Dinwoodie & Rochelle Cooper Dreyfuss, *Patenting Science: Protecting the Domain of Accessible Knowledge*, in GUIBALT & HUGENHOLTZ, *supra* note 5, at 193.

[124] In common law jurisdictions outside of the United States, the most common, relevant doctrine is breach of confidence.

[125] Sherman and Wiseman discuss aboriginal peoples of Australia's perspective on what is in the public domain. *See* Sherman & Wiseman, *supra* note 5. They do this by analyzing the different ways in which western intellectual property law and the aboriginal peoples of Australia structure knowledge. *See id.*, at 267–72.

[126] *See supra* note 19.

[127] *See* Catherine Davis, *Te Matauranga Maori I te Taha o te Mataraunga*, LL.M Research Paper, Victoria University of Wellington (cited in Frankel, *supra* note 27, at 88).

[128] Sherman and Wiseman give similar examples of the use of aboriginal symbols. *See* Sherman & Wiseman, *supra* note 5, at 271.

will need to take account of what is and is not in the indigenous peoples' public domain and in what circumstances those signs and symbols are in the wider public domain.

B. Freedom of expression and language

Trademarks and all intellectual property rights are limitations on free speech. Some form of intellectual-property protection is generally recognized as a justifiable limitation, but often the boundaries of protection are fought out in a free-speech debate. The concept of free speech in the context of indigenous peoples' rights and protection of signs and symbols is complicated, not least of all because the approach to free speech is not uniform worldwide. Primarily the United States approach to appropriate limitations on free speech follows a path quite different from that found in human rights analyses of Europe, Canada, Australia, and New Zealand, all of which differ among themselves.[129]

The right to freedom of expression, as with all human rights, can be limited, but the articulation of those limits varies across borders. In New Zealand, such limitations are permissible provided that they are "reasonable" and "demonstrably justifiable in a free and democratic society."[130] Trademarks are one such permissible limitation.

In the United States, commentators have argued that the cancellation of trademark registrations such as "Redskins" is barred by the First Amendment.[131] Another view is that the legislation allowing opposition to disparaging marks is an important aspect of human rights "because trademarks that are disparaging of Native Americans are a part of a pattern that causes irreparable, substantial harm that has a direct effect on the survival of a culture within the United States."[132]

The free-speech arguments are complicated and cannot be done justice in this chapter. However, the point that trademarks often perform a language function, and therefore use of language should be free, is an important one.[133] Freedom of expression can be construed far more broadly, and more affirmatively. Many indigenous peoples struggle to preserve their language and cultural identity. Language is an important part of cultural identity and the

---

[129] It is beyond the scope of this chapter to analyze the free-speech issues in depth.

[130] *See* Andrew Butler & Petra Butler *The New Zealand Bill of Rights Act: A Commentary*, 6.10 (LexisNexis, 2005).

[131] *See generally* Jeffrey Lefstin, *Does the First Amendment Bar Cancellation of REDSKINS?*, 52 STAN. L. REV. 665 (1999–2000).

[132] Dougherty, *supra* note 68, at 386.

[133] For a general discussion, see Megan Richardson, *Trademarks as Language*, 26 SYDNEY L. REV. 193 (2004).

ability for indigenous peoples to control signs and symbols is, in part, a question of the ability to preserve and develop language. If third parties adopt the language outside its cultural context and therefore alter its meaning, the language might not survive and consequently cultural identity might be threatened.

VIII. Is *sui generis* protection a solution?

An emerging theme from this chapter is that a *sui generis*[134] form of protection of indigenous peoples' cultural intellectual property in signs and symbols should be developed, at both national and international levels. The protection of indigenous symbols and signs, although sometimes possible through trademark law, should not be regarded as a subset of trademark law, but potentially an area requiring a greater extent of protection than trademark law offers. This may mean a *sui generis* system functioning alongside trademark law or a radical rethink of trademark law.

The time has come to protect indigenous peoples' signs and symbols at national and international levels of trademark systems. Many indigenous peoples believe that such protection is long overdue.[135] Ultimately the question of whether and how such protection occurs is a political one. It remains to be seen whether the New Zealand Government, for example, will consider protecting Māori signs and symbols any further by providing a *sui generis* form of protection to complement the trademark opposition provisions.[136]

Internationally, the call for recognition of indigenous peoples' rights in intellectual property is taking place in many forums. There are a number of hurdles for international protection, primarily the diversity of national systems.[137] Therefore, detailed agreements of protection of indigenous designs and symbols at a multilateral level are some way off.[138] Despite these hurdles, when the structure and policy of trademark law is analyzed, as

---

[134] It should be noted that *sui generis* here does not in any way indicate that the system should be similar in format to existing trademark or other intellectual-property regimes. Such a *sui generis* system, particularly at domestic law, could and probably should be based on customary-law understanding of cultural property protection of indigenous peoples' signs and symbols.

[135] One only needs to look at the length of the process for application for removal of "REDSKINS" to see that the goals of the applicants for removal have been in existence for some time. *See supra* note 72.

[136] *See* WAI 262, *supra* note 23.

[137] *See* Dinwoodie, *Traditional Knowledge*, *supra* note 43, at 4. Anthony Taubman, *Saving the Village: Conserving Jurisprudential Diversity in the International Protection of Traditional Knowledge*, in MASKUS & REICHMAN, *supra* note 2, at 521.

[138] *See supra* note 1.

discussed above, there is no real theoretical impediment to creating a system that protects indigenous peoples' rights in their traditional knowledge and cultural intellectual property relating to signs and symbols. All of society grows and benefits from diversity of knowledge and ideas. The public stands to benefit from protecting indigenous peoples' signs and symbols in just the same way that it benefits from the protection of signs and symbols of commerce.[139]

The protection of indigenous signs and symbols at both national and international levels may require a *sui generis* system because its goals and aspirations are not the same as trademark registration. An important aspect of this is the level of control given to indigenous peoples over their signs and symbols; it cannot be that, in protecting their culture, indigenous peoples lose control over their culture. However, that system needs to be related to trademark registrations so that the systems have mechanisms to work out potential clashes between them, rather than being doomed to exist in parallel. In my view, the best way to achieve such a relationship is to have robust objection procedures in trademark registration systems. When indigenous peoples are able to utilize their cultural intellectual property to revive and develop their culture, then the relationship between the systems may also need to change.

---

[139] See Rosemary J. Coombe, *Protecting Cultural Industries to Promote Cultural Diversity: Dilemmas for International Policymaking Posed by the Recognition of Traditional Knowledge*, in MASKUS & REICHMAN, *supra* note 2, at 599, 611–14 (discussing "human rights, cultural diversity and public goods").

17 Culture, traditional knowledge, and trademarks: a view from the South
*Coenraad Visser**

I. Introduction

Here I shall canvass the possible impact of trademark law on traditional knowledge. I shall argue that such impact manifests itself on two levels – the appropriation of items of traditional knowledge and incorporating them as part of registered trademarks, and the use of trademarks to enhance the economic exploitation of, mainly, traditional cultural expressions in order to ensure income streams to the (mainly poor) indigenous communities holding such knowledge. In the process, it shall emerge, especially at the second level, that the collective side of trademark law perhaps best interacts with the collective nature of much of traditional knowledge.

But first, a question of terminology. Without entering into the debate about the precise definition of the term "traditional knowledge",[1] or about whether such a definition is a prerequisite to any legal protection of traditional knowledge, I should merely note that, for present purposes, I shall follow the practice of the World Intellectual Property Organization [hereinafter WIPO][2] of

---

* Professor of Intellectual Property Law, Head of the Department of Mercantile Law, University of South Africa, Pretoria.

[1] Alternative terms in international instruments include, for example, "knowledge, innovations and practices of indigenous and local communities embodying traditional lifestyles relevant for the conservation and sustainable use of biological diversity" (Convention on Biological Diversity, art. 8(j)), "indigenous knowledge (systems and practices)" (United Nations Draft Declaration on the Rights of Indigenous Peoples, preamble); "indigenous cultural and intellectual property" (*id.*, art. 29); "community knowledge" (the Organization of African Unity's Model Legislation for the Protection of the Rights of Local Communities, Farmers and Breeders, and for the Regulation of Access to Genetic Resources); "local and traditional knowledge" (United Nations Convention to Combat Desertification in those Countries Experiencing Drought and/or Desertification, Particularly in Africa, art. 16(g)); and "traditional and local technology, knowledge, know-how and practices", arts. 17.1(c), and 18.2(a) and (b)).

[2] *See Intellectual Property Needs and Expectations of Traditional Knowledge Holders: WIPO Report on Fact-Finding Missions on Intellectual Property and Traditional Knowledge* 25 (2001).

using the term in its widest possible sense,³ to include: traditional and tradition-based⁴ literary, artistic, and scientific works; performances, inventions, scientific discoveries, designs; marks, names, and symbols; undisclosed information, and all other innovations and creations resulting from intellectual activity in the industrial, scientific, literary, or artistic fields.⁵ So categories of traditional knowledge include: agricultural knowledge; scientific knowledge; technical knowledge; ecological knowledge; medicinal knowledge, including knowledge relating to medicines and remedies; knowledge relating to biodiversity; traditional cultural expressions⁶ in the form of music, dance, song, handicrafts, designs, stories, artworks and elements of languages (such as names, geographical indications, and symbols), and movable cultural properties.

---

³ For an analysis that seeks to narrow down the concept of traditional knowledge and distill its defining components, see Daniel J. Gervais, *Spiritual but not Intellectual? The Protection of Sacred Intangible Traditional Knowledge*, 11 CARDOZO J. OF INT'L & COMP. LAW 467, 469–74 (2003); Daniel J. Gervais, *Traditional Knowledge & Intellectual Property: A TRIPS-compatible Approach*, MICH. ST. L. REV. 137, 140–59 (2005).

⁴ The terms "traditional" and "tradition-based" refer to knowledge systems, creations, innovations, and cultural expressions that have, generally, been transmitted from generation to generation, are generally regarded as pertaining to a particular people or its territory, and continuously evolve in response to a changing environment (*Traditional Knowledge – Operational Terms and Definitions*, document prepared by the Secretariat for the Third Session of the Intergovernmental Committee on Intellectual Property and Genetic Resources, Traditional Knowledge and Folklore, Geneva, June 13 to 21, 2002 (WIPO/GRTKF/IC/3/9) ¶ 25; *see also* Wend B. Wendland, *Intellectual Property, Traditional Knowledge and Folklore – WIPO's Exploratory Program*, 33 INT. REV. OF IND. PROP. & COPYRIGHT L. 485, 497 (2002)).

⁵ So knowledge systems, properties, and other materials that are not the result of intellectual creativity in the industrial, scientific, literary, or artistic fields are excluded. Examples are burial sites, languages, spiritual beliefs, and human remains. *Intellectual Property Needs*, *supra* note 2, at 25.

⁶ Sometimes called "folklore" or "expressions of folklore". These terms have been argued to carry negative and Eurocentric connotations, suggestive of "something dead to be collected and preserved, rather than as part of an evolving living tradition." T. Janke, *UNESCO-WIPO World Forum on the Protection of Folklore: Lessons for Indigenous Australian Cultural and Intellectual Property*, 15 COPYRIGHT REPORTER 104, 109 (1997). To Spanish speaking countries, especially, these terms are archaisms, with the negative connotation of being associated with the creations of lower or superseded civilizations. Michael Blakeney, *The Protection of Traditional Knowledge Under Intellectual Property Law*, 22 EUR. INTELL. PROP. REV. 251 (2000). While WIPO is aware that the term "folklore" may have pejorative connotations, it argues that the term has been in use for many years at international level, and so retains its use for the time being. *Intellectual Property Needs*, *supra* note 2, at 25.

II. Developing countries: a clash of intellectual property rights paradigms

Internationally, the TRIPS Agreement[7] mandates the level of protection of intellectual property rights in national law. As a basic premise, the TRIPS Agreement requires that all countries, whether they are developed or developing,[8] adopt the same minimum level of protection for intellectual property rights.

When one concerns oneself with intellectual property protection in developing countries, one has to be conscious that one effectively deals with two systems of legal protection. The first is the system of intellectual property rights enshrined in the TRIPS Agreement. These rights are characterized by the fact that they are individualized – they attach to their holders in the Romantic liberal traditional of rights that attach to individual citizens. Roht-Arriaza,[9] for example, writes of patent law that:

> ... the individual nature of patent law is reinforced in the trade-related intellectual property rights (TRIPS) agreement ... which recognizes intellectual property rights only as private rights. Rights belonging to the public, or a sector of it, do not fit easily.

Coexistent with this system of individual intellectual property rights are indigenous knowledge systems — traditional knowledge, including, as I have indicated at the outset, traditional cultural expressions, and traditional ecological knowledge (sometimes called "ethnobotanical knowledge").

Gudeman[10] explains further:

> Built upon the Cartesian duality of mind and body, intellectual property rights are aligned with practices of rationality and planning. The expression "intellectual property rights" makes it appear as if the property and rights are products of individual minds. This is part of a Western epistemology that separates mind from

---

[7] Agreement on Trade-Related Aspects of Intellectual Property Rights, April 15, 1994, Marrakesh Agreement Establishing the World Trade Organization, Annex 1C [hereinafter, TRIPS Agreement].

[8] There are no World Trade Organization definitions of "developed" and "developing" countries. Members announce for themselves whether they are "developed" or "developing" countries. But other members can challenge the decision of a member to make use of provisions aimed at assisting developing countries.

[9] Naomi Roht-Arriaza, *Of Seeds and Shamans: the Appropriation of the Scientific and Technical Knowledge of Indigenous and Local Communities*, in ESSAYS ON CULTURAL APPROPRIATION 255, 263 (B. Ziff & P.V. Rao eds., 1997).

[10] S. Gudeman, *Sketches, Qualms, and Other Thoughts on Intellectual Property Rights*, in INDIGENOUS PEOPLES AND INTELLECTUAL PROPERTY RIGHTS, 102, 103 (S.B. Brush & D. Stabinsky eds., 1996).

body, subject from object, observer from observed, and that accords priority, control, and power to the first half of the duality. The term "intellectual" connotes as well the knowledge side and suggests that context of use is unimportant. . . . In contrast to this modernist construction, in a community economy innovations are cultural properties in the sense that they are the product and property of a group.

In the same vein, it has been argued[11] that

indigenous [*viz* traditional] knowledge differs from scientific knowledge in being moral, ethically-based, spiritual, intuitive and holistic; it has a large social context. Social relations are not separated from relations between humans and non-human entities. The individual self-identity is not distinct from the surrounding world. There often is no separation of mind and matter. Traditional knowledge is an integrated system of knowledge, practice and beliefs.

The communal nature of traditional knowledge is recognized expressly in legislation in the Philippines and Venezuela, for example.

The Philippine Constitution 1987 expressly mandates the recognition, respect, and protection of the rights of indigenous cultural communities and indigenous peoples.[12] In discharge of this mandate the Indigenous Peoples Rights Act[13] was enacted in October 1997. It protects the following "community intellectual property rights" of indigenous peoples: past, present, and future manifestations of their cultures, such as archeological and historical sites, designs, ceremonies, technologies, visual and performing arts, literature, and religious and spiritual properties; science and technology, such as "human and other genetic resources, seeds, medicines, health practices, vital medicinal plants, animals, minerals, indigenous knowledge systems and practices, resource management systems, agricultural technologies, knowledge of the properties of fauna and flora, and scientific discoveries"; and "language, music, dance, script, histories, oral traditions, conflict resolution mechanisms, peace building processes, life philosophy and perspectives and teaching and learning systems."[14] The extent of these rights appears from section 34:

Indigenous cultural communities/indigenous peoples are entitled to the recognition of the full ownership and control and protection of their cultural and intellectual rights. They shall have the right to special measures to control, develop and protect

---

[11] F. Berkes, C. Folke & M. Gadgil, *Traditional Ecological Knowledge, Biodiversity, Resilience and Sustainability*, in BIODIVERSITY CONSERVATION: PROBLEMS AND POLICIES 281, 283 (C.A. Perrings et al. eds., 1995).
[12] Section 17, art. XIV.
[13] Republic Act No. 8371.
[14] Rules and Regulations Implementing Republic Act No. 8371, section 10, rule VI.

their sciences, technologies and cultural manifestations, including human and other genetic resources, including derivatives of these resources, seeds, traditional medicines and health practices, vital medicinal plants, animals and minerals, indigenous knowledge systems and practices, knowledge of the properties of flora and fauna, oral traditions, literature, designs and visual and performing arts.

Article 124 of the Constitution of the Republic of Venezuela 1999 states succinctly:

The collective intellectual property of indigenous knowledge, technology and innovations is guaranteed and protected. Any work on genetic resources and the knowledge associated therewith shall be for the collective good. The registration of patents in those resources and ancestral knowledge is prohibited.

This distinction between individual intellectual property rights and communal traditional knowledge rights is an oversimplification, of course. While many indigenous and local communities generate and transmit knowledge from generation to generation collectively, and many of these communities are characterized by a strong sharing ethos with respect to their knowledge and resources,[15] there are situations in which individual members of these communities can distinguish themselves and be recognized as informal creators or inventors distinct from their community.[16] And the anthropological literature documents that concepts such as ownership and property rights, or close equivalents, do exist in many indigenous communities.[17] The problem is exacerbated, of course, by the fact that there is no generic communal traditional knowledge rights system:

Indigenous peoples possess their own locally-specific systems of jurisprudence with respect to the classification of different types of knowledge, proper procedures for acquiring and sharing knowledge, and the nature of the rights and responsibilities which attach to possessing knowledge.[18]

---

[15] Graham Dutfield, *TRIPS-Related Aspects of Traditional Knowledge*, 33 CASE W. RES. J INT'L L. 233, 245 (2001).
[16] A. Gupta, statement at the WIPO Roundtable on Intellectual Property and Traditional Knowledge, Geneva, November 1 to 2, 1999.
[17] *See, e.g.,* David A. Cleveland & Stephen C. Murray, *The World's Crop Genetic Resources and the Rights of Indigenous Farmers*, 38 CURRENT ANTHROPOLOGY 477, 477–96 (1997).
[18] Russel Lawrence Barsh, *Indigenous People and Biodiversity, in Indigenous Peoples, Their Environments and Territories*, in CULTURAL AND SPIRITUAL VALUES OF BIODIVERSITY 73 (Darrell A. Posey ed., 1999). *See also* Dutfield, *supra* note 15, at 246–7.

Thus in every transaction involving traditional knowledge, one has to ask questions such as

> [W]ho can speak for what? Who has the authority for what? Whose custom? Whose heritage? Whose culture? And whose identity? All these questions are extremely important.[19]

At the same time, collective marks are known to trademark law, and the TRIPS Agreement itself recognizes geographical indications[20] – both types of intellectual property right protect the interests of a collective.[21]

When these rights paradigms clash, who will emerge the winner? Shiva asks:[22]

> When indigenous systems of knowledge and production interact with dominant systems of knowledge and production, it is important to anticipate whether the future options of the indigenous system or the dominant system will grow. Whose knowledge and values will shape the future options of diverse communities?

Given the reality of economic power, it is not hard to predict that the system of individual intellectual property rights as sanctioned by the TRIPS Agreement will hold sway.[23] But it is precisely its superimposition on traditional knowledge systems that challenges developing countries in two very different ways – to protect their traditional knowledge holders[24] against the

---

[19] Maroochy Barambah & Ade Kukoyi, *Protocols for the Use of Indigenous Cultural Material*, in GOING DIGITAL 2000: LEGAL ISSUES FOR E-COMMERCE, SOFTWARE AND THE INTERNET 133 (Anne Fitzgerald et al. eds., 2nd ed. 2001).

[20] TRIPS Agreement, *supra* note 7, art. 22.

[21] It is wrong, of course, to claim that "not all [intellectual property rights] are individualistic", since "[i]ncreasingly, invention and creation take place in firms where groups or persons may be cited as co-inventors or co-authors, concepts recognized by the [intellectual property] system". *Intellectual Property Needs*, *supra* note 2, at 219. Co-inventors and co-authors jointly still hold individual rights – the content and nature of the right of a patentee or an author do not change by virtue of the fact that such right is held jointly by two or more people.

[22] VANDANA SHIVA, BIOPIRACY: THE PLUNDER OF KNOWLEDGE AND NATURE (1997), quoted by KEMBREW MCLEOD, OWNING CULTURE: AUTHORSHIP, OWNERSHIP AND INTELLECTUAL PROPERTY LAW 158 (2001).

[23] For a compelling integration argument, *see, e.g.*, Chidi Oguamanam, *Localizing Intellectual Property in the Globalization Epoch: The Integration of Indigenous Knowledge*, 11 INDIANA J. GLOBAL LEG. STUD. 135 (2004).

[24] WIPO uses the term "traditional knowledge holders" to refer to all persons who create, originate, develop, and practice traditional knowledge in a traditional setting and context. *Intellectual Property*, *supra* note 2, at 26. Although indigenous communities, peoples, and nations are traditional knowledge holders, not all traditional knowledge holders are indigenous.

470 *Trademark law and theory*

operation of the intellectual property rights systems as embodied in the TRIPS Agreement, and, at the same time, to use those intellectual property rights to protect their traditional knowledge holders, no matter whether they hold individual or communal rights.

III. Protecting traditional knowledge in developing countries: two goal posts

These are some examples of traditional cultural expressions, relevant to the present discussion, for which legal protection has been sought: *(a)* Traditional cultural artistic expressions (such as paintings) have been reproduced without authority on carpets, printed fabric, T-shirts, dresses and other garments, and greetings cards, and have subsequently been distributed and offered for sale. Body paintings and rock paintings (petroglyphs) have also been photographed without authority, and the photos distributed and offered for sale.[25] *(b)* Designs embodied in hand-woven or hand-made textiles, weavings, and garments have been copied and exploited commercially without authority. Examples include the *amauti* in Canada, the *saris* of South Asia, the "tie and dye" cloth in Nigeria and Mali, *kente* cloth in Ghana and some other West African countries, traditional caps in Tunisia, the Mayan *huipil* in Guatemala, the Kuna *mola* in Panama, and the *wari* woven tapestries and textile bands from Peru.[26] *(c)* Sacred or secret traditional cultural expressions have been used, disclosed, and reproduced without authority. Examples include the sacred Coroma textiles of Bolivia,[27] and sacred Aboriginal designs reproduced by an Australian carpet manufacturer.[28] *(d)* Words from the vernacular of indigenous and local communities have been registered as trademarks by people who were not members of these communities. Examples include "Pontiac", "Cherokee", "billabong", "tomahawk", "boomerang", "tohunga", "mata nui", "piccaninny", and "tairona."[29]

As I have indicated at the outset, from these examples it appears that trademark law interacts with traditional knowledge at two levels – the appropriation of items of traditional knowledge and incorporating them as part of

---

[25] *Preliminary Systematic Analysis of National Experiences with the Legal Protection of Expressions of Folklore*, document prepared by the Secretariat for the Fourth Session of the Intergovernmental Committee on Intellectual Property and Genetic Resources, Traditional Knowledge and Folklore, Geneva, December 9 to 17, 2002 (WIPO/GRTKF/IC/4/3) ¶ 36(i).
[26] *Id.* in ¶ 36(v).
[27] Susan Lobo, *The Fabric of Life: Repatriating the Sacred Coroma Textiles*, CULTURAL SURVIVAL QUARTERLY 40 (1991).
[28] Milpurrurru v Indofurn (Pty.) Ltd., (1995) 30 IPR 209.
[29] *Preliminary Analysis, supra* note 25, ¶ 36(xii).

registered trademarks, and the use of trademarks to enhance the economic exploitation of, mainly, traditional cultural expressions. Accordingly, I should now like to look at trademark law from the point of view of, first, the protection of traditional knowledge *against* trade marks, and, then, the protection of traditional knowledge *by* trademarks. Although, at first blush, this distinction seems to mirror the distinction between the "positive" and "defensive" protection of traditional knowledge,[30] the latter distinction signals something different. Some indigenous peoples and traditional communities want *positive* protection of their traditional cultural expressions – they want to benefit from the commercialization of these expressions. But some members of these groups and communities are concerned with the cultural, social, and psychological harm caused by the unauthorized use of their traditional cultural expressions. To them, such use deprives these expressions of their original significance, which, in turn, may disrupt and dissolve their culture. So this group argues for the *defensive* protection of these cultural expressions.[31]

Again, these are not watertight categories. The protection of traditional knowledge for the purposes of exploitation by its holders also entails the protection of such knowledge against misappropriation by "outsiders", against exploitation of traditional knowledge, in other words.

For the sake of brevity, I shall not here consider the protection of the geographical indications of local and indigenous communities.[32]

A. Protection against the exploitation of traditional knowledge

Trademark law may prohibit the registration of distinctive signs and so on as trademarks where such registration may offend sections of the community (including indigenous and local communities), or where it falsely suggests a connection between such sign and an indigenous or a local community.

The first couple of examples below illustrate the use by national legislators of *ordre public* style prohibitions[33] on the registration of trade marks that

---

[30] Wend B. Wendland, *The Legal Protection of Traditional Knowledge*, paper delivered at the International Bar Association Conference 2002, Durban (October 22, 2002).

[31] *Id.*

[32] As to which, see the extensive treatment of Annette Kur & Roland Knaak, *Protection of Traditional Names and Designations*, in INDIGENOUS HERITAGE AND INTELLECTUAL PROPERTY: GENETIC RESOURCES, TRADITIONAL KNOWLEDGE AND FOLKLORE 221, 227–34 235–8 250–54 (Silke von Lewinski ed., 2004).

[33] *See* the Paris Convention for the Protection of Industrial Property, as revised at Stockholm, 1967, art. 6^{quinquies}(B)(3), 21 U.S.T. 1583, 828 U.N.T.S. 305 (trademarks registered in one country of the Paris Union may be denied registration or invalidated in other countries of the Union ". . . when they are contrary to morality of public order . . .") [hereinafter, Paris Convention].

would offend an indigenous or local community in the country of registration. These provisions are often intertwined with others that proscribe the registration of trademarks that could be seen as false attributions of origin, as suggesting a connection between the goods or services to which the trademark will be applied and an indigenous or local community.

In New Zealand, following a proposal by a Māori advisory group, a further absolute ground for the refusal of a trademark application has been added: the Commissioner for Trade Marks must not register a trade mark where "its use or registration would be likely to offend a significant section of the community, including the Māori".[34] Also, the Commissioner may on application by an ". . . aggrieved person (which includes a person who is culturally aggrieved) . . ." declare a trademark registration to be invalid.[35] A committee advises the Commissioner on whether the proposed use or registration of a "mark that is, or appears to be, derivative of a Māori sign, including Māori text and imagery is, or is likely to be, offensive to Māori".[36] During the consultative process preceding the legislative enactment, the Māori advisory group mentioned as an example the Māori word "mana", which can connote a person's honor, sense of prestige, and essence of being. If "mana" were to be registered for beer, the Māori would likely be offended.[37]

In South Africa, the Trade Marks Act[38] states that a trade mark should not be registered, or should be removed from the register where it has been registered, if it ". . . is likely to give offence to any class of persons". The ambit of the phrase "class of persons" is arguably wide enough to include an indigenous or a local community.

In the United States of America, a proposed trademark may be refused registration and a registered trademark canceled if the mark consists of or comprises matter that may disparage, or falsely suggest a connection with, persons (living or dead), institutions, beliefs, or national symbols, or bring them into contempt or disrepute.[39] So the United States Patent and Trademark Office may refuse to register a proposed trademark that falsely suggests a connection with an indigenous tribe or beliefs held by that tribe. According to

---

[34] Trade Marks Act 2002, section 17(1)(c)(i).
[35] *Id.*, section 74(1).
[36] *Id.*, section 177.
[37] *See* Kur & Knaak, *supra* note 32, at 244.
[38] Act 194 of 1993, section 10(12). Compare, for example, art. 124.III of the Lei da Propriedade Industrial N° 9.279, 1996 (Brazil), which states that expressions, figures, drawings, or other signs cannot be registered as trademarks where doing so would offend ". . . idéia e sentimento dignos de respeito e veneração" (". . . ideas or feelings worthy of respect or veneration").
[39] 15 U.S.C. § 1052(a).

Culture, traditional knowledge and trademarks 473

the Office, this provision protects not only Native American tribes but also those of "other indigenous peoples worldwide".[40]

These registration exclusions suffer from two defects.

In the first instance, registration exclusions do not prevent the use of a trade mark that falls within their ambit. Instead, the legislator merely withholds the benefits that would otherwise have resulted from the registration of such a trade mark.[41] So the utility of these exclusions in the present context may be limited, especially if it means that there is no single owner of registered rights who can seek to exclude unauthorized third party uses. By contrast, if the statutory exclusions were to apply also to unregistered rights,[42] the impact of these exclusions on the protection of the traditional knowledge of local and indigenous communities would expand.

Secondly, it may, of course, be difficult for someone not familiar with the traditional knowledge of local and indigenous communities in the country of registration to know whether a particular distinctive sign or word would fall foul of these prohibitions. In such a case, an official database of protected signs (or words) would be useful to applicants and registries.

In the United States of America, the Trademark Law Treaty Implementation Act 1998[43] required the office to complete a study on the official protection of insignia of federally and state recognized Native American tribes. As a direct result of this study, the office established, on August 31,

---

[40] See the *Final Report on National Experiences with the Legal Protection of Expressions of Folklore*, document prepared by the Secretariat for the Third Session of the Intergovernmental Committee on Intellectual Property and Genetic Resources, Traditional Knowledge and Folklore, Geneva, June 13 to 21, 2002 (WIPO/GRTKF/IC/3/10) ¶ 122.

[41] In the United States of America, *see, e.g.*, In re McGinley, 660 F.2d 481, 486 (C.C.P.A. 1981) ("In providing that marks comprising scandalous matter may not be registered, Congress expressed its will that such marks not be afforded the statutory benefits of registration."); Stephen R. Baird, *Moral Intervention in the Trademark Arena: Banning the Registration of Scandalous and Immoral Trademarks*, 83 TMR 661, 663 (1993) ("Importantly, Section 2(a) does not prevent the use of marks that fit the description. Rather, Section 2(a) prevents the government from placing its imprimatur on such marks and denies the statutory benefits that would otherwise result from their federal registration.").

[42] In the United States of America, *see, e.g.*, Baird, *supra* note 41, at 790–93 (arguing that the registration exclusion in section 2(a) of the Lanham Act (*see* 15 U.S.C. 1052(a)) in respect of scandalous and immoral marks should apply also to unregistered marks). Less emphatic is the statement in Two Pesos, Inc. v Taco Cabana, Inc., 505 U.S. 763, 768 (1992), 112 S.Ct. 2753, 2757 (1992) that ". . . the general principles qualifying a mark under § 2 of the Lanham Act are for the most part applicable in determining whether an unregistered mark is entitled to protection under § 43(a)" (*per* White J.).

[43] Pub. L. 105-530, 112 Stat. 3064, section 302.

2001, a searchable Database of Official Insignia of Natives American Tribes that may prevent the registration of a mark confusingly similar to official insignia.[44] (The term "insignia" connotes "the flag or coat of arms or other emblem or device of any federally or State recognized Native American tribe", but it does not include words.[45])

While registrars and applicants may well consult such databases compiled by other registrars, it is difficult for local and indigenous communities to make such information available internationally, for example, by means of a database administered by a body like WIPO. It is against the backdrop of this problem that the recent action of Brazil should be seen.

At the sixteenth session of the Standing Committee on the Law of Trademarks, Industrial Designs and Geographical Indications of the WIPO, Brazil submitted a Non-exhaustive List of Customary Names Used in Brazil Associated with Biodiversity.[46] It is noted that the Government of Brazil had on many occasions, in many different countries, had to institute costly legal proceedings to expunge trademarks that incorporated customary terms such as "açaí" and "cupuaçu" (native fruits of the Amazon region), and "rapadura", a typical unrefined brown sugar traditionally consumed in northeast Brazil.[47] The list, contained in Annex II, then includes some 5000 generic terms in Portuguese relating to Brazilian plant biodiversity and their corresponding scientific names.

While this notification should be seen as an attempt to bring these items of Brazilian traditional knowledge to the attention of trademark registries worldwide, it also highlights the fact that trademarks incorporating items of traditional knowledge (especially, words) should generally be refused registration for lack of a distinctive character.[48] However, where such a mark does manage to get onto the register, it can be expunged by means of proceedings that may be too costly for the relevant local or indigenous community.

The notification also raises the question of the "need to keep free" doctrine – a trademark registration may not foreclose the use of terms (the names of Brazilian plant varieties, for example) required for further commercial use.[49]

---

[44] Establishment of a Database Concerning the Official Insignia and Federally and State Recognized Native American Tribes, 66 Fed. Reg. 44603 (2001).
[45] *Id.*, at 44604.
[46] *Communication from the Permanent Mission of Brazil*, WIPO/SCT/16/7 (September 29, 2006), submitted at the Sixteenth Session of the Standing Committee on the Law of Trademarks, Industrial Designs and Geographical Indications of the World Intellectual Property Organization, Geneva, November 13 to 17, 2006.
[47] *Id.*, in Annex I, ¶ 3.
[48] *Id.*
[49] *See, e.g.*, in Brazil, art. 124.VI of the Lei da Propriedade Industrial; in India,

B. Protection for the exploitation of traditional knowledge

In Australia, for example, the preferred legal technique to protect against nonindigenous people who manufacture and sell indigenous artifacts at the expense of the indigenous artistic community is through the use of certification marks,[50] serving as labels of authenticity. The National Indigenous Arts Advocacy Association [hereinafter NIAAA] registered the first of two proposed national indigenous labels of authenticity as certification marks in Australia. These labels will be applied to goods[51] and services[52] of Aboriginal or Torres Strait Islander origin, which will make it more difficult for non-Aboriginal people to pass off their works as if they were authentically Aboriginal. The first mark – the label of authenticity – will be applied to "products or services that are derived from a work of art created by, and reproduced or manufactured by Aboriginal or Torres Strait Islander people who satisfy the definition of 'authenticity'".[53] An artist who has successfully applied to use this label will be referred to as a certified indigenous creator. The second mark – the collaboration mark – will be applied to "products or services derived from a work of art which has been created by an Aboriginal or Torres Strait person or people who satisfy the definition of 'authenticity'".[54] This mark recognizes that products and services are often produced,

---

section 9(1)(b) of the Trade Marks Act 1999; in South Africa, section 10(2)(b) of the Trade Marks Act. A further practical example: "rooibos", the name of a tea made from a species of shrub growing in South Africa, was registered as a trademark in the United States of America, the Netherlands, and the United Kingdom. DAVID R. DOWNES & SARAH A. LAIRD, INNOVATIVE MECHANISMS FOR SHARING BENEFITS OF BIODIVERSITY AND RELATED KNOWLEDGE, CASE STUDIES ON GEOGRAPHICAL INDICATIONS AND TRADEMARKS 17 (1999).

[50] A certification mark, in terms of section 169 of the Trade Marks Act 1995, is a sign used, or intended to be used, to distinguish goods or services dealt with or provided in the course of trade, and certified in relation to quality, accuracy, or some characteristic (such as origin, material, or mode of manufacture), from other goods or services dealt with or provided in the course of trade, but not so certified. Certification marks symbolize and promote the collective interests of certain groups of traders – by preventing traders whose goods do not comply with the certification process from using the mark, the integrity of those traders whose goods are certified is maintained. Leanne Wiseman, *The Protection of Indigenous Art and Culture in Australia: the Labels of Authenticity*, 23 EUR. INTELL. PROP. REV. 14, 15 (2001). On certification marks generally, *see, e.g.*, Jeffrey Belson, *Use, Certification and Collective Marks*, in TRADE MARK USE, 147, 148–55 (Jeremy Phillips & Ilanah Simon eds., 2005).

[51] Such as fabrics, boomerangs, coolamons, nets, traps, seed and shell necklaces, didgeridoos, musical recordings, sticks, and sculptures. Wiseman, *supra* note 50, at 15.

[52] Such as theatre, dance, concerts, and educational and tourism programs. Wiseman, *supra* note 50, at 15.

[53] NIAAA, *Discussion Paper on the Proposed Label of Authenticity*, 5 (1997).

[54] *Id.*

reproduced, or manufactured under licensing agreements with indigenous people. The collaboration mark will be applied to such products and services, provided that the licensing arrangements are "fair and legitimate".

It has to be admitted that although these labels of authenticity will raise the profile of indigenous artists and help to make sure that they are properly remunerated, they will provide only limited protection to these artists. It is unlikely that, by themselves, they will prevent the production, import, or export of forgeries.[55]

In New Zealand, where Mäori words and symbols can be found in many registered trademarks,[56] *Te Waka Toi* (the Mäori Arts Board of Creative New Zealand), in consultation with Mäori artists, likewise registered a "Mäori made mark" and two companion marks – a "mainly Mäori mark" and a "Mäori co-production mark".[57] These marks are used to promote and sell authentic, quality Mäori arts and crafts, and also to authenticate exhibitions and performances of Mäori arts by Mäori artists. The creation of these marks is a direct response to the burgeoning tourism trade to New Zealand, which often involves the sale of cheap and culturally offensive objects imitating Mäori art, such as plastic tiki.[58] Although the registration of these marks has been lauded in some quarters, in the end they are little more than an initiative for the promotion of authentic Mäori arts and crafts.[59]

In India, too, there are various experiments with certification marks. Two examples: the Policy Sciences Center has been instrumental in implementing, with the Indian Commissioner for Handicrafts, a certification system for products labeled "Handmade in India".[60] And the certification mark "India Organic", owned by the Government of India, is available for use on the basis of compliance with the National Standards for Organic Production. The mark is intended to communicate the genuineness and the origin of the relevant products.[61]

---

[55] Wiseman, *supra* note 50, at 23–4.
[56] GRAEME B. DINWOODIE, WILLIAM O. HENNESEY & SHIRA PERLMUTTER, INTERNATIONAL INTELLECTUAL PROPERTY LAW AND POLICY 1398 (2001).
[57] *See* http://www.toiho.com/about/about/htm.
[58] Tania Waikato, *Hei Kaitiaki Mätauranga: Building a Protection Regime for Mäori Traditional Knowledge*, 8 YEARBOOK OF NEW ZEALAND JURISPRUDENCE, SPECIAL ISSUE – TE PURENGA, 344, 372 (2005).
[59] *Id.*
[60] *See* Frank J. Penna & Coenraad J. Visser, *Cultural Industries and Intellectual Property Rights*, in DEVELOPMENT, TRADE, AND THE WTO: A HANDBOOK, 390, 394 (Bernard Hoekman et al. eds., 2002); Mareen Liebl & Tirthankar. Roy, *Handmade in India: Traditional Craft Skills in a Changing World*, in POOR PEOPLE'S KNOWLEDGE: PROMOTING INTELLECTUAL PROPERTY IN DEVELOPING COUNTRIES 53, 64–70 (J. Michael Finger & Philip Schuler eds., 2004).
[61] *See* http://www.indianspices.com/html/np_organiccert.htm.

IV. Conclusion

It appears, then, that trademark law has limited scope for the protection of traditional knowledge in the form of indigenous names and signs against misappropriation for incorporation into registered trademarks. Largely, this flows from one of the founding principles of trade mark law – the country of protection principle, in terms of which protection is, generally, dependent on the knowledge and the perceptions of the public in the country where protection is sought.[62] This fences in, of course, also the operation of the doctrine of *ordre public*. Even if the *telle-quelle* principle of the Paris Convention[63] (a member of the Convention has to accept for registration any trademark that has been duly registered in its country of origin) were to be adopted more widely in national legislation,[64] this would be mainly cold comfort to traditional knowledge holders – the principle is again subject to the morality and *ordre public* of the country in which the *telle-quelle* registration is sought.[65]

Future efforts at expanding the scope of protection of traditional knowledge against the misappropriation of indigenous names and signs will probably concentrate on developing the supranational information infrastructure, by the development of appropriate databases. For the reasons that I have indicated above, such development may involve major effort for scant reward.

---

[62] Kur & Kraak, *supra* note 32, at 255.
[63] Paris Convention, *supra* note 33, art. 6^{quinquies}(A)(1).
[64] *See* JEREMY PHILLIPS, TRADE MARK LAW: A PRACTICAL ANATOMY, 60 note 6 (2003): "Since '*telle-quelle*' is a French term which has no obvious English translation, it has been to a large extent ignored by English-speaking countries." In respect of the United States, *see*, *e.g.*, *In re* Rath, 402 F.3d. 1207, 1211–14 (Fed. Cir. 2005) (finding that the provision in section 44(e) of the Lanham Act (*see* 15 U.S.C. 1126(e)) that "[a] mark duly registered in the country of origin of the foreign applicant may be registered on the principal register if eligible . . ." meant that the foreign mark was not "eligible" if it did not meet the requirements of section 2 of the Lanham Act"), and United States – Section 211 Omnibus Appropriation Act of 1998: Report of the Appellate Body, WT/DS176/AB/R (January 2, 2002) (finding that section 211(a)(1) of The Omnibus Consolidated and Emergency Supplemental Appropriations Act of 1999, Pub. L. No. 105-277, 112 Stat. 2681 (1999), was not inconsistent with article 2.1 of the TRIPS Agreement read in conjunction with article 6^{quinquies} A(1) of the Paris Convention). On Rath, *see*, *e.g.*, Annette Kur, Comment, *In re Rath and Grupo Gigante v Gallo*, 36 INT. REV. OF INDUSTRIAL PROP. & COPYRIGHT L. 727, 727–8 (2005) (speculating that the finding may well have been different before a more "Convention-friendly" European court). Further on the WTO report, *see*, *e.g.*, Ashley C. Adams, Note, *Section 211 of the Omnibus Appropriations Act: The Threat to International Protection of U.S. Trademarks*, 228 N.C. J. INT'L L. & COM. REG., 221, 231–2 (2002); Annette Kur, *What is "AS IS"? Das telle quelle-Prinzip nach "Havana Club"*, in HARMONISIERUNG DES MARKENRECHTS – FESTSCHRIFT FÜR ALEXANDER VON MÜHLENDAHL ZUM 65. GEBURTSTAG (Verena von Bomhard et al. eds., 2005) 361.
[65] Paris Convention, *supra* note 33, art. 6^{quinquies}(B)(3).

At the level of the exploitation of traditional knowledge, the contribution of trademark law is again modest by offering the vehicles of collective and certification marks. But these vehicles are not only appropriate to the generally collective nature of traditional knowledge and its holders, but, perhaps more importantly, are in line with the origins of trademark law – to protect consumers against deception as to the origin of goods and services. For the protection of their traditional cultural expressions, local and indigenous communities would have to turn to a protection regime closer to copyright,[66] perhaps along the lines of the stillborn Model Provisions for National Laws on the Protection of Expressions of Folklore against Illicit Exploitation and Other Prejudicial Actions,[67] an avenue explored at WIPO by the Intergovernmental Committee on Intellectual Property and Genetic Resources, Traditional Knowledge and Folklore.[68]

---

[66] This is not to deny that traditional cultural expressions fit uncomfortably into the copyright paradigm (*see, e.g.*, Mihály Ficsor, *Attempts to Provide International Protection for Folklore by Intellectual Property Rights*, in UNESCO-WIPO WORLD FORUM ON THE PROTECTION OF FOLKLORE (1998) 213, 217; Gervais, *supra* note 3, at 141–2). Briefly, there are three reasons for this poor fit: (1) traditional cultural expressions are often the result of a continuing and slow process of creative activity exercised by a local or indigenous community by consecutive imitation, whereas copyright usually requires some form of individual creativity; (2) copyright is author-centric, whereas the notion of an author in the copyright sense is usually absent in the case of traditional cultural expressions; and (3) traditional cultural expressions continue to evolve, and have done so over centuries, which does not square with any notion of a fixed term of protection. Still, many developing countries regulate the use of their traditional cultural expressions within the framework of their copyright laws (for a list, *see* Ficsor, *supra*, at 215).

[67] *See* http://unesdoc.unesco.org/images/0006/000637/063799eb.pdf. These Model Provisions were adopted by a Committee of Governmental Experts on the Intellectual Property Aspects of the Protection of Expressions of Folklore, meeting in Geneva from June 28 through July 2, 1982.

[68] Established by the WIPO General Assembly at its Twenty-sixth Session (*Report Adopted by the General Assembly*, WIPO General Assembly, Twenty-sixth (12th Extraordinary) Session, September 25 to October 3, 2000, WIPO Doc. WO/GA/26/10 (October 3, 2000) para. 71). This is effectively a forum for international policy debate and the development of legal mechanisms and practical tools concerning the protection of traditional knowledge and traditional cultural expressions, and the intellectual property aspects of access to and benefit-sharing in genetic resources.

Section D

The Edges of Trademark Protection

18 Of mutant copyrights, mangled trademarks, and Barbie's beneficence: the influence of copyright on trademark law
Jane C. Ginsburg*

In *Dastar Corp. v Twentieth Century Fox Film Corp.*,[1] Justice Scalia colorfully warned against resort to trademarks law to achieve protections unattainable by copyright, lest these claims generate "a species of mutant copyright law that limits the public's 'federal right to "copy and to use,"'" expired copyrights."[2] The facts of that controversy, in which the claimant appeared to be invoking time-unlimited trademark protection to end-run the exhausted (unrenewed) copyright term in a motion picture, justified the apprehension that unbridled trademark rights might stomp, Godzilla-like, over more docile copyright prerogatives. Unfortunately, in the Court's eagerness to forestall Darwinian disaster in intellectual property regimes, it may have engaged in some unnatural selection of its own, mangling trademark policies in the process of conserving copyright. This chapter will first consider how the (mis)application of copyright precepts has distorted trademarks law, then will take up happier examples of beneficent copyright influence. The first inquiry charts the near-demise of moral rights at the hands of copyright-(mis)informed trademark analysis. The second lauds the growing acceptance of copyright-inspired free speech limitations on trademark protection, exemplified by the various "Barbie" cases,[3] and culminating in the "fair use" exemptions of the Trademark Dilution Revision Act of 2006.

---

*   Morton L. Janklow Professor of Literary and Artistic Property Law, Columbia University School of Law. Thanks to Prof. Greg Lastowka, and for research assistance to Zahr Stauffer, Columbia Law School JD class of 2007. Portions of Section I of this article were adapted from Jane C. Ginsburg, *The Right to Claim Authorship in US Trademarks and Copyright Law*, 41 Hous. L. Rev. 263 (2004).
   [1]   539 U.S. 23 (2003).
   [2]   *Dastar*, 539 US at 34 (quoting Bonito Boats, Inc. v Thunder Craft Boats, Inc., 489 U.S. 141, 165 (1989)).
   [3]   *See* Mattel, Inc. v Walking Mountain Prods., 353 F.3d 792 (9th Cir. 2003); Mattel, Inc. v MCA Records, Inc., 296 F.3d 894, 899 (9th Cir. 2002); Mattel, Inc. v Pitt, 229 F. Supp. 2d 315, 318–19 (S.D.N.Y. 2002).

I. Bad influence

In *Dastar Corp. v Twentieth Century Fox Film Corp.*, the Supreme Court announced that a work's entry into the public domain precludes resort to another federal intellectual property statute, the Lanham Trademarks Act, to achieve a *de facto* prolongation of exclusive copyright-like rights. Had that been all the Court held, the decision would have been applauded, and trademark law's remedies against "false designations of origin"[4] could have continued to afford a limited means for the public to be informed about the authorship of creative works. Instead, however, the Court went much farther, holding that section 43(a)(1)(A) of the Lanham Act did not address the intellectual origin of a work of authorship, but rather only the source or manufacture of physical copies of the work.

The Court grounded much of its analysis in a perceived need to maintain separate domains for copyright and for trademarks, but it did not confine this discussion to copyright-expired works. Most perniciously, the *Dastar* Court indicated that the addition to the Copyright Act of a very circumscribed authorship attribution right in the Visual Artists Rights Act[5] promotes a negative inference that VARA is the *only* federal law locus for attribution rights: if the trademark law afforded attribution rights, VARA would be superfluous, and "[a] statutory interpretation that renders another statute superfluous is of course to be avoided."[6] But section 43(a) does *not* make VARA superfluous. There may be narrow areas of overlap, but VARA, in its severely constricted zone, affords a significant right that section 43(a) did not: an *affirmative* right to claim authorship, not merely a right to object to misrepresentations of authorship that confuse consumers as to the work's origin. VARA's beneficiaries are artists, but the beneficiaries of section 43(a) are the consuming public. Moreover, the rationales for copyright and trademarks laws are different. The former seeks to advance knowledge by stimulating creativity, the latter to aid purchasing decisions through truthful attribution of the source of goods or services. Courts addressing overlapping intellectual property claims have acknowledged that differently motivated laws may yield similar results when brought to bear on the same subject matter, yet one does not drive out the other.[7]

---

[4] Lanham Federal Trademarks Act, § 43(a), 15 USC § 1125.
[5] 17 USC § 106A.
[6] *Dastar*, 539 U.S. at 35.
[7] *See, e.g.*, Bach v Forever Living Prods., 473 F. Supp. 2d 1110 (W.D. Wa. 2007) (rejecting *Dastar*-inspired motion to dismiss trademark passing off claim regarding unauthorized copying from JONATHAN LIVINGSTON SEAGULL and use of one of the book's photographs as defendant's corporate logo: "trademark law protects the distinctive source-distinguishing mark, while copyright law protects the work as a whole. *See*

Given the breadth of *Dastar*'s pronouncements about the relationship of copyright and trademarks law, it is not surprising that lower courts have understood *Dastar* to preclude Lanham Act claims related to the authorship attribution of works still under copyright as well as those whose copyrights have expired.[8] This unflinching application of *Dastar* ignores the public interest

---

Whitehead v CBS/Viacom, Inc., 315 F. Supp. 2d 1, 13 (D.D.C. 2004). The fact that the two areas of law protect against different wrongs is reflected in the many cases in which courts have analyzed the same set of facts under both trademark and copyright law without concluding that the trademark claims were 'piggybacking' on the copyright claims [string cite omitted]."); Frederick Warne & Co. v Book Sales, Inc., 481 F. Supp. 1191, 1196–9 (S.D.N.Y. 1979) (stating that a publisher of children's books in the public domain could bring a trademark claim against defendant's copying of particular illustrations from the book, and commenting that "[b]ecause the nature of the property right conferred by copyright is significantly different from that of trademark, trademark protection should be able to co-exist, and possibly to overlap, with copyright protection without posing preemption difficulties"); *cf.* Bonito Boats, Inc. v Thunder Craft Boats, Inc., 489 U.S. 141 (1989) (holding that federal design patent law preempts state laws protecting against copying of boat hull designs but does not preempt state laws protecting consumers against misleading presentations of products). *See also* Viva R. Moffat, *Mutant Copyrights and Backdoor Patents: The Problem of Overlapping Intellectual Property Protection*, 19 BERKELEY TECH. L.J. 1472, 1527 (2004).

[8] *See, e.g.*, Williams v UMG, 281 F. Supp. 2d 1177 (C.D. Cal. 2003) (rejecting "reverse passing off" claim when film writer and director's name was left off the credits of a documentary on which he collaborated; court acknowledged that Ninth Circuit precedent had recognized such claims in similar contexts, but that *Dastar* now "precludes plaintiff's Lanham Act claim" in still-copyrighted as well as public domain works); Hustlers v Thomasson, 73 U.S.P.Q. 2d 1923 (N.D. Ga. 2004) (holding that *Dastar*'s limitation of false designation of origin claims to the producer of physical copies bars not only claims by authors, but also by publishers; the court also follows *Williams v UMG Recordings* in holding *Dastar* not limited to works in the public domain); Zyla v Wadsworth, 360 F.3d 243, 241–51 (1st Cir. 2004) (professor and collaborative author on a college textbook brought suit against a publisher for failing to attribute her authorship properly when she dropped out of the editing process, court read *Dastar* as foreclosing a Lanham Act claim based on the professor's contributions to a copyrighted textbook); Mays & Assoc. v Euler, 370 F. Supp. 2d 362 (D. Md. 2005) (after *Dastar*, no Lanham Act claim for non-attribution of authorship of web design portfolio); JB Oxford & Co. v First Tenn. Bank Nat'l Ass'n., 427 F. Supp. 2d 784 (M.D. Tenn. 2006) (no § 43(a) claim against advertiser who allegedly copied plaintiff's advertisement and substituted its name for plaintiff's.; Carroll v Kahn, 68 U.S.P.Q. 2d (BNA) 1357, 1361–2 (N.D.N.Y. 2003) (quoting *Dastar* and *Williams v UMG Recordings, Inc.* to support dismissal of a "failure to attribute" claim); Chivalry Film Prods. v NBC Universal, Inc., 2006 WL 89944 (S.D.N.Y. 2006) (screenwriter claimed producer of "Meet the Parents" copied his script and misattributed screenplay to third parties; court held *Dastar* required dismissal of misattribution claim); A Slice of Pie Prods. v Wayans Bros. Entm't, 392 F. Supp. 2d 297 (D. Conn. 2005) (same re film "White Chicks"); Beckwith Builders v DePietri, 2006 U.S. Dist. LEXIS 67060; 81 U.S.P.Q. 2d (BNA) 1302 (D.N.H. 2006) (dismissing claim that crediting building to

concern at trademark law's core—accuracy in market information. The author's name is in fact a term that "identifies and distinguishes" goods or services,[9] that allows consumers to choose among works of authorship on the basis of past experiences with other works by the same author or on the basis of the author's reputation. In other words, it functions as a trademark.[10] When the public encounters the author's name, for example, on a book jacket or in film credits, it expects the work to demonstrate certain qualities. A consumer might say, "I liked So-and-So's last novel; I think I'll try the new one." or "This director's films are well-regarded, I think I'll see for myself." This thought process is no different from that of the consumer who purchases shampoo by its brand name or a designer article of clothing. The producer of the shampoo or the clothing designer both endeavor to give their goods a brand image that will enable the consumer to identify the goods and relate them to his past experiences. By the same token, the author's name will convey information about the qualities of literary or artistic expression the reader/viewer/listener may expect from that author.

In confining "origin of goods" to physical goods, *Dastar* (and progeny) thus overlooks the role that the author's name plays in conveying information material to the purchasing decision. This role may underlie *Dastar*'s reference to a related claim under § 43(a). Section 43(a)(1)(B) addresses a "false or misleading description of fact, or false or misleading representation of fact, which . . . misrepresent[] the nature, characteristics, [or] qualities . . . of his or her or another person's goods [or] services" and thus may in some instances preserve a Lanham Act right of action for some authors and performers.[11] Arguably, removing the author's or the actor's name and replacing it with another's constitutes a false or misleading representation of fact (who is

---

another architect violated the Lanham Act, "Beckwith's complaint asserts that the Clark Road home was labeled with a designation of origin – via the signs placed near it. But, because the signs in front of that house accurately identified those who physically produced that tangible object [built the house, as opposed to designed it], the facts alleged by Beckwith fail to state a claim of false designation of origin under the Lanham Act."); Sivak v Versen, 2007 U.S. Dist. LEXIS 22430 (S.D. Cal. 2007) ("Although the [*Dastar*] Court was examining the issue in the context of alleged misuse of material no longer protected under copyright monopoly because the copyright on the material had expired and the material had entered the public domain, the Court's analysis recognized the need to avoid 'over-extension' of trademark and related protections into traditional copyright and patent areas").

[9] See Lanham Act § 45, 15 USC § 1127 (definition of "trademark").

[10] For a more detailed discussion, *see, e.g.*, F. Gregory Lastowka, *The Trademark Function of Authorship*, 85 B.U. L. REV. 1171 (2005); Jane C. Ginsburg, *The Author's Name as a Trademark: A Perverse Perspective on the Right of "Paternity"?*, 23 CARDOZO ARTS & ENT. L. REV. 379 (2005).

[11] *Dastar*, 539 U.S. at 38.

the author of this book; who performed in this film) that misrepresents the nature, characteristics, or qualities (authorship; performance) of the goods (the work). Note that, for purposes of section 43(a)(1)(B), the Court appears to have acknowledged that "goods" can mean a "communicative work," while, for purposes of section 43(a)(1)(A), "goods" would mean only the physical copies. Query whether it makes sense for "goods" to mean two different things in these adjacent sections. In any event, the potential availability of a section 43(a)(1)(B) claim becomes particularly significant if, after *Dastar*, the "origin" of copyrighted works is falsely designated only when physical copies are mislabeled as to their manufacture.

Suppose, for example, that a famous novelist grants film rights in his book. Apart from its title, the resulting movie bears only the slightest resemblance to the underlying literary work. But, recognizing the market value of the author's name, the motion picture company promotes the film (without the author's permission) as "Stephen King's *The Lawnmower Man*."[12] Or suppose that a copyright-licensed U.S. broadcaster airs a truncated version of *Monty Python's Flying Circus*, presenting it as the work of the British comedy troupe even though the troupe did not approve the broadcaster's removal of approximately one-third of the content.[13] In both cases, the attribution to the creators is misleading, not to say, vastly overstated. Presenting the work as "Stephen King's" when virtually the only thing in the film that is still the writer's is the title, or as "Monty Python's" when the editing has garbled it, might falsely describe the nature, characteristics, or qualities of the work. The *Dastar* Court indicated that a claim for false representation of the nature of the work under section 43(a)(1)(B) could lie if Dastar promoted its modestly altered videos as "quite different" from the Fox originals when they in fact are quite the same; by the same token, a claim should remain available if a work is promoted as being "by" an author when its purveyor has in fact made it "quite different" from the work the author created.[14] In both cases, the purveyor has drawn

---

[12] *See* King v Innovation Books, 976 F.2d 824, 826–27 (2d Cir. 1992).
[13] *See* Gilliam v ABC, 538 F.2d 14 (2d Cir.1976).
[14] *See* 4 J. THOMAS MCCARTHY, MCCARTHY ON TRADEMARKS, § 27:77.1, at 27–149.

> The Court hypothesized that if a producer of a video that substantially copied Fox's Crusade television series were, in advertising or promotion, to give purchasers the impression that the video was "quite different from that series," then Fox might have a claim for false advertising for misrepresenting the nature, characteristics or qualities of the creative content of the product in violation of § 43(a)(1)(B). That is, in this hypothetical, the defendant would be making a false statement about the content of its communicative product.

Id. (footnote omitted). McCarthy also notes that the false advertising prong contains a

attention to a commercially attractive feature of the goods (the videos' difference from the Fox original; the film's close association with an author who enjoys substantial market appeal; the television program's authorship by the comedy troupe); if this feature in fact is lacking (or is misleadingly overstated) the consuming public will have been duped.[15]

These examples offer variants of traditional "passing off" claims that had been pursued under section 43(a)(1)(A) (and prior versions of section 43(a)): a version that the author claims is so altered that it no longer represents his work is nonetheless sold as if it were the real thing. Although the "goods" are a work of authorship, this is analytically akin to passing off a fake Fendi bag as though it were the genuine article. If a "false representation" claim remains viable in the case of traditional "passing off," would it also lie against one who engages in "reverse passing off"? Suppose I make copies of a Brad Meltzer legal thriller and sell them under my name. Under *Dastar*, I am the "origin" of the *copies* (or perhaps my publisher is), so a section 43(a)(1)(A) claim against me fails. But I have also made a "false representation of fact which . . . misrepresents the nature, characteristics [or] qualities," that is, the authorship, of my literary work ("goods"). If Brad Meltzer can make out the remaining elements of a claim for "misrepresent[ations of] the nature, characteristics, [or] qualities," then the effects of *Dastar* might be blunted.[16]

This analysis, however, may suggest too simple a sleight of hand: next time, all an author need do is plead section 43(a)(1)(B) instead of section 43(a)(1)(A). Not surprisingly, at least one lower court has perceived a section 43(a)(1)(B) claim to be a mere end-run around *Dastar*, and, accordingly, rejected it. In *Antidote Int'l Films v Bloomsbury Pubishing PLC*,[17] the plaintiff, a film producer, had purchased an option to produce a motion picture based on the novel SARAH, by the elusive cult writer J.T. Leroy, whose personal history outstripped the adventures of his fictional characters. It turns

---

restriction that the "trademark prong" does not: the misrepresentation must be "in commercial advertising or promotion." *Id.* at 27-149 to 27-150 (internal quotation marks omitted). This is "not an insignificant limitation." *Id.* at 27–150.

[15] The Stephen King and Monty Python cases could be made *Dastar*-compatible on another theory: the possessory credit violates § 43(a)(1)(A) not because it is a false designation of *origin*, but because it falsely represents "*sponsorship* or *approval* of [the defendant's] goods, services or commercial activities . . ." (emphasis supplied). *Dastar* itself, however, invites application of § 43(a)(1)(B); a false "sponsorship or approval" claim would not redress the wrongful conduct at issue when an entrepreneur purveys goods as being "quite different" when they are in fact quite the same.

[16] *See, e.g.*, Croson v Eslinger, 455 F. Supp. 2d 256 (S.D.N.Y. 2006) (declining to dismiss § 43(a)(1)(B) claim that film's credits wrongly credited defendant as producer).

[17] 467 F. Supp. 2d 394 (S.D.N.Y. 2006).

out, however, that "J.T. Leroy" was also a fiction, concocted by the actual author, her family, and the publisher. In response to the plaintiff's false advertising claim, the court held: "in the instant case, with respect to claims that sound in false authorship, the holding in *Dastar* that the word 'origin' in § 43(a)(1)(A) refers to producers, rather than authors, necessarily implies that the words 'nature, characteristics, [and] qualities' in § 43(a)(1)(B) cannot be read to refer to authorship. If authorship were a 'characteristic[]' or 'qualit[y]' of a work, then the very claim *Dastar* rejected under § 43(a)(1)(A) would have been available under § 43(a)(1)(B)."

The *Antidote* court's critique, however, overlooks the consumer protection focus of section 43(a). Section 43(a), unlike section 32 of the Lanham Act, does not require that the claimant be a trademark registrant. This is because section 43(a) targets a wider range of deceitful marketplace activity, including misleading imitation of unregistered trade dress, and false advertising. The objective is not primarily to create new rights for unregistered merchants, but to protect the public.[18] This in turn suggests that the application of section 43(a)(1)(B) to misrepresentations regarding the "nature," et cetera, of "communicative goods" should be limited to misrepresentations material to the consumer. As suggested above, knowing who is the actual creator generally is material to the purchasing decision. This observation may also be key to resolving the potential tension in the post-*Dastar* treatment of copyrighted and public domain works.

Dastar and progeny's equation of conduct permissible under the copyright law with activities permissible under trademark law gives rise to additional consumer-unfriendly anomalies. Consider this instance of copyright-permissible material deception: copyright does not protect the ideas, information, or processes that a work discloses. As a result, copyright protection for a work such as a cookbook is typically "thin," covering the chef's literary flourishes, but not the culinary preparations themselves. As a matter of copyright law, therefore, I am free to publish my own cookbook appropriating the ingredients and following the steps needed to produce Nigella Lawson's latest creations. Moreover, because U.S. copyright law says nothing about how I label the *unprotected* material that I copy, any express or implied fair use obligation to

---

[18] See MCCARTHY ON TRADEMARKS, § 27:14, at 27–25 to 27–27.

> The courts have nearly unanimously held that § 43(a) provides a federal vehicle for assertion of infringement of even unregistered marks and names. As the Second Circuit remarked, § 43(a) "is the only provision in the Lanham Act that protects an unregistered mark" and "Its purpose is to prevent consumer confusion regarding a product's source . . . ."

Id. (footnote omitted) (*quoting* Centaur Communications, Ltd. v A/S/M communications, Inc., 830 F.2d 1217, 1220 (2d Cir. 1987)).

credit one's sources would not extend to mere copying of public domain elements. Nonetheless, copyright's free pass on *copying* should not also mean that no law will prohibit me from *representing* that the gastronomy I describe is of my own devising. Section 43(a)(1)(B), with its focus on consumer protection, should supply that prohibition.

But, even if authorship is or can be a "characteristic" of the work, the section 43(a)(1)(B) violation does not occur unless the misrepresentation takes place in "commercial advertising or promotion."[19] Simply mislabeling and selling the work without advertising the name substitution may not constitute "promotion"; the statutory text suggests that the mislabeler has called attention to the false information. One might expect that there would be no market for an unpromoted work, so that in most instances the requisite "commercial advertising or promotion" will occur. But the promotion might not always go to the alleged false representation. For example, if a miscredited actor did not perform in a featured role, his (or his false substitute's) name might not appear on posters and advertisements for the film. In those instances, it is not clear that the spurned performer will have a claim. On the other hand, it may also be questionable whether the misrepresentation of a tertiary actor's name is material to consumer choice. By contrast, scholarly publications afford one area in which mislabeling may matter to the consumer, but the "commercial advertising or promotion" criterion may not be met. If the senior co-author takes sole credit for the scholarly article, the junior participants may have no legal redress, either as a matter of the Lanham Act, or as a matter of copyright law, because co-authors cannot infringe their own joint copyright.[20]

The sparse caselaw on the copyright management information provision included in the 1998 Digital Millennium Copyright Act (DMCA)[21] offers

---

[19] Lanham Act § 43(a)(2), 15 U.S.C. § 1125(a)(1)(B) (2000).

[20] Though, in the absence of a contract to the contrary, they do have a duty to account to each other for the profits of their unilateral exploitation. *See, e.g.*, Thomson v Larson, 147 F.3d 195, 199 (2d Cir. 1998) ("Joint authorship entitles the co-authors to equal undivided interests in the whole work C in other words, each joint author has the right to use or to license the work as he or she wishes, subject only to the obligation to account to the other joint owner for any profits that are made."). If one co-author creates a new work without the other, the former co-author is not entitled to exploit the work in which he did not participate. Moreover, copying that work without crediting its author is unlikely to be considered fair use, even if the copying was done in an academic setting. *See* Weissmann v Freeman 868 F.2d 1313, 1324 (2d Cir. 1989).

[21] 17 USC § 1202, defines copyright management information to include

> any of the following information conveyed in connection with copies or phonorecords of a work or performances or displays of a work, including in digital form, except that such term does not include any personally identifying information about a user of a work or of a copy, phonorecord, performance, or display of a work:

another disturbing illustration of the unfortunate emanations of *Dastar*. In this instance, we are seeing a kind of boomerang effect: *Dastar* sought to purge trademarks law of impure copyright influences, and in so doing largely nullified interpretations of the Lanham Act that would (partially) advance authors' attribution interests. The copyright management information provision protects against the removal or alteration of information identifying a work's author, copyright owner, and/or terms and conditions of licenses, in order to promote electronic commerce by ensuring the reliability of the identifying information.[22] The provision thus can play an indirect role in protecting attribution interests.[23] In *IQ Group, Ltd. v Wiesner Publishing, LLC*,[24] the court ruled that a service mark consisting of the plaintiff company's logo could not be protectable "copyright management information" because *Dastar* "cautioned against blurring the boundaries between trademark law and copyright law." Although the logo identified the copyright owner, and thus came literally within the terms of the DMCA, "[t]he problem is that this construction allows a trademark to invoke DMCA protection of copyrights, eliminating the differentiation of trademark from copyright that is fundamental to the statutory schemes. If every removal or alteration of a logo attached to a copy of a work gives rise [to] a cause of action under the DMCA, the DMCA becomes an extension of, and overlaps with, trademark law. . . . This construction of the DMCA would allow trademarks to invoke DMCA provisions meant to protect copyrights. . . . [T]his turns the DMCA into a species of mutant trademark/copyright law, blurring the boundaries between the law of trademarks and that of copyright."[25] Thus, in this instance of *Dastar* gone feral, not only must trademark law not further copyright interests, but a copyright provision enacted to secure identifying information must not be interpreted to advance that goal if the identifying information happens to be a trademark.

---

(1) The title and other information identifying the work, including the information set forth on a notice of copyright.
(2) The name of, and other identifying information about, the author of a work.
(3) The name of, and other identifying information about, the copyright owner of the work, including the information set forth in a notice of copyright. . . .

[22] *See* Jane C. Ginsburg, *Copyright Legislation for the "Digital Millennium,"* 23 COLUM. VLA J.L. & ARTS 137, 157 (1999).
[23] *See, e.g.,* Justin Hughes, *Art and the Law: Suppression and Liberty, The Line Between Work and Framework, Text and Context*, 19 CARDOZO ARTS & ENT L.J. 19, 21 (2001) ("the copyright management information provisions of the DMCA effectively create a right of attribution in the Internet environment").
[24] 409 F. Supp. 2d 587 (D.N.J. 2006).
[25] 409 F. Supp. 2d at 592.

Fortunately, the mangling of federal trademarks law, related false advertising law, and even para-copyright law by over-vigilant overseers of the copyright genome seems principally to concern authors' (tenuously extant) moral rights of attribution (and, perhaps, integrity).[26] Recent judicial and legislative developments afford a happier example of copyright's recent influence on trademarks law: the growing recognition of free speech-based limitations on the scope of trademarks protection.

II. Good influence

Some years ago, the caselaw on trademark parodies and similar unauthorized "speech" uses of trademarks could have led one to conclude that judges had no sense of humor (or, perhaps, that the Lanham Act cramped whatever sense of fun a judge may have indulged off the bench).[27] Over time, however, courts began to leaven likelihood of confusion analyses with healthy skepticism regarding consumers' alleged inability to perceive a joke.[28] They even suggested that the first amendment might require a more persuasive showing

---

[26] For an analysis of *Dastar's* broader impact on state law passing-off claims, see Tom W. Bell, *Misunderestimating Dastar: How the Supreme Court Unwittingly Revolutionized Copyright Preemption*, 65 MD. L. REV. 206 (2006).

[27] *See, e.g.*, Gucci Shops, Inc. v R.H. Macy & Co., 446 F. Supp. 838 (S.D.N.Y. 1977) ("Gucchi Goo" diaper bags held likely to be confused with Gucci handbags); Mutual of Omaha Insurance Co. v Novak, 836 F.2d 397 (8th Cir. 1987) ("Mutant of Omaha" anti-nuclear protest items such as coffee mugs and posters held likely to be confused with "Mutual of Omaha" insurance services; Anheuser–Busch, Inc. v Balducci Publications, 28 F.3d 769 (8th Cir. 1994) ("Michelob Oily" parody ad in SNICKER humor magazine held likely to confuse the public as to its approval by the producers of Michelob Dry beer); Harriette K. Dorson, *Satiric Appropriation and the Law of Libel, Trademark and Copyright: Remedies Without Wrongs*, 65 B.U.L. REV. 923 (1985).

[28] *See* Cliffs Notes, Inc. v Bantam Doubleday Dell Publishing Group, Inc. 886 F.2d 490 (2d Cir. 1989) ("Spy Notes" parody of Cliffs Notes, no likelihood of confusion found); Yankee Publishing v News America Publishing, 809 F. Supp. 267 (S.D.N.Y. 1992) (New York Magazine parody of cover of Old Farmer's Almanac cover, no likelihood of confusion found); Louis Vuitton Malletier S.A. v Haute Diggity Dog, LLC, 507 F.3d 252 (4th Cir. 2007) (defendant produced "a line of pet chew toys and beds whose names parody elegant high-end brands of products such as perfume, cars, shoes, sparkling wine and handbags. These include – in addition to Chewy Vuiton (LOUIS VUITTON) – Chewnel No. 5 (Chanel No. 5), Furcedes (Mercedes), Jimmy Chew (Jimmy Choo), Dog Perignon (Dom Perignon), Sniffany & Co. (Tiffany & Co.), and Dogior (Dior). The chew toys and pet beds are plush, made of polyester, and have a shape and design that loosely imitates the signature product of the targeted brand. They are mostly distributed and sold through pet stores, although one or two Macy's stores carry Haute Diggity Dog's products. The dog toys are generally sold for less than $20; neither likelihood of confusion nor dilution found).

of likely confusion when expressive works were alleged to infringe.[29] These decisions did not always expressly cite the copyright fair use defense, but the considerations underlying the copyright doctrine seemed to inform trademark analysis as well.[30] The spillover effect may indeed have been inevitable, as several of the cases in which the fair use defense prevailed coupled copyright and trademark claims; it is not surprising that the sardonic expressions that proved fair use for the copyright goose would lead to similar treatment for the trademarks gander, particularly when the avian species at issue was a bird called Barbie.

Lawful unauthorized uses of trademarks of course predate both the Mattel toy company and the Lanham Act. In 1924, in a case concerning the labeling of lawfully purchased and rebottled perfume, Justice Holmes famously declared "When the mark is used in a way that does not deceive the public we see no such sanctity in the word as to prevent its being used to tell the truth. It is not taboo."[31] Lanham Act, section 33(b)(4) codified part of this precept by permitting the use of descriptive terms in a registered trademark for the purpose of description, and not as a trademark. For example, if ZEST is a trademark for a lemon-lime soda, the registrant cannot prohibit a competitor from informing the public that its lemon-lime soda, FIZZUP, includes lemon zests, or that it has a zesty taste. But section 33(b)(4) does not explicitly exempt a competitor's use of ZEST to describe the competitor's product, for example, to proclaim that FIZZUP tastes better than, has more bubbles than, or fewer calories than, ZEST. Nor does section 33(b)(4) explicitly allow a non competitor, such as the (fictitious) magazine Teen Taste, to elicit its readers' beverage preferences by asking them whether ZEST is their most or least favorite soda pop. Judge Kozinski dubbed these latter denominations "nominative fair use," and the sobriquet has stuck.[32] The nominative fair use

---

[29] Rogers v Grimaldi, 875 F.2d 994, 999 (2d Cir. 1989).

[30] *See* Pierre N. Leval, *Trademark: Champion of Free Speech*, 27 COLUM. J.L. & ARTS 187, 208 (2004) (in Federal Anti Dilution Act Congress is saying to courts, "You have shown in your development of fair use in copyright that you know how to limit the scope of a broadly-written exclusivity statute – to keep it in line with the needs of free expression. We are relying on you to do that here. Create appropriate doctrines of 'fair use' to keep the Dilution Act within reasonable bounds.").

[31] Prestonettes, Inc. v Coty, 264 U.S. 359, 368 (1924). *See also* Champion Spark Plug v Sanders, 331 U.S. 125 (1947).

[32] *See* New Kids on the Block v News Am. Publ'g, 971 F.2d 302 (9th Cir. 1992); Playboy Enterprises, Inc. v Welles, 279 F.3d 796 (9th Cir. 2002); Century 21 Real Estate Corp. v Lendingtree, Inc., 425 F.3d 211 (3d Cir. 2005) (following Ninth Circuit). Other circuits reach the same result through similar reasoning, albeit without applying the label "nominative fair use." *See, e.g.*, Universal Commun. Sys. v Lycos, Inc., 478 F.3d 413, 424–5 (1st Cir. 2007). *See generally* J. Thomas McCarthy, Non-

defense to trademark infringement proceeds through an analysis of factors. "First, the plaintiff's product or service in question must be one not readily identifiable without use of the trademark; second, only so much of the mark or marks may be used as is reasonably necessary to identify the plaintiff's product or service; and third, the user must do nothing that would, in conjunction with the mark, suggest sponsorship or endorsement by the trademark holder."[33] As we will see, these factors complement and echo the first, third, and fourth copyright fair use factors.[34]

Although copyright is a property "right in gross," and trademark is not (or is not supposed to be), the trademark and copyright fair use limitations have this in common: the users of the mark or of another author's work are engaged in independent economic or creative activity. They are not simply redistributing another's work of authorship[35] or appending another's mark to the same or confusingly similar goods that the mark owner has not produced. Rather, they are making a new work, or promoting their own goods or communicative activities.[36] By the same token, the uses do not unfairly usurp the copyright or trademark owner's markets. A devastating review may dampen desire for the critiqued work, but that kind of harm is not cognizable in copyright.[37] Similarly, a comparative advertisement may persuade consumers of the superior merits of the competitor's goods or services, but if the advertisement is truthful no Lanham Act claim lies.[38]

Trademark "fair use" may have received its greatest impetus from decisions involving overlapping claims of copyright and trademark infringement, for it

---

Confusing Nominative Fair Use, 4 MCCARTHY ON TRADEMARKS AND UNFAIR COMPETITION § 23:11 (4th ed.).

[33] *New Kids*, 971 F.3d at 306.

[34] *See* 17 USC § 107(1), (3), (4).

[35] In narrow circumstances of "market failure," redistributive uses may be ruled "fair," but the kinds of uses at issue in the copyright/trademark overlap cases are more traditionally "transformative," such as parodies.

[36] Fair use of another's trademark to describe the trademark owner's goods, as lawfully repackaged and resold by the defendant (the situation, for example, in *Prestonettes*), does not, admittedly, involve the same kind of independent economic activity. Permitting the use of the mark, however, is a necessary corollary to the "exhaustion" or "first sale" doctrine, which permits third parties to resell trademarked (or copyrighted) goods once they have been lawfully sold. If the reseller cannot inform the public what the resold goods are, the exhaustion doctrine will, as a practical matter, have little impact. *Cf.* Kellogg Co. v National Biscuit Co., 305 US 111, 118 (1938) (once patent expired, and competitors are free to manufacture the goods, they also are entitled to call the goods "the name by which [they] had become known").

[37] *See, e.g.*, Campbell v Acuff-Rose Music, 510 U.S. 569, 593 (1994).

[38] *See, e.g.*, Smith v Chanel, Inc., 402 F.2d 562 (9th Cir. 1968) (smell-alike perfume); August Storck K.G. v Nabisco, Inc., 59 F.3d 616 (7th Cir. 1995) (competing candies).

is not surprising that once a court has found the use to be "transformative" and to promote speech and/or learning, and thus to be "fair" in the copyright sense, that court is unlikely to find the same activity to violate the copyright holder's trademark in the copied work. Nonetheless, the first of the "Barbie" cases to find trademark fair use did not involve copyright infringement, though it did concern a parody.[39] In that case, the song "Barbie Girl" by the Danish one-hit (at least in the US) group "Aqua" in 1997 foisted on the airwaves lyrics like the following, nasally sung to a catchy refrain: "I'm a Barbie girl, in a Barbie world. Life in plastic, it's fantastic. You can brush my hair, undress me everywhere. Imagination, life is your creation. . . . I'm a blond bimbo girl, in a fantasy world. Dress me up, make it tight, I'm your dolly." To which the bass in the group would interject in a froggish croak (Aqua's album was, after all, called "Aquarium"): "C'mon Barbie, let's go party!"

Holding that "the trademark owner does not have the right to control public discourse whenever the public imbues his mark with a meaning beyond its source-identifying function,"[40] the Ninth Circuit rejected both the likelihood of confusion and the dilution claims. Following Second Circuit precedent, the Ninth Circuit balanced the "public interest in free expression" against the "public interest in avoiding consumer confusion," and accorded the former decisive weight unless the song title's appropriation of Barbie "has no artistic relevance to the underlying work whatsoever, or, if it has some artistic relevance, unless the title explicitly misleads as to the source or the content of the work."[41] Observing that the Barbie doll was the target of the song, the court held the group was entitled to identify the butt of its joke, and had done nothing to mislead the public into thinking that Mattel authorized the song. The court dismissed the dilution claim on the ground that the 1996 Federal Trademark Dilution Act's exception for "noncommercial uses" should be construed to include parodies.

The other Barbie trademark fair use decision challenged irreverent (to say the least) presentations of Barbie dolls, and thus implicated both copyright (the reproduction right in the image of the dolls) and trademarks (use of the Barbie name in the titles of the photographs). The extensive analysis of copyright fair use almost certainly drove the subsequent findings of unlikelihood of confusion and non dilution. In *Mattel, Inc. v Walking Mountain Prods.*,[42] the producer of Barbie tried to enjoin an artist from distributing his series, "Food Chain Barbie," which depicted Barbie victimized by a variety of kitchen appliances

---

[39] Mattel, Inc. v Universal Music International, 296 F.3d 894 (9th Cir. 2002).
[40] 296 F.3d at 900.
[41] *Id*. at 902, *citing* Rogers v Grimaldi, 875 F.2d 994, 999 (2d Cir. 1989).
[42] 353 F.3d 792 (9th Cir. 2003).

(and appearing occasionally to enjoy it). In granting summary judgment on the copyright claim, the court ruled on the first fair use factor (purpose and character of the defendant's use) that the Food Chain series "parod[ies] Barbie and everything Mattel's doll has come to signify. Undoubtedly, one could make similar statements through other means about society, gender roles, sexuality, and perhaps even social class. But Barbie, and all the associations she has acquired through Mattel's impressive marketing success, conveys these messages in a particular way that is ripe for social comment."[43] On the third factor (amount and substantiality of the taking), the court stressed that parodies need not restrict themselves "to take the absolute minimum amount of the copyrighted work possible," and thus that, in context, reproducing the entire doll did not undermine the fair use defense.[44] On the fourth factor (harm to potential market for the work), the court found it unlikely that Mattel would enter the market for "adult-oriented artistic photographs of Barbie."[45]

The Ninth Circuit approvingly cited another Barbie copyright parody decision, *Mattel, Inc. v Pitt*,[46] in which the defendant's "dungeon doll" website offered to customize Barbie dolls in a variety of dominatrix modes, such as a "'Lederhosen-style' Bavarian bondage dress and helmet in rubber with PVC-mask and waspie."[47] The differently accessorized dolls arguably violated Mattel's exclusive right to create derivative works based on Barbie, and the website's photographs allegedly violated the reproduction right. The Southern District of New York considered the statutory fair use factors, and ruled the defendant's use and context of Barbie sufficiently transformative and unlikely to supplant one of Mattel's markets for the work. "A different analysis would apply if Defendant had, for example, dressed Barbie dolls in a different style of cheerleader outfit than those marketed by Mattel. To the Court's knowledge, there is no Mattel line of 'S&M' Barbie."[48]

Having held defendant's use to be "fair" as a matter of copyright law, notably because of the expressive values the parody advanced, the Ninth Circuit effectively sealed the fate of the trademark and dilution claims. When Mattel offered a survey to rebut the copyright fair use argument that the Food Chain series was parodic, the court rebuffed it, ruling that a work's parodic character is objectively determined, that public perception is irrelevant.[49]

---

[43] *Id.* at 802.
[44] *Id.* at 804.
[45] *Id.* at 806.
[46] 229 F. Supp. 2d 315 (S.D.N.Y. 2002).
[47] *Id.* at 322.
[48] *Id.*
[49] 353 F.3d at 801 ("The issue of whether a work is a parody is a question of law, not a matter of public majority opinion.").

Curiously, the court did not address the survey in its trademark analysis, even though public perception normally is highly relevant to the assessment of likelihood of confusion. Rather, with respect to Food Chain's incorporation of Barbie in the title of the series, the court relied on its prior decision in the Barbie Girl song case to reject a likelihood of confusion claim. With respect to Food Chain's alleged violation of Mattel's trade dress rights by reproducing the Barbie figure (largely undressed), the court ruled the copying nominative fair use. "Forsythe used Mattel's Barbie figure and head in his works to conjure up associations of Mattel, while at the same time to identify his own work, which is a criticism and parody of Barbie. Where use of the trade dress or mark is grounded in the defendant's desire to refer to the plaintiff's product as a point of reference for defendant's own work, a use is nominative."[50] "Conjure up," notably, is a standard formulation of the minimum extent of copying that the copyright fair use caselaw permits in a parody.[51] Not surprisingly, then, the court's analysis of the second nominative fair use factor – whether defendant used only so much of a trademark or trade dress as is reasonably necessary – echoed its treatment of the third copyright fair use factor.[52] By the same token, having found as a matter of copyright law that the defendant was not usurping a potential market – "adult" photos – that Mattel was likely to enter, the court ruled on the third nominative fair use factor that "it is highly unlikely that any reasonable consumer would have believed that Mattel sponsored or was affiliated with [defendant's] work."[53] Finally, on the dilution claim, the court again relied on "Barbie Girl" to hold "Food Chain" noncommercial within the meaning of the Federal Trademark Dilution Act, and thus not actionable.[54]

Congress has recently endorsed the judicially-devised nominative fair use limitation, and the resulting exclusion of parodies from the ambit of the dilution claim. In the Trademark Dilution Revision Act of 2006,[55] Congress reaffirmed its expansion of trademarks law in the 1995 Federal Trademarks Dilution Act[56] to protect famous marks, even in the absence of likelihood of confusion, thus continuing to afford famous marks a scope of coverage more akin to a property "right in gross" than the traditional protection limited to

---

[50] *Id.* at 810.
[51] *Id.* at 800, *citing* Dr. Seuss Enters., L.P. v Penguin Books USA, Inc., 109 F.3d 1394, 1400 (9th Cir. 1997).
[52] *Id.* at 811.
[53] *Id.* at 812.
[54] Cf. 17 U.S.C. § 107(1) (copyright fair use factor takes commercial nature of use into account in assessing the "nature and purpose" of the use).
[55] HR 683, 109th Cong., 2d sess. (2006).
[56] Federal Trademark Dilution Act of 1995, 15 USC § 1125(c).

remedying likelihood of deception or confusion.[57] To defuse the potential conflict between invigorated trademarks and expressive interests, Congress set out broad "exclusions," of which the first is "Any fair use, including a nominative or descriptive fair use, or facilitation of such fair use of a famous mark by another person . . . ."[58] The language is striking, because the terms "fair use" and "nominative fair use," though now familiar from the caselaw,[59] do not elsewhere appear in the statute. Nor does "descriptive fair use" as such, although section 33(b)(4) provides a defense regarding "a term or device which is descriptive of and used fairly and in good faith only to describe the goods or services of such party, or their geographic origin."[60] In other words, Congress appears to have taken trademark fair use as a given, perhaps even as a kind of omnipresence brooding over both copyright and trademark rights. As in the Copyright Act, the revised anti-dilution statute does not purport to create fair use; it restates it, in very open-ended fashion.[61]

The statute illustrates the kinds of uses that qualify as trademark fair uses, by providing that fair uses

includ[e] use in connection with –

(i) advertising or promotion that permits consumers to compare goods or services, or
(ii) identifying and parodying, criticizing, or commenting upon the famous mark owner or the goods or services of the famous mark owner.[62]

---

[57] On the dilution claim and its contrast with traditional trademark norms, *see generally*, Robert G. Bone, *Hunting Goodwill: A History of the Concept of Goodwill in Trademark Law*, 86 B. U. L. REV. 547 (2006); Mark A. Lemley, *The Modern Lanham Act and the Death of Common Sense*, 108 YALE L.J. 1687 (1999). On federal dilution's less impressive record in the courts, see Clarisa Long, *Dilution*, 106 COLUM. L. REV. 1029 (2006).

[58] 15 U.S.C. § 1125(c)(3)(A). *See also* H.R. Rep. No. 109-23, 109th Cong., 1st sess. (2005) at 25 (Statement of Rep. Berman).

[59] *See, e.g.*, decisions cited *supra* note 32.

[60] § 1115(b)(4).

[61] *See infra* note 62.

[62] § 1125(3)(A)(i)(ii). The full text reads:

(3) Exclusions. The following shall not be actionable as dilution by blurring or dilution by tarnishment under this subsection:
(A) Any fair use, including a nominative or descriptive fair use, or facilitation of such fair use, of a famous mark by another person other than as a designation of source for the person's own goods or services, including use in connection with –
(i) advertising or promotion that permits consumers to compare goods or services; or
(ii) identifying and parodying, criticizing, or commenting upon the famous mark owner or the goods or services of the famous mark owner.

Of mutant copyrights, mangled trademarks and Barbie's influence 497

Congress codified these fair use concepts in less detail than its codification of copyright fair use in section 107 of the 1976 Copyright Act but in a manner which, with its two "includings," beckons further judicial intervention. The 2006 Congress thus appears to share the 1976 Congress' disinclination to "freeze" fair use, but instead to leave courts "free to adapt the doctrine to particular situations on a case by case basis."[63] Moreover, while Congress endorsed these judge-made limitations in the context of the Dilution Revision Act, it would seem that they remain equally pertinent in the traditional, confusion-based, trademark actions in which courts initially applied them. Trademark fair use, then, shows us that copyright concepts and methodologies can salubriously influence trademarks law, not by cordoning copyright off from trademarks, as in *Dastar*, but by recognizing and drawing the best from the overlap in subject matter and (where relevant) in the rationale for extending or denying protection.

(B) All forms of news reporting and news commentary.
(C) Any noncommercial use of a mark.

It is worth noting that the second and third categories of exclusions involve the kinds of uses that the copyright act considers susceptible to being ruled "fair," see the preamble to 17 USC § 107.

[63] *See* House Report 94-1476, 94th Cong., 2d. sess. (1976) at 66 ("there is no disposition to freeze the doctrine in the statute, . . . Beyond a very broad statutory explanation of what fair use is and some of the criteria applicable to it, the courts must be free to adapt the doctrine to particular situations on a case by case basis. Section 107 is intended to restate the present judicial doctrine of fair use, not to change, narrow, or enlarge it in any way.").

19 Signs, surfaces, shapes and structures – the protection of product design under trade mark law
Alison Firth*

I. Introduction

Design law has sometimes been called the 'Cinderella'[1] of intellectual property. Its territory lies in the border zones between patent law, copyright law and trade marks.[2] It shares this space somewhat uncomfortably with unfair competition[3] and passing off laws. Some years ago the most active border

---

*   Professor of Commercial Law at the University of Newcastle upon Tyne.
[1]   Edward Armitage, *The Copyright, Patent and Designs Bill: Industrial Designs* [1988] EIPR 91; Jeremy Phillips, *International Design Protection: Who Needs It?* [1993] 12 EIPR431; H Cohen Jehoram, *Cumulation of Protection in the EC Design Proposals: The 1994 Herchel Smith Lecture* [1994] 12 EIPR 514; Herman MH Speyart, *The Grand Design: An Update on the E.C. Design Proposals, Following the Adoption of a Common Position on the Directive* [1997] EIPR 603; Howard Johnson, *Communication by Design: Reform of the Law – Cinderella No More* [2002] 7 Comms L 52; Charles-Henry Massa & Alain Strowel, *Community Design: Cinderella Revamped* [2003] EIPR 68. From time to time other aspects are given the epithet, such as performers' rights (Sam Ricketson, reviewing Richard Arnold, *Performers' Rights and Recording Rights*, at [1991] EIPR 311); sound recordings (Owen H Dean, *Sound Recordings in South Africa – the Cinderella of the Copyright Family* (1993) 34 Copyright World 18); copyright (Patrick Wheeler, *Copyright – The Cinderella of Construction Agreements* (1994) 4 Cons L 447 and (1994) 5 Cons L 27); typographical fonts (Stephen Cosby, *Dancing with Cinderella: Challenges and Solutions in Font Licence Management* (2004) 144 Copyright World 14); copyright (Sehgal v Union of India [2005] FSR 39 High Court of Delhi at New Delhi per Pradeep Nandrajog J).
[2]   Jerome H Reichman, *Design Protection and the New Technologies: The United States Experience in a Transnational Perspective* 19 U. Balt. L. Rev. 6 (1989); Uma Suthersanen, *Breaking down the Intellectual Property Barriers* [1998] IPQ 267.
[3]   Both in the sense of passing off or palming off and in the wider senses described by Anselm Kämperman Sanders, *Unfair Competition Law: The Protection of Intellectual and Industrial Creativity* (1997, OUP); F. Beier, *The Law of Unfair Competition in the European Community: Its Development and Present Status* [1985] EIPR 284; and (1985) 16 IIC 139; Christopher Wadlow, *Unfair Competition in Community Law: Part 1: The Age of the "Classical Model"* [2006] EIPR 433; Christopher Wadlow, *Unfair Competition in Community Law: Part 2: Harmonisation Becomes Gridlocked* [2006] EIPR 469.

zone in terms of debate and commentary was probably that between copyright and design – and in particular whether copyright should be expelled from the areas occupied by design law.[4] The areas between copyright, other rights and contract were considered by the Association Littéraire et Artistique at its 2001 Congress.[5] Currently, the border between design law and trade marks/trade dress is attracting the attention of scholars, legislators and judges. This appears to have been caused by several factors. The first is a trend towards the use of non-verbal signs as trade marks for goods and services. Globalisation[6] has encouraged this use of non-verbal signs,[7] with their independence from linguistic differences. Of course, the perception of non-verbal signs, such as colours, may vary from culture to culture; consumer perception also depends upon the patterns of trade. Of these "non-traditional" marks the most "traditional" of them all is product design[8], but it is also the most problematic from a legal point of view because of overlap with utility patents, design patents, and design rights generally. Moves in Australia, Europe,[9] and other jurisdictions towards granting design protection for technically functional design

---

[4] As for example s 51 of the UK's Copyright, Designs and Patents Act 1988 as applied in BBC Worldwide Ltd and Another v Pally Screen Printing Ltd and Others [1998] FSR 665; or Art. 21(2) of the Uniform Benelux Act on Designs and Models, *see* Geert Glas, *The Cumulative Protection of Benelux Designs by Copyright and Design Law: Screenoprints Ltd v Citroen Nederland BV* [1989] EIPR 257.

[5] Jane C Ginsburg & June M Besek, eds, *Adjuncts and Alternatives to Copyright: Proceedings of the ALAI Congress June 13–17, 2001* (2002, ALAI-USA).

[6] Naomi Klein, in *No Logo* (2000) has criticised the role of trade marks in assisting the ills of globalisation and capitalism; challenging this, Olins has suggested that brands act as a two-way conduit and enable consumers/citizens to influence companies (and their social policies) as well as vice versa. Wally Olins, *Who's Wearing the Trousers?* The Economist, 6 September 2001. If this is correct then the spread of non-verbal marks may make this process available to a wider range of citizens.

[7] See Martin Lindstrom, *Brand Sense: Building Powerful Brands through Touch, Taste, Smell, Sight and Sound* (2005, New York, The Free Press); Lionel Bently & Leo Flynn, eds, *Law and the Senses: Sensational Jurisprudence* (1996, Pluto Press, London). Vaver has commented on an expansionist trend in trade mark law; in term of not only the range of signs that may be protected, but also the geographical and legal scope of protection. David Vaver, *Recent Trends in European Trademark Law: Of Shape, Senses and Sensation* (2005) 95 TMR 895. For a US slant on the expansion of trade mark protection see Dana Beldiman, *Protecting the Form But Not the Function: Is U.S. Law Ready For a New Model?* (2004) 20 Santa Clara Computer & High Tech LJ 529.

[8] See Thomas P. Arden, *Protection of Non-Traditional Marks: trademark rights in sounds, scents, colors, motions and product designs in the U.S.* (2000, New York: INTA).

[9] Martin Schlotelburg, *Design Protection for Technical Products* (2006) JIPLP 675.

exacerbates the conflict. The issues may also be triggered by failure to effect legislative change – Dinwoodie opines that a US judicial breakthrough on trade dress protection – the Two Pesos case – was not unconnected with the collapse of draft legislation to expand US protection of designs beyond the patent system to a copyright-type protection for ornamental designs.[10]

Relationships between the creative process, social change and the paradigms of intellectual property law have been charted by many scholars. Reichman has studied the boundaries between traditional intellectual property rights[11] and explored alternative bases for liability.[12] Suthersanen has pointed out the position of design law at the convergence of the scientific, artistic and industrial paradigms[13]. Drahos[14] has charted the distinctions between physical commodities, abstract objects and legal rights.[15] Lury[16] has noted the shift from the cult of the author to the cult of the personality, a shift characterised as one from copyright to trade mark type protection.[17] The expansion of trade mark rights from misrepresentation into misappropriation under dilution laws[18] has been seen as a shift in the other direction, towards copyright-type

---

[10] Coupled with opportunistic litigation: Graeme B. Dinwoodie, *General Report, Session IIA Copyright, Trademarks and Trade Dress: The Overlap (and Conflict?)* in *Intellectual Property Regimes Concerning Designs and Visual Images,* in Jane C Ginsberg & June M Besek, eds, *Adjuncts and Alternatives to Copyright: Proceedings of the ALAI Congress June 13–17, 2001* (2002, ALAI-USA) 497 at 504.

[11] JH Reichman, *Legal Hybrids Between the Patent and Copyright Paradigms,* 94 Columbia L Rev 2432–558 (1994); J. H. Reichman, *Charting the Collapse of the Patent-Copyright Dichotomy: Premises for a Restructured International Intellectual Property System,* 13 Cardozo Arts & Ent. LJ 475–520 (1995).

[12] JH Reichman, *Of Green Tulips and Legal Kadzu: Repackaging Rights in Subpatentable Innovation,* Ch 2 in R Dreyfuss, DL Zimmerman & H First, *Expanding the Boundaries of Intellectual Property* (2001, OUP).

[13] Uma Suthersanen, *Breaking Down the Intellectual Property Barriers* [1998] IPQ 267.

[14] Peter Drahos, *A Philosophy of Intellectual Property* (1996, Aldershot, Dartmouth).

[15] Ibid at p.199, "the existence of physical commodities does not depend on law. The existence of abstract objects does. Commerce in physical commodities and abstract objects depends on a scheme of rights and contract", *cited in* James Mitchiner, *Intellectual Property In Image – A Mere Inconvenience* [2003] IPQ 163.

[16] Celia Lury, *Cultural Rights: Technology, Legality and Personality* (1993, Routledge).

[17] Spyros Maniatis, *Trade Mark Rights – A Justification Based On Property* [2002] IPQ 123.

[18] Handler has suggested that allowing dilution claims only in respect of different products would remove this problem in relation to product design. *See* Milton Handler, *A Personal Note on Trademark and Unfair Competition Law before the Lanham Act* (1996) 59 Law & Contemp Probs 5–11, *cited in* Graeme B Dinwoodie,

protection for trade marks.[19] Lovelady has suggested "revealed preference", a market/perception gauge, as an alternative model to copyright.[20]

That trade marks carry quality and "lifestyle" messages as well as indications of origin is now well understood by the courts[21] as well as brand gurus.[22] However, in the context of product design, legislators and courts are holding on tight to the origin function of trade marks.

How should the law approach this kind of distinguishing sign? Dinwoodie[23] has advocated a teleological approach, based upon the distinguishing function of trade marks. However, courts and legislators in many jurisdictions have clung to a *per se* exclusionary approach, at least in the case of technical functionality. This is especially the case in the European Union, where the rules on registration of shape marks have been construed strictly against trade mark applicants. Trade dress, which distinguishes service providers, has fared somewhat better, the US leading the way with franchising based on the architectural design of outlets[24] and the Two Pesos

---

The Death of Ontology: A Teleological Approach to Trademark Law (1999) 84 Iowa L. Rev. 611 at n74. This was the case under EC law prior to Davidoff & Cie SA v Gofkid Ltd Case C-292/00 [2003] ECR I-389; [2002] ETMR 99 and Adidas v Fitnessworld [2004] ETMR 10.

[19] Megan Richardson, *Copyright In Trade Marks? On Understanding Trade Mark Dilution* [2000] IPQ 66. This trend has been lamented by Jennifer Davis, *To Protect or Serve? European Trade Mark Law and the Decline of the Public Interest* [2003] EIPR 180. See also Hannes Rosler, *The Rationale for European Trade Mark Protection* [2007] EIPR100. On the concept of the 'CopyMark' at the copyright/trade mark boundary, see James Mitchiner, *Intellectual Property In Image – A Mere Inconvenience* [2003] IPQ 163.

[20] Alexander Lovelady, Masters thesis, University of Durham, 2006, citing 'Economics A-Z: Revealed preference', at http://www.economist.com/ research/ Economics/alphabetic. cfm? LETTER=R#REVEALED%20PREFERENCE. *See also* Lior Zemer *Rethinking Copyright Alternatives* (2006) 14 Int JLIT 137.

[21] *See, e.g.* Advocate-General Ruiz-Jarabo Colomer of the European Court of Justice in Arsenal Football Club Plc v Reed [2003] RPC 9 ECJ at para A46 [emphasis added].

> It seems to me to be simplistic reductionism to limit the function of the trade mark to an indication of trade origin. The Commission, moreover, took the same view in its oral submissions to the Court. Experience teaches that, in most cases, the user is unaware of who produces the goods he consumes. The trademark acquires a life of its own, making a statement, as I have suggested, about quality, reputation and even, in certain cases, *a way of seeing life*.

[22] Such as Wally Olins, devisor of the ORANGE brand for mobile telephony.

[23] Graeme B Dinwoodie, *The Death of Ontology: A Teleological Approach to Trademark Law* (1999) 84 Iowa L. Rev. 611.

[24] *See* Jerome Gilson & Anne Gilson Lalande, *Cinnamon Buns, Marching Ducks and Cherry-Scented Racecar Exhaust: Protecting Non-traditional Trademarks* (2005) 95 TMR 773 at 813–16 and citations. For an intriguing view of the fairground origin of many early franchise designs, see Barbara Rubin, *Aesthetic Ideology and*

case.[25] Under European law, trade dress for services is not excluded from trade mark registration. However, unlike in the US, architectural design has enjoyed scant trade mark recognition in the UK[26] and Europe in general.[27]

II. Shape marks – legislation

A. European Community law on designs and trade marks

In Europe, Directive 98/71/EC on the legal protection of designs harmonised the law of Member States relating to registered designs. It expanded eligible subject-matter beyond the traditional sphere of aesthetic or ornamental design to embrace design in the wider sense, with a very limited exclusion for technical designs where design freedom is effectively absent.[28] Echoing the position in many Member States of the EU, the Directive was remarkably liberal about overlap and cumulation of rights. Art 16 states that its provisions shall be without prejudice to any provisions of Community law or of the law of the Member State concerned relating to unregistered design rights, trade marks or other distinctive signs, patents and utility models, typefaces, civil liability or unfair competition, whilst Art 17 allows cumulation with copyright. The Community Design Regulation used the same criteria for protection and added the copyright-style Unregistered Community Design, conferring three-year protection from copying to eligible designs.[29]

Urban Design (1979) 69 Ann Assoc Am Geog 339. Lately, architects and town planners have stressed the need for variety and local style over standardised architecture: Examples of Franchise/Corporate Architecture Design Guidelines available at http://www.ci.kirkland.wa.us/__shared/assets/DRB_RETREAT_ATTACHMENTS_1-95171.pdf.

[25] Two Pesos Inc. v Taco Cabana Inc. 505 US 763 (1992). By contrast recognition of architectural style as indicating the commercial source of services in the old world has been slow.

[26] In passing off cases the judges appeared to look for capricious addition, lacking at least in cases involving domestic buildings: Alison Firth *Passing Off – Get Up – Architectural Design* [1989] EIPR D169 and cases cited.

[27] The case of *Systemhus Norge A/S and Others v Varmbohus A/S* [1994] FCC 137 involved misappropriation of an architectural design.

[28] Procter & Gamble Co v Reckitt Benckiser (UK) Ltd [2006] EWHC 3154 (Ch) [2007] FSR 13, (at para [28] holding that "A Community design right did not subsist in features of appearance of a product which were dictated solely by its technical function. This exclusion was to be narrowly interpreted and only applied where the part of the design in question was the only way to achieve the particular function." (at para [28]); following Landor & Hawa International Ltd v Azure Designs Ltd [2007] FSR 9, CA. The Court of Appeal reversed Lewison J's findings on infringement but not on validity: [2007] EWCA Civ 936.

[29] Qualification for protection depends upon publication in the EU; *see* Richard Plaistowe & Mark Heritage, *Europe v the World: Does Unregistered Community Design Right only Protect Designs first Made Available in Europe?* [2007] EIPR 187.

The shape of goods or their packaging as a class of sign suitable for protection by trade mark registration has been recognised Europe-wide since the promulgation of the Trade Mark Harmonisation Directive[30] and its sister instrument the Community Trade Mark Regulation.[31] The Directive has been implemented in all Member States of the European Union, either by copy-out legislation or by more traditional Parliamentary drafting[32] at national level. Drafts of these pieces of legislation contributed to the drafting of the WTO TRIPs agreement.[33] Probably for this reason, a number of states outside the European Union have followed EC legislation and case law,[34] or that of its Member States.[35]

Burrell, Beverly Smith and Coleman[36] identify a number of causative factors which may have led to the provisions on shape marks:

---

[30] Council Directive 89/104 of 21 December 1988 to approximate the laws of Member States relating to trade marks.

[31] Council Regulation (EC) no 40/94 of 20 December 1993 on the Community Trade Mark.

[32] This can cause problems of interpretation; national courts often refer directly to the provisions of the European legislation, *see, e.g.* Boehringer Ingelheim KG v Swingward Ltd [2004] EWCA Civ 129; [2004] 3 CMLR 3, [2004] ETMR 65 (Eng CA).

[33] For drafting history, see Daniel Gervais (2003), *The TRIPS Agreement: Drafting History and Analysis*; *see also* Christopher Wadlow, *Including trade in counterfeit goods: the origin of TRIPS as a GATT anti-counterfeiting code* [2007] IPQ 350.

[34] See, eg, Mike Reynolds' presentation, *Evolution of EC and UK Case Law: Relevance to HKSAR*, available at http://www.ipd.gov.hk/eng/trademarks.htm (Hong Kong). In Triomed (Pty) Ltd v Beecham Group Plc [2003] FSR 27 the Supreme Court of Appeal in South Africa applied the decision of the European Court of Justice in Case C-299/99 Philips Electronics NV v Remington Consumer Products Ltd [2003] RPC 2, ECJ as regards the technical functionality of the tablet shape in issue and as to distinctiveness. Relevant provisions were s 10(5) and 10(11), South African Trade Mark Act which exclude the "shape, configuration, colour or pattern" of goods which are "necessary to obtain a specific technical result" or "result from the nature of the goods themselves", or are "likely to limit the development of any art of industry".

[35] For example, Hong Kong trade mark law is now independent of UK law but follows UK and EC jurisprudence. Examples may be found in the Examination Manual and decisions at http://www.ipd.gov.hk/eng/trademarks.htm.

In Unilever's application (Taco shaped ice cream) available at http://www.ipd.gov.hk/eng/intellectual_property/trademarks/trademarks_decisions/decision/DEC199801908R.pdf, the Hong Kong Registry refused the application on technical functionality grounds, referring to UK and EC case law but giving no weight (in the absence of the relevant decisions) to the fact that the mark had been registered in New Zealand, Australia and the UK.

[36] Robert Burrell, Huw Beverley Smith & Allison Coleman, *Three-dimensional Trade Marks: Should the Directive be Reshaped?* in Norma Dawson & Alison Firth, eds, *Trade Marks Retrospective* (Vol 7, Perspectives on Intellectual Property, 2000, Sweet & Maxwell).

- the tendency of EC legislation to harmonise rights[37] coupled with the fact that shapes of products and their packaging were protected in a number of Member States;
- evidence of consumer recognition that shapes could be distinctive as to origin; the European courts have, however, been sceptical about this;
- an expanded view of trade mark function as extending beyond origin to quality;
- protection of the advertising or merchandising function of distinctive shapes.

Burrell et al regard the exclusion from registration in these legislative texts for 'natural', functional and aesthetically valuable shapes as not providing sufficient safeguard. Although those authors stopped short of recommending repeal of the provision allowing registration of shape marks, it appears that at least for product shapes conferring technical advantage or non-trade-mark value (usually aesthetic value and in any event not merely brand premium),[38] the European courts have shown great strictness in excluding functional shapes from protection – as suggested by the structure and wording of the provisions, the exclusions are applied without any alleviation for distinctiveness for both technical and aesthetic product shapes.[39] Unlike with the design laws, the fact that the technical effect could be achieved by another shape does not save the mark from exclusion.

The text relevant to shape marks appears at Arts 2 and 3 of the Trade Mark Directive. Art 2 would appear at first glance to support a teleological interpretation:

> 2. Signs of which a trade mark may consist
> A trade mark may consist of any sign capable of being represented graphically, particularly . . . the shape of goods or their packaging, providing such signs are capable of distinguishing the goods and services of one undertaking from those of other undertakings,

---

[37] Art 295 of the EC Treaty provides that it is without prejudice to national systems of property ownership, which discourages the legislator from diminishing intellectual property rights.

[38] Estimated at about 20–25% in 1964. *See* Hannes Rosler, *The Rationale for European Trade Mark Protection* [2007] EIPR 100 at n74.

[39] Philips v Remington C-299/99 [2002] ECR 1 5475; Linde C53-55/01 [2003] ECR I-0000; Laboratoires Irex v Ste Roche Case 02-12.335, (2004) 180 Dalloz 14/7155 p1015 (criticised as "questionable" at (2006) 96 TMR 402 but consistent with earlier case law).

However, Art 3 listing the so-called "absolute grounds" for refusal or invalidity[40] states

> 3. Grounds for refusal or invalidity
> 1. the following shall not be registered or if registered shall be liable to be declared invalid:
> ...
> (e) signs which consist exclusively of:
> – the shape which results from the nature of the goods themselves,[41] or
> – the shape of goods which is necessary to obtain a technical result,[42] or
> – the shape which gives substantial value to the goods.

This suggests a categorical exclusion, regardless of distinctive character.[43] The first indent of Art 3(1)(e) applies to both the shape of goods and their packaging;[44] the second refers only to the shape of the goods themselves. Burrell et al criticise this limitation.[45] However, in Henkel KGAA v Deutsches

---

[40] The equivalent provision of the Community Trade Mark Regulation, Art 7(1)(e), was successfully invoked to cancel Community registration of the shape of LEGO bricks in Lego Juris A/S v Mega Brands Inc Case R 856/2004-G [2007] ETMR 11. For LEGO marks in different jurisdictions, see Thomas Helbling, *Shapes as Trade Marks? The Struggle to Register Three-dimensional Signs: A Comparative Study of United Kingdom and Swiss Law* [1997] IPQ 413; Lego System A/S v Mega Bloks Inc [2004] ETMR 53 (Switzerland).

[41] Sometimes called the "natural" shape, although this limb was argued in relation to VIENETTA ice cream – a highly artificial product. *Société des Produits Nestlé SA v Unilever Plc, Aka Unilever Plc's Trade Mark Applications* [2003] ETMR 53; [2003] RPC 35. Burrell et al assert (p165) that this has been "interpreted out of existence". Under Japanese trade mark law, Art 3(1)(3) prohibits the registration of marks indicating the shape of goods or packaging "in a common manner", suggesting that this provision is designed to exclude generic shapes (Japanese TM law, translation thanks to (2007) 22 Yusara and Hara IP News 1).

[42] Although an earlier patent would not be a bar to registration *per se*, it would be "virtually irrefutable" evidence of this: LEGO [2007] ETMR 11; European patents have no utility requirement as such, but must be capable of industrial application and are regarded as displaying non-obvious solutions to technical problems. European Patent Convention, Art 57. On the problem-solution approach, see George SA Szabo, *Letter re Paul Cole's article* [1999] EIPR 42 and citations.

[43] Alison Firth, Ellen Gredley & Spyros Maniatis, *Shapes as Trade Marks: Public Policy, Functional Considerations and Consumer Perception* [2001] EIPR 86. A contention rejected in relation to aesthetic functionality by Lloyd J in *Dualit* [1999] RPC 304 (TM Registry); [1999] RPC 890 (ChD) but ultimately confirmed by the European Court of Justice in Philips v Remington.

[44] Of course the product and packaging may share the same distinctive (or non-distinctive) shape, e.g. TOBLERONE triangular chocolate bars. See Marie-Christine Janssens, *The "Toblerone" Chocolate Bar Case In Belgium* [2004] EIPR 554.

[45] Burrell et al. at 162.

Patent- und Markenamt,[46] the European Court of Justice gave a wider interpretation of "shape of goods" for products, such as liquids, which necessarily take up the shape of their container. On a referral from Germany concerning the shape of a tall bottle for liquid wool detergent,[47] the court held

> (1) For three-dimensional trade marks consisting of the packaging of goods which are packaged in trade for reasons linked to the very nature of the goods, the packing thereof must be assimilated to the shape of the goods, so that that packing may constitute the shape of the goods within the meaning of Art.3(1)(e) of the First Council Directive 89/104 . . . and may, where appropriate, serve to designate characteristics of the packaged goods, including their quality, within the meaning of Art.3(1)(c) of that directive.

This ruling goes also to distinctiveness.

The third indent mentions only "shape" and again could refer to packaging as well as to the shape of goods.

The second indent relates to the technical functionality of the goods. In Philips v Remington[48] the European Court of Justice held that the question of exclusion took precedence over any distinctiveness enquiry. Nor can the prohibitions of Art 3(1)(e) be avoided by registering a graphic mark showing the product[49] rather than the shape itself. If the essential functional character-

---

[46] Case C-218/01 [2005] ETMR 45.
[47] Which narrowed towards the top, with an integral handle, a small pouring aperture and a two-level stopper, which could also be used as a measuring cup.
[48] Case C-299/99 Koninklijke Philips Electronics NV v Remington Consumer Products Ltd [2001] RPC 38, (Advocate General); [2003] RPC 2, ECJ, [2002] ECR I-5475, [2002] ETMR 81.
[49] In Case C-299/99 Koninklijke Philips Electronics NV v Remington Consumer Products Ltd [2003] RPC 2, the Court of Justice stated at [76]:

> If any one of the criteria listed in Art.3(1)(e) is satisfied, a sign consisting exclusively of the shape of the product or of a graphic representation of that shape cannot be registered as a trade mark.

This was echoed by Jacob J in Philips v Remington in the English High Court, [1998] RPC 283 at 290:

> Even though it is only a picture which is formally the subject of the registration, both sides, in my judgment rightly, treated it as a registration covering also a three-dimensional shape. It would be quite artificial to regard a straight picture of a thing, and the thing itself, as significantly different under a law of trade marks which permits shapes to be registered.

This issue was not explicitly dealt with on appeal and has been criticised by Burrell et al, *supra*. at n36.

In Nation Fittings (M) Sdn Bhd v Oystertec Plc [2005] SGHC 225; [2006] FSR 40 High Court of Singapore, it was ingeniously but unsuccessfully argued that the transi-

istics of product shape are attributable solely to the technical result achieved, it is irrelevant that a similar result could be achieved by other shapes.[50] In this the exclusion from registration of a shape as a trade mark is more absolute than the exclusion from design registration under EC design law.[51] The Advocate-General[52] deduced this after an exercise in literal interpretation of the design and trade mark legislation:

> 34 The wording used in the designs Directive for expressing that ground for refusal does not entirely coincide with that used in the trade marks Directive. That discrepancy is not capricious. Whereas the former refuses to recognise external features "which are solely *dictated* by its technical function", the latter excludes from its

---

tional provisions of Singapore's Trade Marks Act 1998 had converted a two-dimensional mark depicting pipe fittings into a three-dimensional mark. See Yakult Honsha KK's Trade Mark Application [2001] RPC 39; Interlego AG's Trade Mark Applications [1998] RPC 69, Dualit Ltd's (Toaster Shapes) Trade Mark Applications [1999] RPC 890; Procter & Gamble Ltd's Trade Mark Applications [1999] RPC 673; Joined Cases C-53/01–C-55/01 Linde AG v Deutsches Patent-und Markenamt [2003] RPC 45 ECJ; Joined Cases C-456/01 P and C-457/01 P Henkel KGAA v Office for Harmonisation in the Internal Market [2005] ETMR 44, ECJ and Bongrain SA's Trade Mark Application [2005] RPC 14. Under Japanese TM law (translation thanks to (2007) 22 Yusara and Hara IP News 1), the use of the phrase "mark indicating" suggests that the sign can be the shape itself or a pictorial mark depicting shape.

[50] Philips v Remington at [83], applied in Lego Juris A/S v Mega Brands Inc Case R 856/2004-G [2007] ETMR 11 at [56]–[63] and Koninklijke Philips Electronics NV v Remington Consumer Products Ltd [2006] EWCA Civ 16; [2006] ETMR 42; [2006] FSR 30. See Julia Clark, *Adorning Shavers with Clover Leaves: Koninklijke Philips Electronics NV v Remington Consumer Products Ltd* [2006] EIPR 352–5. This aspect of the ECJ's ruling in Philips was significant in the successful Swedish appeal which led to a finding of invalidity of Swedish registrations depicting the three-headed shaver. Koninklijke Philips Electronics NV v Rotary Shaver Sweden AB [2005] ETMR 103 Svea Court of Appeal. Prior to *Philips*, the Swedish court had found the registration of the Tripp Trapp baby's high chair to be valid over an expired patent and subsisting copyright in the chair design as a work of applied art on the ground that other shapes could be, and were, used to perform the same function: Stokke Fabrikker and Another v Playmaster of Sweden AB (Ltd) and Another [1998] ETMR 395 Ljungby District Court.

[51] Whereby only those functional designs which uniquely permit of a technical result are excluded. Council Regulation (EC) No. 6/2002 of 12 December 2001 on Community Designs Article 8(1) ("A Community design shall not subsist in features of appearance of a product which are *solely dictated* by its technical function); equivalent in Art 7(1) of Directive 98/71/EC of the European Parliament and of the Council of 13 October 1998 on the legal protection of designs, "A design right shall not subsist in features of appearance of a product which are *solely dictated* by its technical function" (emphasis added). Such exclusions are permitted by Art 25(1) of the WTO TRIPs agreement and interpreted in *Landor & Hawa International Ltd v Azure Designs Ltd* [2007] FSR 9, CA.

[52] *Philips v Remington*, n. 48 at para [AG34].

protection "signs which consist exclusively of . . . the shape of goods which is *necessary* to obtain a technical result". In other words, the level of "functionality" must be greater in order to be able to assess the ground for refusal in the context of designs; the feature concerned must be not only *necessary* but *essential* in order to achieve a particular technical result – form follows function. [The semantic contrast which exists in the German version between the adjectives "erforderlich" and "bedingt" is particularly telling.] This means that a functional design may, nonetheless, be eligible for protection if it can be shown that the same technical function could be achieved by another different form.[53]

For A-G Ruiz-Jarabo Colomer, this was consistent with the respective purposes of design/patent law and trade mark law – protecting the substantial value of good by design protection, or the value which derives from their technical performance by patents, whilst protecting the origin function and the trader's goodwill in the case of trade marks. This suggests that the purpose of the prohibition is to protect the legal purity of the design and trade mark regimes,[54] but is not necessarily inconsistent with a teleological approach. Alternatively, the exclusion may serve to protect the public domain once design protection has expired;[55] Folliard-Monguiral and Rogers[56] stress the fact that design protection

---

[53] This view is consistent with Recital 14 of the Directive 98/71/EC on the legal protection of designs:

> Whereas technological innovation should not be hampered by granting design protection to features dictated solely by a technical function; whereas it is understood that this does not entail that a design must have an aesthetic quality; whereas, likewise, the interoperability of products of different makes should not be hindered by extending protection to the design of mechanical fittings; whereas features of a design which are excluded from protection for these reasons should not be taken into consideration for the purpose of assessing whether other features of the design fulfil the requirements for protection.

It is cited by the Office for Harmonisation of the Internal Market in relation to Community Design registration, *see* Martin Schlotelburg, *Design Protection for Technical Products* (2006) JIPLP 675, and by the UK Intellectual Property Office in its Designs Practice Notice (DPN) 5/03 *Designs dictated by their technical function*, available online at http://www.ipo.gov.uk/design/d-decisionmaking/d-law/d-law-notice/d-law-practicenotice/d-law-practicenotice-dpn503.htm.

[54] The authority of the A-G's opinion and of this line of argument have been doubted by Suthersanen. Uma Suthersanen *The European Court of Justice in Philips v Remington – Trade Marks and Market Freedom* [2003] IPQ 257.

[55] In Koninklijke Philips NV v Remington Consumer Products Ltd [2006] F.S.R. 30 at [93] the English Court of Appeal stressed the need to prevent the impairment of competition by the registration of shape marks incorporating technical solutions or functional characteristics.

[56] Arnaud Folliard-Monguiral & David Rogers, *The Protection of Shapes by the Community Trade Mark* [2003] EIPR 169.

is limited in time whereas trade mark protection is not. In *Lego Juris A/S v Mega Brands Inc*[57] OHIM state a market freedom imperative:

> Art.7(1)(e)(ii) CTMR pursues an aim which is in the public interest, namely to bar from registration shapes whose essential characteristics perform a technical function, and were chosen to fulfil that function, hence allowing them to be freely used by all [Remington/Philips at [79] and [80]].

This must be read in conjunction with the fact that many product shapes will be (or have been) eligible for design protection. In fact, a problem with the distinctiveness of a functional product shape is that it may have been acquired during a period of *de facto* monopoly conferred by another right, such as a patent or design registration.

The third limb will usually be triggered by the aesthetic value conferred by the shape of goods. This has been distinguished from what might be described as the "trade mark value" of goodwill in the shape.[58] In some product sectors the distinction may be difficult to determine.

Is there any evidence that the methodology of enquiry under Art 3(1)(e) has differed as between the second and third indent, so that evidence of distinctiveness could overcome an objection under the third limb (substantial value), but not the second (technical function)? There was the decision of Lloyd J in Dualit,[59] deciding the fate of toaster shape marks on distinctiveness rather than functionality grounds. That decision, however, predated the European Court of Justice's decision in Philips v Remington. According to the later approach of Kitchen J[60] in Julius Sämaan Ltd v Tetrosyl Ltd the prohibition is equally mandatory across all limbs. In Benetton v G-Star[61] the Dutch court[62] made a

---

[57] Case R 856/2004-G [2007] ETMR 11 (OHIM) at para. [34] in relation to the exclusion of functional shape marks from Community Trade Mark protection.

[58] Or "brand premium". Thus in Philips v Remington in the English Court of Appeal [1999] RPC 809 at 822–33 Aldous LJ stated "In the present case, the shape registered by Philips has a substantial reputation built up by advertising and reliability and the like. That in my view is not relevant. What has to be considered is the shape as a shape."

[59] Dualit [1999] RPC 304 (TM Registry); [1999] RPC 890 (ChD). Arden shows Dualit's four-slot toaster as a published US Federal mark. See Thomas P Arden *Protection of Non-Traditional Marks: Trademark Rights in Sounds, Scents, Colors, Motions and Product Designs in the U.S.* (2000, New York, INTA), at 183.

[60] For many years Mr Justice Kitchen was an editor of the trade mark practitioner's bible *Kerly on Trade Marks*.

[61] Benneton Group SpA v G-Star International BV (C-371/06) [2008] ETMR 5.

[62] Hoge Raad, 8 September 2006; *see* Charles Gielen, *Netherlands: Trade marks – shape marks* [2006] EIPR N237. For criticism of the Dutch Supreme Court's decision on copyright claims in the litigation between Benetton and G-Star, *see* Herman

reference to the European Court of Justice concerning the relationship between the first and third limbs of Art 3(1)(e) in the context of designer jeans. There was evidence that the features of the two trade mark registrations in suit[63] had become distinctive of G-Star before registration. The Amsterdam Regional Court of Appeal indeed held that the attractiveness of the jeans derived from recognition of the trade mark rather than aesthetic appeal. The European Court of Justice gave short shrift to this subtle distinction, regarding the situation as analogous to Philips. A mark which was unregistrable under the third indent could not be saved by proof of acquired distinctiveness.[64]

However, in order to bar a shape from registration any aesthetic surplus has to be substantial. In Julius Sämaan Ltd v Tetrosyl Ltd[65] the outline 'pine tree' shape of air freshening cards for hanging on the rear-view mirrors of cars did not confer substantial value within the meaning of the second indent, although it might be an attractive feature to purchasers.

According to Folliard-Monguiral and Rogers, this indent prevents trade mark law from subverting design laws.[66] The law in Europe is thereby in contrast to that in many jurisdictions,[67] where an absolute exclusion is only applied to functional designs and decorative designs may be registered as trade marks for the products in question if acquired distinctiveness can be shown.

If the enquiry under Art 3(1)(e) or its equivalents shows that there is no bar to registration, of course there is still the hurdle of distinctiveness to overcome. This of course must be assessed by reference to the goods or services for which registration is sought. A trade mark will be refused registration if it is incapable of distinguishing, inherently or in fact. The requirement of distinctiveness

---

Cohen Jehoram, *The Dutch Supreme Court recognises 'dilution of copyright' by degeneration of a copyright design into unprotected style: the Flying Dutchman: all sails, no anchor* [2007] EIPR 205.

[63] Respectively "sloping stitching from hip height to the crotch seam, kneepads, yoke on the seat of the trousers, horizontal stitching at knee height at the rear, band of a contrasting colour or of another material at the bottom of the trousers at the rear, all on one garment" and "seams, stitching and cuts on the kneepad of the trousers, slightly baggy kneepad".

[64] In the words of the court's ruling, 'The third indent of Art. 3(1)(e) of Directive 89/104 to approximate the laws of the Member States relating to trade marks is to be interpreted as meaning that the shape of a product which gives substantial value to that product cannot constitute a trade mark under Art. 3(3) of that Directive where, prior to the application for registration, it acquired attractiveness as a result of its recognition as a distinctive sign following advertising campaigns presenting the specific characteristics of the product in question.'

[65] [2006] EWHC 529; [2006] FSR 42 (Ch).

[66] Arnaud Folliard-Monguiral and David Rogers, *The Protection of Shapes by the Community Trade Mark* [2003] EIPR 169.

[67] Such countries include the U.S. and Japan.

pursues an aim which is in the public interest, namely that descriptive signs or indications relating to the characteristics of goods or services in respect of which registration is applied for may be freely used by all, including as collective marks or as part of complex or graphic marks.[68]

Distinctiveness is viewed through the eyes of the hypothetical average consumer, who is reasonably well informed and reasonably observant and circumspect.[69] The European Court of Justice held in Philips v Remington and in Linde AG and Others v Deutsches Patent- und Markenamt[70] that the standard of distinctiveness is the same for shape marks as for other marks. However

> it may in practice be more difficult to establish distinctiveness in relation to a shape or product mark than a word or figurative trade mark. But whilst that may explain why such a mark is refused registration, it does not mean that it cannot acquire distinctive character following the use that has been made of it.[71]

The provisions are not completely symmetric as between the shapes of goods and that of their packaging. In the case of packaging the case law is driven to a far greater degree by distinctiveness concerns.[72] The courts repeatedly state that the standard for distinctiveness is not higher for three-dimensional marks than for any other, but that it may be harder to attain because consumers are less likely to perceive shapes as indications of origin.[73]

Thus, in practice it may be necessary to establish acquired distinctiveness before registering a shape mark[74] which has passed the hurdles of technical function and substantial value. Although the distinctiveness enquiry[75] is separate

---

[68] Linde at [73].
[69] Gut Springenheide and Tusky (C-210/96), [1998] ECR I-4657 at [31], [1999] 1 CMLR 1383; Philips (C-299/99) (2002) ECR I-5475, [2002] 2 CMLR 52 at [63].
[70] Joined Cases C-53/01 (Linde, fork-lift trucks) C-54/01 (Winward, torch shape), C-55/01(Rado, wrist watch) [2005] 2 CMLR 44. On torch shapes, see also Mag Instrument Inc v Office for Harmonisation in the Internal Market (Trade Marks and Designs) (OHIM) (C136/02 P) [2004] ECR I-9165, [2004] ETMR 71.
[71] Linde at [48].
[72] See e.g. (bottle shape with lemon in neck) Eurocermex [2005] ETMR 95 ECJ.
[73] See e.g. (stand-up pouches) Deutsche SiSi Werke v OHIM C173/04P [2006] ETMR 41 ECJ.
[74] Since shape marks are most often used in conjunction with other marks, the decision of the European Court of Justice in Société des Produits Nestlé SA v Mars UK Ltd (C353/03) [2006] All ER (EC) 348, [2005] ECR I-6135, [2005] 3 CMLR 12, [2006] CEC 3; [2005] ETMR 96; [2006] FSR 2 is important – that distinctiveness may be acquired notwithstanding the mark in suit is part of a larger mark (HAVE A BREAK – HAVE A KIT-KAT).
[75] In Betafence Ltd v Registrar of Trade Marks aka Betafence Ltd's Trade Mark Applications (Nos. 2303706 and 2309201) [2005] EWHC 1353, the fence panels were held to be devoid of distinctive character.

from, and subordinate to, the exclusion enquiry, the fact that the shape has functional features may be relevant to the distinctiveness enquiry, for example because the technical features might be common to the trade.[76] Packaging shape may be combined with another feature which confers distinctiveness, such as the matt white surface of the bottle for sparkling wine in Freixenet.[77] As well as the visual aspect, the matt finish of the bottle could be regarded as a tactile sign; the registration of tactile marks has recently attracted comment.[78]

In Julius Sämaan Ltd v Tetrosyl Ltd,[79] Kitchen J doubted whether the provision[80] allowing for cancellation of marks which have become generic after registration applied to shape marks. However, this may disregard the fact that the first limb of the exclusion is apt to describe generic shapes; if so, generic shapes are doubly precluded from registration, in that they contravene the first limb of the exclusion and necessarily lack distinctiveness. In view of such strictness before registration, it would be surprising to find that shapes which have become generic due to the fault or default of the proprietor cannot not be expunged from the register.

Folliard-Monguiral and Rogers list a number of factors which are considered unpersuasive by the Office for Harmonisation in the Internal Market when assessing the distinctiveness of shape marks for the Community trade mark register:

- The creative merit of a mark
- The process of creation of the shape
- Distinctiveness does not require novelty
- The ownership of national registrations[81]

---

[76] Linde at [69]; Case C-456/01 P and C-457/01 P Henkel KGM v OHIM (2005) ETMR 44, ECJ; Maasland NV's Application for a 3-Dimensional Trade Mark [2000] RPC 893 (AP) (decided before Linde but, it is submitted, not inconsistent). *See also* Arnaud Folliard-Monguiral & David Rogers, *Significant Case Law from 2004 on the Community Trade Mark from the Court of First Instance, the European Court of Justice and OHIM* [2005] EIPR 133 (noting Community trademark decisions).
[77] T-190/04 Freixenet SA v OHIM [2006] ECR II-79.
[78] Alexander Gonzalez, *Feel the Difference – German Federal Supreme Court Provides some Guidance on Registrability of Tactile Mark* [2007] 36(7) CIPAJ 402.
[79] [2006] EWHC 529, [2006] FSR 42 (Ch).
[80] Section 46(1)(c) of the UK Trade Marks Act 1994, corresponding to Art 12 of the Directive and Art 51 of the CTM Regulation, refers to the "common *name* in the trade".
[81] In Bongrain SA's Trade Mark Application [2004] EWCA Civ 1690, [2005] ETMR 47; [2005] RPC 14, CA (fancy cheese shape, application rejected), the English court pointed out that the fact of registration in other jurisdictions would not usually assist unless the basis for such registrations was clear. *Cf* Josef Rupp GmbH's

- The stability of the shape[82]

Conversely, the following are relevant:

- The geographical extent of the use[83]
- The public concerned[84]
- Methods of use

This list is consistent with para 51 of Windsurfing Chiemsee,[85] where it was held by the European Court of Justice that, assessing the distinctive character of a mark, one could consider

- The market share held by the mark;
- How intensive, geographically widespread and long-standing use of the mark has been;
- The amount invested by the undertaking in promoting the mark;
- The proportion of the relevant class of persons who, because of the mark, identify goods as originating from a particular undertaking;
- Statements from chambers of commerce and industry or other trade and professional associations.[86]

Ultimately the question is not whether the shape mark has been used, even extensively, but whether it has become distinctive through use. Thus the manner of use and in particular whether it educates the public to regard the mark as a source identifier will be a crucial aspect.

The perception of the relevant public is key to the question of distinctiveness. In relation to three-dimensional marks, the European Court has shown itself reluctant to exclude end consumers from the enquiry, for example in skein-shaped sausage casing[87] it was argued that a sausage casing sold by the

---

Community Trade Mark [2002] ETMR 35 (Community Trade Mark registration of doughnut shape for cheese not invalid).

[82] Decision BoA R 820/1999-3, 14 November 2000, §20: flexible net-bag could be registered if all other criteria satisfied.

[83] Use in one Member State is sufficient under the Directive, *see* Linde, *supra*.

[84] The relevant public may vary according to the type of good or service for which registration is sought.

[85] Windsurfing Chiemsee Produktions- und Vertriebs GmbH v Boots- und Segelzubehör Walter Huber (Joined Cases C-108 and 109/97) [2000] Ch 523, 555.

[86] On the problems of survey evidence in the UK courts, see Gary Lea, *Masters of All They Survey? Some Thoughts upon Official Attitudes to Market Survey Evidence in U.K. Trade Mark Practice* [1999] IPQ 191.

[87] T-15/05 Wim De Waele v OHIM 31 May 2006 (CFI).

applicant to charcuterie manufacturers might become unique to one of the manufacturers after registration. In 'shape of cheese box'[88] an attempt to limit the specification of goods to exclude consumers from the enquiry was unsuccessful. Here the sign was described in elaborate terms; the CFI took the view that consumers would simply not observe the detail, so distinctiveness was lacking.

From the above, it is clear that EC law and the law of Member States of the European Union on shape marks are underpinned by an ideal of market freedom.[89] In fact a distinctive trade mark is accepted to be an essential element of a system of undistorted competition in the EC.[90] For this reason it is likely that trade mark jurisprudence in Europe generally will be influenced by that on shape marks. Nonetheless, a 'keep free' competitive aspect did not conclusively militate against registration in the 'stand-up pouches' case.[91]

An extreme example of application of the consumer perception test to keep a design free from trade mark protection is the case of *Dyson*[92], where registration was sought for the transparent dust collection bin of Dyson Ltd's bagless vacuum cleaners.[93] It was accepted that the application was not to register a shape, because a variety of shapes were possible[94] and two quite different shapes were shown in the application. On appeal from the UK Registry's refusal to register the mark, the English court referred

---

[88] T-360/03 Frischpack GmbH v OHIM 23 November 2004 (CFI).

[89] Uma Suthersanen, *The European Court of Justice in Philips v Remington – Trade Marks and Market Freedom* [2003] IPQ 257.

[90] Gillette Co v LA Laboratories Ltd OY [2005] FSR 37 ECJ, (citing *Hag, Merz & Krell, Arsenal v Reed*).

[91] Deutsche SiSi Werke v OHIM C173/04P [2006] ETMR 41 ECJ rejecting appeal against finding that consumers would not perceive the shapes of the pouches as trade marks. Conversely in the US TrafFix case, it was held that a finding of competitive necessity was not essential to a functionality refusal: *TrafFix*, 532 US 23, 58 USPQ 2d 1001.

[92] Dyson Ltd v Registrar of Trade Marks (C321/03) [2007] 2 CMLR 14; [2007] CEC 223; [2007] ETMR 34; [2007] RPC 27. See Mike Walmsley *Too Transparent? ECJ Rules Dyson Cannot Register Transparent Collection Chamber as a Trade Mark* [2007] EIPR 298.

[93] The mark was described in the following way "the mark consists of a transparent bin or collection chamber forming part of the external surface of a vacuum cleaner". *See* ECJ decision at [15]. This decision related to an application to register in the UK. An application to register as a Community Trade Mark (no 522144) was withdrawn prior to the hearing of an appeal, Dyson v OHIM Case T-278/02 [2002] OJ C 289/29.

[94] Although in the flexible net-bag case the OHIM Board of Appeal took the view that stability of shape was not essential. *See* Board of Appeal Decision R 820/1999-3, 14 November 2000, *supra*. n.82 above.

questions[95] relating to the assessment of distinctiveness to the European Court of Justice. However, in its ruling, the European Court addressed a somewhat different question posed by the European Commission and supported by Advocate-General Leger: was the transparency of the bin a "sign" within the meaning of the trade mark legislation,[96] or merely a concept?[97] In his opinion, A-G Leger referred to aspects of Philips v Remington and continued:[98]

> In my opinion it is clear that this reasoning applies legitimately to a functional feature which forms part of the appearance of a product. Although that article refers only to signs which consist *exclusively* of the shape of a product, I think that the general interest which underlies that provision requires that registration of a functionality like that at issue in the main proceedings be refused.

He expressed the view that registration would confer exclusivity of the technical solution to a single operator for an indefinite time[99] and went on to enumerate the ways in which registration of the transparency concept would frustrate the system of free competition which the EC Treaty sought to establish.[100] A-G Leger also referred to the patentability of such a technical solution and the need to keep trade mark law from straying.[101]

---

[95] 1. In a situation where an applicant has used a sign (which is not a shape) which consists of a feature which has a function and which forms part of the appearance of a new kind of article, and the applicant has, until the date of application, had a de facto monopoly in such articles, is it sufficient, in order for the sign to have acquired a distinctive character within the meaning of Article 3(3) of [the Directive], that a significant proportion of the relevant public has by the date of application for registration come to associate the relevant goods bearing the sign with the applicant and no other manufacturer?
2. If that is not sufficient, what else is needed in order for the sign to have acquired a distinctive character and, in particular, is it necessary for the person who has used the sign to have promoted it as a trade mark?

The applicant had previously enjoyed patent protection for the operative features of the bagless vacuum cleaner, so during this period consumers came to recognize the transparent bins as indicating the type and origin of the cleaners. The questions are of great interest, but in the end the court found it unnecessary to answer them.

[96] The not-a-sign argument had been used in Philips v Remington [1998] RPC 283 at 298.

[97] Another example of a concept mark, British Airways' use of decorative art work in the corporate livery on the tail fins of aircraft, seems to have suffered from unpopularity rather than legal challenge.

[98] Advocate General's opinion at 88.

[99] Echoing the comments of Patten J in Dyson Ltd v Registrar of Trade Marks [2003] EWHC 1062; [2003] 1 WLR 2406; [2003] ETMR 77; [2003] RPC 47 at para 26: "It is not the function of a trade mark to create a monopoly in new developments in technology".

[100] Advocate General's opinion at 97.

[101] Advocate General's opinion at 95–96.

516 *Trademark law and theory*

The full court handed down a rather briefer opinion confirming the view that Dyson's application did not constitute a "sign".[102] Again, there was stress on the need to prevent "the abuse of trade mark law in order to obtain an unfair competitive advantage".[103]

In a number of the EC cases cited, consumer perception of the significance of the shape mark is said to have been affected by the presence of other, more traditional, forms of mark on the goods or packaging, usually to diminish the trade mark significance of the shape mark. However this is not conclusive; in Golden Rabbit TM[104] it was held that "There does not exist any rule of experience according to which the overall impression of a three-dimensional mark consisting of a shape, a colour, word and figurative elements as well as further features is regularly determined by the word element regardless of the concrete arrangement and get-up of those elements." By contrast, in Japan, the presence of additional word or device marks is likely to be seen as fatal to distinctiveness of the shape.[105]

Having considered in detail the law of the most restrictive regime, it is time to turn to other jurisdictions.

B. US Federal law

Although the influential doctrines of technical and aesthetic functionality[106] have long been recognised in US case law, especially in the interpretation of Federal trade mark legislation under the Lanham Act,[107] their enshrinement in statutory language at the Federal level came comparatively recently with the Technical Corrections to Trademark Act of 1946.[108] This amending legislation introduced specific references into Section 2 of the Lanham Act,[109] relating to the Principal Register:[110]

---

[102] *Dyson, supra.,* note 92 at para. [35]–[39].
[103] At [34], citing Heidelburger Bauchemie [2004] ECR I-6129 at [24], a case concerning the colours blue and yellow.
[104] [2007] ETMR 30 Case I ZR 37/04 Bundesgerichtshof, Germany.
[105] Yukis Yagyu, 'Protection of Three-dimensional Trademarks in Japan', *Yuasa and Hara Intellectual Property News,* August 2007, **22**, p. 1 at 3.
[106] The conceptual category of aesthetic functionality has been doubted by the USPTO; *see* Trademark Manual of Examining Procedure (TMEP) – 5th edition, para 1202.02(a)(vi) Aesthetic Functionality, available online at http://tess2.uspto.gov/tmdb/tmep/.
[107] Under ss 1, 2 and 45 of the Trademark Act, 15 USC §§1051, 1052 and 1127.
[108] Pub L No 105-330, §201, 112 Stat 3064, 3069, effective from 30 October 1998.
[109] US Code 15, para 1052.
[110] Section 23(c) of 15 USC §1091(c) is amended to similar effect for the Supplemental register.

No trademark by which the goods of the applicant may be distinguished from the goods of others shall be refused registration on the principal register on account of its nature unless it

. . .

(e) Consists of a mark which

. . .

(5) comprises any matter that, as a whole, is functional.

The next subsection makes functionality an absolute prohibition, regardless of distinctiveness:[111]

(f) Except as expressly excluded in subsections (a), (b), (c), (d), (e)(3), and (e)(5) of this section, nothing in this chapter shall prevent the registration of a mark used by the applicant which has become distinctive of the applicant's goods in commerce.

In relation to marks already registered, Section 14(3)[112] allows functionality to be raised in cancellation proceedings more than five years after registration, the usual period for incontestability, while Section 33(b)(8)[113] provides a defence of functionality where infringement of an incontestable mark is alleged.

Thus the statutory amendments have crystallised TrafFix functionality as a pre-emptive enquiry which takes precedence over any amount of acquired distinctiveness. The United States Patent and Trademark Office's (USTPO) Manual of Examining Practice for trade marks[114] gives the competitive imperative as the basis for this exclusion, defining the traditional functionality of a feature which is "essential to the use or purpose of the product or affects the cost or quality of the product"[115] and citing from Qualitex Co v Jacobson Products Co, Inc:[116]

The functionality doctrine prevents trademark law, which seeks to promote competition by protecting a firm's reputation, from instead inhibiting legitimate competition by allowing a producer to control a useful product feature. It is the province of patent law, not trademark law, to encourage invention by granting inventors a

---

[111] As decided in relation to technical functionality in TrafFix Devices, Inc v Marketing Displays, Inc, 532 US 23, 34–35, 58 USPQ 2d 1001, 1007 (2001). However, in Wal-Mart Stores, Inc v Samara Bros, Inc. 529 US 205, 120 SCt 1339, 146 LEd2d 182, 54 USPQ 2d 1065, the Supreme Court held that decorative trade dress could be protected under the Lanham Act on proof of factual distinctiveness.
[112] 15 USC §1064(3).
[113] 5 USC §1115(b)(8).
[114] Para 1202.02, available at http://tess2.uspto.gov/tmdb/ tmep/1200.htm#_T120202.
[115] See Dinwoodie, *Death of Ontology*, at 686, 694.
[116] 514 US 159, 164, 34 USPQ 2d 1161, 1163 (1995).

monopoly over new product designs or functions for a limited time, 35 U.S.C. §§154, 173, after which competitors are free to use the innovation. If a product's functional features could be used as trademarks, however, a monopoly over such features could be obtained without regard to whether they qualify as patents and could be extended forever [because trademarks may be renewed in perpetuity].

However, it becomes clear from the Manual that the USPTO does not regard the prohibition on functional shapes or other marks as extending to those conferring purely ornamental[117] advantage, what may in the past have been referred as "aesthetic functionality." Rather, there seems to be a very limited notion of the "aesthetic functionality" which would disqualify a mark under s 2(e)(5) on the basis of competitive need.[118] The manual[119] goes on to describe the doctrine of aesthetic functionality as "the subject of much confusion."[120] The examples given[121] of valid use of the term relate mainly to the use of colour. In Dippin' Dots, Inc v Frosty Bites Distrib LLC,[122] the colours of popular flavours of ice-cream were considered functional even when used in particular combinations and style.

In the case of purely ornamental product design, even where substantial value is conferred and the protection of a design patent has been enjoyed,[123] it seems that a showing of acquired distinctiveness will enable registration to be achieved, unlike the position in the European Community. In a number of cases[124] the shape of guitar heads has been protected by registration – Yamaha Intl Corp v Hoshino Gakki Co;[125] Gibson Guitar Corp v Paul Reed Smith Guitars LLP.[126] A case involving the "Beast" pointy guitar shape has been considered under European Law.[127] However, the Office for Harmonisation in

---

[117] Gerard N Magliocca, *Ornamental Design and Incremental Innovation* (2003) 86 Marq L Rev 845.
[118] Or significant non-reputation-related disadvantage.
[119] At para 1202.02(a)(iii)(C).
[120] See also Mark Alan, *Thurmon: The Rise and Fall of Trademark Law's Functionality Doctrine* (2004) 56 Fla L Rev 243.
[121] *Qualitex*, 514 US 165; *Brunswick Corp v British Seagull Ltd*, 35 F3d 1527 (Fed Cir 1994); *M-5 Steel Mfg, Inc. v O'Hagin's Inc*, 61 USPQ 2d 1086 (TTAB 2001).
[122] 369 F3d 1197 (2004).
[123] J Thomas McCarthy, *McCarthy on Trademarks*, para 7.91, citing In Re Mogen David Wine Corp 328 F2d 925, 140 USPQ 575 (CCRA 1964).
[124] Karen Feisthamel, Amy Kelly & Johanna Sistek (2005), *Trade Dress 101: Best Practices for the Registration of Product Configuration Trade Dress with the USPTO* 95 TMR 137 providing fascinating tables of product configurations registered for food products, furniture and furnishings and musical instruments.
[125] 231 U.S.P.Q. 926 (TTAB 1986).
[126] 311 F. supp 2d 690 (M.D. Tenn 2004).
[127] T-317/05, *Kustom Musical Amplification, Inc v Office for Harmonisation in the Internal Market* [2007] ERMTR 72.

the Internals Market (OHIM – the Community trademark and design registry) had done an internet search and in its decision communicated the links to the applicant but not copies of the web pages consulted. OHIM's argument that this was consistent with applicant's right to be heard was undermined by the fact that when the appeal court tried the links, many did not work. Accordingly the CFI annulled OHIM's decision on procedural grounds and did not consider the substantive merits of the application.

Returning to technical functionality, US case law shows that this objection will be upheld even if other product designs share similar technical advantages. In Thomas Betts Corp v Panduit Corp[128] and Keene Corp v Panaflex Industries Inc[129] the product design in issue was one of a dozen or so alternatives on the market, albeit not all optimal. A suggestion in Vornado Air Circulation systems v Durcraft Corp[130] that the presence of alternative designs could overcome the evidence of functionality provided by a utility patent was rejected in TrafFix.[131] Cases cited by Arden[132] suggest that the applicant's advertising of the technical advantages of its wares is not always taken at face value; sometimes the courts will dismiss it as "mere puffery", whilst on other occasions giving it weight in a finding of functionality.[133]

Considering the options of design patent, utility patent and trade dress protection, Valenzuela[134] recommends that both utility and design patents be sought for new product configurations, in the hope that decorative features can be shown to be distinctive through use in the period between expiry of design patent (14 years) and utility patent (20 years).

Another difference between jurisdictions is the weight given to the applicant's or proprietor's advertising. As the USPTO manual puts it, "The applicant's own advertising touting the utilitarian aspects of its design is often strong evidence supporting a functionality refusal."[135] However, in the US, Canada

---

[128] 65 F 3d 654 (7th Cir 1995); on remand, 835 F Supp 1399 (ND Ill 1996); see Thomas P Arden, *Protection of Non-Traditional Marks: Trademark Rights in Sounds, Scents, Colors, Motions and Product Designs in the U.S.* (2000, New York, INTA) 109–12.

[129] 653 F 2d 822 (3d Cir 1981).

[130] 58 F 3d 1498 (10th Cir 1995).

[131] TrafFix Devices, Inc v Marketing Displays, Inc, 532 U.S. 23, 34–5 (2001).

[132] Thomas P Arden, *Protection of Non-traditional Marks: Trademark Rights in Sounds, Scents, Colors, Motions and Product Designs in the U.S.* (2000, New York, INTA) 112–13.

[133] As in Re Schafer Machine Inc., 223 U.S.P.Q. 170 (TTAB 1984).

[134] Daniel A Valenzuela, *Can an Inventor Continue Protecting an Expired Patented Product Via Trade Dress Protection?* (2005) 81 N.D. L. Rev. 145.

[135] Para. 1202.02(a)(v)(B) (Advertising, Promotional or Explanatory Material in Functionality Determinations.)

and elsewhere, publicity vaunting the technical value of a product is often viewed as "mere puffery" and disregarded whereas in Europe such "puffs" are taken seriously as admissions against interest. It could be that European consumers take product information more seriously; after all trade mark law is ultimately about consumer perception,[136] so one must be cautious in comparing different markets. However the contrast is quite striking in cases involving the embossing of paper kitchen towels, considered in the next section.

C. Canadian Federal law

Canadian law emphasises that a trade mark is not a product but the symbol of a connection between the product and source. The doctrine of technical functionality was explored in Kimberley-Clark Tissue v Fort James[137] and Kirkbi v Ritvik.[138] In Kimberley-Clark, involving an application to register an embossing design for paper kitchen towels, the opponent argued technical functionality – the applicant had asserted in advertising that the embossing made the towels more absorbent, stronger, and softer. Opposition was rejected on this ground; the applicant's claims were regarded as "mere puffery." However, opposition succeeded on the ground that the design was decoration; Canadian law regards ornamentation features as incapable of registration as a valid trade mark unless the feature is shown to have acquired distinctiveness. Here it was relevant that the embossing was often obscured by packaging and not readily visible to consumers.

In Kirkbi, the plaintiff's LEGO brick indicia were held to consist solely of technical and functional characteristics. These had been protected by the plaintiff's expired patents. The court discussed the decision in Kimberley Clark and the doctrine of functionality generally. A finding of technical functionality would be fatal to a claim based upon a registered or unregistered mark.[139] Section 13(2) of the Canadian Trade Marks Act provides that no registration of a distinctive guise may interfere with the use of any utilitarian feature embodied in the distinguishing guise.

The distinction between technical and decorative features seems consonant with that in the USA, the defence under s 13(2) seeming to deal with issues embraced in the limited US doctrine of aesthetic functionality. The attitude of the court to the applicant's advertisements in Kimberley-Clark is in contrast to

---

[136] *Linde* (Directive Art 23(1)(b)); *Mag* (Regulation Art 7(1)(b)).
[137] (2005) 37 CPR (4th ed.) 559 (TM0B).
[138] [2005] 3 SCR 302.
[139] Section 7 of the Trade Marks Act 1985 Act merely codified the law of passing off.

that of the European Courts in the Philips v Remington[140] cases; in the latter, great stress was laid upon advertisements vaunting the technical advantages of the three-headed shaver.

By contrast, another EC example concerned paper kitchen towels. In Georgia-Pacific Sarl v Office for Harmonisation in the Internal Market (Trade Marks and Designs) (OHIM),[141] the application was for a three-dimensional mark consisting of four concentric circles, the outer circle interlocking with the outer circles of adjoining motifs.[142] The application was rejected by OHIM as being devoid of distinctive character for kitchen towels and the like, contrary to Art (1)(b) of Reg 40/94. The design was held to be neither inherently distinctive, nor to have distinctiveness acquired as a result of use. In upholding this decision, the Court of First Instance held that the relief pattern did not operate as an indication of source according to the perception of the relevant public,[143] here consumers. Rather these consumers would regard the pattern as connoting quality, that of absorbency.[144] This was reinforced by the fact that a word mark and the descriptor "super absorbent grâce à son gaufrage spécial"[145] were used on the packaging.

D. Other jurisdictions

New Zealand law seemingly avoids a categorical approach to functional features, even when previously protected by patent. In Fedco Trading v

---

[140] Case C-249/99 *Koninklijke Philips Electronics NV v Remington Consumer Products Ltd* [2001] RPC 38, Advocate General, [2003] RPC 2, ECJ, [2002] ECR I-5475; [2002] ETMR 81 ECJ.

[141] Case T283/04 (Unreported, 17 January 2007) (CFI). See case comment by Katharine Stephens & Zoe Fuller at (2007) 36 CIPAJ 91.

[142] In assessing distinctiveness, the court observed that there were two aspects, the fact of embossing and the particular pattern used, but looked at the overall effect of these. Case T283/04, *supra*. note 141 at para. [45] referring to Stihl T234/01 [2003] ECR II 2869 at [32] on the proposition that this did not preclude separate and successive consideration of the individual aspects.

[143] Nestlé Waters France v OHIM (bottle shape), T-305/02, ECR II-5207 at [29]; Eurocermex/OHMI, C-286/04P, ECR I-5797; such average consumer was reasonably well informed and attentive; Axions et Belce/OHMI (Forme de cigare de couleur brune et forme de lingot doré), T-324/01 & T-110/02, ECR II-1897, point 31, but such consumer was possessed of imperfect recollection. Procter & Gamble/OHMI (Forme d'un savon), T-63/01, ECR II-5255, point 41.

[144] There was some evidence that consumers had been educated to regard embossing generally as conferring superior absorbency, *see* Case T283/04, *supra*. note 141, at para. [47].

[145] Which can be roughly translated as "super absorbent thanks to its special embossing."

Miller[146] a previously patented horticultural vine tie was held to be registrable under the Trade Marks Act 2002 in view of evidence of extensive use and consumers' perception of the tie as indicating source.

Thai law appears to place few fetters on the registration of shape marks which have acquired distinctiveness. In Société Bic v Department of Intellectual Property,[147] the Thai Intellectual Property and Information Technology Court recognised the Bic ballpoint pen shape as a famous mark whose non-functional features included the hexagonal body and cone shaped tip.

Art 4(1)(18) of Japan's Trade Mark Act 1997 states that where a trade mark consists solely of the three-dimensional shape of goods or their packaging, the mark cannot be registered if the shape is "indispensable for the goods or packaging properly to function".[148] This applies the doctrine of technical functionality to packaging as well as product shapes but appears to be a higher test than that used in Europe and the USA.

III. What (if any) correlations can be identified between scope of design laws and treatment of shape marks?

It has been argued that the case of Europe shows an inverse relationship between the liberal scope for protecting product shapes under design law and their limited registrability under trade mark law. A strictness militating against trade mark registration may manifest itself in categorical exclusions or in reluctance to find that shape signs are capable of distinguishing. Although due caution must be exercised in comparing the rules applicable to different markets, it does appear that jurisdictions with narrower criteria for design protection, such as the USA, do have a more generous approach to registration of shapes. This could be due to a decreased likelihood that the shape in question was previously protected by design laws, or due to a more relaxed policy. A telling example is that of "retro" toaster designs; Dualit's shape mark applications were refused in the UK, whilst Sunbeam's retro design shapes have been registered as trade marks in the USA.[149] This resonates with Dinwoodie's ascription of the Two Pesos decision to narrow design protection in the US.

---

[146] High Court, 16 December 2004, noted at (2006) 180 TMR 486.
[147] IP and IT Court, No. 38–41/2547, noted at (2006) 96 TMR 530.
[148] Translation thanks to (2007) 22 Yusara and Hara IP News 1.
[149] See *supra*. at n59.

Index

abandonment 6, 84, 92–4
Abercrombie & Fitch v Hunting World (1976) 54–6
Acomplia Report 427–8
acquisition 101
acte clair doctrine 184
Action Plans 200
actionable use 269–73
activation theory 287–8
Adams, F.M. 27–8
Adidas/Fitnessworld Trading (2003) 157
Advantage-Rent-A-Car v Advantage Car Rental (2001) 129–30
advertising 72, 407, 488, 520
   informative view 329
   persuasive view 329
   third party 406
   trademark owner's 406
   see also comparative advertising; false advertising; truth and advertising
aesthetic functionality 518, 521
affiliation products 270
Africa 199
African, Caribbean and Pacific Group of States 199
Agreement on Trade-Related Aspects of Intellectual Property Rights 34, 250–52
   bilateral free trade agreements 232–5, 238
   bureaucracies 104
   European Court of Justice, jurisdiction of to interpret 180–82
   exclusive rights pursuant to 186–7
   harmonization: WTO Appellate Body and ECJ 177–80, 183, 188–9, 192–3, 195–8, 200, 203
   Lanham Act and commercial speech doctrine 315–16
   legal framework 239–40
   legal standards 236–8, 252, 255
   non-visually perceptible trademarks 240–42
   product design protection 503
   trade names as an exception under Article 17 190–91
   traditional knowledge and cultural property 434, 435n, 436, 443, 445, 451, 466, 469–70
Agreement on Trade-Related Aspects of Intellectual Property Rights-plus provisions: well-known trademarks, additional protection for 242–8
Ainsworth v Walmsley (1866) 33
Albania 199
Algeria 200
all-or-nothing rules 84, 87
allusion to trade marks, restriction of 324–41
   expressive autonomy 331–7
   limiting protection against allusion 337–40
   protection against allusion and justification of other intellectual property regimes 329–31
   protection against allusion as protection against confusion 326–8
   protection against allusion and trademarks as property 328–9
American Civil Liberties Union 145
Anheuser Busch/Budejovicky Budvar (Budweiser case) (2004) 174–6, 178, 180–81, 183–4, 187–90, 194, 196–7, 200–201, 202
Anheuser-Busch Inc. v Balducci Publications (1994) 282
anti-dilution statutes 369
Antidote Int'l Films v Bloomsbury Publishing (2006) 486–7
appropriate use 439–40
Arden, T.P. 519

524 Trademark law and theory

Armenia 200
Arsenal Football Club plc v Matthew Reed (2001) 187–8, 202, 326–7, 338, 354
  expressive values 272–3, 276, 285–6, 291, 293
Asia 199
assignment doctrine 49
assignments in gross 82–3
Association Littéraire et Artistique 499
Austin, G.W. 368–403
Australia 240, 248, 249, 250, 251, 252, 253
  bureaucracies 101, 103, 111, 116, 118, 119
  Corporations Act 2001 116
  Intellectual Property 120–23
  product design protection 499
  Securities and Investment Commission 116
  Trade Marks Act 1995 103
  traditional knowledge and cultural property 434, 454, 461, 470, 475
authenticity 440–41
automobiles 215, 223–4
Azerbaijan 200

bad faith 276–7
bad influence 482–90
Bahrain 240, 248, 249, 250
'Barbie' cases 481
  see also Mattel
Baudrillard, J. 61–2, 64
Beebe, B. 42–64, 382
behavioral approaches 287–92
Belarus 200
Bell, T. 46
Benelux countries 151, 156
Benetton v G-Star (2008) 509–510
Benkler, Y. 319
Bently, L. 3–41
Beverly Smith, H. 503–4
bilateral free trade agreements 229–55
  Agreement on Trade-Related Aspects of Intellectual Property Rights 249, 250–52, 255
  Australia 248, 249, 250, 251, 252, 253
  Bahrain 248, 249, 250

Chile 249, 251, 252, 253
Colombia 248, 249, 250
intellectual property standards and free trade agreements 232–6
international trade 229–32
Korea 249, 251, 252, 253
Malaysia 248
Morocco 248, 249, 250
Panama 248, 249, 250
Peru 248, 249, 250
scent marks and/or sound marks 249
Singapore 249, 251, 252, 253
South African Customs Union 248
Thailand 248
United Arab Emirates 248
United States 249, 251–3, 255
visual perceptibility 249
World Trade Organization 251
BioID/OHIM (2005) 163
Blackstone, Sir W. 4, 194, 198
Blanchard v Hill (1742) 9
Blofield v Payne (1833) 8–9
blurring 58–9
  bilateral free trade agreements 244
  confusion and fair use 385
  expressive values 278
  Lanham Act and commercial speech doctrine 314, 316, 319
  political economy of dilution 136, 144
  restricting allusion to trademarks 340
  search-costs theory of limiting doctrines 72
BMW/Deenik (1999) 166, 191
BMW/Hölterhoff/Freiesleben (2000) 167
Bolivia 470
Bone, B. 36
Bosland, J. 340–41
Bosley Med. Inst. Inc. v Kremer (2005) 417–18, 420
Bosnia-Herzegovina 199
Boy Scouts of America v Dale (2000) 331–2
Boyle, J. 361–2
brand 47
  name 476
  perception 410
Brazil 474
breach of confidence 110

Brennan, D. 113–14, 115
Bulgaria 199, 200
bundle of privileges 362
bureaucracies 95–131
  constructing trade mark office client 123–9
  courts, role of and bureaucratic resistance 129–31
  financial imperative 118–20
  IP Australia and new public management 120–23
  property argument 113–16
  protection prior to use 110–113
  reform 116–18
  see also clearance cost argument for registration
Burrell, R. 95–131, 503–5

Campina v Benelux-Merkenbureau (2004) 163, 360
Canada 234, 434, 461, 470, 520–21
category dominance 287–9
Central Hudson test 296, 305, 309, 313, 322
certification marks 475, 476
Chancery courts 5
Chile 240, 245–9, 250, 251, 252, 253
City of Cincinnati v Discovery Network (1993) 321–2
Clark v Freeman 11
Class International v Colgate-Palmolive (2006) 224–5
clearance cost argument for registration 98–109
  false negatives 100–102
  false positives 102–7
  quality concerns 107–9
  search costs argument 109
Coca Cola Trade Marks (1986) 353
Coca-Cola v Nehhi (1944) 364–5
Code of Conduct 127–8
cognitive approaches 287–92
Coleman, A. 503–4
Collins Co. v Brown (1857) 12–13
Colombia 240, 248, 249, 250
colour marks 164, 358, 359–60
Combined Interest Group 124
Comedy III Productions Inc. v Gary Saderup (2001) 282
commentary advertising 72
Commerce Clause 379, 415–16

commercial advertising or promotion 488
commercial speech doctrine *see* truth and advertising: Lanham Act and commercial speech doctrine
Commissioner of Trade Marks 450, 472
Common Commercial Policy 199, 199n
Common Law 4–5, 7, 8, 13, 14, 15, 36
  action for deceit 9
  courts 10
  free movement of protected goods in Europe 220, 221
  harmonization, concerns of 151
commons 361–4
comparative advertising 75–9
  expressive values 265, 279
  Internet and trademark law 427
  Lanham Act and commercial speech doctrine 320, 322
  restricting allusion to trademarks 338
  search-costs theory of limiting doctrines 72, 76
compelled speech 332–6, 341
compelled subsidy of speech 332, 333, 341
competition enhancement 455–6
complementary view 327
confusion:
  policies and fair use 368–403
  consumers, necessity of 372–80
  fair use 389–403
    development of trademark law 399–403
    KP Permanent 395–9
  growing brands 386–9
  knowing consumers 381–5
  post-sale 326–7, 378, 387
  protection against 326–8
  and restricting allusion to trademarks 339
  see also initial interest confusion; likelihood of confusion
Congress:
  confusion and fair use 379, 396
  copyright influence on trademark law 495, 496–7
  Internet and trademark law 415–16, 419
  Lanham Act and commercial speech doctrine 320, 322

political economy of dilution 132,
    133–5, 140–41, 142, 143–7
connotative aspect of a trademark 340
consent for resale 219, 220, 221, 223
Consolidated Revenue Fund 120
constitution-based solutions 280–83
constitutionalization of adjudication
    200–201
consumer confusion
    copyright influence on trademark law
        493
    discounting of in favor of free
        movement 192–3
    expressive values 274–5
    minimization 455
    restricting allusion to trademarks
        324, 328
    search-costs theory of limiting
        doctrines 86–7, 88
    surveys 57
    see also likelihood of confusion
consumer welfare 378–80
content source confusion 425–6
Cooperation Agreement 199
Copenhagen criteria 199
copyright 30, 481–97
    bad influence 482–90
    bilateral free trade agreements 231
    expressive values 263
    good influence 490–97
    product design protection 498, 499,
        502
    search-costs theory of limiting
        doctrines 73–4
    traditional knowledge and cultural
        property 436, 444, 447, 456
Copyright Act 1976 482, 496, 497
Copyright Clause 361, 379, 380
Cotonou Agreement 199
counterfeiting cases 143, 440–41
County Court 39
Court of Appeal 40, 41, 132, 201, 202
    confusion and fair use 381, 392–3,
        400
    harmonization: WTO Appellate Body
        and ECJ 193
    Netherlands 510
    product design protection 510
    public domain delineation 349, 357
Court of Chancery 10, 12
Court of Customs and Patent Appeals
    402

Court of Equity 21, 23, 25
Court of First Instance 154, 163, 514,
    519, 521
Court of King's Bench 8
courts, role of and bureaucratic
    resistance 129–31
Croatia 199
Croft v Day (1843) 11–12
cultural identity 452
cultural tastes and preferences 217
cyberpiracy 267
cyberspace 286
cybersquatting/domainers 404

*Dallas Cowboys Cheerleaders Inc. v
    Pussycat Cinema Ltd* (1979) 325
Daniel, E.M. 29
Danone trademark 170
*Dastar Corp. v Twentieth Century Fox
    Film Corp.* (2003) 50–52, 481,
    482–7, 489, 497
Database of Official Insignia of
    Native American Tribes 474
Davidoff/Gofkid (2003) 157, 221,
    225–6
Davis, J. 345–67
Day v Day (1816) 9–10
deception, likelihood of 496
deception, problems in determining
    305–6
decorative use 167
defenses 279–80
defensive protection 471
Denmark 173, 217, 219
denotative aspect of a trademark 340
deposit system 99
descriptive marks 78, 346, 352, 355
descriptive terms 233, 237
design 30, 99, 499
detriment:
    by allusion 325
    to reputation 325
Deutsche Grammophon v Metro (1971)
    208
differentiation 63
Digital Millennium Copyright Act 1998
    488–9
dilution 43, 52, 58–9, 132–47, 312–22
    actual 244, 245, 278–9, 383–4
    bilateral free trade agreements 244

cognitive model of and
  noncommercial uses 317–20
confusion and fair use 370–71,
  376–7, 379, 384, 385, 401
contributory 89–90
expressive values 267, 271, 277–9,
  289
Federal Trademark Dilution Act
  134–8
Federal Trademark Dilution Act,
  Congress's reinvigoration of
  143–6
Federal Trademark Dilution Act,
  courts' reaction to 138–43
First Amendment implications
  320–22
likelihood of 139–40, 244, 278–9,
  383–5
new basis for 314–16
restricting allusion to trademarks 326
search-costs theory of limiting
  doctrines 72
  see also blurring; tarnishment
Dinwoodie, G.B. 388, 415, 419, 500,
  501, 522
*Dippin' Dots Inc v Frosty Bites
  Distrib LLC* (2005) 518
disclaimers 311–12
disparaging marks 448–50
Dispute Settlement Understanding 193,
  198
dissimilar goods 157
dissimilar marks 236–7
distinctiveness 43, 52–9, 61, 63
  acquired 52, 364, 522
  bureaucracies 118
  differential 52, 54–9
  from other marks 59
  inherent 52
  loss of 325–6
  political economy of dilution 141
  product design protection 510–512,
    513–15, 516, 520
  public domain delineation 352, 359
  signification and value 52–3
  source 52, 54–9
  statute-based factual solutions 268–9
  traditional knowledge and cultural
    property 444, 456–8
  see also factually distinctive marks

distinguishing through nature 357
Dixon v Fawcus (1861) 15
DKV/OHIM (COMPANYLINE) (2002)
  163
Dogan, S.L. 65–94
dominant mark 288–9
double identity 168
Drahos, P. 362, 500
Dreyfuss, R.C. 261–93
Dualit (1999) 509, 522
Dunns Trade Marks (Fruit Salt case)
  (1889) 347–8
dyadic model 44–5
Dyrberg, P. 208
Dyson Ltd v Registrar of Trade Marks
  (2007) 514, 516

Economic Partnership Agreements
  199–200
economic theory 66–70
Edelsten v Edelsten (1863) 20–21
Edelsten v Vick (1853) 14
Edenfield v Fane (1993) 302
editorial content 408–9
Egypt 200
Eighth Circuit 79
ejusdem generis rule 190
Eldred v Ashcroft (2003) 307–8
Emperor of Austria v Day and Kossuth
  (1861) 38
enclosure of the common 354–60
endorsement 387
Eno v Dunn (Solio case) 348–9,
  350–51
equitable action 9, 14
equitable jurisdiction 13, 15
equity 7, 10, 36
  in fraud 11
Esso trademark 170
Europe 199, 436, 461
  product design protection 499, 518,
    520, 521, 522
European Atomic Energy Community
  (Euratom) 151
European Commission 171, 184, 197,
  208, 211, 515
European Community Customs Code
  224–5
European Community Design Regulation
  502

European Community law on designs
    and trade marks 502–516
European Community Trade Mark
    Regulation 152–6, 159, 163, 165,
    169, 170, 172–3, 176, 209, 503,
    509
European Community Treaty 151, 172,
    199, 219, 515
  Art. 28 204–5, 206
  Art. 30 205, 206, 207
  Art. 81 208, 210–212, 226
  Art. 82 212–14, 226
  Art. 234 154, 223
  Art. 295 206, 207, 228
  Art. 307 207
European Constitutional Treaty 170
European Council 184, 197, 199
European Court of Justice 107
  expressive values 272, 276
  free movement of protected goods in
    Europe 207–220, 223, 225,
    227–8
  harmonization, concerns of 152, 154,
    155–9, 160, 162, 163–8,
    174–5, 176
  product design protection 506, 509,
    510, 511, 513, 515
  public domain delineation 347, 354,
    356, 357, 358, 359, 360, 364,
    367
  restricting allusion to trademarks
    326–7, 330, 338
  see also harmonization: WTO
    Appellate Body and ECJ
European Directive 48/2004/EC 171–2,
    226
European Directive 97/71/EEC 502
European Economic Area 206, 208, 209,
    210, 214, 217, 218, 221–2, 225
European Neighbourhood Policy 200
European Patent Litigation Protocol
    (EPLA) 172
European Union 346, 451–3, 501–2,
    514, 519
Evans, G.E. 177–203
exchange value 62
Executive Relationship Group 124
exhaustion of consent 222–3
exhaustion doctrine 492
exhaustion of rights upon a first sale
    doctrine 208, 219, 220n, 221–2,
    223, 224, 492n
experience goods 324
expressive autonomy 331–7
expressive values 261–93
  cognitive and behavioral approaches
    287–92
  constitution-based solutions 280–83
  normative assessment 283–6
  see also statute-based factual
    solutions

factually distinctive marks 353, 356–8,
    360
fair use 237
  copyright influence on trademark law
    481, 491, 492–4, 497
  defenses 426–8
  descriptive 496
  expressive values 269, 279–80
  Internet and trademark law 419, 422
  nominative 269, 279–80, 390, 392,
    394, 426–8, 491–2, 495, 496
  restricting allusion to trademarks
    332
  search-costs theory of limiting
    doctrines 87, 88
  see also confusion: policies and
    fair use
false advertising 296–312, 406
  infringement 298–307
  deception, problems in determining
    305–6
  First Amendment precedents
    298–303
  intent 306–7
  partially useful information 303–4
  non-trademark 307–312
  Supreme Court discussions of truth
    versus falsity 296–8
false negatives 100–102, 106, 107
false positives 102–7
famous marks 140–41, 144–6, 244
Fedco Trading v Miller (2006) 522
Federal Circuit 132, 201
Federal Court 129
Federal Express/FedEx 93
Federal Trade Commission 308
Federal Trademark Dilution Act 134–8
  Congress's reinvigoration of 143–6

copyright influence on trademark law 493, 495
courts' reaction to 138–43
expressive values 277–8
political economy of dilution 132–3
search-costs theory of limiting doctrines 81
Fiat cars 440
Fifth Circuit 306
film distribution 223–4
financial imperative 118–20
Financial Management and Accountability Act 1997 120
Finland 183, 189–90
  Supreme Court 174, 178, 181, 184, 202
First Amendment 145, 461
  confusion and fair use 390, 392, 394, 395, 400
  and dilution 320–22
  false advertising 298–303
  Lanham Act and commercial speech doctrine 294–6, 301–4, 306–9, 312, 314, 316, 318, 323
First Circuit 142
Firth, A. 498–522
fixation 447
'folklore'/'expressions of folklore' 465
Folliard-Monguiral, A. 508, 510, 512
Food and Drug Administration regulations 311–12
Foreign Office 19
France 151, 154, 170, 184, 284
Frankel, S. 433–63
Franks v Weaver (1847) 11–12
fraud 10–11, 12, 13, 15, 16, 21, 23
free movement 192–3, 204–228
  Community interpretations on national laws 219–24
  Community law 204–214
  parallel goods, market for 217–18
  parallel importation paradox 224–6
  parallel trade 214–17
  and parallel trading, future of 227–8
free riding 144, 316, 321–2, 373
free trade agreements 232–6
  see also bilateral free trade
freedom of expression 262, 340, 461–2, 493

freedom of speech 461, 481
  see also expressive autonomy
Friedman v Rogers (1979) 298–300, 301–2
FTC v QT Inc (2006) 308–9
functionality 50, 84, 90–92

gadfly products 270
General Agreement on Tariffs and Trade 232
genericide 85–90, 339
genericness 84, 85–90, 94, 346, 355
Genesee Brewing Co. v Stroh Brewing Co. (1997) 88
geographical distances and associated costs of transporting goods 217
geographical extent of trading area 140
geographical indications 436, 451–3
Georgia 200
Georgia-Pacific Sarl v OHIM (2007) 521
Germany 19
  Federal Supreme Court 164, 169–70
  free movement of protected goods in Europe 220–21
  harmonization 151, 155, 160, 172, 184
  product design protection 506
  Trade Mark Act 184
Gerolsteiner Brunnen GmbH & Co v Putsch GmbH (2004) 191–2
Ghana 470
Gibson Guitar Corp v Paul Reed Smith Guitars LLP (2004) 518–19
Gillette/LA Laboratories (2003) 168
Ginsburg, J.C. 481–97
Girl Scouts of the United States of America v Personality Posters Manufacturing Co (1969) 334–5
Golden Rabbbit TM (2007) 516
Goldman, E. 404–429
good faith 280, 304, 308
goodwill 36, 46, 47, 49, 51, 57
  bilateral free trade agreements 231, 232, 244, 254
  bureaucracies 114, 115
  confusion and fair use 369, 371, 375, 379
  harmonization 173, 175, 182, 184–5, 190

530 *Trademark law and theory*

political economy of dilution 135, 136
search-costs theory of limiting doctrines 66, 68, 73, 76, 77, 84, 93
spill over 112
traditional knowledge and cultural property 454
governmental policies 218
'gray goods' 231
Greenough v Dalmahoy (1769) 8
Greenough v Lambertson (1777) 8
growing brands 386–9
Guatemala 470
Gudeman, S. 466–7

HAG II 187
Hall v Barrows (1863) 21–2, 39
Hampton, P.G. II 138
harm 143, 273–9
harmonization 151–76, 223, 225–6, 227
  actors and stages 153–5
  bilateral free trade agreements 254
  likelihood of confusion (including association) 156–9
  new areas 173–5
  procedures, sanctions and institutions 171–3
  provision, structure of 159–63
  public domain delineation 354
  threshold setting 163–5
  use as a mark 165–71
  WTO Appellate Body and European Court of Justice 177–203
  Appellate Body case law 198
  constitutionalization of adjudication 200–201
  EC Trademark Directive 184
  European Court of Justice case law 198–200
  European Court of Justice and TRIPS Agreement 180–82
  judicial activism 193–7
  potential disadvantages 201–3
  see also protection of trade names
Havana Club (2002) 185, 195, 197, 198, 200
Hays, T. 204–228

Henkel KGAA v Deutsches Patent- und Markenamt (2005) 505–6
Henson court 290
Hewlett-Packard v Expansys (2005) 226
Heymann, L. 318
High Court 155, 202, 357
high-technology industry 230
historical aspects 3–41
  commentators' responses 25–8
  internationalisation 19–20
  judicial activity 20–25
  law prior to 1860 6–15
  legislative activity 16–19
  legislative activity: Trade Marks Registration Act 1875 28–30
  significance of trade marks as property 30–33
Holloway v Holloway (1850) 11–12
honest concurrent use 174–5
honest practice in industrial or commercial matters 191
Honoré, Professor 4
Hormel Foods Corp. v Jim Henson Productions Inc. (1996) 274
House Judiciary Committee 144
House of Lords 32, 35, 41, 184
  public domain delineation 348, 351, 352
Hurley v Irish-American Gay, Lesbian and Bisexual Group of Boston (1995) 331
hypermark 60–61

Ibañez v Florida Department of Business & Professional Regulation (1994) 297–8
Iberian countries 217–18
icons *see* traditional knowledge and cultural property
identical signs 236
imagination costs 369, 378
imperceptible uses 421
implied consent doctrine 219, 220
in gross rights 48, 49
In re Rath (2005) 201
inappropriate use 440
incontestibility doctrine 99
indexical function 338–9
India 476
Indigenous Peoples Rights Act 1997 467

Index 531

industrial property law 6
infringement 52, 56–7
    bureaucracies 101, 108, 109
    expressive values 267
    see also under false advertising
initial interest confusion 275, 378, 387, 422, 425–6
injunctive relief 9
instance dominance 287
intangible rights 437
Intel Corporation 241
intellectual property 30
    bilateral free trade agreements 230, 231, 234, 235, 239, 242, 255
    bureaucracies 98, 118, 119
    copyright influence on trademark law 481
    expressive values 282
    free movement of protected goods in Europe 206–7, 210, 212–17, 220–27
    harmonization 152, 166, 179, 185, 196
    piracy 232
    product design protection 500
    public domain delineation 353, 361, 362, 366
    restricting allusion to trademarks 324, 328
    rights 96
    search-costs theory of limiting doctrines 69–70
    standards and free trade agreements 232–6
    see also Agreement on Trade-Related Aspects of Intellectual Property Rights
Intellectual Property Clause 415
Intellectual Property and Information Technology Court (Thailand) 522
intent-to-use 103–4, 110, 117, 306–7
International Court of Justice 182
    Statute 198
International Order of Job's Daughters v Lindeburg & Co. (1990) 395
international trade 229–32
internationalisation 19–20
Internet:
    contextual advertising 50
    expressive values 265–6, 274–5, 283–4, 291–2

search-costs theory of limiting doctrines 80
see also Internet and online word of mouth
Internet and online word of mouth 404–429
    amplification of word of mouth 411–12
    consumer word of mouth 409–410
    editorial content 408–9
    fair use defenses 426–8
    likelihood of confusion 424–6
    product experiences 405–6
    retail interactions 406–7
    search engines and competition for attention 412–13
    third party advertising 406
    trademark owner control and brand perception 410
    trademark owner's advertising 406
    use in commerce 414–24
interrelationship of trademarks and trade names 187–90
I.P. Lund Trading ApS v Kohler Co. 142
IQ Group Ltd v Wiesner Publishing (2006) 489
Ireland 153
Israel 200
Israelite House of David v Murphy (1934) 345–6
Italy 173
ius in rem 27, 40

Jacoby, J. 284–5
Janis, M. 415, 419
Japan 516, 522
Jenkins, H. 27
JG v Samford (1584) 7
Johanns v Livestock Marketing Association (2005) 333–4
Joint Recommendation Concerning Provisions of the Protection of Well-Known Marks 242
Jordan 200, 240, 242, 245, 247–9, 250, 251, 252, 253
judicial activity 20–25, 193–7
Julius Sämaan Ltd v Tetrosyl Ltd 509, 510, 512

Keene Corp v Panaflex Industries Inc (1981) 519

keyword triggering 423–4
Kimberley-Clark Tissue v Fort James (2005) 520–21
Kirkbi v Ritvik (2005) 520
Knott v Morgan (1836) 10, 11
Korea 245–7, 249, 251, 252, 253
KP Permanent Make-Up Inc. v Lasting Impression I Inc. (2004) 286, 288–9, 395–9, 415
    confusion and fair use 372, 389–90, 400–401, 402–3
KPN&PTT/Benelux Merkenbureau (Postkantoor) (2004) 163
Kur, A. 151–76

Lamparello v Falwell (2005) 417–18, 420
land common 350–51, 366
Land Registry for England and Wales 125
Landes, W. 65, 77, 83, 327, 330, 336
Langdale, Lord 10
language 461–2
Lanham Act:
    bilateral free trade agreements 244
    bureaucracies 100
    confusion and fair use 369, 384, 387, 390, 393, 396, 399
    copyright influence on trademark law 482–4, 487–92
    expressive values 273, 286
    harmonization: WTO Appellate Body and ECJ 201
    Internet and trademark law 414, 415, 416, 417, 418
    political economy of dilution 132, 134–5, 137, 139, 142, 143
    product design protection 516
    public domain delineation 364
    and scandalous or disparaging marks 448–50
    search-costs theory of limiting doctrines 66, 82n, 88, 90–91
    traditional knowledge and cultural property 450, 453, 454
    see also truth and advertising: Lanham Act and commercial speech doctrine
Laugh It Off Promotions CC v SAB Int'l (Finance) BV (2005) 281–2, 285

Leather Cloth Co v American Leather Cloth (1865) 22, 25, 26, 32, 36, 39
Lebanon 200
Lego 439
Lego Juris A/S v Mega Brands Inc. (2007) 508
Lemley, M.A. 41, 65–94, 145
libel 295, 302, 307
Libertel Groep BV/Benelux Merkenbureau (2003) 162, 359
Libya 200
licensing doctrine 49
likelihood of confusion 156–9
    bilateral free trade agreements 233, 236, 238, 242, 243, 246
    confusion and fair use 370–71, 377, 381–2, 385–6, 387, 389, 395, 400–403
    copyright influence on trademark law 490–91, 495, 496
    expressive values 273, 276, 277
    harmonization, concerns of 175, 176
    Internet and online word of mouth 418, 422, 424–6
    political economy of dilution 139
limited exceptions 237, 238
Linde case (2003) 358, 360, 511
Litman, J. 361
L.L. Bean v Drake Publishers Inc. (1987) 282
Lloyd, E. 25–6
Long, C. 132–47, 277–8
Lovelady, A. 501
Lowry Whittle, J. 30
Ludlow, H. 27
Lury, C. 500

'Mc' suffix 319
McCarthy, J.T. 415
Macedonia 199
Madison, M. 332
Madrid Protocol 239
magazine copy 394
Malaysia 248
Mali 470
M'Andrew v Bassett (1864) 33
Manhattan Oil 241
Māori Advisory Committee 450–51, 472
Māori Arts Board of Creative New Zealand (*Te Waka Toi*) 476

Māori people 437, 439–41, 446, 450, 460, 462
'marchio di fatto' doctrine (Italy) 173
marketing 371
Mattel Inc. v MCA Records Inc. (2002) 271–2, 290, 338–9
Mattel Inc. v Pitt (2002) 494
Mattel Inc. v Walking Mountain Products (2003) 338–9, 493–4
me-too marketing 338
media industry 230
merchandising cases 71
merchandising doctrine 50–52
metaphors 349
metatag usage 421
Mexico 234
Michelin & Cie v C.A.W.-Canada (1996) 270–71, 272, 291
Microsoft Corporation 89, 241
Millington v Fox (1838) 5, 13–15, 21, 26
Minister for Industry Tourism and Resources 127–8
misrepresentation 175, 176
Miss World Ltd. v Channel 4 Television Corp. (2007) 282
Moldova 199, 200
monadic structure 61
Montenegro 199
moral rights 437–8, 481
Morocco 200, 240, 248, 249, 250
Moseley v Secret Catalog (2003) 133, 139–40, 143–4, 244, 245, 383–4
Moskin, J.E. 138

naked licensing 49, 82–3
National Indigenous Arts Advocacy Association 475
national laws of contract 224
Native Americans 449, 461, 473
need to keep free doctrine 160, 176
negative association 72
NERA Report 217, 218
Netherlands 156, 217, 509–510
New Kids on the Block v News America Publishing Inc. (1990) 392–5, 400
new public management 120–23
New Zealand 448
   Government 462
   Intellectual Property Office 446
   Museum of 457
   offensive trademarks 450–51
   product design protection 521–2
   Registration Office 451
   shape marks-legislation 521–2
   traditional knowledge and cultural property 434, 436, 454, 461, 472
   see also Māori
news reporting and commentary 279
Nigeria 470
Nike v Kasky (2003) 308–9
Ninth Circuit 381–2, 390–93, 396, 398, 400–401, 425–7, 493–4
non-distinctive signs 346, 352, 355
Non-exhaustive List of Customary Names Used in Brazil Associated with Biodiversity 474
non-use 103–5, 118
non-visually perceptible trademarks 240–42
normative assessment 283–6
normative level 277
North American Free Trade Agreement 234, 235
novelty 444

objective values 215–16
offensive trademarks in New Zealand 450–51
Office for Harmonisation in the Internal Market 153–4, 508, 512, 519
   Appeal Board 154
OHIM v Wrigley Jr. Co. (2004) 360
Oman 240, 245–9, 250
Ong, B. 229–55
ordre public doctrine 477
originality 444

Pacific Gas and Electric Company v Public Utilities Commission of California (1986) 331
Palestinian Authority 200
Panama 240, 248, 249, 250, 470
parallel goods 217–18, 221
parallel importation 152, 205–6, 208, 211, 213, 219, 222–4, 231
   paradox 224–6
parallel trading 210–211, 214–17, 227–8

Paris Convention 6
    bilateral free trade agreements 233, 237, 238, 242, 243
    harmonization: WTO Appellate Body and ECJ 180, 183, 185, 189, 193, 195–6, 201
    harmonization, concerns of 163, 173, 174
    traditional knowledge and cultural property 436, 477
    parodies 276, 280–82, 285, 319, 416, 427
    copyright influence on trademark law 490, 493–4, 495
    target 339
    weapon 339
Paris Union, assembly of for the Protection of Industrial Property 242
partially useful information 303–4
Partnership Agreements 199, 200
passing off 130, 306–7
Patent Clause 379, 380
Patent and Trademark Office 305–6
patents 30
    bilateral free trade agreements 231
    bureaucracies 96–7, 99
    expressive values 263
    free movement of protected goods in Europe 213
    product design protection 498, 508
    search-costs theory of limiting doctrines 73–4
    traditional knowledge and cultural property 433, 436, 444, 447, 456, 466
Patents, Designs and Trade Marks Act 1883 347
Patents, Designs and Trade Marks Act 1888 347, 348
pay-to-play 408
Pearson v Shalala (1999) 310–312
Peel v Attorney Registration and Disciplinary Commission (1990) 298
Permanent Court of International Justice 182
Perry v Truefitt (1842) 11, 14
Pertursson, G. 208
Peru 240, 248, 249, 250, 470

PETA v Doughney (2001) 416–17, 420
pharmaceuticals 214, 223–4, 230
Philippines 467
Philips v Remington 356–8, 360, 506, 509, 510, 511, 515, 521
Piazza's Seafood World LLC v Odom (2006) 305
placebo effect 308–9
placement 407
plain meaning rule 194, 195–6, 197
Planned Parenthood v Bucci (1997) 417, 420
positive protection 471
Posner, R. 65, 77, 83, 314–16, 327, 330, 366, 377
post-sale confusion 326–7, 378, 387
potentially and actually misleading concept 306
pricing 406–7
procedural considerations 422
Procter & Gamble/OHIM (BABY DRY judgment) (2002) 163
product:
    characteristics 25
    design protection 498–522
    see also shape marks-legislation
    experiences 405–6
    review websites 422–3
Professional Standards Board for Patent and Trade Mark Attorneys 127–8
Promatek 425
property argument 113–16
property right 339
protection prior to use 110–113
protection of trade names 182–93
    consumer confusion, discounting of in favor of free movement 192–3
    exclusive rights pursuant to Agreement on Trade-Related Aspects of Intellectual Property Rights 186–7
    honest practice in industrial or commercial matters 191
    interrelationship of trademarks and trade names 187–90
    trade names as an exception under Agreement on Trade-Related Aspects of Intellectual Property Rights 190–91

proving harm 136
proxies 379
public awareness 173, 175
public choice theory 137, 146, 283, 284
public domain 345–67, 453
 bundle of rights 362
 and commons, comparison of 361–4
 negative 361–2
 perseveration 456
 scope 459–61
 trade mark common 347–53
 Trade Marks Directive and enclosure of the common 354–60
public interest 359–60
public trust doctrine 365

Qualitex Co v Jacobson Products Co. Inc. (1995) 517–18
quality concerns 107–9

Re Joseph Crosfield & Sons Ltd. to Register a Trade Mark (Perfection for soap case) (1909) 349, 351, 353
Re Morton-Norwich Prods. Inc. (1982) 402
'Redskins' trademarks 449, 461
redundancy rule 195
Reed Executive plc Ors v Reed Business Information Ltd. (2004) 193
referent 44, 45, 46–7, 49, 50, 56, 57, 58, 61
referential function 339
referential use 167, 420–21
reform 116–18
regional economic development 217–18
Registrar of Trademarks 150
registration 95–7, 109–110, 111, 114–15
 see also clearance cost argument
reputation 108, 190
restrictiveness of national governmental policies 217–18
retail interactions 406–7
reviews 320
Richardson, M. 329
Robelco NV and Robeco Groep NV (2001) 187
Robertson, W. 26–7, 40

Robins v Pruneyard Shopping Center (1980) 283
Rogers, D. 508, 510, 512
Roht-Arriaza, N. 466
Romania 199, 200
Royal Commission 37
royalty-collecting societies 223
Rumsfeld, D. 290

Sabel/Puma (1997) 156–8
Salaman, J.S. 29
salesperson-consumer interactions 407
same or similar products 157
San Francisco Arts & Athletics Inc. v United States Olympic Committee (1987) 301–2, 400
SAT.1/OHIM (2004) 163
satire 276, 394
satisficing behavior 288
Saussure, F. de 42, 52–3, 60, 62
Saxlehner v Wagner (1910) 76
scandalous marks 448–50
Scandecor Development AB v Scandecor Marketing (2001) 184
Scandinavian countries 218, 220
scent marks 164, 241–2, 249
Schechter, F. 58, 62–3, 135, 289
search engines 412–13, 421, 423–4, 425
search-costs 109, 318, 455–6
search-costs theory of limiting doctrine 65–94
 abandonment 92–4
 comparative and other truthful advertising 75–9
 economic theory 66–70
 functionality 90–92
 genericide 85–90
 limiting rules 70–75
 naked licensing, prohibitions on and assignments in gross 82–3
 trademark use 79–82
Second Circuit 142, 301, 303, 397–8, 493
secondary meaning 55
Select Committee 5, 16–19
semiotic account of trademark doctrine and culture 42–64
 distinctiveness 52–9
 floating signifier and hypermark 60–61

536 *Trademark law and theory*

semiotic sign structurations 44–5
sign value 61–3
sign value and consumer culture 63–4
triadic structure 45–8
triadic structure, breakdown of 48–52
Serbia 199
Seventh Circuit 377
shape marks-legislation 358, 502–522
   Canadian Federal law 520–21
   European Community law on designs and trade marks 502–516
   Japan 522
   New Zealand 521–2
   Thailand 522
   United States Federal law 516–20
Sheffield Bill (1862) 16–18, 28
Sherman, B. 30
Shiva, V. 469
Sieckmann v Deutsches Patent- und Markenamt (2002) 107
sign 45, 47
   value 61–4
signification 52–3, 54, 56, 57
signified 44–5, 47, 49–51, 54, 56–7, 59, 61, 340
signifier 44–52, 54, 56–9, 61
   expressive values 262
   floating 60–61
   restricting allusion to trademarks 340
   search-costs theory of limiting doctrines 77
signs, similar 236
signs and symbols *see* traditional knowledge and cultural property
Silhouette case (1998) 209–210, 221
Singapore 237, 240, 242, 244–5, 247–53
Singer Mfg. Co. v June Mfg. Co. No. 6 (1896) 361, 363
Singer Mfg. v Wilson (1876) 40
Singer v Loog (1879) 31–2, 40
Singleton v Bolton 8
Sirena SRL v Eda SRL (1971) 330
Sixth Circuit 427
Smead Manufacturing Company 241
Smith, T.E. 138
Smith v Chanel Inc. (1968) 76–7
social harm 137
Société Bic v Department of Intellectual Property (2006) 522

sound marks 241–2, 249
source
   designation and intermediaries 422–4
   designation requirement 419
   identification 440–41
   of the product 47
South Africa
   Constitutional Court 281
   Customs Union 248
   Trade Marks Act 472
South Asia 470
South Korea 240, 247–9
Southern v How (1618) 7, 8
Spalding v Gamage (1915) 35–6
Spence, M. 324–41
sponsorship 387, 392–3
Standing Committee on the Law of Trademarks, Industrial Designs and Geographical Indications (of WIPO) 474
statute-based factual solutions 267–80
   actionable use 269–73
   defenses 279–80
   distinctiveness 268–9
   harm 273–9
strength 55
sui generis system 436, 452, 462–3
Sunbeam 522
supplementary material rule 197
Supreme Court 50
   bilateral free trade agreements 244, 245
   confusion and fair use 369, 372, 375–6, 379, 383, 389–90, 395–7, 399
   copyright influence on trademark law 482
   discussions of truth versus falsity 296–8
   expressive values 278, 280, 283, 286
   Finland 174, 178, 181, 184, 202
   Internet and trademark law 415, 416
   Lanham Act and commercial speech doctrine 294–5, 301, 303, 308, 317, 321
   political economy of dilution 133, 139, 144
   public domain delineation 363, 364
   restricting allusion to trademarks 333–5

search-costs theory of limiting doctrines 76, 90–91
Suthersanen, U. 500
Sykes v Sykes (1824) 8
symbols *see* traditional knowledge and cultural property
Syria 200

tangible product 50–51
tangible rights 437
tangible symbol 46
tarnishment 244
  expressive values 278–9
  Lanham Act and commercial speech doctrine 315–16, 319
  political economy of dilution 136, 140, 146
  restricting allusion to trademarks 325–6, 340
  search-costs theory of limiting doctrines 73
tastes 241
technical requirements 217
telle quelle provision 269, 477
textures 241
Thailand 248, 522
Third Circuit 381, 386, 390
third parties 108
Thomas Betts Corp v Panduit Corp (1995) 519
three-dimensional objects 164
Tiffany & Co. v Tiffany Productions Inc. (1933) 325
trade associations 223
trade dress 501–2
Trade Marks Act 116, 123, 127, 363
  1875 30
  1905 349
  1938 184, 352
  1946, technical corrections to 516
  1994 171
  1995 (Australia) 103
  1997 (Japan) 522
  1998 244
  2002 522
  Canada 520
  Germany 184
  Ireland 153
  South Africa 472

Trade Marks Directive (1989) 34, 354–60, 504, 506, 510
  free movement of protected goods in Europe 208, 210, 224, 225
  harmonization: WTO Appellate Body and ECJ 178–80, 181, 184, 187–8, 190, 192, 197, 201
  public domain delineation 347, 351, 352, 360, 364
Trade Marks Harmonisation Directive 503
Trade Marks Registrar 351
Trade Marks Registration Act 1875 5, 28–30, 347
Trade Marks Registration Bill 1861 5
trade names as an exception under Agreement on Trade-Related Aspects of Intellectual Property Rights 190–91
Trade Practices Act 1974 101
Trade-mark cases (1879) 379
Trademark Dilution Revision Act 2006 133, 144–7, 384–5, 481, 495, 497
Trademark Law Treaty (1994) 104, 239
Trademark Law Treaty Implementation Act 1998 473–4
trademark owner control and brand perception 410
trademark rights 47
Trademark Trial and Appeals Board 449
trademark use doctrine 49–50, 79–82
traditional knowledge and cultural intellectual property 433–63, 464–78
  authenticity and source identification 440–41
  competition enhancement and search costs, reduction of 455–6
  consumer confusion, minimization of 455
  developing countries: clash of intellectual property rights paradigms 466–70
  distinctiveness 456–8
  existing intellectual property law 441–2
  freedom of expression and language 461–2
  geographical indications 451–3

538   *Trademark law and theory*

limitations of trade mark
    registration 445–8
offensive trademarks in New Zealand
    450–51
protection against exploitation of
    traditional knowledge 471–4
protection for exploitation of
    traditional knowledge 475–6
public domain perseveration 456
public domain, scope of 459–61
recognition, preservation, use,
    control and development
    438–40
scandalous or disparaging marks and
    the Lanham Act 448–50
sui generis protection 462–3
utility of trademark registration
    443–5
*TrafFix Devices Inc v Marketing
    Displays Inc.* (2001) 517, 519
tragedy of the commons 366
Treaty of Rome 151, 204
triadic model 44, 45–52
truth and advertising: Lanham Act and
    commercial speech doctrine
    294–323
    dilution 312–22
        cognitive model of and
            noncommercial uses 317–20
        First Amendment implications
            320–22
        new basis for 314–16
    see also false advertising
Tunisia 200, 470
Turkey 199, 199, 200
Tushnet, R. 294–323
Twentieth Century Fox Film Corporation
    241
Two Pesos Inc v Taco Cabana Inc
    (1992) 500, 501–2, 522
Ty Inc. v Perryman (2002) 314

Ukraine 199, 200
unauthorized biography 394
Underdown, E.M. 26–7
Unfair Commercial Practices Directive
    (29/2005/EC) 169
Uniform Commercial Code procedure
    116

Uniform Domain Name Dispute
    Resolution Policy 276
unilateral trade sanctions 232
United Arab Emirates 248
United Kingdom:
    bureaucracies 115–16
    free movement of protected goods in
        Europe 217, 219–20, 219,
        220, 221, 226
    harmonization 151, 154, 171, 183,
        184
    Land Registry 125–6
    product design protection 502, 522
    public domain delineation 346–7,
        350–52, 355–8, 360–62,
        364–5, 366
    Registry 514
    traditional knowledge and cultural
        property 454
United States 20, 36, 41
    bilateral free trade agreements 232,
        234–7, 239–40, 242, 244–9,
        251–3, 255
    bureaucracies 98, 100, 104–5, 110,
        111, 114, 116
    confusion and fair use 401
    Constitution: Copyright Clause 361
    copyright influence on trademark law
        487
    courts 55, 56
    expressive values 265, 269, 271, 273,
        276, 277–80, 282
    Federal law 516–20
    harmonization 159, 185, 186, 195
    Patent and Trademark Office 116,
        201, 241, 472–3, 517, 520
    political economy of dilution 145
    product design protection 500,
        501–2, 519, 521, 522
    public domain delineation 346, 347,
        361, 363, 364–5
    restricting allusion to trademarks
        331, 338
    search-costs theory of limiting
        doctrines 69
    semiotic account of trademark
        doctrine 43
    traditional knowledge and cultural
        property 434, 436, 448, 449,
        451

Treaty (1877) 19–20
see also Native Americans
United States v United Foods Inc. (2001) 332
Universal City Studios Inc. v Ideal Publishing Corp. 394
unjust enrichment and desert 330
Unregistered Community Design 502
Uruguay Round Agreements 232
use in commerce 414–24, 427
    imperceptible uses 421
    no goods/services 419–20
    procedural considerations 422
    referential uses 420–21
    source designation and intermediaries 422–4
use as a mark 165–71
use value 62

Valenzuela, D.A. 519
value 52–3, 54, 56
Van Doren 222, 226
Venezuela 467–8
Vienna Convention on the Law of Treaties (1969) 181–2, 186, 195, 197
Virginia State Board of Pharmacy v Virginia Citizens Consumer Council Inc. (1976) 296, 300–301
Visser, C. 464–78
Visual Artists Rights Act 482
visual perceptibility 249
Volkswagenwerk Aktiengesellschaft v Church (1969) 391, 395
Vornado Air Circulation Systems v Durcraft Corp (1995) 519

W. and G. du Cros Ltd.'s Application (1913) 351, 352–3
Waitangi Treaty 451
Wal-Mart Stores Inc. v Samara Bros (2002) 364
'warehousing' marks 92
Warner Brothers 138
Welch v Knott (1857) 15
well-known trademark 108, 242–8
West Africa 470
Windsurfing Chiemsee/Attenberger (1999) 160, 356–8, 360, 513
Winter v DC Comics (2003) 282
word of mouth *see* Internet and online word of mouth
World Intellectual Property Organization 464–5
    International Bureau 239, 474, 478
    Joint Recommendation 242–3, 245–7
World Trade Organization 232, 240, 251, 264, 503
    Dispute Settlement Understanding 181, 237
Wotherspoon v Currie (1872) 35

Yamaha Intl Corp. v Hoshino Gakki Co. (1986) 518
York Trailer Holdings decision (1981) 353, 360
Yorkshire Copper Works Ltd.'s Application for a Trade Mark (1954) 352–3, 355

Zauderer 303
Zino Davidoff v A&G Imports (2002) 220